Unity and Diversity in the New Testament

JAMES D. G. DUNN

Unity and Diversity in the New Testament

An Inquiry into the Character of Earliest Christianity

SECOND EDITION

SCM PRESS
London

TRINITY PRESS INTERNATIONAL
Philadelphia

First published 1977
Second edition 1990

SCM Press
26–30 Tottenham Road
London N1 4BZ

Trinity Press International
3725 Chestnut Street
Philadelphia, Pa. 19104

334 02436 6

Library of Congress Cataloging-in-Publication Data
Dunn, James D. G., 1939–
Unity and diversity in the New Testament: an inquiry into the
character of earliest Christianity/James D. G. Dunn.
p.   cm.
Includes bibliographical references.
ISBN 0–334–02436–6
1.   Bible. N.T.—Theology.   2. Theology, Doctrinal—History—Early
church, ca. 30–600.   I. Title.
BS2397.D85   1990
270.1—dc20   89–20659

Printed in Great Britain at
The Camelot Press, Southampton

To
CHARLIE MOULE
Christian, scholar, friend

CONTENTS

CONCLUSIONS

PREFACE

Eight years ago I was privileged to be a member of a study group in Edinburgh which spent some time discussing the questions raised by Walter Bauer's *Rechtgläubigkeit und Ketzerei im ältesten Christentum* ([2]1964, ET *Orthodoxy and Heresy in Earliest Christianity*, 1971). In the summer of 1970 I participated in another study group at Tyndale House, Cambridge, which took as its theme 'Diversity and Development in NT Theology'. The interest these seminars aroused in me resulted in a series of ten lectures on the subject of 'Unity and Diversity in the NT' as the final section of an undergraduate Part I course on NT Theology at the University of Nottingham in 1971–72. After three years, syllabus changes made it feasible to transfer the already too tightly packed series to Part II (third year undergraduate). It is these lectures which are now written up with the necessary detail and documentation.

The book has several purposes. First, it seeks to explore the issues raised by Bauer with reference to the NT. Can we properly speak of 'orthodoxy and heresy in *earliest* Christianity'? What is 'the unity of the NT'? How broad is the diversity within the NT? The issues are clarified and sharpened in the Introduction. There have been many contributions on this theme, of course, but they have been all either too brief and too popular, or too narrow and too specialized. What has become increasingly necessary is a single study which brings together the different aspects of the investigation in sufficient detail within the covers of one book. This I have attempted to do in the following pages. It is my hope that as a result, the issue of the NT's unity and diversity will come into clearer focus, and its implications and ramifications will become a subject for further investigation and debate. I have taken the liberty to include a few remarks at the close of several chapters relating the conclusions to the present day, and have outlined some of the corollaries for our understanding of 'the Authority of the NT' in the final section (§76).

Second, it seeks to bridge the gaps which too often exist between literary critical study of the NT documents, historical sociological inquiry into the beginnings of Christianity, and theological investigation of the beliefs and practices of the first-century Christians. Only when all these different disciplines are integrated can we have any real hope of getting inside the situations which gave rise to the NT writings; only so can we even begin to grasp the reality of first-century Christianity. No one study of course can do anything like justice to the complexity of historical reality. But the theme chosen, Unity and Diversity in the NT, does provide both a tool of analysis and a focus for synthesis which enables us both to penetrate to some depth and to hold the different issues and insights together. To emphasize the interlocking character of the various discussions I have indulged in fairly extensive cross-referencing between chapters.

Third, as a by-product of the first two purposes, the book should also serve as a kind of advanced introduction to the NT and to first-century Christianity. Introductions to the NT we have aplenty. But when the student has completed his appointed stint on form-criticism, the who wrote what, when, why and where questions, exegetical method, etc., he often has little choice but to narrow his sights and to plunge into particular areas and specialist monographs and commentaries. What is needed is a volume which provides an overview of areas and issues that go beyond the usual run of introductory questions, which introduces the advanced student to particular problems without requiring him at once to entangle himself in a maze of detailed discussion, and which stimulates him to feel after the reality of Christian origins for himself at a deeper level. It is my hope that this present volume will fill such a need and provide such a stimulus. It is dedicated to Professor C. F. D. Moule with deepest respect and warmest affection – his *Birth of the New Testament* (1962) was something of a pioneer in this area.

The material which follows was written up with a view primarily to third year undergraduates who have already completed two years in NT studies. No doubt it could serve also as a text or starting point in some programmes for a Master's degree. In addition it will I hope not be without relevance to the higher ranks of scholarship, while at the same time the detail it handles and issues it raises should not be beyond the competence of 'the informed layman'. Each chapter can stand by itself to provide the jumping-off point for an independent study, even though all are linked by the overarching theme.

I toyed with the idea of presenting the material in a much more popular format, like Ernst Käsemann's *Jesus Means Freedom* (ET 1969). But without documentation and argumentation, controversial statements can be too readily ignored and dismissed. On reflection I felt it better to stick to a format which provided sufficient detail to indicate the grounds for my conclusions and such support as they commend from fellow scholars. At the same time, since the area covered is so large I could not hope to meet every objection or discuss each alternative interpretation, either in the text or in the notes. I have therefore attempted a not altogether satisfactory compromise – cutting notes to a minimum, but offering sufficient variety in the bibliographies to enable students to come to terms with the alternatives for themselves and to reach their own conclusions.

Since the book has undergraduates primarily in mind I have confined the bibliographies largely to English language items or those in translation. The only exceptions I have allowed are classic studies and recent contributions of some note. For the same reason I have avoided the use of Greek in both text and notes. Although advanced study of the NT cannot progress very far without a working knowledge of the original language, the student without Greek is by no means incapable of coming to grips with the historical and theological issues examined in the following pages.

A book like this owes many debts to the comments and advice of others. Here I wish to express my gratitude to the members of the original study groups in Edinburgh and Cambridge, and to my students of several years whose questions and discussion have helped sharpen up issues and eliminate several weaknesses. Most of all my sincere thanks to those who gave up valuable time to comment on an earlier draft of the book in whole or in part – to Dr G.I. Davies and the Rev. S. G. Hall, my colleagues here at Nottingham, to Professor Moule of Cambridge, who also kindly allowed me to read his *Origin of Christology* (1977) at proof stage, and particularly to Robert Morgan of Oxford and Dr Graham Stanton, Professor-elect of King's College, London. Above all my wife's encouragement and consideration enabled me to maintain a too tight schedule when wiser men would probably have settled for a slower pace. Last but not least my thanks are due to my youngest daughter, Fiona, for not cutting up more than six pages of the typescript last Christmas – 'for snowflakes, Daddy'!

JAMES D. G. DUNN

29 May (Pentecost) 1977
Nottingham

FOREWORD TO SECOND EDITION

The trouble with an introductory text book is that it soon becomes dated – particularly if it attempts to provide an overview and synthesis of recent scholarship, including bibliographies. One of the major objectives of *U&D* was to provide such a text book. Not as yet one more example of busy lecturers pushing their first year 'Introduction to the NT' lecture courses before a wider public; there are more than enough of these! But as a second level introduction, designed for the third year student, or for those who want a specialist Masters course which takes them through the NT material at a deeper level, or for such as may desire a broad yet challenging refresher course some years after completing their degree or earlier study of the NT. But it is now twelve years since *U&D* was first published, and, such has been the rapid movement in NT scholarship over that period, it certainly has become dated.

Fortunately the imminent need of a fresh (5th) reprint has coincided with the near completion of a German translation, commissioned by Vandenhoeck & Ruprecht, Göttingen.[1] The coincidence spurred my faint enthusiasm to review the possibility of a revision. And SCM Press encouraged me to revise at least to the extent of writing a new, updating Foreword and new, updated bibliographies. But could revision be contained within these limitations? Certainly I was in no doubt that major revision was impossible, at least for the English edition, not least because it would take far more time than I could afford. But would it not be necessary to ask for some selective and minimal revisions of the text itself, always within the limitation of keeping the same English pagination? Otherwise dated text might repeatedly jar with updated bibliography.

One intriguing way of resolving my dilemma quickly suggested itself – to ask the NT Postgraduate Seminar at Durham for its help. The response was warm and encouraging. And so for the past fifteen meetings of the seminar we have gone through *U&D* chapter by chapter in critical (and I mean critical!) review. It has been a fascinating and (for the most part) exhilarating experience. Most of the time I have felt as though I was in the dock, being forced by sharp and persistent questioning to justify and defend myself, now on points of detail, now on terms and categories used, now on issues where the debate has moved on, now on oversimplifications, now on gaps in bibliography. At most points, somewhat to my surprise, I found that I wanted to defend myself, and often could do so, since in framing the original text I recalled having taken several similar considerations into account. At many others the brevity of treatment meant that the text was insufficiently nuanced or qualified; but to meet these points would have required a more substantial expansion of the text than was practical. And at not a few others I could only concede that the text was now inadequate and should be amended if at all possible.

So far as the extent of revision was concerned, therefore, the conclusion to which the meetings of the seminar repeatedly pointed was that if major revision was ruled out, then at least some minimal revision of the text was more or less essential, together with the updating Foreword and updated bibliographies. I could not but agree, and in what follows I attempt to implement that conclusion and to explain its rationale.

As I familiarized myself with the text once again, both prior to, during and after each seminar, one of the main impressions was, How quickly the agenda has changed. In my inaugural lecture at Durham, only seven years after publication, I was to note three major trends in NT studies.[2] All of them in the force of their impact postdate *U&D*. They still constitute the main agenda changes and so can serve as a summary of the shift of perspective and interest since *U&D* was first published.[3]

At the time I completed the original manuscript the new wave of sociological studies, heralded particularly by the work of G. Theissen,[4] was just getting under way. Even then I was already convinced of its importance and rather overoptimistically had indicated my hope in the Preface that *U&D* itself would incorporate a sociological dimension, although I must confess the manuscript was in penultimate draft before this particular light had fully dawned. But since then the wave of sociological interest has gained in strength[5] and were I to contemplate a complete revision of *U&D* I would have to rework most of the material more thoroughly than is possible in this second edition. The impact on Part II in particular would have been considerable, indicating the social complexity of the several trends and developments outlined there. As a second best I have indicated at several points in the following paragraphs where a fuller,

including sociological perspective, would have influenced the formulation of the chapters in question.

U&D was published in the same year, and by the same publisher,
as E. P. Sanders, *Paul and Palestinian Judaism.*[6] Sanders' work has
marked a decisive shift or stage in the reappraisal of relationships
between the earliest Christians and the Judaism of which they were
part, a reappraisal stemming from a combination of factors,
including revulsion at the Holocaust, a growing awareness of the
long history of Christian anti-Semitism, the discovery of the Dead
Sea Scrolls, J. Neusner's work on rabbinic traditions,[7] and renewed
interest in the so-called intertestamental literature or Jewish pseudepigrapha.[8] This reappraisal has resulted in a fresh reassertion of
the Jewishness of Jesus and occasioned what some now call 'the third
quest of the historical Jesus'.[9] It has also sparked off a vigorous
debate on Paul and the law, in which I have been privileged to
participate.[10] On rereading several passages of *U&D* I realized how
'pre-Sanders' were some of my brief characterizations of Jesus and
the law in particular. These I could not leave unchanged in any, even
minor revision.

A third new wave of research relating to the NT has been on what
I may describe simply as 'the literary criticism' front.[11] Although I
recognize its importance in the hermeneutical quest for meaning in
the NT texts, I have felt much less compulsion to take it into account
in preparing this revision than in the first two cases. This is
principally because a major driving force in the literary criticism
movement has been the desire to free the NT texts from the
restrictive and often question-begging concerns of historical inquiry.
Whereas my concern in *U&D* is thoroughly historical, as its subtitle
clearly indicates – *An Inquiry into the Character of Earliest Christianity*. At
the historical level, of course, questions of genre and literary form are
of major importance. But in fact, and somewhat surprisingly, they
have not impinged to any great extent on *U&D*, with the principal
exception of the chapter on 'Apocalyptic Christianity'. And although diversity of genre is an important feature of NT diversity, my
concern in *U&D* has been more to explore the commonality of
themes and beliefs and practices and trends running through and
across documents, rather than particular documents as such.
Consequently, given the limited revision of the second edition, I
must leave it to others to develop this further dimension of unity and
diversity.

If then the agenda has changed so much, and if this second edition
can incorporate only a limited revision, is it worth while proceeding?

This was a question which I and the seminar considered seriously. The conclusion was firm and clear: a second edition was desirable and should proceed. The main reasons were as follows.

First, on a purely pragmatic note, the German edition was nearly complete. It would be a great pity if it consisted simply of a translation of the dated 1977 English version. And even if the English edition would find revision of the text difficult, there were no such constraints in the case of the German edition, since the translator's manuscript had not yet been typeset. At the same time it would be undesirable for the German edition to be at significant variance from the second English edition. The most obvious solution was a minimally revised text which would update where necessary and possible, without altering the English pagination. As I reviewed each chapter, following the discussion of the seminar, I was relieved to find that I could accomplish all essential and most desirable revision even while operating within these constraints.

Second, despite a degree of datedness, there is a great deal of continuing value even in the original version of *U&D*. The issues and themes examined within Part I and the trends examined within Part II are still of importance in any inquiry into the character of earliest Christianity. It would be a grave disservice to both current and past NT scholarship to suggest that the three new waves of interest discussed briefly above constitute the whole agenda for modern NT study. There is much of perennial interest and of enduring significance in the material gathered and ordered in the following chapters, which remains unaffected by developments over the past twelve years. There is solidly packed and packaged data which I hope still provides one of the most useful brief introductions and starting points for discussion and further study of the topics and trends. The presentation should still challenge and provoke readers to see the NT and earliest Christianity in a fresh and hopefully illuminating light, and, if the Durham seminars are anything to go by, provide fresh stimulus and insight for those working in diverse parts of the NT. And if a minimal revision can increase that value, by eliminating more dated features and by updating the bibliography, then its useful life might well be extended for a further generation of students of the NT.

Third, above all there is the importance of its theme – Unity in Diversity. The primary objective was not to provide a second level introduction to the NT, but to explore the historical reality of first-century Christianity and the Christianity of the NT documents, to explore the historical and theological tension between their unity and their diversity. As I lived with these issues for eight years prior to publication in discussion, teaching, reflection and writing, I became more and more convinced of *the positive function of diversity* within Christian unity.[12] The point has become increasingly important for me in the subsequent twelve years, as I have come to see more and more clearly that Christian unity is impossible *without* diversity, that without sufficient diversity Christian unity will be (heretically) narrow, squeezing out what is also the life of the Spirit and what also expresses the grace of God in Christ, that without diversity of type and function Christian unity will be as ludicrously lopsided and grotesque as the body which consists only of an eye or of an ear (I Cor. 12.17–20).

One of the most heartening consequences of *U&D* has been a number of invitations to participate in ecumenical consultations and conferences, precisely with the charge to bring out and reflect further on what the unity and diversity of the NT may say to ecumenical concerns today.[13] I have been more than happy to do so, since I believe that the conclusions of chapter XV are of first importance for anyone who takes seriously the historical character of Christianity and the definition of it which the NT provides.[14] If an updated second edition can help to bring home to more students of the NT and Christians generally the reality and importance of unity in diversity (equal emphasis on both words), then I most certainly wish to proceed with it.

Fourth, a new edition gives me opportunity to clarify the intention, the scope and the limitations of *U&D*. For example, it should have been sufficiently clear that I set out on the quest of unity in Part I by asking what historically has served to unify Christianity, or been regarded as part of its distinctive core or essence. To that extent the agenda was provided by the subsequent history of Christianity. Similarly in Part II the strands and trends examined became most clearly developed in their distinctiveness in the post-NT period – in effect the main alternatives for would-be Christians in the second century. The inquiry therefore was not a random exploration of the NT or first-century Christianity, and certainly in no sense an attempt to treat the NT and beginning period of Christianity in isolation from Christianity thereafter. The result was, not altogether surprisingly, a more integrated and coherent survey than might otherwise have emerged. Which made it more difficult to consider adding fresh chapters (I had long wondered about one on ethics),[15] or shifting the focus and imagery away from 'unity and diversity' to, say, J. C. Beker's helpful 'coherence and contingency' schema, which serves to make a similar point.[16]

On the other hand, perhaps I should have brought out more clearly that I am deliberately moving on two levels in *U&D*. One is the historical reality of the churches spoken of in the NT. The other is the NT itself. The latter is, of course, contained within the former, but they are not the same. The fact that the diversity of the NT documents is narrower than the diversity of the earliest churches should not be allowed to cloak the fact of the diversity of the NT itself. But neither should we ignore the fact that the narrower diversity of the NT documents functioned as a check on and limitation to the larger diversity.

Again, the character of the following chapters as introductory or summary treatments needs to be recalled. In every case the topics chosen provide sufficient subject matter for several monographs. Frequently in the course of the Durham seminar we had to accept that, of course, more could be said and needs to be said on this point or that, but only at the cost of considerable expansion of the text. The data and the treatment provided is only a starter for discussion, a tool in the hands of the wise discussion leader. The subdivisions of the text are designed to facilitate corporate use. The degree of repetition is an attempt to ensure that each chapter is as compact and self-contained as possible. While the cross-referencing should make possible expanded discussion of particular points where desired. The bibliographies do not consist simply of items which document points made, but also items which dispute them or which carry the discussion forward in other directions. My hope, need I say, is that a discussion which uses *U&D* as a starter, and whose members both study the NT texts cited and the suggested bibliography for themselves, will achieve a fuller and more fully rounded picture than was possible to achieve in *U&D* itself.

As part of my objective, to provide stimulus for discussion, I have been deliberately provocative in posing the questions to be asked and the corollaries to be drawn. At not a few points during the course of the revision I wondered whether I should temper some of the bolder or more challenging statements, and in some instances I have concluded that the question posed did push too hard. But for the most part the objective of stimulating and challenging 'safer' conclusions is one I have continued to pursue. If the cost of opening up windows for some minds is the occasional overstatement I am content. And if the end result is a clearer grasp of the historical reality of earliest Christianity and of the character of the NT, I am more than content.

Other clarifications will be incorporated in revisions to the text or the notes, or in the new introductions to each chapter below. Fifth, a revised edition gives me opportunity to defend myself against those who have criticized the first edition in inappropriate ways. Several reviewers of *U&D* charged me with narrowing the unity and emphasizing the diversity far too much.[17] I wonder if they read pp. 370f. and 382f. with sufficient closeness, and have considered the full importance of the christological centrality of the uniting core.[18] I confess I also find myself wondering whether such readers have fully considered with sufficient seriousness the plain fact of the diversity which was, is and always will be Christianity, uncomfortable as that fact may be for those who lust for the security of having others believe and act just as they believe and act.

Another surprisingly frequent attack from the conservative side was the accusation that I found the NT to be full of contradictions.[19] Not so! The word 'contradiction' never passed my lips (or typewriter). And deliberately so. For that was not the point; and the accusation betrays a failure to grasp that point. The point, as expressed clearly enough already in chapter II, is that any and every statement of the gospel in the NT is historically conditioned and context specific. The word of God speaks to the human condition in its diverse specificity. That is why it is diverse and different in its varied expressions. Recognition of this fact in the NT should be something liberating and exciting, since it undergirds the affirmation that God continues to speak to the diverse and specific situations of today. Failure to recognize the difference and diversity of the gospel in the diverse situations of past and present simply succeeds in imprisoning the gospel in less than meaningful forms and formulae.[20]

The charge of anti-Catholic bias from one or two Roman Catholic reviewers I will return to below in the new introduction to chapter XIV.[21]

Finally, perhaps it also needs to be said, not least for the sake of future reviewers, that the main question to be asked with regard to *U&D* is not whether the opinions and characterizations offered in the following pages are correct or command consensus in every particular. That would be hardly likely, especially when so many exegetical decisions have had to be made without sufficient detail and justification. The main question is whether the broad picture is right and overall a fair reflection of the NT and of the character of earliest Christianity. Whether I am right or wrong on several, or even many details, what is important is the *fact* that the unifying and distinctive core of Christianity in the beginning centred irreducibly on Jesus Christ, the *fact* of diversity as something inescapable in every attempt to bring that unifying core to concrete expression, and, not least, the *fact* that the unity of the Christianity of the NT consisted in and through that diversity.

In the light of all the above considerations, revision of *U&D* for the new edition has been limited to the following: (i) completely revised bibliographies for each chapter; (ii) expanded and additional notes to add occasional clarifications or qualifications to the text, and to take account of the most relevant of more recent literature, including further studies of my own which provide more substantial underpinning at various points; (iii) usually small corrections to the text itself, to remove minor infelicities and occasionally inadvertant sexist language, and to reflect change of perspective or opinion; the most substantial of these come at pp. 135f. and in chapter XIII, the chapter with which I became dissatisfied most quickly; the difficulty of keeping such revisions within the established structure and pagination of the paragraphs was considerable, but I hope I have achieved the aim without introducing too much awkwardnesses; (iv) fresh introductions to each chapter to give opportunity for further clarification as necessary and to indicate where a fuller, particularly sociological perspective would have given opportunity for a much more thorough revision had that been possible. These new introductions follow immediately.

In reference to *chapter I*, since it functions simply as an 'Introduction', I need hardly add to what I have already said above. The discussion of Bauer's thesis has continued in the interim,[22] and H. Koester has posed the issue in still more extreme terms.[23] But chapter I focused the study in its own terms (unity and diversity); and given the range and character and historical conditionedness of the NT documents, the question of unity and diversity is one which cannot be avoided by serious students. It may bear repeating, that the chapters which follow are in no sense intended as an exhaustive survey of the NT or of first-century Christianity. The chapters of Part I are simply a sequence of 'bore holes' through the variegated mass and strata of the traditions which make up the NT; while Part II attempts to trace in sketchy overview the major Christian continuities and discontinuities between the first century and the early patristic period.

In view of some responses in reviews and other comment, it is perhaps necessary to remind readers that *chapter II*, 'Kerygma or Kerygmata?', has a limited objective. This was indicated already at pp. 6–7, 13 and 33. It is a superficial survey of the NT material – and deliberately so. Its purpose was simply to show that the issue of unity and diversity is there, clearly visible, even on a quick read. It is not something forced unnaturally on the text by sceptical scholars.[24] Consequently, for example, there is no need at this point to justify the use of Synoptic traditions as evidence of Jesus' teaching, since our concern in chapter II is simply with the fact that it is presented as Jesus' teaching. So when in §3 I speak of 'the kerygma of Jesus' I mean simply the preaching of Jesus as reported by the Synoptics.

Chapter III, 'Primitive Confessional Formulae', turns by natural progression to confessional formulae. Not because the response of faith to the kerygma is primarily cerebral or finally reducible to concepts; we turn to other responses in the subsequent chapters. But simply because verbal confession has been a fundamental and prominent feature of Christianity as it grew and developed. A historical perspective is bound to ask whether it was so in the beginning and how this basic instinct of faith (to 'confess with the lips') came to expression. The chapter limits the discussion to confessional formulae, since, once again, Christianity has always found it necessary to express its faith in brief definitional formulae. This, however, is not to say that verbal confessions of faith cannot take much fuller and larger forms. Recent literary study of the biblical texts, for example, has properly emphasized the role of narrative theology; the tradition of making confession by telling a story is one well established in the OT. Consequently the Gospels themselves can quite properly be regarded as confessional statements. And if the passion narratives were retold in part or whole during early Christian worship they would certainly function as confessional within the terms of §13. Here again the limited scope of the discussion is not intended as any kind of claim that only this material is eligible for discussion under this head. On the contrary, the hope in attempting such a concise summary presentation was to provoke precisely such broader ranging reactions and reflections.

Chapter IV, 'The Role of Tradition', is one example of where a fuller sociological perspective would have helped clarify the greater complexity of the historical situation, particularly as regards Jesus' attitude to the law and the halakah. The rather more simplified terms of the discussion are, in point of fact, closer to the terms used within the NT text itself; but even so, they may not reflect the social reality of the period in sufficient detail. Thus in the case of Jesus' reaction to tradition, a more nuanced treatment would have noted that Jesus' own interpretation of the Torah, from one aspect, was quite within the range of debate on halakah current among the Pharisees themselves, and, from another, was itself a kind of tradition. I hope it is sufficiently clear from §§15 and 17–18 that Christianity was not against 'tradition' per se; §16 is about *Jewish* tradition; and the main ongoing thesis is that such tradition was *not* a unifying point within earliest Christianity.

Chapter V, 'The Use of the Old Testament', needs more refinement with regard to Jesus and the law and on methods of exegesis. The terms in which the former was posed in the first edition were simply the received tradition of the time, but that tradition has itself been amended (a nice example of how tradition develops); and I would wish to join my voice with those pressing for a fuller setting of Jesus *within* the Judaism of his day.[25] As to the latter, discussion of terms could have been greatly expanded, and the definitions modified or reshaped. However, the objective of the chapter was not to achieve precision of definition, but rather to document that there was a range and diversity of exegetical usage, both in first-century Judaism and in earliest Christianity, and to explore the ramifications of that fact. The chapter continues to serve that objective well, with only minor revision required.

The topic of *Chapter VI*, 'Concepts of Ministry', is one where sociological analysis has proved particularly fruitful.[26] And more interaction with such discussions would have been valuable, particularly in bringing the issue of authority and legitimation to sharper focus, and in tightening up categories like 'charismatic' and 'institutional'. Suffice it to say here that on balance I still prefer to use 'charismatic' in the sense given us by Paul, and *not* so much or so directly in the reminted definition so central for Weber; principally because the Weberian category can so easily be used without regard to the more specifically Pauline usage and thus miss the intrinsically theological character of the term ('charisma' as the expression of 'grace'), thereby losing something fundamental for the discussion of the Pauline 'model' in particular. So too I continue to prefer 'institutionalization' rather than a term like 'routinization' (Weber), not because I think the Pauline vision of community lacked structure, including institutional structure, but because the force of the word 'institutionalization' is fairly self-evident in describing developments from the more spontaneous worship and organization of the early Pauline churches.[27]

In writing chapter VI, I was conscious that the focus on 'ministry' was very limiting and did not allow sufficient discussion of other categories like community and organization.[28] The choice, as throughout the book, was determined by the fact that ministry was such a fundamental factor in developing Christian self-definition over the early centuries, a decisive factor in determining the 'shape' of the catholic tradition, and remains central in ecumenical discussions today.[29] Here again it would have been possible to raise the same or further issues by posing the questions differently. But it is equally obvious that the well recognized and long established category of 'ministry' catches hold of one of the most important strands in the whole sweep, past and continuing, of Christian history. As an example of one major 'bore-hole' into earliest Christianity it continues to serve a useful purpose within the overall theme of the book which could hardly have been neglected. I have taken the opportunity of a largely blank final page to add a paragraph on the question of priesthood and the ministry of women.

In *Chapter VII*, 'Patterns of Worship', the main need was twofold. First to modify the section on Jesus to reflect a clearer appreciation of contemporary Jewish spirituality. And second to modify the treatment of 'Christ-hymns' (§35.3), particularly Phil. 2.6–11: in the interim, the mirage-like character of the pre-Christian Gnostic redeemer myth has been still more widely recognized, and my own work on the beginnings of christology was sufficient to convince me that Adam christology was much the most obvious factor in the formulation of the Philippian hymn.

It seemed and still seems to me obvious that *chapter VIII*, 'Sacraments', had to take as its starting point and focus the historic significance of the two (almost) universal Christian sacraments, even while recognizing that the definition of 'sacrament' is among the points at issue. Of course I leave myself open to the criticism that the discussion has been too much dictated by later perspectives. Should I not, as in chapter III, have refused to limit the exploration to the categories which dominated later thought in this area – by asking simply how Christian faith and spirituality came to ritual expression in the beginning? Alternatively, if later categories are allowed to set the agenda, why limit the discussion solely to baptism and Lord's Supper? However, I remain unrepentent here. It is clear, even from a fairly cursory study of the NT, that baptism and the Lord's Supper (including here last supper traditions) have a significance across a range of NT material which is not paralleled in other cases, such as foot-washing, or the kiss of peace, or even the laying on of hands. It is probable, in fact, that the reason why just these two ritual acts became 'sacraments' is that they were able to embody a richer christological significance than any of the others.

Since I may be criticized for using 'sacramentalist' as a somewhat pejorative term I should simply point out that I use the word in the dictionary sense – 'one who attaches great importance to the sacraments' – with the implication that there is a danger of attaching too much importance to them, that is, to the extent that they come to be regarded as exclusive means of grace. I still believe that the ministries of Jesus, Paul and John constitute vigorous protests against just such narrowing and limiting of the grace of God.

In *chapter IX*, 'Spirit and Experience', a fuller preliminary definition of 'enthusiasm' might have been desirable. Perhaps I was assuming too much the 'identikit picture' of the 'enthusiast' which I had drawn in *Jesus and the Spirit* (p. 157). But the final sentence of the first paragraph of §43 should have been a sufficient starting point, and the rest of §43 sufficient to fill out the first preliminary sketch. Certainly those who understand 'enthusiasm' in the classic terms provided by Ronald Knox[30] would have little difficulty in recognizing the characteristic features being indicated. I should add that I do not wish 'enthusiasm' to be regarded solely in negative terms. It should also be recognized as having a positive dimension. Or at least I would prefer its meaning to be seen as more of a spectrum – from the more desirable (liberation of repressed emotions and harnessing of deep-rooted motivation) to the less desirable (unrestrained emotions and self-promoting elitism). My preference for 'charismatic' reflects both my own earlier work in this area[31] and the continuing influence of the positive and (for me) determinative Pauline usage. Phenomenologically, of course, 'charismatic' and 'enthusiastic' overlap as types and I should perhaps have spelled out the way I was distinguishing them more explicitly; but I hope the discussion on pp. 185–6 will remain sufficient for the purpose.

The focus of *chapter X*, 'Christ and Christology', is, of course, determined both by the question left hanging at the end of chapter II (p. 31) and by the repeated finding of the preceding chapters (that the unity at each point surveyed was christologically centred). It functions therefore as a conclusion to the discrete series of investigations which have constituted Part I. As such its objective is limited. There are of course other factors in the continuity between pre- and post-Easter, and I have had to be content to document the *fact* of unity and diversity rather than attempt to explore *why* earliest christology developed as it did. One important aspect of the latter became the principal concern of my next major study project.[32] But the concern here is simply to mark out the fact of unity and diversity within the unifying core itself. Given that limited objective, only modest revision has been necessary here too.

In comparison with the other three chapters of Part II, *chapter XI*, 'Jewish Christianity', came through the sieve of the seminar requiring surprisingly little revision. I hope it is sufficiently clear from §53 that the titles used in each of these four chapters are unsatisfactory in one degree or other.[33] They function simply as labels to denote areas of inquiry, not definitions as such. Nor should they be regarded as describing coherent or clearly distinct movements. They simply denote major trends and facets within much more complex movements, and one or more could certainly have been present in greater and less degree in particular churches and areas. It should also be clear that, as before, I took my lead from developments in the second century. It is a matter of fact that in the second half of the second century, there were, in very simplified terms, four main claimants to the title 'Christian'. My question is simply, How did this come about? What does this tell us about the character of first-century Christianity? To what extent can all four alternatives properly be described as 'Christian'? The seminar on this chapter evoked a fascinating discussion on the issue, Why was Ebionism wrong? And why was 'development' right? My own tentative short answer would be that the main body of earliest Jewish Christianity in the event allowed a diversity which both held to the christological centre and reflected Jesus' own openness, whereas 'heretical' Jewish Christianity was condemned precisely by its failure to recognize and respect that diversity. In this chapter I am unable to address the vexed question of anti-semitism in the NT, where the debate since the first edition of *U&D* has been particularly lively,[34] but I will return to it in a later publication.

As the introductions to chapters XI and XII make clear, the objective of *chapter XII*, 'Hellenistic Christianity', is to explore the interface between the movement stemming from Palestine and wider Hellenistic religion. That interaction was fantastically complex and to examine it adequately even within the aims of the present inquiry would require a sequence of interrelated studies of infant Christianity's relationships with the old Graeco-Roman religions, magic and astrology, current religious philosophies, mystery cults, not to mention the broader social structures. That is obviously an impossible undertaking for this volume. The original chapter, of course, reflected the interest in first-century Gnostic and proto-Gnostic influences which has been a major feature of NT studies for most of the present century. And though that interest is fading, the theses of Koester and those afflicted with the 'Nag Hammadi fever' keep the issue sufficiently and challengingly alive for the thrust of the chapter to be retained. More important, Gnosticism in its manifold forms was quickly to become the major challenge to (catholic) Christianity in the second century. So it continues to be appropriate to ask whether and to what extent this challenge was foreshadowed in the NT period – especially as both sides in the subsequent disputes made bold to claim NT texts for themselves.

On the other hand, since the second-century Gnostic movements were prime examples of religious syncretism, most of the questions posed in chapter XII could just as well be reformulated in terms of 'syncretistic Christianity'. For Christianity to speak to the Hellenistic world some degree of syncretism was inevitable; this is simply an application of the conclusion drawn as far back as chapter II, that in order to be heard, the gospel must be put in terms which can be appreciated by the particular audience addressed. But how far did that adaptation to particular and changing contexts go? And how far could it go before it ceased to be 'Christian', unacceptably diverse? Despite its limitations, therefore, the attempt to trace one or two of the strands of that first-century diversity, which demonstrate the problem of unity in syncretistic diversity and which with some plausibility may be placed on (what with hindsight can be described as) a gnosticizing trajectory, retains its value within the revised edition.

As already mentioned, *Chapter XIII*, 'Apocalyptic Christianity', was one chapter with which I became dissatisfied quite soon after publication. The characterization of 'apocalyptic' to which I was heir and on which I structured the chapter was quickly overtaken by the new wave of interest in Jewish pseudepigrapha and by the ground-breaking and more detailed analyses particularly of J. J. Collins and C. Rowland. I was well aware that the issue of whether a 'touch-up and patch' revision was to be adequate would be decided here. In the event the seminar agreed that the issue largely boiled down to one of definition. The catch-all use of 'apocalyptic' should be abandoned, and the confusion and overlap between 'apocalyptic' and 'eschatology' resolved by making it clear that the main focus of the chapter was on 'apocalyptic eschatology' – that is, not merely concern with (the events of) the end (eschatology), but that concern as characteristically though not exclusively expressed in apocalyptic literature.[35]. However, the characterizations of apocalypse and apocalyptic eschatology (§66.2 and 66.3) remain valid as characterizations, so all that was required was a rewriting of p. 310 to clarify the question of definition, and a consistent implementation of these definitions throughout the rest of the chapter. Since the point was raised in one or two reviews, it perhaps should be reiterated that 'apocalyptic Christianity' did not exist as a separate entity within earliest Christianity. It was a trend or facet or dimension, characteristic of all earliest Christianity in greater or less degree. It is, and always was, precisely my point that apocalyptic eschatology was too integral a part of first-century and NT Christianity to be ignored or easily disparaged.

With *chapter XIV*, 'Early Catholicism', the principal problem was the title itself. 'Early Catholicism' is becoming an outmoded term, the product of Lutheran confessionalism, and it has a distinctly pejorative ring.[36] This comment from a Lutheran member of the seminar chimed in with the criticism of one or two Roman Catholic reviewers of the first edition that in *U&D* I betrayed an 'anti-Catholic bias'.[37] Certainly, on reading through the chapter again, I could see how it could give rise to the insinuation 'that Early Catholicism was a distortion of true Christianity'.[38] That, however, was not my intention. I hope I stressed sufficiently that the several 'notes' of early catholicism are present already within the NT, which I do regard as providing the normative definition of 'true Christianity'. As I indicate in chapter XIV, I go along with the older F. C. Baur thesis at least to the extent that emerging catholicism was a catholic synthesis of several strands and tendencies (and factions) within earliest Christianity. The critical note which emerges I do not deny, but it is not a criticism of catholicism (or Catholicism) as such. Rather my concern is to point up the danger of *a catholicism which is not catholic enough*. When 'catholicism' makes a monopolistic claim and thereby excludes other elements which are *also* legitimate heirs of earliest Christianity, it becomes sectarian (whatever its breadth) rather than truly catholic.[38a] By saying this I do not mean to pass a negative judgment on catholic rejection of Gnosticism or Ebionism. But I do want to ask whether a catholicism which embraced anti-Semitism and condemned the Montanists and Messalians was sufficiently catholic. I am fully aware of the danger of playing with words here. How can a catholic church not include all Christians, since 'catholic' means 'universal'? The danger, however, remains, that in the event 'catholic' becomes a party name or factional claim which excludes others who have legitimate right to the title 'Christian'.[39] The problem of early catholicism is precisely that of the majority seeking to draw boundaries which both include and exclude round the whole body of Christian believers.

How then to avoid the pejorative ring of 'Early Catholicism'? There is no easy answer.[40] 'Early orthodoxy' might have served; but that would simply mean jumping from the frying pan into the fire, since 'Orthodoxy' became the collective name for eastern Christianity, just as 'Catholicism' became the collective name for western Christianity. Moreover, 'early catholicism' does 'plug in' to an important strand of discussion running through most of the twentieth century. In the end I decided to stay with the original term, with the single modification of using lower case for the initial letters (early catholic/catholicism, in place of Early Catholic/Catholicism), in the hope that possible confusion between early catholicism and Roman Catholicism might thereby be reduced. But also with the hope that the ambiguity embodied in the title might serve as a constant reminder of the historical problem of retaining the full sweep of legitimate diversity within the recognized forms of the church universal.

Finally, in *chapter XV*, 'The Authority of the New Testament', it is important to recognize the deliberately limited nature of the discussion. I had no intention of raising questions about the propriety of a 'canon' or legitimacy of including some writings and not others. That would have broadened the discussion far beyond the scope of the chapter. In fact I accept the legitimacy of having a canon, a definition or yardstick by which to measure Christianity (the constitutional documents of Christianity), and would be prepared to defend the inclusion of almost if not indeed all of the present documents and the exclusion of (almost all of) the rest. But in chapter XV it was more important to take the discussion a step beyond that: given the fact of the NT canon and what is in it, notice what that means. It means unity and diversity. It means that the catholic church in its wisdom recognized the normative authority of a range of writings which actually document what true catholicity embraces – unity in and through diversity.

But is the NT canon sufficiently catholic? In polemical terms, was it not the winning factions which chose just these documents to bolster and authenticate their claims to be the true heirs of the apostles? Does the canon truly represent the full diversity of first-century Christianity? The answer is No! I have already made the point that in *U&D* I move between two levels – the historical diversity of the earliest churches, and the more limited diversity of the NT writings. Two points should be emphasized. First, the extent of NT diversity needs to be reiterated: if I am right, it has to be recognized that Paul and John, to name only the most prominent, were engaged in exploring the circumference round the new movement and in pushing it back. But second, they both insisted that a line had to be drawn, a line, or lines, between acceptable and unacceptable diversity. The claim I would wish to defend, therefore, is that the canon reflects the breadth of acceptable diversity which the leading figures Peter and Paul and John recognized (and to a lesser extent, James). The canon therefore continues the guidelines which were already being drawn in the first century – guidelines drawn so as to include James as well as the early Paul, the Apocalypse as well as Acts, John as well as the Synoptics.

But did not the church select the canon? And does that not mean that early catholicism is the norm rather than the NT as such?[41] No! To say the church chose the canon is a misleading half-truth. A closer approximation would be to say that the church *recognized* the canon. That is to say, early catholicism recognized that there were certain documents which had been exercising authority within a widening circle of churches since they were delivered to their first readers. It was the fact that the Gospels and Paul were being acknowledged and were already functioning as 'canonical' more or less from the beginning which made it inevitable that they would be recognized as canonical when the idea of a closed canon became important.[42] In most cases, the formal act of canonization (itself a too formal way of describing what happened) did not bestow an authority on the NT documents which they did not already possess.[43] In a very real and important sense the major NT documents chose themselves; the NT canon chose itself! But that also means that early catholicism was not at liberty to pick and choose within these documents, though of course interpretative glosses could be and were added to some versions. They were 'chosen', canonized as they were, in all their diversity, despite the range of their diversity. I do not hesitate to claim that it was the leading of the Spirit which enabled catholicism to acknowledge as canonical a range of documents, which so richly embody the diverse vitality of that Jewish messianic renewal movement during the first two or three generations of its existence, as an inspiration and resource for similar renewal in the centuries ahead.

This too is a point which I have found needing to be made in the ecumenical discussions in which I have participated: the canonical authority of the NT needs to be reaffirmed. Despite the care with which it was formulated, it has to be asked whether the Montreal statement on 'Scripture, Tradition and Traditions', has not, after all, had the unfortunate side-effect of de-canonizing the canon.[44] If scripture is simply an expression of Tradition (the Gospel) and cannot be understood except within the tradition(s) of the church-(es), then there is a real danger that the inspired genius which recognized just these, but all these documents as canonical will be subverted and rendered of too little effect. This is in no way to dispute the problems of how these texts may or should be interpreted. It simply means that to affirm scripture as the criterion of the truth of the gospel must also mean that scripture be allowed to function in criticism of church tradition. If that principle be lost in practice, the canon of scripture has become a dead letter. *Unless the NT functions in a critical role within tradition but also over against the rest of tradition it has ceased to be canonical!* My final plea, then, in revising *U&D* is that the church once again should let the canon be the canon, as a force and measuring rod for that unity in and through diversity which is the only true unity.[45]

It remains my pleasant task to express my thanks to reviewers who welcomed and/or criticized the first edition of the book and to individual readers who had the graciousness to write and let me know when they found the theme of the book helpful. My warmest thanks, however, go to the members of the Durham postgraduate NT seminar for the magnificent help they gave me in preparing the revision, particularly those who led off the seminar on individual chapters – Jane Allison, John Chow, Ellen Christiansen, David Kupp, Bruce Longenecker, Nicholas Taylor, Ray Witbeck, and my colleague Stephen Barton. Ellen Christiansen also gave me invaluable help in revising the bibliographies. Finally, spare a thought, kind reader, for an author who finds that the most quoted words he ever wrote are those which conclude the original Preface to this book. One reviewer indeed wondered whether 'the simple-minded Christian' might not wish 'that Fiona Dunn had destroyed rather more than six pages of the typescript'! Such is fame!

University of Durham   JAMES D. G. DUNN
July, 1989

NOTES

1. Trans. Ilse von Loewenclau, Vandenhoeck & Ruprecht, forthcoming.
2. *Testing the Foundations. Current Trends in New Testament Study.* University of Durham 1984.
3. On the other hand, J. A. T. Robinson's attempt at *Redating the New Testament,* SCM Press 1976, prior to AD 70 has not carried much conviction within the guild of NT scholars; though see E. E. Ellis, 'Dating the New Testament', *NTS* 26, 1979–80, pp. 487–502.
4. G. Theissen, *The First Followers of Jesus. A Sociological Analysis of the Earliest Christianity,* SCM Press 1978 = *Soziologie der Jesusbewegung,* Kaiser 1977; *Studien zur Soziologie des Urchristentums,* WUNT 19, Tübingen 1979 = reprint of series of articles going back to 1973. J. Z. Smith, 'The Social Description of Early Christianity'. *Religious Studies Review* 1, 1975, pp. 19–25 and A. J. Malherbe, *Social Aspects of Early Christianity,* Louisiana State University 1977, alerted English readers to the importance of Theissen's work.
5. See e.g. H. C. Kee, *Christian Origins in Sociological Perspective,* SCM Press 1980; B. J. Malina, *The New Testament World. Insights from Cultural Anthropology,* SCM Press 1981; W. A. Meeks, *The First Urban Christians. The Social World of the Apostle Paul.* Yale University 1983; J. H. Elliott, ed., *Social-Scientific Criticism of the New Testament and its Social World, Semeia* 35, 1986. Further bibliography in D. J. Harrington, 'Second Testament Exegesis and the Social Sciences. A Bibliography', *Biblical Theology Bulletin* 18, 1988, pp. 77–85.
6. London: SCM Press 1977.
7. J. Neusner, *The Rabbinic Traditions about the Pharisees before 70,* Brill 1971; *From Politics to Piety. The Emergence of Pharisaic Judaism.* Prentice-Hall 1973; *Judaism. The Evidence of the Mishnah,* University of Chicago 1981; *Judaism in the Beginning of Christianity,* Fortress/SPCK 1984.
8. G. W. E. Nickelsburg, *Jewish Literature between the Bible and the Mishnah.* Fortress/SCM Press 1981; J. H. Charlesworth, ed., *The Old Testament Pseudepigrapha,* 2 vols., Darton, Longman & Todd 1983, 1985; H. F. D. Sparks, ed., *The Apocryphal Old Testament,* Clarendon 1984; M. E. Stone, ed., *Jewish Writings of the Second Temple Period.* Van Gorcum/Fortress 1984; R. A. Kraft and G. W. E. Nickelsburg, ed., *Early Judaism and its Modern Interpreters,* Scholars 1986; E. Schürer, *The History of the Jewish People in the Age of Jesus Christ,* revised and ed., G. Vermes, et al., T. & T. Clark, Vol. 3, 1986, 1987.
9. Particularly T. Wright in S. Neill and T. Wright, *The Interpretation of the New Testament 1861–1986,* 2nd edition, Oxford University 1988, pp. 381ff. Wright refers to B. F. Meyer, *The Aims of Jesus,* SCM Press 1979; A. E. Harvey, *Jesus and the Constraints of History,* Duckworth 1982; M. J. Borg, *Conflict, Holiness and Politics in the Teachings of Jesus,* Mellen 1984; and E. P. Sanders, *Jesus and Judaism,* SCM Press 1985. Others who could be mentioned as pursuing a third quest, from different perspectives, include B. Chilton, *A Galilean Rabbi and his Bible. Jesus' Own Interpretation of Isaiah,* SPCK 1984; F. G. Downing, *Jesus and the Threat of Freedom,* SCM Press 1987; R. A. Horsley, *Jesus and the Spiral of Violence. Popular Jewish Resistance in Roman Palestine,* Harper & Row 1987; R. Leivestad, *Jesus in His Own Perspective,* Augsburg 1987; G. Theissen, *The Shadow of the Galilean,* SCM Press 1987;

S. Freyne, *Galilee, Jesus and the Gospel*, Gill & Macmillan 1988; I. M. Zeitlin, *Jesus and the Judaism of his Time*, Polity 1988; J. H. Charlesworth, *Jesus within Judaism. New Light from Exciting Archaeological Discoveries*, SPCK 1989.

10. J. D. G. Dunn, *Jesus, Paul and the Law: Essays on Mark and Galatians*, London: SPCK, 1990, with bibliography.

11. See e.g. D. Rhoads and D. Michie, *Mark as Story. An Introduction to the Narrative of a Gospel*, Fortress 1982; R. A. Culpepper, *Anatomy of the Fourth Gospel. A Study in Literary Design*, Fortress 1983; E. V. McKnight, *The Bible and the Reader. An Introduction to Literary Criticism*, Fortress 1985; R. C. Tannehill, *The Narrative Unity of Luke–Acts. A Literary Interpretation. Vol. 1: The Gospel according to Luke*, Fortress 1986; D. Jasper, *The New Testament and the Literary Imagination*, Macmillan 1987; N. R. Petersen, *Literary Criticism for New Testament Critics*, Fortress 1978. For what we may call historical literary criticism see particularly D. E. Aune, *The New Testament in its Literary Environment*, Westminster 1987. For a positive critique see R. Morgan & J. Barton, *Biblical Interpretation*, Oxford University 1988, ch. 7.

12. One of the most surprising reviews of *U&D* criticized me for not taking the diversity of the NT seriously enough and for making it of peripheral importance (T. Radcliffe, *New Blackfriars*, July 1978, pp. 334–6)! The point being made eludes me.

13. The principal point about unity being consistent with and consisting in diversity has been taken in ecumenical discussion; see e.g. M. Kinnamon, *Truth and Community*, World Council of Churches/Eerdmans 1988, pp. 1–7.

14. Only one of my papers has so far been published – 'Die Instrumente kirchlicher Gemeinschaft in der frühen Kirche', *Una Sancta* 44.1, 1989, pp. 2–13. One aspect of what I have attempted to say is summed up in my protest against overuse of the metaphor of 'convergence', since 'convergence' means, by definition, narrowing: the traffic of two motorways which 'converge' is then restricted within the limits of one motorway. A better metaphor would be that of 'confluence': two rivers merging become one river, but a broader and/or deeper river than either of the two tributaries. See further below n. 15.

15. The issue has now been addressed by W. Schrage, 'Zur Frage nach der Einheit und Mitte neutestamentlicher Ethik', *Die Mitte des Neuen Testaments. Einheit und Vielfalt neutestamentlicher Theologie*, E. Schweizer Festschrift, hrsg. U. Luz and H. Weder, Vandenhoeck 1983, pp. 238–53.

16. J. C. Beker, *Paul the Apostle*, Philadelphia: Fortress, 1980.

17. So also Robinson (n. 22 below) p. 25 n. 62; but see also his own affirmation of the need to recognize the diversity within earliest Christian unity (p. 29); and contrast R. A. Markus, 'The Problem of Self-Definition: From Sect to Church'. *Jewish and Christian Self-Definition. Vol. One: The Shaping of Christianity in the Second and Third Centuries*, ed. E. P. Sanders, SCM Press 1980, p. 8.

18. See also ch. XV, n. 7. K. Berger in his review of the first edition (*ThR* 53, 1988, p. 366) chides me for proposing 'a pale, humanistic ecumenism, whose greatest virtue is tolerance, for which one should wish something more of the – positively understood – intolerance of the OT and Jewish belief in God . . .'. In defence I would simply say: (*a*) tolerance in itself is not the virtue, but tolerance in the face of intolerance; (*b*) Jesus himself is the model of such tolerance (e.g. Mark 9.38–40; Matt. 11.19) – another aspect of the centre determining the circumference; (*c*) it is such acceptance (i.e. dynamic tolerance) within the framework of the common faith (see again ch. XV n. 7) which is still needed in modern ecumenism. Nevertheless, I recognize that there is an uncomfortable tension to be maintained

here, between whole-hearted commitment and openness/tolerance, and should like
to reflect further on it as being one of the greatest challenges confronting Christian
(as indeed any) claim to truth.

19. See e.g. those cited in my *The Living Word*, SCM Press 1987, p. 175 n. 6.

20. See further *The Living Word* (n. 19).

21. In fairness I should perhaps also note that in general Roman Catholic
reviews were among the most positive and welcoming.

22. See particularly D. J. Harrington, 'The Reception of Walter Bauer's
Orthodoxy and Heresy in Earliest Christianity During the Last Decade', *HTR* 73, 1980,
pp. 289–98; T. A. Robinson, *The Bauer Thesis Examined. The Geography of Heresy in the
Earliest Christian Church*, Edwin Mellen 1988.

23. H. Koester, *Introduction to the New Testament. Vol. 2. History and Literature of Early
Christianity*, Fortress 1982.

24. Perhaps I could refer to the similar comment and pleas which I make in *The
Evidence for Jesus*, SCM Press 1985, ch. 1.

25. See chs. 1–3 (above n. 10), and most of those cited in n. 9.

26. See J. H. Schutz, *Paul and the Anatomy of Apostolic Authority*, SNTSMS 26,
Cambridge University 1975; B. Holmberg, *Paul and Power. The Structure of Authority in
the Primitive Church as Reflected in the Pauline Epistles*, CWK Gleerup 1978; R. Banks,
Paul's Idea of Community, Paternoster 1980; Meeks (n. 5 above) particularly ch. 4;
M. Y. MacDonald, *The Pauline Churches. A socio-historical study of institutionalization in
the Pauline and Deutero-Pauline Writings*, SNTSMS 60, Cambridge University 1988.

27. Cf. the discussion of Holmberg, *Paul and Power*, and M. Y. MacDonald,
Pauline Churches, who both wish to distinguish degrees of institutionalization –
'cumulative institutionalization' (Holmberg), 'community-building institutionalization' – Paul, 'community stabilizing institutionalization – Colossians and Ephesians, and 'community-protecting institutionalization' – Pastorals (MacDonald).

28. See ch. VI n. 26. It is the discussion of community as focused in ministry
which explains why the emphasis on Johannine 'individualism' can still stand; not
as a denial of what we can call Johannine community (or communities), but as a
way of characterizing the spirituality inculcated in these communities (see also
pp. 358–9).

29. The historical importance of ministry as a category in catholic tradition and
ecumenical discussion is clearly shown by the prominence it receives in such
documents as *Lumen Gentium*, the Vatican II statement on the Church, 1965; the
Anglican–Roman Catholic International Commission's *Agreed Statement on Ministry
and Ordination*, 1973; *Baptism, Eucharist and Ministry*, World Council of Churches
1982.

30. See Knox as in ch. IX n. 2, pp. 1–4.

31. *Jesus and the Spirit*, SCM Press/Westminster 1975.

32. *Christology in the Making*, SCM Press/Westminster 1980.

33. See particularly R. Murray, 'Jews, Hebrews and Christians: Some Needed
Distinctions', *NovTest* 24, 1982, pp. 194–208. On the other hand, I should perhaps
point out that the conclusion to chapter XI (p. 265 below) in large measure
anticipated the fourfold categorization suggested by R. E. Brown, 'Not Jewish
Christianity and Gentile Christianity but Types of Jewish/Gentile Christianity',
CBQ 45, 1983, pp. 74–9.

34. See particularly S. Sandmel, *Anti-Semitism in the New Testament*, Fortress 1978;
A. T. Davies, ed., *AntiSemitism and the Foundations of Christianity*, Paulist 1979;
J. Koenig, *Jews and Christians in Dialogue. New Testament Foundations*, Westminster

1979; F. Mussner, *Tractate on the Jews. The Significance of Judaism for Christian Faith*, 1979, ET Fortress/SPCK 1984; J. G. Gager, *The Origins of Anti-Semitism. Attitudes Towards Judaism in Pagan and Christian Antiquity*, Oxford University 1983; N. A. Beck, *Mature Christianity. The Recognition and Repudiation of the Anti-Jewish Polemic of the New Testament*, Associated University Presses 1985; P. Richardson, ed., *Anti-Judaism in Early Christianity. Vol. I. Paul and the Gospels*, Wilfrid Laurier University 1986; S. G. Wilson, ed., *Anti-Judaism in Early Christianity. Vol. 2. Separation and Polemic.* Wilfrid Laurier University 1986; M. R. Wilson, *Our Father Abraham. Jewish Roots of the Christian Faith*, Eerdmans 1989.

35. See the more careful statement in J. J. Collins, *The Apocalyptic Imagination*, Crossroad 1984, p. 9. I thus accept the main point of Rowland's strictures on the first edition (*The Open Heaven*, SPCK 1982, pp. 354–6), though he does not give enough weight to the fact that 'resurrection of the dead' is itself an apocalyptic category in the sense that it first emerged in apocalyptic writing and is a feature of several major apocalypses.

36. 'A German Protestant construct, of more use in ecumenical anatomy than in new Testament study' (Murray, 'Jews, Hebrews and Christians' p. 197). See also F. Hahn, 'Das Problem des Frühkatholizismus', *Exegetische Beiträge zum ökumenischen Gespräch*, Göttingen 1986, pp. 62–6; W. Trilling, 'Bemerkungen zum Thema "Frühkatholizismus". Eine Skizze', in J. Rogge and G. Schille, hrsg., *Frühkatholizismus im ökumenischen Gesprach*, Berlin 1983, pp. 62–70.

37. R. Kugelman, C.P., in *Theological Studies*, December 4, 1978, p. 780.

38. *Ibid.* On the other hand, as F. Hahn notes, Roman Catholic scholars have quite naturally seized upon the term for its value as evidence of the Catholic beginnings of Christianity in what might be called a riposte apologetic (F. Hahn, 'Frühkatholizismus als ökumenisches Problem', *Beiträge* pp. 59–60). For a positive and eirenic discussion see H. Schürmann, 'Auf der Suche nach dem "Evangelisch-Katholischen". Zum Thema "Frühkatholizismus" in J. Rogge and G. Schille, *Frühkatholizismus im ökumenischen Gespräch*, Berlin 1983, pp. 71–107.

38a. I hope this restatement of my point meets the criticism of Berger in his *ThR* 53, 1988, review (p. 366).

39. O. Cullmann reports that the written outline of a speech given by Pope John Paul II during the 1980 anniversary celebration of the Augsburg Confession contained the statement: 'The Spirit of God has allowed us to recognize anew that as long as the church has not realized the fullness of its God-willed catholicity there are authentic elements of Catholicism existing outside its visible community' (*Unity through Diversity*, Fortress 1988, p. 21).

40. Integral to the problem is the fact that 'Early Catholicism' is an English translation of the German Frühkatholizismus, and that in German Katholik and katholisch refer to Roman Catholic. There is no real German equivalent to the English 'catholic' = universal. In the German version of the creeds the equivalent phrase to 'holy catholic church' is 'heilige christliche Kirche' (holy Christian Church).

41. 'The fundamental weakness of D.'s position is neglect of the implications that flow from the historical fact that it was the Early Catholicism of the second century which selected the NT writings and constituted that selection as the canon, the norm and measure of genuine Christianity' (Kugelman p. 781).

42. See also my 'Levels of Canonical Authority', *Horizons in Biblical Authority* 4, 1982, pp. 13–60, reprinted in *The Living Word*, SCM Press 1987, pp. 141–74.

43. The statement is arguably true, however, for some of the documents which

were accepted only after lengthy debate.
44. Republished in *Apostolic Faith Today*, ed. H.-G. Link, World Council of Churches Geneva 1985, pp. 79–83.
45. Cf. the valuable agenda of questions posed by Schürmann, 'Suche', pp. 90–91.

ABBREVIATIONS

AHGFFB	*Apostolic History and the Gospel: Biblical and Hisorical Essays Presented to F. F. Bruce,* ed., W. W. Gasque and R. P. Martin, Paternoster 1970
Arndt-Gingrich	W. F. Arndt and F. W. Gingrich, *A Greek-English Lexicon, of the New Testament,* ET Chicago 1957
BJRL	*Bulletin of the John Rylands Library*
BNTE	*The Background of the New Testament and its Eschatology: Studies in Honour of C. H. Dodd,* ed., W. D. Davies and D. Daube, Cambridge University Press 1954
BZ	*Biblische Zeitschrift*
CBQ	*Catholic Biblical Quarterly*
CINTI	*Current Issues in New Testament Interpretation,* ed., W. Klassen and G. F. Snyder, SCM Press 1962
CSNT	*Christ and Spirit in the New Testament: Studies in Honour of C. F. D. Moule,* ed., B. Lindars and S. S. Smalley, Cambridge University Press 1973
ed.	editor
EKK	Evangelisch-Katholischer Kommentar zum Neuen Testament
ENTT	E. Käsemann, *Essays on New Testament Themes,* ET SCM Press 1964
ET	English translation
EvTh	*Evangelische Theologie*
ExpT	*Expository Times*
FRP	*The Future of our Religious Past: Essays in Honour of Rudolf Bultmann,* ed., J. M. Robinson, SCM Press 1971
HE	Eusebius, *Historia Ecclesiastica*
Hennecke, *Apocrypha*	E. Hennecke, *New Testament Apocrypha,* ed.,

	W. Schneemelcher, ET ed., R. McL. Wilson, SCM Press, Vol. I. 1973, Vol. II 1974
HNT	Handbuch zum Neuen Testament
HTR	*Harvard Theological Review*
IDB	*The Interpreter's Dictionary of the Bible*, Abingdon 1962, 4 vols.
IDBS	*IDB* Supplementary Volume 1976
JBL	*Journal of Biblical Literature*
JCHT	*Jesus Christus in Historie und Theologie: Neutestamentliche Festschrift für H. Conzelmann*, ed., G. Strecker, Tübingen 1975
JSJ	*Journal for the Study of Judaism*
JSNT	*Journal for the Study of the New Testament*
JSOT	*Journal for the Study of the Old Testament*
JThC	*Journal for Theology and Church*
JTS	*Journal of Theological Studies*
JuP	*Jesus und Paulus: Festschrift für W. G. Kümmel*, ed., E. E. Ellis and E. Grässer, Göttingen 1975
KEK	Kritisch-exegetischer Kommentar über das Neue Testament
KuD	*Kerygma und Dogma*
LXX	Septuagint
LTK	*Lexikon für Theologie und Kirche*
MBBR	*Mélanges Bibliques en hommage au R. P. Béda Rigaux*, ed., A. Descamps and A. de Halleux, Gembloux 1970
NEB	New English Bible
NIDNTT	*The New International Dictionary of New Testament Theolgy*, Paternoster 1975f.
NovTest	*Novum Testamentum*
ns	new series
NTD	Das Neue Testament Deutsch
NTETWM	*New Testament Essays: Studies in Memory of T. W. Manson*, ed., A. J. B. Higgins, Manchester University Press 1959
NTK	*Neues Testament und Kirche: für R. Schnackenburg*, ed., J. Gnilka, Freiburg 1974
NTQT	E. Käsemann, *New Testament Questions of Today*, ET SCM Press 1969
NTS	*New Testament Studies*

par.	parallel
RB	*Revue Biblique*
*RGG*³	*Die Religion in Geschichte und Gegenwart,* ³1957ff.
SBL	Society of Biblical Literature
SBLMS	Society of Biblical Literature Monograph Series
SJT	*Scottish Journal of Theology*
SLA	*Studies in Luke Acts*, ed., L. E. Keck and J. L. Martyn, Abingdon 1966, and SPCK 1968
SNT	Supplement to *Novum Testamentum*
SNTSMS	Society for New Testament Study Monograph Series
Strack-Billerbeck	H. L. Strack and P. Billerbeck, *Kommentar zum Neuen Testament aus Talmud und Midrasch*, 1920ff.
TDNT	*Theological Dictionary of the New Testament*, ET of *Theologisches Wörterbuch zum Neuen Testament*, ed., G. Kittel and G. Friedrich, 1933ff.
ThR	*Theologische Rundschau*
TZ	*Theologische Zeitschrift*
WUNT	Wissenschaftliche Untersuchungen zum Neuen Testament
ZKG	*Zeitschrift für Kirchengeschichte*
ZKT	*Zeitschrift für Katholische Theologie*
ZNW	*Zeitschrift für die neutestamentliche Wissenschaft*
ZTK	*Zeitscrift für Theologie und Kirche*

I

INTRODUCTION

§1. IS 'ORTHODOXY' A MEANINGFUL CONCEPT WITHIN THE NEW TESTAMENT PERIOD?

The relation between orthodoxy and heresy has always been important in the history of Christianity. Orthodoxy has traditionally been thought of as conformity to 'the apostolic faith'. Up until the twentieth century the tendency has always been for each church, denomination or sect to claim a *monopoly* of this faith, to deny it to others, to ignore, denounce or persecute the others as heretics. A particular line of interpretation (rarely recognized as such) proves the apostolicity of the faith held, and the rest are denied apostolicity – because, so the polemic usually runs, they have added to, subtracted from or in some way corrupted 'the faith'. The test or criterion of apostolicity has been variously the apostolic writings, 'the gospel', secret apostolic traditions, the developing tradition of the Church, the ecumenical creeds; or, in more institutional terms, apostolic succession, the Church in council, the Pope; or, in more individualistic terms, the immediate inspiration of the Spirit, an 'inner light'.

There is an immediate problem with terms. 'Orthodoxy' implies that a clear distinction can be drawn between truth and error. 'Orthodoxy' implies that there is a pure, uncontaminated faith, a correct teaching; all variations from it are then at once 'heretical' in greater or less degree. In the simplest form of the antithesis, 'orthodoxy' means God's absolute truth revealed to the Church, and 'heresy' denotes any deviation from that single, clearly defined faith. Two problems at once arise.

(*a*) First, a *theological* problem, *the problem of interpretation,* summed up in the question, *Whose* orthodoxy? It is a simple fact that there is no single orthodoxy in modern Christianity: the concept of orthodoxy in Eastern Christianity is very different from that prevalent among Western Christians; Roman Catholic orthodoxy is not the same as Protestant orthodoxy, and Pentecostal orthodoxy is something different again; the orthodoxy of the 'anglo-catholic' is not the orthodoxy of the 'evangelical', and neither would satisfy the 'liberal' and the 'radical'. Quite clearly each understands and interprets the concept 'orthodoxy' in his own way. Even those who agree on one criterion of orthodoxy find interpretation a problem. For example, Protestants have generally agreed that the Bible must have the central and fundamental role in determining faith and life (*sola scriptura*); but the fragmentation of Protestantism and Protestant sects demonstrates that no agreed orthodoxy has emerged.

The problem of interpretation thus raises the basic question: *Is there a final expression of Christian truth whose meaning is unequivocal? Can* there be such a final expression? Is truth finally reducible to a formula or a statement or a way of doing things which is eternal and unchangeable? Or does the subjectiveness of our apprehension and the relativeness of our situation mean that such finality can never be achieved? Is it not significant that even for traditional Christianity the final revelation of truth was made in a person, Jesus of Nazareth, and not in a statement? – can a man ever be reduced to a statement?[1a] The ramifications of this problem stretch far and wide through Christianity and theology. We will have to keep it at the back of our minds throughout the following chapters and return to it at the end.

(*b*) The second problem about the very idea of a Christian orthodoxy is the one which provides the agenda for the present study – a *historical* problem. *Was there ever in fact such an orthodoxy?* – a single clearly defined faith which separated Christian from heretic? The traditional answer from within Christianity has been that there was. The classical view of orthodoxy is that there always has been a single, pure faith reaching right back to the apostles, that the Church has kept the teaching of Jesus and the apostles undefiled. In the fight against heresy from the latter decades of the second century onwards the typical picture presented by orthodoxy was that heresy was a corrupt offshoot from the true faith; in all cases the pure teaching of orthodoxy had been established first; only at a later stage did the wolves and false teachers appear to disturb the flock and distort the faith. Thus, for example, Eusebius quotes Hegesippus to the effect that 'godless error' only began to penetrate into the Church in the second century when all the apostles had passed on, before which time the Church 'had remained a virgin, pure and uncorrupted' (*HE*, III.32.7–8). Similarly Tertullian, one of the earliest and doughtiest champions of this view of orthodoxy and heresy:

> Were Christians found before Christ? Or heresy before true doctrine? But in everything truth precedes its counterfeit. It would be absurd to regard heresy as the prior doctrine since it is prophesied that heresy should arise (*prae. haer.*, 29).

And the same writer castigates and characterizes Marcion as 'a deserter before he became a heretic' (*adv.Marc.*, 1.1).

This had been the generally accepted view of orthodoxy until this century. But the important work of W. Bauer, *Orthodoxy and Heresy in Earliest Christianity*,[1] has demonstrated how slight a foothold this view has in historical fact and it can no longer seriously be maintained. Bauer has shown that second-century Christianity was a very mixed bag. There was no 'pure' form of Christianity that existed in the beginning which can properly be called 'orthodoxy'. In fact there was no uniform concept of orthodoxy at all – only different forms of Christianity competing for the loyalty of believers. In many places, particularly Egypt and eastern Syria, it is more likely that what later churchmen called heterodox Christianity was the initial form of Christianity, the dominant force in the early decades of Christianity's establishment in these areas. The concept of orthodoxy only began to emerge in the struggle between different viewpoints – the party that won claimed the title 'orthodox' for itself! Our viewpoint today is distorted because we hear the voice of only one of the parties – Clement, Ignatius, Polycarp, Irenaeus, etc. – and only echoes and quotations from the Ebionites, Marcion, the Montanists, etc.

Bauer confined his researches more or less to the second century. What of first-century Christianity? Here the myth of the virgin Church has been compounded with a belief in the initial period of Christianity as a time of unique (apostolic) inspiration – with the sub-apostolic period often represented as a sort of fall from primeval purity. This idealized view of a 'canonical' age of earliest Christianity, in which the apostles spoke with one authoritative voice on all matters of importance, had already been rudely challenged a century before W. Bauer by his near namesake F. C. Baur. Where Catholic orthodoxy had secured its picture of primitive purity by (in effect) subordinating Paul to Peter, and Protestant orthodoxy by making Paul the integrating focus of earliest Christianity, Baur postulated a *conflict* between Petrine and Pauline Christianity, as evidenced particularly by Galatians, and argued that the whole course of earliest Christianity was shaped by the opposition between these two parties. Baur attempted to force the stream of early Christian history into too narrow a channel. But his recognition that there was more than one current in that stream and that its course was far from calm and untroubled was of lasting importance. Since then we have come to realize that the stream of first-century Christianity was much broader than Baur had imagined, that there were many currents and crosscurrents running in it, and that its banks crumbled away at many points. In particular, two major new disciplines of the twentieth century – history of religions research (*Religionsgeschichte*), and the study of the history of earliest Christian traditions (*Traditionsgeschichte*) – have confirmed that the antithesis of Jewish (Petrine) Christianity and Hellenistic (Pauline) Christianity was too sharp; at many points we have to recognize a Hellenistic Christianity prior to Paul and to distinguish Palestinian Jewish Christianity from Hellenistic Jewish Christianity – without, of course, allowing these to become rigid categories in turn. To put it another way, *Religionsgeschichte* and *Traditionsgeschichte* have brought home to NT scholarship *the historical relativity of first-century Christianity* and *the fragmentary nature of our knowledge of it*. No longer is it possible to conceive of first-century Christianity as a clearly defined entity, easily extractable from its historical context like a nut from its shell; the historical reality was much more complex, and our view of it much less clear than once we thought.[2]

It obviously follows that the traditional concept of first-century Christian orthodoxy cannot remain unaffected by these developments. This has been seen most clearly by R. Bultmann and his pupils. For example, Bultmann himself in the last part of his magisterial *Theology of the New Testament*[3] draws attention to the considerable diversity of theological interests and ideas in the earliest period, and points out that 'a norm or an authoritative court of appeal for doctrine' is lacking throughout this period.

> In the beginning, *faith* is the term which distinguishes the Christian Congregation from Jews and the heathen, not *orthodoxy* (right doctrine). The latter along with its correlate, *heresy*, arises out of the differences which develop within the Christian congregations.[4]

Bultmann's pupils have carried the discussion forward with some bold claims. H. Braun maintains that 'the essentially Christian element, the constant . . . in the New Testament' is the 'self-understanding of faith'.[5] E. Käsemann regards the Fourth Gospel not as the voice of orthodoxy, but as an expression of a 'naive docetism' – a way of presenting Jesus which developed into the heresy of Docetism proper.[6] Even bolder was his earlier treatment of III John: the author ('the presbyter') is not the defender of orthodoxy attacking the heretic Diotrephes; on the contrary, Diotrephes is the 'orthodox' leader of the community addressed, while the presbyter is a 'Christian Gnostic'! Diotrephes acts as a 'monarchial bishop' defending himself against a false teacher.[7] And H. Koester, in extending W. Bauer's method to an investigation of first-century Christianity, writes:

> We have to do here with a religious movement which is syncretistic in appearance and conspicuously marked by diversification from the very beginning. What its individuality is cannot be taken as established *a priori*.[8]

The question therefore becomes more and more insistent: *Was there ever a single orthodoxy within primitive Christianity, within the New Testament?* Even more basic, *can we properly use the concepts 'orthodoxy' and 'heresy'?* Is it meaningful to speak of 'orthodoxy' within the context of first-century Christianity? H. E. W. Turner attempted to defend the concept in his 1954 Bampton Lectures, *The Pattern of Christian Truth: A Study in the Relations between Orthodoxy and Heresy in the Early Church*.[9] He rejected the major thrust of Bauer's thesis and argued in contrast that second century Christianity could be seen in terms of an orthodoxy surrounded by a 'penumbra' or fringe where the borderline between orthodoxy and heresy was still blurred (pp.81–94). In the earliest period 'orthodoxy was a matter rather of instinctive feeling than of fixed and definable doctrinal norms' (pp.9f.). Before the written creed there was a *lex orandi*, 'a relatively *full* and *fixed* experimental grasp of what was involved religiously in being a Christian' (p.28 – my emphasis). But is this satisfactory? Does it pay sufficient heed to the large scale diversity (and disagreement) within earliest Christianity of which NT scholarship has become increasingly aware since F. C. Baur? At the opposite extreme J. Charlot maintains that 'No theological position . . . is common to all writers and levels of tradition in the New Testament'.[10] But is this any more satisfactory? Did the earliest Christians hold *nothing* in common?

In attempting to examine this whole issue afresh it would seem wiser to avoid the use of the terms 'orthodoxy' and 'heresy' at least as the basic categories of discussion: the concepts beg too many questions, are too emotive, provide categories that are far too rigid, and tend to close off avenues of investigation rather than to open them up. What alternative terminology is there? One possibility is to use the metaphor introduced into the discussion by J. M. Robinson. He calls on NT scholarship to break out of its old, rather static categories and for a reinvestigation of NT and other first- and second-century material more in terms of 'trajectory' or direction of movement. The deficiencies of the metaphor are obvious, and Robinson is aware of them,[11] but the language of trajectory does bring out the fact that primitive Christianity was a living, moving process, developing all the time in different ways and different directions in response to diverse influences and challenges. The metaphor will prove to be of some value in Part II of the present study, but less so in Part I where we will be examining a series of cross-sections through the NT material. The more useful terminology for our purposes is the language of our title – 'unity' and 'diversity': it is both less colourful and less emotive and will, I think, permit a greater flexibility in the discussion.

Our basic question thus becomes: *Was there a unifying strand in earliest Christianity which identifies it as Christianity?* If so, how well defined was it? Was it a broad or a narrow strand? Was it defined in different ways? Was there a *diversity* of faith and practice? – diversity *within* the unity, diversity *around* the unifying centre? If so, how broad was the range of diversity? Where did valid or acceptable diversity fall over into unacceptable conduct or teaching? What agreement was there about such boundary marks on different issues, in different environments? Throughout the discussion we will have to remind ourselves that the problem of unity and diversity does not refer solely to earliest Christianity proper, but becomes if anything more pressing when we include within it the relation of earliest Christianity to Jesus himself. Does a unity exist between Jesus and the different post-Easter developments? Does Jesus' own concept and practice of religion and his own self-understanding stretch the diversity of first-century Christianity even further? In short, what was the unity, the unifying element, the uniting force in earliest Christianity? And what breadth of diversity existed in Christianity from the first?

The study which follows is intended to be provocative rather than definitive, to demonstrate the unity and diversity rather than to document them in any comprehensive way. We begin by asking what were the characteristic emphases in the gospel as presented by the four figures whose teachings or writings form the bulk of the NT – Jesus, Luke, Paul and John. We will see that even when we take the NT documents at face value the breadth of diversity is not inconsiderable, though it is possible to speak of a unifying core for the post-Easter kerygma at any rate (ch. II). Thereafter in Part I we will endeavour to penetrate below the surface of the NT documents, sinking, as it were, a series of exploratory shafts into the NT material at various key points. Our task in each case will be to examine the diverse strands and layers thereby uncovered in order to ascertain whether the same unifying element or indeed any unifying element is present throughout. We will examine first the area of primitive Christianity's preaching and teaching, the various oral and/or written formulations whereby its distinctive faith came to expression in words or wherein it found inspiration and authority for that faith – primitive confessional formulae (ch. III), various oral traditions some inherited and some created by the first Christians (ch. IV), and the OT itself (ch. V). Secondly we will turn to the area of primitive Christianity's organization and worship, its concepts of ministry and community (ch. VI), its patterns of worship (ch. VII), its ritual acts (ch. VIII). Part I will conclude with a study of the two most obviously common and foundational elements in first generation Christianity, experience of Spirit (ch. IX) and faith in Christ (ch. X). Even here there is no little diversity – but unity too?

In Part II our objective changes. Where previously we sought the unity within the diversity, now we seek to map out in a limited way the range and scope of that diversity. Accordingly our procedure changes too, and we attempt to identify and trace the major currents within the stream of first and second generation Christianity, to see how Christianity developed through the first century and how first-century Christians reacted to developments both within and around Christianity. Without forgetting what was said above (p.4) our study here is most conveniently pursued under the headings of Jewish Christianity (ch. XI), Hellenistic Christianity (ch. XII), Apocalyptic Christianity (ch. XIII) and Early Catholicism (ch. XIV). This investigation of unity and diversity in the NT inevitably raises many questions about the status of the NT itself within Christianity, and in the Conclusions we will look at some of the repercussions of our findings on the idea of the NT canon and its authority for Christians today (ch. XV).

PART ONE

UNITY IN DIVERSITY?

II

KERYGMA OR KERYGMATA?

§2. INTRODUCTION

Preaching has a role of quite fundamental importance in the NT. Jesus' public ministry is regularly characterized in terms of preaching. Preaching is always the means to conversion in Acts. Preaching features prominently as Paul's mode of evangelism. John too links the 'word' with the 'Spirit' as the recreative power of God. And James and I Peter likewise attribute spiritual regeneration to the word preached. So proclamation of the gospel, or kerygma, to use the technical term of modern debate, is a key area to examine.

The problem which confronts us can be posed simply: Can we speak of 'the NT kerygma'? or ought we rather to speak of NT *kerygmata*? Was there one single, normative expression of the gospel in the earliest days of Christianity? Or were there many different expressions of the gospel, with no one having a better claim to be *the* gospel than any other, but *all* were the gospel?

The first problem is that of *definition*. 'Kerygma' can mean either *what* is preached, or the *act* of preaching (cf. Rom. 16.25, I Cor. 1.21 and 2.4 where it could have either sense). In the debate about the kerygma in the NT, C. H. Dodd has focused attention on kerygma as *content*, R. Bultmann on kerygma as *preaching*.[1]

In his well known study, *The Apostolic Preaching and its Developments*[2] Dodd drew from an analysis of the speeches in Acts and the Pauline epistles the following outline as the core of the primitive kerygma:

> The prophecies are fulfilled, and the new Age is inaugurated by the coming of Christ.
> He was born of the seed of David.
> He died according to the Scriptures, to deliver us out of the present evil age.
> He was buried.
> He rose on the third day according to the Scriptures.

He is exalted at the right hand of God, as Son of God and Lord of quick and dead. He will come again as Judge and Saviour of men (p.17).

This he considers to be 'a fairly clear and certain outline sketch of the preaching of the apostles' (p.31). He recognizes that 'within the NT there is an immense range of variety in the interpretation that is given to the *kerygma*'; but is equally convinced that 'in all such interpretation the essential elements of the original *kerygma* are steadily kept in view . . . . With all the diversity of the New Testament writings, they form a unity in their proclamation of the one Gospel' (p.74). Dodd's position is clear: despite diversity, there is still something he can call '*the* kerygma', 'the one Gospel'.

The so-called kerygmatic theologians on the other hand have focused attention primarily on the kerygma as *preaching,* on the act of proclamation in the immediacy of the present rather than on the record of what was proclaimed in the past. The kerygma, claims Bultmann,

is neither an enlightening *Weltanschauung* (world view) flowing out in general truths, nor a merely historical account, which, like a reporter's story, reminds a public of important but by-gone facts. Rather . . . it is, by nature, personal address which accosts each individual, throwing the person himself into question by rendering his self-understanding problematic, and demanding a decision of him.[3]

In so far as Bultmann's case depends on the use of the word *kerygma* in the NT he is building on a firm foundation; for of the seven occurrences of the word some are best understood as denoting the *act* of preaching (particularly Matt. 12.41/Luke 11.32; I Cor. 15.14) and none requires reference to content. A point of some importance therefore at once emerges: that *kerygma in the NT probably includes the idea of proclamation at a particular time and place.* That is to say, kerygma is always situational to some degree – to some degree conditioned by the circumstances which called the proclamation forth. This in turn makes it very unlikely that the kerygma can simply be abstracted from these different contexts as a fixed formula which can be applied without change or modification in any and every situation. Our question thus becomes, Can we find an absolute form of the kerygma in the NT? or will it always be relative to some extent? And if so, *how* relative? Is there underlying the different forms a common element, however differently conceived and expressed? It is worth noting that Bultmann, like Dodd, is quite happy to speak of 'the kerygma'. But can we properly so speak? – kerygma or kerygmata? one gospel or many gospels?

In tackling this question there is a constant danger of losing sight of the wood because of the trees. It seems wiser therefore not to plunge too quickly into the analysis of particular texts, but to concentrate on building up a broader picture. Our method then in this chapter is to make as it were an aerial survey of the most important proclamations of the gospel in the NT, concentrating on picking out the characteristic features of each kerygma rather than attempting a fully balanced treatment of the whole. The answers to our questions which this method provides will inevitably be first approximations; but at least by the end of the chapter we should see more clearly that the diversity of the NT writings is a factor of considerable importance in our evaluation of first-century Christianity and that it has many facets and ramifications. Then, having shown that there is a *prima facie* case for our study, we can go on to examine it with much greater care and in much greater detail.

§3. THE KERYGMA OF JESUS

All three Synoptic Gospels[4] characterize Jesus' public ministry in summary statements as 'preaching the gospel of God' (Mark 1.14), 'preaching the gospel of the kingdom' (Matt. 4.23; 9.35), 'preaching the good news of the kingdom of God' (Luke 4.43; 8.1; 16.16). The key word here obviously is 'kingdom of God'; for Mark too goes on to define Jesus' proclamation of the gospel of God in terms of 'the kingdom of God': 'The time is fulfilled, and the kingdom of God is at hand; repent, and believe in the gospel' (Mark 1.15). In this one sentence the main features of Jesus' kerygma are encapsulated.

3.1 *'The kingdom of God is at hand'* (Mark 1.15; Matt. 10.7; Luke 21.31). 'The kingdom of God' here denotes the manifest rule of God whose intervention will bring to an end the history of this world as we know it and its judgment (Matt. 10.15/Luke 10.12; Matt. 24.37–44/Luke 17.26–36). The kingdom is at hand – it will come within the lifetime of Jesus' own generation (Mark 9.1; 13.28–30; Matt. 10.23). This is why 'the poor' are blessed, because they belong to the coming kingdom (Luke 6.20/Matt. 5.3), when God will soon set right all men's injustices (Luke 16.19–31; 18.7f.; Matt. 23.33). This is the gospel to 'the poor' (Matt. 11.5/Luke 7.22; Luke 4.18). It is for this that Jesus' disciples have to pray – 'May your kingdom come' (Matt. 6.10/Luke 11.2).

The imminence of the end-time rule of God sharpens the challenge of Jesus' kerygma to the point of crisis. In the light of the coming kingdom men must decide, and decide now. Hence among the parables, Jesus' most distinctive mode of preaching, we find a number of parables of crisis, where the note of warning sounds loud and clear – in particular, the parable(s) of the absent householder, for whose return the servants have to be prepared (Mark 13.34–36; Luke 12.36–38; Matt. 24.42,45–51/Luke 12.42–46); the parable about the thief coming unexpectedly (Matt. 24.43f./Luke 12.39f.); and the parable of the ten virgins (Matt. 25.1–12). See also Mark 13.14–20 (and further below pp. 73, 320).

The failure of these expectations to materialize, at least in the most obvious way, has always been a problem for Christian theology (see below §§7.2; 50.3). But we must recognize this expectation of the kingdom of God's imminence to be part of Jesus' kerygma, otherwise we do scant justice to a key and characteristic emphasis of his public proclamation (see more fully below §67.2). But even more distinctive of his kerygma was his proclamation that the kingdom of God was in some way already being realized through his ministry.

3.2 'The time is fulfilled.' According to the Synpotics, Jesus also proclaimed that the end-time rule of God was already manifesting itself through his own words and actions. The long cherished hope of the messianic age was already beginning to be fulfilled (Matt. 11.5/Luke 7.22; Matt. 11.11/Luke 7.28; Matt. 11.12/Luke 16.16; Matt. 12.41f./Luke 11.31f.).

> Blessed are your eyes, for they see, and your ears, for they hear. Truly, I say to you, many prophets and righteous men longed to see what you see, and did not see it, and to hear what you hear, and did not hear it (Matt. 13.16f./Luke 10.23f.).

In specific terms, the kingdom was already in the midst of his hearers (Luke 17.20f.); the binding of Satan was expected at the end of the age, but Jesus claimed that Satan was already being routed (Mark 3.27; Luke 10.18); Jesus' power over evil spirits in exorcism was proof positive that the kingdom of God had already come upon them (Matt. 12.28/Luke 11.20).

The same note of fulfilment comes through in several of Jesus' other parables – the picture of the wedding feast (Mark 2.18f.), the parables of the new patches on old garments and the new wine in old wineskins (Mark 2.21f.), the parables of the treasure hidden in the field and the pearl of great value (Matt. 13.44–46), and the metaphor of the end-time harvest (Matt. 9.37f./Luke 10.2).

The tension in Jesus' proclamation of the kingdom between hope already fulfilled and not yet imminence is also a problem for NT theology. It is most simply resolved by recognizing a close tie-up between the two in Jesus' own understanding of his mission. The certainty that the end-time rule of God was already operative in and through his ministry brought with it the conviction that its full manifestation could not long be delayed (see further below §§45.3, 50.5).

3.3 *'Repent, and believe in the gospel.'* In the Synoptics the response which Jesus looked for in his hearers can be summed up in these two words – repent, believe. The importance of *repentance* is marked in several places (Matt. 11.21/Luke 10.13; Matt. 12.41/Luke 11.32; Luke 13.3, 5; 15.7, 10; 16.30). That the call here is for something radical, a complete turn round of the basic direction of his hearers' lives and attitudes, is clearly indicated in some of his parables, particularly the prodigal son (Luke 15.17), and by some of his encounters particularly with the rich young man (Mark 10.17–31) and Zacchaeus (Luke 19.8); perhaps above all in his demand that would be followers convert and become like children (Matt. 18.3; Mark 10.15/Luke 18.17).

The other side of this childlike dependence on God is *faith.* In the Synoptics faith is usually spoken of in relation to miracles, where Jesus encourages that openness to the power of God which will make a healing possible (Mark 5.36; 9.23f.; Matt. 9.28), or commends the faith that reaches out for wholeness (Mark 5.34; 10.52; Matt. 8.10/Luke 7.9; Matt. 15.28; Luke 7.50; 17.19; contrast Mark 6.5f.). We must notice that in no recorded instance did Jesus call for faith *in himself.* The faith which he looked for was faith in the end-time power of God acting through him. Here we will find a further problem when we come to compare Jesus' proclamation with the post-Easter kerygma (see below §§7.2, 50.4).

3.4 The *offer* which Jesus' message held out to repentance and faith was of participation in the end-time reign of God and its blessings: 'Blessed are you poor, for you share in God's reign' (Luke 6.20/Matt. 5.3). In particular, this included the blessings of forgiveness and acceptance (Mark 2.5; Luke 7.36–50) – an offer which is presented in several parables, for example, the parable of the giant debt and the unmerciful debtor (Matt. 18.23–35 – 'the kingdom is like . . .'), the parable of the two debtors (Luke 7.41f.), the parable of the pharisee and taxcollector (Luke 18.9–14) and the parable of the prodigal son (Luke 15.11–32).

In his own ministry Jesus embodied this forgiveness and acceptance of the end-time kingdom, particularly in his table fellowship. These gatherings, from which Jesus excluded no one, even open sinners, expressed the heart of his message, for they were the foretaste of the messianic feast of the new age (Luke 14.13,16–24). Hence Mark 2.17 – 'I came not to invite the righteous (that is, to the wedding feast) but sinners' (see also below p.162). So too his immediate band of disciples included two or three taxcollectors and ex-prostitutes. This was why he was so disparagingly called 'a friend of tax-collectors and sinners' (Matt. 11.19/Luke 7.34; Luke 15.1f.; 19.7).

3.5   Finally, we may simply note the *ethical corollary* of Jesus' message. In a context where the written, and increasingly the oral law determined the whole of men's relationships, both with God and with other men (see below §16.1), Jesus' message was simple but revolutionary. He *radicalized* the claim of God: it reaches into the innermost recesses of man's hidden motivation (Matt. 5.21–32). Consequently, to live only at the level of rules and regulations is to avoid the claim of God (Mark 7.1–23); the repentance Jesus looked for takes that claim seriously (Matt. 23.26). At the same time, he *reduced* the claim of God to one word – 'love'. The first and greatest command is, 'love God with your whole being and your neighbour as yourself' (Mark 12.28–31); anything which hinders the expression of that love, even the law itself, is to be set aside and ignored (Matt. 5.38–48).

3.6   To *sum up*. The characteristic features of Jesus' kerygma are these: (1) the proclamation of the kingdom of God, both its imminence and its presence – Jesus saw himself as the instrument of this end-time rule, but he did not put himself forward as the content of his kerygma; (2) the call for repentance and faith in face of the end-time power and claim of God – Jesus himself was not the object of faith; (3) the offer of forgiveness and a share in the messianic feast of the new age, with its ethical corollary of love.

§4. THE KERYGMA IN ACTS

We have already outlined the summary of the kerygma which Dodd drew largely from the sermons recorded in Acts. Here however we are not concerned, as Dodd was, to uncover the proclamation of the primitive churches. Our task is simpler: we will use the sermons in Acts quite straightforwardly as Luke's portrayal of the kerygma of the earliest believers and focus attention on their *distinctive* features. We will have occasion to inquire into their historical value when we dig more deeply later on. But here we ask simply, what is the kerygma of the earliest Christians as portrayed by Luke in Acts?

4.1   Jesus proclaimed the kingdom. The sermons in Acts *proclaim Jesus*. Jesus has become the content of the message; the proclaimer has become the proclaimed. In particular, *the principal focus falls on the resurrection of Jesus*; again and again it forms the central thrust of the message, both to Jew and to Gentile (e.g. 2.24–32; 4.1–2,33 – a summary passage; 10.40f.; 13.30–37; 17.18,30f.). As we shall see, this coincides with the emphasis of the message inherited and passed on by Paul (see below p.22), but it is in striking contrast with the message of Hebrews, where the resurrection appears only at the last minute in the concluding doxology (Heb. 13.20).

In contrast, in the Acts sermons *hardly any concern is shown for the historical Jesus*: his ministry hardly features at all; the only references are in 2.22 and 10.36–39. More striking still, the actual sermons in Acts contain remarkably few echoes of Jesus' own message and teaching (though cf. 8.12; 14.22; 19.8; 20.25,35; 28.23,31). A key question therefore at once arises: is there any unity, any continuity between Jesus' proclamation of the kingdom and the Acts' proclamation of the resurrection of Jesus?

4.2   An important corollary to the Acts sermons' concentration on the resurrection is the absence of any theology of *the death of Jesus*. His death is mentioned, but only as a bare fact (usually highlighting Jewish responsibility). The historical fact is not interpreted (2.23,36; 3.13–15; 4.10; 5.30; 7.52; 10.39; 13.27f.). It is never said, for example, that 'Jesus died on our behalf' or 'for our sins'; there are no suggestions that Jesus' death was a sacrifice. The few brief allusions to Jesus as the Servant (of Second Isaiah) pick up the theme of vindication following suffering, not of vicarious suffering as such (3.13,26; 4.27,30; so also 8.30–35). Similarly the allusion to Deut. 21.22f. in Acts 5.30 and 10.39 ('hanging him on a tree' – cf. 13.29) seem to be intended (by Luke) to highlight Jesus' shame and disgrace, and so to serve the same humiliation-vindication motif; to draw the theology of Gal. 3.13 from them is to read more into the text than sound exegesis permits.[5] And even 20.28 ('the church of the Lord – or of God – which he obtained with his own blood – or with the blood of his own'), not properly speaking part of an evangelistic proclamation, remains more than a little puzzling and obscure. In short, *an explicit theology of the death of Jesus is markedly lacking in the kerygma of the Acts sermons.*

Here again we are confronted with a striking variation; for the vicarious sufficiency of the cross is a prominent feature of Paul's gospel (Rom. 3.25; I Cor. 15.3; II Cor. 5.14–21), as it is in I Peter and Hebrews, not to mention Mark 10.45. Whether this is a true representation of the primitive kerygma or a reflection of Luke's own theology is not entirely clear. The presence of 'for our sins' in the kerygma handed down to Paul (I Cor. 15.3) and the fact that Luke omits Mark 10.45, or at least prefers a significantly different version of the saying (Luke 22.26), suggests the latter.[6] One possible explanation is that Luke was somewhat influenced by the diaspora Judaism of his time which also sought to play down the concept of atonement by sacrifice.[7] Be that as it may, so far as the kerygma of the Acts sermons is concerned, we have to say that it lacks a theology of the cross, it makes no attempt to attribute a definite atoning significance to the death of Jesus. Here then is another important element of diversity between the different kerygmata contained within the NT.

4.3 *Completely lacking* in the sermons of Acts is *the tension between fulfilment and imminent consummation* which was such a prominent feature of Jesus' proclamation of the kingdom and which is equally strong in Paul's message (below p.23). The parousia, or second coming of Jesus, the nearest equivalent to the coming of the kingdom in Jesus' message, is noticeable by its *lack* of prominence. The sense of its imminence barely squeezes through Luke's formulation in Acts 3.20f., and the day of judgment hardly seems to offer more than a distant threat – certainly not an immediate crisis such as Jesus envisaged (10.42; 17.31; 24.25). Also lacking is a strong note of realized eschatology, the conviction that the last days are here (despite Dodd – above p.11); it is present in 2.15–21 and 3.24, but otherwise wholly absent. Here the contrast is utterly astonishing. For we have seen that Jesus proclaimed the presence of the end-time blessings and the imminence of the kingdom as an important part of his message (above §§3.1,2). Likewise Paul strongly believed that Jesus' resurrection and the gift of the Spirit were the beginning (the first-fruits) of the end-time harvest (I Cor. 15.20,23; Rom. 8.23); and for most of his ministry Paul proclaimed the imminence of the parousia and the end (I Thess. 1.10; 4.13–18; I Cor. 7.29–31).

Particularly worthy of notice is his preservation in I Cor. 16.22 of an Aramaic cry from the earliest church – 'Maranatha, Our Lord, come!'. It is scarcely possible that the earliest communities in Jerusalem and Palestine lacked this same sense of eschatological fervour and urgency. Indeed, as we shall note later, the community of goods of which Luke tells us in Acts 2 and 4 is best explained as an expression of this kind of eschatological enthusiasm – property being sold without much thought for the needs of a year hence, for the Christ would have returned before then (see further below §§51.1, 67.3). Consequently, the conclusion seems inevitable that Luke has suppressed or ignored this element of the early kerygma, presumably because the lapse of time and delay of the parousia made it less appropriate (see further below §71.2).

4.4   Despite the sense that a long time gap had opened up between the resurrection and parousia of Jesus, and despite the emphasis on the resurrection of Jesus, there is hardly any role attributed to the exalted Jesus in Acts – beyond the bestowal of the Spirit at Pentecost, the beginning of this new epoch of salvation history (Acts 2.33), and his role as judge at the end (10.42; 17.31). Jesus was presumably thought of as the authorization behind those who acted 'in the name of Jesus' (2.38; 3.6; 4.10,30; 8.16; 10.48; 16.18; 19.5 – and cf. 9.34), and he appears in not a few visions (7.55f.; 9.10; 18.9; 22.17f.; 23.11; 26.16,19), but there is nothing of the rich sense of union between believer and exalted Lord which is such a feature of the messages of Paul and John.[8] In particular, the relation between exalted Lord and Holy Spirit which Paul and John handle so sensitively (Rom. 1.3–4; 8.9–11; I Cor. 12.3–13; 15.45; John 14.15f.,26; 16.7–15) is only hinted at in Acts (16.6f.). Even more striking, indeed astonishing, is the total absence from Acts of the concept and experience of sonship which was so central both for Jesus (see particularly Mark 14.36; Luke 11.2/Matt. 6.9; Matt. 11.25f./Luke 10.21; and below §45.2) and for Paul, who preserves for us the Aramaic prayer of the early churches and something of the intensity of their experience of sonship (Rom. 8.15f.; Gal. 4.6).

4.5   Finally under the heading of the proclamation of Jesus in Acts, we should notice the strong 'subordinationist' element within the sermons of Acts. Only rarely is Jesus depicted as the subject of the action described; everything he does, ministry, resurrection, exaltation, etc., is attributed to God (e.g. 2.22,32; 3.26; 5.30f.; 10.38,40). The sole reference to the parousia is framed in terms of God *sending* the Christ (3.20); and in the two references to Jesus as judge it is specifically stated that God appointed him to this office (10.42; 17.31 – where Jesus is not even mentioned by name). Moreover, on at least two occasions we should speak more precisely of an 'adoptionist' emphasis within the Acts kerygma – where the resurrection introduces Jesus to a new status as Son, Messiah and Lord (2.36; 13.33). This agrees very well with other probably early forms of kerygma (Rom. 1.3f.; Heb. 5.5) and so very likely reflects the emphasis of the earliest communities (see further below §§11.2, 12.3, 51.1 and p.243). But it contrasts markedly with the cosmic view of Christ which we find particularly in the later Paulines and in Revelation.

4.6   Like the proclamation of Jesus the kerygma of the Acts sermons issues in a *call for repentance and faith*. Here the diversity is rather interesting. For, on the one hand, the demand for repentance in Acts (2.38; 3.19,26; 14.15; 17.30; 26.20) is closely parallel to that of Jesus, but is in marked contrast to Paul and John. Paul in fact has little or nothing to say about repentance as such (only Rom. 2.4; II Cor. 7.9f.; 12.21) and John makes no use of the word whatsoever. But in the call for faith the similarity and dissimilarity run in the opposite direction. Luke's emphasis on faith (2.44; 4.32; 5.14; 10.43; 13.12,39,48; 14.1; etc.) is closely paralleled by both the Fourth Evangelist, who uses the verb 'believe' 98 times, and the Pauline epistles, which use verb and noun nearly 200 times. But the call is specifically for faith *in the Lord Jesus* (Acts 9.42; 11.17; 14.23; 16.31) and this marks off the kerygma in Acts clearly from the kerygma of Jesus himself (see above p.15). One other aspect of Luke's presentation of faith in the earliest communities should perhaps also be mentioned, since it is so distinctive of Acts and sets Acts apart from the rest of the NT writings. I refer to the way in which Luke portrays faith in Christ as the effect of miracle without apparently any misgivings on the point (5.14; 9.42; 13.12; 19.17f.) whereas elsewhere in the NT this evangelistic, propagandist value of miracle is rather disparaged (Mark 8.11f.; Matt. 12.38f./Luke 11.16, 29; John 2.23–25; 4.48; 20.29; II Cor. 13.3f.).

4.7   With the demand is coupled a *promise* – in Acts usually in terms of *forgiveness* (2.38; 3.19; 5.31; 10.43; 13.38f.; 26.18), *salvation* (2.21; 4.12; 11.14; 13.26; 16.31) or *the gift of the Spirit* (2.38f.; 3.19; 5.32; cf. 8.15–17; 10.44–47; 19.1–6). Here the overlap is rather more extensive with the other kerygmata of the NT. Jesus' kerygma held out the offer of forgiveness and acceptance (see above §3.4), and Paul's idea of justification is not so very far removed from that of forgiveness (see below pp.22f.), though the word 'forgiveness' itself occurs only in Eph. 1.7 and Col. 1.14, and not at all in the Johannine writings. The idea of salvation (noun or verb) is frequently attributed to Jesus in the Synoptic Gospels (Mark 3.4; 5.34; 8.35; 10.52; etc.) and is regularly used by Paul (Rom. 1.16; 5.9f.; 8.24; 9.27; 10.1,9f.,13; etc.), though it appears little in the Johannines (7 times). With the promise of the Spirit the overlap is different. Jesus spoke very little about the Spirit as such, at least according to our evidence; only Mark 13.11 could be taken as a promise of the Spirit, and then not as part of the kerygma but as a promise to disciples in time of trial.[9] But the Spirit is very clearly part of the basic kerygma for both Paul and the Johannine circle (see e.g. Rom. 2.29; 8.2,9,15; I Cor. 6.11; 12.13; II Cor. 1.22; Gal. 3.2f.; John 3.5–8; 7.39; 20.22; I John 2.27; 3.24).

Where again Acts is rather remarkable is in the absence of any ethical corollary to the kerygma it portrays. Luke does imply that believers held together in mutual dependence: there are no isolated Christians in Acts (here is part of the significance of the episodes in Acts 8 and 18.24–19.7). But there is little in Acts of a moral obligation stemming from the acceptance of the proclamation. Most astonishing is the fact that the word 'love' (noun and verb) occurs not at all in Acts; whereas it was integral to the messages of Jesus (see above p.16), of the Pauline epistles (108 times) and of the Johannine Gospel and epistles (95 times). Here the contrast is wholly striking.

4.8   To *sum up*, can we speak of a single kerygma in Acts? Can we recognize within the different sermons reproduced by Acts a regular outline which may be said to provide a solid core and which we can call the basic or core kerygma of the earliest Church, at least in Luke's presentation of it? The answer is, Yes. The most regular and basic elements are these: (1) the proclamation of the resurrection of Jesus; (2) the call for a response to this proclamation, for repentance and faith in this Jesus; (3) the promise of forgiveness, salvation, Spirit to those who so respond.

§5. THE KERYGMA OF PAUL

So far we have been able to draw on material which is specifically presented as kerygma, as missionary proclamation. It is less easy to uncover Paul's missionary preaching from his letters, since they are directed to those already converted and only occasionally refer to the preaching which brought about the conversions. But our task is not so difficult as it might seem, since, on the one hand, we have various kerygmatic and confessional formulae which Paul preserves and which he must have used in bringing his readers to the point of commitment. And, on the other, we can draw on the great distinctives of his message as a whole and be fairly certain that they featured in Paul's initial proclamation of the gospel in greater or less degree as circumstances determined. In fact we have already alluded to much of the Pauline kerygma by way of comparison with the kerygma in Acts. Here we need make only a few brief summary remarks; we will then draw in other material from the Pauline epistles of immediate relevance to our theme.

5.1   Paul, like the sermons in Acts, *proclaimed Jesus*. We know from the kerygmatic and confessional formulae passed on by Paul that Jesus as risen was probably the most prominent feature of Paul's gospel (Rom. 1.3f.; 4.24f.; 8.34; 10.9; I Cor. 15.3–11; I Thess. 1.10; cf. II Tim. 2.8). As in Acts also the historical Jesus hardly features at all in Paul's message. We learn only the barest details of Jesus' life from the Pauline letters (birth, Davidic descent, Last Supper and betrayal – Gal. 4.4; Rom. 1.3; I Cor. 11.23–25), and Paul makes hardly any (explicit) use of the tradition of Jesus' own preaching (though see below §§17.2,3). Here again the question of unity and continuity between the kerygmata of Jesus and of Paul is thrust upon us in a forceful manner. On the other hand the death of Christ receives far more prominence than in Acts (Rom. 3.24f.; 4.25; I Cor. 1.23; 2.2; 15.3; II Cor. 5.14–21; Gal. 3.1), and I Thess 1.10 and II Thess. 2.5 are sufficient proof that the imminent parousia was an integral part of Paul's missionary proclamation, during the first half of his missionary career at any rate (see below §71.1). However, the most distinctive and characteristic expressions of Paul's gospel are to be found in his emphasis on Jesus as Lord (see below p.50), and on the exalted Christ as representative of a new humanity ('the last Adam' – see particularly I Cor. 15.20–23,45–49), so that conversion means entering into union with Christ (e.g. Rom. 6.3; I Cor. 12.13; Gal. 2.19f.; Col. 3.1,3), and so that believers are his body (Rom. 12.5; I Cor. 12.27) and live, worship, conduct themselves 'in Christ', 'in the Lord' (phrases which occur more than 160 times in Paul's writings). For Paul the essence of Christianity is acceptance by God (justification) in an intimate relationship, entered into and lived in by faith on man's side, made possible and empowered by the gift of grace, the gift of the Spirit (see particularly Rom. 3.21–5.21; Gal.

2.16–4.7). This seems to be the core of Paul's kerygma, distinctive both in its central emphases and in its developed expression.

As in the case of Jesus, so too implicit in Paul's kerygma is a tension between 'already' fulfilment and 'not yet' consummation. The belief in Jesus' resurrection as an event of the past and the experience of the Spirit as already given creates an eschatological tension in believers who are themselves still 'in the flesh', not yet raised from the dead, not yet fully controlled by the Spirit ('spiritual bodies') – a tension expressed most forcefully in the warfare between 'flesh' and 'Spirit' (Rom. 8.12ff.; Gal. 5.16f.), in the tug-of-war between 'old nature' and 'new' (Rom. 7.22–25; Eph. 4.22–24; Col. 3.5–10).[10]

The scope and range of Paul's writings thus enable us to gain a fair idea of what the basic kerygma was for Paul. But they also reveal the diversity of proclamation which Paul recognized as kerygma. Since in this chapter we are attempting only a preliminary survey we will confine ourselves to the most obvious points.

5.2   In *Galatians* Paul speaks of no less than *three* gospels. First, his own – the gospel for the Gentiles, 'for the uncircumcision' (Gal. 2.7): it brings liberty from the curse of the law and from subjection to the law as a means to righteousness (2.16–5.12). Paul characterizes his gospel in this way because he wants to distinguish it clearly from the other two gospels (cf. particularly 3.1–14). Second is the gospel for the Jews, 'for the circumcision' (2.7), represented by the 'pillar apostles', Peter in particular, centred on Jerusalem. Paul recognizes this Jewish version of the gospel as a legitimate form of Christian kerygma, appropriate to the Jews.[10a] Presumably it was not so very different from Paul's gospel in content (2.2, 6–9), though Paul certainly jibbed at its corollaries, since in his view it involved a greater subjection to the law than he himself thought right (2.11–21). However, so long as the proponents of each of these two gospels recognized the validity of the other and did not seek to impose their own gospel on those who held to the other, Paul was content. But evidently the churches in Palestine had a legalistic right wing which opposed the law-free Gentile mission. Theirs is the 'other gospel' which Paul attacks in fierce language in 1.6–9. It is not finally clear whether Paul denied Christian status to this third gospel (1.7 probably means: it is not another gospel but a perversion of the gospel of Christ). But he leaves us in no doubt as to what he thought of the so-called 'Judaizers'' attempts to force their understanding of the gospel on others: it is no good news, the way of bondage; those who

preach it are 'sham Christians', they have missed the full truth and
ought to castrate themselves (2.4f.; 5.12)!

Paul launches a similar sounding attack in *II Cor. 10–13*. Clearly
those attacked regarded themselves as Christians, indeed as 'servants of Christ' and 'apostles of Christ' (11.13,23). But in Paul's
view they preached a 'different gospel', 'another Jesus'; they were
'servants of Satan', 'false apostles' (11.4,13ff.) (see further below
§§56.1,2).

These two letters of Paul are sufficient indication in themselves
that there was more than one kerygma sponsored among and within
the earliest churches. *Where the very concept of and claim to apostleship was
the subject of controversy, what meaning can we give to the phrase 'the apostolic
faith'?*

5.3   From other letters of Paul it becomes clear that so far as he was
concerned there was *no standardized pattern, no extended outline of Christian proclamation*. The basic outline of Paul's kerygma in I Cor. 15.3ff. is
limited to a statement about Jesus' death and the assertion of his
resurrection. He insists that the Corinthians adhere to that. But
when it comes to diversity of belief about whether or not there is a
general resurrection to come (15.12 – a question central to the kind of
salvation offered in the kerygma), Paul does not denounce those who
hold the contrary view to his own as apostates and renegades; he
merely argues against it. He is quite scathing, but not denunciatory
(15.12–57).[10b] Similarly he accepts a diversity of belief about baptism
(1.10–16; 15.29). He does not insist on the sole legitimacy of his own
view or of a particular view of baptism. Instead he plays down the
role of baptism; it is kerygma that matters not baptism (1.17). And
though in 10.1–12 he is probably arguing against a magical view of
baptism, in 15.29 he shows no disapproval of the belief in vicarious
baptism, baptism for the dead; on the contrary he uses the practice
as an argument for the belief in resurrection (see also below §39.5).

I Corinthians reveals a Christian community full of strains and
tensions, of diverse beliefs and practices all in the name of Christ
(1.11f.; 3.1–4; 4.6–21; etc.), and we can recognize similar disagreements indicated in the Thessalonian epistles (I Thess. 5.19–22; II
Thess. 2.2; 3.14f.), in Romans (particularly 14.1–4; 16.17f.), in
Philippians (1.15–18; 3.2,12–19) and in Colossians (2.8,16–23).
These suggest that the picture of a wholly unified primitive Church
belongs more to the realm of dogmatic wishful thinking than to
historical reality. We cannot pursue that issue now, but will return to
it in Part II.

5.4   We should notice also the extent to which *Paul varied his procla-mation of the gospel according to circumstances.* I Cor. 9.19–23 clearly implies that Paul allowed circumstances and situations to determine the statement of his kerygma to a considerable degree. Thus we recognize a different emphasis as to the source of his gospel in Gal. 1.1, 11–17 and I Cor. 15.3ff. (see below §17.1). And in one remark-able passage Jesus hardly features at all, where his gospel appears to take the form of a works (doing the law) righteousness (Rom. 2.6–16); though here, as he himself says, he is talking about those who have never heard the law, let alone the gospel.[11] In some circumstances he set his face firmly against the gospel proclaimed by the Palestinian Christians: his own gospel is fiercely defended and Peter is denounced for his compromise at Antioch (Gal. 2); or again missionaries from Jerusalem (as it would appear) are outrightly condemned as counterfeit apostles (II Cor. 10–13) (see below §§56.1, 2), and a gospel of law is strongly repudiated (Gal. 5.1–13; Col. 2.16–23). In other circumstances he is happy for the gospel for the circumcision to remain in effect in his own churches (I Cor. 8; cf. Rom. 14) and happy that the gospel is proclaimed even by those who do so in opposition to and out of spite for Paul (Phil. 1.15–18).

Also worthy of note under this heading is *the degree of development evident in Paul's message over the years.* The clearest example is its eschatological orientation. In I and II Thessalonians the imminence of the parousia is very real; and the imminent parousia formed an important element in Paul's proclamation, if the situation which developed in Thessalonica from his preaching is anything to go by (see particularly I Thess. 1.9f.; 4.13–18; II Thess. 2.5). The same emphasis shines clearly through I Cor. 7.29–31, 15.51f. But in Phil. 1.20ff. Paul reckons seriously with the likelihood of his death before the parousia, and in Colossians the focus has swung from future to past. Where in Rom. 6.5, 8.11 Paul thinks of resurrection with Christ as something still future, in Col. 2.12, 3.1 resurrection with Christ is something already past (see further below p.345). These are not simply the different expressions of the same message in different circumstances.[12] The line of development is too clear and consistent for that : from the expectation of a parousia which is proclaimed as so imminent that the death of some believers prior to it comes as a shock to his converts, to the clear recognition that some will die before the parousia though he will probably be spared, to the calm acceptance that many will die including probably himself before the parousia; from the earlier statement of faith where the metaphor of 'resurrec-tion with Christ' is forward looking, reserved for the imminent not

yet, to the later reverse emphasis, where the metaphor of 'resurrection with Christ' looks back to that which has already been accomplished – a clear shift in perspective (see below §71.1).

5.5   We can *summarize* our findings here as follows. (1) Paul had a
very clear idea of what the gospel of Christ was. But his understanding and expression of it did not take any final or fixed form. For, (2)
he recognized the validity of other proclamations and called them
also 'gospel'. And (3) his own kerygma took diverse forms as circumstances determined and it developed over the years altering in
emphasis and tone. (4) Most striking of all, in several situations he
resolutely opposed forms of gospel which other believers regarded as
authentic and called them 'no gospel'. Indeed it is somewhat doubtful whether Paul could ever have given wholehearted approval to the
two NT documents which most clearly express the Jewish Christian
understanding of kerygma – Matthew and James.[13] Certainly Paul
could never have spoken of the law simply as 'the law that makes us
free' (James 1.25 NEB); it was a claim completely untrue to his own
experience, and one almost always inappropriate in the circumstances of the Gentile mission. But then, James would no doubt have
been equally unhappy with Paul's kerygma (see further below §55).

A point of crucial importance begins to emerge here: that *within the
NT itself we have not simply diverse kerygmata, but in fact kerygmata which
appear to be incompatible* – that is, gospels which are incompatible when
compared directly with each other without reference to their different life-settings.

§6. THE KERYGMA OF JOHN

The Fourth Gospel gives as its purpose: 'that you may believe that
Jesus is the Christ, the Son of God, and that believing you may have
life in his name' (20.31). We may take this as the evangelist's own
concise summary of his gospel.

6.1   It aims to stimulate *faith* – that is, to bring the unbeliever to
faith or to encourage the believer in his faith (the verb could be taken
either way), or both. John heavily underscores the importance of
believing. The verb 'believe' occurs far more in the Fourth Gospel
(98 times) than in any other NT writer. This is the one thing
required of hearers (we recall that John never speaks of repentance) if
they are to experience 'life in Christ's name'. 'Believing' here means

both accepting the veracity of the claim that 'Jesus is the Christ, the Son of God' (belief *that* – e.g. 6.69; 8.24; 11.27; 16.27; 20.31; I John 5.1, 5), and commitment to this Jesus (belief *into* – the predominant and characteristic Johannine usage – e.g. John 1.12; 3.16; 6.29; 11:25f.; 17.20; I John 5.10). Distinctive also of Johannine usage is the extent to which the verb 'know' (56 times) has become a near equivalent to 'believe'.

6.2   The content of faith is that 'Jesus is the Christ, the Son of God'. We can tell what this meant for John by the way in which he presents Jesus in his Gospel. Two aspects in particular mark out the distinctiveness of John's kerygma at this point. First, the extent to which the historical Jesus and the exalted Jesus overlap in the Fourth Gospel – the extent to which the historical Jesus is seen in terms of the exalted Christ. It is this which almost certainly accounts for the striking differences between the Jesus of the Fourth Gospel and the Jesus of the Synoptics. I am thinking here especially of the following features: of the roll-call of christological titles which confronts us right away in John 1 – Lamb of God, Messiah, Son of God, King of Israel, Son of Man – whereas in the Synoptics such recognition as Jesus meets with only comes to expression much later in his ministry; of the famous 'I am' claims of Jesus in the Fourth Gospel (6.35; 8.12; 10.7, 11; 11.25; 14.6; 15.1), which would hardly have been ignored so completely by the Synoptics if they had belonged to the original tradition of Jesus' sayings; and of Jesus' striking self-consciousness particularly of pre-existence which confronts us regularly throughout the Fourth Gospel (e.g 3.13; 6.38; 8.38, 58; 10.36; 17.5, 24) and which again must have left some equivalent mark in the Synoptic tradition had such sayings been part of the historical Jesus' message. Such differences cannot be reconciled on the strictly historical level. The best explanation is that John is not attempting to give a historical picture of the man Jesus, but what he sees to be a true picture of the historical Jesus – the historical Jesus as John now sees him to be, the historical Jesus with the glory that was to be his by virtue of his death, resurrection and ascension already visible in his earthly life (see particualry 1.14; 2.11; 11.4; 12.23; 13.31; 17.5).[14] Other kerygmata in the NT keep the historical Jesus and exalted Christ much further apart: Acts and Paul seem hardly interested in the historical Jesus; the Synoptics, though presenting Jesus in the light of Easter faith, do not let the two pictures merge to anything like the same extent. John's proclamation of Jesus is therefore quite distinctive – as distinctive as Paul's 'last Adam' christology and Hebrews' High Priest christology (see further below pp.223, 299f.).

Second, at the same time John marks a much increased emphasis on the historical actuality of Jesus' earthly life, as compared with Paul and Acts. This no doubt in large part is due to the growing influence and challenge posed by emerging Gnosticism. The particular form current at the time of John we know as Docetism. Since Gnostic dualism regarded matter, flesh, the physical as evil, Docetism denied that the divine redeemer could have wholly embraced the physical, become incarnate in matter. The humanity of Jesus must have been only an appearance, a seeming (*dokei* – it seems). Hence the Johannine writings stress the reality of Jesus' humanity; the fleshness of Jesus is emphasized in a way which has no real comparison in the kerygmata of Acts and Paul (John 1.14; 6.51–58; 19.34f.; I John 4.1–3; 5.6–8). Here is clear evidence that the changed circumstances and challenges at the end of the first century AD played a large part in shaping the kerygma addressed to them (see further below pp.300ff.).

6.3   Believing that Jesus is the Christ, the Son of God, leads to *life*. Here is another important and characteristic theme in John: verb and noun ('live', 'life') together occur 67 times in the Johannine Gospel and letters. The words occur as regularly in the Pauline letters (96 times), though less frequently in Acts (20 times). John makes little or no use of the concepts of forgiveness, justification and salvation, but he does link the promise of life closely with the Spirit (4.10–14; 6.63; 7.38f.; 20.22), and his talk of mutual abiding (e.g. 6.56; 14.18–23; 15.4–7; I John 2.27f.; 3.24; 4.12–16) has close parallels to Paul's idea of union with Christ (see above p.22), although John's conception is much more individualistic in its outworking (see below §31.1). Perhaps then we ought simply to recognize all these as broadly equivalent expressions of kerygmatic promise. Their diversity as between Acts, Paul and John was presumably determined more by the personal preferences of the proclaimer and the appropriateness of the language to the situation addressed, than by differences of substance and content in the promise itself.

Where the Johannine kerygma becomes distinctive is in the way it presents the promise of life as a sharp 'either-or'. Hearers must choose life or death, and if they choose life they pass at that moment from death to life, leaving death and judgment behind (3.36; 5.24; 11.25f.; I John 3.14; 5.12). Such clear-cut antitheses are typical of John's message – between light and darkness, sight and blindness, truth and falsehood, Spirit and flesh, etc. (1.5; 3.6, 19–21; 6.63; 8.12,

44f.; 9.39–41; etc.). There is no room here for compromise, for an in-between position of indifferent shades. There is no idea of life as a process, of an already which is only a beginning, of the not-yetness of life in the Spirit which characterizes Paul's message. In the Johannine circle the distinction between believer and unbeliever is clear-cut (see e.g. I John 2.4, 23; 3.6, 9f., 14f,; 4.5f.). This is clearly an ethical dualism, the antithesis of decision – the Johannine writer(s) want to pose the challenge of the gospel as sharply and as clearly as possible. But it does leave us with a rather simplistic view of reality. It divides humankind into two classes; whereas in Paul the division passes through the heart of the believer as such (above p. 23). Clearly then, the eschatological tension characteristic of the kerygmata of Jesus and Paul has slackened and become the all-or-nothing of John's realized eschatology. Nowhere is this more apparent than in the various 'tests of life' which I John offers to its readers – indwelling Spirit, love, right confession, obedience (e.g. 2.4; 3.24; 4.2f., 7). Evidently the author assumed that those who love are those who make a right confession. It is not at all evident what the author would make of the person who displays a Christ-like love and who yet refuses to believe in Christ. The sharp Johannine antithesis provides no answer to the (Christian) 'problem' of the good pagan, the loving atheist. Paul, on the other hand, with his recognition of the divided state of each individual and his yearning over unbelieving Israel would at least understand the problem and be able to volunteer some answer. Whereas I John has nothing to say.

§7. CONCLUSIONS

We have not examined all the NT writings, only made a surface survey of the kerygma of Jesus, the kerygma of the first Christians as depicted in Acts, and the kerygmata presented by the two other most important theologians in the NT – Paul and John. Do they share a common kerygma? Can we speak of *the* kerygma? Leaving the message of Jesus aside for the moment we compare first the three samples of post-Easter kerygma.

7.1   Do the Acts sermons, Paul and John share a common kerygma? If we think of the individuality of their proclamation, the distinctiveness of their emphases, the answer has to be No! But on closer examination it becomes evident that *there is a common element present in these different proclamations*; they give expression in their different ways to something we can call 'a common kerygma'. There are three components to this *core* kerygma.

First, the proclamation of the risen, exalted Jesus – expressed by the Acts sermons' emphasis on the resurrection of Jesus as such, by Paul's emphasis on the present Lordship and representative significance of Jesus, and by John's presentation of the historical Jesus in the full illumination of Easter faith.

Second, the call for faith, for acceptance of the proclamation and commitment to the Jesus proclaimed. This is the most consistent feature in all three cases, and to that extent it supports Bultmann's claim that 'faith' is the term which most clearly distinguishes earliest Christianity, rather than 'orthodoxy' (see above p.4).

Third, the promise held out to faith – whether it be put in terms of Spirit, or of its various aspects (forgiveness, salvation, life) or of a continuing relation thus established between exalted Christ and believer (union with Christ, mutual indwelling). Not always so clearly drawn out is the corollary that the relation of faith towards Christ involves a community of faith, and the responsibility of love within (and beyond?) that community.

This is the *unity* of the post-Easter kerygma. But beside it stands the considerable *diversity* of the different kerygmata. It must clearly be understood that the unified core kerygma outlined above is an *abstraction*. No NT writer proclaims this kerygma as such. No NT writer reduces the kerygma to this core. The basic kerygma in each of the cases examined above is larger than this core. They share these common elements, but in different proportions. And *in the event of proclamation no two kerygmata were exactly the same*. Not only so, but *the diversity meant difference and disagreement* – differences for example over the significance of Jesus' earthly ministry and his death, disagreement over the continuing relevance of the law, on the eschatological dimension of the gospel, and on its ethical outworking. These differences and disagreements often ran deep, but the kerygmata involved could nevertheless be put forward (and accepted) as valid expressions of Christian kerygma in the appropriate circumstances. Exponents of different kerygmata may not always agree on 'the kerygma'. Indeed they may strongly disagree on what the kerygma is in a particular situation. But in different circumstances they can agree to differ and respect these differences as acceptable and valid.

We must therefore beware when we talk of 'the NT kerygma'. For if we mean the core kerygma, then we are talking about a kerygma which no evangelist in the NT actually preached. And if we mean one of the diverse kerygmata, then that is only one form of kerygma, and not necessarily appropriate or acceptable to the different evangelists in the NT or their circumstances. To put it another way, *if we insist on the unity of the kerygma in the NT, we must insist also on the diversity of kerygmata in the NT.* One can sometimes say in a particular situation, in response to a particular challenge: This is the gospel; there is no other (cf. Gal. 1.6–9). But, if the NT is any guide, one can never say: This particular formulation is the gospel for all time and for every situation.

7.2 If we can speak of the unity of the post-Easter kerygma it is much more difficult to speak of a unity between the post-Easter kerygma and the kerygma of Jesus. At the level of public proclamation the differences are stark: Jesus proclaimed the kingdom, the first Christians proclaimed Jesus; Jesus called for repentance and faith with respect to the kingdom, the first Christians called for faith in Jesus; Jesus held out the offer of God's forgiveness and acceptance, the first Christians held out a similar offer but as mediated through Jesus. Quite clearly Jesus stands at the centre of the post-Easter kerygma in a manner which is not really paralleled in Jesus' own kerygma. So far, of course, we have only made the comparison at the level of public proclamation, in terms of the characteristic emphases of each kerygma. The question is whether a degree of continuity between the two can be traced at a deeper level, whether Jesus saw himself as integral to his own kerygma, whether he saw a close tie-up between the kingdom and himself, that is, between the kingdom he proclaimed and his proclamation of it, or between the kingdom's coming and his own destiny. In short, *can we discern sufficient continuity between Jesus the proclaimer and Jesus the proclaimed to enable us to affirm that the kerygma of Jesus and the kerygma of the first Christians are ultimately one and the same?* This question will underlie much of our discussion throughout the following chapters and we will have to return to it in the light of that discussion at the end of Part I.

In the meantime we should recognize and underline the most obvious difference between the pre-Easter proclamation and the post-Easter proclamation – and that is *Easter* itself, belief in the resurrection of Jesus. This needs to be said in view of the still strong tendency to try to return to the pre-Easter kerygma, to sum up Christianity in terms of the Sermon of the Mount or the parable of the Prodigal Son. But *there can be no going back to the proclamation of Jesus as such.* The kerygmata of Acts and Paul, and in a different way of John, demonstrate that *the first Christians were not concerned simply to reproduce the message of Jesus.* In the view of the earliest churches a decisive development had taken place which *itself* became the good news *par excellence* – that Jesus had been raised from the dead and exalted to heaven. It is this new development which forms the distinctive essence of the post-Easter proclamation, which gives it its distinctively *Christian* character. As Paul explicity states, a kerygma without the proclamation of Jesus as risen or exalted would not be Christian proclamation, it would cease to be valid as gospel (I Cor. 15.14–19). In short, *the Christian Church is built round the post-Easter kerygma, not the teaching of the historical Jesus*, or at least not that teaching as independent of the post-Easter kerygma.

7.3   To *sum up*. (1) There is a unifying strand which holds all the NT kerygmata together and enables us to grasp the distinctive character of the earliest Christian gospel. (2) In the concrete situation the actual gospel was much more closely defined and larger in content – a definition and content largely determined by the situation addressed. (3) In different situations the actual gospel was different, and could be as different as the situations themselves. These differences were often considerable, and incompatible when transposed to other situations. (4) These differences were often *integral* to the gospels in their different situations; it would not have been possible to abandon them in the situation which called forth that particular form of proclamation without altering its character as good news to that situation.

Two important corollaries follow whose application extends to the present day. (*a*) Any attempt to find a single, once-for-all, unifying kerygma is bound to fail. For the concrete situation *always* calls forth a more closely defined and larger kerygma – a form of proclamation which in the concrete situation cannot be boiled down to the unifying core without losing its meaning and its relevance to the concrete situation. And it is in this fuller proclamation that the differences and disagreements lie. (*b*) Christians will simply have to accept the fact of different expressions and interpretations of 'the kerygma' and live with them – accepting the *necessity* and the *validity* of these different expressions, and not being upset over them or grieving over them as 'sinful divisions' or 'heretical schisms'. At the same time the abstraction (and it is an abstraction) of the core kerygma does give clear enough indication of the distinctive character of Christianity – a clear enough basis for common action, service and worship. To demand more as the indispensable minimum is tantamount to asking Paul to excommunicate James or Luke to excommunicate John!

III

PRIMITIVE CONFESSIONAL
FORMULAE

§8. INTRODUCTION

From the study of kerygma we turn to the study of confessional formulae. As the first Christians proclaimed their new faith, so they also confessed it. In seeking to push a little way below the surface which we have so far only skated over, it is natural to look first for the confession of faith which lay behind the proclamation and which the proclamation produced in the convert. How did the first Christians confess their faith? What form of words did they choose to distinguish themselves from other and similar religious belief all around?

This area has been subjected to considerable research since the beginning of the twentieth century. The studies in question have highlighted several dangers of which the careful student should be aware from the start.

(a) *The danger of reading back the great ecumenical creeds into the NT.* The investigation of primitive creeds is probably the best example of the way in which the pattern of orthodoxy has been read back into the first-century Christian writings. Up until the early 1940s, with a few honourable exceptions, the starting point for such investigations was almost always the standard creeds of Eastern and Western Christianity. Given the basic statements of Christian faith in the Apostles' Creed, the Nicene Creed, etc., the task seemed clear: to find out whether primitive or latent expressions of these credal formulae are present in the NT itself.[1] The governing but unwritten assumption seemed in many cases to be the axiom that Christianity *is* the creeds, they are the normative expression of confessing Christianity; therefore, the NT writings must express that credal faith, if not in so many words at least in a hidden or yet unclarified, formless manner. The danger here is obvious – the danger of squeezing the NT material into a later unified pattern so that the distinctive character of that material (and its diversity?) is lost to us.

(b) The second is *the danger of looking for a single unified creed* – the danger of making a patchwork quilt of bits and pieces from here and there in the NT and hailing it as a seamless robe. This was a weakness of Dodd's reconstruction of the primitive kerygma. And A. Seeberg fell into the same trap in his pioneering study in our present area of concern.[2] The temptation here is to pick out confessional forms from diverse strands of the primitive tradition and to group them together into a single formula, disregarding questions about their original life-settings. In such a case 'the Church's primitive confession of faith' is nothing more than an uneven amalgam of disparate elements bonded together by twentieth-century methodology.

(c) If the second danger is that of looking for a single unified formula, the third danger is *that of looking for a single uniform life-setting for the earliest confessions*. It is a striking fact that the great majority of scholars researching into this field have assumed or concluded that one and only one life-setting produced and preserved the earliest confessional formulae – and that one life-setting, baptism. Here again the inevitable tendency is to squeeze the shape of the NT material into a pre-determined mould – to let the high sacramental theology of later centuries determine our understanding of earliest Christianity.

(d) Fourth, we should also beware of the opposite tendency evident in some tradition-history investigations – that of overfussily stratifying the material into different layers (Palestinian Jewish Christianity, Hellenistic Jewish Christianity, pre-Pauline Gentile Christianity, etc.), and then expecting to find a coherent chronological development in the confessional formulae from layer to layer, stage to stage. We should not forget that a significant section of the *earliest* Jerusalem community spoke, worshipped and theologized in Greek from the start ('the Hellenists' – Acts 6.1; see below §60). Nor can we readily divide the NT writings into such clearly distinct pigeon-holes; in a very real and important sense all the NT writings are Jewish Christian documents.[3] In fact I believe that we do have to recognize different emphases within the NT material which can appropriately be labelled 'Jewish Christian', 'Hellenistic Jewish', 'Gentile'. But we must beware always of imposing such categories on the evidence and seek always to let the text dictate its own categories to us (see also below p.236).

As a starting point, all we need to assume here is that the earliest believers formulated their new found faith in words expressing that faith, and that some at least of these primitive confessions have been preserved for us. If we are to recognize and properly to understand these confessions we must put all the later creeds and categories to one side and come to the NT writings with an open question: *How did the earliest believers express their new faith in a confessional way*? And in pursuing that question we must avoid imposing on our material either the unities of ecumenical or sacramental Christianity or the diversities of a pre-packed tradition-history approach. Only so can we hope to let the material speak for itself.

As the main studies of primitive confessional formulae have shown, the earliest forms focus on Jesus; that which is confessed is *faith in Jesus*. This is what we would have expected anyway from our finding in the last chapter, that the kerygmata of earliest Christianity were basically a proclamation of Jesus and a calling to faith in Jesus. Our study therefore divides up most straightforwardly into an examination of *the different ways in which Jesus was confessed*. We will concentrate on what appear to have been the principal formulae used.

§9. JESUS IS THE SON OF MAN

Over 60 years ago W. Bousset suggested that the confession of Jesus as the Son of Man was the first Christian confession and the focal point of the earliest Christian community.[4] A decade or so later E. Lohmeyer maintained that the Christianity which originated in Galilee (as distinct from Jerusalem Christianity) was expressed distinctively in Son of Man christology.[5] More recently research has concentrated on Q and produced the thesis that Q embodies an early expression of faith in Jesus as the heavenly Son of Man, distinct from and not yet merged with the latter passion-centred presentation of Jesus (as most clearly in Mark).[6] May we then say that 'Jesus is the Son of Man' was one of the earliest, perhaps the earliest form of words which the first Christians used to confess their faith?

9.1   As is well known the title 'the Son of Man' belongs almost exclusively to the Gospels (Synoptics 69, John 13, rest of the NT 1), and in all these cases it appears to all intents and purposes *only on the lips of Jesus*. Jesus is never addressed as Son of Man in the narratives, or hailed or confessed as Son of Man by his disciples. Our question would appear therefore to be quickly answered – in the negative: 'the Son of Man' is a phrase used by Jesus, not a confession used by the early churches. But it is not quite so simple. Throughout this century leading NT scholars have examined the Son of Man sayings and come to the conclusion that it is impossible to refer all of them back to Jesus; some at least must have reached their present form in the post-Easter situation. The chief reasons are as follows: (1) A whole block of Son of Man material is absent from Q. That is to say, there are no references in Q to the suffering (and resurrection) of the Son of Man such as we find most clearly in Mark 8.31, 9.12, 31, 10.33f., 45. It could plausibly be argued therefore that Q comes from a stage prior to the merging of the Son of Man tradition with the passion kerygma as in Mark, and that suffering Son of Man sayings as such did not emerge until after the Q material reached its present form. (2) Comparison of parallel Synoptic traditions suggests other instances where the phrase 'the Son of Man' is a later addition – Matt. 16.28 (cf. the earlier form in Mark 9.1/Luke 9.27); Matt. 24.30a looks like an addition to Mark 13.26; and Matt. 26.2 could well be an editorial expansion of Mark 14.1; other occasions where 'the Son of Man' may be the product of editing are Mark 9.9, Luke 19.10 and Matt. 13.37, 41. Moreover, almost all the Johannine Son of Man references lack any close parallel in Synoptic usage, and some are so obviously linked with specifically Johannine language and themes that they must be counted as part of developed Johannine theology (particularly 3.13, 6.62 – ascending/descending theme; 3.14, 8.28, 12.34 – Jesus' being lifted up; 12.23, 13.31 – Jesus' glorification). (3) Nowhere in the Synoptic tradition do we find a Son of Man saying as a constituent part of Jesus' proclamation of the kingdom. Granted that the latter is the most distinctive feature of Jesus' message it is quite possible to conclude that the two distinct strands of material were in fact originally independent – the kingdom material stemming from authentic Jesus' tradition, the Son of Man material stemming from the earliest community.[7] On the other hand, this last argument cuts both ways: it is more likely that sayings of Jesus which emerged from the prophetic inspiration of the earliest communities would have entwined themselves round or been developments of the already accepted Jesus-tradition; prophetic sayings which were a completely new departure were less likely to be accepted as sayings of the risen Jesus.[8] All in all however there is sufficient indication that *the Son of Man tradition underwent some development at least within the earliest community.* This strongly suggests that the earliest churches thought of Jesus as the Son of Man in a creative way, that *the conviction that Jesus was the Son of Man was an important part of their faith.*

9.2   Can we be more specific? How important was this belief for them? To what extent is our present Son of Man sayings material the work of the earliest community as such? That is, to what extent is the Son of Man material an expression of the first Christians' faith chosen by them to be such? Do the Son of Man sayings reflect a confessional faith in Jesus as the Son of Man? The basic problem here is that the evidence is amenable to several different interpretations and it is not possible to achieve certain conclusions. The following are the most important of the alternative interpretations.[9]

(*a*) *All* the Son of Man sayings come from *the early churches*; none of them goes back to Jesus at all. In which case the belief that Jesus was the Son of Man was probably the earliest expression of the new and distinctive post-Easter faith of Jesus' disciples. Moreover, it has played a creative role in the development of Christian faith, in particular in the development of the tradition of Jesus' sayings, unequalled by any of the other formulations of faith. On the other hand it is difficult on this view to explain why the first Christians took the step of identifying Jesus with the Son of Man;[10] and even more difficult to understand *why this new faith produced the present pattern of the tradition, where all the Son of Man affirmations appear on the lips of Jesus himself and none is preserved in another context.* Why does the belief that Jesus is the Son of Man not appear in any kerygmatic statements? Why such a total absence of the title from any primitive teaching or liturgical formulae? The fact is that there is no comparable development in the cases of the other 'titles of majesty'. On the contrary, comparison with the development of the titles examined below tells firmly against this hypothesis.

(*b*) *Some* of the Son of Man sayings go back to *Jesus* more or less in the form preserved for us in the tradition. These are the sayings where Jesus looks to the future coming of the Son of Man as someone distinct from himself – in particular Mark 8.38, Luke 12.8f.; see also Matt. 24.27/Luke 17.24; Matt. 24.37, 39/Luke 17.26, 30; Matt. 24.44/Luke 12.40; Matt. 10.23; Luke 11.30; 17.22. The basic reason why these sayings can be referred back to Jesus with some confidence is the unlikelihood that the earliest community would have distinguished the exalted Jesus from the Son of Man in this way. The creative role of the earliest churches in this case started with the identification of the Son of Man with the now exalted Jesus himself. Not only was Jesus identified with the Son of Man in those sayings where Jesus had looked forward to the Son of Man's coming, but new sayings emerged in the Jesus-tradition – further sayings describing the Son of Man's heavenly activity and coming in glory, and then sayings involving Jesus' earthly activity and suffering.

The key question here is *whether Jesus did in fact look for the coming of someone greater than himself*. And the difficulty under which this hypothesis labours is that these Son of Man sayings mentioned above are the only real evidence for it. Is it strong enough? Do Luke 12.8f. and Mark 8.38 require us to recognize a distinction between Jesus and the Son of Man? In fact such an interpretation runs counter to the realized element of Jesus' proclamation in which Jesus contrasted the eschatological fulfilment of his own ministry with the preparatory nature of what went before, and in which the Baptist filled the role of the forerunner (see particularly Matt. 11.11/Luke 7.28; Matt. 12.41f./Luke 11.31f.). Moreover, once again we may ask why and how it was that belief in Jesus as the heavenly Son of Man should have led to the development of tradition where Jesus' *earthly* activity was referred to with an apocalyptic title – why particularly such inconsequential sayings as Matt. 8.20/Luke 9.58 should have appeared as expressions of faith in Jesus the glorious one in heaven. Nothing similar happened with the other titles of exaltation; indeed, in contrast, Luke's use of 'Lord' in his Gospel is *clearly editorial* and reflects his post-Easter standpoint unmistakably (see below p.51).

(c) A third view is that *some* at least of the Son of Man sayings go back to *a (non-titular) speech idiom of Jesus* – that Jesus sometimes used the Aramaic phrase *bar 'enāšā* ('the son of man') in the sense of Ps. 8.4b (cf. Heb. 2.6) = 'man' in general, that is, without distinctive self-reference.[11] This would be the original sense behind certain Synoptic sayings, particularly Mark 2.10, 2.28 ('the Sabbath was made for man . . . therefore the son of man = man is lord of the Sabbath'), Matt. 8.20/Luke 9.58 and Matt. 11.18f./Luke 7.33f. Some support for this view is given by the Gospel of Thomas which preserves only one Son of Man saying – Logion 86, a close parallel to Matt. 8.20/Luke 9.58 (cited below p.284). Several of the Thomas logia seem to stem from an independent and early Aramaic source.[12] This could therefore be taken as confirmation that the earliest stage of the Son of Man tradition was a non-titular *bar 'enāšā* usage.

The role of the earliest community in shaping Son of Man sayings would then have been as follows. The search through the OT for language to express faith in Jesus as exalted would have picked up the heavenly son of man figure in Dan. 7.13, and sayings which identified the risen Jesus with this figure would have emerged, either on the basis of the original Ps. 8.4 type of saying or independently of it. In the developing tradition these original sayings became titular sayings ('the son of man' became 'the Son of Man'); this is the stage we find crystallized in Q. Subsequently the whole tradition continued to expand and merged with the developing (Pauline) kerygma of the cross to form the so-called suffering Son of Man sayings in Mark.[13] The Fourth Gospel cemented this connection by linking Son of Man language with the peculiarly Johannine themes of Jesus being lifted up and glorified (see below p.75), and further expanded the tradition to embrace the implication of pre-existence (John 3.13; 6.62).[14]

However, the Gospel of Thomas's support here is of questionable value, since the eschatology of Thomas is hardly typical either of Jesus' proclamation or of the early kerygmata, so that it may well reflect a *post*-apocalyptic stage in the development of the Jesus-tradition (rather than a *pre*-apocalyptic stage) from which apocalyptic Son of Man sayings have been eliminated (see below p.286). Of greater weight is the consideration that those sayings which have been identified as Ps. 8.4 type sayings *hardly make sense except as self-references*. In particular, it is simply not true that 'man in general has nowhere to lay his head'; as it stands that logion is only really intelligible as a reference to Jesus' own mission as a wandering preacher (Matt. 8.20/Luke 9.58). The point is even clearer in the case of Matt. 11.18f./Luke 7.33f. If original to Jesus these sayings reflect a manner of Jesus' speech in which he referred to himself in the third person idiom, *bar* *ᵉnāšā*.

(*d*) A fourth view is a variation of the third – that *Jesus used bar ᵉnāšā, but of himself, and in a deliberately ambiguous way = 'one'*. There is some dispute on the question whether there are any parallels to this use of *bar ᵉnāšā* in the Palestine of Jesus' day.[15] Be that as it may, *the best evidence that Jesus used bar ᵉnāšā as a self-reference comes from the Synoptic tradition itself*: it is the best explanation of the texts mentioned above (beginning of (*c*)); the present divergent forms of certain other texts are best explained if we recognize a common original *bar ᵉnāšā* form (particularly Mark 3.28/Matt. 12.31f./Luke 12.10);[16] it is the best explanation of why in parallel versions one reads 'I' and the other 'the Son of Man' since *bar ᵉnāšā* could be taken either way (particularly Matt. 5.11/Luke 6.22; Matt. 10.32/Luke 12.8; Matt. 16.13/Mark 8.27).

The problem which this thesis has to wrestle with is the question, At what point did the overt influence of Dan. 7.13 begin to exert itself on the Son of Man sayings? We noted how difficult it is to accept that an original apocalyptic Son of Man imagery drawing on Dan. 7.13

expanded to embrace distinctively non-apocalyptic material like Matt. 8.20/Luke 9.58. It is almost as difficult to accept that Jesus used a *bar 'ᵉnāšā* form which embraced both the Ps. 8.4 idiom and the Dan. 7.13 imagery within itself. Nevertheless, *an ambiguous bar 'ᵉnāšā form which in at least some instances Jesus used with allusion to Dan. 7.13 seems to be the least objectionable of the four hypotheses.*[17] The problem is substantially eased if we see the influence of Dan. 7.13 as more pervasive on Jesus' *bar 'ᵉnāšā* language, and *at the same time*, recognize that Dan. 7.13 is itself not a titular usage but speaks only of a human figure who represents or symbolizes the persecuted loyalists of the Maccabean days in their ultimate vindication in the court of heaven.[18] In such a case it becomes quite possible that (some of) the suffering Son of Man sayings also go back to an ambiguous *bar 'ᵉnāšā* formulation of Jesus – despite their absence from Q.[19]

The most likely view of the earliest community's role in the development of the Son of Man tradition is therefore as follows. The first Christians inherited a number of *bar 'ᵉnāšā* sayings spoken by Jesus, (almost?) all with reference to himself and some at least (most? all?) alluding to or influenced in greater or less degree by the Dan. 7 vision, and thus containing an implicit christology. In almost every case the early communities removed the ambiguity either by taking *bar 'ᵉnāšu* as first person singular, or by elaborating it into the full blown title 'the Son of Man' with explicit or implicit reference to Dan. 7.13.

9.3   Thus, in *conclusion*, we can say that *the conviction that Jesus was the Son of Man was part of the earliest church's faith.* But decisive evidence that the first Christians used a Son of Man christology to confess the distinctiveness of their faith to others or to achieve a clearer self-understanding of it for themselves is lacking. The fact remains that, so far as our evidence takes us, *the activity of the earliest church at this point was confined to elaborating the tradition of Jesus' sayings.* Faith in Jesus as the Son of Man had no real life outside that tradition (Acts 7.56 is the only real exception). Son of Man christology did not provide a growing point for the distinctive theology of the earliest churches. In so far as any confession characterized earliest Palestinian communities it was that 'Jesus is Messiah'. And though Jesus was recognized as the coming Son of Man this forward looking faith found its expression much more clearly in the confession of Jesus as Lord.

§10. JESUS IS MESSIAH

This seems to have been *a key expression of faith within the early Jewish mission* and the affirmation that Jesus was Messiah probably formed the decisive step of faith for Jewish converts. This is certainly the testimony of Acts 2.31f., 3.18, 5.42, 8.5, 9.22, 17.3, 18.5, 28, and there is no reason to doubt Luke's account at this point, since these passages reflect the (early) titular usage rather than the (later) proper name usage. Elsewhere in the writings of the NT (apart from the Jesus-tradition preserved in the Synoptics) 'Christos' usually serves as a proper name, a way of referring to Jesus rather than an actual confession of faith in Jesus as the Christ (particularly Paul and the Church or 'Catholic' Epistles; though note passages like Rom. 9.5 and 15.3). However, somewhat surprisingly perhaps, the Fourth Gospel preserves the primitive use of Christos. Though written late in the first century John only rarely uses Christ as a proper name (Jesus Christ); whereas he regularly speaks of 'the Christ' (e.g. 1.20; 3.28; 7.26, 41; 10.24) and even preserves the Hebrew (or Aramaic) form 'Messias' (1.41; 4.25). His avowed aim, as we have seen, (p. 26), is to demonstrate that 'Jesus is the Christ, the Son of God' (20.31). And in 11.27 Martha becomes the model for full Christian confession – 'I believe that you are the Christ, the Son of God' (cf. the Baptist – 3.28).

10.1   The history of this confession within the first century is fairly clearly marked. *In essence it goes back to Jesus' own life-time.* The decisive evidence comes from the circumstances of his death. Without diminishing the serious historical problems relating to the trial of Jesus, it is nevertheless hardly less than certain that Jesus was put to death as a messianic pretender – one who posed a nationalist threat to the political authorities (Mark 15.26; Matt. 27.37; Luke 23.38; John 19.19 – where 'king of the Jews' is simply the messianic pretender charge rephrased for the benefit of the Roman governor). Traces of an enthusiasm towards Jesus as such a claimant to political messiahship are visible in the episode underlying the feeding of the 5000 (Mark 6.30–45), especially when we compare it with the probably independent account preserved in John 6.1–15 (cf. Mark 6.45 with John 6.15). The confession itself probably also goes back to the context of Jesus' ministry (Mark 8.29); but if so, the confession of Peter very probably envisaged a messiahship in the same nationalist and political terms.

What is clear from all three episodes is that Jesus *rejected* such a role. Indeed, never once in the earliest Synoptic tradition does Jesus use the title Messiah of himself; never once does he unequivocally welcome its application to himself. The reason presumably is that the concept of messiahship inextricably bound up with the title Messiah, at least in popular hope and imagination, was one which Jesus did not himself embrace. For Jesus, then, the confession of himself as Messiah meant a *misunderstanding* of his mission. Consequently he *discouraged* such confession.

On the other hand, we cannot say that Jesus denied a messianic role altogether. His entry into Jerusalem and attack on the abuse of the temple may well have contained deliberate messianic overtones. Mark 12.35–37, if it originated with Jesus, would probably have been understood as having some sort of self reference (see also below p.51). The main weight of the charge against Jesus at his trial probably rested on the obscure saying about the destruction and eschatological reconstruction of the temple, which must go back to Jesus in some form (Mark 14.58/Matt. 26.61; Mark 15.29/Matt. 27.40; John 2.19; cf. Mark 13.2 pars.; Acts 6.14; Gosp. Thos. 71), and which would have constituted some sort of claim to messiahship (II Sam. 7.12–14 as interpreted by Qumran;[20] I Enoch 90.28f.; IV Ezra 9.38–10.27; cf. Ezek. 40–48; Jub. 1.17, 27f.; T. Ben. 9.2; II Bar. 32.4; Sib. Or. V.423f.). And Jesus' response to the specifically messianic charges of Caiaphas and Pilate are best taken in the sense, 'If you want to put it that way' (Mark 14.62; 15.2),[21] implying that it was hardly Jesus' own choice of expression. According to our evidence then (Mark 8.29–33; 14.61f.), *Jesus' primary concern at this point was to explain his role in terms of suffering and eschatological consummation rather than to dispute concepts of messiahship.*

10.2   It is at this point that *the earliest community* seems to have taken over. Where Jesus shows a marked ambivalence in his attitude to the title Messiah, because of its political connotations, the earliest Christian apologists found it necessary to fight for the retention of the title, but suitably redefined in terms of the suffering Jesus had anticipated and the death he had died. *It is this redefinition of the title Messiah in terms of Jesus' suffering and death which seems to have dominated its earliest use as a confession.* In the earliest days of Christianity when the new sect was not yet distinct from Judaism, the confession 'Jesus is the Messiah' was obviously a key point in the debate with more traditional Jews – the point at issue being the death of Jesus. How could a Jew believe that a crucified man was God's Messiah? – 'Christ crucified . . . a stumbling block to Jews' (I Cor. 1.23). Hence it became of cardinal importance for these first Christians to demonstrate that 'Christ crucified' was not a contradiction in terms. Scriptures were searched and passages brought to light (no doubt including Isa. 53) which could be taken to show that Messiah must suffer (Acts 3.18; 17.2f.; 18.28; 26.23; I Cor. 15.3; cf. above pp.17f.). Luke 24.26, 46 may at least be taken as an indication that this recognition of a suffering Messiah within scripture was an important element in the developing self-understanding of the earliest faith. At the same time Acts 3.20f. certainly counts as evidence that the earliest Palestinian churches spoke of Jesus as Messiah in connection with his imminently expected *parousia*. But even so the weight of evidence suggests that for the period prior to Paul this was not the primary focus of its usage. Rather we see what appears to be a degree of *continuity* between Jesus and the earliest church, namely on *the basic association of messiahship with suffering*. The problem for Jesus in the pre-Easter situation was to link suffering and death with the given concept of messiahship – a problem Jesus apparently never solved, at least during his life. The problem for the earliest church in the post-Easter situation was to link messiahship with the given facts of a man's suffering and death – a problem with which they had greater success, though probably at the cost of largely restricting the title to this specific function (of surmounting Jewish antipathy to the proclamation of a crucified Messiah).

10.3 *Paul's* use of the Christ title reflects the same emphasis – Christ *crucified* is the Messiah Paul proclaims (see particularly I Cor. 1.23; 2.2; Gal. 3.1). But his use of it also implies that this was a battle already long won for Paul. He makes no attempt to prove that Jesus really is 'the Christ' despite his suffering and death. 'Christ' is no longer a title whose fitness in its application to Jesus has to be demonstrated. The belief in Jesus as the Christ has become so firmly established in his mind and message that he simply takes it for granted, and 'Christ' functions simply as a way of speaking of Jesus, as a *proper name* for Jesus (so even in I Cor. 15.3).

The evidence of the Pauline letters therefore is that *the confession, 'Jesus is the Christ' had little relevance to or life within a Gentile or predominantly Hellenistic environment* – as we might have expected. This conclusion is supported by two other observations. First, the way in which the Christ title has to be supplemented and defined in terms of 'Son of God' in Hellenistic Jewish Christian writings (see below p.47). That is to say, even within Hellenistic Jewish Christianity the confession seems to have faded in significance. Second, the alternative messianic confession, 'Jesus is the Son of David', also seems to have had little currency outside Palestine and to have been largely 'subordinated' to the Son of God language.[22] Matthew alone makes very much of it (Matt. 1.1; 9.27; 12.23; 15.22; 20.30f.; 21.9, 15 – contrast 21.9 with Mark 11.9f.), and echoes of its early significance are preserved in Acts 13.23, II Tim. 2.8 and Rev. 5.5, 22.16. But elsewhere, even among Hellenistic Jews, the very few allusions to such a confessional faith seem to imply a certain degree of embarrassment with the claim (Mark 12.35–37; John 7.42 – on the lips of the fickle, wavering crowd; Rom. 1.3f. – 'according to the flesh' regularly sounds a negative, even pejorative note in Paul;[22a] cf. Acts 2.29–31; and note Barnabas 12.10). The reason presumably was that the title was already too clearly defined in nationalist, political terms, and even less capable than 'Messiah' of being remoulded within the wider context of Hellenism (cf. Acts 17.7 and the spiritualization of the concept of Jesus' kingship in John 18.33–38 and Heb. 7.1f.).

Of greater importance for us at this point of our study is the fact that also preserved in Paul we see *the beginnings of a fuller confessional formula* – Christ died (for us), but was raised or rose again (see particularly Rom. 4.24f.; 8.34; 14.9; I Cor. 15.3–5; II Cor. 5.15; 13.4; I Thess. 4.14).[23] But whether this was a confessional formula as such, or merely a standard dual emphasis in proclamation, is not clear. And even if it was a confessional formula we are still a very long way indeed from the second article of the Apostles' Creed.

10.4   If the confession 'Jesus is the Christ' lost its significance outside the borders of Palestine, it certainly seems to have *retained* its importance *within more distinctively Jewish circles*. This is suggested by the preservation of the titular usage in Matthew's special material and redaction of Mark (Matt. 1.17; 2.4; 11.2; 16.20; 23.10; 24.5). But the point is most vividly demonstrated by the tension set up within Jewish Christianity by the fall of Jerusalem and the reconstitution of the Sanhedrin at Jamnia, when Judaism began to turn in upon itself, and Christianity and Judaism began to pull apart. Where previously Christians could remain Jews and continue to worship regularly in the synagogue, from about the middle of the 80s onwards Jewish Christians were faced with the stark choice either of conforming to the new, more narrowly defined Judaism or of being excommunicated from the synagogue. This is one of the situations which seems to lie behind the Johannine writings.[24] In these circumstances 'Jesus is the Christ' appears to have become the test formula. For the Christians it became the test of true faith (I John 2.22; 5.1). For the synagogue it became the test of heresy (John 9.22). In short, we may say that *where the confrontation between Judaism and Christianity remained a factor of importance in the development of confessional Christianity, the confession 'Jesus is the Christ' retained its significance and importance* (cf. Justin, *Dial.* 35.7; 39.6; 43.8; 47.4; 48.4; 108.2; 142); *but almost nowhere else.*

§11. JESUS IS SON OF GOD

11.1   It is becoming increasingly probable that *the Son of God language of early Christianity has its roots within Jesus' own ministry.* (1) Whereas it earlier appeared that 'Son of God' had no messianic significance within the Judaism of Jesus' time, the evidence from the Dead Sea Scrolls now begins to point in the other direction. Not only are II Sam. 7.14 and Ps. 2 linked together and interpreted messianically,[25] but a recently translated fragment from Cave 4 specifically applies the title 'Son of God' to a human being in an apocalyptic setting (4Qps Dan A).[26] It is quite possible therefore that any messianic speculation which attached to Jesus during his ministry also caught up the title Son of God (hence the plausibility of the question in Mark 14.61 par.; see above p.42 n.20). (2) There are some indications that Jewish *Hasidim* who were recognized to possess charismatic powers were also called sons of God, or holy men (of God).[27] If this was so, then it is quite possible that some of the possessed individuals, to whom Jesus ministered, hailed him as 'Son of God' or 'Holy Man of God' – as some of the narratives of his exorcisms suggest (Mark 1.24; 3.11; 5.7; cf. John 6.69). (3) Probably the firmest root is Jesus' own distinctive habit of addressing God as *abba* (Father) in all his prayers (see particularly Mark 14.36; Matt. 11.25f./Luke 10.21). Evidently Jesus thought of himself as God's son in a distinctive sense, and he seems to have conveyed something of this sense to his disciples (Matt. 6.9/Luke 11.2; Luke 22.29). We should, however, beware of reading too much back into Jesus' self-consciousness at this point.[28]

11.2   *The earliest churches do not seem to have made much use of the title 'Son of God' as a confession.* Heb. 1.5 suggests that they took over (from the Qumran community?) the association of Ps. 2.7 and II Sam. 7.14 in reference to the exalted Jesus. It should be noted that this earliest use of Ps. 2.7 was clearly *'adoptionist'* in sense: Jesus was begotten by God as his Son through his resurrection and exaltation (so explicitly Acts 13.33; note also Rom. 1.3f. and Heb. 5.5).[28a] Even if he already had been God's son during his life, his status as son had been greatly

enhanced by his resurrection (Rom. 1.3f). Here *the fundamental impor-*
tance of the resurrection of Jesus as the starting point for and principal catalyst
in christological reflection is underlined (see also below pp.217 and 243).
That the primary reference of the title at this stage was to Jesus'
exaltation to kingly power and to the imminent consummation of his
parousia is clearly suggested by these references (cf. Mark 13.32;
14.61f.; Luke 1.32f.; I Cor. 15.24–28; I Thess. 1.9f.).

Also probably early was the forging of the link between Jesus as
God's son and the Servant language of Second Isaiah (with the
concept of Jesus' messiahship presumably providing the common
denominator). This may lie behind (or be the result of) the link
between Ps. 2.7 and Isa. 42.1 in the words of the heavenly voice
addressed to Jesus at Jordan (Mark 1.11), and may possibly also
explain the ambiguity of the language in Acts 3.13, 26, 4.27,30.[29] In
view of the discussion above (§11.1) it is worth noting that in the last
of these Acts references Jesus is described as 'your holy child/servant
Jesus'.

11.3   If the confession of Jesus as Son of God plays little role in the
witness of the earliest Christians it certainly *came to full flower within*
the widening mission of Hellenistic Jewish Christianity. According to Luke,
Paul's first proclamation in the synagogues of Damascus could be
summed up in the confession, 'He is the Son of God' (Acts 9.20). In
Rom. 1.3f. Paul clearly uses an older and more widely acceptable
formula as guarantee of his good faith to commend himself to the
Roman Christians; in this affirmation it is the sonship of Jesus which
is most prominent. I Thessalonians 1.9f. may very well be a summary of such Hellenistic Jewish Christian preaching to the Gentiles[30] – 'You turned to God from idols, to serve a living and true
God, and to wait for his Son from heaven . . .' – an association of
Jesus' sonship with his parousia unique in the Pauline literature.
Elsewhere, although Paul makes relatively little use of the title, it
does appear most frequently in those letters where he is most closely
in dialogue with Christianity's Jewish tradition (Romans 7, Galatians 4). In Hebrews the central concept is, of course, the High-
priesthood of Christ. But that belongs more to the writer's own
distinctive christology, not so much to his common faith. The basic
confession common to his readers and himself is more likely to be
'Jesus is the Son of God' (4.14; see also 6.6; 7.3; 10.29). Most striking
of all is the way in which the Father-Son language so sparingly used
in Mark, Q and Luke, positively blossoms in Matthew and particularly John ('Father' = God in the words of Jesus – Mark 3, Q 4, Luke

4, Matthew 31, John 100).[31] Notice also how the begetting of Jesus'
sonship, originally associated with Jesus' resurrection-ascension is
now traced back in some cases to his experience at Jordan (Mark
1.11; Q ? – cf. Matt. 4.3, 6/Luke 4.3, 9), in others to his birth (Luke
1.32, 35), and in others to eternity (John 1.14, 18; cf. Rom. 8.3; Gal.
4.4; Col. 1.15; Heb. 1.2f. – see also below §51.2).

One of the most interesting developments is the clear way in which
the Son of God confession is brought in to *supplement and define the
confession of Jesus' messiahship.* John as we saw preserves the primitive
way of speaking of Jesus as 'the Christ'. But in the Fourth Gospel the
phrase usually appears on the lips of the crowd – that is, as a
question, a confession of doubt, not a confession of faith (cf. his use of
the title 'prophet' – particularly 6.14; 7.40). Evidently 'Mes-
siah/Christ' did not provide a wholly adequate confession of John's
faith. The primary confession for the Johannine circle is rather 'Jesus
is the Son of God' (John 1.34, 49; 10.36; I John 4.15; 5.5). The
Johannine writers certainly retain the confession of Jesus' messiahship (see above §10.4), but evidently they also felt the need to
redefine it and transform it into the confession 'Jesus is the Son of
God'. Hence John 11.27, 20.31, where we have to translate, 'You are
the Christ, that is, the Son of God', '. . . believe that Jesus is the
Christ, that is, the Son of God' – *not* '. . . Christ *and* Son of God' – (so
I John 2.22f. 5.1, 5–12).

With Matthew it is much the same. He retains the confession that
Jesus is the Messiah, David's son – still important no doubt for
his (Palestinian) Jewish readers (see above p.44). But with a view
to his wider readership he too takes up the Son of God language. The
importance of the Son of God confession for Matthew is clear from
14.33 – the episode of Jesus walking on the water. His source, Mark,
ends by noting the disciples' astonishment and hardness of heart
(Mark 6.51f.). Matthew has transformed this into the outright and
clear-cut confession: 'Truly you are the Son of God' (cf. also Matt.
27.40, 43's redaction of Mark 15.30). And in the account of Peter's
confession at Caesarea Philippi he does precisely what John does: he
explains the confession 'You are the Christ' (Mark 8.29) by adding,
'that is, the Son of the living God' (Matt. 16.16) – quite clearly an
interpretative addition. Like John in John 11.27 and 20.31, Matthew
says in effect, 'This is the way you have to understand the confession
"Jesus is the Christ"' (see also 2.15; 4.3, 6; 11.27; 28.19; and cf.
8.29's redaction of Mark 5.7 and 26.63's redaction of Mark 14.61).[32]
An interesting conclusion suggests itself from Matthew's use of both
the Son of David and the Son of God formulae: viz. that this Gospel

was intended as something of a bridge document between a more narrowly defined Jewish Christianity (and Judaism) on the one hand, and a Jewish Christianity much more informed by Hellenistic categories on the other (see further below p.384). When we add the evidence of John and Hebrews, the three together being probably the clearest expression of Hellenistic Jewish Christianity in the NT, the further conclusion seems to be firmly established, that 'Jesus is the Son of God' was the most meaningful confession in Hellenistic Jewish Christian circles.

Why was this? Probably because the title 'Son of God' was more meaningful to a Gentile audience than Messiah could ever be. Moreover, it could serve as a good *bridge between Jewish and Gentile thought*: both societies were familiar with the idea that a good or great man might be called a son of God, and in both societies 'son of God' could have connotations of divinity. Perhaps there was also a tendency to avoid *kyrios* (Lord) in some Jewish Christian circles because it threatened Jewish monotheism (*kyrios* is never used in the Johannine letters). Son of God would be an obvious and attractive alternative. And by filling it with distinctively Christian content it could become as exalted a confession as 'Jesus is Lord' (see below §12.4). This is certainly what has happened in the usage of the Johannine corpus (John 1.14, 18; 3.16, 18; 10.36; I John 4.9). At the same time it had special overtones for the Christian which *kyrios* could not have, and offered a link with Jesus' own self-understanding which *kyrios* could not provide.

11.4   The confession of Jesus as Son of God was also of considerable significance within *Gentile Christianity*. This is particularly clear from its use in Mark, where the title 'Son of God' plays a central role (note especially Mark 1.1, 11; 3.11; 5.7; 9.7; 12.6; 13.32; 14.61; 15.39). We should not overemphasize the distinction between Hellenistic Jewish Christianity and Gentile Christianity at this point however. Bearing in mind our earlier comments (above p.34), it would probably be more accurate to describe Mark (like Matthew) as something of a bridge document – in Mark's case between Gentile Christians and Christians from the Jewish diaspora. The tradition that it was written by the Jew Mark, and the impression that it was written in a Gentile situation would support this suggestion. The point for us to note is that in the words 'Jesus is the Son of God' we have *a confession which had the ability to cross over cultural and national boundaries and still remain meaningful* – an attribute which marks off the Son of God confession from those examined above.

However, this same attribute can easily become a weakness and a danger to the faith confessed. For the word or phrase which slips easily from one language to another never in fact remains the same, despite appearances; for in that new culture it tends to draw its meaning from the language context of that culture rather than from its previous context. And so a quite different range of meaning can be imparted to a word or phrase even though it itself remains unchanged. Something like this probably happened to the Son of God confession within the churches of the Gentile mission; for there are some indications that 'Jesus is the Son of God' became a vehicle within Hellenistic Christianity[33] for rather *disparate and divergent christologies*. Reading between the lines in Mark, Son of God language seems to have been used to present Jesus simply as a great miracle worker, what has been called (misleadingly) a 'divine man' conception (see particularly Mark 3.11; 5.7; 9.7).[34] More clearly behind John stands a docetic understanding of Christ (see below pp.70f.). Both Mark and the Johannine circle resolutely oppose such christologies. Mark does so by his presentation of Jesus as the Son of God who is also the suffering Son of Man. The Johannines do so by presenting us with another confessional formula: 'Jesus Christ came in the flesh' (I John 4.2; II John 7; cf. John 1.14; I John 5.6) – clearly a polemical slogan against docetic ideas of Christ, and against any misunderstanding of his Son of God confession. As we have already noted (p.27) John allows his faith in Jesus as exalted Son of God to colour his presentation of the earthly Jesus to a remarkable degree – far too much, some would say. At times he draws perilously close to pushing his faith in Jesus over the brink into outright myth (see further below pp.299f.). It was I John's explicit confession that Jesus Christ came in the flesh which makes it finally clear that the Johannine circle never falls over the edge. Both John and I John firmly maintain the reality of Jesus' earthly life, and so maintain the unity and continuity between the earthly, fleshly Jesus and the exalted Son of God (see below pp.300–305).

Looking beyond the documents of first-century Christianity we should simply remind ourselves that the confession of Jesus as Son of God became the key description of Jesus in the classic creeds, the chief language vehicle to confess both Jesus' divinity and his difference from God the Father – 'the Son of God, begotten from the Father, only-begotten . . . begotten not made . . .'. To what extent this Nicene confession can claim to be according to the scriptures examined above, or to be a proper extension of the earliest confession of Jesus as Son of God is an important question and worth pondering. If nothing more, it reminds us that the recognition of the unity and diversity of the NT writings has ramifications which extend far beyond the NT itself (see further below chs X and XV).

§12. JESUS IS LORD

12.1   This is undoubtedly *the principal confession of faith for Paul and for his churches.* The Pauline epistles use the title Lord (*kyrios*) of Jesus nearly 230 times. That Jesus is Lord, is a central affirmation of the Pauline kerygma (II Cor. 4.5; Col. 2.6). 'Jesus is Lord' is the basic confession at conversion-initiation (Rom.10.9). 'Jesus is Lord' is the distinguishing mark of inspiration by the Spirit of God (I Cor. 12.3). 'Jesus is Lord' is the climactic expression of the universe's worship in Phil. 2.11. *Kyrios* is also greatly used with reference to Jesus by the authors of Luke-Acts and of the Church Epistles, less frequently elsewhere, and surprisingly not at all in the Johannine epistles. Not least in importance is the early Aramaic invocation preserved by Paul in I Cor. 16.22, 'Maranatha', 'Our Lord, come!', where *mara(n)* is the equivalent of *kyrios*.

The history of this confession of Jesus as Lord in earliest Christianity largely revolves round the question, How significant is the application of this title to Jesus? What role or status does this confession attribute to Jesus or recognize as belonging to Jesus? The answers of earliest Christianity vary and we cannot always be sure if we are hearing them correctly. The problem is that 'lord' can denote a whole range of dignity – from a respectful form of address as to a teacher or judge to a full title for God.[35] Where do the early Christian references to the lordship of Jesus come within this spectrum? The answer seems to be that *over the first few decades of Christianity the confession of Jesus as 'Lord' moved in overt significance from the lower end of this 'spectrum of dignity' towards the upper end steadily gathering to itself increasing overtones of deity.*

12.2   According to Matthew and Luke *Jesus was regularly addressed as 'Lord' during his ministry* – in Matthew chiefly within the context of miracle stories (Matt. 8.2, 6, 8, 25; 9.28; 14.28, 30; etc.), in Luke chiefly in teaching contexts (Luke 9.59, 61; 10.40; 11.1; 12.41; etc.). We need not doubt that the Aramaic *mari* underlies the Greek *kyrie* (vocative) in at least some of these instances. *Mar* was used of the first-century BC holy man Abba Hilkiah, presumably in recognition of the charismatic powers attributed to him.[36] Moreover, 'lord' was largely synonymous with 'teacher' at the time of Jesus, and Jesus was certainly recognized to have the authority of a rabbi or teacher (Mark 9.5, 17, 38; 10.17, 35, 51; etc.). This equivalence of 'teacher' and 'lord' is probably reflected in John 13.13f. and may well lie behind the use of *kyrios* in Mark 11.3 (cf. Mark 14.14). We can say therefore that *the confession of Jesus as Lord was rooted within the ministry of Jesus to the extent that he was widely acknowledged to exercise the authority of a (charismatic) teacher and healer* (cf. Mark 1.22, 27; 6.2; 11.28). Whether 'Lord' already had a higher significance for Jesus himself during his ministry depends on how we evaluate Mark 12.35–37. Even if it contains an authentic word of the historical Jesus (as is quite possible) it need only mean that he understood Messiah to be a figure superior to David in significance and specially favoured by Yahweh. It does not necessarily imply that he thought of Messiah as a divine figure (Psalm 110 after all probably referred originally to the king; see also p.53 n.43 below).

12.3 *As a confession 'Jesus is Lord' stems primarily from the post-resurrection faith of the first Christians.* It was evidently the belief that Jesus had been raised from the dead which gave 'lord' the decisive nudge along the 'spectrum of dignity' towards a connotation of divinity. According to both Acts 2.36 and the hymn cited by Paul in Phil. 2.9–11, *kyrios* was the title given to Jesus at his resurrection/exaltation and by virtue of it. A striking confirmation of the resurrection's significance at this point is Luke's own use of the title. In his Gospel, when he is narrating some episode, he quite naturally refers to Jesus as 'the Lord'. But never do the characters in these episodes speak in this way. The first time Jesus is called 'the Lord' by one of his contemporaries is immediately after his resurrection (Luke 24.34).[37] Similarly in the Fourth Gospel. Despite the high christology of John's presentation of the incarnate Logos (including the roll-call of titles in John 1 and Jesus' consciousness of pre-existence) *kyrios* is not used by Jesus' contemporaries until John 20.28, and the Evangelist himself, unlike even Luke, shows a marked reserve in his own use of the title for Jesus prior to the resurrection.[38] In other words, what we have preserved here, as explicitly elsewhere, is the conviction that *Jesus became Lord as a consequence of his resurrection and exaltation.*

It is not wholly clear what status was affirmed of Jesus as risen Lord at this earliest stage. If I Cor. 16.22, James 5.7f., Rev. 22.20, and I and II Thessalonians (the earliest Pauline epistles, where *kyrios* is used frequently) are any guide, the dignity and authority of Jesus' Lordship was that of *soon returning judge*. Here 'Lord' had

begun to absorb the significance of the Danielic 'Son of Man', quite
possibly through the combination of Ps. 110.1 and Dan. 7.13 in early
Christian apologetic.[39] We cannot say how far 'Lord' had thereby
moved along the 'spectrum of dignity' or whether overtones of
divinity were yet present to those who thus confessed Jesus (cf. after
all Matt. 19.28/Luke 22.29f.). On the other hand, the sense of 'Lord'
used of Jesus by his contemporaries had already been left far
behind[40] (though it could be argued that the resurrection of Jesus
was regarded in part as the divine seal of approval on the authority
he exercised as teacher and miracle worker; see further below §50.3).
What we can say with more confidence is that the *mara* confession
was probably not the most important confession of the earliest
churches. In particular it does not seem to have provided a medium
of evangelism in the Jewish mission, as did the Messiah confession
and the Son of God confession (with Hellenistic Jews)[41] – though
Mark 12.35–37 and Barn. 12.10f. may well imply that it featured
within Christian Jewish apologetic from quite an early period.
I Corinthians 16.22, Rev. 22.20 and Didache 10.6 suggest however
that the *mara* confession of the first Christians *belonged primarily to their
own worship* where it has left its most enduring mark. Only within
Hellenistic Christianity did the confession 'Jesus is Lord' come fully
into its own.

12.4   In *Hellenistic circles* the *mara* confession would naturally be
translated by the Greek *kyrios*. Indeed, according to Acts 11.20, it
was the *kyrios* language which was chosen by those who first
preached the gospel to pagans. With this transition the confession
'Jesus is Lord' gathered to it still greater significance. For one thing
kyrios was well established as a title for the cult deity in several of the
mystery religions (particularly Isis and Serapis), and was in process
of becoming the key title in Emperor worship ('Caesar is Lord'). But
even more important, in the Greek versions of the OT used by Paul
and his churches, *kyrios* was the translation of the divine name,
Yahweh. In other words, *it was only at this point of transition from* mara
to kyrios *that the confession 'Jesus is Lord' clearly became an assertion of the
exalted Jesus' divinity*. And this was quite consciously done. Indeed, it
is quite astonishing how Paul uses OT texts speaking of *Yahweh* with
clear reference to *Jesus* (e.g. Rom. 10.13; I Cor. 2.16). Most striking
of all is the application of one of the sternest monotheistic passages of
the OT (Isa. 45.23) to the exalted Jesus in Phil. 2.10f. – a hymn
already in circulation before Paul took it up (see below pp.134f.).
Here quite clearly 'Jesus is Lord' has become a confession not just of

divinely given authority, but of *divinity* itself.

  Should we then say that Jesus was confessed as *God* from earliest
days in Hellenistic Christianity? That would be to claim too much.
(1) The emergence of a confession of Jesus in terms of divinity was
largely facilitated by the extensive use of Ps. 110.1 from very early on
(most clearly in Mark 12.36; Acts 2.34f.; I Cor. 15.25; Heb. 1.13).

> The Lord says to my lord:
> 'Sit at my right hand,
> till I make your enemies your footstool'.[42]

Its importance here lies in the double use of *kyrios*. The one is clearly
Yahweh, but who is the other? Clearly *not* Yahweh, but an exalted
being whom the psalmist calls *kyrios*.[43] (2) Paul calls Jesus *kyrios*, but
he seems to have marked reservations about actually calling Jesus
'God' (Rom. 9.5 is the only real candidate within the main Pauline
corpus, and even there the text is unclear). Similarly he refrains from
praying *to* Jesus. More typical of his attitude is that he prays *to God*
through Christ (Rom. 1.8; 7.25; II Cor. 1.20; Col. 3.17).[44] (3) 'Jesus is
Lord' is only part of a fuller confession for Paul. For at the same time
that he affirms 'Jesus is Lord' he also affirms 'God is one' (I Cor.
8.5–6; Eph. 4.5–6). Here Christianity shows itself as a developed
form of Judaism, with its monotheistic confession as one of the most
important parts of its Jewish inheritance; for in Judaism the most
fundamental confession is 'God is one', 'There is only one God'
(Deut. 6.4). Hence also Rom. 3.30, Gal. 3.20, I Tim. 2.5 (cf. James
2.19). Within Palestine and the Jewish mission such an affirmation
would have been unnecessary – Jew and Christian shared a belief in
God's oneness. But in the Gentile mission this Jewish presupposition
within Christianity would have emerged to prominence, in face of
the wider belief in 'gods many'. The point for us to note is that *Paul*
can hail Jesus as Lord not in order to identify him with God, but rather, if
anything, to distinguish him from the one God (cf. particularly I Cor.
15.24–28; see also below pp.225f.). So too Jesus' Lordship could be
expressed in cosmic dimensions without posing too many problems
to monotheism, since Wisdom speculation provided a ready and
appropriate terminology (particularly I Cor. 8.6; Col. 1.15–20; Heb.
1.3f.; see below pp.220f.).

12.5   *The confession of Jesus as Lord is thus at first only an addition to the*
confession of the one God. Here we see the beginnings of a two-clause
confession: God is one, Jesus is Lord. So long as the early Church
was happy to live with the ambiguity of the *kyrios* confession there

were no problems. But from the first there was an inbuilt tension between the two clauses, and one which came increasingly to the surface: *how to affirm the oneness of God without detracting from the Lordship of Jesus; how to affirm the Lordship of Jesus without detracting from the oneness of God*. The NT writers did not attempt to investigate it very far. Was Paul content to rest with the solution outlined in I Cor. 15.24–28? Eph. 1.20–23 and Col. 1.15–20 would have put that solution under some strain. The author of Hebrews seems to have been content to juxtapose strong adoptionist language with a psalm hailing the exalted Christ as 'God' (Heb. 1.9 – see further below pp.222f., 259f.). Only the Fourth Evangelist makes anything like a sustained attempt to grapple with the issue in his Father-Son christology. His Gospel comes to a striking climax in Thomas's acclamation of the risen Jesus, 'my Lord and my God' (John 20.28). Here certainly *kyrios* has moved in its overt significance right along the spectrum of dignity to its upper end – though the words of Thomas may perhaps be better described as the extravagance of worship rather than the careful formulation of a confession (see also John 1.1, 18; I John 5.20; cf. Titus 2.13).

In the following centuries of course the tension between the Lordship of Jesus and the oneness of God became the central problem of theology. And to this day it remains the chief stumbling block in Christian-Jewish, Christian-Muslim dialogue. To an important degree also it is the basic problem which underlies much of modern Christian theology: how to speak of God and of Jesus today?

§13. THE LIFE-SETTINGS OF THE EARLIEST CONFESSIONAL FORMULAE

In the material surveyed above several quite clear confessional situations are apparent – situations which called for the earliest Christians to put into a concise and explicit form what was the central element in their new faith, what now marked off their faith as distinctive.

13.1   The most obvious life-setting is *proclamation*: 'Jesus is the Christ' – Acts 5.42, 9.22, 17.3, 18.5, 28, I Cor. 1.23; 'Jesus is the Son of God' – Acts 9.20, Rom. 1.3f.; 'Jesus is Lord' – Acts 2.36, 10.36, 11.20, Rom. 10.9, II Cor. 4.5, Col. 2.6. It is wholly to be expected that the distinctive character of the Christian gospel should find expression in confessional-type formulations – especially when that proclamation is presented in summary form.

As we noted at the beginning of this chapter, most scholars have regarded baptism as the predominant and almost exclusive life-setting for these confessions (p.34). And of course one naturally expects that confessional statements would play a prominent part in the process of becoming a Christian, particularly at the point of commitment. The fact is, however, that there is no firm association between baptism and the confessional formulae in the NT. The clearest example is the Western text of Acts 8.37, where the Ethiopian eunuch confesses, 'I believe that Jesus Christ is the Son of God' before being baptized. But the Western text is not original; consequently Acts 8.37 has to be recognized as a baptismal formula of a later generation (see also below pp.144ff.). In the NT itself the nearest thing to a baptismal confession as such is Rom. 10.9: conversion and public confession are linked together – and that naturally suggests a baptismal scene. Otherwise *there are no intrinsic grounds for linking any of the confessional formulae within the NT to a specifically baptismal context*.[45]

13.2   *Worship*. It is somewhat surprising that a number of the most explicitly confessional formulae are found in a worship context – John 20.28, I Cor. 12.3, Phil. 2.11, I John 4.1–3 (see also I Cor. 16.22). It would be easy to speak of the liturgical origin of these confessions, but misleading to do so. For 'liturgy' implies something thought out beforehand, structured, established; whereas these worship contexts are noticeable for their spontaneity. In particular, two of the confessions (I Cor. 12.3; I John 4.1–3) are thought of as spoken under the immediate inspiration of the Spirit, perhaps as ecstatic utterances (though 'ecstasy' also tends to be a misleading word). In both cases the situation envisaged is the assembly at worship, when the inspired utterance could be tested by the rest of the congregation. Nor need we assume, because of Didache 10.6, that I Cor. 16.22 ('Our Lord, come!') belonged originally or even at all to a eucharistic context at the time of Paul. There is nothing whatsoever in the letter itself (or in Rev. 22.20) to suggest such a specific context.[46] In particular, that Paul would have expected the reading of his letter to lead at once into the Lord's Supper (the conclusion to his letter serving as the introduction to the Supper!)[47] hardly accords with our knowledge either of Paul's churches or of his relationship to them. It would presuppose a degree of regularity in order and form in the Corinthian worship which is hardly borne out by I Corinthians itself (I Cor. 11.24–25 – the bread and wine as part of a complete meal). And would Paul expect his letter simply to be read out (like a scripture reading at a modern eucharist!) without any time for reflection and/or discussion (cf. 14.29)? In short, what was true of baptism (above §13.1) applies as much here (see also below p.215 n.20).

It would appear then that confessional-type exclamations and cries quite often punctuated the worship of the earliest churches. Enraptured believers (or congregations?) spoke out that rallying cry which at one and the same time summed up their faith, expressed their worship and identified them with the congregation. Here the confessional formula played an important role in developing the self-consciousness and self-understanding of the church; and no doubt served also on not a few occasions as a form of evangelism (cf. I Cor. 14.23–25).

13.3   *Confrontation*. In confrontation with other faiths a confessional formula obviously has an important role in marking out the distinctiveness of the faith confessed by Christians. It is not surprising then that much of the material belongs to *apologetic or polemical contexts*: Acts 9.22, 17.3, 18.28 – a more apologetic situation; John 9.22, 12.42 – a situation where the confrontation with Judaism has become very sharp; I Cor. 8.5f. – which presupposes confrontation with the polytheistic religions of Greek paganism; I John 2.18–23, 4.1–3, II John 9–11 – where the confession of Jesus is the distinguishing criterion of true faith in a debate occasioned by syncretistic forces within the Johannine community (cf. I Cor. 12.3); I Tim. 6.12f., Heb. 3.1, 4.14, 10.23 – where the confession of Jesus is the distinctive mark of the Christian in a time of persecution, the firm pillar to which he clings when faith is threatened by the flood of temptation and tribulation.

§14. CONCLUSIONS

14.1   The chief function of a confession is to lay bare the *distinctiveness* of the faith expressed. What is the distinctiveness of the confessional formulae examined above? It is, I suggest, *the conviction that the historical figure, Jesus the Jew, is now an exalted being* – that this Jesus is and continues to be the *agent of God*, supreme over all other claimants to the titles, Lord and Son of God. There are several points here worthy of notice.

(*a*) First, it is *Jesus* who is confessed – not his ideas, faith or teaching in itself. It is not the faith *of* Jesus which here comes to expression, but faith *in* Jesus. The NT knows no confession which is a confession merely of the significance of the historical Jesus. What Jesus did or said never provides the central or sole element in confessional faith.

(*b*) Second, it is the *present* status of Jesus which is confessed – not what he was, but what he *is*. This is most obvious in the case of the *kyrios* confession, since it is a title of exalted majesty, only applied to Jesus in a more than ordinary way after his resurrection. But it is true also of Son of Man, Son of God and even Messiah. Son of Man began to approach a confessional role only when the *bar 'ᵉnāš* language of Jesus was crystallized into a statement, explicit or implicit, of the exalted Jesus' present apocalyptic significance. Similarly, the early belief that 'Son of God' and 'Christ' was a status into which Jesus entered, or at least fully entered, only at Easter, is reflected in Rom. 1.3f., Acts 13.33 and Acts 2.36, 3.20. Only with the confession, 'Jesus Christ came in the flesh' does the confession confine itself to a historical retrospect – and even there it is the present, glorious Jesus Christ of whom the confession is made. But with the three basic confessions it is always the present tense which is used: 'Jesus *is* . . .'.

(*c*) Third, V. Neufeld has reminded us that in each case *Jesus* is the subject of the confession;[48] *it is the historical person who is so confessed*. In other words, each confession itself maintains the vital link between the historical person and the one who is the present author of life, justification, power. *Jesus*, the Jesus who was, *is*, now is and continues to be Christ, Son of God, Lord. Here emerges an important conclusion in our quest for a unifying element within earliest Christianity: viz., the distinctive feature which comes to expression in all the confessions we have examined, the bedrock of the Christian faith confessed in the NT writings, is *the unity between the earthly Jesus and the exalted one who is somehow involved in or part of our encounter with God in the here and now*. More specific conclusions arising from this chapter on the question of the continuity between Jesus' own message and self-understanding and the faith of the first Christians must await a later stage in our discussion (below §50).

14.2   The confessions lay bare the distinctiveness of the faith confessed in *different particular situations*. We have uncovered no single, final confession appropriate to all circumstances and all times. Any attempt to find a single primitive confession will almost certainly fail. Our investigation has revealed at least three confessions, all of which deserve the epithet 'basic and primitive'. Three *different* confessions – different because the Christians who used them were different, and they used them in different circumstances. In oversimplified terms, and leaving aside the Son of Man tradition which was an important expression of the eschatological faith of the earliest community, we may say that 'Jesus is the Messiah' appears to have been the chief confession of Palestinian Jewish Christians, 'Jesus is the Son of God' of Hellenistic Jewish Christians, 'Jesus is Lord' of Gentile Christians. Or in rather more precise terms, 'Jesus is the Messiah' was the most important confession in Jewish Palestine, 'Jesus is the Son of God' in a Hellenistic-Jewish situation, 'Jesus is Lord' among Gentiles.

Why was it that they were each important in their own spheres? Presumably because each was the most *relevant* and *meaningful* expression of Christian faith in that situation. They were the most important, because they were the most relevant and meaningful. But this also means that the situation in which faith was confessed had a determinative say in the shaping of the confession. The situation called forth the confession. It helped provide the language content of the confession and contributed something to its meaning. Thus we find that language which was important and meaningful in one context became meaningless and redundant in another (Son of Man), or a confessional formula broadened in significance as it moved from one language to another (Jesus is Lord). The development of the 'Christ confession' is perhaps the best example of all. Initially spurned, or at least not welcomed by Jesus, because of its connotations in the Palestine of Jesus' day, it became the key confession of a Palestinian Christianity seeking to mark out its distinctive faith within the context of Judaism, first apologetically, then polemically. But as Christianity moved more and more outside Judaism the confession 'Jesus is the Messiah' became less and less relevant. 'Christ' became little more than a proper name, and the confession had to be explained, supplemented, and so in effect superseded, by the confession 'Jesus is the Son of God'. But then in a confrontation with docetic views 'Jesus is the Son of God' ceased to be an adequate expression of Christian faith (many gnostics could make that confession too), so it in turn had to be supplemented by the confession 'Jesus Christ came in the flesh'. And so it goes on. The fact is, quite simply, that *confessions framed in one context do not remain the same when that context changes. New situations call forth new confessions. A Christianity that ceases to develop new confessional language ceases to confess its faith to the contemporary world.*

14.3 Notice, finally, the *simplicity* of the confessions we have examined – Jesus is the Christ, Jesus is the Son of God, Jesus is Lord.

It is important that faith can be reduced to such simple assertions or claims. To be able to sum up the distinctiveness of one's faith in a single phrase; to be able to express one's worship in a single word; to be able to unite round a single banner; to be able to cling to simply stated conviction in the face of persecution and testing – that is important. NT confessions do not lose themselves in philosophical abstractions or theological profundities. They are not hedged around with qualifications. They are confessions which the so-called 'simple believer' can use as well as the Christian of more sophisticated faith. They are like advertising slogans, brief epigrammatic formulae which sum up the large claim being made. Such slogans are necessary, for without them a faith can never be the faith of the masses. But they are epigrams, with all the oversimplifications and lack of closer definition of epigrams, with all the strengths and dangers of epigrams (a slogan presumably is strong when it is a vital expression of a fundamental principle; a slogan is dangerous when it becomes merely the instrument of a mindless fundamentalism or a divisive factionalism – cf. Matt. 7.22f.; I Cor. 1.12).

It is important also to realize that the *unity* of faith in a particular situation depends to a large extent on the simplicity of the confession. Any slogan is an *over*simplification. But fuller definition quickly becomes divisive – *unnecessarily* divisive. The faith of the earliest churches is reducible to these standard formulae, appropriate to different situations; but the interpretation of these formulae is never rigidly defined – nor do they permit of a standardized credal expansion or require a uniform pattern of conduct.

Here again then a pattern of unity and diversity begins to emerge: *unity* in the different basic confessions in that the earliest believers thereby confessed the *exaltation* of the *man* Jesus and a *continuity* between Jesus of Nazareth and the one who enabled them to come to God; *diversity* in the different basic confessions themselves, in the different life-settings that called them forth, in the way faith was confessed in different situations, and in the way confessions were interpreted, supplemented and changed.

IV

THE ROLE OF TRADITION

§15. INTRODUCTION

Few would dispute the importance of 'the gospel' or of 'the creeds' in a study relating to the unity of Christianity. But many would be disposed to deny that tradition is a possible focus of unity. For 'tradition' by definition means that teaching and practice of the Church inherited from the past, which is formally distinct from the words of scripture. And many Protestants in particular would react strongly against any suggestion that tradition might rival scripture in determining Christian teaching and practice, perhaps recalling with some antipathy that the Council of Trent (1546) opposed the Protestant idea of the sole sufficiency of scripture by ordering that tradition was to be received by the Church together with scripture as of equal authority.[1] But, of course, the fact is that *every church and every denomination, Protestant or otherwise, has been shaped to a considerable extent by tradition* – the tradition of a particular way of interpreting scripture, the tradition of a particular (limited) range of emphases drawn from the Bible, the tradition of a particular manner of worshipping, the tradition of a particular mode of church government. It is the acceptance of these particular traditions within a denomination which is the practical bond of unity for that denomination. So too the difficulty which one tradition finds in fully recognizing another has been a major stumbling block for the ecumenical movement. Those who fail or refuse to recognize the role of tradition in shaping their own teaching and practice are in far greater danger of being enslaved by that tradition than those who make no secret of their indebtedness to tradition.[2] Clearly then a study of unifying and diversifying factors within the period of Christianity's beginnings must inquire after the role of tradition in shaping the teaching and practice of Christianity during that period.

The question here posed is peculiarly intriguing, particularly when tradition is defined by distinguishing it from scripture (as above). For, of course, in the first century there was no New Testament as such. The only ‘scripture’ for the first Christians was the Old Testament (more or less – see below p.81). All that we now know as the New Testament was in the process of formation. In fact it took the form of *traditions*, traditions relating to Jesus, traditions relating to Peter and Paul, and so on. This is something we have come to recognize more clearly through the discipline of *Traditionsgeschichte* (the study of the history of the earliest Christian traditions) – viz. that *the various NT documents are themselves traditions, developing traditions caught at various moments in time in the course of their development.* However much they are the work of creative inspiration, the NT writings also embody teaching and practice fixed in writing at particular points in their development. This of course is why *Traditionsgeschichte* is so important: by trying to reconstruct the particular historical conditions of situation and context for each tradition the hope is that the tradition will be seen again as a living force in the history of first-century Christianity. It is precisely this ‘living force’ of tradition in general that we want to uncover in the present chapter.

Our task then is to inquire into the role of tradition in earliest Christianity. How did the earliest Christians regard what was handed over to them by those longer in the faith? How, for example, did Paul respond to what he heard from Ananias, Peter, etc. about Jesus and the gospel? In particular, was the tradition received by the first Christians the basis of their unity, the practical bond of their community life? In one sense we are already well into this inquiry; for what we have done in chs II and III is to examine the diversity and development of particular traditions – viz. kerygmatic and confessional traditions. And in a later chapter we will take up the question of liturgical and catechetical traditions (below §36). In the present chapter it is the role of tradition as such which holds our attention: *what part did tradition play in earliest Christianity? how much of a force for unity was it?*

§16. ‘THE TRADITION OF THE ELDERS’

Since Jesus was a Jew and Christianity began as a Jewish sect we must first look at first-century Jewish tradition. How did Jesus and the first Christians respond to the religious traditions which must have played a part in their own upbringing as Jews?

16.1   *The role of tradition within Judaism.* It is not unimportant for us to note that this was a subject of dispute within the Judaism of Jesus' time. Basically it was a dispute between Pharisees and Sadducees. For Pharisees the Torah was both written (the Pentateuch) and unwritten (oral tradition). Whereas the Sadducees regarded only the written Torah as authoritative.[3] Since the Pharisees have generally received a 'bad press' on this count we ought to realize why it was that they ranked oral tradition so highly. The Pharisees recognized that no written law could cover all the exigencies of life; unless it was to become an archaic relic the written Torah had to be interpreted and supplemented to meet the changing conditions of society. For the Pharisees the Torah was something greater and holier and more immediately relevant to life than the written word by itself. What this meant in practice was the growth of precepts and ordinances able to meet the demands of situations not covered by the written law. For the Pharisees these were authoritative; but not in their own right – only if they could be regarded as interpretations of the written law, as a rendering explicit what had all the time been implicit in the written Torah.[4] But if the tradition was a justifiable interpretation of the written Torah then it was part of Torah and authoritative as such. Whereas in the eyes of the Sadducees, because it was not part of the written Torah, it could not be authoritative.

The interpretation took two forms – Halakah and Haggadah. *Halakah* was a specific declaration of God's will in a particular case, a rule of right conduct to guide the inquirer in the way he should go. As one generation gave way to another the rulings of earlier teachers were preserved and passed on, so that over the generations a considerable case law developed covering the whole of practical life, matters civil and criminal as well as religious. This lengthening chain of transmitted teaching, a series of halakoth linked together, is what Mark and Matthew call 'the tradition of the elders'. It was first codified and written down in the Mishnah (second century AD); the Mishnah in turn became the subject of study which resulted in the Talmud. But the process was already well under way before AD 70.[4a]

Haggadah is the term used for interpretation of scripture which is designed for edification and not for regulating conduct. It was much freer than Halakah, the result of allowing imagination free range over the contents of scripture with the aim of developing religious or moral lessons conducive to piety and devotion. Some Haggadah has been preserved in the Talmud, but most of it was preserved separately in the various Midrashim. In this chapter we are concerned primarily with Halakah. In chapter V we will have occasion to look at some of the methods employed by the teachers of Jesus' time to derive their interpretations and lessons from the written law (§21).

16.2 *Jesus' attitude to tradition.* It is quite clear that Jesus rejected much of the prevailing Halakah. Whatever his attitude to the written law (see below pp. 97f.), there can be no doubt that he reacted strongly against several well established rulings of the oral law. It would not be true to say that he rejected all tradition, for he regularly attended the synagogue on the sabbath (Mark 1.21; Luke 4.16; 13.10; and cf. Matt. 23.3). But the fact remains that *the only references to tradition as such in the Gospels show Jesus as radically opposed to it* (Mark 7.1–13/Matt. 15.1–9). In this passage Jesus sets 'the tradition of the elders' in direct antithesis to 'the commandment of God' and 'the word of God'. The Pharisees might see the Halakah as part of God's Torah and delight in it – obedience to it was obedience to God. But evidently Jesus found such tradition irksome and alien to a spirit motivated by love of God and love of neighbour, a sequence of detailed rulings which stifled rather than stimulated a free loving obedience.

Jesus' radical questioning of the oral tradition comes to clearest expression over three issues – the sabbath, ritual purity and the corban vow. In their interpretation of the sabbath commandment the rabbis were to distinguish 39 different kinds of work which were forbidden on the sabbath (including '. . . making two loops . . . sewing two stitches . . . writing two letters . . .').[5] In Jesus' view this attitude made people slaves of the sabbath. Such sabbath tradition prevented them from fulfilling the commandment to love. The sabbath Halakah did not explain the will of God but in fact ran counter to God's will (Mark 2.23–3.5). Similarly with the Pharisaic regulations about the ritual washing of hands before meals (Mark 7.1–8). 'The tradition of men' encouraged the worshipper to remain at the level of the merely outward, the superficial, and so encouraged hypocrisy.[5a] Even fiercer was his attack on the *corban* casuistry that made it possible for a son to avoid all obligations to his parents by fictitiously dedicating to the temple all the support he owed them, even though he acted out of spite or anger (Mark 7.9–13). Tradition which started as a way of interpreting the law had become in practice more important than the law.

Had Jesus appeared at an earlier stage, before the tradition had become so extensive, before the tendency to control and restrain acceptable conduct had become so pronounced, his attitude to tradition as a whole might have been more positive. But in the circumstances of his ministry the effect of such rulings caused him to reject completely many of the traditions which governed the religion of his Pharisaic contemporaries and to oppose resolutely the attitude which made the conduct of religion and of personal relationships dependent on the observance of such tradition.

16.3   If Jesus' attitude to tradition was radical *the attitude of the earliest Jerusalem Christians seems to have been much more conservative*. The concern shown by the Jerusalem believers over Peter's eating with uncircumcised Cornelius (Acts 11.2f.) clearly implies that the ritual purity of the meal table remained important for the Jerusalem Christians. The essential historicity of Acts on this point at least is confirmed by the fact that the same concern is evident among the Jerusalem Christians who occasioned the confrontation between Peter and Paul in Antioch (Gal. 2.12; see further below §56.1). Acts 21.20f. further characterizes many of the Jerusalem believers as 'zealous for the law', that is, in particular, for the continued observance of circumcision and 'the customs'. And similarly the clear implication of Acts 6.14 is that prior to Stephen the Jerusalem Christians were faithful both to the temple and to 'the customs which Moses delivered to us' (cf. n.4 above). It was presumably this loyalty to and observance of the Torah, both written and oral, which transformed the Pharisees' opposition to Jesus into a much more tolerant acquiescence towards the activities of his followers (Acts 5.33–39) and which attracted many Pharisees into the new sect while still remaining Pharisees (Acts 15.5; 21.20; see further below §54).

16.4   Markedly different is the attitude of another Pharisee (or ex-Pharisee) – *Paul*. Paul had once been wholly devoted to the traditions of his fathers (Gal. 1.14), but his conversion and subsequent mission to the Gentiles forced him to the conclusion that the traditions of Judaism were shackles which imprisoned faith; they did not bring faith to expression, rather they hindered and destroyed its liberty. Hence the only traditional obligation he accepted from the Jerusalem apostles was a practical concern for the poor (Gal. 2.10). Hence too the strong words of Gal. 4.8–11 and the warnings against 'the traditions of men' in Col. 2:

> Why let people dictate to you: 'Do not handle this, do not taste that, do not touch the other' . . . That is to follow merely human injunctions and teaching. True, it has an air of wisdom, with its forced piety, its self-mortification, and its severity to the body; but it is of no use at all in combating sensuality (Col. 2.21–23, NEB).

Here Paul is rejecting outright the views of a syncretistic Christianity influenced by Pharisaic Judaism – the view in particular that Gentile Christians must observe an elaborate oral tradition (Halakah) (see further below pp. 280f.). He was more tolerant when it was a Jewish Christian who felt that he had to remain faithful to the traditions of his fathers, for example in matters of diet and holy days (I Cor. 8; Rom. 14). To be sure, he thought such a believer was 'weak in his faith' and rejoiced in his own liberty (Rom. 14.1, 14; I Cor. 10.25f.); but he did not insist that faith in Christ required a Jew to abandon all his traditions any more than it required a Gentile to embrace them. So far as he was concerned, such traditions were of no value in themselves (cf. I Cor. 8.8; Gal. 6.15); and he himself was quite willing to go along with his old traditions when in the company of orthodox Jews without thereby renewing his commitment to them (I Cor. 9.19–22; Acts 21.23–26; cf. Rom. 14.19–15.2; I Cor. 8.9–13). What he did object to was any attempt to force one individual's tradition (or one individual's freedom from tradition) on another.

In short, Paul's attitude to Jewish tradition was plain: *faith in Christ could not and must not be made to depend on the observance of certain traditions.* If inherited tradition hindered the liberty of Christ and the worship of God they should be abandoned. A strong faith might observe or ignore halakic rules equally, without peril. A weak faith might find that remaining within or falling in with the traditional ways of Judaism was some sort of support, but it confessed its weakness thereby.

16.5   Thus we see *within first generation Christianity a striking diversity of attitude towards Jewish tradition* – from continued and fierce loyalty to it at one end of the spectrum to complete rejection of it at the other. In particular, it is quite clear that *Jewish tradition did not prove a force for unity in the earliest Christian churches*: the Hellenists soon began to react against it in the earliest Jerusalem church itself (see further below §60), and in the churches which included Gentiles as well as Jews it was more a matter of dispute than the basis of community. Paul certainly did not commend Jewish tradition as something worthy of every Christian's loyalty. Moreover, on this point there is a greater degree of *dis*continuity than continuity between Jesus and the first Christians.

§17. TRADITIONS OF THE EARLIEST COMMUNITIES

What then about the more specifically Christian traditions which circulated among the earliest believers? Did they serve as the basis of unity among the first Christian communities? In this section we focus attention on the Pauline corpus, since these letters contain the fullest evidence of early community tradition (outside the Gospels), and since Paul himself consciously grapples with the question of tradition's role in the life of a Christian community. Did Paul see tradition as a unifying strand within the diversity of earliest Christianity? The traditions in question divide conveniently into three categories – kerygmatic tradition, church tradition, and ethical tradition – though naturally there is no hard and fast division between any of them.

17.1 *Kerygmatic tradition.* We have already noted the various kerygmatic and confessional formulae which Paul inherited and used in his own preaching (above p.22). In I Cor. 15.1–3 he explicitly states that he passed on to the Corinthians what he himself had received (*parelabon*). How does this square with his insistence in Gal. 1.11f.,

> that the gospel which was preached by me is not man's gospel. For I did not receive (*parelabon*) it from man, nor was I taught it, but it came through a revelation of Jesus Christ (cf. also 1.1, 16f.)?

On the one hand, he clearly expresses his gospel in the language of tradition handed over to him by his predecessors in the faith, while on the other he insists that his gospel came directly from God and not as inherited tradition. How can we explain this tension in Paul's thought?

The best explanation is that Paul regarded the kerygmatic tradition as *confirming* his own convictions about Jesus which stemmed immediately from his conversion and commissioning on the Damascus road, and also as providing an invaluable way of expressing what was his gospel anyway, because it was a widely accepted formulation and not just his own idiosyncratic mode of expression. To put the point more clearly, what was at issue between Paul and those against whom he writes in Galatians, was not the traditional formulation of the gospel, but Paul's *interpretation* of it. Paul was convinced that the risen Jesus had appointed him apostle to the Gentiles and that the gospel for the Gentiles was free from Jewish law, written and oral. It was this interpretation of his apostleship and of the kerygmatic tradition which incited the opposition of many of the Jewish Christians. *Kerygmatic tradition for Paul then was interpreted tradition – interpreted in the light of his own encounter with the risen Jesus.* The same point emerges from his own description of his preaching. The gospel which he preached was effective not because his words were correct tradition, but rather because his words were given him by the Spirit (cf. particularly I Cor. 2.4f.; I Thess. 1.5; 2.13). In other words, even when his preaching used the language of the traditional kerygma, it was *pneumatic tradition*, tradition re-expressed, re-formulated in the inspiration and power of the Spirit.[6] We may conclude, therefore, that *kerygmatic tradition was a unifying bond among the earliest Christian communities, but that it was subject to diverse interpretations.* Many Jewish Christians interpreted it in the light of 'the tradition of the elders', whereas Paul interpreted it in the light of the 'revelation of Jesus Christ' given to him outside Damascus.

17.2   *Church tradition.* Paul uses the language of tradition in one passage where he is talking about the Lord's Supper:

> For I received (*parelabon*) from the Lord what I also handed on to you, that the Lord Jesus on the night when he was betrayed took bread . . . (I Cor. 11.23–25).

Here is a tradition of Jesus' words which Paul clearly believes should govern the common meals of the Corinthians. At the same time he has no compunction about adding what appears to be his own interpretation to the received formula ('For as often as you eat this bread and drink the cup, you proclaim the Lord's death until he comes' – 11.26).[7] Moreover he specifically designates the source of the Last Supper tradition as 'the Lord'. This seems to mean not so much that the earthly Jesus was the original source of the tradition, but rather that Paul understood the present, exalted Jesus to be the immediate source of the historical formula – that is to say, that *it was authoritative not because it was a tradition but because it was received and accepted on the direct authority of the exalted one* (cf. and note the present tense in I Cor. 7.10).[8] Here again evidently we are back with the idea of 'pneumatic tradition', tradition which is authoritative because of its immediate inspiration and its direct relevance.

Paul also appeals on several occasions in I Corinthians to the practices of other churches in the Gentile mission (I Cor. 4.17; 7.17; 11.16; 14.33). Here evidently a form of church tradition was growing up which could be appealed to as some sort of unifying bond. But if

I Cor. 7, 11 and 14 are any guide these were simply practices which served to commend the new Christian groups to the societies in which they lived. And Paul as the creator of that tradition certainly did not regard it as having an independent authority. Rather it served only in a confirmatory role – to confirm that the instruction and guidance he gave in one church was the same as in others.

17.3   *Ethical tradition*. Paul uses the language of tradition most often when talking about his converts' conduct and moral responsibilities (I Cor. 7.10; 9.14; 11.2; Phil. 4.9; Col. 2.6; I Thess. 4.1; II Thess. 2.15; 3.6). One of the most striking features of this ethical tradition is that *it seems to draw its force very largely (perhaps even entirely)*[9] *from the life of Jesus*, that is, from *the Jesus-tradition*, both his words (I Cor. 7.10–Matt. 5.32; I Cor. 9.14–Luke 10.7) and his conduct (Rom. 6.17; I Cor. 11.1; II Cor. 10.1; Phil. 2.5; Col. 2.6; Eph. 4.20).[10] Even where the immediate appeal is to follow Paul's own example (I Cor. 4.16f.; 11.1f.; Phil. 3.17; 4.8f.; II Thess. 3.6–9) the appeal only has force because Paul regarded that conduct as modelled on Christ's (I Cor. 11.1; cf. I Thess. 1.6).

It would appear then that Paul is able at these points to draw on quite an extensive tradition about Jesus, and to assume that his converts were also familiar with it – a conclusion which is probably confirmed by the amount of Jesus' teaching which Paul seems (consciously) to echo, particularly in the sections of his letters devoted to ethical teaching (e.g. Rom. 12.14; 13.9; 16.19; I Cor. 9.4; 13.2; Gal. 5.14; Phil. 4.6; I Thess. 5.2, 13, 15). This suggests in turn that *the traditions which Paul passed on when he first established a new church* (I Cor. 11.2; II Thess. 2.15; 3.6) *included a fair amount of tradition about Jesus*, though whether in fragmentary form or already gathered in various topical collections we cannot say.[11]

This common heritage of Jesus-tradition obviously served as a unifying factor of some significance among the earliest communities. Paul is even able to speak of it as *the 'law of Christ'* (Gal. 6.2; cf. I Cor. 9.21).[12] But this should not be misinterpreted as though Paul regarded this tradition as a regulation of binding force on all his converts. Paul's ethic was much too charismatic for that, much too conscious of the Spirit's immediate direction (Rom. 8.4, 14; Gal. 5.16, 18, 25), much too liberated from a rule book mentality (Rom. 6.14; 7.6; 8.2; II Cor. 3.3, 6, 17; Gal. 5.16), much too dependent on the Spirit's gift of discernment in matters of doubt or dispute (Rom. 12.2; Phil. 1.9f.; Col. 1.9f.; Eph. 5.10).[13] This is evidenced clearly by the way in which he himself *disregards* one of the explicit words of

Jesus preserved in the Jesus-tradition (I Thess. 2.6, 9; II Thess. 3.7–9; cf. I Cor. 9.14). It would appear then that he regards the ethical tradition drawn from the traditions about Jesus not as a series of *laws* which have to be *obeyed whatever* the circumstances, but more as a set of *principles* which have to be *applied in the light of* the circumstances. In other words, what we have once again is pneumatic tradition, that is to say, *tradition which is not something independent of the Spirit or of independent authority, but tradition which has to be interpreted under the guidance of the Spirit and followed only in so far as it is recognized to be a direction of the Spirit.*

17.4   *Tradition in the Pastorals.* Quite another attitude to tradition is a dominant feature of the last members of the Pauline corpus. Evidently by the time the letters to Timothy and Titus were written (late first century?) a coherent body of tradition had become established to serve as a clearly defined touchstone of orthodoxy. This is variously described as 'the teaching' (I Tim. 4.16; 6.1; II Tim. 3.10; Titus 2.7, 10) or more specifically 'sound teaching' (I Tim. 1.10; II Tim. 4.3; Titus 1.9; 2.1), 'the good teaching' (I Tim. 4.6), or 'the teaching which accords with godliness' (I Tim. 6.3), 'the faith' (11 times), 'sound words' (I Tim. 6.3; II Tim. 1.13), or 'that which has been entrusted' (I Tim. 6.20; II Tim. 1.12, 14). The content of the tradition is not very clear, but if the 'faithful sayings' are any guide, it includes all three categories distinguished above – kerygmatic tradition (I Tim. 1.15; II Tim. 2.11; Titus 3.5–8), church tradition (I Tim. 3.1; cf. Titus 1.9), and ethical tradition (I Tim. 4.8f.; II Tim. 2.11–13) – and presumably included traditions about Jesus(?). The attitude towards tradition is wholly conservative: it is to be kept (I Tim. 6.14; II Tim. 4.7), clung to (Titus 1.9), guarded (I Tim 6.20; II Tim 1.12, 14), protected (I Tim. 6.1) and passed on faithfully from one generation to another (II Tim. 2.2). Very typical is the passage II Tim. 1.12–14:

> . . . I am sure that he is able to guard until that day what has been entrusted to me. Follow the pattern of the sound words which you have heard from me, . . . guard the truth that has been entrusted to you by the Holy Spirit who dwells within us.

Notice particularly that even Paul himself is depicted more as the keeper of tradition than as its author, and that the Spirit is thought of not as the interpreter or re-creator of tradition but simply as the power to preserve the heritage of the past.[14] With the Pastorals then we have come almost full circle, for *here we seem closer to the Pharisees' attitude towards the oral law than to the attitudes of Jesus and Paul towards the tradition of their time.*

§18. TRADITIONS ABOUT JESUS

We have seen that kerygmatic traditions and traditions about Jesus served as some sort of unifying strand linking the different early Christian churches together. We have seen something of the diversity of *role* and *authority* attributed to these traditions, as between Paul himself and his more conservative disciple in the Pastorals. As to the *content* of these traditions, we have sufficiently demonstrated the diversity of forms taken by the kerygmatic and confessional traditions in chapters II and III. But now more needs to be said about the content and shape of the traditions about Jesus. To what extent was there an agreed body of traditions about Jesus which were passed from one Christian to another and provided a sort of common court of appeal? Was there perhaps even a fixed tradition carefully preserved from the first and of regulative force for teaching and resolving disputes, as the Pastorals seem to suggest?

18.1   So far as we can tell, the traditions about Jesus were brought together in different ways. The *passion narrative* seems to have been the only substantial block to be shaped early on into a connected account. Here is reflected the earliest community's concern to understand and portray Jesus the crucified one as Messiah (see above §10.2). The existence of a source (Q) of the Synoptic Gospels containing only *sayings of Jesus* has been disputed. But the already strong indications from within the Synoptics themselves have been greatly strengthened by the discovery of the Gospel of Thomas, which is precisely such a document. The point of significance is that Q certainly lacks a passion narrative. That is to say, here we have evidence of an early Christian interest in the sayings of Jesus as such, and not in what he did or in his death and resurrection (see further below §62). The suggestion of an extensive overlap between the Q traditions and the ethical tradition to which Paul refers (above §17.3) obviously commends itself.

More recently there has been a growing body of opinion that behind both Mark and John there was some sort of *'miracle source'* – that is to say, a cycle of miracle stories used by some early Christian preachers to portray Jesus as a great miracle-worker, as one authenticated before God and men by his mighty works. Paul seems to be reacting against such a presentation of Jesus in his second letter to the Corinthians – assuming a correlation between the false apostles' proclamation of 'another Jesus' (II Cor. 11.4), and their over evaluation of miracles, visions and striking speech (10.10; 11.16–20; 12.1, 12 – see below pp.179f.); hence his emphasis that the power of God only comes to its full expression in weakness (II Cor. 4.7–12; 12.9; 13.3f.), adding a deeper dimension to his earlier stress on 'Christ crucified' (I Cor. 1.23; 2.2). And Mark seems to make a similar response to a similar portrayal of Jesus as miracle-worker *par excellence*; hence his emphasis on the Son of Man as one who suffers and dies (Mark 8.29–33; 9.31; etc.), which serves as a corrective to any presentation of Jesus in terms only of the miracle stories used by Mark in the first half of his Gospel (particularly 4.35–5.43; 6.31–56).[15] The clearest evidence that something like a miracle source was actually in circulation comes from the Fourth Gospel, where there is evidence both of a 'Signs Source' (particularly John 2.11; 4.54) and also of the Fourth Evangelist's correcting its emphasis even while incorporating its material (4.48).[16] Here then is evidence of another use of the Jesus traditions within earliest Christianity, again without any direct link with the death and resurrection of Jesus – a concentration by some early believers on Jesus as a miracle-worker.

One of the most surprising features of the earliest NT writings is *the lack of overt interest displayed by Paul in the traditions about Jesus*. As we have seen, he seems to be familiar with and alludes to a fair amount of material (above p.68), but he refers *explicitly* to only one episode from Jesus' ministry (I Cor. 11.23–25 – betrayal and last supper) and quotes *explicitly* only two other sayings which have come to him in the tradition (I Cor. 7.10; 9.14). What we should conclude from this is not at all clear, but taken with the evidence cited above, it does give some hint of *the diversity of use and non-use of the traditions about Jesus among the first Christians*.

18.2   What actually happened to particular traditions when they were passed on and put to use? Is there any evidence that the Jesus-tradition was fixed from the earliest date and passed on without significant change from one community to another? Like so many of the questions we have to ask in the course of our study this one requires a much fuller treatment than we can afford here. We will therefore concentrate most of our attention on that stage of *Traditionsgeschichte* which is easiest to analyse – from Q and Mark to Matthew and Luke.[16a]

First *narrative traditions*. (1) Some narratives seem to have been transmitted with *little change* beyond that of editorial convenience and style (e.g. Mark 1.16–28; 2.1–12; 5.21–43; 8.1–9). (2) With others we see a certain development or *diversity of tradition* which is of no great moment: for example, Jesus' experience at Jordan ('You are my son . . .' – Mark 1.11; 'This is my son . . .' – Matt. 3.17; but also the expansion of Matt. 3.14f.); the healing of the centurion's servant (did he come to meet Jesus personally – Matt. 8.5f.? or did he send friends – Luke 7.6f.?); the healing of Bartimaeus, or was it two blind men, on entering Jericho, or was it on leaving Jericho (Mark 10.46–52 pars.)? (3) Greater freedom in handling the Jesus-tradition is indicated by the fact that there is a certain *chronological inconsistency* between the respective settings of some of the narratives: Mark has the cursing of the fig tree before the 'cleansing of the temple', Matthew the day after (Mark 11.12–25; Matt. 21.12–22); John sets the cleansing of the temple at the beginning of Jesus' ministry, the Synoptists at the end (John 2.13–22); and the difficulty of reconciling the chronology of John's as against the Synoptists' account of the last supper and the crucifixion is well known. (4) Many scholars think that Mark's double account of a feeding miracle (Mark 6.30–44; 8.1–9) and Luke's portrayal of two missions sent out by Jesus (Luke 9.1–6; 10.1–12) resulted from *two divergent traditions of the same episodes* coming to Mark and Luke from separate sources (cf. the two versions with their Synoptic parallels). (5) A more *theologically calculated development of tradition* is seen in a number of cases where the Evangelist has quite clearly amended or corrected his source. For example, where Mark says, Jesus '*could* not perform any miracle except that he laid his hands upon a few sick people and healed them' (Mark 6.5), Matthew has altered this to, 'He *did* not perform many miracles there' (Matt. 13.58). Mark's conclusion to the walking on the water episode reads thus: 'They were utterly astounded, for they did not understand about the loaves, but their hearts were hardened' (Mark 6.51f.); but, as we noted above (p.47), Matthew has transformed this into, 'Those in the boat worshipped him, saying, "Truly you are the Son of God"' (Matt. 14.33). (6) In one case the different versions of an episode have diverged so far from each other that it is well-nigh impossible to discern its earliest form. I refer to the two accounts of Judas's death (Matt. 27.3–10; Acts 1.18f.). On the variant accounts of the 'twelve' see below (p.108 n.6). In none of these cases do I wish to deny that there was an 'actual event' underlying the divergent traditions – rather the reverse. The point to be noted here, however, is the fact that *different accounts of the 'actual event' seem in many cases to have diverged from each other in the course of transmission*, whether by natural causes or by theological design, and that in some cases *the degree of divergence is too significant to be ignored*.

18.3　　From narrative traditions about Jesus we turn to *the traditions of Jesus' sayings*. Here we see a range of diversity in transmission similar to that outlined above (§18.2). (1) Many of Jesus' sayings are preserved with *a striking degree of verbal agreement* between different Evangelists (e.g. Mark 2.19f.; Matt. 8.9f.; 12.41f.; 24.43–51). We may note in passing how many of the logia preserved in the Gospel of Thomas have close parallels in the Synoptic tradition (see below p.284 n.39). (2) Some sayings are preserved in *different contexts*. For example, the saying about finding and losing one's life is set in two or three different contexts (Matt. 10.39; Matt. 16.25/Mark 8.35/Luke 9.24; Luke 17.33; John 12.25); Luke reproduces the saying about the lamp twice (Luke 8.16; 11.33); the 'by your fruits' saying has been either squeezed into one by Luke 6.43–5 or separated into two by Matthew (7.16–18; 12.33–35); perhaps more significant variant doublets are the warnings of Mark 8.38, Matt. 10.32f., Luke 9.26, 12.8f. (see also below p.217). (3) We should note also sayings with a good claim to be authentic Jesus' logia which have been *preserved outside the Gospels*, and which therefore provide evidence of particular traditions which have by-passed or been omitted by the Evangelists. Good examples here are Acts 20.35; the codex D version of Luke 6.5 (to a man working on the sabbath) – 'Man, if you know what you are doing you are blessed; but if you know not, you are cursed and a transgressor of the law'; and the Gospel of Thomas logion 82 – 'He who is near me is near the fire, and he who is far from me is far from the kingdom'.[17] (4) Some sayings have been *interpreted differently* in the course of transmission. Thus an Aramaic original translated differently into Greek seems to be the source of the significantly divergent versions: Mark 3.28f. ('sons of men'), but Matt. 12.32/Luke 12.10 ('the Son of Man') (see above p.39 n.16); Mark 4.12 ('in order that'), but Matt. 13.13 ('because').[18] So too there is much to be said for the view of C. H. Dodd and J. Jeremias that various parables have been given a different sense in the course of transmission than that intended by Jesus. Particularly noteworthy here is the transformation of the 'parables of crisis' into parables about the second coming (Mark 13.34–36 and various pars.; Matt. 24.43f./Luke 12.39f.; Matt. 25.1–13).[19] Compare too the different ways in which the proclamation of the Baptist is presented – the preacher of fiery judgment of Q (Matt. 3.7–10/Luke 3.7–9) is only a preacher of repentance in Mark (1.4–8 – no fire, no judgment), is only a witness to Jesus in John (1.19–34; 3.27–30 – no fire, no judgment, no call to repentance). Perhaps most striking here is the tradition history of Jesus' saying about the destruction and eschatological restoration of the temple. It is preserved only as a false testimony in Mark 14.58/Matt. 26.61, but John attributes it to Jesus himself (John 2.19; see above p.42). How the first Jerusalem believers understood it is not quite clear (as a false testimony? or as a promise that the temple would be the focus of eschatological renewal for Israel? – see below p.324). Be that as it may, the implication of Acts 6.14 is clearly that Stephen understood it as a word of judgment on the temple (see below pp.98, 271f.). (5) We must note also how some sayings of Jesus have been *deliberately altered* in the course of transmission – altered in such a way as to give a *clearly different* sense from the original. For example, the opening interchange between the rich young man and Jesus: Mark 10.17f. – '*Good* teacher, what must I do to inherit eternal life?' 'Why do you *call me good*? No one is good except God'; but Matt. 19.16f. – 'What *good deed* must I do to have eternal life?' 'Why do you *ask me about what is good*? Only one is good'. Note also the way in which Jesus' clear cut verdict against divorce preserved in Mark 10.11 has been softened by the addition of the unchastity clause in Matt. 19.9, and by a more lenient ruling in the case of mixed marriages in I Cor. 7.15 (see further below p.247). Or again consider how Luke has neatly avoided the need to portray resurrection appearances in Galilee by omitting Mark 14.28 and by transforming the promise of Galilee appearances in Mark 16.6f. into a reminiscence of words spoken by Jesus *while still in Galilee* (Luke 24.6f.; see further below p.354). (6) Finally there are clear indications in several, though not very many cases that a particular saying has *originated* in the early churches and been *added* to the Jesus-tradition during the course of its transmission. Thus, for example, Matt. 18.20 is almost certainly a promise spoken in the name of the exalted Jesus by an early Christian prophet and accepted by the churches as a saying of Jesus. Similarly, though not quite so certain, Luke 11.49–51. Matt. 11.28–30 is probably a prophetic interpretation of the Q saying 11.25–27, in which the exalted Jesus who spoke on earth as Wisdom's messenger is now understood to speak as Wisdom itself (see further below pp.258f., 285). And one of the best examples of interpretative addition, consequent upon the changed perspective brought about by the mission to the Gentiles, is Mark 13.10 (peculiar to Mark, disturbing the flow of thought, and use of 'the gospel' – particularly Markan). Indeed Mark 13 as a whole affords some of the most fruitful material for tradition history investigations (see below pp. 323f., n. 21).

We must conclude therefore that *the earliest churches had no conception of the Jesus-tradition as something fixed, a body of tradition whose content and outline was firmly established from the first.*[20] The fact that so many traditions of Jesus' words and deeds were preserved indicates that they were treasured by the earliest communities, and must therefore have played an authoritative role in shaping their teaching and practice (see above p.36, n.8). But the traditions themselves were not thought of as already cast in a final or finally authoritative form, and their authority was subject to the adaptation and interpretation called forth by the prophetic Spirit in changing circumstances (cf. Matt. 13.52).

18.4   The clearest demonstration of this last point is the tradition about Jesus as it reappears towards the end of the first century in the *Fourth Gospel*. Even a superficial comparison of John with the Synoptics reveals that Jesus is portrayed in a very different way, that *the traditions about Jesus*, we have to say, *have undergone a striking development*. By this I do not mean that the Johannine presentation of Jesus has lost touch with historical reality – for there are sufficient indications at points where John parallels the Synoptics that he is drawing on good tradition (e.g. John 1.19–34; 2.13–22; 6.1–15).[21] Consequently we may presume with some confidence that even where parallels are lacking there is a solid traditional foundation anchoring the Johannine superstructure in history (cf. e.g. Luke 13.34 and Mark 14.13f. which support John by suggesting that Jesus had fuller contact with Jerusalem than the Synoptics otherwise indicate).

The point which must be noted here however is the extent to which that traditional material about Jesus has been elaborated by John. I have already drawn attention to various features of John's christology which illustrate the point (see above pp.27, 39, 44, 47). Two other features of the Johannine presentation, more directly relevant to the present chapter, demonstrate the degree to which John has moulded the Jesus-tradition to meet the requirements of his own situation. First, he sets all his material within and as part of *a dramatic structure*, so that the whole Gospel moves forward towards the climax of 'the hour', the hour when Jesus will be 'glorified', 'lifted up', 'ascend' whence he descended,[22] and so that the movement towards that climax is characterized by the increasing 'judgment' or 'separation' (*krisis*) brought about by Jesus' very presence (see particularly 3.17–19; 5.22–24; 7.43; 9.16; 10.19; 12.31; 16.11).[23] In order to fit and explain this unfolding drama John has tailored both deeds and words of Jesus in such a way that their distinctively Johannine colouring can scarcely be denied (see e.g., the extended sections, 4.1–42; 9; 11).

Secondly, we should note the distinctive character of *Jesus' discourses* in the Fourth Gospel. A comparison of the various discourses reveals a striking *regularity of pattern*, where the thought seems to progress in a series of concentric circles, usually beginning with a statement by Jesus which is misunderstood by his hearers and which then provides the starting point for a fuller re-statement by Jesus, and so on.[24] Since the pattern is maintained whatever the audience – for example, intellectual Jew (3), Samaritan prostitute (4), Galilean crowd (6), the hostile Jewish authorities (8), the disciples (14) – and since it also lacks any real parallel in the Synoptics, it is hard to escape the conclusion that that pattern is a *literary product*, John's way of presenting his own deepened understanding of the original Jesus-tradition. In short, the best explanation of the Johannine discourses is that they are a series of *extended meditations or sermons on original sayings of Jesus, or on original features of his ministry*.

Here then quite clearly there is no conception of the traditions about Jesus as an established entity only to be guarded and passed on, as being already in a fixed and final form. On the contrary, *the Jesus-tradition is apparently preserved in and by the Johannine community only in an interpreted and developed form*; or rather it is part of the community's ongoing life, living and maturing as they live and mature, responding with them to the challenges of each new situation – more like the pneumatic tradition of Paul than the 'sound teaching' of the Pastorals.

§19. CONCLUSIONS

19.1 *Tradition formed a unifying strand of some importance within the diversity of earliest Christianity*. Not the traditions distinctive of Judaism, since Paul and his Gentile converts rejected or ignored most of them, whereas the church in Jerusalem thought them to be of continuing importance and remained largely loyal to them. But *the kerygmatic tradition and the traditions about Jesus* – that is to say, those kerygmatic and confessional formulae and various (collections of) narratives and sayings of Jesus which were common currency among the different churches. Here a new strand of unity emerges which is of no little significance. For we are already familiar with the proclamation and confession of the death and resurrection of Jesus as a bond of unity.

But now we see also bound up with it *a common acceptance of traditions about Jesus*, that is traditions of Jesus' earthly ministry and teaching.

19.2   Within this unifying strand there are *several marked features of diversity*. Enough has already been said about the diversity of use and form of kerygmatic and confessional traditions (chs II and III). We have now seen that the *use* made of the Jesus-tradition is similarly diverse. Q seems concerned to preserve the actual words of Jesus in a way and to an extent not true of Paul. Mark uses the narratives of Jesus' ministry in a way which clearly sets him over against those who might wish to portray Jesus primarily as a miracle-worker. There are fundamental differences regarding the role of tradition between Paul and the Pastorals. So too the *shape and content* of the Jesus-tradition is very different. The stage of transmission between Q and Mark on the one hand and Matthew and Luke on the other reveals something of the *liberty* as well as the *respect* with which the tradition was handled. And the Fourth Gospel shows how *extensive* that liberty was felt to be, demonstrating a freedom in interpreting and developing the tradition from the earlier generation which seems to be poles apart from the conservatism of the Pastorals – even though the authors probably belonged to the same generation of Christianity. Certainly there is no evidence prior to the Pastorals of tradition being seen as something fixed, to which the teacher was wholly subservient, his role being confined to preserving and passing it on. On the contrary, the evidence of Paul and of all the Evangelists, but particularly the Fourth, is that *each community and each new generation accepted a responsibility laid upon it (implicitly or explicitly by the Spirit) to interpret the received tradition afresh and in relation to its own situation and needs*.

19.3   A little more should be said about this particularly Pauline and Johannine (though also Synoptic) concept and use of tradition as *interpreted or pneumatic tradition* and its repercussions on the authority attributed to tradition. For Paul and John the kerygmatic and Jesus traditions are authoritative, but *not in themselves*, not independently authoritative. They are *authoritative only when taken in dynamic conjunction with the present inspiration of the Spirit*. Tradition which has ceased to be relevant is either abandoned (Jewish tradition) or interpreted and adapted (kerygmatic and Jesus traditions). This could be done because for both Paul and John the focus of revelation is not simply the past (earthly Jesus) but the present as well (the

Spirit of Jesus). Consequently authority revolves round not one, but two foci – tradition *and* Spirit – and the authoritative expression of preaching or teaching in any particular case takes the form of interpreted tradition.[25]

John gives what appears to serve (partly at least) as his apologia for this in two of the Paraclete passages in John 14–16. For in 14.26 and 16.12–15 the Paraclete has the double function of *recalling the original message* of Jesus and of *revealing new truth*, and thus of *re*proclaiming the truth of Jesus. In other words, John himself regards his own extensive elaboration of the Jesus-tradition as nevertheless still controlled by the original tradition. There is a similar balance clearly intended in I John between the present and continuing role of the Spirit as teacher (2.27; 5.7f.) and the teaching which was given 'from the beginning' (2.7, 24; 3.11). We will have to return to this subject later and look at it from the other side (below pp.192f., 198), but for the moment we can say by way of summary that tradition from the past was authoritative for Paul and John when it was interpreted tradition, interpreted by the present Spirit for the present situation.

19.4   Throughout the chapters of Part I we are gathering material on the relation of the message of Jesus to the gospel(s) of the earliest churches. From the present chapter two points of relevance emerge. First, the fact that the early churches regarded the traditions about Jesus as at all authoritative indicates that *the message of the earthly Jesus had a continuing importance for them*. But since it was authoritative for them only as *interpreted* tradition, *its authority lay not in its historical point of origin so much as in the fact that it was spoken by the one who was now present Lord of the community and that it could be regarded as expressing his present will*. In other words, even in the matter of inherited tradition the key unifying factor was *the continuity between the earthly Jesus* (the historical source of the Jesus-tradition) *and the exalted Lord* (the present source of the interpreted tradition). This conclusion strengthens the conclusions reached in chapters II and III.

Second, this continuing importance of the Jesus-tradition should *not* be taken to signify a substantial overlap between the kerygma of Jesus and the kerygmata of the first Christians. The fact is that while the language of tradition is used by Paul for both the Jesus-tradition and the kerygmatic tradition, the Jesus-tradition is cited by Paul *only in matters ethical* and with reference to the Lord's Supper, whereas the kerygmatic tradition as such uses *only the tradition of Jesus' death and resurrection*.[26] This confirms that Paul had no thought of the kerygma as simply re-expressing the message or teaching of Jesus. *The kerygma proclaimed the crucified and risen one, not the past teaching of the earthly Jesus*. The question about the relation of Jesus' proclamation to the proclamation of the first Christians has been partly answered, but remains largely unresolved.

19.5   For those who value tradition or the tradition of first-century Christianity in particular, some important corollaries follow from the above investigations which are of contemporary relevance. First, we should not be alarmed by the marked difference of opinions regarding tradition which are current in modern Christianity, for we have seen how marked was the degree of diversity of attitude towards and use of tradition within earliest Christianity. In particular, those who find more congenial the conservative attitude of the early Jerusalem church to early Jewish tradition and of the Pastorals to early Christian tradition should bear in mind that Paul and John, not to mention Jesus himself, were much more liberal towards the tradition of the past; and those who are more liberal themselves should bear in mind that the Pastorals are also part of the NT. Both conservative and liberal would do well to follow Paul's advice to 'weak' and 'strong' (in questions of tradition) in Rom. 14.1–15.6 and I Cor. 8–10: not to attach undue importance to matters of tradition and fully to respect the opinions and practices of those who differ, with neither the conservative condemning the liberal for his exercise of liberty, nor the liberal despising the conservative for his scruples (particularly Rom. 14.3; see further below pp. 377f.).[27] There is no such thing as uninterpreted tradition, even in and from the beginning. The real question then is how the diversity of interpretation should be handled.

   Second, if it is *interpreted* tradition which becomes the authoritative expression in any given situation, what about the whole series of interpreted traditions which fill the pages of church history throughout the centuries? Do they retain a continuing authority since the work of interpretation has already been done, or was that interpretation authoritative only for its own day because it was relevant only to its own day? Or do they become part of the tradition which has to be interpreted afresh? If so, does interpretation in the present have to take into account the whole of the preceding interpreted tradition, or does some element within it serve as a *norm* for the rest? Or again, does the interpretative process bypass, or even disregard previous interpretations and work only with the original tradition? If so, what is the 'original tradition'? Does it include John and the Pastorals, or even Clement, Ignatius, etc.? Or is it the tradition which lies *behind* Paul and the Gospels, Synoptic as well as John? These are questions of importance for twentieth-century Christianity's concept and practice of authority. But they raise wider questions, particularly about the NT and its canonicity which we cannot go into here and must reserve for our final chapter.[28]

For the moment we may simply repeat by way of summary, that much the same pattern of unity and diversity emerges from our study of early Christian tradition as we found in chapters II and III – *unity in the traditions of Jesus' death and resurrection and in the traditions about Jesus*, and *diversity on the need to reinterpret the tradition afresh and in the range of interpretation which actually confronts us*.

V

THE USE OF THE OLD TESTAMENT

§20. INTRODUCTION

One of the most important unifying factors in Christianity has been mutual recognition of certain writings as foundational and normative, or, in a word, as scripture. Moreover, those who have most vigorously contested the role of tradition have done so in defence of the primary and unequalled authority of the Bible. Was the same true of the earliest churches' Bible? The only Bible they knew and recognized were the Jewish scriptures, that is the Law and the Prophets, together with other Writings whose authority and whose number were not yet fully agreed, but which coincided more or less with what Christians call 'the Old Testament'. We will use this last term (OT) for convenience. But we must recognize that in the first century AD it is both too precise a delimitation and an anachronism, since *Old* Testament presupposes that there is already a *New* Testament, which of course did not yet exist as such.

We need spend little time demonstrating that *the OT is an important unifying element in earliest Christianity and in the earliest Christian literature*. This is obviously true in the more specifically Jewish Christian writings: notice the frequent use of the phrase 'in order that it might be fulfilled' in Matthew and John and the important role played by scriptural quotation in the early speeches in Acts, in Rom. 9–11 and in Hebrews. But it is also true throughout the NT. A glance at a Nestle Greek text shows on almost every page words in different type, denoting a direct scriptural reference (the Johannine epistles are a striking exception) – and that does not include the less clear-cut allusions. In this sense all Christianity in the NT is Jewish Christianity; that is to say, the influence of the OT pervades the whole, determines the meaning of its categories and concepts.

C. H. Dodd made much the same point in his significant book,

According to the Scriptures, by subtitling it, *The Substructure of New Testament Theology*:

> This whole body of material – the passages of OT scripture with their application to the gospel facts – is common to all the main portions of the NT, and in particular it provided *the starting point for the theological constructions* of Paul, the author to the Hebrews, and the Fourth Evangelist. *It is the substructure of all Christian theology and contains already its chief regulative ideas.*[1]

This is a bold claim. If it is true then we have indeed a unifying element of primary significance, perhaps as important a unifying factor as faith in Jesus itself – not just 'gospel facts' but 'OT scripture', not just Jesus but OT. So far we have seen that in kerygma, in confession and in tradition, Jesus alone gives unity and coherence to the diversity of formulations. Do we now have to add another block to the foundation of Christianity – the OT? Is the real basis of early Christian unity Jesus *and* the OT?

The relation between NT and OT, and vice-versa, is one which has fascinated scholars for centuries, and the mass of literature which has appeared in recent years indicates that the debate has been particularly lively over the past two decades. Fortunately the concerns of the present study enable us both to narrow the question down and to sharpen it as well. For the key question is not so much whether the Jewish scriptures were authoritative, as *how their authority was understood in practice*. The same is true of the modern debate about biblical authority: what is the Bible's authority when the meaning of a text cannot be fully determined but has to be left ambiguous? what is the Bible's authority when on the same topic one author says one thing and another something else? We have already seen a fair amount of that kind of diversity in the last three chapters, and the diversity of denominations within Christianity is living testimony to the diversity of interpretation possible in biblical exegesis. The key question for us then is not whether the OT was regarded as authoritative, but what was its authority in practice? How were the Jewish scriptures actually handled in the first years of Christianity? How did the first Christians actually use the OT?

§21. JEWISH EXEGESIS AT THE TIME OF JESUS

It is generally accepted that contemporary Jewish exegesis is the proper background to early Christianity's use of the OT. It is here that we must start. For the purposes of this discussion five broad categories of Jewish exegesis can be distinguished – targum, midrash, pesher, typological and allegorical. There is considerable controversy over the last three. It should be stressed at once therefore, that these are by no means hard and fast categories, simply useful ways of characterizing the range of Jewish exegesis and interpretation and that it is often very difficult to draw a dividing line or to classify a particular mode of exegesis with confidence. But the justification for making the five-fold distinction will I hope become apparent as we proceed.

21.1   *Targum* means basically *translation (into Aramaic)*. Between the return from Exile and the second century AD, Hebrew was gradually superseded by Aramaic as the *spoken* language of the Jews. Hebrew survived for a long time particularly as the *learned* and *sacred* tongue, and so was used in written works of this period. But by the first century AD Aramaic was probably the only language which many (most?) Palestinian Jews actually spoke.[2] This meant that in the synagogue the readings from the Law and the Prophets had to be *translated* so that people could understand. For a long time oral translations were sufficient, but eventually written translations were made. A number of different Targumim (Targums) survive.[3]

Notice that the targum is *not a literal translation*. It is often more like a paraphrase or explanatory translation. It often involves expanding the text, and not infrequently alters the text. This is not surprising, since the LXX does it as well, particularly in the translation of I Kings. But the Targumim are not so restrained as the LXX; the translation on several occasions embodies an interpretation distinctly at odds with the original – an *interpretative* translation. The most striking example is the Targum of Isa. 53, where the translation has been deliberately framed to rule out a Christian interpretation. That is to say, it is a tendentious translation:

Who hath believed these our tidings? and to whom hath the power of the mighty arm of the Lord been so revealed? [2]And the righteous shall grow up before him even as budding shoots; and as a tree that sendeth forth its roots by streams of water, so shall the holy generation increase in the land that was in need of him: his appearance shall not be that of a common man, nor the fear of him that of an ordinary man; but his countenance shall be a holy countenance, so that all who see him shall regard him earnestly. [3]Then shall the glory of all the kingdoms be despised and come to an end; they shall be infirm and sick even as a man of sorrows and as one destined for sickness, and as when the presence of the Shekinah was withdrawn from us, they (or we) shall be despised and of no account. [4]Then he shall pray on behalf of our transgressions and our iniquities shall be pardoned for his sake, though we were accounted smitten, stricken from before the Lord, and afflicted. [5]But he shall build the sanctuary that was polluted because of our transgressions and given up because of our iniquities; and by his teaching shall his peace be multiplied upon us, and by our devotion to his words our transgressions shall be forgiven us. [6]All we like sheep had been scattered; we had wandered off each on his own way; but it was the Lord's good pleasure to forgive the transgressions of us all for his sake.[4]

21.2   *Midrash* means *exposition of a passage or text*, an exposition whose aim is to bring out the relevance of the sacred text to the present. It was concerned not so much with the literal or plain meaning, as with the *inner* or *hidden* meanings of the text over and above the obvious meaning. The typical midrash consisted in drawing out such hidden meanings contained in a particular text.

> Midrash starts from a (sacred) text or often a single word; but the text is not simply explained – its meaning is extended and its implications drawn out with the help of every possible association of ideas.[5]

By the time of Jesus rules of interpretation had already been agreed – the seven *middoth* (rules) of Hillel. (1) Inference drawn from the less important to the more important, and vice-versa. (2) Inference by analogy, where two passages were drawn together by means of a common word or words. (3) Constructing a family, a group of passages related by context, where a feature peculiar to one member is taken to apply to all. (4) The same as (3), but where the family consists of only two passages. (5) The general and particular, the particular and general; that is, the detailed determination of a general application from a particular occurrence, and vice-versa. (6) Exposition by means of a similar passage elsewhere. (7) An inference deduced from the context. The rules were later extended to thirty-two.[6] The two basic kinds of midrash, Halakah and Haggadah, we have already touched on above (pp.62f.).

21.3   *Pesher* can be described as a narrower form of midrash, though many scholars would refuse to recognize it as a separate category.[7] Pesher means simply *'interpretation'*. It gains its characteristic sense from Daniel, in the Aramaic portion of which (2.4–7.28) it occurs 30 times, and where it is used for Daniel's interpretation of the dreams of Nebuchadnezzar and Belshazzar and for Daniel's interpretation of the writing on the wall at Belshazzar's feast. It tends to be much more precise an interpretation than midrash. In much over-simplified terms midrash expands the *relevance* of a text, whereas pesher explains the *meaning* of a text with a one-to-one correspondence. Thus, for example, each element in the dream, each word on the wall has a precise meaning – a precise meaning in terms of the present.

> *Mene, mene, tekel* and *parsim*. This is the interpretation (*pesher*) of the matter: *Mene*, God has numbered the days of your kingdom and brought it to an end; *tekel*, you

have been weighed in the balance and found wanting; *peres*, your kingdom is divided and given to the Medes and Persians (Dan. 5.25–28).

Pesher has become an important word in this area of study in recent years because of its use in the Qumran commentaries. The Dead sea community regarded itself as the new covenant faithful living in the final days before the eschaton. They believed therefore that certain prophecies of the OT referred to themselves and to themselves exclusively – prophecies which had remained unillumi-nated mysteries until the Teacher of Righteousness provided the necessary interpretation.[8] Several of their commentaries have been preserved in fragments – for example, commentaries on Isaiah, Hosea and Nahum. The most completely preserved is the Commen-tary on Habakkuk. The method of exposition is to quote the text and then append the interpretation. Thus:

> For behold, I rouse the Chaldeans, that cruel and hasty nation (1.6a). The explanation (*pesher*) of this concerns the Kittim (that is, the Romans) . . .

Note how bold the interpretation is – 'Chaldeans' means 'Kittim (Romans)'.

> O traitors, why do you look on and keep silence when the wicked swallows up the man more righteous than he? (1.13b). The explanation of this concerns the House of Absalom and the members of their council who were silent at the time of chastisement of the Teacher of Righteousness . . .

> But the righteous will live by faith (2.4b). The explanation of this concerns all those who observe the Law in the House of Judah. God will deliver them from the House of Judgment because of their affliction and their faith in the Teacher of Righteousness.

Thirteen principles of interpretation have been adduced from the Qumran pesher technique. These are most conveniently to be found in K. Stendahl's book, *The School of St Matthew*[9].

21.4   *Typology* is a form of interpretation much abused by Christ-ians in the past, particularly in post-Reformation Protestantism, and still in some modern sects, whereby, for example, details of the patriarchal histories or the furniture of the wilderness tabernacle are seen as types of Christ and of Christian salvation. Partly for this reason many scholars would dispute whether typology is an appropriate category to use in such a discussion as this. But, rightly defined, typological exegesis can be recognized within both pre-Christian Judaism and the NT.

Typology sees *a correspondence between people and events of the past and of the future (or present)*. The correspondence with the past is not found within the written text but *within the historical event*. That is to say, typology is to be distinguished both from predictive prophecy, where the text functions only as a prediction of the future, and from allegory, where the correspondence is to be found in a hidden meaning of the text and not in the history it relates. For its part typology does not ignore the historical meaning of a text, but rather takes that as its starting point. Typological exegesis then is based on the conviction that certain events in the past history of Israel, as recorded in earlier scriptures, thereby revealed God's ways and purposes with men and did so in a typical manner. In particular, certain high moments of revelation in the history of salvation, especially events of the beginning, whether of the world (creation and paradise) or of Israel (exodus, wilderness), and events from the high period of Israel's national life (kingdom of David), manifest a pattern of God's acts and so prefigure the future time when God's purpose will be revealed in its fullness in the age to come. In this sense typology can appropriately be defined as '*eschatological analogy*'.

There are some clear examples of typology within the OT itself. Paradise is probably understood as the type of eschatological bliss (Isa. 11.6–8; Amos 9.13). The exodus and the wilderness become the type of eschatological deliverance (e.g. Isa. 43.16–21; 52.11f.; Hos. 2.14–20). David is the type of the coming deliverer (Isa. 11.1; Jer. 23.5; Ezek. 34.23; 37.24). Later on Moses is seen as the type of the eschatological prophet (on the basis of Deut. 18.15), and in the apocalyptic writings of the intertestamental period paradise vies with Jerusalem as the type of God's consummated purpose in the new age imminent.[10]

21.5   *Allegory*. The most prominent allegorizer within pre-Christian Judaism was Philo of Alexandria. The distinctive mark of the allegorical method is that *it regards the text as a sort of code or cipher*; the interpretation is simply the decoding of the text in question – in other words a more extreme form of midrash, not unlike the pesher. For the allegorist there are (at least) two levels of meaning in a text – the literal, superficial level of meaning, and the underlying meaning. The literal meaning is not to be wholly despised or disregarded; but it is comparatively unimportant beside the deeper meaning – as shadow to substance. Those who remain with the literal meaning alone are 'uncritical' (*Quod Deus Imm.*, 21; *Quis Her.*, 91). Thus in various places Philo says things like: 'the literal story is symbolical of a hidden meaning which demands explanation' (*De Praem.* 61); 'when we interpret words by the meanings that lie beneath the surface, all that is mythical is removed out of our way, and the *real* sense becomes as clear as daylight' (*De Agric.*, 97 – allegorizing was the earliest form of demythologizing); 'let us not, then, be *misled* by the actual words, but look at the allegorical meaning that lies beneath them' (*De Cong. Quaer.*, 172).[11]

As R. Williamson points out, the value of allegorical exegesis for Philo was four-fold. (1) It enabled him to avoid taking literally the anthropomorphic descriptions of God; (2) it enabled him to avoid the trivial, unintelligible, nonsensical or incredible meanings of some OT passages when interpreted literally; (3) it provided a means of dealing with the historical difficulties of the OT – for example, where did Cain find his wife? (4) it enabled him to read out of the OT conclusions which harmonized with the Hellenistic philosophies, and so to vindicate the OT to his fellow philosophers.[12]

§22. EARLIEST CHRISTIAN EXEGESIS OF THE OT

All five types of Jewish exegesis occur within the NT.

22.1　*Targum.* NT writers usually use the LXX, but quite often they or their sources have made their own translation direct from the Hebrew. There is no need to quote examples. The question of targumic translation, or pesher quotation, requires fuller treatment and we shall return to it below (§23).

22.2　*Midrash.* We have several good examples in the NT of more extended midrashim. John 6.31–58 is a midrash on Ps. 78.24 – 'he gave them bread from heaven to eat' (6.31). In it the Johannine Jesus explains that the 'he' of the text is not Moses, but the Father. The 'bread from heaven' is he who came down from heaven, that is Jesus, that is his flesh given for the life of the world. And those who eat therefore are not the fathers in the desert eating manna and dying, but those who hear Jesus: if they eat his flesh and drink his blood, that is if they believe in him and receive his Spirit, they will never die.[13]

Romans 4.3–25 is a midrash on Gen. 15.6 – 'Abraham believed (*episteusen*) God, and it was counted (*elogisthē*) to him for righteousness'. Note how Paul quotes it at the beginning (v.3) and again as the conclusion (Q.E.D. – v.22). Verses 4–8 are his exposition of *elogisthē* – where he shows that it can be understood in the sense of attributing a *favour*, rather than of paying a *reward* (using the second rule of Hillel to link Gen. 15.6 with Ps. 32.1f.). Verses 9–22 are his exposition of *episteusen* – where he presents three arguments to prove that Abraham's *pistis* (faith) has to be understood as faith in the Pauline sense, not faithfulness in the rabbinic sense (vv.9–12, 13–17a, (17b–21).[13a] Similarly Gal. 3.8–14 (or even 8–29) can be regarded as a midrashic interpretation of Gen. 12.3, 18.18.

II Corinthians 3.7–18 can be classified as either a midrash or an allegory. Paul expounds Ex. 34.29–35 – expounding first the meaning of the *shining* of Moses' face (vv.7–11), then the meaning of 'the *veil*' which Moses used to cover his face (vv.12–15), then the meaning of the *Lord* to whom Moses spoke unveiled (vv.16–18). Notice that in his interpretation Paul goes beyond, perhaps even contradicts the sense of Exodus: Exodus says nothing about the glory fading away; and Moses used the veil to hide the brightness from the people, not its fading.[14]

Similarly it has been shown that some of the speeches in Acts (particularly Acts 2 and 13) take the form of Christian midrashim,[15] and even Matt. 4.1–11 can be regarded as a midrash on Deut. 6–8, as B. Gerhardsson has demonstrated (see above n.5).

22.3   *Pesher.* The nearest equivalents to the pesher of the Qumran type are Rom. 10.6–9 and Heb. 10.5–10. Romans 10.6–9 is an interpretation of Deut. 30.12–14, where each verse is quoted in a very free translation with its explanation added in pesher fashion:[16]

> The righteousness that comes by faith says, [12]'Do not say to yourself, "Who can go up to heaven?" ' (this means to bring Christ down), [13]'or, "Who can go down the abyss?" ' (this means to bring Christ up from the dead). But what does it say? [14]'The word is near you, on your lips and in your heart'. This means the word of faith which we proclaim. For if 'on your lips' is the confession 'Jesus is Lord', and 'in your heart' the faith that God raised him from the dead, then you will be saved.

Hebrews 10.5–10 is an interpretation of Ps. 40.6–8, though here the whole passage is quoted first in the LXX version, which is itself an interpretative paraphrase of the Hebrew text. Following the quotation the key features of it are taken up and explained in pesher fashion:

> Sacrifice and offering thou didst not desire,
>   but thou hast prepared a body for me.
> Whole offerings and sin-offerings thou didst not delight in.

> Then I said, 'Here am I: as it is written of me in the scroll,
> I have come, O God, to do thy will'.
> First he says, 'Sacrifice and offerings, whole-offerings and sin-offerings, thou didst not desire nor delight in' – although the law prescribes them; and then he says, 'I have come to do thy will'. He thus annuls the former to establish the latter. By that 'will' we have been consecrated, through the 'offering' of the 'body' of Jesus Christ once and for all.

Other examples of pesher exegesis are Rom. 9.7f., I Cor. 15.54–56, II Cor. 6.2, Eph. 4.8–11, Heb. 2.6–9, 3.7–19. And see further below, §23.

22.4   *Typological exegesis* in the sense defined above (§21.4) can also be found in the NT, though how extensively is a matter of dispute. Paul seems to use the very word (*tupos* – type) with this sense implied in two passages. In Rom. 5.14 he calls Adam 'a type of him who was to come'. Notice that the typological correspondence is limited: Adam is a type of Christ only to the extent that he shows how in God's purpose the single act of one man can decisively affect the divine-human relationship of the race that he begets. Beyond that the correspondence between Adam and Christ is better described as a converse type (Rom. 5.15–19). In I Cor. 10.6 he speaks of the events which followed the exodus as *tupoi*. God's dealings with the tribes of Israel in the wilderness are 'typical' (v.11): as the blessings of redemption (from Egypt) and of miraculous sustenance in the desert did not prevent them falling under the judgment of God for their subsequent idolatry and sin, so baptism into and communion with Christ will not prevent judgment falling on the Corinthian believers.

  The writer to the Hebrews uses the language of type in a highly distinctive way much influenced by Hellenistic philosophy. The instruction given to Moses in Ex. 25.40 – 'See that you make everything according to the pattern (*tupos*) shown you on the mountain' – enables him to tie together Hebrew eschatology of two *ages* (present age and age to come, or old age and new age) with Platonic cosmology of two *worlds* (the heavenly world of reality and the earthly world of copy and shadow). The tabernacle in the wilderness and its attendant ritual was but a 'shadow' (10.1) or 'antitype' (9.24) of the heavenly sanctuary. But Christ has now entered the real sanctuary and made it open to believers. He is the real priest and sacrifice, and no mere copy or shadow. That is to say, as the old age was the age of shadow and antitype, so the new age is the age of reality and type. Christ has banished the shadows once for all and brought the heavenly realities into earthly experience. What believers now experience is the real thing – real cleansing, real access into the presence of God. In short, the OT priesthood, sacrifice, sanctuary and covenant are typical of Christ's ministry and its blessings, in that the heavenly reality of which they were only an imperfect copy has become the reality of Christian experience here and now.

The only other occurrence of the word 'antitype' in the NT is I Peter 3.21, where Noah's deliverance is taken as the type of baptism (the antitype). The typological correspondence is strained since deliverance from a flood is not altogether typical of God's way of saving men. The only real link is the water involved in both the flood and in Christian baptism. And I Peter rather forces through the correspondence by speaking of Noah's salvation *'through* water'. Here we are not so very far from the more bizarre typological exegesis of later centuries.

Other examples of NT exegesis which imply some form of typology would include Jesus' representation as the paschal lamb (John 19.36; I Cor. 5.7), as indeed the whole sacrificial imagery of the NT in its application to Jesus. The danger is that the wider we extend the range of typological correspondence between OT and NT the more we trivialize the idea of type and the closer typological exegesis comes to the less edifying kind of allegorizing.

22.5   *Allegory.* Some scholars would deny outright that there is any allegorical exegesis in the NT.[17] The more balanced judgment is that there is some, but not much – though it should be said that what there is for the most part differs markedly from the allegorizing of Philo. The only really clear examples are I Cor. 10.1–4, Gal. 4.22–31 and probably II Cor. 3.7–18. The exegesis of I Cor. 10.1–4 is based on the recognition of a typological correspondence between the situations of the Israelites in the wilderness and the Christians in Corinth (see above p.89). But it has clear-cut allegorical features: the passage through the Red Sea is taken as an allegory of baptism into Christ ('baptized in the cloud and in the sea into Moses' = allegorically, baptized in the Spirit into Christ – cf. 12.13); manna and water from the rock are allegories of the Christian's supernatural sustenance (*pneumatikos* in vv.3–4 is almost equivalent to 'allegorical' – cf. Rev. 11.8); the rock itself is an allegory for Christ (the allegory is decoded explicitly for the first time by means of the explanation, 'The rock was/= Christ').[18]

Even clearer is Gal. 4.22–31, where Paul explicitly claims to be indulging in allegorical exegesis (v.24). Here the decoding is slightly complex, but the difficulties do not affect the sense too greatly: Hagar = the covenant of the law from Mount Sinai, the present Jerusalem, bearing children in slavery to the law; Sarah = the covenant of promise, the Jerusalem above which is free; Ishmael = the children by law, those who are born 'according to the flesh'; Isaac = the children by promise, those born 'according to the Spirit'.[19]

I have already dealt with II Cor. 3.7–18 under the heading of Midrash to which it more closely belongs (§22.2). The clearest allegorical features are to be found in v.14, where Paul describes the veil over Moses' face as still covering the minds of the Jews today when they read the law – 'the *same* veil'! and v.17, where Paul gives the decoding key to the verse from Ex. 34 just quoted – ' "The Lord" (of whom this passage speaks) = the Spirit'. I Cor. 9.8–10 could also merit the title 'allegory' since Paul seems to take the Mosaic injunction, 'You shall not muzzle an ox when it is treading out the grain' (Deut. 25.4), as a command to communities to provide support for their apostle or other missionaries. Paul's dismissal of the literal sense of the original regulation makes I Cor. 9.9f. the nearest thing we have to Philonic allegorizing in the NT (*cf. Ep. Aristeas 144*).

§23. PESHER QUOTATION

So far the diversity in earliest Christian use of the OT simply reflects the similar diversity within Jewish exegesis of that time – and, we may infer, reflects a closely similar respect for the authority of the Jewish scriptures. But there is another type or aspect of exegesis in Qumran and the NT which helps to focus and clarify the issues for us, and which therefore deserves separate treatment.

In the case of midrash, pesher (and allegory) the OT text is usually quoted and then the interpretation added. But in this other type of exegesis *the actual quotation of the text embodies its interpretation within the quotation itself* – what is perhaps therefore best described as a targumic translation or (as I prefer) a *pesher quotation*. The incorporation of the interpretation within the text itself sometimes leaves the text verbally unaltered, but usually it involves modifying the actual text form.[20]

23.1 Quotations where the text is given *a different sense from the original*, with *little or no alteration of the text form* – for example:

Micah 5.2: 'You Bethlehem Ephrathah who are least among clans of Judah . . .';
Matt. 2.6: 'O Bethlehem, who are *by no means least* among the rulers of Judah'.

Hab. 2.4: 'the righteous shall live by his faith/faithfulness';
LXX: 'He that is righteous shall live by my faith', that is, God's faithfulness;
Rom. 1.17: 'those justified by faith will live'.

Ps. 19.4: the testimony of creation;
Rom. 10.18: the same words referred to the gospel.

Probably the most striking example here is Gal. 3.16, which refers to Gen. 12.7 (LXX) – the covenant made with Abraham and his seed, that is his descendants. Paul seizes on the fact that LXX uses *sperma*, a collective singular, and interprets it of Christ. To take *sperma* (seed) as singular of course makes nonsense of the *original* promise; but in Paul's debate with the Judaizers this type of rabbinic exegesis enables him to make his point in a way which would carry some force with those he was addressing. For other examples see Acts 1.20, 4.11, Rom. 12.19. We should also recall how not just obviously messianic scriptures are referred to Jesus (beloved Son of the Psalms, Servant of Isaiah, Stone passages), but also passages originally addressed to Yahweh (see above p.52).

23.2   Quotations where *the sense of the text is significantly modified by means of altering the text form* – for example, II Cor. 3.16 (see above n.14) and Eph. 4.8 (Ps. 68.18).

Ps. 68.18	Eph. 4.8
Thou didst ascend the high mount,	When he ascended on high
leading captors in thy train	he led a host of captives,
and receiving gifts among men.	and gave gifts to men.

In the Hebrew and LXX the king *receives* gifts of *homage from* his captives. In Paul the exalted Jesus *gives* gifts of the *Spirit to* his disciples. There is however also a targum on Ps. 68 which refers the verse to *Moses* and which paraphrases 'you received gifts' by 'you have learned the words of the Torah, and gave them as gifts to the sons of men'.[21] Whether Paul knew this version or not, his own targumic translation is as bold.

The clearest example of pesher quotation is probably Matt. 27.9–10 (Zech. 11.13, with clauses rearranged to make comparison easier).

Zechariah	*Matthew*
I took the 30 shekels of silver – the	*They* took the 30 pieces of silver, the

splendid price at which *I* was priced/paid off by them –

price of *him* on whom a price had been set by some of the sons of Israel,

and *cast* them in the house of Yahweh *unto the potter*, as Yahweh had commanded me.

and *they gave* them *for the potter's field*, as the Lord directed *me*.

Throughout Zechariah the actor is the prophet, 'I'; the 30 shekels are his wages; he casts them down in the house of the Lord. In Matthew the 'I' becomes 'they' (priests) and 'him' (Jesus) – though for some reason Matthew retains the 'me' at the end, bringing the quotation to an oddly jarring conclusion. The 30 pieces of silver become the blood money paid to *Judas*. The prophet's casting down in the house of the Lord becomes the priests' buying the potter's field.

Note also that Matthew refers the passage to Jeremiah, though he quotes from Zechariah. This is probably because he wants to include in his quotation a reference to Jeremiah. Two famous incidents in Jeremiah's life were his encounter with the potter and his prophetic act in buying a field (Jer. 18–19, 32). So the Matthean text is properly to be regarded as a combination of texts – primarily of Zechariah, but with implicit reference to Jeremiah.

Other examples of combination of texts are Matt. 21.5, 13, Rom. 9.33, 11.8, II Cor. 6.16–18, Gal. 3.8, Heb. 10.37f., 13.5.[22]

23.3   On a number of occasions the pesher quotation involves *the development of a text which has no real parallel*. A clear example of this is Matt. 2.23. There is in fact no prophecy which says, 'He shall be called a Nazarene'. The text is probably formed by combining a reference to Judg. 13.5 with a reference to Isa. 11.1. Samson is taken as a type of Jesus – so, 'he shall be a Nazirite' is referred to Jesus; Isa. 11.1 speaks of the branch (*nēzer*) of Jesse. Matthew's pesher *nazōraios* (Nazarene) is established by a play on *nazir(aion)* (Nazirite) and *nēzer* (branch).[23] Other examples of quotations which have no parallel in the OT and must be formed by a combination of references and allusions are Luke 11.49, John 7.38, I Cor. 2.9, James 4.5 (cf. Eph. 5.14).

§24. PRINCIPLES OF INTERPRETATION

It has become increasingly clear that when we talk of the OT within earliest Christianity we are not talking of something *in itself*. When we talk of the NT's use of the OT we are not talking of a straight-forwardness of correspondence and fulfilment which gave the OT a wholly objective authority. The last two sections have shown beyond dispute that NT quotations from the OT are *interpretations* of the OT. The OT was quoted only because it could be interpreted in favour of the point being made, in relation to the situation addressed; and quite often this interpretation could only be achieved by modifying the textual form. In short, *the first Christians valued the OT not as an independent authority so much as an interpreted authority.*

What then are the principles which governed their interpretation? Was it completely arbitrary? or was their freedom of interpretation restricted within certain bounds?

24.1   The first thing to be said is that the choice of OT text as a rule was not arbitrary. The NT writers did not simply seize on *any* text, or create texts *ex nihilo*. There is a *givenness* in the passages they quote. They are for the most part passages which had already been accepted as messianic (like Ps. 110.1), or which in the light of Jesus' actual life have a *prima facie* claim to be messianic (like Ps. 22 and Isa. 53). This is true even of the allegories of Gal. 4.22–31 and II Cor. 3.7–18. Even before the Christian interpreter had gone into detailed interpretation it was plausible to take Ishmael and Isaac as pictures of two types of relation to Abraham, plausible even to take the glow on Moses' face as a picture of the glory of the Mosaic covenant. Likewise in the case of texts like Matt. 2.23 and John 7.38; they were not conjured out of the mind, but even now we can have a fairly good idea of what texts the author had in mind – the different passages which were the *starting*-point for his thinking and which merged together in his mind to form the new text. In short, there is *a certain givenness in the choice of the text interpreted.*

24.2   Second, the interpretation was achieved again and again by reading the OT passage or incident quoted *in the light of the event of Christ*, by viewing it from the standpoint of the new situation brought about by Jesus and of the redemption effected by Jesus. The technique is best illustrated in Gal. 3.8, 4.22–31, II Cor. 3.7–18 and Matt. 2.23.

> Gal. 3.8: The scripture, foreseeing that God would justify the Gentiles by faith, preached the gospel beforehand to Abraham, saying, 'In you shall all the nations be blessed'.

Abraham did not in fact hear the gospel itself. The promise, 'In you shall all nations be blessed' can be called 'gospel' only when inter-preted in the light of Christ; only because it was fulfilled in Jesus in some sense can it be called 'the gospel'; it draws its significance as gospel for Paul from Jesus and his redemptive acts. So with Isaac and Ishmael in Gal. 4. The meaning Paul sees in their births is drawn from his own key categories – *kata pneuma* and *kata sarka* (according to the Spirit, according to the flesh). Isaac and Ishmael were significant at this point because they could be interpreted allegorically in terms of the current debate. Likewise the veil of Moses referred to in II Cor. 3. It had none of the significance which Paul sees in it for the old dispensation. Its significance lies wholly in the new dispensation – the veil of Moses understood and interpreted as the veil over the hearts of the Jews *now* (3.14 – it is the *same* veil). In other words, the significance Paul attaches to the veil was drawn not so much from the text as from his own theology. Similarly in the case of Matt. 2.23. The text, 'He shall be called a Nazarene' would not have emerged had Jesus not come from Nazareth. Neither Nazirite nor *nēzer* (branch) in themselves or together suggested 'Nazarene'. The interpretation emerged as much, if not much more from the gospel tradition as from the OT. In short, we can see here something of *the extent to which interpretation of the OT was determined by the present and not the past.*

24.3   We can now say simply what the principle of interpretation was, how pesher quotation was achieved. *The pesher emerged from the bringing together of given text and given gospel tradition.* The process is probably best illustrated in the case of Matt. 27.9f. First, there was the givenness of the text in Zechariah. Zechariah 11 is unquestion-ably messianic: it speaks of the flock and the shepherd. The flock is presumably Israel. The shepherd is the prophet himself who at God's command becomes the shepherd. He speaks throughout in the first person. This is clearly messianic and was accepted as such. So, first, there was the messianic passage. Second, there was the tradi-tion of the Jesus event and the Christian belief that Jesus is Messiah. This involved belief that messianic scriptures were fulfilled in Jesus. So there was a natural impulse to bring together the messianic passage and the Jesus-tradition.

In this case the immediate relevance of the Zechariah prophecy to the Jesus-tradition is clear. In Zech. 11 the shepherd in some sense fails and is rejected by the flock, and there is talk of 30 shekels as his wage/price. In the Jesus-tradition the Messiah is rejected by Israel and betrayed for 30 pieces of silver. Clearly then there was an obvious and immediate 'fit' between OT prophecy and the Jesus-tradition. Moreover, in Zechariah the shepherd throws the money down in the temple and the Hebrew adds 'unto the potter' (Syriac – treasury); and this can be explicated by reference to Jeremiah, famous both for his association with a potter and for buying a field as a prophetic act. In the Jesus-tradition, Judas throws the 30 pieces of silver down in the temple and it is used for buying a potter's field.

Clearly the points of contact between Zechariah/Jeremiah and the Jesus-tradition relating to Judas are *sufficiently close* to justify the conclusion that these events were the fulfilment of the Zechariah/Jeremiah prophecy. If this is agreed, then it is merely a matter of jockeying with the *exact* details of the one until they fit more or less with the *exact* details of the other. In the event this involves applying some actions to different actors; ignoring certain details on either side (Judas does not actually appear in the pesher – to introduce him would complicate the pesher too much); incorporating certain elements from Jeremiah into Zechariah to make a corporate whole; leaving some details uncorrelated ('as the Lord directed *me*').

This whole issue – of pesher quotation – requires of course a much fuller examination. But Matt. 27.9f. is probably the clearest example of an OT text which as quoted owes much more to the theological intention of the NT writer than to any possible alternative version available to him. Had we more space the procedure could be illustrated by various other examples showing how often the OT text and the original Jesus-tradition came together to form a new text, an interpreted text, or to give the original text a meaning which its original wording could hardly bear.[24]

24.4   The importance of the interpreter's situation for his interpretation is further illustrated by the fact that *in some cases the same OT text is interpreted differently by different NT writers*. For example, (1) Genesis 15.6. As we have seen, Paul cites Gen. 15.6 as proof that Abraham was justified by faith alone and not by works (Rom. 4.3ff.; Gal. 3.6). But James cites the same passage to prove almost precisely the opposite! – that Abraham was justified by works and not by faith alone (James 2.23; see further below p.251). (2) Psalm 2.7 – in Paul's sermon in Pisidian Antioch it is referred to Jesus' resurrection (Acts 13.33; so probably Heb. 1.5; 5.5); but in the Synoptics it is referred to Jesus' experience of the Spirit's descent upon him at Jordan (Mark 1.11 pars.; see also below p.220). (3) Isaiah 6.9f. – 'Hear and hear, but do not understand; see and see, but do not perceive . . .' – the classic explanation for the unbelief of the Jews. As B. Lindars notes:

In John 12.39f. it appears as the reason why the response to the mission of Jesus, especially to his signs, was so small; in Acts 28.25–28 it suggests the change of St Paul's policy, turning from the Jews to the Gentiles; while in Mark 4.11f. and pars. it is advanced as the reason for our Lord's method of teaching by parables. All these are of course concerned with response. But none of them is quite the same, and from the point of view of apologetic the Markan example has strayed into an entirely different field.[25]

(4) Isaiah 8.14–18. Isaiah 8.14f. is one of the famous Stone passages, where Yahweh is depicted as a stone of offence and a rock of stumbling. Romans 9.33 and I Peter 2.8 refer this passage to Jesus: Jesus is equated with Yahweh, the stone. Isaiah 8.17f. speaks of Isaiah's trust in Yahweh and of the children Yahweh has given him. Hebrews 2.13 refers *this* passage to Jesus: Isaiah's trust in Yahweh is seen as *Jesus'* trust in Yahweh. In other words, within five verses Jesus is identified both with Yahweh and with Isaiah in his trust in Yahweh. (5) Daniel 7.13 – Perrin argues that the NT preserves traces of three exegetical traditions using Dan. 7.13, in the course of which application of Dan. 7.13 is gradually shifted from ascension to parousia.[26] This is certainly plausible (though I am not wholly convinced of it). (6) More clear-cut is the shift in application of Zech. 12.10 from parousia (Matt. 24.30; Rev. 1.7) to passion apologetic (John 19.37). (7) Compare too Ps. 110.1 which is usually used of Jesus' session at God's right hand (e.g. Mark 14.62; Acts 2.33–35; Col. 3.1; Heb. 8.1), but also in support of particular christological titles (particularly Mark 12.35–37; Acts 2.33–36; 7.56), to affirm the subjection of the powers to Christ (particularly I Cor. 15.25) and in regard to Jesus' heavenly intercession (Rom. 8.34; cf. Heb. 7.25).[27]

24.5 The clearest examples of the way in which the revelation of the OT was reinterpreted by the revelation of Jesus are those cases where *the OT is actually set aside and abandoned* – cases where the new revelation was so at odds with the old that no amount of interpretation could reconcile the two and the old had to give way and stand abrogated.

We see this happening with Jesus, where *Jesus clearly sets his own revelation and insight into God's will over against the Torah* – not just the oral Torah (see above §16.2) but even the written Torah itself. Thus in Matt. 5.21f., 27f. he sets himself up as the determinative interpreter of the law, proposing a very radical interpretation of the sixth and seventh commandments. And in other passages gathered together in the Sermon on the Mount he does not merely reinterpret the law, he radically qualifies it; in Matt. 5.33–37 he in effect sets aside the regulations about swearing (Lev. 19.12; Num. 30.2; Deut. 23.21), and in 5.38–42 he abolishes the *ius talionis* (Ex. 21.24; Lev. 24.20; Deut. 19.21). In Mark 10.2–9/Matt. 19.3–8 he devalues the Mosaic permission for divorce (Deut. 24.1). Perhaps most striking of all, his teaching on the causes of impurity as recalled in Mark 7 in effect cuts at the root of the *whole* ritual law (as Mark perceives – 7.19b). Of course, the openness of his table fellowship to the 'sinner' had the same effect – hence the fierceness of the Pharisaic opposition to Jesus.[27a]

An instructive example of radical reinterpretation is Stephen's attack on the temple (Acts 7 – particularly vv.41–50). It appears to have been inspired by the tradition of Jesus' saying about the destruction and reconstitution of the temple (Acts 6.14), a saying apparently ignored or interpreted otherwise by the Jerusalem believers (see above p.74). He seems to have read the history of Israel's worship in the light of that saying, producing what is in fact a highly tendentious interpretation of that history. Using Isa. 66.1–2, one of the few OT passages which seem to denounce the temple root and branch, he argues in effect that the building of the temple in the first place, a permanent, stationary sanctuary, was the mark of Israel's apostasy from God – and that despite II Sam. 7.13, etc. (see more fully below pp.271f.). In other words, viewing the OT *in the light of Jesus' words Stephen used one part of scripture to justify the abandonment of the clear teaching of many other scriptures.*

Paul of course provides some of the clearest examples of a first-century Christianity which rejected and abandoned much of its Jewish heritage, much in the OT which the Jews (and Jewish Christians) regarded as still of binding force and relevance. In particular, the central role of the law in Judaism: 'Christ', he says, 'is the end of the law as a means to righteousness'; the Mosaic prescription of Lev. 18.5 ('covenantal nomism' – Sanders) is no longer valid – Deut. 30.12–14 is more to the point. And he proceeds to interpret what was also intended as an encouragement to *law-keeping* (Deut. 30.11, 14), in terms of righteousness/salvation through *faith* (Rom. 10.4–9)! In other words, the law was only temporary, a kind of 'baby-sitter' until the coming of faith (Gal. 3.19–25). But now that faith has come, now that Christ has come, the law has been abrogated and set aside (II Cor. 3.13f., NEB; Eph. 2.15).

In all these cases Jesus and his followers evidently found themselves so at odds with the plain sense of certain key scriptural passages and themes that they had to set them aside, had to regard their period of relevance as past. The experience of Christ, the freedom brought by Christ called for such a radical reinterpretation of the OT that some of its revelatory functions had to be consigned to an era dead and gone.

24.6   One other issue deserves brief consideration. We have seen the extent to which the revelation of the past was subordinated to the revelation of the present in earliest Christianity. Was the opposite tendency also present? Were elements actually introduced into the current traditions in order to provide a correspondence with and fulfilment of OT expectations or themes? In particular, did the desire to establish 'proof from prophecy' result in the actual *creation* of details in the Jesus-tradition, as various scholars from D. F. Strauss onwards have suggested?[28]

The difficulty in testing this hypothesis is that many of the details in question are too brief and appear only in the context of fulfilment (for example, the tradition of the crucifixion – Mark 15.36 (= Ps. 69.21?); Luke 23.46 (= Ps.31.5?); John 19.33 (= Ps. 34.20?); etc.). Consequently one cannot determine whether such details were already present in tradition (or eye-witness memory) independently of the proof from prophecy motif. However, in cases where some sort of check can be made the evidence suggests that *the tendency to create Jesus-tradition out of messianic expectation was limited*. The subject again requires a much more extensive treatment; here we can give only one or two brief examples.

One clear example of detail created out of prophecy is Matthew's account of Jesus' entry into Jerusalem riding on both the ass *and* the colt of Zech. 9.9 (Matt. 21.2–7; contrast Mark. 11.2–7). But this is a trivial case. More important, but more contentious examples would be the location of Jesus' birth in Bethlehem and the virgin birth itself. There are several indications that Jesus could have been born elsewhere (Nazareth being the most obvious alternative) – for example, the substantial question mark against the historicity of a Roman census that affected Galilee and took place before the death of Herod the Great (Luke 2.1ff.), and the suggestion in Mark 12.35–37 that Jesus or the first Christians queried the belief that Messiah had to be of Davidic descent (cf. Barn. 12.10f.). However disturbing he may find it, the Christian historian nevertheless cannot ignore the possibility that the whole Bethlehem birth narrative stems ultimately from the conviction that Jesus the Messiah ought to be shown fulfilling Micah 5.2. Indeed many Christian scholars find themselves unable to deny or ignore the possibility (even more disturbing to traditional Christian faith) that the account of the virginal conception of Jesus originated in the apologetic desire to show Jesus as the fulfilment of as many OT prophecies as possible (in this case Isa. 7.14).[29]

On the other hand, two other important examples from one of the most disputed areas (the passion narrative) point in the other direction. Our study of Matt. 27.9f. above (pp.95f.) clearly indicates a process whereby OT prophecy and Jesus-tradition were brought together and married, the form of the Jesus-tradition imposing itself on the citation of the OT. Of course a more precise fulfilment could have been achieved by altering or creating details in the tradition of Judas. But this happened at most with the specification of the blood price as *thirty* pieces of silver (Zech. 11.12). Otherwise the details of the OT prophecy did not lead to a reformulation of the Jesus-tradition – rather the reverse. In this case at least the proof from prophecy motif did not mean the subordination of Jesus-tradition to OT.

The other example is the Gethsemane narrative (Mark 14.32–42 pars.). M. Dibelius claimed that this tradition was largely determined by the desire to present Jesus as the ideal martyr whose sufferings correspond to those spoken of by the psalmist.[30] But vv.33,35 are hardly martyr-like, and v.34 contains only an echo of Pss. 42.5, 11, 43.5. More important, the actual prayer itself (v.36) is not framed in words from the Psalms. Here again the more probable explanation is that we have authentic Jesus-tradition which permitted a correlation with OT language but which at no point of significance was determined by it.

In short, the evidence suggests that *where Jesus-tradition was already circulating and accepted it served as a check and limitation on any tendency to supplement it with details or items from messianic prophecies of the OT.* But where firm Jesus-tradition was meagre or lacking there may have been more scope for those early Christian apologists who thought it important to present Jesus as the one who fulfilled OT expectation completely, at every point of his life, from birth to resurrection (see also above p.36 n.8).

§25. CONCLUSIONS

It is obvious that *the Jewish scriptures were important for Jewish Christianity; it was important for the first Christians to establish the continuity between the OT and their new faith, to identify Jesus with the messianic figure(s) prophesied.* Had Jesus not fulfilled any of the OT hopes, then presumably one of two things would have happened: either he would have won no lasting following, or his disciples would have abandoned the OT more or less *in toto* from the first. But Jesus fulfilled too many prophecies, or at least too many OT passages can be referred to him with little difficulty. Consequently the OT was too valuable a means of evaluating Jesus and of presenting him to fellow Jews for it to be ignored.

Thus there developed within earliest Christianity *the interpretative process whereby the OT text and the Christian convictions about Jesus were brought together*. Neither wholly dominated the other, imposing its meaning completely on the other, swamping the other. But neither did they mesh completely. There was considerable correlation; and some passages could be taken straight over with a minimum of readjustment. But usually the Jewish scriptures had to be *adapted* to some degree in the light of the Jesus-tradition, in the light of their estimate and faith in Jesus, in the light of the new situation he had brought about. The adaptation was sometimes only in the *meaning* given to the text. But often it involved some *modification* of the text itself as well, sometimes a *considerable* modification and *conflation* of different texts. And sometimes it meant *abandoning* various precepts integral to the religion of the OT, the Jesus-tradition having wholly superseded them.

We can conclude therefore that the Jewish scriptures remained authoritative, particularly for Jewish Christians, but *not in themselves, only as interpreted*. For many others of the first Christians we have to put it more sharply: *the Jewish scriptures remained authoritative only to the extent that they could be adequately re-interpreted by and in relation to the new revelation of Jesus*. The event of Jesus, the Jesus-tradition, the belief in Jesus exalted, the new experience of the Spirit – these were the determinative elements in the process of interpretation. In this the earliest Christians could claim to be true followers of their Master. For the same respect for Jewish scripture combined with a sovereign freedom towards it in the light of his own experience of God and of God's Spirit is reflected in the earliest Christians' *respect* for the OT combined with a *radical liberty* in interpreting it in the light of the Christ event.

In short, in terms of our study of unity and diversity, we have to conclude that the OT provided a bond of unity within first-century Christianity – but not the OT as such, not the OT in itself, rather the OT *interpreted*. *It was the OT as interpreted in the light of the revelation of Jesus which helped to unify the different Christian churches in the first century –* just as it was *their differences of interpretation which again underlay the diversity within first-century Christianity*. Jesus again stands at the centre

– the traditions about him and the Christians' present relation to him through the Spirit. The OT therefore does not rival Jesus as the foundation of Christian unity, for the first Christians read it only from the perspective of the Jesus revelation. Thus it served as an indispensable prolegomenon and supplement to the Jesus- and kerygmatic tradition, crucial to their own emerging self-identity, a vitally important apologetic tool in the Jewish mission particularly. But where the old revelation did not fit with the new there was little question for the mainstream of first-century Christianity but that the old had to be adapted to the new or else abandoned.[31]

Here, naturally, a contemporary question arises by way of corollary. It can be posed simply: If the first Christians so handled their scriptures, how ought Christians today to treat the scriptures of today? Jesus' and the first Christians' acceptance of the OT's divine inspiration is often taken as paradigmatic for Christians' acceptance of the divine inspiration of the whole Bible. Ought we not to add that Jesus' and the first Christians' liberty in interpreting the OT is paradigmatic for Christians' interpretation of the NT today? These are questions to which we must return in the concluding chapter.

VI

CONCEPTS OF MINISTRY

§26. INTRODUCTION

As has often been pointed out, the emergence and consolidation of orthodoxy in the second century largely depended on two factors: the development of the idea of a 'rule of faith' (particularly Tertullian) and the emergence of monarchical episcopacy. To what extent were these second-century developments rooted in the first century? The last four chapters have in effect been attempting to answer that question in relation to 'the rule of faith'. There we have seen something of the extent both of the unity and diversity of first-century Christian faith as it came to expression in kerygma and confession and in relation to tradition and scripture. And we have concluded that the focus of unity was much less carefully defined and the diversity much more extensive than we might have expected.

Now we must turn to the second factor decisive for second-century orthodoxy – *monarchical episcopacy*. We know that certainly by the time of Cyprian the bishop was the real focus of unity and the bulwark against heresy. But even as early as Ignatius we find this exhortation:

> You should all follow the bishop as Jesus Christ did the Father . . . Nobody must do anything that has to do with the Church without the bishop's approval . . . Where the bishop is present, there let the congregation gather, just as where Christ is, there is the catholic Church. Without the bishop's supervision, no baptisms or love feasts are permitted. On the other hand, whatever he approves pleases God as well . . . It is a fine thing to acknowledge God and the bishop . . . (*Smyrn.*, 8.1–2).

This is the second century, the early second century, and not yet typical by any means of the second century as a whole. But Ignatius's exaltation of the bishop is the thin edge of a very large wedge indeed.

What about the first century? What concepts of *ministry* emerge there? What was the focus of *authority* within the common life of the earliest churches? Was there already in the first century, perhaps even from the start, a standard pattern of ministry, which served to bind the earliest Christian congregations into a unity? Such questions have been debated vigorously for the past 100 years, particularly in the 50 years spanning the end of the nineteenth century and the beginning of the twentieth.[1] One way of tackling them would be to review the different positions taken up in the debate over the whole period; but probably the simplest way to answer these questions is to examine the different writings and periods embraced by the NT documents to discover what form or forms of ministry are reflected there.[2]

§27. JESUS AND HIS DISCIPLES

There were a variety of groupings within the Judaism of Jesus' time. The Sadducees were in effect the dominant political party, the aristocratic and conservative 'establishment'. Much more a sectarian organization, but still basically a religious-political party, were the Zealots who appeared later – fervently nationalist and prepared to achieve their aims by violence. Somewhere in the middle of this religious-political spectrum came the Pharisees; but they were much more concerned with the task of interpreting the Torah than with politics. They were certainly a distinct party (Pharisees = 'the separated ones'?), but not greatly organized as such and characterized more by a series of teacher-pupil relationships. The Essenes on the other hand, coming somewhere between the Pharisees and the Zealots in the spectrum of sectarian Judaism, were much more organized internally and formed a very tightly structured community at Qumran.

Where do Jesus and his disciples fit within this context? Probably the nearest parallel to the relationship between Jesus and his disciples was that of the rabbi and his pupils. This is borne out by the fact that Jesus was widely known as a teacher, one who had disciples (Mark 9.5, 17, 38; 10.17, 35, 51; etc.). But *can we go on to speak of the community of Jesus?*[2a] Can we see the later Church already mirrored in the disciples gathered round Jesus? Did Jesus regard his disciples as a community? The evidence most clearly in favour of an affirmative answer is as follows. (1) The use of *ekklēsia* (assembly of God's people, later 'church' – Matt. 16.18; 18.17). (2) He chose *twelve* disciples, and almost certainly regarded the twelve as in some sense representative of Israel (twelve tribes – note particularly Matt. 19.28/Luke 22.29f.). (3) He spoke of his disciples as God's flock (Luke 12.32; cf. Matt. 10.6; 15.24; Mark 14.27 par; and the shepherd metaphors), a metaphor for Israel which appears a number of times in Jewish literature (Isa. 40.11; Ezek. 34.11–24; Micah 4.6–8; 5.4; Ps. Sol. 17.45). (4) Jesus thought of his disciples as a family (Mark 3.34f.); the disciples were those who had converted and become as little children, members of God's family as well as sharers in his kingdom (Matt. 18.3). (5) At the last supper Jesus explicitly described their fellowship in terms of the (new) covenant (Mark 14.24 par.; I Cor. 11.25); that is to say, he saw his disciples as 'founder members' of the new covenant, as the new Israel (see further below p.166). (6) We should note also the degree of organization among the followers of Jesus implied by Luke 8.3 and John 12.6. So there are grounds for speaking of the community of Jesus, or community round Jesus.

However, other considerations point in a different direction.

(a) *Discipleship of Jesus did not entail joining anything that could be properly called a community*. There was no clear dividing line between those who actually left home to follow Jesus and the much wider circle of disciples which must have included many who stayed at home: membership of Jesus' family was dependent on doing the will of God, not on following Jesus (Mark 3.35). Similarly, the Lord's prayer was not the badge of a closed ecclesiastical community but the prayer of all who truly desired the coming of God's kingdom. Again, Jesus practised no rituals which would mark out his disciples from their contemporaries. He abandoned John's baptism, presumably because he did not want any cultic or ritual act which might become a hurdle or barrier to be surmounted. Certainly his table-fellowship was in no sense a ritual or ceremony from which non-disciples were excluded (see further below §§39.3, 40.1). It was the *openness* of the circle round Jesus which distinguished the following of Jesus so sharply from the community at Qumran.[3] Jesus 'founds no new Church; for there is no salvation even by entering a religious society, however radically transformed'.[4]

(b) The role of the disciples as the new Israel appears to have been reserved for the future, a role not yet entered upon. It would be a feature of the imminent end time, part of the new covenant, the new age which Jesus believed would be initiated by his death and vindication (cf. below pp.210f.). Thus most clearly with the twelve (Matt. 19.28/Luke 22.29f.); their role as twelve while Jesus was still present was only symbolical of the future eschatological people of God. There is no evidence that they were regarded or acted as functionaries, far less a hierarchy, constituting a community gathered round Jesus in Palestine (note Matt. 23.8; Mark 10.43f.). In particular, there is no hint whatsoever of them playing 'priest' to the other disciples' 'laity'. What power and authority they did exercise was not within a community of discipleship for its upbuilding, but was given to enable them to share in Jesus' mission (Mark 3.14f.; 6.7 pars.; Luke 10.17ff.). If one word must be chosen to describe the circles round Jesus it would be 'movement' rather than 'community'.

(c) It is important to realize that this movement centred and depended wholly and solely on Jesus himself. Discipleship meant 'following' Jesus. He alone was prophet and teacher. The only real authority, the only real ministry was his. And if he encouraged his disciples on some occasions at least to exorcise demons and to preach the good news of the kingdom, this was no more than Jesus pursuing his mission by proxy. There was no community as such functioning alongside or around Jesus, but only larger or smaller groups of disciples either observing his mission or hindering his mission or participating in some small way in his mission.

It would seem wiser therefore to refrain from speaking of the community of Jesus or the community round Jesus. Any concept or pattern of ministry must be derived from Jesus alone, since it cannot be derived from the disciples or the twelve round Jesus. And if we choose to speak of the disciples of Jesus as the 'church' then we should recognize the character of church thereby denoted – namely, a group or groups of disciples gathered round Jesus with each individually and together *directly* dependent on Jesus *alone* for all ministry and teaching.

§28. MINISTRY IN THE EARLIEST COMMUNITY

Two pictures of ministry within the earliest Palestinian church are possible. Both can be derived from a reading of Acts: the one appears more straightforward but is probably more contrived; the other is less obvious but is probably more historical.

28.1   On the former view the twelve apostles constituted the leadership of the Jerusalem community from the first and oversaw its mission – Matthias having been divinely elected (by lot) to restore the apostolic twelve after Judas's defection (e.g. 1.15–26; 2.42f.;

4.33–37; 6.2, 6; 8.1, 14; 15.22). At an early stage their office was supplemented by the appointment of seven others to a secondary office to take over some of the administrative chores from the apostles (6.1–6) – just as Moses had appointed seventy to share his administrative burden (Num. 11.16–25) and Jesus had appointed seventy to assist him in his mission (Luke 10.1ff.). 'Elders' are first mentioned in 11.30, but thereafter appear on several occasions, exercising authority together with the apostles (particularly 15.2, 4, 6, 22f.). On this reading, then, at an early date the classic three-fold order of ministry was quickly established: bishop (successor to apostle), priest (= elder) and deacon (the seven). Moreover, so it is sometimes implied or argued, this was the pattern of ministry which became the norm for other churches and congregations as they sprang up in different places round the eastern Mediterranean.

But there are several difficulties with this view. Here are the most important. (*a*) According to the primitive tradition(s) of I Cor. 15.3–7 *'the apostles' are not to be identified with 'the twelve'*. Paul himself (I Cor. 9.1; 15.8f.), James (Gal. 1.19), Barnabas (Gal. 2.9), Andronicus and Junia(s) (Rom. 16.7), and probably Apollos and Silvanus (I Cor. 4.9; I Thess. 2.6f.) were also reckoned apostles. Consequently, *'the apostles' must have been a much wider group than 'the twelve'*. Moreover, for Paul apostleship consisted primarily in mission (I Cor. 9.1f.; 15.10f.; Gal. 1.15f; 2.9). This accords well with the primitive sense of apostle as 'missionary' preserved in Matt. 10.2, Mark 6.30 (only in the context of mission are the disciples called 'apostles') and Acts 14.4, 14. It does not accord so well with the picture of 'the apostles' as resident leaders of the Jerusalem church implied particularly in Acts 8.1 – 'the apostles' are the only ones *not* to go out from Jerusalem!

(*b*) The suggestion that the seven appointed in Acts 6 were subordinates of the twelve and that they are the forerunners of the deacon is based only narrowly in the text. *Their election was much more a recognition of a charismatic authority already in evidence than an institution to an office*: their fullness of Spirit was neither lacking before the laying on of hands nor bestowed by it (6.3, 5, 8, 10). Besides, according to the more natural sense of the Greek, it was the crowd of disciples and not 'the apostles' who laid their hands on the seven (6.6). And their authority was certainly not confined, if directed at all, to 'serving tables'. As the sequel indicates, their charismatic authority was much more important and found its expression most fully in evangelism and mission (6.8ff.; 8.4ff.) (see further below p.270).

(*c*) Elders certainly played an important role in the Jerusalem church (cf. James 5.14), and Luke suggests that the Jerusalem pattern was reproduced elsewhere by Paul (14.23; 20.17). But this is not borne out by Paul himself: 'elders' are nowhere mentioned in the Pauline writings prior to the Pastorals, which are most probably post-Pauline. Perhaps most striking of all, even according to Luke's own account, the leadership of the church at Antioch lay in the hands of prophets and teachers (Acts 13.1–3) – a hint of a very different kind of community structure and ministry in the churches of the Hellenistic mission, which we will find fully borne out by Paul's own account of things below (§29).

As will be confirmed later (§72.2), the probability is therefore that Luke has attempted to portray earliest Christianity as much more unified and uniform in organization than was in fact the case.

28.2   On the other view of Acts, *ministry and authority within the earliest Jerusalem community were much more spontaneous and charismatic in nature, and leadership took several diverse forms before a form of administration following the pattern of Jewish synagogue government became established.*

Ministry was evidently undertaken at the immediate behest of the Spirit or of a vision – and that was regarded as authority enough. This was certainly the case with the church at Antioch and with Paul (13.2, 4; 16.6f., 9f.; 18.9; 22.17f.). So too with the Hellenists and with Ananias of Damascus (6.8, 10; 7.55; 8.26, 29, 39; 9.10). So too with Peter and John and 'the brothers' in Judea (4.8; 10.10–16, 19; 11.18; cf. 15.28). Thus Philip ministered to the Ethiopian eunuch, Ananias to Paul and Peter to Cornelius, without prior consultation with fellow missionaries or local church or the church at Jerusalem; and those who were, according to Luke, to 'wait at table' at the appointment of the community, exercised rather a ministry of evangelism at the urging of the Spirit. Ministry was certainly not confined to a few, and even priests who were converted (6.7) seem to have held no special position or performed any particular ministry within the church.

Leadership probably focused initially in the twelve, in their role as representatives of eschatological Israel (Matt. 19.28/Luke 22.29f.; Acts 1.6, 20–26; 6.2).[5] But for some reason or other their place at the centre of things diminished, and, apart from two or three obvious exceptions, they began to disappear wholly from view – presumably at least because their role was thought of more in relation to the resurrection and return of the Christ (I Cor. 15.5; Matt. 19.28/Luke 22.29f.) and was less suited to the continuing community of the interval.[6] Be that as it may, so far as we can tell, Peter (and probably the brothers James and John) quickly emerged as the most prominent, and so we may assume, leading figures (Acts 1.13; 3–4; 12.1f.; and note their prominence in the Gospel tradition). The episode of the .Hebrews and the Hellenists in 6.1–6 reveals another side of things: the seven chosen were probably all Hellenists, and so quite likely they were the leading lights among the Hellenists – already marked out by their spiritual maturity and authority (6.3) (see also below p.270). The relation of the leadership of the group round Peter to that of the seven is not at all clear – Peter does not figure at all in the central episode, 6.7–8.4.

It was only after about ten years of the Jerusalem church's life, that is after Herod Agrippa's death in AD 44, that a firm and final pattern of leadership took shape and authority became rather more institutionalized. The key figure here was James the brother of Jesus. When did he first emerge among the Jerusalem leadership? We have no clear answer. But certainly by the time Paul went to Jerusalem for his second visit (AD 46 at the earliest) he was already the most prominent of the three 'pillar apostles' (Gal. 2.9). The other James had been killed some time earlier by Agrippa (Acts 12.2), and Peter and John were steadily fading from the Jerusalem leadership scene – Peter because presumably he was under threat from Agrippa and anyway was more concerned with 'the mission to the circumcision' (Acts 12.3–17; Gal. 2.8), John we do not know why (he appears for the last time in Acts in 8.14; see also below p.385). At all events James soon attained a position of complete dominance which lasted till his death in AD 62 (Acts 15.13ff.; 21.18; Gal. 2.12), and it was probably he who adopted the pattern of synagogue government for the Jerusalem church by gathering round him a body of elders (11.30; 15.2, 4, 6, 22f.; 16.4; 21.18). Within this more rigid community structure we may suppose that there was (progressively) less room for the earlier charismatic authority that depended solely on Spirit and vision, though on important issues the whole congregation was apparently still consulted (Gal. 2.2–5; Acts 15.22) and prophets were still associated with Jerusalem (Acts 15.32; 21.10).

§29. MINISTRY IN THE PAULINE CHURCHES

29.1   *The body of Christ as charismatic community*. Paul's concept of ministry is determined by his understanding of the church as the body of Christ. This understanding comes to clearest expression in Rom. 12, I Cor. 12 and Eph. 4. To appreciate the force of Paul's imagery at this point we must note the following important aspects.

(*a*) In Rom. 12 and I Cor. 12 Paul is describing *the local church*. Paul does not yet speak of 'the (worldwide/universal) Church' in his earlier letters, rather of 'the churches' (Rom. 16.16; I Cor. 7.17; 16.1, 19; etc.). So too 'the body' in Rom. 12 and I Cor. 12 is not the universal Church, but the church in Rome and the church in Corinth. It is particularly clear from the way he develops the metaphor of the body in I Cor. 12 that the body referred to was the Corinthian body of believers (v. 27 – 'you are Christ's body' in Corinth).

(*b*) The body of Christ was for Paul a *charismatic community*. The 'functions' of the body are precisely the charismata of the Spirit (Rom. 12.4). The members of the body are precisely individual believers as charismatics, that is, as functioning members of the body, manifesting particular spiritual gifts, speaking some word or engaged in some activity which expresses the Spirit of the community and serves its common life (Rom. 12.4–8; I Cor. 12.4–7, 14–26).

(*c*) It follows that *each* member of the Christian community has *some* function within the community; 'to each' is given some charisma or other (I Cor. 7.7; 12.7, 11). All, strictly speaking, are charismatics. No member lacks some manifestation of grace (= charisma). Each is a member of the body only in so far as the Spirit knits him into the corporate unity by the manifestation of grace through him. At no time did Paul conceive of two kinds of Christian – those who have the Spirit and those who do not, those who minister to others and those who are ministered to, those who manifest charismata and those who do not. To be Christian in Paul's view was to be charismatic. One cannot be a member of the body without being a vehicle of the Spirit's ministry to the body.

(*d*) The members of the body have *different* functions, *different* ministries (Rom. 12.4; I Cor. 12.4ff.) – otherwise the body would not be a body (I Cor. 12.17, 19). It is for each member to recognize when and what charisma it is that the Spirit would bring to expression, through him. And he must co-operate with the Spirit in bringing that charisma to expression, otherwise the functioning of the whole body will be impaired. Because it is the *Spirit's* gift and not his own he can take no credit for himself. Consequently he has no cause to feel ashamed or inferior if his charisma seems to him less important; and he has even less cause to feel proud or superior if his charisma seems to him more important. *All* the body's functions are important, indeed *indispensable* to the health of the whole (I Cor. 12.14–26; Rom. 12.3). The body metaphor is and remains the classic illustration of unity in diversity, that is, a unity which does not emerge out of a regimented conformity, but *a unity which results from the harmony of many different parts working together, and which depends on the diversity functioning as such.*

In short, *ministry in the Pauline churches belonged to all*, and each depended for his life within the body of Christ not just on some special ministry of a few, but on the diverse ministries of all his fellow members.

29.2 *Acts of ministry and regular ministries.* Charisma in Paul properly means a *particular* expression of charis (grace), some particular act of service, some particular activity, some particular manifestation of the Spirit. It is an *event* not an aptitude, a transcendent gift given in and for a particular instance, not a human talent or ability always 'on tap'.[7] The unity of the body of Christ thus consists in the interplay of these diverse charismata. *Christian community exists only in the living interplay of charismatic ministry*, in the concrete manifestations of grace, in the actual being and doing for others in word and deed.

But as well as individual charismatic acts and utterances Paul recognized that some members of the body have more *regular ministries* and that in addition there was the unique role of the apostle.

(*a*) The *apostle* had a *unique* ministry within the Pauline church: he had been personally commissioned by the risen Christ in a resurrection appearance (I Cor. 9.1; 15.7; Gal. 1.1.15f.); he was a successful missionary and church founder (I Cor. 3.5f., 10; 9.2; 15.9ff.; II Cor. 10.13–16); his was a distinctively eschatological role (Rom. 11.13–15; I Cor. 4.9). As the founder of a particular church, that is as one whose divinely given authority in ministry had been demonstrated and validated by his success in founding that church, he had a continuing responsibility to counsel its members and give guidance in its affairs (hence Paul's letters to Thessalonica, Galatia, Corinth, etc.). This was why the apostle is ranked first among the ministries within the local church (I Cor. 12.28) and first indeed in a more general list of ministries (Eph. 4.11). In particular it was his responsibility to pass on the gospel given him by the risen Lord in his commissioning, as confirmed by his fellow apostles (Gal. 1.11f., 15f.; 2.2, 6–10), and the various traditions shared by all the churches (see above §17). It should be stressed however that he was not an apostle of the universal Church, one whose authority would be recognized by all churches. His authority was confined to his sphere of mission (Gal. 2.7–9; II Cor. 10.13–16), to the churches he had founded (I Cor. 12.28 – 'God has set in the (local) church . . .'; see above p.110). Paul certainly contested vigorously claims by other apostles to exercise authority within his churches (II Cor. 10–13) and made no attempt to throw his own weight around within the Jerusalem church (Acts 21; cf. 15.12f.).[8] Furthermore we should also note that because of the uniqueness of the apostle's role and authority no category of church 'office' is adequate to describe his function: he was not appointed by the church, and Paul certainly did not conceive of any succeeding to his apostleship (I Cor. 15.8 – 'last of all'; 4.9 – the last act in the world arena before the end).

(b) Less fundamental (in the strict sense) but of first importance among the regular ministries within the Pauline churches were the *prophets* and *teachers* (I Cor. 12.28). In oversimplified terms, the role of the prophet was to transmit new revelations to the church, that of the teacher to transmit old revelations to the church. There is no suggestion in the Pauline letters that these were church 'offices', only entered upon by appointment, and certainly prophecy was not confined to prophets nor teaching to teachers (I Cor. 12.10; 14.1, 5, 26, 39). It follows from Paul's concept of charismatic ministry that the prophets were recognized as prophets because they prophesied regularly. That is to say, they did not prophesy because they were prophets, rather they were prophets because they prophesied, because that is the way the Spirit regularly manifested himself through them within the church. Similarly with the teacher, though by the nature of his ministry we may well infer that much of his ministry had a more formal character (giving instruction in the traditions of the churches – Gal. 6.6).

(c) There was also *a wide variety of other regular but less well defined ministries* within the Pauline churches. They included preaching, a wide range of services, administration and/or some kinds of leadership, and acting as a church delegate or serving in the Gentile mission as a co-worker with Paul (see particularly Rom. 12.7–8; 16.1, 3, 9, 21; I Cor. 12.28; 16.15–18; II Cor. 8.23; Phil. 1.1; 2.25; 4.3; Col. 1.7; 4.7; I Thess. 5.12f.). These diverse forms of ministry were by no means clearly distinguishable from one another – for example, the ministry of exhortation overlaps with that of prophecy (Rom. 12.6–8) and the ministry of 'helping' (I Cor. 12.28) with the 'sharing, caring and giving' of Rom. 12.8. The explanation of this diversity is obvious: any form of service etc. which any individual member of the charismatic community found himself regularly prompted to by the Spirit and which benefited the church was (or at least should have been) recognized as a regular ministry by the church (I Thess. 5.12f.; I Cor. 16.16, 18). Consequently these ministries should not be thought of as established or official ministries, and they were certainly not ecclesiastical appointments or church offices. Indeed we are told specifically in the case of Stephanas and his household that 'they *took upon themselves* their ministry to the saints' (I Cor. 16.15). The only ones which took a form which may have provided the beginnings of a pattern for the future were the 'overseers (bishops) and deacons' of Philippi (Phil. 1.1). There it would appear that some of the less well defined areas of administration and service mentioned above had begun to be grouped together or to cohere into more clearly outlined forms of ministry, so that those who regularly engaged in them could be known by the same name (overseer or deacon). But whether these Phil. 1.1 ministries were indeed the direct forerunners of the second-century offices of bishop and deacon must remain doubtful; if only because neither Ignatius nor Polycarp know of any bishop's office in connection with Philippi. The 'evangelists' and 'pastors' of Eph. 4.11 may also denote more clearly defined ministries, though in Ephesians the (universal) Church is possibly viewed from a later (post-Pauline?) perspective (see below pp.351f.). Yet even here the words seem to denote functions rather than offices and are not yet established titles.

(*d*) We should note finally the ministry of *the congregation* in Paul's vision of charismatic community. It is clear from his concept of the body of Christ that each member and all members of the body together have a responsibility for the welfare of the whole. So we are not surprised when Paul exhorts *all* the members of different communities to teach, admonish, judge, comfort (Rom.15.14; I Cor. 5.4f.; II Cor. 2.7; Col. 3.16; I Thess. 5.14). Indeed, it is noticeable that Paul's instructions and exhortations are generally addressed to the community as a whole. Nowhere in his letters, with the probable exception of Phil. 1.1, does he address a single group of people as though responsibility lay primarily or solely with them for the organization, worship and general welfare of the rest. This is clearest in I Corinthians where, despite a sequence of situations and problems which might seem to cry out for a well structured leadership, no such individual or group is called upon. The implication is plain: if leadership was required in any situation Paul assumed that the charismatic Spirit would provide it with a word of wisdom or guidance through some individual (cf. I Cor. 6.5; 12.28). The community as a whole certainly had the responsibility of testing all words and acts claiming the inspiration and authority of the Spirit (I Cor. 2.12, 15; I Thess. 5.20f.), even those of Paul himself (cf. I Cor. 7.25, 40; 14.37). It was part of their responsibility to give assent, to say the

'Amen' to the inspired utterances (I Cor. 14.16), to recognize the authority of the Spirit in these ministries undertaken at his compulsion (I Cor. 16.18; I Thess. 5.12f.).

29.3   *To sum up*, the Pauline concept of church and ministry *differs from the discipleship of Jesus' earthly ministry* in that it was a concept of charismatic *community*, characterized by mutual interdependence where each though knowing the Spirit directly must depend on fellow members for teaching and all sorts of other ministries. So too the Pauline concept of church and ministry *differs from the pattern which evolved at Jerusalem* in that it was essentially a concept of *charismatic* community and nothing else, 'of free fellowship, developing through the living interplay of spiritual gifts and ministries, without benefit of official authority or responsible "elders" '.[9] In particular, this means that the Pauline church cannot be described as sacerdotal with only some having ministry and particular ministries confined to a few. For Paul the Spirit had surmounted the old Jewish distinction between priest and people and left it behind – *all* have ministry and any member may be called upon to exercise any ministry. Some would have a more *regular* ministry which the congregation should recognize and encourage. But the idea of mono-ministry or ministerial autocracy – that is, of all the most important gifts concentrated on one man (even an apostle) or in a select group – is one which Paul dismissed with some ridicule (I Cor. 12.14–27).

§30. TOWARDS IGNATIUS

30.1   *The Pastorals*. If we glance back a few pages and compare Paul's vision of charismatic ministry with the exhortations of Ignatius to the Smyrneans (p.103 above), we might be tempted to conclude that the two concepts of ministry are poles apart, even irreconcilable. And yet when we turn to the latest members of the Pauline corpus (the Pastoral epistles) we see *an understanding of church structure which seems much closer to Ignatius than to Paul*! This degree of development in ecclesiastical organization is one of the chief indicators that the Pastorals as they now stand are post-Pauline, reflecting the situation in the Pauline churches probably in the last quarter of the first century, but possibly even later.

Here are the chief features. (1) Elders appear for the first and only time in the Pauline corpus (I Tim. 5.1f., 17, 19; Titus 1.5). (2) 'Overseers' (bishops – I Tim. 3.1–7; Titus 1.7ff.) and 'deacons'

(I Tim. 3.8–13) appear now as descriptions of established offices (I Tim. 3.1 – 'office of overseer'). The presentation of I Tim. 3 suggests that deacons were subordinate officials, though we cannot tell from this chapter what their respective functions were. (3) The role of Timothy and Titus within this hierarchy is not very clear either, though they certainly rank above the elders, overseers and deacons. What is significant is that the letters are addressed to them and they seem to exercise a responsibility and degree of authority in regulating the community's affairs which Paul himself never exercised directly or through his immediate co-workers (see further below p.352). (4) Most strikingly, the Pauline concept of charisma has been narrowed and regulated: it is a single gift given once-for-all in the course of ordination; Timothy now possesses it within himself and it equips him for his different responsibilities. In short, from being an event which carries its authority in itself, charisma has become the power and authority of *office* (I Tim. 4.14; II Tim. 1.6).

Perhaps the best explanation of this form of ministry and church organization is that *the Pastorals represent the fruit of a growing rapprochement between the more formal structures which Jewish Christianity took over from the synagogue and the more dynamic charismatic structure of the Pauline churches after Paul's death*. The central evidence for this hypothesis is that in the Pastorals we find both elders on the one hand and overseers and deacons on the other. Elders, we noted as a feature of the Jewish Christian congregations (above pp.107f., 109 – also James 5.14f.); overseers and deacons (the names at least) featured in what is probably one of the last letters written by Paul as a development in church organization evidenced only in Philippi. The suggestion is, therefore, that after Paul's death the name (and form?) of those regular ministries at Philippi were copied by other Pauline churches,[10] or at least became more widespread among the Pauline churches, while at the same time the functions of overseer and deacon began to be more clearly defined and regulated (cf. Didache 15.1–2). At this stage in the process the attempt began to be made to merge the two patterns, to assimilate the organization of the Jewish Christian churches to that of the Pauline churches (or vice-versa). The Pastorals (and I Clement) seem to have been written at a stage when this process of assimilation or integration was well advanced, but not yet complete. In particular, the roles of overseer and elder were probably being assimilated to each other, but it is not clear from the Pastorals whether the two words were yet quite synonymous, or whether, alternatively, 'overseer' had already become the title of a particular leadership function within the eldership (why are elders not mentioned in I Tim. 3?); cf. Acts 20.17, 28; I Clem. 42.4; 44.4f.; 47.6; 57.1.

30.2   If this hypothesis truly mirrors the actual historical developments, then we may be able to detect *earlier and different stages in this rapprochement* between the Jewish Christian churches and those of the Pauline mission in some of the other NT documents. I am thinking here of I Peter and Matthew.[11] The evidence is much slighter and more allusive, so we must proceed with due caution and cannot hope to achieve anything like a full picture. But what evidence there is seems to support the hypothesis outlined above.

I Peter seems to come from a Pauline milieu, or at least to be heavily influenced by Pauline theology (for example, the use of distinctively Pauline language and thought in 2.5, 3.16, 4.10f., 13, 5.10, 14). Notice particularly that the Pauline concept of charisma is still intact: he speaks of *each* having received some charisma and of 'the grace of God that manifests itself in various ways' (4.10); and he summarizes the charismata in terms of speaking and serving, a summary that is nevertheless wide enough to embrace the diversity of the Pauline lists in Rom. 12 and I Cor. 12, while maintaining the Pauline emphasis on charismata of the word and on charisma as service. Note also that the title of priest is given not to any individual Christian (never so in the NT), but to the church as a whole, and their ministry as a whole can be described in terms of priestly service (2.5, 9), just as with Paul (Rom. 15.27; II Cor. 9.12; Phil. 2.17(?), 25, 30). So too the title of 'pastor and overseer' is referred to Jesus alone (I Peter 2.25). At the same time the only prophets mentioned are spoken of in the past tense (1.10–12 – probably referring to or at least including early Christian prophets). Moreover, I Peter seems to envisage a clearly defined circle of elders with relatively well defined responsibilities (5.1–5). On this evidence we have to regard I Peter as reflecting *that stage when the Pauline churches*, or those most influenced by Paul, *had already begun to adopt and adapt the model of Jewish Christian church order, without yet losing the flexibility and freedom of the Pauline charismatic community*.[12]

30.3   *Matthew* seems to reflect an even earlier stage in the rapprochement, but from the side of Jewish Christianity. Thus, for example, on the one hand there is a strong emphasis on the continuing validity of the law (particularly 5.17–20 – see below §55.1); only in Matthew do we find preserved the logia restricting Jesus' concept of mission to the Jews (10.6, 23); and it is Peter who is singled out in the words about the church's firm foundation and 'the keys of the kingdom of heaven' (16.18f.). On the other hand there were evidently Christian scribes (= teachers) in the Matthean church (cf. 7.29 – 'their scribes') whose role it was not merely to pass on the law and the traditions about Jesus, but to interpret them afresh (13.52 – see above ch.IV); the Matthean church was much more open and committed to mission than the earliest Jerusalem church was (28.19f.); and it is not James who is singled out, but Peter,[13] who in first-century tradition is as closely identified with mission as Paul (particularly Gal. 2.8f.).[14]

The most interesting passages for our study are 7.15–23, 18.1–20 and 23.8–12. In 7.15–23 it is evident that the Matthean church had suffered somewhat from the ministry of wandering prophets – that is, they had experienced a type of charismatic ministry which, in Matthew's view at least, was wedded to antinomianism (7.22f.; cf. 24.11, 24). In this passage Matthew does not reject such ministry (cf. 10.7f., 41; 17.20), but wishes rather to integrate it with a fuller loyalty to the law. In 'the community rule' of 18.1–20 it is noteworthy that there are no special leaders distinguished from the ordinary church member, not even elders or overseers, to whom special exhortations are addressed. It speaks only of 'these little ones' – obviously the membership as a whole, since to enter the kingdom of heaven each must become such a one (18.1–6, 10). The 'rule' goes on to lay responsibility on every one of them to find the lost sheep, to win back the erring brother, to bind and loose (18.12–20). That is to say, it was not simply Peter or some single individual or group of office-bearers who had the authority to 'bind and loose', to teach and to discipline, but every member of the church was so authorized by Jesus (18.18–20).[15] *In Matthew Peter is picked out not so much as a hierarchical figure but more as the representative disciple* – as again in 14.28–31, where he typifies 'little faith' discipleship (cf. 6.30; 8.26; 16.8; 17.20)[16] – just as the twelve are also probably understood as representative of the church as a whole (19.28; cf. I Cor. 6.2f.). Finally, in 23.8–10 there is the quite explicit warning to the Matthean church against conferring any rank or title or special status on any individual member – God alone is 'father', and Jesus alone is 'teacher' and 'master'. The greatness to which they are all encouraged is not that of executive power and authority but that of humble service (20.25–27; 23.11f.).

The Matthean community is perhaps best described as a *brotherhood* (5.22–24, 47; 7.3–5; 18.15, 21, 35; 23.8) grouped round the elder brother Jesus (12.49f.; 18.20; 25.40; 28.10), striving to develop a form of outgoing life and all-member ministry amid Jewish hostility (with the most prominent ministries those of Peter, prophets and teachers), and conscious of the opposite dangers both of a hierarchical structure which inhibits the manifold ministry of the brothers[17] and of a charismatic prophetism which divorces miracles and revelation too sharply from a proper loyalty to the law – in other words, *trying to develop a form of Pauline 'churchmanship' within and more appropriate to a Jewish context.*[18]

§31. THE JOHANNINE ALTERNATIVE

If the Pastorals evince a development within first-century Christianity towards the greater institutionalization of Ignatius and the great Church of the second century onwards, we must also recognize a counter-tendency within the first century which seems to run in the opposite direction. The clearest witness to this *resistance to institutionalization* is the Fourth Gospel and the Johannine epistles; but we can also detect signs of it in Hebrews and Revelation.

31.1 *The individualism of the Fourth Gospel* is one of the most striking features of this remarkable document. Like Paul the author sees worship in charismatic terms (see below p.131), but unlike Paul there is no concept of charismatic *community*. Certainly there is a sense of community both in the Gospel and in the first epistle (John 10.1–16; 15.1–6; 17.6–26; I John 1.7; 2.19; 3.13–17), but not of a community charismatically interdependent. And of course the 'horizontal' responsibility is laid on each to love the brethren; in both writings, as in Paul, this is the real mark of the Christian believer (John 13.34f.; I John 3.10–18, 23f.; 4.20f.). But for John the 'vertical' relationship with God the Spirit is essentially an *individual* affair. Thus, in particular, there is mutual belonging to Christ, but not a mutual interdependence in that belonging: each sheep hears the shepherd's voice for himself (John 10.3f., 16); each branch is rooted directly in the vine (15.4–7). The talk of munching Jesus' flesh, drinking his blood, or of drinking the water from his side, is addressed more to a sequence of individuals than to a community which is itself the body of Christ (6.53–58; 7.37f.). And the climax of the 'Gospel of Signs' (1–12) is the resuscitation of a single individual, symbolizing a one-to-one salvation (11) rather than the general resurrection of the dead. Jesus does pray for the *unity* of believers, which again speaks of community, but even here the unity John has in mind is comparable to the unity of the Father and the Son and is both rooted in and dependent on the individual believer's union with

Jesus (17.20–23).[19] Perhaps most striking of all, the small group left round Jesus after the tremendous sifting (*krisis*) of faith and loyalty (a dominant motif – see above p.75) do not form some hierarchy or particular office which sets them apart from other disciples: they are never called 'the apostles' (cf. 13.16) and presumably include some of the women who feature so prominently in this Gospel (4; 11; 20); there is no thought of them having special ministries *within* the community of disciples; they are simply 'the disciples' and are most likely intended to represent all (including future) disciples in their common responsibility of mutual love and mission (14–16; 20.22).[20] The same is probably true of 'the beloved disciple' in particular. That is to say, whatever the historical reality underlying his presentation (cf.21.20–24), John probably intends him to symbolize the individual believer in the immediacy and closeness of his relationship to Jesus (13.23–25; 20.2–8). Similarly in I John 2.27, the anointing of the Spirit obviates the necessity of teachers: the Spirit indwelling each believer is teacher enough. In short, *throughout these writings there is no real concept of ministry, let alone of office*. Everything is seen in terms of the individual's immediate relationship to God through the Spirit and the word.[21]

31.2   Of all the NT letters outside the Pauline corpus, *Hebrews*, next to I Peter, has the closest affinities to Paul. But whereas I Peter is something of a half-way house between Paul and the Pastorals, Hebrews is more of a half-way house between Paul and John. To be sure there are 'leaders' active in the Hebrews' church (13.7, 17, 24), but they are defined more in terms of pastoral function than of office (13.17). The same is even more clearly true of the ministry of teaching in 5.11–6.8, where the only qualification mentioned is spiritual maturity evidenced by skill in discriminating good from bad – a skill gained by experience and practice (5.14); compare the qualification for recognition as a prophet or teacher in Paul (above p.112). No other ministries are referred to individual members. Instead, responsibility for service and exhortation is laid on the whole membership (6.10; 10.25; 12.15). Here too are distinct parallels with the charismatic community of Paul (see above pp.113f.).

The most striking feature of Hebrews at this point however is the way in which *ministry focuses in Christ in a complete and final manner*. He alone is called 'apostle' (3.1). He completes the fragmentary revelation given through the prophets of old (1.1f.). Above all, he is priest, high priest, priest according to the order of Melchizedek (2.17; 3.1; 4.14f.; 5.1; etc.). His priesthood is so complete and exalted, his priestly ministry so perfect and final, that *there is no role or room left for any priestly intermediary within the Christian community*. A distinct priesthood belonged only to the past, to the era of shadow. But Christ has brought the reality thus foreshadowed to every believer (7–10). As *the* priest he has offered the once-for-all and final sacrifice and opened up the Holy of Holies to every believer, so that *each* can experience *for himself* the reality of what the high priest alone experienced in shadow for his people (4.16; 6.19f.; 10.19–22). In short, those ministries which typified the old covenant have been wholly fulfilled by Christ and therefore abolished for the people of the new covenant. Here then is a close parallel with the Johannine concept of church and ministry, where ministry is focused in an all but exclusive way in Jesus and *each believer can 'draw near' the presence of God for himself without depending on other believers or any human intermediary*.[22]

31.3   The concept of ministry hinted at in *Revelation* seems also to belong somewhere between Paul and John. Here too is a striking absence of any idea of hierarchy and office. All believers are kings and priests (1.6; 5.10; 20.6), all are God's servants (7.3). Apostles are mentioned, but as belonging to the founding era of the Church (21.14). Elders appear in the heavenly throne room, but if they represent human counterparts at all (rather than the OT council of Yahweh) it would be the whole Church and not just particular office bearers within it – twelve perhaps representing the Israel of God of the old era, twelve the present Church (4.4, 10; 5.8; 11.16; 19.4; cf. 3.21). So too the 'angels' of the churches in 1.20, 2–3 should not be taken to represent bishops (overseers) or particular leaders; since the words addressed to each angel clearly apply to each church as a whole, the angels are best taken as heavenly counterparts of the various churches. In short, *there is no mention in Revelation of bishops, deacons, teachers or pastors, and 'priests' and 'elders' are designations for the whole Church*.

The only distinctive ministries mentioned by Revelation are those of *prophet* (2.20; 10.7; 11.10, 18; 16.6; 18.20, 24; 22.6, 9) and *witness* or martyr (2.13; 11.3; 17.6; cf. 1.2, 9; 6.9; 11.7; 12.11, 17; 19.10; 20.4). These words seem sometimes to denote particular individuals within the church (2.13, 20; 22.9), but in 11.3, 10 it is probably the church as a whole which is symbolized as two witnesses or prophets. It is not clear whether the twin terms 'saints and prophets/martyrs' (11.18; 16.6; 17.6; 18.24) refer equally to the entire community, or distinguish prophets/martyrs from the rest of the saints (as presumably in 18.20). But certainly there is no suggestion of a prophetic hierarchy, and in so far as all believers are called upon to bear testimony to Jesus so all experience the Spirit of prophecy (12.11, 17; 19.10; cf. 6.9–11; 20.4). Here we have something of a parallel with the Pauline concept of ministry: in principle every saint is a witness and prophet, though some are called upon to exercise that ministry in a fuller way than others. The writer of Revelation is sometimes singled out as claiming a unique authority (1.3; 21.5; 22.6, 18f.), but this is simply the authority of prophetic inspiration which any prophet believes to belong to his prophecy, and 22.18f. is little more than a literary convention to ensure faithful transmission of the author's original (cf. e.g. *Ep. Aristeas* 310f.); John the seer does not distinguish himself from those to whom he writes either as witness or as prophet (1.2, 9; 19.10). In short, so far as Revelation is concerned, *the Church is pre-eminently a church that lives through and out of prophecy*.[23]

§32. CONCLUSIONS

32.1   In our study of first-century Christianity *we have discovered no greater diversity than that apparent in the various concepts of ministry and community reviewed above.* In the stage of pre-Easter discipleship we could not easily use the word 'community' to describe the circles round Jesus, and ministry was centred exclusively in Jesus himself. In the second stage, the first generation of Christianity itself, we were confronted with two diverging patterns: on the one hand, the early and somewhat chaotic charismatic freedom of the Jerusalem church settled down into a more conservative pattern of church order borrowed from the synagogue; on the other, Paul vigorously advocated a much freer vision of charismatic community, where unity and maturity grew out of the living interplay of gifts and ministries without dependence on any office or hierarchy. In the third stage, the second generation of Christianity, the patterns became both intermingled and more divergent: on the one hand we see a certain growing together of the forms of Jewish Christianity and those of the Pauline churches after his death which in the Pastorals at any rate is beginning to harden into the more rigid structures of future Catholicism; on the other we see what is best understood as a reaction against such institutionalizing trends, where in different ways John, Hebrews and Revelation protest against the emergence of a church structured round office and intermediaries and insist on the immediacy of the individual believer's relation to God through Christ and on the corporate nature of priesthood and prophecy – John in particular seeming to hanker after the pattern of discipleship which characterized the first stage, to preserve what we would call now a kind of conventicle or camp-meeting or convention Christianity.

32.2   This means that out of the 'spaghetti-junction'[24] of first-century Christianity *only one road led towards the orthodox church order of Ignatius; others led in at least one other very different direction.* To be sure we have examined only one aspect of NT ecclesiology, but we have surely seen enough to recognize the justice of E. Käsemann's famous claim: 'the New Testament canon does not, as such, constitute the foundation of the unity of the Church. On the contrary, as such . . ., it provides the basis for the multiplicity of the confessions'.[25] This conclusion has not been sufficiently reckoned with in the twentieth-century ecumenical movement, and its possible corollaries for modern denominational diversity need to be thought through with much greater care and thoroughness. We will have to return to this issue in the concluding chapter (particularly §76.2).

32.3   Does any focus of unity hold these divergent patterns of ministry and community together, or are they simply scattered fragments lacking essential coherence? *Only one focus of unity can be detected with any consistency* – that is, once again, *Jesus and faith in him.*[26] In the pre-Easter movement Jesus alone was minister, prophet, teacher. In the initial period following Easter, authority and direction came from visions of Jesus, from those who acted 'in his name', from the Spirit given by the exalted Jesus; and even James's elevation to leadership was due partly at least to the fact that he was Jesus' brother. In the Pauline vision the charismatic community was nothing if it was not also the body of Christ, living by his Spirit, manifesting the character of his self-giving love. Even when we begin to move into the second generation of Christianity the focus remains the same: it is Christ alone who is described as 'shepherd and overseer of our souls' in I Peter 2.25; it is Christ alone who may be called teacher and master in Matt. 23.8–10; it is Christ alone who is priest and highpriest in Hebrews; and for the seer of Revelation the Church is presented as the bride of Christ (21.2f., 9). Even in the Pastorals it is specifically stressed that the man Christ Jesus is the one mediator between God and man (I Tim. 2.5), while in John the centrality of Jesus the incarnate and exalted Logos and the immediate dependence of every disciple on him is one of the most dominant features. Here again then, and in a striking way, *the one unifying strand that unites the divergent patterns is Jesus*, the man of Nazareth now exalted, still providing the essential focus of authority and still serving as the pattern of ministry.

32.4   Two other features deserve brief comment, since, despite an obvious potential relevance to present day issues, they have usually been ignored. One is the uniform fact that within the NT there is no place for a continuing distinction between priest and people, between 'clergy' and 'laity'. The sense of eschatological fulfilment consistent within the first two generations of Christianity means that *any thought of an order of priesthood* within *the body of believers, setting some believers apart from others, has been left wholly behind as belonging to the age before Christ.* Christ alone is designated 'priest' (Heb.; cf. Rom. 8.34). Several NT writers speak of believers as a whole having priestly ministry (I Peter 2.5, 9; Rev. 1.6) and Paul describes ministry in service of the gospel or of other believers as priestly service (Rom. 15.16; Phil. 2.25). But there is now no sacred space into which only some can enter (John 4.20–24), and the sacrifice to be offered by believers is the sacrifice of themselves in the bodily relationships of the everyday world (Rom. 12.1). The cult has been secularized. There is no place for an order of priesthood distinct in character or kind from the priesthood of all believers. This consistent feature of Christianity's canonical documents does not seem to have been given enough weight in all the contemporary discussions, whether of 'the ministry' or of 'the ministry of the whole people of God'.

Equally striking within the context of the times would have been the prominent role played in the beginnings of Christianity by *the ministry of women disciples.* Their role in the Gospels is marked – Matt. 28.1–10, Mark 15.40–41 and Luke 8.1–3, and still more in John (2.3–5; 4.25–30, 39; 11.24–27; 20.1–18). In the Pauline epistles the discussion has focused far too much on the one hand on I Cor. 11.2–16 and 14.34–35 (not to mention I Tim. 2.11–12), and on the other on Gal. 3.28. And much too little attention has been paid to the clear evidence of women exercising prominent ministry and bearing authority of leadership in the Pauline churches. To cite only Rom. 16, notice Phoebe (16.1), the first to be designated 'deacon' within the NT, and also a 'patron' of the church in Cenchreae. Then Prisca (16.3), one of Paul's co-workers and evidently more prominent than her husband Aquila in leadership and ministry. Then Junia (16.7 – *not* Junias), probably wife of Andronicus, and a leading apostle before Paul. And not least Mary, Tryphaena, Tryphosa and Persis (16.6, 12), all described as 'hard-workers' – a description which elsewhere is usually taken as an indication of leadership (I Cor. 16.16; I Thess. 5.12). As these are the only ones so described in the list of greetings in Rom. 16, we should presumably conclude that women were particularly prominent in the leadership of the earliest churches in Rome.

VII

PATTERNS OF WORSHIP

§33. INTRODUCTION

Worship is one of the great unifying forces in Christianity. For in worship there is room for an extravagance of language, for a freedom of literary form which is absent in kerygmatic and confessional statements. The liturgies of the various denominations, particularly their hymns, are a treasury of worship drawn from many diverse traditions past and present and transcending denominational and national boundaries. Even hymns intended to express particular doctrinal standpoints (like Wesley's 'Love divine, all loves excelling') or hymns by Unitarians have become vehicles of a Christian worship which often makes differences and divisions seem of little consequence. Indeed a slogan which gained some currency in ecumenical discussions of the present century – born no doubt of the frustrations of cross-denominational dialogue – was 'Worship unites, doctrine divides'. It should also be noted that Eastern Christians have always tended to place a far higher (relative) importance on worship than their Western brothers: for the Orthodox 'orthodoxy' is not so much about doctrine and much more about worship. To be an Orthodox Christian is to belong to that community which praises and glorifies God in the right spirit.

Here then is another important area deserving investigation in our inquiry into the unity and diversity of first-century Christianity. What patterns of worship characterized the churches of the NT period? Was there a single pattern, or were there as many diverse patterns of worship as there were of ministry (ch. VI)? How much of a force for unity was worship, how diverse were its forms? We will look first, and fairly briefly, at a cross-section of the NT, concentrating particularly on Jesus, the earliest Church, Paul and John. Then we will focus more specifically on the *hymnody* of the NT churches, where NT scholarship has proved particularly fruitful in the past 50 years. Finally we will ask whether there were *extended liturgical and catechetical forms* already in use in the first century AD and already providing a much broader unifying strand than we have so far uncovered.

§34. DIVERSITY OF ATTITUDE AND FORM

34.1   *Jesus.* It is not altogether clear what Jesus' attitude was to the worship of his own day. This is one of the many subjects in research into Christian origins on which scholars are divided. Certainly we must regard his eschatological perspective as basic to the whole question: Jesus experienced the power of the end-time kingdom as already in operation and expected the consummation of the kingdom imminently (see above §§3.1, 2). Consequently his whole understanding and worship of God was at some remove from the typical attitude of his contemporaries. For most of them God was the high and holy one, to be addressed with the utmost reverence, and the immanence of God was expressed in terms of the name of God, or the Wisdom of God, etc. But for Jesus God was the God who is near in his own person. He was Father, not in terms of original creation or adoption, but in the intimate individual and family sense expressed in the address *abba* (dear father, 'dad') (see below §45.2). This attitude recognized a *continuity* with the past – Jesus saw this revelation given as the climax to what went before (cf. Matt. 5.17; Matt. 11.25f./ Luke 10.21); but it also implied a *discontinuity* with the past – something new had entered which could not be contained and retained within the old framework (Mark 2.21f.). We see this working itself out most clearly in Jesus' attitude to temple and synagogue, in his attitude to the law, and in his practice of prayer.

(*a*) *Jesus' attitude to the temple and synagogue.* We do not know how often Jesus visited the temple (note particularly Matt. 23.37–39/Luke 13.34f., as well as the several visits in John's Gospel). On the one occasion that we certainly know of, we know also what he did – the so-called 'cleansing of the temple'. But what was the significance of his action? If we take Mark 11.17 with its citation of Isa. 56.7 as authentic, then we must conclude that Jesus looked on the temple as the focal point of God's eschatological renewal – an interpretation which is supported by the attitude of the first Christians to the temple (see below pp.127, 238f.). But it could also be argued that the expulsion of the sellers of sacrificial animals etc. implied a rejection of the traditional sacrificial cult, since his action would in effect make its continuation impossible; compare his critique of the ritual purity laws (see below). Here we have to recall again the saying of Jesus preserved in Mark 13.2, 14.58 (see above p.42), which seems to indicate that for Jesus the temple (and its sacrificial cult) belonged to the old age already passing away – in the coming kingdom a new (heavenly) temple would be provided (cf. the interpretation of John 2.21 and Acts 6.14 – see below p.128).[1] So we are left in some doubt about Jesus' attitude to the temple (cf. also Matt. 5.23f. with 9.13, 12.7; and Mark 1.44, Luke 17.14 with Luke 10.31f.); also John 5.14, 7.14, 28; 8.20; 10.23; and the *ambiguity* of his preserved teaching is reflected in the diverse paths followed by Hebrews and Hellenists in the earliest Jerusalem community (see below §34.2). As for his attitude towards the synagogue, we are told that he attended it and may assume that he did this regularly, though according to our evidence his primary purpose in so doing was to teach his own message (Mark 1.21–27, 39; 3.1; 6.2; Matt. 9.35; Luke 4.15–21; 13.10), not merely to read the Torah and join in the prayers.

(*b*) We have already examined *Jesus' attitude to the law* oral and written (see above §§16.2, 24.5). We need only recall here his rejection of the Sabbath halakah, the corban casuistry and the regulations on ritual washing. His attitude to fasting also caused comment (Mark 2.18; Matt. 11.19/Luke 7.34), though he may have expected his disciples to practise it in the interval before the coming of the kingdom (Mark 2.20; Matt. 6.16–18). Even more striking is the sovereign manner in which he handled the written law, determining in what manner and to what extent its regulations were to be obeyed. In particular, we noted how 'his teaching on the causes of impurity as recalled in Mark 7 in effect cuts at the root of the *whole* ritual law' (above p. 98). Here again then there is continuity (he restates at a deeper level the commandments against murder and adultery), but here too there is striking discontinuity.

(*c*) *Jesus' practice of prayer.* J. Jeremias believes that Jesus observed the Jewish times of prayer, 'the morning prayer at sunrise, the afternoon prayer at the time when the afternoon sacrifice was offered in the temple, the evening prayer at night before going to sleep'.[2] But prayer for Jesus was something much more spontaneous and fresh – as again becomes most evident in the word with which he regularly addressed God, *abba*, an expression of confident trust and obedience, whereas the manner in which his contemporaries addressed God, so far as we can tell, was much more formal (see further below §45.2).

To be sure the prayer which he taught his disciples (Matt. 6.9–13/Luke 11.2–4) has echoes of ancient Jewish prayers in two or three of its petitions,[3] but remains distinct precisely in its sense of intimacy and in its sustained note of eschatological urgency.

34.2   *The earliest community.* There was sufficient ambiguity in Jesus' teaching about worship for *divergent interpretations and practices* to emerge almost from the first.

(*a*) So far as we can tell the earliest Christians in Palestine maintained the traditions of Jewish worship virtually unchanged. They attended the temple daily (Acts 2.46; 3.1; 5.12, 21, 42), probably expecting it to be the place of Jesus' return (Mal. 3.1 – see below p.324). That this continuing prominence of the temple is not simply a consequence of Lukan theology (cf. below p.354) is confirmed by Matt. 5.23f. whose preservation also suggests that the sacrificial cult continued to be observed by the first Christians. It would appear then that the idea of Jesus as the end of the temple had not yet become established. They seem also to have observed the traditional hours of prayer (Acts 3.1; 5.21; 10.9(?)) at temple and/or synagogue (cf. Acts 6.9; John 9 – see above p.44). And they continued to observe the law and the 'tradition of the elders' (including the sabbath) with faithfulness – as such passages as Matt. 23.3, 23, 24.20, Acts 21.20, Gal. 2.3ff.,12, 4.10 (cf. Rom. 14.2, 5; Col. 2.16, 20f.) clearly indicate (see above §16.3). It was apparently not until the Cornelius episode that the continued importance of ritual purity was even called in question by the Palestinian Christians (Acts 10.14; 11.3) (see also below p.238f.).

(*b*) However, at the same time *new forms of worship* seem to have been developing, and that from the first. These centred on gatherings in private houses (Acts 2.46; 5.42). We hear of different elements entering into these meetings – worship and prayer (1.14; 2.42; 4.23–31; 12.12), teaching – that is, presumably, both the scriptures (OT) and the Jesus-tradition, both passing them on and interpreting them (2.42; 5.42), and common meals (2.42, 46). There is nothing to indicate that these fell into a regular pattern or formed a unified service of worship. It is more likely that there were *at least two different kinds of gathering*, one (more formal?) for prayer and teaching, following somewhat the pattern of the synagogue service, and the other for fellowship meals, which may also have included other elements, such as singing, introduced as appropriate in more spontaneous manner (cf. the note of exuberance in 2.46f.). The new patterns of worship which began to emerge in these meetings were not wholly different from what had gone before: we do not know whether they recited the *Shema* (Deut. 6.4–9; 11.13–21) which every individual Israelite was obliged to repeat twice daily;[4] but they must have read from the scriptures (though we lack direct evidence of this); and no doubt they continued to use some of the typical forms of thanksgiving and blessing and the 'Amen' (cf. I Cor. 14.16). But there were also distinctively Christian elements: the Lord's prayer, the use of *abba* in prayers, the recollection of the words and mighty acts of Jesus (all of which must have been transmitted through the earliest communities), not least the centrality of Jesus in his presence (Matt. 18.20)[5] and expected soon return (I Cor. 16.22), and those elements in the common meal which recalled the table-fellowship of Jesus' ministry, the last supper in particular, and which were to develop into what we now know as the Lord's Supper (see below §40).

(*c*) For some time this dual pattern of worship, temple and house-meeting, continued side by side, with no tension felt between them. But with *the Hellenists and Stephen* we come to a parting of the ways: the continuing role of the temple for followers of Jesus was put sharply in question, and old worship (temple) and new were set in clear-cut antithesis.[6] The key evidence here is Acts 6–7, whose historical status is somewhat in question, but which probably represents fairly accurately, on this point at least, the views of the Hellenists which led to the first persecution of Christians. The charge against Stephen was that he spoke against the temple cult (6.13f.), and the clear implication of 6.14 is that he had taken up Jesus' word about the destruction of the temple (Mark 13.2; 14.58) and interpreted it as a rejection of the temple as the locus of the divine presence (see above pp.74, 126). Even more explicit is the latter part of the speech preserved in Acts 7, which climaxes in an outright attack on the temple in which Stephen calls Isa. 66.1f. as testimony (see above p.98f.) and describes the temple as 'made with hands' (Acts 7.48–50) – the very epithet which in Jewish polemic against paganism characterized idolatry (references on p.271). If this is a fair representation of Stephen's and/or the Hellenists' views, and the sequel strongly suggests that it is (8.1–4; 11.19–21), then we must conclude that from a very early date *the main focus of the Hellenists' worship was the house meeting*, where the distinctively Christian elements were the chief force in shaping a new pattern of worship. Moreover, we should not ignore the fact that Stephen's attitude was a *rejection* not only of the Jewish attitude to the temple but also *of the worship of the Aramaic/Hebrew speaking Christians so far as it continued to centre on the temple*. It is not clear whether it was at this time or later that the Palestinian Christian attitude to the law was also called in question: it was evidently zeal for the law and the traditions which made Paul a persecutor of the Hellenist Christians (Gal. 1.13f.; Phil. 3.5f.; and note Acts 6.13); but the speech of Acts 7 never really extends to an attack on the law (cf. 6.14). Be that as it may, it is clear that from an early date there was a *diversity of attitude to and practice of worship* and a *fairly sharp divergence of opinion* which must have imposed severe strains on the unity of the first Christian community (see further below §60).

34.3   *Paul*. Of the two early patterns of worship Paul was apparently more influenced by the free house churches of the Hellenists, though to what extent is not clear. Certainly house churches were an important locus of community life in Paul's mission (Rom. 16.5; I Cor. 16.19; Col. 4.15; Philemon 2), as well of course as the larger (weekly?) gatherings of the whole community (I Cor. 11; 14; cf. 16.2). But his concept of worship is more than a rationalizing of inherited forms and stems primarily from his concept of the local church as the body of Christ. We recall that the body of Christ is for Paul the charismatic community, that is, the community functioning charismatically. The body of Christ comes to expression, lives and moves, through the mutual interplay of gifts and ministries, the diversity of manifestations being integrated into a unity of purpose and character by the controlling Spirit of Christ (see above §29). But this means that *the body of Christ comes to visible expression pre-eminently in and through worship*: it is most clearly in worship that the diversity of functions (= charismata) demonstrate their mutual interdependence and unifying force (hence the discussion of charismata in I Cor. 12–14 centres on the assembly at worship).

How did this work in practice? The clearest answer is given in I Cor. 14.26–33a: 'When you meet for worship, each of you contributes a hymn, a word of teaching, a revelation, an utterance in tongues, an interpretation . . .'. Here, beyond dispute, *Paul conceives of worship as a very spontaneous affair, without regular structure or form, and wholly dependent on the inspiration of the Spirit*. The only regulations he gives are: that there should not be an unbroken sequence of glossolalic utterances – an utterance in the vernacular, an interpretation, must follow each utterance in tongues, otherwise tongues should be wholly excluded; that each prophetic utterance should be evaluated by the prophets and/or the whole community (cf. I Cor. 2.12–15; I Thess. 5.19–22); and that no more than two or three glossolalic and two or three prophetic utterances should be allowed in any meeting.

The period of worship then would consist in a sequence of contributions in which those with regular ministries would participate (prophets and teachers), but where any member might experience the urging of the Spirit to manifest a particular charisma (including a prophecy or teaching). The regular ministries were not expected to dominate the meeting or necessarily to provide leadership. Leadership would be provided by the Spirit, possibly through a regular ministry of leadership, but possibly also through an occasional gift of guidance or word of wisdom (I Cor. 6.5; 12.28). As we noted above (p.113), in I Corinthians anyway Paul does not seem to envisage any established leadership as such.[6a]

Whether *women* participated in this charismatic worship is not clear. I Cor. 14.33b–36, if original, appears to exclude any contribution from women, but a less rigorous interpretation is possible (for example, it forbids only their interrupting the process of evaluating prophetic utterances (14.29–33a) by asking unnecessary questions), and should probably be accepted in view of I Cor. 11.5 which clearly envisages women prophesying. Compare Acts 2.17–18, 21.9, Col. 4.15 and Rom. 16.1–12 (see above p. 123).

Finally we might note that there is no hint in I Cor. 11 or 14 as to how the meeting for worship was related to the common meal. The discussion of each does not seem to embrace the other or to leave much room for the other, and we best assume that Paul envisages *two separate gatherings* for the different purposes (cf. particularly Pliny, *Epp.*, X.96.7).

34.4   When we move beyond the first generation of Christianity we discover *a divergency of patterns in worship* similar to that in concepts of ministry. Once again the Pastorals and John seem to mark out the divergent pathways most clearly. We will follow the same procedure as in chapter VI though more briefly.[7]

(*a*) In the *Pastorals* the leadership of worship seems to be much more restricted, as we might expect. In particular, exhortation and teaching are no longer thought of as charismata which anyone might be called upon to exercise, but seem to belong to the responsibility and authority of office (I Tim. 2.12; 3.2; 4.13; Titus 1.9). Prophecy is spoken of, but only as an authoritative voice from the past (I Tim. 1.18; 4.1, 14) – was prophecy too spontaneous, too creative a gift to be permitted room within the church bent on maintaining good order and preserving the inherited tradition (see further below p.361)? Of other elements in the patterns of worship outlined above only prayer seems to be a general congregational activity (I Tim.

2.8). Here evidently is *a much more regulated and ordered style of worship* than that implied in I Cor. 11–14.

(*b*) *Matthew* again seems to represent some sort of earlier rapprochement between the original pattern of Palestinian Christian worship (Matt. 5.23f.) and the freer charismatic worship of the Pauline churches (7.22; 10.7f.; 17.20). In particular, we must note that in 18.15–20 responsibility for exercising discipline lies with the church as a whole (cf. I Cor. 5.4f.; 6.4f.). Similarly the authority of 'binding and loosing', whether it is a teaching function that is envisaged (see below p.360) or the declaration of sins forgiven (cf. John 20.23), belongs not to Peter alone (Matt. 16.19) but once again to the whole congregation (18.18). Where *any* two believers exercise their faith or celebrate their faith God acknowledges it and Jesus is present (18.19–20). Here is *a believer and community centred understanding of worship*, not a worship regulated by officebearer and tradition.

(*c*) Moving in the opposite direction from the Pastorals *John* seems to be reacting against a growing formalism and institutionalization in worship (as well as in ministry). Here the key passage is John 4.23f. – 'God is spirit, and those who worship him must worship in Spirit and truth' – where John is able to achieve his purpose by setting Christian worship over against the traditions of Jewish and Samaritan worship – that is, by setting worship in Spirit and truth over against the sort of concerns in worship typified by the Jerusalem/Gerizim conflict.[8] John is saying in effect that Jesus has left far behind that sort of issue and attitude, just as he has superseded the temple (2.19), the Jewish feasts and sacrifices (1.29; 6.4, 25–58; 7.37–39; 19.36), the law (1.17; 4.10, 14; 6.30–35) and the Jewish rituals (2.6; 3.25–36) – *worship of God no longer depends on sacred place or sacred tradition or sacred ceremony.* The worship that God seeks is a worship not frozen to a sacred building or by loyalty to a particular tradition or rite, but a worship which is living, the ever new response to God who is spirit as prompted and enabled by the Spirit of God in the light of the truth of Jesus. John 4.23f. therefore is probably intended by John as an implied rebuke to all who want to continue worshipping God in terms of institution, tradition and ritual. That worship in Spirit and truth meant for John and the Johannine churches a sort of *individualistic pietism* is probably implied by the passages mentioned in §31.1 above and by I John 3.24, 4.13.

(*d*) *Hebrews* seems to reflect a not dissimilar sort of reaction against the ritualistic worship of the old covenant. That was all only a mere shadow of the reality which Jesus has made possible for his followers – the immediate and direct entry into the heavenly tabernacle, the very presence of God (10.1). Here too worship is conceived in somewhat pietistic terms: where all priesthood and ministry focuses on Jesus (see above §31.2) each member of the community is dependent only on him for the reality of renewal in worship (4.16; 6.19f.; 10.19–22; 13.15).

34.5   Here again then we see a considerable degree of diversity: in particular, diversity about the patterns of worship inherited from the past, whether they should be maintained or whether the Spirit should be trusted continually to create new forms more appropriate to the people of God in their different and changing situations, with all that that involves in terms of breaking with past traditions; and diversity as to whether worship is primarily the affair of the individual soul before God or rather something which can only come to full expression for the individual when he is functioning as part of a structured worshipping community. A further factor making for diversity will become more apparent when we look more closely at one particular expression of earliest Christian worship – its hymnody.

§35. EARLY CHRISTIAN HYMNS

Some hymns or hymn-like forms have been obvious more or less from the first – the psalms of Luke 1–2 and the great ascriptions of praise in Revelation. Others have been recognized only within this century – hymns in praise of Christ, particularly within the Pauline literature.

35.1   *Luke 1–2.* The Christian Church has long been familiar with the four psalms of Luke 1–2 as part of its own worship.

(*a*) The *Magnificat,* the song of Mary – Luke 1.46–55. This was probably modelled on Hannah's song in I Sam. 2.1–10. It is noticeable that there are *no specifically Christian ideas in it*; it is typically Hebraic in character and content. But equally clearly and from the earliest days of the new faith, Christians have been able to take it over fully as an expression of their own praise.

(*b*) The *Benedictus,* the song of Zechariah – Luke 1.68–79. The canticle is full of OT allusions, particularly to the Psalms, Genesis, Isaiah and Malachi. The first part (vv.68–75) in particular is very Jewish in character, although in the second part (vv.76–79) more distinctively Christian ideas enter. Many scholars believe that it was originally a messianic psalm – note particularly vv.68f., 76 and 78:

... he has turned to his people, saved them and set them free
and has raised up a deliverer of victorious power
from the house of his servant David;

... you, my child, shall be called Prophet of the Highest

for in the tender compassion of our God
the morning sun from heaven will rise/has risen upon us ... (NEB).

One of the figures or titles in Jewish messianic expectation was 'prophet' (Deut. 18.18f.; Isa. 61.1ff.; Mal. 4.5; Test.Levi 8.15; Test.Ben. 9.2(?); 1QS 9.11; 4QTest. 5–8); and the Greek word used in v.78 for sunrise (*anatolē*) may well be an allusion to the LXX of Jer. 23.5, Zech. 3.8, 6.12, where it translates the messianic metaphor 'Branch'. If the song of Zechariah was originally a messianic psalm (referring to the Baptist as Messiah?), then the Christians who first took it over were easily able to make it their own by interpreting the Baptist's role as 'forerunner of the Lord' as forerunner of *Jesus*.

(*c*) *Gloria in excelsis* – Luke 2.14. This had become a well established feature in Christian morning worship according to the fourth-century *Apostolic Constitutions*. It contains nothing specifically Christian in itself, that is, outside of its context.

(*d*) *Nunc dimittis* – Luke 2.29–32. A psalm of praise for the coming of the Messiah, it expresses the calm ecstasy of faith at the realization of a life-long yearning and hope. It must have served over and over again to express the wonder of deliverance experienced by the earliest Christians, and their consequent abandonment to God's will.

These are all hymns which sprang directly from the soil of pious Judaism; a distinctively Hellenistic influence is wholly absent. In two of the four there is not even anything distinctively Christian. And even the remaining two are more messianic than Christian – that is, they rejoice that the Messiah has already come, but the Messiah remains unidentified. Whatever their ultimate origin and derivation, Luke has almost certainly drawn them from the living worship of the earliest congregations (rather than from memories reaching back to events 80 years earlier). In other words, they are *the psalms of the early Palestinian communities*, which reached their present form in a period when there were not yet any 'Christians', only Jews who believed that the Messiah had come.[9]

35.2   In *Revelation* there are many psalms or doxologies, or perhaps more accurately shouts of praise: acclamations of God – 4.8, 11; 7.12; 11.17f.; 15.3f.; (16.7; 19.1–3, 5); acclamations of the Lamb – 5.9f., 12; acclamations of God and of the Lamb/Christ – 5.13; 7.10; 11.15;

(12.10–12); 19.6–8. These are also Jewish in flavour (note particularly the use of 'Hallelujah' and 'Amen'), but less traditional in form and content than the psalms of Luke 1–2. The influence here seems to come more from the synagogues of the diaspora, where the holy and righteous God of Judaism was praised as Creator and Sustainer of the world and Judge of all – the themes which occur most frequently in the worship of the Johannine apocalypse. The overlap between Christianity and Judaism is again marked, and consequently we should probably see in them *typical expressions of the praise of Hellenistic Jewish Christians*. The acclamation of the Lamb seems to be more peculiarly the author's formulation, but is modelled on the acclamations of God and may well have been part of the language and worship of the community to which the seer belonged.

Notice the *excitement and sheer exuberance* of the praise. It is depicted as the praise of heaven, but very probably is modelled on or represents the worship and language with which the seer himself was familiar. If so it is difficult to imagine the worshippers speaking these words solemnly while sitting formally in rows as part of a set liturgy! There is an enthusiasm and vitality here – indicated also by the absence of any longer psalms like the Magnificat – the shorter form, their frequency and variation implying greater spontaneity. One can readily imagine gatherings for worship in early Hellenistic Jewish Christian communities where after a prophecy or psalm or prayer an exuberant worshipper cried out, 'Victory to our God who sits on the throne, and to the Lamb!' (7.10); or where an individual began a familiar doxology and all joined in, 'Amen! Praise and glory and wisdom, thanksgiving and honour, power and might, be to our God for ever and ever! Amen!' (7.12).

35.3   Discovery of various *Christ-hymns* embedded within the NT material has set many hares running in NT scholarship of which we can take only the briefest cognizance here. We will look first at the three longest hymns.

(a) *Phil. 2.6–11.* Since E. Lohmeyer's study of the passage in 1928[10] there has been increasing recognition that this is an early Christian hymn which Paul has deliberately quoted. The balance and rhythm of the clauses certainly support this view, although the actual structure of the hymn is still in dispute. The strongest clue is probably the parallelism which becomes evident when the verses are set down in couplets, since it is the style of Hebrew poetry to repeat the thought of one (half-)line in alternative language in the next. An almost perfect parallelism comes to light if three phrases are regarded as explanatory glosses: v.8 – 'the death of the cross'; v.10 –

'in heaven, on earth and beneath the earth'; v.11 – 'to the glory of God the Father'. Perhaps the most satisfactory way of setting it out is to follow the pattern suggested by R. P. Martin:[11]

> Who being in the form of God
>> did not count equality with God something to be grasped.
>
> But emptied himself,
>> taking the form of a slave.
>
> Becoming in the likeness of men.
>> And being found in form as man.
>
> He humbled himself
>> becoming obedient to death . . .
>
> Wherefore God has exalted him to the heights
>> and bestowed on him the name which is over every name.
>
> That at the name of Jesus every knee should bow . . .
>> and every tongue should confess that 'Jesus Christ is Lord'.

More important for us are the disputes about the background and theology of the hymn. Some would see that background as strongly Hellenistic: the hymn seems to operate with a Greek world view of two simultaneous spheres rather than a Jewish eschatology of two successive ages; and not a few have argued that behind the hymn lies the Heavenly Man of an already pre-Christian Gnostic redeemer myth[12] – a thesis, which was greatly overworked in the middle decades of this century, but which is now widely seen as a 20th century construction on a most questionable historical foundation. In this case it is much more justified to recognize *a strong Jewish influence*: the Hebraic poetic form even suggested to Lohmeyer that an Aramaic original lay behind the Greek; there is probably some influence from Jewish reflection on the suffering and vindication of the righteous. But much the strongest single influence on the whole is the speculation within many Jewish circles about the sin of Adam, its consequences and God's remedy. The Christian version of this is of Jesus' *obedience* which more than counteracts Adam's *disobedience* (cf. particularly Rom. 5.12–21). Here the contrast is clear: Adam being in the divine image grasped at equality with God; though man he exalted himself and was disobedient; therefore he was condemned to an existence under the power of sin and death. In contrast, Christ being in the form of God did *not* grasp at equality with God; he took the form of a slave, accepted the condition of (fallen) humanity, and humbled himself in obedience to death; therefore God exalted him and gave him a title and honour due to God.

One other issue is whether we have here a three-stage christology. Does the hymn speak no longer simply of the earthly and exalted Christ, but now also of an earlier stage of mythic pre-history or preexistence? We should probably not make too much of this however.

The primary motif is the humility-exaltation contrast, and the first two lines do not evince any speculative interest in divine being and essence in the pre-history stage. The language is drawn from the Adam narrative and is used primarily to stress Christ's humility, how great was his self-humbling. This deepening of the idea of Christ's earthly humility is matched by a corresponding heightening of the idea of exaltation – God *super*-exalted (literally) him and gave him the divine title *kyrios* (see also below p. 222).

(*b*) *Col. 1.15–20.* The recognition of the hymnic form of these verses goes back to E. Norden, in 1913.[13] The hymn as it now stands clearly divides into two main stanzas – the first dealing with Christ and creation, the second with Christ and the Church.

A *Who is* the image of the unseen God, the *firstborn* of all creation,
   For in him were created all things in heaven and on earth, seen and unseen,
   Whether thrones or dominions or powers or rulers,
   All things were created *through him* and *to him*,
   And he is before everything and all things in him cohere,
   And he himself is the head of the body (the Church).

B *Who is* the beginning, the *firstborn* from the dead,
   That he might become in all things himself pre-eminent,
   For in him willed all the fullness to dwell,
   And *through him* to reconcile *all things to him*,
   Making peace (through the blood of his cross) through him,
   Whether those on earth or those in heaven.

The parallelism between the stanzas is indicated by the underlining and is obviously deliberate. The brackets indicate probable Pauline additions.

The origin of the hymn is again the chief bone of contention, in particular the degree and type of Hellenistic influence. E. Käsemann has noted that if only eight of the 112 words in vv.15–20 are removed, then every specifically Christian motif is eradicated. He goes on to argue that underlying the hymn is the Gnostic redeemer myth – the myth of the archetypal man who is also Redeemer.[14] Now it is true that in the hymn we have concepts which could be said to have come from a Hellenistic Judaism in which some elements of later full blown Gnosticism are already present – '*image* of the unseen God', '*firstborn* of all creation', 'things seen', 'thrones', 'dominions', 'cohere' (these last four all more or less unique in Paul), 'fullness'. But the theory shatters on one phrase – 'firstborn from the dead'. This is manifestly integral to the hymn; and it is too specifically Christian to be attributed to a pre-Christian source. Much more plausible is the view that the Colossian hymn emerged from a Christian community composed mainly of diaspora Jews (or indeed Gentiles influenced by Jewish ideas) who *had been accustomed to theologize in terms of Hellenistic-influenced Wisdom speculation*. Here is quite sufficient explanation of the two most distinctive elements in the hymn – the clear affirmation that Jesus is to be identified with the pre-existent agent of creation, and the cosmic role attributed to the exalted Jesus. For them and for Paul Christ had taken over and filled out all the concepts and categories previously applied to Wisdom (see also below pp.220f.) – and, as the letter goes on to argue, had taken them over so completely as to prevent them being applied to others: Christ is not one (gnostic or Jewish) mediator among many, but *the* Mediator (note particularly 2.9, 17). On this point we should not fail to observe how breathtakingly bold is the language of the hymn – 'all things in him cohere . . . reconcile all things through him and to him' – the language of theological speculation caught up in adoration and praise (see further below pp. 194f.)[14a]

(c) *John 1.1–16* seems also to incorporate what is probably an earlier Logos hymn, or better, poem; note particularly the brief rhythmical clauses and limpid style. The poem probably consisted of vv.1, 3–5, (9), 10–12b, 14, 16, with vv.6–8 or 9 and v.15 obvious prose insertions serving as some sort of polemic against a Baptist sect, and vv.2, 10b, 12c–13, 17–18 as explanatory expansions.[15] Once again the origin of the poem is greatly disputed. Bultmann, for example, argued that the Fourth Evangelist drew it from a Gnostic source – that it was originally a hymn in praise of the Gnostic redeemer.[16] But the language and thought of the poem seem to belong to an earlier stage in the melting pot of ideas and concepts, a stage in which the most prominent elements were the Stoic concept of Logos and (once again) Hellenistic Jewish speculation about Wisdom.[17] Distinctively Gnostic words and themes are absent. Rather we should say that both Gnosticism and the Logos poet drew and developed ideas from the same pot.

It is also questionable whether we should see here a *pre*-Christian poem at all. Some or most of the specifically Christian lines can be excised from the last two stanzas (vv.10–16) without much disruption. But is it plausible to remove the line: 'And the Logos became flesh'?[18] The first two lines of v.14 (stanza 4) are the lynch-pin of the whole poem. Moreover they are fully integrated into the whole poem in style and in the clear allusion to Wisdom (Ecclus. 24.8). The removal of the fourth stanza (vv.14, 16) mutilates the poem. Once again therefore we have to see in the Logos poem evidence of a Christian community *thoroughly familiar with the syncretistic religious thought of the time and using that language to praise Jesus.*

Notice that here there is even greater attention focused on the pre-existence stage of the christology. The poem ends with the incarnate Jesus; it does not extend to his death and resurrection/exaltation. This is both Johannine and non-Johannine. To speak of the incarnate Jesus as full of grace and truth and of his 'fullness' reminds us of John's readiness to see the earthly Jesus in terms of his exaltation (above §6.2). But the strong movement of John's Gospel towards the salvation climax of death, resurrection, ascension and Spirit is lacking (see above p.75 and below p.301). Probably therefore the poem first emerged in the Johannine community at an earlier stage in its development.

(*d*) Three shorter hymns in praise of Christ have plausibly been identified within the NT writings; these we need only look at briefly. First, *Heb. 1.3*:

> Who being the reflection of his glory
> And the stamp of his nature,
> Upholding all things by the word of his power;
> When he had made purification for sins,
> He sat down at the right hand of the majesty on high.

The opening 'who', the participles, and the rather ceremonious style, are all indications of hymnic form. The use of words like 'reflection' and 'stamp', and the third line, all remind us of Col. 1.15–20 and indicate the influence of Hellenistic Jewish thought about Wisdom (cf. particularly Wisd. 7.26f.).[18a]

(*e*) *I Tim. 3.16:*

> He was manifested in the flesh,
>   Vindicated in the Spirit,
> Seen by angels,
>   Preached among the nations,
> Believed on in the world,
>   Taken up in glory.

The lines are obviously built on a series of contrasts – flesh/Spirit, angels/nations, world/glory. A chronological progression is not intended here, though the hymn certainly includes a contrast between Jesus' earthly state in humility (in the flesh), and his exaltation. What we have here basically is a simple and neat expression of the humility-vindication theme so prominent elsewhere (including Phil. 2.6–11).

(*f*) *I Peter 3.18f., 22* is very similar in form.

> (Who suffered once for sins
>   that he might bring us to God)

> Put to death in the flesh,
>   made alive in the Spirit,
> (Wherein also he preached to the spirits in prison)
> Having journeyed/gone into heaven
>   he sits at God's right hand,
> With angels, authorities and powers subject to him.

The hymn is incomplete: probably it is only partly quoted, and perhaps adapted. Notice again the flesh/Spirit, death/resurrection contrast, and the emphasis on Jesus' exaltation over the powers. The theology and ideas determining the language of these last two hymns is different from those which we examined earlier, of a more Pauline type, if I may put it thus, and certainly Hellenistic in background.

(g) Other passages suggested as Christ-hymns are Eph. 2.14–16, Col. 2.13–15[19] and I Peter 1.20, 2.21ff. – though I am not yet persuaded that these are any more than 'purple passages' of the letter writers themselves. R. Deichgräber also classifies several passages as *God-hymns* – Rom. 11.33–36, II Cor. 1.3f., Eph. 1.3–14, Col. 1.12–14, Peter 1.3–5; see also for example the doxologies of I Tim. 1.17, 6.15f.[20] In none of these cases however are there sufficient grounds for isolating an earlier form which the writer has incorporated. Purple passages in a Pauline or Petrine letter do not necessarily indicate a borrowing.

There is one other hymn-fragment which should be mentioned – Eph. 5.14. It is generally agreed to be a hymn, since the introductory formula is much less likely to be explained as a reference to scripture – 'Wherefore it says:

> Awake, sleeper,
> Rise from the dead;
> And Christ will shine upon you' (NEB).

It is obviously very different from the Christ-hymns – it is not in praise of Christ. Rather it is a call to the Christian summoning him to action. The hymn books which emerged in Britain in the first half of the present century are familiar with this type of hymn: it would take its place within the section headed 'Gospel Call'.

(h) We should also recall that the Pauline churches in particular knew yet another form of hymnody – '*spiritual songs*' (I Cor. 14.15; Eph. 5.19; Col. 3.16) – probably spontaneous hymns sung by an individual or the assembly as a whole in glossolalia – a kind of praise which has re-emerged as a feature of the modern charismatic movement.

To sum up, there are many common elements in the first six

hymns discussed in this section. Three of the first four in particular all come from a fairly similar background and reflect similar influences and thought. Common to them is the language of pre-existence and humiliation; only the Logos poem does not go on to include the thought of resurrection/exaltation and consequent cosmic significance. The hymns of Colossians, John and Hebrews emphasize the pre-existent one's role in creation; the Johannine prologue speaks of incarnation in clear terms. The Philippian hymn is determined by the Adam parallel. The other two hymns (I Timothy, I Peter) also belong in a Hellenistic milieu, but show no indebtedness to the Logos-Wisdom circles of thought. They too emphasize exaltation, but the contrast is more the simple one with earthness/fleshness than with humiliation as such.

35.4   Our study of the hymns which have been preserved for us from the NT period has revealed further facets of the diversity of first-century Christianity – in particular, *the diversity which arises when worship reflects the moods and background of each particular group of worshippers* or which reflects their *concern to use the language and thought forms of their contemporaries and environment*, to worship in ways that speak most meaningfully to their time. (1) The Lukan psalms reflect an *early Palestinian Jewish Christianity* – the praise of simple Jewish Christian piety. The fact that they were preserved for Luke to transcribe indicates that the Palestinian Christians continued to use them, that they were able to express their worship (fully) through psalms which are so markedly lacking in distinctively Christian (that is, distinct from Jewish) theology. (2) The Philippian hymn reflects a different but also characteristically *Jewish* (apocalyptic, Wisdom, rabbinic) theological reflection on how Adam's sin is to be undone. (3) The Revelation hymns reflect a form of *Hellenistic Jewish Christianity* – more inspirational and prophetic, more influenced by enthusiastic and apocalyptic religion. (4) The hymns of Colossians, John and Hebrews reflect a *very different form of Hellenistic Jewish Christianity* – more sophisticated, more influenced by philosophical and religious speculation about the cosmos, linking Hellenistic Jewish speculation about the relation between God and the world with Jesus. (4) The hymns of I Timothy and I Peter reflect yet another side of *Hellenistic Christianity* – emphasizing the contrast between Jesus' fleshly state and his exaltation.

Notice how different these various hymns are. The simple Jewish piety is quite a far cry from the theological sophistication and profundity of the Johannine and Colossian hymns, characterized as they are by their philosophical language and awareness of contemporary religious thought. Different again is the apocalyptic exuberance of the hymns in Revelation. Different also the enthusiastic glossolalic hymnody of the Pauline churches.

The more sophisticated hymns are found in quite a range of literature – Paul, John, Hebrews, plus the Pastorals and I Peter if we include the last two. This suggests that they were typical of a form of worship fairly widespread through the Hellenistic Jewish congregations – a more thoughtful, intellectual type of Christianity. At the same time 'spiritual songs' were also familiar to the Pauline communities which appear to have cherished intellect and wisdom most highly (I Cor., Col.). The other two categories are confined to Luke and Revelation respectively – and these are the only sort of hymns these writings contain. They reflect therefore a rather more distinctive worship, and presumably rather distinctive worshipping communities: on the one hand a Jewish Christianity which at several points remained more Jewish than Christian, on the other an apocalyptic Christianity where prophecies and enthusiastic utterances of praise typified the worship. We shall have to examine these diverse types of Christianity more closely in Part II.

§36. 'PAN-LITURGISM'?

Where in all this diversity can we find unity? One answer which has come to increasing prominence over the past half century is that there were in fact quite extensive unifying elements linking together the lives and worship of the different Christian communities. This is the thesis that at an early date liturgical and catechetical forms began to be developed for the worship and teaching of various churches and soon spread widely among the rest. If this is true then we have an important answer to our question: common liturgy and catechism served as a stabilizing unity within the restless diversity of first-century Christian community and worship. But how valid is the thesis? We have already seen that various kerygmatic, church and ethical traditions circulated among the early churches, especially traditions about Jesus (§§17–18 above). Do we now have to go further and conclude that not merely particular traditions or groups of traditions, but structured and coherent catechetical and liturgical forms circulated as well? The thesis has gained sufficient support for us to give it some attention.

36.1   *I Peter* has provided an important focal point in these investigations. In 1940 P. Carrington noted that there was a significant
amount of material common to Colossians, Ephesians, I Peter and
James – namely, the exhortations to *put off* evil, to *submit* themselves
(to God and elders), to *watch and pray* and to *resist* the devil. He
concluded that each of these writers was drawing from a common
pattern of teaching, a baptismal catechism, not yet written, but in
widespread oral use – 'a series of formulae which tended to be
emphasized in dealing with candidates for baptism in the various
apostolic traditions, and derived from an original mode of procedure
which spread widely through the New Testament church and
developed along divergent lines'.[21]

E. G. Selwyn, taking his cue from Carrington, cast his net wider,
in particular drawing material from Romans and I Thessalonians.
He discovered a baptismal catechism with five different sections. (1)
The entry into the new life at baptism: its basis – the Word, truth,
gospel; and its nature – rebirth, new creation, new manhood. (2) The
new life: its negative implications and renunciations ('Put off'). (3)
The new life: its faith and worship. (4) The new life: its social virtues
and duties. (5) Teaching called out by crisis: watchfulness and
prayer ('Keep awake'); and steadfastness ('stand firm . . .'). He
dates this pattern to AD 50–55, and thinks it circulated in a number
of written versions for use by teachers in different districts and
groups of communities.[22]

Others have gone a good deal further. In particular, H. Preisker
and F. L. Cross have argued that I Peter incorporates not just a
baptismal catechism or a baptismal sermon (another popular view)
but is in fact an elaborate liturgy more or less as it stands.[23]

The development of form criticism and its apparent success in the
case of I Peter sparked off others to ransack the NT for liturgical
forms. *Ephesians* was an obvious candidate because of its
catechetical-type parallels with I Peter. The most ambitious thesis
here has been J. C. Kirby's. He argues that 'when the epistolary
sections of Ephesians are removed, we are left with a document
complete in itself which could be used in an act of worship' – an act of
worship which 'may have had a close connection with baptism,
though not necessarily with the administration of the sacrament
itself'. More likely it was 'a Christianized form of the renewal of the
covenant; the Ephesian leader decided to use this pentecostal ceremony as the basis of his letter'.[24] At the same time A. T. Hanson was
discovering 'elements of a baptismal liturgy' in *Titus 2–3*, based
primarily on parallels between Titus on the one hand and I Peter

and Ephesians on the other.[25]

On a smaller canvas, several of the hymns examined above have been specifically identified as baptismal. P. Vielhauer regards the Benedictus as a baptismal hymn.[26] Lohmeyer thought the Philippian hymn belonged to a eucharistic context; but others are more inclined to the view that the Philippian hymn is a solemn reminder to Christians of the significance of their baptism.[27] Käsemann takes Col. 1.12–20 as 'a primitive Christian baptismal liturgy',[28] while G. Bornkamm links Heb. 1.3 with the celebration of the Lord's Supper.[29] Others have argued, for example, that I Thess. 1.9f. is a baptismal hymn,[30] that Col. 2.9–15 contains another,[31] that I John is a 'recall to baptism',[32] and that Rev. 1.5 uses established baptismal terminology.[33]

The *Gospels* of course have by no means escaped the net, although their role in early Christian worship is reckoned differently. Thus, in particular, Carrington has interpreted Mark as a lectionary laid out in accordance with a liturgical year.[34] G. D. Kilpatrick regards Matthew as 'a liturgical book' designed for (selected) public reading and exposition.[35] M. D. Goulder greatly elaborates a similar position – regarding all three Synoptics as lectionary books, Mark for half a year, Matthew for a full year following the festal cycle, Luke for a year but following the sabbath cycle.[36] And A. Guilding has suggested that one of the Fourth Evangelist's aims was to preserve a tradition of Jesus' discourses and synagogue sermons in a form suitable for liturgical use in the churches.[37]

36.2 *Assessment.* I must confess that I find many of these theses unconvincing – at two points in particular. First, I am not sure how valid it is to argue from similarities in teaching to established catechetical forms. Certainly there is a significant amount of common teaching material – particularly the calls to put off, to be subject, to watch, to stand or resist. But we know how quickly different individuals with a common enthusiasm and loyalty can develop a common language, with its own jargon or technical terms in words and phrases. With a fair degree of mobility between different Christian communities a common language of exhortation and style of exhorting the assembled believers could quickly spread. That different authors use the same or similar words and ideas to describe the great change of conversion in its basis, nature and outworkings is also striking, but hardly surprising. The fact is that these authors were to a large extent drawing from a fund of metaphors and symbols common to the various religions of the day, as parallels with the Hellenistic mysteries and the Dead Sea scrolls have made clear. And once ideas of re-birth, new creation, light and darkness, discarding the old life and its evil, accepting the gospel message, and taking up the new life and its practices, had become current among Christians, they would naturally lend themselves to the type of exhortations so frequent in the NT epistles. So before we make too much, for example, of the repetition of a word like *apothesthai* (put off), we should ask what other word would have done so well to express a metaphor so natural and common in such talk. Consequently I am not altogether convinced by attempts to erect these *similarities* of language and style into one or two *established* and widely acknowledged catechetical forms.

Second, my unease grows when these catechetical forms become explicitly *baptismal* catechisms.

(*a*) The fact is that we just do not know how developed was the ceremony of baptism at the time of the NT documents. To draw lines from later writers like Hippolytus (third century) as does Cross, or Theodore of Mopsuestia (fourth to fifth century)[38] proves nothing for a letter like I Peter. The fact is that *there is no express reference to a catechumenate before about the year 200*.

(*b*) Within the NT itself I would have thought the evidence is very much against these theses. *Acts knows nothing of a course of instruction given to enquirers before baptism* – a fact which grows in significance the more we think Luke reads back later practices into his history of the early Church (though see below pp.356f.). Acts 8.37 is sometimes cited as an example of pre-baptismal instruction; but it is a late 'Western text' addition and does not derive from the first century, and so hardly supports the theory which sees evidence of developed and established forms of ethical instruction in Colossians and I Peter. Moreover, there is nothing formal about what is set forth as a spontaneous question and answer; rather it is much closer to Acts 2.37–39 than to catechetical instruction. Indeed Acts 2.37–39 suggests that anything which might be called pre-baptismal instruction in the earliest churches was nothing more than the concluding application and exhortation of the sermon (cf. John the Baptist's preaching – Luke 3.7–14). The more one looks for parallels to the instruction given to proselytes prior to baptism in Judaism, [39] the more striking is the complete absence of any mention of such instruction in any of the baptisms recorded in Acts (see also p.55f.).

(*c*) Rom. 6.17 is often cited as the most likely indication of an established catechesis. But *tupos didachēs* ('pattern of teaching') is more probably to be identified with the gospel. The distinction frequently made (by Dodd and others) between kerygma and didache (teaching) is essentially an artificial one and non-Pauline: converting obedience in Paul is regularly obedience to the gospel (e.g. Rom. 1.5; 16.26). And *tupos* elsewhere in the Pauline literature always refers to a person or to particular individuals' conduct (Rom. 5.14; I Cor. 10.6; Phil. 3.17; I Thess. 1.7; II Thess. 3.9; I Tim. 4.12; Titus 2.7). All of which suggests that in Rom. 6.17 we have a thought very similar to that of Col. 2.6, the probability being that 'the pattern of teaching' is another reference to the Jesus-tradition (see above particularly §17.3).

(*d*) In so far as the distinction between kerygma and didache is valid, Matt. 28.19f. suggests that *any systematic teaching followed baptism,* and that the summons to baptism was simply the conclusion of the preaching.[40] Likewise the list of Heb. 6.1–2 probably refers to the content of the preaching which resulted in the readers' conversion: all six elements (except laying on of hands) appear in the evangelistic preaching of Acts; and Paul certainly 'laid the foundation' (I Cor. 3.5–11) by means of his preaching. The Corinthians received (*parelabete*) and Paul delivered (*paredōka*) the 'common deposit of instruction' by means of his evangelistic preaching (*euēggelisamēn*) (15.1–3).

(*e*) The evidence of the Gospels themselves is that elements of the Jesus-tradition were retained and passed on in recognized forms and that these forms were grouped together to a certain extent in topical collections, but also that the forms were *freely combined and recombined in diverse ways to serve a wide variety of teaching situations* (cf. e.g. Matthew's and Luke's use of the Mark and Q material which they share). It would be unjustified therefore to assume that such Jesus-tradition as the young converts early received (above §17.3) was passed on in any established or even necessarily regular pattern.[40a]

36.3   As for the suggestion that elaborate baptismal *liturgies* were already in existence in the NT period, the evidence here is even more flimsy.

(*a*) There is really no evidence whatsoever for the view that in the first two generations of Christianity baptisms were organized ceremonies at which the gathered congregations sang established hymns. The information we have in the NT suggests that for the first 50 years or so at least initiation ritual was still simple and spontaneous, still flexible and not yet hardened into a rigid pattern – consisting basically of the baptisand's confession, an immersion with the baptismal formula ('in the name of Jesus'), and (in many places and on many occasions) a laying on of hands. Beyond that we leave firm ground and enter the realm of speculation. The fact that *different* baptismal rites developed in Eastern and Western Christianity does not mean that one was original and the other not, but indicates rather the fluidity and formlessness of initiation procedures in the beginning – out of which the different forms developed.

(*b*) The clearest evidence within the NT in fact is that of Acts, which goes quite against the liturgical hypothesis – again a fact of greater significance for those who think that Luke was reading later church practice (of the 80s or 90s) back into the primitive period. Note particularly Acts 8.36, 38 – the request for baptism answered immediately and without demur; 16.14f. – Lydia's heart was opened to receive Paul's word and she was baptized (apparently forthwith); 16.33 – baptized in the middle of the night!; 18.8 – many were believing and being baptized. J. Munck evaluates the evidence fairly when he writes: 'In Acts, as in the rest of the New Testament, there seems to have been no hesitation about baptizing. In a way that is remarkably casual compared with the modern formal ceremony, one baptizes and goes on one's way'.[41]

(*c*) Against this firm evidence of Acts all that has been so far offered are possible inferences and allusions – inferences and allusions which are usually caught in a circular argument, since they depend on the assumption that baptism was a formal liturgical occasion. One might be forgiven for concluding from the tenor of such arguments that, for example, baptism was the only occasion when the early churches gave thanks for forgiveness of sins, or that the love of Christ was a theme exclusive to baptismal language. W. C. van Unnik has given a valid warning here – against 'a certain "pan-liturgism" which sees everywhere in the Pauline epistles the background of the liturgy whenever a simple parallel in wording between them and the *much later* liturgies is found'.[42]

(*d*) As for I Peter in particular, it is more likely that it is simply a *letter* addressed to young converts – a letter in which the writer often looks back to the beginnings of their Christian experience. The perfect tenses of 1.22f. seem to look back to an event which took place some time ago. 1.5–7 likewise suggests a present and continuing experience of God's keeping power following from a commitment made earlier. And his description of them as children (1.14) and new born babes (2.2) implies no more than a fairly recent conversion, if as much. Other features which are usually taken to indicate a sermon (the seven 'nows' are made much of, and 1.8 can readily conjure up a picture of the preacher addressing radiant converts) can adequately be understood as part of such a letter.[43]

(e) Our earlier findings also have bearing here. It is noticeable that the most fertile ground for the pioneers of 'pan-liturgism' have been the Pauline letters and those which belong within the Pauline circle (including I Peter). But, as we have seen, in the Pauline churches *spontaneity and flexibility* was a *dominant* feature of their common life; worship was an *ad hoc* combination of more established forms (psalms, hymns, readings, etc.) and more spontaneous utterances (spiritual songs, prophecies, etc.) (see above §34.3). It is within this context that the sort of teaching and exhortation which Carrington and Selwyn, etc., have focused on must be evaluated; and *against that background it is very difficult to give any credence to the thesis that the churches of the Pauline mission observed any well known liturgy, let alone an established baptismal liturgical ceremony.*

36.4   As to the *lectionary* hypotheses regarding the Gospels, they are probably the least convincing of all.

(a) There is no evidence that the Jewish lectionary cycles presupposed especially by Guilding and Goulder were already in existence in the first century AD. Particular readings from the scriptures were probably associated with the feasts at that time, but there is no evidence that there was an established festal lectionary.

(b) The theses usually presuppose that the early Christian churches wanted to continue celebrating the Jewish year. The evidence relating to the Pauline churches is to the contrary: Paul was distinctly unsympathetic to the view that his converts should observe the Jewish feasts (Rom. 14.5ff.; Gal. 4.10f.; Col. 2.16f.); but cf. Acts 20.16. There would be justification for assuming that it was otherwise in the more conservative Jewish Christian communities. But where is the evidence that Mark or Matthew is at all interested in the Jewish feasts? John's interest in the feasts he mentions (Passover, Tabernacles, Dedication) is to demonstrate that Jesus is the fulfilment of them (see above p. 131); any attempt to demonstrate lectionary links beyond that makes exceeding hard work of the text.

(c) Again the lectionary hypotheses necessarily imply a concern for a degree of regularity and order in the distinctively Christian worship of the first-century churches of which we have found no real evidence. The testimony of the Pauline letters certainly gives them no support – Matthew and John if anything even less. And Justin Martyr's description of second-century worship is both pertinent and revealing: 'the memoirs of the apostles or the writings of the prophets are read *as long as time permits*' (*Apol.*, I. 67 – my emphasis).

In other words, even in the middle of the second century there was as
yet no prescribed length for the readings – and consequently no place
for a lectionary.

§37. CONCLUSIONS

37.1   *Of the diversity of earliest Christian worship there can be little doubt.*
We have seen clear evidence of the range of this diversity – diversity
over the continuing relevance of Jewish traditions of worship and the
extent to which form and order should be left to the creative inspiration of the Spirit in each assembly; diversity as to whether worship is
primarily an individual or communal affair (above §34.5); the diversity of hymns whose style reflects different modes and moods of
worship and whose language and concerns reflect the different
apologetic environments of the worshippers (§35.4).

Where in all this diversity can we find unity? Not in established
catechetical and liturgical forms. There were certainly a number of
hymns in fairly widespread currency, at least among the churches
influenced by Paul. Traditions of Jesus provided a unifying bond at
least in so far as they were repeated, interpreted and discussed
within the worship. And similar styles and metaphors are clearly
detectable, again particularly within the literature of the Hellenistic
Jewish and Gentile churches. But precisely in these churches the
liberty of worship in the Spirit meant that these more regular forms
only complemented much more spontaneous contributions from the
worshippers, and were themselves used in very individual and
diverse combinations in the spontaneity of inspiration and praise.

37.2   *One clearly unifying element does seem to appear* – and that is *Christ*.
In the earliest community both Hebrews and Hellenists could justify
their patterns of worship by appealing to the words and actions of
Jesus. The features of earliest Christian worship which were preserved into the Greek speaking churches are precisely those most
clearly derived from the earthly Jesus – particularly the *abba* prayer
(Rom. 8.15f.; Gal. 4.6) and the Lord's prayer (Matt. 6.9–13/Luke
11.2–4) – or centred on the exalted Jesus (Maranatha – I Cor.
16.22). In Paul it is precisely the worshipping assembly that Paul
thinks of as the body of Christ, precisely the charismatic community
of which he says, 'so it is with Christ' (I Cor. 12.12). The only hymn
in the Pastorals is a Christ-hymn (I Tim. 3.16) and three of the five
'faithful sayings' are about Christ (I Tim. 1.15; II Tim. 2.11–13;

Titus 3.5–8), focusing attention equally on his earthly and now heavenly mission. In Matthew worship is enabled and community constituted precisely by the presence of (the exalted) Jesus in the midst – thus Matt. 18.20, a saying retained within the context of the (earthly) Jesus-tradition – and mission likewise (Matt. 28.18–20). In John the worship which the Father looks for is precisely worship in the Spirit of/from Jesus (the 'other Paraclete') and according to the truth revealed in Jesus (John 4.23f.). Finally in Hebrews it is precisely the man Jesus, the same flesh and blood as us, who has gone ahead as pioneer to open the way into the Holy of Holies, the very presence of God, for those who come after him (Heb. 2.5–15; 10.19–22); it is precisely this Jesus who as high priest in the heavenly temple brings aid to the tempted worshipper (2.17f.; 4.14–16).

The same is true of the early Christian hymns examined above. There are of course God eulogies in Revelation and doxologies to God in Paul. This is what we would expect in Gentile communities, just as we find confessional formulae which confess not only the Lordship of Christ but also the unity of God (above p.53). Otherwise the distinctive and unifying theme of all the hymns is the significance they attach to Jesus – and this includes Eph. 5.14, and the Lukan psalms where Mary and John the Baptist are the main subjects, for Mary and John draw their significance precisely from their relation to Jesus, as mother and forerunner. The Lukan psalms concentrate in the deliverance brought by the Messiah. But in the rest the most common element is the exalted Jesus. It was the awareness of his *present* status and of his exalted presence which evidently was the chief inspiration for almost all of these hymns. In particular it was this belief in his present exaltation which led the Christian worshipper to praise him in the language of pre-existent Wisdom. Just as prominent and regular, though expressed in different ways, is the identity of the present exalted Lord with the human Jesus – the Lamb that was slain, the Man (Obedient Adam) become Lord of all (eschatological Adam), the first born from the dead, the incarnate Word the source of grace, the man of flesh vindicated in the Spirit, put to death but made alive.

37.3   In short, when we examine the worship of the first-century Christian churches we discover *the same sort of pattern of unity and diversity* as came to light in the other areas of our investigation – a unity centring on faith in the man Jesus now exalted, but round that unity a diversity which displays almost endless variety wherever we have looked.

VIII

SACRAMENTS

§38. INTRODUCTION

The note therefore of the true Kirk of God we believe, confess and avow to be, first, the true preaching of the Word of God in which God has revealed Himself unto us, as the writings of the prophets and apostles do declare. Secondly, the right administration of the Sacraments of Christ Jesus, which must be annexed unto the Word and promise of God, to seal and form the same in our hearts. Last, ecclesiastical discipline uprightly ministered, as God's Word prescribed, whereby vice is repressed and virtue nourished . . . (*The Scots Confession*, 1560, Article 18).

No one would deny that of these 'the Word of God' and 'the Sacraments of Christ Jesus' are of central importance as foci of unity in Christianity past and present – though the question of what is 'the *true* preaching' of the one and 'the *right* administration' of the other has made more for division than unity, and the proper interrelation of the two has never finally been resolved. The centuries prior to the Reformation were marked by a growing tendency to focus grace, authority and unity more and more exclusively through the sacraments, with a consequent diminution of the role given to the word preached. At the Reformation these roles were sharply reversed and the word was exalted above the sacraments. Thus the Heidelberg Catechism – 'faith is produced in our hearts by the preaching of the Holy Gospel, and confirmed by the use of the Sacraments' (Question 65). And Calvin, more trenchantly – 'Nothing is more absurd than to extol the sacraments above the Word, whose appendages and seals they are'.[1] This changed emphasis was reflected in ecclesiastical architecture, with the pulpit given central position in the typical Reformation church. Since then the debate has proceeded in less strident tones, but with differences that still run deep. The liturgical movement has gained increasing influence, most clearly marked by the way in which the communion table has been brought much more into the centre of the worship with the pulpit reduced in prominence. At the same time a still lasting impact has been made by the theology of the word which gained its chief stimulus from Karl Barth: 'The presupposition which makes proclamation to be proclamation, and therewith the Church to be the Church, is the Word of God'.[2] Many would maintain that a much happier balance between word and sacrament has been achieved in recent years, but this seems sometimes to have been gained at the cost of blurring some of the theological issues more clearly seen in earlier centuries: in particular, What are 'the means of grace' (properly speaking) – *how does God minister grace to man*? What are the roles of the symbol and of rationality in this process? What sort of communication or integration of the divine and human does it involve?

Here again then we find some prompting from the disagreements of later centuries to investigate how things stood in the first century. We have already looked with some care at the importance of preaching and the role of the word kerygmatic and written during that period (chs II–V above). Now we must inquire into the role of the sacraments within the unity and diversity of the earliest churches. Baptism and the Lord's Supper were certainly unifying factors of some significance:

> Spare no effort to make fast with bonds of peace the unity which the Spirit gives. There is one body and one Spirit . . . one Lord, one faith, one baptism . . . (Eph. 4.3f.);

> Because there is one loaf, we, many as we are, are one body; for it is one loaf of which we all partake (I Cor. 10.17).

But what did these claims mean in practice? round this unity what diversity? What meaning attached to the ritual acts at each stage of Christian expansion, in each centre of Christian community? What prompted the earliest Christians to single out just these two?[3] To what extent and in what form do they derive from Jesus? What influences shaped their development? What role did they play in the divine-human encounter? Can we speak properly of them as 'sacraments' from the beginning? We will proceed by attempting to trace briefly the development in form and significance of baptism and Lord's Supper in turn; though since the Fourth Evangelist's attitude to both is rather distinctive (and much disputed) we will treat John's Gospel separately.

§39. BAPTISM

39.1   *Origins of baptism*. There have been various suggestions as to
the origins of Christian baptism – Jewish ceremonial washings,
Qumran purification rites, proselyte baptism, the baptism of John.
Of these the last named, the ritual act which gave John the Baptist
his nickname, is almost certainly to be regarded as the immediate
antecedent of Christian baptism. A direct link is established through
Jesus' own baptism by John; and the Fourth Gospel confirms what
we might have guessed anyway, that some of Jesus' earliest disciples
had formerly been disciples of the Baptist (John 1.35–42). John's
baptism itself is probably best understood as an adaptation of the
Jewish ritual washings, with some influence from Qumran in particular.[4]

If then Christian baptism derives from the baptism of John we
must attempt to grasp the meaning which the rite had for John
himself. So far as we can tell, John's baptism had a two-fold significance for his hearers.[5] (*a*) First, it was a baptism of *repentance – an
act by means of which the baptisand expressed his repentance*. This is how
Mark and Luke describe it (Mark 1.4; Luke 3.3; Acts 13.24; 19.4);
Mark and Matthew tell how all were baptized in Jordan, confessing
their sins (Mark 1.5; Matt. 3.6); and Matthew reports the Baptist as
proclaiming, 'I baptize you in water for or *into* repentance' (Matt.
3.11), which is best understood to mean that the actual acting out of
the resolve to be baptized helped to crystallize repentance and to
bring it to full expression. We should add that Mark and Luke use
the fuller phrase, 'a baptism of repentance for (or into) the forgiveness of sins' (Mark 1.4; Luke 3.3). But this should *not* be taken to
imply that either John or the Evangelists thought of his baptism as
achieving or mediating forgiveness. Even if John thought that forgiveness could be enjoyed there and then rather than awaiting the
ministry of the Coming One, which is disputed – Matthew's editing
at 3.2, 11 and 26.18 indicates that he for one thought that forgiveness
came only through Jesus' ministry – the Greek is best taken to mean
that the forgiveness was the result of the repentance not of the
baptism as such (cf. Luke 24.47; Acts 3.19; 5.31; 10.43; 11.18; 26.18).
That is to say, *John's baptism was seen as the means of expressing the
repentance which brought forgiveness of sins*.

   (*b*) Secondly, John's baptism was *preparatory for the decisive ministry
of the Coming One*: John baptized in water, but he would baptize in
Spirit and fire (Matt. 3.11/Luke 3.16). This latter would be a minis-

try of judgment – of fire (Matt. 3.10–12/Luke 3.9, 16f.), of wind and
fire, or better, of fiery spirit (cf. Isa. 4.4). But also a ministry of mercy
and salvation, for John holds it out as a promise more than as a
threat to those who undergo his baptism: 'I baptize you . . . but he
will baptize you . . .' – John's baptism was a preparation for the
baptism in Spirit and fire. The implication then is that the baptism
in Spirit and fire would be purgative, an act or process of refining,
which would destroy the impenitent but purify the penitent.[6] In
other words, *'baptism in Spirit and fire' is John's metaphor for the messianic
woes*, the period of great tribulation, suffering and destruction which
was expected to precede the establishment of the messianic kingdom
(see e.g. Zech. 14.12–15; Dan. 7.19–22; 12.1; I Enoch 100.1ff.;
Sib.Or. III.632–51; 1QH 3.29–36).[7] 'Baptize' was a metaphor
which was particularly expressive here, especially when drawn from
a rite of baptism in a river, since the river and the flood are familiar in
the OT as metaphors for being overwhelmed by calamity (cf. particularly Ps. 69.2, 15; Isa. 43.2; and note particularly Isa. 30.27f.).
Clearly then John used this metaphor for the ministry of the Coming
One because he saw his own baptism as both symbolizing its effect
and preparing for it.

39.2   *Jesus' baptism by John.* Granted the significance which attached
to John's baptism, we inevitably must ask whether John's baptism
became something else when Jesus was the baptisand. (*a*) Was it still
a baptism of repentance? It is quite clear that the tradition of Jesus
undergoing a baptism of *repentance* was a source of some embarass-
ment to many early Christians (cf. Matt. 3.14f.; Jerome, *contra Pelag.*,
III.2). But why did Jesus choose to accept baptism at the hands of
John? – in order to become a disciple of John? – with a view to the
coming of the kingdom? – as dedication to the ministry he believed
himself called to? The answer is not clear; but at least we can say that
Jesus' baptism by John must have been *an expression of Jesus' resolve one
way or another*, and to that extent at least it was not so very different
from John's baptism of repentance (see above p.152).

(*b*) Was it still a preparatory baptism? The difficulty here is that
according to our records the Spirit came upon Jesus straightaway,
and not in the way that John's metaphor of Spirit and fire baptism
anticipated. On the other hand, we have to recognize that the
descent of the Spirit was not thought of as a constituent part of John's
baptism of Jesus. The language of the Gospels indicates that *the
baptism was already completed when the Spirit descended*. Moreover it is also
clear in all four Gospels that the chief element in the whole episode is

the descent of the Spirit (Matt. 3.16; Mark. 1.10; Luke 3.21f.; John 1.32–34). It looks therefore as though the Evangelists want us to recognize that *the Spirit was given to Jesus in response to his baptism*, that is, presumably, in response to his dedication expressed in baptism. And to that extent we can say that *even in the case of Jesus, John's baptism was still essentially preparatory*. Not only so, but since Jesus clearly thought of the power of the Spirit operating through him in proclamation and healing as the power of the end-time (see above p.14 and below §45.3), we can also say that even in the case of Jesus, John's baptism was preparatory to the *eschatological* ministry of the Spirit. The relationship between the two was chronologically closer but not essentially different from that envisaged by John.

39.3   *Baptism in Jesus' ministry.* Did Jesus baptize? John 3.22, 26, 4.1 look very much like a tradition to that effect. If true then the tradition also implies that he was simply carrying on John's baptism (John 3.22f., 26). But Jesus' own administration of baptism is denied by John 4.2, and we lack confirmatory evidence elsewhere. At most therefore we have to say that Jesus and/or his disciples may have baptized converts at the beginning, but if so they soon gave it up. Why? Why did they abandon the practice of baptizing so quickly, or indeed not baptize at all? The answer appears again to be two-fold. (*a*) Because Jesus probably saw his own ministry as a fulfilment of John's expectation. He himself was already experiencing the end-time Spirit (see below §§45.3, 50.5), and his whole ministry was building up to the fiery judgment prophesied by John in his metaphor of Spirit and fire baptism (Luke 12.49f.; cf. Mark 9.49; 10.38; 14.36; Gosp. Thos. 10, 82).[8] (*b*) Because *he was unwilling to erect a ritual barrier which had to be surmounted before people could join his company or be his disciples.* Jesus could accept no ritual exclusion from the kingdom. Those outside were outside by choice (cf. above p.105f.).

39.4   *Baptism in earliest Christianity.* There have been some attempts to argue that baptism (in water) was not practised in the first Christian communities but was introduced later by the Hellenists: Spirit-baptism alone had been regarded as sufficient (Acts 1.5; 11.16); there is no mention of baptism in relation to the outpouring of the Spirit at Pentecost; early baptismal references (particularly 2.38, 41) were introduced later; and the narratives in Acts 8.12–17, 10.44–48, 19.1–7 indicate the difficulty in integrating the two kinds of baptism in the early mission.[9] On the other hand, baptism was already well established prior to Paul's conversion – he simply takes it for granted in Rom. 6.4, I Cor. 1.10–17, etc.; and we know of no unbaptized Christian in earliest Christianity – though in some instances John's baptism was deemed sufficient (those at Pentecost and Apollos – 18.24–28). Had Christian baptism originated with the Hellenists then we would have expected it to feature more in controversies between Jewish Christianity and Hellenistic Christianity, the latter setting baptism over against circumcision as the necessary rite, whereas in these controversies it is faith and Spirit which are set against circumcision, not baptism (Gal. 3.1–5; 5.1–6; and see below pp.159f.). So Acts is most probably right – *baptism was an integral part of Christianity from the first*. And almost certainly the baptism they adopted was the baptism of John, the rite which some of them had themselves undergone and earlier used, the rite which Jesus himself had undergone and perhaps for a brief period administered. The inspiration for taking it up is attributed to the risen Jesus (Matt. 28.19; cf. Luke 24.47).

The significance of these first Christian baptisms seems to have been fourfold. (*a*) Baptism was *an expression of repentance and faith*: notice the close interrelation between repentance/faith and baptism in 2.38, 41, 8.12f., 16.14f., 33f., 18.8, 19.2f. It is not surprising that I Peter 3.21, the nearest thing that we have to a definition of baptism in the NT, defines Christian baptism as 'an appeal or pledge to God for or from a clear conscience'. Probably from the first baptism served as the 'Rubicon' *step of commitment*[9a] for would-be Christians from which there was no going back and without which they remained uncommitted. (*b*) Baptism appears also to have retained its *preparatory*, forward looking aspect, its *eschatological orientation*. This is largely hidden in Acts, where Luke has chosen to ignore or conceal most of the eschatological fervency of the earliest Christian communities (see below §71.2). But there is certainly a hint of it in Acts 3.19–21, and more than a hint of it in Heb. 6.1–2, not to mention I Thess. 1.9f.

These two elements of significance are what we would expect and confirm that *Christian baptism was derived directly from John's baptism*. But there are also two new and distinctive elements which seem to have belonged to Christian baptism from the first. (*c*) Christian baptism *was administered 'in the name of Jesus'* (Acts 2.38; 8.16; 10.48; 19.5). The use of the phrase means either that the baptizer saw himself acting as a representative of the exalted Jesus (cf. particularly 3.6,16; 4.10 with 9.34), or that the baptisand saw his baptism as his act of commitment to discipleship of Jesus (cf. I Cor. 1.12–16 and below p.158f.). Quite probably both were implied. Incidentally the evidence just cited strongly suggests that the triadic formulation of

Matt. 28.19 is a late expansion of the simpler and earlier formula 'in the name of Jesus'. (*d*) Baptism served as *a rite of entry or initiation into the local Christian community*. On the one hand, part of the 'Rubicon' significance of baptism was that it expressed the baptisand's commitment to the congregation of Jesus' disciples, with all that this meant in terms of breaking with the previous way of life, social ostracism and possible persecution. On the other hand, baptism, together with laying on of hands when practised, no doubt expressed also *the community's acceptance of the convert*. This last aspect is most apparent in Acts 10.47f., where public initiation into and acceptance by the church must have been the principal reason for Cornelius's baptism.

These last two aspects of earliest Christian baptism ((*c*) and (*d*)) may explain why the first Christians baptized when Jesus did not: they needed *a tangible way of expressing faith towards one who was no longer visibly present* (cf. e.g. Luke 7.37f., 48–50); and they felt themselves to be more of a *community* than was the case with the disciples of the earthly Jesus (see above §27). The decision of course involved the risk of Christianity erecting the sort of cultic and ritual barrier against the 'outsider' that Jesus had rejected, a risk that has seriously threatened Christian theology and practise of the sacraments on not a few occasions since then.

One other question which requires clarification is *the relation of baptism to the gift of the Spirit* at this period. Many have argued that baptism from the first was regarded as the means of receiving the Spirit, of bestowing the Spirit. But it is certainly not true that early Christian baptism was understood as baptism in the Spirit: the antithesis between the rite of water-baptism and the metaphor of Spirit-baptism, which the Baptist first coined, was carried over into Christianity (Acts 1.5; 11.16); and nowhere in Acts can it be said that the Spirit was given in, with or through baptism (Acts 2.4, 38; 8.12–17; 10.44–48; 18.25; 19.5f), unless 'baptism' is given a much more extended sense than any of these passages warrants. What is clear is that, for Luke at least, *the gift of the Spirit was the most important, the decisive element in conversion-initiation, the gift of the Spirit was the mark of God's acceptance*: 2.17 – the Spirit is the decisive initiation to 'the last days' (cf. 11.17); 8.12–17 – baptism insufficient without the Spirit; 10.44–48 – the Spirit decisive, baptism serves as man's acknowledgment of the divine acceptance; 18.25–28 – Apollos has the Spirit, so John's baptism suffices; 19.1–7 – the Spirit is lacking, so the whole process must be gone through. In other words, baptism did not serve as the expression or channel of God's action – that was the Spirit's role (see further below pp.356f.). Consequently we cannot say, either from Luke's or the earliest churches' perspective, that the direction of baptism changed when John's baptism was taken over by the first Christians. *Christian* baptism *remained primarily the expression of man's action* (repentance/faith) *towards God, whereas it was the* Spirit *that was recognized as the expression of God's action towards men.*

Notice finally *the diversity of form and pattern* in conversion-initiation in Acts – baptism prior to Spirit, Spirit prior to baptism, Spirit without baptism, baptism followed by laying on of hands. We may conclude with some confidence that the primary concern, whether of the first Christians or of Luke, was *not* to establish a particular ritual procedure, far less to determine the action of God in accordance with a cultic action (see further below p.357). On the contrary, the evidence of Acts serves to underline the freedom of God to meet faith when and as he pleases, and *what we see in Acts is the early churches adapting themselves and their embryonic ritual in accordance with God's manifest action through the Spirit* (see also below §44.1).

39.5 *Baptism in Hellenistic Christianity apart from Paul.* Here we must simply note that if the church at Corinth was in any way typical of Hellenistic Christianity, then Hellenistic Christianity embraced some views of baptism very different from those so far outlined. It is clear from I Cor. 1.10–17 that baptism had been a catalyst of division in Corinth. At the very least parties were being formed on the basis of who baptized whom (1.12–15). Quite probably many Corinthians thought that baptism created a mystical bond between baptizer and baptisand – in which case *quasi-magical properties* were probably being attributed to baptism. This is borne out by I Cor. 10.1–12 where the implication of Paul's exhortation is that the Corinthians viewed baptism (and the Lord's Supper) as a sort of talisman which ensured salvation. I Cor. 15.29 probably refers to a practice of vicarious baptism whereby the baptism of one was thought to secure the salvation of another already dead. Here then is indication of influences shaping the theology of baptism and developing views of baptism which are far removed from anything we have already examined. And yet Paul addresses those who held such views as members of the Christian community in Corinth – these views were held also by Christians. In other words, *as soon as we move outside that sphere of Christianity most influenced by the Baptist's inheritance the diversity of Christian thinking about baptism broadens appreciably.*

39.6   *Baptism in Pauline theology.* The last paragraph naturally raises
the key question: Did Paul also hold a quasi-magical view of baptism? Were his views also influenced by the mystery religions? How
broad must the diversity of baptismal theology be to incorporate
Paul? Many would hold that Paul was so influenced: (*a*) his view of
baptism as a dying with Christ shows the influence of the cults of the
dying and rising god; (*b*) Paul's phrase 'baptized into Christ'
describes what baptism accomplished, since baptism 'into Christ' is
a shorter form of baptism 'in the name of Christ' which certainly
describes the act of baptism; (*c*) the washing metaphors, particularly
those in Eph. 5.26 and Titus 3.5 specifically attribute a spiritual
cleansing and renewal to the ritual act.[10]

I find myself unconvinced by these arguments. (*a*) Paul certainly
links baptism with the death of Jesus in Rom. 6.4 and Col. 2.12. But
in Rom. 6.4 it is important to note that Paul links baptism only with
the idea of death, not with resurrection, which is still future (6.5; cf.
8.11). Paul clearly thinks of baptismal immersion as symbolizing
burial with Christ; but the thought of emergence from the water as
symbolizing resurrection with Christ is not present in Rom. 6.
Similarly in Col. 2.12 the structure of the clauses seems to imply that
baptism is linked primarily with burial, which it symbolizes so well,
and not immediately with resurrection.[11] This suggests that Paul
does not think of baptism as accomplishing a dying and rising in
union with Christ (an initiation into a mystery cult), but rather as
symbolizing death and burial. This suggests in turn that the more
important influence on Paul's thought stemmed from *Jesus'* own
attitude to his death (Mark 10.38; Luke 12.50 – see above p.154). If
Jesus spoke of his coming death as a baptism, then it would help
explain why Paul spoke of baptism as a means to sharing in that
death. In which case baptism, symbolizing burial for Paul, really
expressed *the baptisand's desire to identify himself with Jesus* (the one who
had successfully endured the messianic woes) in his death. Instead of
the fiery baptism that John foretold and Jesus experienced in reality,
the initiate experienced only the baptism which John himself had
used, only the symbol which in the same sort of way embodied the
faith of the baptisand towards what was symbolized.

(*b*) 'Baptized into Christ' should not be taken as an abbreviation
of the fuller formula, 'baptized into the name of Christ'. The latter is
a straightforward reference to the baptismal act. The Greek account-
ing formula, 'into the name of', meant 'to the account of', and
strengthens the suggestion that baptism was recognized as *a deed of
transfer, an act whereby the baptisand handed himself over to be the property or*

disciple of the one named; hence Paul's line of argument in I Cor. 1.12f. –
'I am (a disciple) of Paul' implies, I was 'baptized in the name of
Paul'. The former phrase, 'baptized into Christ', is better under-
stood as a *metaphor*, rather than as a description of the ritual act. Thus
I Cor. 12.13 seems to hark back to the second half of the Baptist's
antithesis between the rite of water baptism and the metaphor of
Spirit (-and-fire) baptism, and Rom. 6.3f. seems to hark back to
Jesus' own metaphorical use of the verb 'baptized' in relation to his
death (Mark 10.38; Luke 12.50). And in Gal. 3.27 we have the
complementary metaphors of baptism and putting on clothes, in
I Cor. 12.13 of baptism and rain, in Rom. 6 of baptism, burial and
crucifixion. That the idea of dying with Christ is in no way anchored
in or dependent on baptism is confirmed by the use of the motif
elsewhere in Paul where it is quite independent of any thought of
baptism (e.g. II Cor. 4.10; Gal. 2.19f.; 6.14; Phil. 3.10). The
metaphor of baptism is particularly appropriate for conversion
because it symbolizes burial so well, and because baptism itself as
the rite of initiation and expression of commitment holds an important place in the total event of conversion-initiation; but to say more
runs beyond the testimony of Paul.

(*c*) I doubt whether the metaphors of cleansing can particularly
strengthen the case for seeing the influence of Hellenistic mystery
religions on Pauline baptismal thought. Ephesians 5.25–27 is dominated by the portrayal of the Church as Christ's bride; part of this is
the metaphor of the bridal bath, which in this case represents the
cleansing and renewal effected by the word of preaching (cf. Acts
15.9; I Cor. 6.11; Titus 2.14; Heb. 9.14; 10.22). Even in Titus 3.5 the
'faithful saying' seems to envisage 'a washing . . . of the Holy Spirit',
that is, a washing which the Spirit effects and whereby he regener-
ates and renews the inner nature and mind of the convert (cf. Rom.
12.2; II Cor. 4.16; Col. 3.10). It is quite possible, however, that the
author of the Pastorals read the faithful saying in a more strongly
sacramental sense (see below p.352).

(*d*) Furthermore, we should observe that *Paul did not give to baptism
the role which circumcision played in the Judaism of his time*. Had Paul
understood baptism in the way it was understood in Corinth (above
§39.5), or in much sacramental theology today, he would not have
been able to discuss circumcision in the way he does, particularly in
Galatians, where in effect he argues against the sacramentalism of
the Judaizers. To be sure he argues against a ritualism without
reality, but *not* in favour of a ritualism *with* reality, rather directly in
favour of the reality itself. It was this reality of the experience of the

Spirit in their lives to which he recalled his readers (Rom. 5.5; II Cor. 1.21f.; Eph. 1.13f.). It was the common experience of the one Spirit which bound them in unity (I Cor. 12.13; II Cor. 13.14; Eph. 4.3; Phil. 2.1). It was circumcision of the heart, not baptism, which had replaced the ritual act of the old Israel (Rom. 2.28f.; II Cor. 3.6; Phil. 3.3; Col. 2.11 – 'made without hands'). For Paul baptism was relatively unimportant (I Cor. 1.17). When he countered those who had misunderstood it and treated it as a quasi-magical act, he did not even pause to correct their theology of baptism. He preferred rather to push it into the background. To do otherwise would presumably have given it the sort of importance that the Corinthians attached to it, and for Paul it evidently was not so important.

To sum up. (1) Paul agreed with his predecessors in the Christian faith: baptism is baptism 'in the name of Jesus', that is, it is baptism into discipleship of Jesus, *the means of expressing commitment to Jesus as Lord* (cf. Rom. 10.9). (2) Paul deepens the symbolical significance of baptism: it now provides *a metaphor for union with Christ*, baptism into Christ, the rite itself symbolizing burial, a self identification of the baptisand with Christ in his death. Here he uses language which could be given an *ex opere operato* connotation – many did so take it (and still do). But there is no real indication that Paul himself ever changed the basic direction of baptism and its role in the divine-human encounter: baptism was still the expression of man's faith, and the manifestation of God's grace was clear enough at the time of baptism – or at any other time – in the gift and gifts of the Spirit. (3) Paul did however change the direction of baptism in another sense. With Paul the act of baptism clearly looks backward to the death of Christ,[12] and it seems to have lost its forward look to the eschaton almost entirely.

39.7   A few brief comments are perhaps called for on the subject of *infant baptism*. It is one of the standing ironies of the diversity of Christian theology and practice that the chief means of accomplishing regeneration for so many centuries has had so little foothold in the NT, and has not clearly been encompassed even within the wide-ranging diversity of first-century Christian practice. For it has to be recognized that *infant baptism can find no real support in the theology of baptism which any NT writer can be shown to espouse*. And the more we recognize that a primary function of baptism throughout the first decades of Christianity was to serve as a means of expressing the initiate's faith and commitment, the less justified in terms of Christian beginnings would the practice of infant baptism appear to be.

The strongest support from within the NT period would probably come from the Corinthians (above §39.5), but that is not a precedent many would want to argue from.

A more circuitous justification can be attempted with greater promise through the concept of family solidarity – that the child of a believing parent by virtue of that fact stands within the circle of (the parent's) faith (I Cor. 7.14). And no one would want to deny that Jesus blessed infants during his ministry (Mark 10.13–16). *The real question is whether Christian baptism is the appropriate expression of this status within the family of faith,* or whether baptism is the means whereby the children of today are brought to Jesus and blessed by him. The household baptisms of Acts 16.15, 33, 18.8 and I Cor. 1.16 might provide sufficient (NT) precedent; but the case is hardly proved, since it is far from certain that the households included small children: Acts 16.15 – was Lydia married? 16.34 – all rejoiced in the middle of the night; 18.8 – all believed; I Cor. 16.15 – all served. The supporting argument from circumcision's being administered to Israelite (male) infants as part of the covenant people of Yahweh depends on how one assesses the relation between the old Israel and the new: as we have seen, the new covenant equivalent of old covenant circumcision is the circumcision of the heart, the gift of the Spirit, not baptism; and membership of the new covenant is through faith in Christ Jesus, not by natural descent (see particularly Gal. 3). The weakness of the family solidarity argument then is that it explains the child's status within the circle of faith, without necessarily justifying the further step that he/she ought therefore to be baptized – for certainly that status is not dependent on baptism, nor is the blessing of Christ. Consequently if baptism is to retain its regular significance within the NT, as the expression of the baptisand's faith, it should probably be reserved for that time when it can serve to express the child's own commitment, a practice which can be followed without detracting in any way from the status of the child of a believing parent within the circle of faith. In short, for all the diversity of faith and practice in first-century Christianity it remains doubtful whether it stretches so far as to include infant baptism.

§40. THE LORD'S SUPPER[13]

40.1   The *origin* of the Lord's Supper is less disputed and is certainly to be found within Jesus' ministry – in particular in two features of his ministry: (*a*) Jesus' fellowship meals, and (*b*) the last supper with his disciples.

(*a*) During his ministry Jesus was often a guest at meals (Mark 1.29–31; 14.3; Luke 7.36; 11.37; 14.1; John 2.1–11), and at least on some occasions did his own entertaining (Mark 2.15; Luke 15.1f.). Indeed his habits here became a by-word – 'a glutton and a drunkard, a friend of taxcollectors and sinners!' (Matt. 11.19) – which obviously implies that he frequently took his meals in company, and questionable company at that. Other indications that his table companions constituted quite a large circle include Luke 8.1–3, 24.33, Mark 6.32–44 and 8.14; cf. John 4.8, 31; 21.12.

It is important to realize how significant this was for Jesus and his contemporaries. For the oriental, table-fellowship was a guarantee of peace, trust, brotherhood; it meant in a very real sense a sharing of one's life. Thus, table-fellowship with tax collector and sinner was Jesus' way of proclaiming God's salvation and assurance of forgiveness, even for those debarred from the cult. This was why his religious contemporaries were scandalized by the freedom of Jesus' associations (Mark 2.16; Luke 15.2) – the pious could have table-fellowship only with the righteous. But *Jesus' table-fellowship was marked by openness, not by exclusiveness*. That is to say, Jesus' fellowship meals were invitations to grace, not cultic rituals for an inner group which marked them off from their fellows (see also above p. 105).

We must note also *the eschatological significance* of Jesus' fellowship meals. That is, we must set Jesus' practice of table-fellowship within the context of his proclamation. Here it becomes clear that so far as Jesus was concerned, to share in table-fellowship with him was to anticipate the messianic banquet (Mark 2.19; 10.35–40; Matt. 22.1–10/Luke 14.16–24; Matt. 25.10; Luke 22.30; cf. Isa. 25.6; 65.13; I Enoch 62.14; II Bar. 29.8; 1QS[a]2.11–22) (see also above p.16).[13a]

(*b*) *The last supper* which Jesus enjoyed with his disciples was the final expression of that communal fellowship which had been such an integral part of his whole mission. In particular, it brought into sharper focus the character of his mission as one of service (Luke 22.24–27; cf. John 13.1–20); it foreshadowed his death with starker clarity (note especially the motif of the 'cup' running through Mark 10.38, Luke 22.20, Mark 14.36); and in it the eschatological note reached its highest pitch, with the supper itself a last anticipation of the feast of consummation (Mark 14.25; Luke 22.16, 18 – probably a vow to fast in view of the imminence of the kingdom).

Was the last supper a passover meal? Here opinions are divided.

An affirmative answer is suggested by the fact that the meal was eaten in Jerusalem (not Bethany), and at night, that wine was drunk, and by the words of interpretation (Mark 14.17f. etc.).[14] On the other hand, the execution of Jesus was unlikely to take place on Passover day, and the oldest traditions do not speak of the meal as a passover. Perhaps the simplest explanation is that Jesus viewed the supper as a special passover meal, or that he deliberately heightened the significance of what was otherwise an ordinary meal.[15]

40.2   *The Lord's Supper in earliest Christianity.* Can we properly speak of a Lord's Supper in earliest Christianity? We are told that the first Christians participated in daily fellowship meals (Acts 2.42, 46). These were probably seen as *the continuation of Jesus' fellowship meals*, for they were often conscious of his presence in their midst, particularly at the beginning (Luke 24.30f., 35; John 21.12–14; Acts 1.4; cf. Rev. 3.20), and the meals were almost certainly an expression of their eschatological enthusiasm (cf. Acts 2.46),[16] and so, like Jesus' table-fellowship, a foretaste of the eschatological banquet.

What relation did these meals have to the last supper? The answer is not clear. Most probably however they were ordinary meals: only bread is mentioned (Acts 2.42, 46) and wine was not usually drunk at ordinary meals; the same phrase in 20.11 and 27.35f. can surely denote only an ordinary meal; and no words of institution or interpretation are mentioned, or even hinted at. In a situation dominated by expectation of the imminent consummation there would be little incentive to establish forms or to create a ritual of remembrance. At the same time the fact remains that the words of interpretation over the bread and wine, which go back to Jesus in some form or other (see above §17.2 and below §40.4), were preserved by and transmitted through the earliest community. In the absence of any firmer data probably the best explanation is that the Lord's Supper was initially *an annual celebration* – the Christian equivalent of the Passover: the first Christians were Jews after all; and the Ebionites, whose beliefs closely parallel those of the primitive Jerusalem community at other points (see below §54), celebrated it in this way, as an annual festival.[17] We should not assume however that there was a clear distinction in the minds of the first Christians between the regular fellowship meals and that (or those) in which they specifically recalled the words of the last supper.

40.3   *The Lord's Supper in Paul.* Paul speaks of the Lord's Supper only in I Cor. 10.14–22, 11.17–34, but these few paragraphs are enough to show us where the communion celebrated in the Pauline churches was continuous with earlier tradition and where it had developed. The *continuity* with earlier tradition is most evident at three points. (1) Paul cites old tradition as the basis for his understanding of the Supper (I Cor. 11.23–25) – a tradition which stems ultimately from the last supper of Jesus and his disciples. This is tradition which must have been handed on to Paul from earlier believers, even though its authority for Paul lay in the fact that he received it 'from the Lord' (see above p.67). (2) The continuing eschatological emphasis of the Supper – I Cor. 11.26: '. . . until he comes'. Though we should also note that the emphasis is not so strong: indeed v.26 ('For . . .') looks very much like an explanatory note added by Paul himself rather than part of the tradition he received. (3) The Supper is still seen as a fellowship meal: in I Cor. 10.18–22 he draws a double comparison between the sacrificial meal in Israel's cult (Lev. 7.6, 15), the Lord's Supper and the feast in a pagan temple – and the point of comparison is that each is an expression of fellowship (*koinōnoi*, 'partners' – 10.18, 20);[18] and in I Cor. 11.17–34 the Lord's Supper is clearly thought of as taking place within the context of a meal.

At the same time certain *developments* are also evident.

(*a*) The relation between the fellowship meal and the words of interpretation over the bread and the wine is now somewhat clearer, since the partaking of the bread and the wine seems to be in process of becoming something in itself and to come at the end of the meal. This is somewhat speculative on the basis of a few clues, but the probability is that the rich Corinthian Christians were going ahead with their meal, while the poor (slaves, etc.) were usually able to arrive only in time for the Lord's Supper itself (11.21, 33). Hence the rebukes of 11.27, 29: 'not discerning the body' probably means an eating and drinking which does not express fellowship with the poor and weak; 'guilty of the body and the blood of the Lord' is probably a re-expression of 8.11f. and means sinning against the weaker brother.[19]

(*b*) Although the eschatological note is present, the backward look to Jesus' death is much stronger in 11.26. Here a shift in emphasis again becomes evident – from the fellowship meal as a whole as a symbol of the messianic feast, to the Lord's Supper as such as a proclamation of Jesus' death.

(*c*) Has Paul also allowed himself to be influenced by syncretistic thought so that the Lord's Supper has become something of a magical rite? The case has been argued on the basis that *pneumatikos*

in 10.4 should be understood to mean 'conveying *Pneuma* (Spirit)',
that 10.16f. reveals a much closer equation between bread and body
of Christ and between wine and blood of Christ than that of symbolism alone, and that 11.29f. is evidence of Paul's own superstition
at this point.[20] Paul's language is certainly open to such an interpretation. But it is clear from 10.1–13 that Paul is warning *against*
precisely such a sacramentalism on the part of the *Corinthians* – such
a view of the Lord's Supper is a corruption of the Lord's Supper. And
since 10.1–4 is an allegory ('the rock' in the tradition is to be
interpreted allegorically as 'Christ', etc.) *pneumatikos* is better understood in the sense 'allegorical' (see above p.90). The passage 10.16f.
could be taken as implying the Hellenistic idea of union with the cult
deity (Christ) through eating his body. But v.20 shows that Paul is
thinking rather in terms of fellowship or partnership – a fellowship
expressed through participating in the same meal, at the same table.
The emphasis is not so much on what was eaten and drunk as on the sharing
(koinōnia) of the same bread and cup (v.16); believers were one because they
shared the same loaf (v.17) not because of some efficacy in the bread itself (see
above p.164 and n.18). And in 11.29f., since the Corinthians made
too much of the Lord's Supper rather than too little (10.1–13), Paul
is probably thinking of the illness and death as a result of sinning
against the *community* (the body of Christ – cf. 5.5) rather than as an
effect of the elements themselves.[21]

40.4   *Possible variations within earliest Christian usage*. What we now
call the Lord's Supper, the Eucharist, Holy Communion, the mass,
may be *the end result of a conflating or standardizing of a number of divergent*
traditions.

(*a*) We know of different kinds of meals, each of which has
influenced the development of the Lord's Supper. (1) The Jerusalem
fellowship meal at which probably only bread was used and no wine
(see above §40.2). (2) An annual (?) passover(?)-type of meal, with
the bread and wine as part of the complete meal, the bread either at
the beginning (ordinary meal) or middle (Passover), and the wine at
the end (I Cor. 11.25 – 'after supper'). (3) A complete meal in which
the cup came first and the bread later – this may be implied by I Cor.
10.16, the shorter Lukan text (with Luke 22.19d–20 omitted),[22] and
Didache 9.

(*b*) The textual traditions also suggest divergent forms and
developing practice. There are at least two different textual traditions of the words of interpretation at the last supper.

A *Mark 14.22–24/Matt. 26.26–28*	B *I Cor. 11.24–25/Luke 22.19–20*
This is my body;	This is my body (which is for you);
This is my blood of the covenant which is poured out for many.	This cup is the (new) covenant in my blood (which is poured out for you).

In the word over the bread the phrase 'which is for you' in tradition B is probably later, hard to derive from Aramaic, absent from tradition A, and the sort of form that liturgical usage would develop.

The differences in the second word are more striking: in tradition A the emphasis is on the *blood*, in tradition B on the *covenant*. In this case it is probably tradition B which is earlier: 'my blood of the covenant' is a grammatical form unnatural or at least very unusual in either Hebrew or Aramaic; the drinking of blood was an abhorrent idea to Jews (see particularly Lev. 17.10–14; cf Acts 15.20, 29); and the closer parallelism of the two words in tradition A is probably the result of liturgical usage.[23] Bearing in mind that the words over bread and cup were originally *two separate words spoken at different points of the meal* (see above p.165), the probability is that the form of the second word was assimilated to that of the first only when the bread and the wine became a separate ritual at the end of the meal (cf. also I Cor. 10.16); whereas, had tradition A been earlier it becomes very difficult to explain how the originally parallel formulations came to diverge. It appears then as though *the earlier form of the second word* (over the cup rather than over the wine) *put the emphasis on the covenant* – and this would certainly harmonize with the eschatological note in the last supper (see above p.162). The 'in my blood . . .' could be a later addition, but even so it may already be implied – the covenant being established by sacrifice, Jesus seeing his own imminent death as the sacrifice in question (cf. Ex. 24.8; Heb. 9.20; Luke 12.49f. – see above n.8); the phrase 'poured out' certainly has strong sacrificial overtones.

It would appear then that we have a twofold tradition in the second word of interpretation. The one tradition interpreted the last supper in terms of the new covenant; the earlier fellowship meals of Jesus had been tokens of the messianic banquet of the coming kingdom; now with the last of these meals the imagery of interpretation changes to covenant, and the meal is seen to foreshadow also the means by which the covenant would be established, the kingdom come – namely, his death, as the fiery baptism, the messianic woes foretold by the Baptist. But the emphasis is on the covenant itself; the cup is the cup of promise of what lies beyond his death (Luke

22.18/Mark 14.25); the eschatological note predominates over the soteriological. This is the form of the tradition which probably derived most directly from Jesus himself, and its preservation probably reflects the continuing eschatological emphasis of the meal in the gatherings in which the words were repeated. The other tradition focuses much more on Jesus' death as such, and the soteriological note predominates; it involves only a shift of emphasis rather than a change of content, but probably reflects an early stage of the development of the Lord's Supper as a separate entity with the perspective beginning to become more of a backward look to redemption accomplished than a forward look to the eschatological feast.

John 6.53–56 may reflect yet another tradition, where the first word of interpretation was rendered, 'This is my flesh', rather than 'This is my body'. That such a variant tradition existed is certainly supported by Ignatius (*Phil.*, 4.1; *Smyrn.*, 6.2), although it may only have been developed late, as a counter to a docetic view of Christ.

40.5 *The probable developments in the celebration of the Lord's Supper* may be summarized therefore as follows.

(*a*) The relation of the Lord's Supper to the complete meal: (1) in earliest Christianity it was probably a constituent part of the whole meal (Christian Passover, I Cor. 11.25 – bread word earlier in the meal); (2) in the Pauline churches, or Corinth at least, it seems to have formed a distinct element at the end of the meal; (3) the balanced liturgical formulation of the words of interpretation in Mark and Matthew seem to indicate a further stage when the Lord's Supper was becoming or had already become a separate, distinct event.

(*b*) This probable overall development is reflected also in the development in the *significance* attached to the actions and words which came to constitute the Lord's Supper proper. Originally the two actions and words would have been understood separately and not in parallel. They came at different points within the context of the complete meal, so that each of them *individually* would have been understood as an expression of the whole meal, rather than them together. That is to say, *the fellowship reality of the new covenant was expressed in the whole meal*, and at separate points in the meal that expression would come to particular focus, first in the bread and then in the cup.

Subsequent developments seem to have transformed this original understanding in three ways. (1) The fellowship meal, where the sacramental reality lay in the act of table-fellowship, was apparently *transformed into a ritual act* which was more open to a magical interpretation (I Cor. 10). The bread and the cup seem to have become less a focus of the whole meal's significance, and more significant in themselves, separate from the meal, with more significance attached to the actual eating and drinking ('Do this in remembrance of me' – I Cor. 11.24, 25). That is, *the sacramental reality probably began to focus more on the elements of bread and wine*, on that which was consumed, *than on the meal as such*. (2) In particular, the earlier emphasis on the meal as a *covenant* meal expressed especially in *the common cup* (tradition B) probably began to give way to *a strengthening emphasis on the element of wine* as a symbol of Jesus' blood and sacrifice (tradition A). If so, the predominant note of a covenant fellowship enjoyed in the here and now would have begun to give way to the representation of an initiating sacrifice. (3) Consequently, also, the eschatological significance of the meal as an anticipation of the messianic banquet presumably began to fade, and the elements of bread and wine became *more backward looking to the death of Jesus*, so that in Paul the Supper is essentially a re-telling of the decisive redemptive event of the past and the eschatological dimension is preserved only in that the Supper will serve as such a proclamation of Jesus' death until the parousia. In short, thus we see even within forty years of the last supper developments which do not yet cause any NT writer to regard the Lord's Supper as a distinctive means of grace as such, far less as the main or exclusive means of grace to believers, but which do appear to show us the beginning of that process whereby in later years the Lord's Supper came to be more and more the principal focus for the divine-human encounter between God and the believer through Christ.

§41. THE SACRAMENTS IN THE FOURTH GOSPEL

In recent years opinions about the role of the sacraments in John's theology have been sharply divided. They can be classified in a rough and ready way in three categories. (1) The *ultrasacramental* interpretation[24] where a water reference is always accorded sacramental significance (including 2.1–11; 4.7–15; 5.2–9; 7.37–39; 9.7, 11; 13.1–16; 19.34), and where the Lord's Supper is seen to be mirrored in 2.1–11 and 15.1–11. Sacramental allusions have even been detected in the 'cleansing of the temple' episode (2.13–22), in the account of Jesus walking on the water (6.16–21) and in the Good

Shepherd discourse (10.1–18). (2) The *non-sacramental* interpretation:[25] the rest of the Gospel is so obviously *anti*-sacramental that the
clearly sacramental references in 3.5 ('water and'), 6.51–58 and
19.34 must be regarded as the work of an ecclesiastical redactor.
(3) A *modified sacramental* interpretation,[26] which sees only a few
sacramental references – 3.5 and 6.51–58 certainly, 19.34 likely but
not definite, with several others such as 2.1–11 and 13.1–16 only
graded as 'possible'.

The answer probably lies somewhere between the last two alternatives. (*a*) Notice first *the complete absence of any account of Jesus' baptism*
(John 1) *and of the 'institution' of the Lord's Supper* (John 13). This
silence can be adequately explained only in one of two ways. Either
John wants to place no emphasis on the two sacraments, but rather
to draw attention away from them; or he wants to set them in the
context of Jesus' whole ministry. In view of 6.51–58 the latter is
certainly possible (John uses some far-reaching symbolism), but
otherwise it requires a tremendous amount to be read into the text.
Overall the former seems to have greater plausibility.

(*b*) Wherever we find '*water*' mentioned in the Fourth Gospel it is
used in one of two ways. Either *it symbolizes the blessings of the new age, or
the Holy Spirit in particular*: 4.10, 14 – 'the gift of God' is almost a
technical term for the Holy Spirit in earliest Christianity (Acts 2.38;
8.20; 10.45; 11.17; II Cor. 9.15; Eph. 3.7; 4.7; Heb. 6.4),[27] and
welling or springing up' is probably intended to recall the action
of the Spirit in Judg. 14.6, 19; 15.14; I Sam. 10.10 where the same
word is used; 7.37–39 – explicit equation with the Spirit; 19.34 – the
primary reference is anti-docetic, hence the emphasis on the blood
(he really died; see below pp.301f.), while the water is probably
intended as a symbolical fulfilment of 7.38; in 9 and 13 water is not
mentioned, and in 9.7 anyway the pool is explicitly explained as
symbolizing 'the one who has been sent' (that is, Jesus). Alternatively, water *represents the old dispensation in contrast to what Jesus now offers*:
1.26, 31, 33 – repeated emphasis that John's baptism is only in water
heightens the contrast with Jesus' Spirit-baptism; 2.6 – the water
represents the Jewish purification rites, in contrast to Jesus' wine of
the new age; 3.25–36 – as John the Baptist is from below so is his
baptism, in contrast to Jesus who is from above and who has and
gives the Spirit not by measure; 5.2–9 – the point is that the water
did *not* provide healing, whereas Jesus did. The probability is therefore that John will have intended the remaining water reference (3.5)
to be understood in one of these two ways, *as symbol of Spirit or in
contrast to Spirit* – and if it can be so interpreted, in a way that makes

sense within its context, then the grounds for regarding it as a secondary addition will be removed. In fact both interpretations of 'water and' in 3.5 make plausible sense. Either the reference is to the cleansing, renewing effect of the Spirit from above, echoing such prophetic passages as Isa. 44.3–5 and Ezek. 36.25–27 (cf. 1QS 4.20–22). Or the reference is to water-baptism (either John's or Christian), or even to the breaking of the waters at natural birth (as 3.4), in contrast to the birth from the Spirit (the subject of the passage – 3.6–8): to enter the kingdom of God one must be born of water and *Spirit*, that is, *one must experience not just physical birth but the renewal of the Spirit, not just water baptism but baptism in the Spirit* (cf. 1.33; 3.26–34). We should perhaps just add that there is no justification for interpreting the hendiadys *'born* of water and Spirit' as equivalent to *'baptized* in water and Spirit' (particularly in view of John's emphasis on the Baptist's antithesis between baptism in water and baptism in Spirit – 1.26, 31, 33). More likely the hendiadys treats both water baptism and Spirit baptism as integral parts of conversion-initiation (born of water baptism and Spirit baptism), while giving the latter the primary emphasis (just as Jesus could be called the 'hendiadys' between the Logos become *flesh* and the life-giving *Spirit* – cf. 3.6 and 6.63; and see the next paragraph).

(c) John probably takes up the language of the Lord's Supper in 6.51–58,[28] as the parallel with Ignatius seems to imply (see above p.167). But if so, then we must note how he uses it and to what purpose. First, he uses the language of 'eating', 'munching', 'drinking' as *metaphors for believing in Jesus*: the need to believe in Jesus is the central emphasis of the whole passage (vv.29, 35, 36, 40, 47, 64, 69 – see also above §6.1). Second, he wants to insist that this Jesus is not merely the exalted Christ but the one who also came down from heaven (vv.33, 38, 41f., 50f., 58), that is, the truly incarnate and crucified as well as now ascended Jesus. That is to say, the passage incorporates *a strongly anti-docetic polemic,* which comes to its bluntest expression in vv.51–56 where 'flesh' is substituted for 'bread' (v.51) and the cruder 'munch' for 'eat' (v.54): to munch Jesus' flesh and drink his blood is to believe in Jesus as the truly incarnate one (cf. again Ignatius, *Smyrn.*, 6.2; and see also below pp.300f.). Third, John also believes that it is *only through the Spirit of the ascended Jesus* that this vivifying new relation with this Jesus is effected (3.3–8; 4.10, 14; 6.27; 20.22) – 'faith' is met by the gift of the Spirit (7.39). Moreover, he seeks to avoid the impression that this relation is achieved through or is dependent upon participation in the Lord's Supper. Having used the eucharistic terminology of flesh (and blood) in vv.51–56 to underscore his rejection of docetism, he at once goes on to warn that 'the flesh does no good whatever, it is the Spirit that gives life' (6.63). In other words, if vv. 51–58 do use eucharistic language, it is very hard to read vv.62f. as anything other than *a protest against sacramental literalism,* that is, as a protest against the view that the life of which John so often speaks is mediated through the eating and drinking of sacramental elements.[29]

It looks very much as though John is reacting against a kind of sacramentalism current in his own day. Just as John felt it necessary to protest against such institutionalizing trends as are already present in the Pastorals and I Clement (see above §§31.1, 32.1), so he evidently felt it necessary to protest against a growing tendency towards sacramentalism such as we find a little later in Ignatius (particularly *Eph.,* 20.2). He does *not* adopt an anti-sacramentalist stance properly speaking, nor does he turn his back on the sacraments, for he alludes to them in 6.51–58 (most probably) and 3.5 (quite likely). But John's Gospel must be read in part at least as a protest against a (presumably) increasing sacramental literalism.[30]

§42. CONCLUSIONS

42.1   We are now in a position to answer some of the questions posed at the end of §38, and to appreciate something of the diversity of theology and form which must be encompassed by any attempt to discuss the role of the sacraments in first-century Christianity.

(*a*) Perhaps most striking of all is *the complete absence from Jesus' own ministry of any sustained parallel to the later churches' sacramental practice*: he himself administered no baptism (at least for the bulk of his ministry) and his table-fellowship was the very opposite of a restricted or 'closed communion'.[31] If we wish to describe Jesus' ministry as 'sacramental' in a broader sense, then we must note that this broader sacramental significance had a wide range of expression, both ritual (laying on of hands, washing disciples' feet, etc.) and non-ritual (personal relationships).

(*b*) When did the two sacraments become part of Christianity? Baptism more or less immediately, but the Lord's Supper proper not for some years – the common and/or Passover meal of the earliest Jerusalem community can be described at most as no more than an embryonic sacrament, and *the Lord's Supper as we would recognize it is the end product of quite a long process.*

(*c*) *Initially the central emphasis was eschatological* – baptism as being a direct takeover of John's baptism, and the common meal as a continuation of Jesus' practice and an expression of the new covenant fellowship. But as Christianity moved out more and more into the wider Hellenistic world the eschatological emphasis diminished and was *increasingly replaced by the backward look to Jesus' death* – baptism as an expression of burial with Christ, the Lord's Supper as a proclamation of Jesus' death.

(*d*) Among some Christians at least (certainly in Corinth) the developing sacraments came to be understood in *semi-magical terms* – as effecting or securing salvation and union with the exalted Lord – an emphasis which Paul strenuously contested.

(*e*) At the other end of the spectrum we have the *Johannine protest against sacramentalism* or sacramental literalism towards the end of the first century – a protest which in the event was unavailing when the sacramentalist tendency in Ignatius became the dominant one.

42.2   When we look for a *unifying focus* within this diversity we find it once again in Jesus, and precisely in *the continuity between the earthly Jesus and the exalted Christ which the sacraments embody and express*. From the first, baptism was performed 'in the name of Jesus', with the baptizer representing the exalted Jesus and/or the baptisand entering into discipleship of the exalted Lord. At the same time Paul was able to stress, as something which no one would deny, that baptism also spoke of the dying of Jesus and provided a metaphor for union with Christ in his death. There is however no explicit attempt to link Jesus' baptism by John with Christian baptism. Christian baptism expresses a continuity not so much between pre-Easter and post-Easter discipleship as *between Jesus' death and the subsequent Christian communities*.

The Lord's Supper on the other hand provides a continuity on both levels. On the one hand the fellowship meals of the earliest Christian communities (out of which the Lord's Supper as such grew) were themselves probably *the continuation of Jesus' own table-fellowship*; indeed, the continuity was perhaps even more marked, since they may well have eaten these meals in the consciousness of Jesus' presence, the Lord of the covenant (cf. Luke 24.35; Acts 1.4; I Cor. 10.21), the words of interpretation being understood as spoken by the earthly and exalted one himself (through a prophet? – cf. Didache 10.7). On the other hand, the tradition of *the words of the last supper* always played a part in shaping the Lord's Supper as a sacrament, and in the event had the most decisive effect, and these provide the continuity precisely with Jesus' passion and death.

42.3   The importance of the sacraments within the NT, therefore, is *not* that they provide some sort of exclusive focus or channel of grace – such interpretations seem to be more resisted by Jesus and the NT writers than welcomed. On the contrary, where the sacraments are valued within the NT it is because *they embody in a strikingly symbolical way the heart of the Christian belief in Jesus,* the man who gave his life for many and who is now exalted, and because *they enable faith in this Jesus to find appropriate expression.*

IX

SPIRIT AND EXPERIENCE

§43. INTRODUCTION

Traditionally Christianity has found its unity in creed, ministry and liturgy. But there has always been one strand or stream of Christianity (often little more than a trickle) which has tended to play down the centrality of written creed, of properly ordered ministry and of structured worship – stressing rather *the immediacy of experience*. For the proponents of experiential Christianity, in its more vigorous expression more usually called 'Enthusiasm', what matters is direct experience of God – some feeling or awareness of God, a conversion experience, some significant experiences of revelation, of inspiration or of commissioning, or some ultimate mystical experience of union with God.

A few examples from the history of Christianity chosen more or less at random will illustrate the importance of experiential Christianity in previous centuries. The sect called the Messalians flourished between the fourth and seventh centuries: according to John of Damascus, when priests used to say to Messalians, 'We profess in faith that we have the Holy Spirit, not by experience', they would reply, 'Come and pray with us, and we promise you the *experience* of the Spirit'. Symeon the New Theologian (tenth to eleventh centuries), the most outstanding of the Byzantine medieval mystics, maintained that a baptism without genuine conversion is a baptism only in water; it is only the 'second baptism', baptism 'of the Spirit', or the 'baptism of tears', which actually makes one a real Christian, an experience of enlightenment which Symeon refused to reduce to mere intellectual knowledge.[1] St Vincent Ferrar (fourteenth to fifteenth centuries) lists among the perfections 'essential to those who serve God, . . . constantly to *taste* and to *experience* the divine sweetness'. The Recogidos, an influential group in the Spanish church in the first half of the sixteenth century, practised a form of prayer called 'recollection' through which they sought to experience within themselves the truth of their faith, allowing God to come into the soul; their prayer could and often did lead to ecstatic phenomena like trances, crying out with joy and groanings. Martin Luther wrote in the preface to the Magnificat: 'No one can understand God or God's word unless he has it revealed immediately by the Holy Ghost; but nobody can receive anything from the Holy Ghost unless he experiences it'. As is well known George Fox set the 'inner light' above Scripture in matters of authority, in one famous incident interrupting a preacher at Nottingham by saying: 'It is not the Scripture, it is the Holy Spirit by which holy men of old gave forth the Scripture, by which religions . . . are to be tried'. Count Zinzendorf, founder of the Moravian settlement at Herrnhut, understood the process of salvation 'as an immediate and joyful apprehension of a loving Father'.[2] The influence of Moravian pietism is evident both in F. D. E. Schleiermacher's understanding of religion as the 'feeling of absolute dependence', and more obviously in John Wesley's experience of his heart being 'strangely warmed' and in the importance he placed on assurance: 'The testimony of the Spirit is an inward impression on the soul, whereby the Spirit of God directly witnesses to my spirit that I am a child of God'.[3] Finally, in the past twenty years Pentecostalism has gained increasing recognition within the world Church as the twentieth-century expression of experiential Christianity, a vital and valid form of Christianity distinct from Catholicism and Protestantism – the present day embodiment of the conviction 'that if we would answer the question "Where is the Church?", we must ask "Where is the Holy Spirit recognizably present with power?" '[4]

To be sure, the Church catholic has usually sought to restrict and divert this stream of Christianity, hemming it in behind high banks or channelling it underground, fearful lest a flood of 'enthusiasm' devastate its flocks and folds – and sometimes with good reason. Luther, for all that he recognized the importance of religious experience, complained vigorously against the spiritualist Anabaptist who talks facilely about 'Geist, Geist, Geist', and then 'kicks away the very bridge by which the Holy Spirit can come . . . namely, the outward ordinances of God like the bodily sign of baptism and the preached Word of God'.[5] Bishop Butler's famous remark to John Wesley reflects the rationalist's disparagement of religious experience: 'Sir, the pretending to extraordinary revelations and gifts of the Holy Ghost is a horrid thing, a very horrid thing'.[6] More measured and more immediately relevant to our study is the recent claim of Alan Richardson 'that the Bible itself places little emphasis upon subjective experiences . . . It is impossible to translate "religious experience" into NT Greek'.[7]

Here then is as vigorous a cross-current of controversy as any we have so far met. Is religious experience a focus of Christian unity or a dangerous diversion from the central issues? How important was religious experience in earliest Christianity – in shaping its character, in forming its self-understanding? Behind the outward expressions of kerygma and creed, of ministry and worship, was there some great passion or common experience(s) which gave rise to diverse manifestations but which bonded the diversity together in a unity at the centre? And if religious experience is an important component among the basic building blocks of first-century Christianity, what experience – any experiences, or just a certain kind? the enthusiasm of the Anabaptists, or the 'cooler' experience of Luther? What is the tale of unity and diversity in the matter of the religious experience of the first Christians? We will pursue these questions by noting first that earliest Christianity was largely enthusiastic in nature (including Luke's account of it), and then attempt to highlight the role of religious experience, so far as it can be discerned, in Jesus, Paul, and more briefly in the Pastorals and John.[8]

§44. ENTHUSIASTIC CHRISTIANITY

Enthusiastic Christianity, the third, or better, fourth main strand or stream of Christianity (beside Orthodoxy, Catholicism and Protestantism) is sometimes assumed to be a tangential development of Christianity in later centuries, more influenced by Gnosticism or Montanism than by orthodox Christianity, or even a peculiarly Protestant aberration spawned by the Reformation and largely confined to the seventeenth and eighteenth centuries.[9] In fact, however, *the earliest form of Christianity seems to have been nothing other than such an enthusiastic sect*.

44.1   It is not easy to penetrate back through our sources to *the earliest communities in Palestine* – Acts as often obscures as illuminates. But we can recognize several features characteristic of enthusiasm. If Acts contains any history at all, then it is difficult to deny that experiences of vision and ecstasy, or miracles and of immediate inspiration in speaking were characteristic of the first Christian churches.

(a) *Vision and ecstasy.* The resurrection appearances have to be classified as some form of visionary experience. Paul's understanding of the resurrection body ('spiritual' not 'natural') certainly implies that he understood Jesus' mode of risen life as different from physical existence (I Cor. 15.42–50); consequently his 'seeing' the risen Jesus (I Cor. 9.1) must have been of a different order from 'physical' seeing – that is to say, it must have been some mode of visionary seeing (cf. Gal. 1.16 – 'to reveal his Son in me'). Indeed this is just how Paul himself describes it in one of the Acts accounts of his conversion (Acts 26.19 – 'heavenly vision; though see below n.16). The nature of the earlier resurrection appearances described in the Gospels is less clear; but they too are best understood as some kind of vision, in which, to be sure, all who saw Jesus were convinced that Jesus was there to be seen, risen and alive with new life.[10]

The first great communal experience of the Spirit at Pentecost, described by Luke in Acts 2, has to be recognized as an ecstatic experience which at least included elements of audition (sound like a strong wind), vision (tongues like fire) and automatic speech (glossolalia). That this was understood as an experience of the Spirit (and presumably not just by Luke) tells us something both about the importance of such experiences in the first years of the new sect and about the character attributed to the Spirit by the first Christians – the Spirit of *enthusiasm*. This is borne out by the significance of the other ecstatic experiences specifically attributed to the Spirit, in 4.31, 8.17ff. (by implication), 10.44ff. and 19.6. In each case Luke is obviously describing men caught up out of themselves, that is, in ecstasy.

That visions were frequently experienced within the first Christian communities is the clear testimony of Acts, and it is confirmed by Paul's testimony in II Cor. 12.1, 7. There is little artifice in Luke's account at this point and little reason to question his claim that visions were experienced by all the key figures in the earliest development of the new sect – Peter, Stephen, Philip, Ananias, Paul. Not only so, but according to Luke at least, these visions played a significant part in directing the course of the earliest mission (particularly 9.10; 10.3–6, 10–16; 16.9f.; 18.9; 22.17f.). Two of them are explicitly described as 'ecstatic' (10.10; 11.5; 22.17). *Where important decisions are determined by visions we have enthusiasm pure and simple.*

(b) *Miracles.* It can scarcely be doubted that the course of earliest

Christianity was marked by many out of the ordinary happenings and reports of many miracles. The record of Acts is here adequately confirmed by the first hand testimony of Paul (Rom. 15.19; I Cor. 12.10, 28f.; Gal. 3.5). These included healings of lameness, blindness and paralysis (Acts 3.1–10; 8.7; 9.18, 33f.; etc.), and the account of Peter restoring Tabitha from death (9.36–41; cf. 20.9–12). Such 'mighty works' have appeared or at least have been reported wherever enthusiasm has gripped a meeting or a community throughout the history of religion. Particularly noteworthy are the claims to healings through Peter's shadow (5.15f.) and through handkerchiefs and scarves touched by Paul (19.11f.), and the 'miracles of judgment' in 5.1–11 (the death of Ananias and Sapphira) and 13.8–11 (the blindness of Elymas). Such are the claims of enthusiasm – where the spirit has become so elevated and the imagination so fired that the experience of supernatural power becomes readily anticipated and claims to the manifestation of such power cause no surprise.

(c) *Inspiration*. Experiences of inspired speech were also frequent in earliest Christianity. Paul certainly wanted all his Corinthian readers to experience prophecy (I Cor. 14.5) and warned his Thessalonian converts against restricting the prophetic Spirit (I Thess. 5.19f.). Indeed it would appear from Acts that the experience of inspired utterance was so widespread among the first believers that they could readily believe that Joel's prophecy had been wholly fulfilled – *all* were prophets, young and old, parents and children, masters and servants (Acts 2.17f.). The Spirit was experienced as giving words to say, words of praise, words of testimony (Acts 2.4; 4.8, 31; 5.32; 6.3, 5, 10; etc.). They felt themselves under divine direction that was immediate and not to be gainsaid (5.3, 9; 8.29, 39; 9.31; 10.19; 13.2, 4; etc.). They acted and spoke boldly, with authority, believing that they did so 'in the name of Jesus', that is as the direct representatives of the risen Christ and as his plenipotentiaries (2.38; 3.6, 16; 4.10, 13, 29–31; 5.28, 40f.; etc.). *In the history of Christianity such claims have been most characteristic of enthusiasm.*

The intensity and frequency of these various experiences claimed for this earliest form of Christianity indicate that we are here dealing not with a few isolated instances of poetic vision or charismatic potency or prophetic rapture, but with a community where such experiences were characteristic, a community which largely depended on such experiences for its spiritual sustenance and sense of direction. Such a community has to be called an *enthusiastic* community.

44.2   There are clear indications in various NT writings of *a very strong* (many would say too strong) *enthusiastic tendency or stream within first-century Christianity.*

(*a*) Some of Paul's chief headaches were caused by enthusiastic factions – particularly at *Corinth*. From I Cor. 1.18–4.21 it becomes evident that some of the Corinthian Christians thought of themselves as 'the spiritual ones' (*pneumatikoi* – see particularly 3.1); they had achieved a higher plane of spirituality, they knew a higher wisdom, they despised the low-level Christianity of Paul among others (see particularly 4.8–10). Here clearly is a kind of spiritual elitism typical of the less attractive forms of enthusiasm. Similarly in I Cor. 8 we hear of those (probably the same group) who thought they possessed a superior knowledge which justified action that was selfish and inconsiderate to those who did not share the same insights. In I Cor. 14 Paul addresses those (the *pneumatikoi* again) who seemed to think that spirituality was to be measured by the volume of ecstatic speech – the more unintelligible, the more inspired (14.6–25)! Their conduct was too reminiscent of the frenzied worship of devotees of Dionysus (12.2); they desired spirits (14.12) – that is, they put themselves out for experiences of inspiration; their worship was characterized by confusion and disorder (14.23, 33, 40). Here again clearly are the marks of *unrestrained enthusiasm.* In I Cor. 15.12 we meet the view that 'there is no resurrection of the dead' – that is, no *future* resurrection, no resurrection of the body. This was probably another facet of the same elitist spirituality: there could be no resurrection to come, because they already experienced *fullness* of resurrection life through the Spirit (cf. 4.8; 15.45f.). Notice that this strand of enthusiasm was *part of the church at Corinth,* not merely some external threat (see further below §61.1).

The situation addressed in II Cor. 10–13 had developed from that reflected in I Corinthians. But there too we hear of men held in high regard within the Corinthian church because they displayed manifestly enthusiastic traits: their speech was impressive, that is, probably, inspired and ecstatic (10.10; 11.6); they evidently boasted of their visions and revelations (12.1); their 'signs and wonders and mighty works' were regarded as proof positive of their apostleship. Since they evaluated themselves in such terms, their gospel presumably reflected the same emphasis; that is, the 'other Jesus' whom Paul accuses them of preaching (11.4) was probably Jesus presented as a man mighty in such spiritual powers, a divine miracle worker who thereby showed himself superior to all other like figures in Hellenistic religion, just as they themselves demonstrated their superiority over Paul in matters of religious experience (cf. above pp.70f.).

The evidence of enthusiastic tendencies within the Pauline churches is clearest in the Corinthian letters. But the situation of Corinth was not untypical of other Pauline churches, as II Thess. 2.2 and Col. 2.18 clearly show. In the former we have another instance of a (probably) prophetic word about the parousia being taken uncritically as divine guidance for present conduct (cf. II Thess. 3.6–13). And in the latter it would appear that there were those within the Colossian assembly who boasted of their visions experienced at initiation and regarded them as justification for the practice of angel worship (see also below p.281).

(b) *Mark* too may well have constructed his Gospel to counter a christology similar in type to that which Paul denounced in II Cor. 10–13, an apologetic or evangelism which presented Jesus primarily as a pre-eminent miracle worker (cf. above pp.49, 71). If so, then the implication is that within the situation or community addressed by Mark there were strong influences towards enthusiasm similar to those in Corinth.

(c) Other evidence of the less desirable forms of enthusiasm within first-century Christianity may be found in Matt. 7.21–23, where Matthew evidently has in mind enthusiastic charismatics with a dangerous tendency towards antinomianism, and Jude 19, where Jude seems to be attacking a group who like those in Corinth, regarded themselves as *pneumatikoi*, a spiritual elite (see further below p.282).

44.3   *Luke* himself has to be regarded as something of an enthusiast (though not an elitist). As he looks back to the beginnings of Christianity in Acts, it is the enthusiastic features which he picks out again and again – just as among the Synoptic Gospels it is Luke alone who mentions the one clearly ecstatic experience of Jesus (Luke 10.18; cf. 10.21; 22.43). Moreover, in highlighting the phenomena of enthusiasm he does so in a surprisingly uncritical way.

(a) It is clear from his presentation of the Spirit (particularly in Acts) that *he shares something at least of the enthusiast's desire for the dramatic in spiritual experience, for the divine to become opaque and tangible.* For Luke *the Spirit is most clearly seen in extraordinary and obviously supernatural phenomena*, and in Acts is hardly present anywhere else. The Spirit is the power that comes with a sound like a mighty wind and in visible tongues like fire (2.3), the power that is clearly manifested in glossolalia (2.4; 10.46; 19.6), the power that affects its recipients in such a manner as to excite the wonder and envy of an accomplished magician (8.18f). That is to say, when the power of the Spirit first takes hold of someone in Luke's narrative it manifests itself typically and directly in ecstatic experience. This is why he uses such dramatic language to describe the coming of the Spirit – 'baptized into' (1.5; 11.16), 'came upon' (1.8; 19.6), 'poured out' (2.17f., 33; 10.45), 'fell upon' (8.16; 10.44; 11.15). This is why the question can be asked in 19.2 – 'Did you receive the Spirit when you believed?' – for the coming of the Spirit would be something tangible, unmistakable. This is why in 2.33 'the promise of the Holy Spirit' can be further described as 'this which you see and hear', where the ecstatic behaviour and speech of the disciples is *identified* with the outpoured Spirit! *Luke's understanding of the Spirit is that of the enthusiast.*

(*b*) *Ecstatic visions* occur frequently in Acts – twelve at least, and that is not counting resurrection appearances in Acts 1 or the Pentecost experience of Acts 2 (see above p.177). There are more visions recorded in Acts than in the rest of the NT put together (Revelation apart). Luke clearly delights in the fact that the early churches were guided in their mission directly by visions, and particularly at decisive moments (9.10; 10.3–6, 10–16; 16.9f.; 18.9; 22.17f.; 26.19f.). He shows no consciousness of the problem that an authority rooted in vision can be grossly abused; he seems to share none of Paul's reservations on this point (cf. II Cor. 12.1; Col. 2.18). We know from these two Pauline passages that the problem arose in acute form at least twice during the time span covered by the Acts history. But Luke registers no disquiet on the subject, and offers no cautionary tales of visionary experiences being used to justify questionable practices or attitudes. Such unquestioning acceptance of all visions as directly from God, *such uncritical treatment of authority vested in visionary experiences clearly betrays the hand of the enthusiast.*

(*c*) The same uncritical attitude towards claims among the first Christians to direct experience of the supernatural is if anything even more pronounced in Luke's treatment of *miracles* in Acts. He regularly calls them 'wonders and signs' (9 times). But this is a phrase which is usually used elsewhere in the NT in a more negative sense – 'signs and wonders' characterize the work of the false prophet, the attitude of unfaith, the boasting of counterfeit apostles, the deceit of anti-Christ (Mark 13.22/Matt. 24.24; John 4.48; II Cor. 12.12; II Thess. 2.9) – that is, they are not something to be trusted or commended, but acts to be wary of. Yet Luke boasts of the early churches' 'wonders and signs' as acts which demonstrated God's hand in the churches' mission. To be sure, there is a certain restraint in the miracles he records, and he sharply contrasts the miraculous progress of the 'word of God' with magic (Acts 8.18–24; 13.6–12; 19.13–20). But nevertheless, he clearly thinks of the early Christian mission's miracles as more spectacular than those of any rivals – '*great* signs and wonders', '*extraordinary* miracles' (8.13; 19.11) – and all the more valuable and creditable for that.

Another significant pointer to Luke's own attitude is his portrayal of *the relationship between miracles and faith*. Luke seems to think more of the faith which miracles produce than of the faith which makes a miracle possible in the first place (5.12–14; 9.42; 13.12; 19.13–18). Whereas elsewhere in the NT the attitude is completely the reverse: the publicity, propagandist value of miracles is disparaged and a faith based on miracle is usually treated with reserve and disapproval (Mark 8.11f.; Matt. 12.38f./Luke 11.16, 29; John 2.23f.; 4.48; 20.29 – see also below p.303; II Cor. 13.3f.). In short, what other NT writers see as at best ambiguous ('signs and wonders'), Luke glories in. What Jesus and other NT writers saw as something to be discouraged (faith based on miracles), Luke sees as something that may be encouraged. *He who glories uncritically in miracles for their propaganda effect and values faith rooted in miracle may quite properly be designated an enthusiast.*

(*d*) Much the same attitude is reflected in Luke's emphasis on the earliest communities' experience of *inspired utterance*. He sees this as *the great mark of the Spirit-filled individual and community* (he makes no similar effort to link the Spirit with the 'wonders and signs' he records); see Acts 2.4, 17f. ('and they shall prophesy' has been added to the Joel citation to emphasize the point); 4.8, 31; 5.32; 6.10; 7.55f.; 10.44–46; 11.28; 13.2, 9–11; 18.25; 19.6; 20.23; 21.4, 11. Two features of Luke's presentation deserve attention. First, *he makes no real effort to distinguish prophecy from ecstatic utterance*: he runs the two together in 19.6 (cf. 10.46) and seems to equate them in Acts 2, where the *glossolalia* of 2.4 fulfils Joel's expectation of the outpouring of the Spirit in *prophecy* (2.16–18). This implies that Luke is more interested in or impressed by the fact of inspiration rather than by its character (intelligible or unintelligible utterance – cf. the Corinthians above p.179). Second, he shows no *awareness of the problem of false prophecy*. The only 'false prophet' we meet is outside the church, its declared enemy (13.6). That it could be a problem *within* a Christian congregation is hardly envisaged. Even when two inspired utterances/convictions contradict each other, he attributes both to the Spirit without qualm or question (20.22; 21.4). *This unquestioning acceptance of all inspired utterance within the community as inspired by the Holy Spirit is certainly the attitude of the enthusiast.*

(e) One counterbalancing consideration should however not be ignored. Luke shares many of the traits of enthusiasm, but *he is no elitist.* He is an enthusiast – he sees Christianity as a higher form of spirituality. But he is no elitist – he has no conception of a higher spirituality *within* Christianity. To be sure, the account of Acts 8.12–17 offers itself as a proof text for a kind of Christian elitism – the Samaritans as the type of baptized believers who yet lack the Spirit. But an alternative exegesis is that Luke intends here to emphasize the importance of the gift of the Spirit as that which makes anyone a Christian (as clearly in 10.44–48; 11.15–18; 15.8f.; 19.2f.) – in the last analysis the one thing needful. It is the gift of the Spirit which tells whether there has been a genuine belief in God and commitment to Christ rather than simply a belief that the preacher was saying something important and a desire to please him (as Luke's language in 8.12f. implies: they believed Philip, not *God* or *in* Christ, Luke's regular description of conversion). Luke's enthusiasm as reflected in Acts 8 can therefore best be characterized thus: not Christians who yet lack the Spirit, but lacking the Spirit not yet Christians.[11]

We may conclude therefore that *Luke is one of those believers for whom spiritual experience must be visible, tangible, able to serve as a proof to others*: the Holy Spirit descends on Jesus 'in bodily form' at Jordan (Luke 3.22); the three inner circle disciples really witnessed Jesus' transfiguration, they did not dream it (Luke 9.32); the resurrection appearances provided 'many convincing proofs' of Jesus' resurrection (Acts 1.3; cf. Luke 24.39); the angel who released Peter from prison was real and not a vision (Acts 12.9); the Spirit is actually to be seen in the effects of his coming (Acts 2.33); the miracles of Christianity are more impressive, carry more conviction than any others; guidance in moments of indecision or stress can be expected through vision or inspired utterance; ecstasy and inspiration within the church is always the work of the Spirit. There are other aspects of Luke's presentation of earliest Christianity to which we must return (see below §72.2). But enough has been said here to demonstrate that what impressed Luke most about earliest Christianity were its enthusiastic features. Yet his enthusiasm focuses on Christianity as a whole; unlike the enthusiasts Paul had to encounter, he does not seek to encourage a higher form of spirituality within Christianity – that would be divisive and destructive to the unity of the church, and Luke would certainly not wish to encourage that (see below §72.2). It is enthusiastic Christianity as such that Luke portrays – and he draws his materials and colours from the reality itself. In short, as well as recognizing Luke as evangelist, historian and theologian, and with the qualifications outlined above, we must also name him, 'Luke the enthusiast' (see further below pp.356f.).

§45. THE RELIGIOUS EXPERIENCE OF JESUS

The stream of enthusiastic Christianity flowed from the very beginnings of Christianity through the first generation churches and into the second generation, finding its first and perhaps classic written expression in the Acts of the Apostles. The question naturally arises for us, Did Jesus himself stand within that stream? Does it first appear in his own ministry?

It is of course exceedingly difficult to reach back to Jesus' own religious experience. Many would say that it is impossible, given the nature of our sources and their lack of interest in Jesus' own experience as such. And the endeavours of nineteenth-century NT scholarship to produce lives of Jesus and to uncover his 'messianic self-consciousness' are a standing warning of the hazards threatening any such attempt. Certainly it is true that we can no longer hope to write a (modern) biography of Jesus, or to trace any developments in his self-awareness, etc. But we have at least some historical reminiscences of Jesus' ministry and we have the actual words of Jesus preserved in at least a few instances. And a person's self-understanding is bound to come to expression in some degree or other in what he or she says and does. So we can entertain some hope of penetrating back to Jesus' understanding of his religious experience at one or two points in his ministry.

We will look first at the evidence most similar to the outline of enthusiastic Christianity sketched above, then examine more closely the material which reflects Jesus' consciousness of sonship and of the Spirit of God working through him.

45.1 *Was Jesus an enthusiast?* There are a number of points at which Jesus' ministry shows clear parallels to the enthusiastic Christianity described above.

(a) Jesus may well have had *one* or *two ecstatic experiences*.[11a] One likely example is Luke 10.18 – the vision of Satan falling like lightning from heaven. The accounts of Jesus' anointing with the Spirit at Jordan probably go back to Jesus himself in one form or another (Mark 1.10 pars.); quite likely the experience involved both vision (Spirit descending like a dove) and audition (the voice from heaven). The temptation narratives possibly go back to some visionary experiences which Jesus had in the wilderness (Matt. 4.1–11/Luke 4.1–12). Beyond that we cannot go with any confidence. Was the 'transfiguration' originally a vision? – but if so, it was a vision experienced by the inner circle disciples rather than by Jesus (Mark 9.2–8 pars.). The appearance of an angel in Gethsemane (Luke 22.43f.) is another possible candidate; but here the text is uncertain. All told we have a minimal element of enthusiasm – hardly to be compared with the strong visionary and ecstatic element in Acts.

(b) Jesus was certainly a *miracle worker*, in the sense at least that he brought about many extraordinary healings and exorcisms – a feature of his ministry confirmed from Jewish sources.[12] However we understand or explain what happened (the hypnotic impact of his personality, the illnesses as hysterical disorders, the healings as the effect of divine power, etc.), it is clear enough that there was a charismatic or enthusiastic dimension to his ministry. That is to say, there was a power in his words and actions which was not something conferred upon him by the authorities of his day, nor a technique learned at some school, but an authority which he and others recognized and which he himself attributed to the Spirit working through him (see below pp.185f. and §45.3).

At two points, however, Jesus' attitude to miracle sets him apart from Luke. First, *he seems to have rejected outright the idea that miracles were valuable for their propaganda or sign effect* (Mark 8.11f. pars.; cf. Matt. 4.5–7 par.; Luke 16.31), even though he almost certainly regarded his exorcistic power as the inevitable outworking and expression of God's kingly rule (Matt. 12.28/Luke 11.20). Second, one of the most characteristic features of Jesus' healing ministry was *the emphasis he placed on the faith of the one requesting healing* (see particularly Mark 5.34, 36; 10.52; Matt. 8.10/Luke 7.9; Matt. 9.28f.; 15.28; Luke 7.50; 17.19). With such faith all things were possible (Mark 9.23f.; 11.23 pars.); without it he could do next to nothing (Mark 6.6). This sense of being able to exercise effective healing power marks out Jesus as a charismatic healer; but his sense that this power was dependent on the faith of the recipient and his unwillingness to value it for its publicity potential prevents us from calling him either enthusiast or magician.

(c) Jesus almost certainly regarded himself as a *prophet* (see particularly Mark 6.4 pars.; Luke 13.33; and below §45.3), and various instances of prophetic insight (see particularly Mark 2.8; 9.33–37; 10.21; 12.43f.; 14.18, 20; Luke 7.39ff. 19.5) and prophetic foresight (see particularly Mark 10.39; 13.2; 14.8, 25, 30) are attributed to him. Moreover his teaching possessed an otherly authority which was widely recognized and commented on (see particularly Mark 1.27; 6.2; 11.28; Matt. 8.9f./Luke 7.8f.), and which comes to clearest expression in the ' . . . but *I* say' words of Matt. 5, and in the use of 'Amen' to give weight to his words (34 times in the Synoptic tradition).[13] What was astonishing about this implicit claim to authority was that he thereby set himself critically over against the accepted authorities of Israel and Judaism past and present, even Moses himself (see above §16.2 and pp.97f.). His well-spring of authority was not the law, the fathers, the tradition or the rabbis, but his own certainty that he knew the will of God. Here is a teaching which can properly be called 'charismatic'. Here is a claimed authority which could well be called 'elitist' since only he seemed to possess it. But it was the teaching itself which provoked the surprise, not any overtly inspired delivery; and there is no evidence that Jesus valued ecstatic speech or experienced glossolalia. So even here it would be more appropriate to call Jesus *a charismatic rather than an enthusiast*.

In short, when we begin to come into touch with Jesus' own religious experience we find *several features which can justifiably be called charismatic* in that his ministry was characterized by a power and authority which was neither learned in any school nor bestowed by any human agency but which came to him and through him in direct and spontaneous manner. But since that power and authority was neither rooted in ecstasy, nor expressed in ecstatic speech, but depended rather on the response of those to whom he ministered, they cannot so readily be regarded as the manifestations of enthusiasm. In fact however, a discussion about charismatic and/or enthusiastic phenomena in the ministry of Jesus takes us only so far; they certainly do not bring us to the heart of Jesus' religious experience. For that we have to penetrate rather more deeply.

45.2 *Jesus' experience of God as Father*. We can be fairly confident that Jesus often resorted to prayer – not just the set prayers of synagogue worship or of Jewish piety – but times of prayer when he unburdened himself to God in his own words (cf. above p.126). The evidence here is not so strong as we might think, but strong enough (Mark 1.35; 6.46; 14.36; Matt. 11.25f./Luke 10.21; Luke 3.21; 5.16; 6.12; 9.18, 28f.; 11.1). We can even hope to answer the question, Why did he find it necessary to supplement the prayers of Jewish worship with such times alone with God? The answer seems to be, Because in those times of prayer he experienced God as Father in a very personal, intimate sense.

The justification for this claim rests almost entirely on one word – *abba*. Again the evidence is not so strong as we might wish, but again probably strong enough: Mark 14.36 – 'Abba, Father, all things are possible to you; take this cup from me; yet not what I want but what you want'. In the other prayers of Jesus recorded in the Gospels, the Aramaic *abba* presumably lies beneath the Greek *pater* (Matt. 6.9/Luke 11.2; Matt. 11.25f./Luke 10.21; Luke 23.34, 46; Matt. 26.42; 9 times in John). The conclusion that here we are in touch with Jesus' own prayer mannerism is strengthened by the fact that it appears in all five strata of the Gospel tradition (Mark, Q, Luke, Matthew, John), and that *abba* is used in every prayer that is attributed to Jesus except one (Mark 15.34) – but that exception only serves to strengthen the case, as we shall see in a moment.

The fact that Jesus used *abba* in addressing God enables us to say with some confidence that Jesus experienced God as Father in a very personal and intimate way. Why so? Because, as J. Jeremias has demonstrated with sufficient clarity,[14] *abba* was the language of family intimacy: it was a word with which children, including tiny children, addressed their fathers – a word therefore of courtesy and respect, but also of warm intimacy and trust. Moreover, so far as our evidence goes, it was hardly used by Jesus' contemporaries in their prayers if at all – presumably because it was too intimate, too lacking in reverence and awe before the exalted and holy One. Jewish prayers certainly spoke of God as Father, but in a much more formal mode of address – God as Father of the nation – and without the directness and simplicity of Jesus' prayers. How people pray when alone reflects their understanding of their relation to God and their experience of God. What Jesus experienced of God in his moments of solitude and prayer comes to its most characteristic expression in the word *abba*. It is not unjustified therefore to conclude from that one word that *Jesus experienced God as Father with an immediacy and an intimacy which could find expression only in that cry, 'Abba'*. And this is if anything confirmed by the one prayer of Jesus which does not begin with 'Abba' – Mark 15.34 – for that is Jesus' cry of dereliction on the cross; in the awful experience of abandonment by God he could not cry 'Abba'.

There still remain questions to be answered. But the conclusion seems firm enough. And given the conclusion it is hard to resist the corollary that *through this word abba we have touched one of the tap roots of Jesus' authority and power* – that through this sense of sonship to God, of

God as his Father, Jesus drew the convictions which in very large part governed his life and determined his mission.

45.3   *Jesus' experience of Spirit.* It belongs to the accepted bedrock of Jesus-tradition that Jesus had no little success as an exorcist (cf. above p.185). What is more to the point here is that also in the Jesus-tradition we have two or three sayings of Jesus where Jesus himself speaks about his exorcistic ministry, and where he indicates what he sees as the reason for its success. These sayings have been preserved in two separate but overlapping blocks of material in Mark and Q – Mark 3.22–29 (a group of three sayings) and Matt. 12.24–28, 30/Luke 11.15–23 (four sayings). Q's version of a fifth saying (a variation of Mark 3.28f.) very likely belonged to a different context in Q (Luke 12.10/Matt. 12.32). At all events, it can scarcely be doubted that this material derives ultimately from controversy over Jesus' ministry of exorcism, and few would deny that it contains at least a core of authentic Jesus-tradition.[14a]

The key sayings indicate beyond dispute that for Jesus the reason for his success was the Spirit or power of God: Matt. 12.28/Luke 11.20 – 'Since it is by the Spirit (Matthew)/finger (Luke) of God that I cast out demons, then has come upon you the kingdom of God'; the implication is the same in Mark 3.27, 28f. and their Q parallels. In the saying quoted the emphasis (in the Greek at least) falls on two phrases – 'Spirit of God' and 'the kingdom of God': it was through *the Spirit or power of God* that Jesus achieved his success, even though the Spirit was popularly thought to have been withdrawn from Israel (cf. Ps. 74.9; Zech. 13.2–6; I Macc. 9.27), and even though the rabbinic exorcists do not mention the Spirit of God in connection with exorcisms; and his success through this divine power was a sign that *the kingdom of God* was already present, that is the *eschatological* kingdom, that exercise of divine rule which would mark out the end-time. How could he make such bold and audacious claims? – not simply because he was a successful exorcist, for others among his contemporaries had at least some success in casting out demons (Matt. 12.27/Luke 11.19). How then? The answer probably lies in *his own* experience when he ministered to demoniacs. In such ministry he was conscious of spiritual power operating through him, of that power which God seemed to have withdrawn from Israel for many generations, of such power as he could ascribe only to the end-time rule of God – it was by that power that he cast out demons, and that power was the visible manifestation of God's eschatological reign. In short, these sayings imply *a clear sense on the part of Jesus of the eschatological distinctiveness of his power*, they indicate *how deeply rooted in his own experience were the claims he made regarding his ministry*, and they suggest something of his perception of his own role within that ministry.

Another group of important sayings in the Jesus-tradition are those which echo Isa. 61.1f. – Luke 4.18f.(?), Luke 6.20f./Matt. 5.3–6 and Matt. 11.5/Luke 7.22. These make it sufficiently clear (and it is not greatly disputed) that Jesus' understanding of his mission as a 'proclamation of good news to the poor' was drawn at least in large part from the Isaiah prophecy. The relevance of Isa. 61.1 is that there it is the anointing of the Spirit which provides the authority and source for that proclamation. The implication is then, particularly in Matt. 11.5/Luke 7.22, that Jesus understood his whole ministry, both its healings (not just its exorcisms) and its preaching, as the outworking of the Spirit of God upon him. The power which he sensed and whose effect he saw in exorcism and healing, the authority which he sensed and whose effect he saw in his hearers, these sprang from *Jesus' own consciousness or conviction that the eschatological Spirit of God had anointed him*, was making him aware of the will of God, was working through him.

Here again then it would appear that we have touched another tap root of Jesus' authority and power – and that in appreciating something of Jesus' sense of God as Father and his sense of the Spirit of God upon him we have gone at least some way towards entering empathetically into Jesus' own experience and understanding of his mission. We need venture no further, even if it were possible.

Two points should be made by way of summary. First, even the brief study possible to us here should have been sufficient to demonstrate *the importance of Jesus' own religious experience*: his experience of God as Father and of the Spirit's anointing was *the immediate source of those features of his ministry which made the greatest impact on his contemporaries*. Second, with Jesus' sense of sonship and of Spirit we have been able to penetrate to *a deeper level of religious experience than that which characterizes enthusiasm*. Where enthusiasm typically experiences God in the visible and tangible manifestations of ecstasy, vision, miracle and inspired utterance, Jesus' experience of God was at a profounder level, in a much more immediately personal relationship, in a more direct individual disclosure 'below the surface'.

§46. THE RELIGIOUS EXPERIENCE OF PAUL

We have now seen how strongly the stream of enthusiasm ran through earliest Christianity. We have also concluded that Jesus must be regarded as something other than an enthusiast, for all that his mission and message sprang directly from his own religious experience and even though he can properly be called a charismatic. But what of Paul, the most dominant figure of first generation Christianity – at least so far as our literary records go? How important was religious experience in Paul's practice of and reflection on Christianity? Was he also caught up in that strong stream of enthusiasm? Or did he turn his face totally against a Christian faith and conduct rooted in religious experience? Or does he stand somewhere in the middle – like Jesus himself? Part of the answer will already be evident from what was said above (pp. 177–180); now we must sketch it in more fully.

46.1   There can be little doubt that *Paul's whole conception and practice of Christianity sprang in a direct way from his own religious experience*. This observation can be substantiated without too much difficulty. It was the experience of seeing Jesus risen and exalted on the road to Damascus which stopped him dead in his tracks and turned his whole life into a new channel (I Cor. 9.1; 15.8; Gal. 1.13–16); for Paul this was not merely a flash of insight or intellectual conviction, but a personal encounter, the beginning of a personal relationship which became the dominating passion of his life (Phil. 3.7–10; cf. p.22 above). To put it another way, it was his own *experience of grace* which made 'grace' a central and distinctive feature of his gospel – grace as not merely a way of understanding God as generous and forgiving, but grace as the experience of that unmerited and free acceptance embracing him, transforming him, enriching him, commissioning him (e.g. Rom. 5.2, 17; 12.6; I Cor. 1.4f.; 15.10; II Cor. 9.14; 12.9; Gal. 2.9; Eph. 1.7f.; 3.7f.). Or again, Christianity was evidently characterized for Paul by his own experience of being enabled to offer a worship that was real, direct, from the heart (Rom. 2.28f.; Gal. 4.6; Phil. 3.3), of a love and joy even in the midst of suffering (Rom. 5.3–5; I Thess. 1.5f.), of liberty from a rule-book mentality of casuistry and fear (Rom. 8.2, 15; II Cor. 3.17), of immediacy of guidance in every day conduct (Rom. 7.6; II Cor. 3.3; Gal. 5.25). Such experience he could only attribute to the Spirit of God, and therein recognize that the new covenant had come into effect (the law written in the heart – II Cor. 3.3), the harvest of the end-time had begun (Rom. 8.23). It is such experience of the Spirit that he evidently regards as *quintessentially Christian* (Rom. 8.9, 14); it is to the first such experience or beginning of such experiences (and not baptism as such) that Paul refers his readers when he recalls them to the start of their lives as Christians (e.g. Rom. 5.5; I Cor. 12.13; II Cor. 1.21f.; Gal. 3.2–5; Eph. 1.13f.). In short, it is abundantly evident that Paul's own religious experience was as fundamental to his mission and message as was the religious experience of Jesus to his mission and message. But was Paul also an enthusiast?

46.2   *Paul, enthusiast or charismatic?* Paul can certainly be described as a charismatic. In point of fact we owe the word 'charisma' almost wholly to him. It occurs hardly at all before Paul's time. In the NT, outside the Pauline corpus, it occurs only in I Peter 4.10 (a letter which falls within the Pauline 'sphere of influence' anyway – see above p.116). And after the NT its characteristic Pauline sense is almost entirely lost.[15] In other words, it was Paul who took up this unimportant word and gave it a specifically and distinctively Christian connotation – *charisma* as the expression, embodiment of *charis* (grace). Charisma is, in Paul's definition, *the experience of grace coming to particular expression through an individual believer in some act or word usually for the benefit of others* (see also above pp.110f.). Now the point is that within these experiences of grace Paul includes experiences such as those which characterized earliest Christianity, or at least Luke's account of it. And it is quite clear that he himself enjoyed not a few such experiences in the course of his missionary activity.

(*a*) *Visions and revelations.* In II Cor. 12.1–4 Paul is obviously speaking of his own experience – though one which took place all of fourteen years earlier. Equally clearly it was an ecstatic experience, with out-of-the-body and mystical features not untypical of such experiences. II Corinthians 5.13 and 12.7 also imply that this was not an isolated instance for Paul.[16] Not so very far removed from such claims to ecstatic revelation were those made by the faction at Corinth to a higher wisdom and superior knowledge (see above p.179.). What we must note here is that Paul claims to have experienced a wisdom deeper than that of his disputants (I Cor. 2.6–13) and to share their knowledge (I Cor. 8.1, 4; II Cor. 11.6).

(*b*) *Miracles.* Paul was certainly of the opinion that he had worked miracles in the course of his mission (Rom. 15.19; II Cor. 12.12) and he takes it more or less for granted that his converts experienced miraculous powers whether at and since their conversion (Gal. 3.5) or specifically as charismata, within the community (I Cor. 12.9f., 28–30).

(c) *Inspired speech* too was a regular part of Paul's experience. He vividly recalled the impact of his evangelistic preaching in Thessalonica and Corinth and attributed its success to the direct inspiration and power of the Spirit (I Thess. 1.5; I Cor. 2.4f.; cf. Eph. 6.17). He understood prophecy as inspired utterance and valued it in part at least as a kind of supernatural mind-reading (I Cor. 14.24f.). To those who presumably wished to keep prophecy on a much tighter rein he urged, 'Do not quench the Spirit; do not despise prophecy' (I Thess. 5.19f.). And he valued glossolalia for its self-edification, even though it left the mind unfruitful (I Cor. 14.4, 14, 18f.).

So clearly *there were some enthusiastic features about Paul's own religious experience*. But that is by no means the whole story.

46.3　　Paul is also very much aware of *the dangers of enthusiasm*. As the importance of religious experience is more evident in Paul than in any other NT writer, so it is Paul who is most alert against a Christianity which puts too much stress on religious experience. This is most clearly to be seen in his attitude towards the enthusiasts whose presence in his churches we noticed briefly above (pp.179f.). Although he shared several of their emphases (e.g. the liberty of the Christian, the importance of prophecy) his primary concern in almost every instance seems to have been to warn against the excesses of enthusiasm, to confine the stream of enthusiasm strictly within its banks.

In particular *he stresses the need for his churches to treat the claims of religious experience critically, with discernment*, and employs several *criteria* by which the genuineness and value of charismata can be tested.

(a) One test is provided by *the kerygmatic and Jesus traditions* which he passed on to his converts when they formed themselves into a new church – the traditions, that is, which served as a sort of constitution for the Pauline churches (see above §§17.1–3). It is to these traditions that he turns again and again in I Corinthians to provide the basis for a ruling on matters of controversy involving the Corinthian enthusiasts (so particularly I Cor. 9.14; 11.23; 12.3; 15.3). So too in II Thessalonians the excesses of apocalyptic enthusiasm (see below pp.326f.) are countered by an appeal to the founding traditions (II Thess. 2.15–3.6). In Galatians it is the basic keynote of gospel liberty which provides a check against possible enthusiastic licence (Gal. 5.13–25) as it does against the greater threat of Judaizing nomism (2.3–5; 5.1–12). And Phil. 3.16f., 4.9 seem to be another recall to the fundamental character of the kerygmatic and Jesus traditions against a kind of enthusiastic perfectionism alluded to in 3.12–19 (see below p.280). This is not so straightforward a test as it might at first appear, since tradition for Paul was not something frozen and fixed but living, an original word which had to be interpreted afresh as circumstances changed; Paul never lets tradition become simply law (see above §19.3). Nevertheless, we can still say that for Paul, *only that experience was to be recognized as experience of the Spirit which accorded with the founding traditions.* The Spirit of Christ must accord with 'the law of Christ' (I Cor. 9.21; Gal. 6.2).

(*b*) Another test is provided by *love*. I Corinthians 13.1–13 is obviously directed against a kind of enthusiasm, where zeal for the more spectacular charismata, particularly prophecy, glossolalia and knowledge, had provoked jealousy, arrogance, irritability, and kindred sins. Love had been the loser, and love provides the test (13.4–7). No matter how outstanding the gifts exercised, if they produced a loveless character, Paul counts them of no value whatsoever. By the same criterion he turns his back on all elitism in I Cor. 2–3, 8; those who claim to be 'the spiritual ones' (see above p.179) but provoke only jealousy and strife and have no concern for others show thereby their unspirituality (3.1–4; 8.1). For Paul 'the spiritual ones' are all those who have received the Spirit and who walk by the Spirit, not giving way to self-conceit, unkind criticism or envy (Gal. 5.25–6.3). *The criterion of spirituality is not the degree of inspiration but love.*

(*c*) A third test is that of *community benefit*, denoted by the word *oikodomē* in Greek. Paul uses the verb and noun seven times in I Cor. 14 (vv.3–5, 12, 17, 26). This is the criterion which shows clearly for Paul the superiority of prophecy over glossolalia. Similarly it is noticeable that when he lists various charismata in I Cor. 12.8–10 it is not the experience of revelation as such which he counts as the charisma but the '*utterance* of wisdom' and the '*utterance* of knowledge' (so 14.6). For Paul charismatic experience is characterized less by ecstasy and profundity of insight (cf. II Cor. 12.2–4) and more by the intelligible word spoken through one believer which brings understanding and guidance to another (I Cor. 14.3–5, 16–19, 24f.). If the would-be 'spiritual ones' in Corinth evaluate his directions by this test they will surely recognize that he speaks from the Lord (14.37). *All charismata stand under this rubric – 'for the benefit of others' – and are to be judged thereby* (12.7). This is why acts of service, however *un*inspired they appear, may well have higher claim to be recognized as charismata than the most manifestly inspired utterance (Rom.

12.6–8). By this criterion Stephanas should be recognized as a man to be followed (I Cor. 16.15f.). What does not benefit others cannot be for the good of the church.

We should not underestimate the importance Paul attaches to spiritual discernment. Whenever he speaks explicitly about charismata he speaks also about rightly evaluating what is good and what is of benefit (see particularly Rom. 12.2; I Cor. 2.14–15; 12.10; 14.29). He who himself rejoiced so fully in the rich experiences of the Spirit (above §46.1) and for whom the body of Christ was essentially a charismatic community (above §§29, 34.3), was also the one to insist so emphatically on the need for checks and safeguards against the dangers of enthusiasm. One of his earliest exhortations on the theme remains as balanced a pronouncement as we could wish for: 'Do not stifle inspiration, and do not despise prophetic utterances, but bring them all to the test and then keep what is good in them and avoid the bad of whatever kind' (I Thess. 5.19–22, NEB).[17]

46.4   *Christ-mysticism. The most profound safeguard which Paul offers against enthusiasm is the touchstone of Christ – the character of his ministry as attested in the gospel.* The Spirit for Paul is essentially the Spirit of Christ (Rom. 8.9; Gal. 4.6; Phil. 1.19). The experience of the Spirit which is quintessentially Christian for Paul is the experience of the Spirit of the Son crying 'Abba! Father!' (Rom. 8.15f.; Gal. 4.6) – that is, reproducing that most intimate experience and relation which characterized Jesus' own life on earth (above §45.2), and bringing the believer a share in it ('fellow heirs with Christ' – Rom. 8.17; Gal. 4.7; see further below §50.4). Or again, the experience of the Spirit is the experience of being moulded by a life-giving power to take on more and more the character of Christ (I Cor. 15.45–49; II Cor. 3.18; 4.16–5.5). The grace in which believers rejoice and which manifests itself through them in grace's gifts (charismata) is essentially that grace most fully manifested in Christ – 'the grace of our Lord Jesus Christ' (Rom. 5.15; II Cor. 8.9; 13.14; Gal. 2.21; Eph. 1.6f.). The revelation which had transformed Paul's life most fundamentally, as it had the whole of salvation history, is the revelation of Christ (Rom. 16.25f.; II Cor. 4.4–6; Gal. 1.12, 16; Eph. 3.2–12; Col. 1.26f.). And so on. It is against this yardstick that all claims to Spirit, grace, revelation, etc. must in the end be measured. Religious experience for Paul is basically experience of union with Christ ('in Christ' – see above p.22).

Now the point is that experience of union with Christ is experience of life being moulded by Christ, taking its characteristic features from Christ, manifesting the same character as was manifested in the ministry of Christ. That is to say, union with Christ for Paul is *characterized* not by lofty peaks of spiritual excitement and ecstasy, experiences of vision, revelation, extraordinary power or high inspiration, but more typically by self-giving love, by the cross – union with Christ is nothing if it is not union with Christ in his death (**Rom.** 6.3–6; **Gal.** 2.19f.; 6.14; **Phil.** 3.10; **Col.** 2.11f.). Nowhere more emphatically than in the Corinthian correspondence does Paul emphasize that Jesus is the *crucified* (**I Cor.** 1.23; 2.2; **II Cor.** 13.4); the wisdom of God, though it appeals neither to intellectual sophistication nor to spiritual enthusiasm, is Christ crucified, the event of the cross, and the gospel of the cross (**I Cor.** 1.17–25, 30; 2.6–8).

Thus we come to understand that *for Paul the distinctive characteristic of the religious experience of the disciple of Christ is experience of sharing in Christ's sufferings as well as of sharing in his life* (**Rom.** 8.17; **II Cor.** 1.5; 4.10; **Phil.** 3.10f.; **Col.** 1.24) Against the enthusiasts of II Corinthians Paul insists that the experience of the Spirit is not of power alone, nor of power that transcends and leaves weakness behind, but of *power in weakness* (**II Cor.** 4.7; 12.9f.; 13.3f.). To put it another way, religious experience for Paul is characterized by *eschatological tension*, by tension between the new life which he shares as being 'in Christ' and the old life which is his 'in the flesh' (**II Cor.** 10.3f.; **Gal.** 2.20; **Eph.** 4.20–24; **Phil.** 1.21–24; **Col.** 3.9f.), by warfare between Spirit and flesh (**Rom.** 7.14–23; **Gal.** 5.16f.), by the frustration of having to live out the life of the Spirit through the 'body of death' (**Rom.** 7.24f.; 8.10f., 22f.; **II Cor.** 4.16–5.5).[18] No religious experience however profound or spiritual or inspired or glorious sets believers free from the limitations of their present existence. On the contrary it is precisely that experience which most clearly manifests the paradox of power in weakness, of life through death, of greatness as serving, which is to be recognized as typically Christian.

In short, *Paul is a charismatic* who regards the experience of grace (*charis*) as fundamental to Christian living and the experience of *charisma* as fundamental to Christian community, but *who sets his face against enthusiasm* by insisting that all charismata must be tested and that only that charisma which manifests the grace (*charis*) of Christ is to be welcomed.

§47. DIVERGENT PATHS

47.1   Second generation Christianity is marked by a divergence of paths so far as the importance of religious experience and attitudes to enthusiasm are concerned. The majority seem to be striving for something like the Pauline balance – though their treatment is for the most part either too brief or (for us) too allusive to provide more than a few pointers. Mark, as we have noted before (above p.71), following in Paul's train, achieves his balance by wedding the traditions of Jesus' miracle working to his suffering Son of Man christology. I Peter, like Paul, seems to be insisting that 'the Spirit of glory (and of power)' is most surely present (not in mighty works and ecstatic speech but) when the believer is suffering for the name of Christ, that is, 'sharing Christ's sufferings' (I Peter 4.13f.). Jude too pursues a line similar to Paul's in Jude 19f. – warning against an elitist spirituality, but calling for prayer 'in the Holy Spirit' (cf. I Cor. 14.15–17; Eph. 6.18). Hebrews in its turn harks back to the miracles and gifts of the Spirit of the early mission as attesting God's approval (Heb. 2.3f.), but hastens to remind those who presume too boldly on their experience of the Spirit that they are still far short of 'the promised land' and by their presumption may well fail to attain it (3.7–4.13; 6.4–8; 10.26–31; cf. e.g. Rom. 8.13; I Cor. 10.1–12). Finally, in Revelation, where the Spirit is most clearly experienced in visions and ecstasy (Rev. 1.10; 4.2; 17.3; 21.10), we find the same insistence – that the Spirit is the Spirit of Jesus (3.1; 5.6), so that his (inspired) words are the words of Jesus (2–3), and so that prophecy must accord with 'the testimony of Jesus' (19.10; contrast 2.20).

Matthew also strives for a balance but from a different angle and in different terms. Coming from his confrontation with Pharisaic Judaism (see below §55.2) he certainly encourages a miracle-expecting faith (particularly Matt. 17.20), but he also insists that the desired expression of righteousness is the law interpreted through love (contrast Gal. 5.18, but cf. 5.22f.) rather than charismatic ministry (cf. particularly Matt. 22.34–40 with 7.15–23; and cf. I Cor. 13). In contrast Luke in his account of Christian beginnings is much less inhibited and less circumspect in his admiration for enthusiasm than any of the above (see above §44.3).

Heading in a very different direction are the Pastorals, while the Johannine writings attempt to plot still another path through the middle ground. If we follow these last two a little way we will have done enough to gain a sufficiently clear perspective on the unity and diversity of the NT on the subject of religious experience.

47.2   The striking feature about the *Pastorals* at this point is that although they bear the name of Paul they contain only a few echoes of the powerful and characteristic expressions of Pauline thought which we examined briefly above (§46). Two of the clearest echoes reverberate in II Tim. 2.11 and Titus 3.4/5–7; but these are 'faithful sayings', that is, sayings which did not originate with the writer but were passed on to him from the past. II Tim. 1.7 and 8 also echo the thought of the earlier Paul, though they use language which is not characteristic of the earlier Paul. Beyond these the echoes grow faint indeed. Here in other words there is reflected *little or nothing of that vigorous religious experience which shone so clearly through so very much that Paul wrote*. Instead, as we have seen, all seems to be subordinated to the primary task of preserving the traditions of the past (§17.4); and, whereas in Paul ministry grew to such a large extent from the vitality of religious experience and from the spontaneous interplay of charismata, in the Pastorals ministry has already become much more institutionalized with charisma subordinated to office (see above §30.1 and below §72.1).

Why this should be so is not entirely clear. Perhaps the enthusiast faction became the dominant influence in some of the Pauline churches after his death, and others within the Pauline tradition drew the conclusion that the position Paul had attempted to maintain was inherently unstable, not a viable long term solution to the threat of enthusiasm. Perhaps the Pastorals, like I Clement, were written to counter the threat to good order and established tradition from a group of younger enthusiasts, who rather like Luke, hankered after the clear cut supernatural powers of the early days. We cannot tell. At all events, whatever the precise circumstances which occasioned the writing of the Pastorals, this much seems clear: the Pastorals are a classic example of the transformation which afflicts so many movements of religious awakening in the second generation. That is to say, whereas in the first generation the vitality of fresh experience breaks through older forms and formulae to express itself in new ways, in the second generation these new ways (or some of them) become regarded as the pattern and norm, become in other words a new dogma and set form to which religious experience must be subordinated and to which the expression of religious experience must conform.[18a]

In short, *the author of the Pastorals can properly be regarded as the first churchman to deal with enthusiasm by rejecting it totally and shutting it out wholly from the life of the Church.* But in so doing he stood in grave danger of discounting the religious experience of his own generation or at least of failing to give it a creative role in the life of the church.

And that means he stood in danger of shutting out the Spirit, or at least of shutting the Spirit up in the past.

47.3   In contrast to the Pastorals, *the Johannine writings* (Gospel and letters) demonstrate that elsewhere in the closing decades of the first century there was a very positive attitude towards religious experience. The vitality of the religious experience of the Johannine community is clearly reflected in words like 'life', 'loving', 'knowing', 'believing', 'seeing', all of which appear regularly in both the Gospel and the letters, and by such passages as John 3.5–8, 4.10–14, 6.63, 7.37–39, 14.17, I John 2.20, 27, 3.24, 4.13 and 5.6–10. The Johannine theological evaluation of this religious experience is similar to Paul's at two points, but also different from Paul's at two other points.

Like Paul, the Johannine circle marks out the parameters of religious experience (*a*) by defining the Spirit in terms of Christ, and (*b*) by correlating the experience of revelation with the Jesus-tradition. (*a*) In the 'farewell discourses' of John 14–16 the Spirit is characterized as the '*other* Paraclete' or Counsellor (14.16), with Jesus clearly understood as the *first* Paraclete (cf. I John 2.1); and the clear implication of John 14.15–26 is that the coming of the Spirit fulfils the promise of Jesus to come again and dwell in his disciples (cf. 7.38f.; 15.26; 19.30; 20.22). In other words, the Johannine community had no sense of being historically distant from Jesus or of having to live out of the experience of earlier generations as mediated now only through sacrament or office. On the contrary, *each generation is as close to Jesus as the first, and religious experience retains its vitality and immediacy because the Spirit is the presence of Jesus.*

(*b*) As we have already seen (above §19.3) the Johannine writings achieve *a balance between present inspiration by the Spirit and the tradition of the past* (kerygmatic and Jesus traditions) similar to that in Paul – the new truth of revelation being set in correlation with the original truth of Jesus, 'the anointing (which) teaches you about everything' being set in correlation with 'that which you heard from the beginning' (John 14.26; 16.14–15; I John 2.24, 27). Clearly there is a concern here lest tradition become petrified, stifling the creative reinterpretation of a vital religious experience – the danger already apparent in the Pastorals; at the same time there is equal concern lest new revelation be thought wholly to supersede and make irrelevant the revelation of the past – the danger inherent in enthusiasm.

On the other hand, (*c*) the Johannine evaluation of religious experience is *different* from Paul's in that John sees little or no need to emphasize the corporate dimension of worship: John's individualism (see above §31.1) gives too little place to the mutual interdependence of charismatic community, and so also too little place to the spiritual discernment of religious experience which Paul counted an indispensable part of the charismatic community (§46.3; but note 1 John 4.1–3). (*d*) Different again from Paul *is the almost total absence in the Johannine writings of the eschatological tension* so fundamental to Paul (see above pp. 23, 195). In the Johannine writings there is no suggestion that flesh and death continue to threaten the believer and might finally triumph. He is born of the Spirit and under the Spirit's power (John 3.6; cf. 6.63); he is of God and no longer of the world (John 15.18f.; I John 4.5f.); he has passed from death to life (John 5.24). In other words the tension is resolved, the eschatology 'realized', the crisis of judgment a thing of the past for the believer (3.18f.; see above pp. 28f.). Consequently a kind of perfectionism emerges (most clearly expressed in I John 3.6–9; 5.18) which is apparently closer to the enthusiasm of Paul's opponents (particularly I Cor. 4.8) than to the circumspection of Paul (e.g. Rom. 8.13; I Cor. 9.27; Phil. 3.12–14). Yet John is no enthusiast: he is not a protagonist of tangible spirituality. And he is no elitist either: his 'realized' eschatology embraces all who are 'born of God' (I John 2.20 – 'you *all* know' – probably directed against a form of early Gnosticism). His is more the spirituality of pietism, whose clearest parallel in Christian history is probably the nineteenth-century Holiness Movement – non-ecclesiastical (see above pp. 118f., 122), emphasizing the spiritual experience of the individual, and perfectionist in tendency.

§48. CONCLUSIONS

48.1   It should now be clear enough that *religious experience was a factor of fundamental importance in the beginnings of Christianity* – that many of the distinctive features of first-century Christianity grew out of and were shaped by the religious experience of the leading participants – Jesus' experience of sonship and of Spirit, the first Christians' various enthusiastic experiences, Paul's experience of the risen Jesus, of accepting grace, of charismatic Spirit, John's experience of life-giving Paraclete. It should be clear too how important a factor was the religious experience of the first Christians in drawing them together into *unity* and *community*. It is probably no accident that the word *koinōnia* (participation, fellowship) first occurs immediately after Luke's account of Pentecost (Acts 2.42); and certainly in Acts it is the experience of the Spirit which brings the individual disciples into real participation in the new community (Acts 2.38f.; 8.14–17; 10.44–48; 11.15–17; 19.1–6). The fundamental importance of the shared experience of the Spirit in bringing about Christian community is even clearer in Paul (see particularly I Cor. 12.13; II Cor. 13.14; Phil. 2.1; Eph. 4.3). And in the Johannine writings we need recall only that one of the tests of life within the brotherhood was the experience of the Spirit (I John 3.24; 4.13).[18b]

48.2 *The diversity of religious experience and of attitudes to religious experience within first-century Christianity* has also become obvious – from the enthusiasm of the earliest Palestinian communities and of Luke's presentation of Christianity's early history, to the much more austere and formalized attitude of the Pastorals. Somewhere in between come Jesus and most of the other NT writings (and writers), in particular Paul and John, for all of whom experience of the Spirit is fundamental, but who all fight shy of enthusiasm. But here too there is diversity: Paul can give significance to religious experience only in the context of the Christian community, the body of Christ, while John's is primarily the religious experience of individualist pietism; Paul understands religious experience as a tension and warfare between Spirit and flesh, life and death, while John thinks the battle of faith is already won and the believer's experience is of Spirit and of life. As for Jesus, he and Paul can both properly be called charismatics so far as religious experience is concerned, and Jesus' experience certainly knew something of the same eschatological tension as Paul's: he announced the kingdom's presence, as evidenced by his exorcisms in the power of the Spirit; but he proclaimed also the imminent coming of the kingdom, since, presumably, if the eschatological Spirit was already active, the eschaton itself could not long be delayed (above §§3.1, 2). On the other hand, there are not the same community dimensions in Jesus' experience which Paul counted so important – there was an aloneness and uniqueness in Jesus' experience, which we saw particularly in his understanding of his exorcisms (only in *his* own exorcisms does he recognize the eschatological Spirit's power and the kingdom's presence), and which we shall have to investigate more fully in chapter X (§50).

48.3 When we inquire within this diversity for *the distinctive features of the religious experience which marked it out as Christian* the answer comes in varying forms, but all emphasizing that there must be some *correlation between present experience and past tradition, between the exalted Christ experienced now through the Spirit and the earthly Jesus of the kerygmatic and church traditions.* It is precisely the threat of enthusiasm that it cuts off the Jesus who is experienced now in glory from the Jesus of history, that it holds to a 'theology of glory or triumphalism' without reference to the historical reality of Jesus of Nazareth. Paul and John counter the threat by refusing to let the two fall apart: only that charisma is to be welcomed which is consistent with the founding traditions, only that Spirit is to be followed who is recognizably the Spirit of Christ, the other Paraclete is precisely he who proclaims the same truth as the incarnate Logos (cf. I Peter 4.13f.; Rev. 19.10). The Pastorals tend to meet the danger by sacrificing present experience to past tradition – a policy of safety first. Luke on the other hand is uncritical of enthusiasm, but he is no elitist, and he does write two volumes, the Gospel as well as the Acts, so that the imbalance of the latter can be corrected to some extent by the Jesus of the former; that is to say, even with Luke the Gospel about Jesus provides something of a check to his portrayal of the enthusiasm of the earliest church. In short, the answer to the important question, 'Does the New Testament kerygma count the historical Jesus among the criteria of its own validity?'[19] is Yes!: the central NT theologians *do* count the character of Jesus' life and ministry (available to them in the traditions about Jesus) as one of the chief criteria for evaluating their self-understanding, religious experience and conduct as believers in Christ.[20] Whether we can relate the actual religious experience of Jesus more closely to the religious experience of first-century Christianity is a question we take up in the next chapter.

48.4   Our introductory paragraph (§43) in effect posed the question, *Can Christianity preserve a creative role for religious experience in its continuing life and worship without giving way to enthusiasm?* Three answers (at least) came through very loudly from the closing decades of the first century. The verdict of the Pastorals, as indeed of the dominant voice of orthodoxy through most of Christianity's history has been in effect No! – the spontaneity of the Spirit must be firmly subordinated to the authority of office and tradition – yet all too often at the cost of forcing vital Christian experience to find expression outside the main Christian traditions, that is *forcing it into enthusiasm* because it lacks the checks which tradition would afford! The Lukan presentation of earliest Christianity gives the opposite answer: its portrayal of enthusiasm in the raw certainly excites, but it leaves too many questions unanswered which need to be answered if enthusiasm is not to get out of hand. The Johannine alternative also answers in the affirmative – an alternative to which those who seek to live creatively out of their religious experience without abandoning their traditions have often been forced – that of personal mysticism or individual pietism; yet it provides too narrow a basis for full Christian community. Perhaps then we have to go back behind the second generation and listen to the dominant voice which still reaches us from the first generation – that of Paul. His balance in religious experience between the already and not yet, between present revelation and past tradition, between individual and community, may have been too difficult for the first generation to hold, but it is probably such an answer that our questions demand, such a balance that each new generation must seek to hold for itself.

In short, once again we have seen something of the scope of first-century diversity and once again the central unifying factor is to be found in the holding together of the exalted Christ (experienced through the Spirit) and the earthly Jesus (through the Jesus-tradition).

X

CHRIST AND CHRISTOLOGY

§49. INTRODUCTION

Thus far we have investigated eight important areas of first-century Christian faith and life; we have sketched out something of the diversity within each area; and we have inquired whether within that diversity there is some focus or strand of unity. In each case *the unifying factor* which has emerged, though not always with the same clarity, has been *Christ* – in particular, *the unity between the exalted Christ and Jesus of Nazareth*, the crucified who is also the risen one. At the heart of the diverse kerygmata of the early Christians we found the proclamation of the resurrection and exaltation of Jesus, of the earthly Jesus as the contemporary Christ of faith. Common to the various confessions of faith was the conviction that Jesus, that is Jesus of Nazareth, is now Messiah, Son of God, Lord. In so far as tradition had a role in shaping the faith of the early congregations, the basic traditions concerned were the traditions about Jesus, his words, deeds and passion, and the kerygmatic traditions interpreting his passion and proclaiming his resurrection. The Jewish scriptures were fundamental to the self-understanding of every first-century Christian church, but the focus of revelatory significance lay in the whole 'event of Christ'; in the last analysis, it was only as interpreted in relation to and in the light of 'the revelation of Christ' that the OT provided 'the substructure of NT theology'. Less clear was the element providing a unifying bond to the diverse concepts of ministry; but even here too it was possible to trace out a common conviction that Jesus should still be recognized as head of the community and that the character of his own ministry should still provide the pattern for all ministry. Likewise early Christian worship was characterized by and centred on the recognition of what Jesus had done, that by his life, death and resurrection a new relationship with God had become a reality and that only by his continuing life was the church's worship possible and effective. More clear was the christological unity expressed in the sacraments – unity between the Jesus who died, in which death they somehow shared, and the Lord alive from the dead, in whose life they somehow shared. Clear too was the christological unity expressed in early Christian understanding of the Spirit and of their religious experience, since it was precisely the character of Jesus as embodied in the Jesus-tradition which they found reflected in their own experience (the Spirit of Jesus) and which became in greater or less degree the norm for evaluating their experience.

Christ is the focus of unity in first-century Christianity – the Christ who was and now is, the Christ of the Jesus-tradition and the Christ of faith, worship and experience, one and the same. The conclusion is hardly surprising, since after all it is *Christ*ianity that we are investigating. But that is not the end of the matter. For with this conclusion we have not by any means resolved the problems of unity and diversity in earliest Christianity; what we have done is simply to uncover the *central* problem. The problem has two main facets. On the one hand, traditional Christianity wants to say much more about Christ than merely to affirm the unity and continuity between the earthly Jesus and the exalted Christ: it wants to affirm his role as the unique revelation of God, his being as divine, the second person of the Trinity, the God-man. A striking expression of this is the simple statement adopted initially by the World Council of Churches: for the participating churches the minimal Christian confession meant accepting 'our Lord Jesus Christ as *God* and Saviour'.

On the other hand, the advance in NT studies over the past two centuries has made it increasingly difficult to affirm even the modest conclusion reached above, let alone the more weighty claims of Christ's deity. And it is precisely the unity and continuity between the earthly Jesus and exalted Christ which has become so problematical. (1) There seems to be more *dis*continuity between the proclamation of Jesus and the faith of the early churches than continuity – 'Jesus proclaimed the kingdom, the first Christians proclaimed Jesus' (above p.31). Among those NT scholars who have thought they could reach back to the historical Jesus the dominant conclusion seems to be that Jesus did not count himself as part of the good news he preached. (2) There is such a diversity in the NT authors' talk of Christ that it is by no means clear what the continuity is that is being affirmed. In other words, we need to look more carefully at the conclusion, 'Christ is the focus of unity', since it is not clear what can be affirmed about the historical Jesus, it is not clear what the first Christians were affirming about the Christ of faith, and it is not clear whether traditional christology has firm roots in earliest Christianity. These are the questions with which we must now grapple: How are we to correlate the centrality of Christ in the faith and life of the earliest churches with what we know of Jesus' own message and self-understanding? How are we to correlate with each other the diverse assertions made by the first Christians about Christ? And how are we to correlate the NT's different assertions about Christ with the christological claims of traditional Christianity? In short, *does the christology of first-century Christianity provide a stable unifying centre within the diverse expressions and forms of first-century Christianity?*

Before proceeding we should perhaps just repeat the warning given at the beginning of chapter III – that in trying to reach back to the beginnings of christological thought in the first century we must not read back the later conclusions of the classic christological debates; we must not *assume* that everywhere we will find a latent orthodoxy waiting to be brought to light; otherwise we cannot handle the NT material without prejudice. He who enters the period of Christian beginnings with the classic formulations of Christian orthodoxy ringing in his ears is hardly in a position to catch the authentic tones of first-century Christian thought (should they be different). We must rather put ourselves as best we can in the position of first-century Jews, with their strong tradition of monotheism, and try to hear with their ears the claims of Jesus and of the first Christians.

§50. THE CONTINUITY BETWEEN THE HISTORICAL JESUS AND THE KERYGMATIC CHRIST

What role did Jesus have in his own message? Did Jesus proclaim a christology? It is one thing to assert that the exalted Christ was presented as one and the same as the earthly Jesus. It is another to assert that the earthly Jesus *himself* saw his role as one and the same as that attributed to the exalted Christ. Can we indeed speak of the continuity between the historical Jesus and the kerygmatic Christ and claim that the links bonding the two together are as strong on the side of the historical Jesus as they are on the other?

50.1   The reality and seriousness of the problem is underlined by *the inadequacy of so many of the answers which have been given in previous generations.* For traditional christology the Christian gospel was of God become man in order that man through the work of the God-man, or better God-in-man, might be enabled to participate again in the divine life. For traditional dogmaticians our problem was no problem at all: as God, the God-in-man knew himself to be God and knew what his work would accomplish. In so far as they attempted to base this judgment exegetically the Gospel of John provided sufficient proof texts for the purpose. And when in the nineteenth century the issue was posed in terms of Jesus' self-consciousness, the Fourth Gospel again provided the exegetical foundation. This was certainly true of what is perhaps the classic restatement of the traditional position in H. P. Liddon's 1866 Bampton Lectures, *The Divinity of our Lord and Saviour Jesus Christ* (Lecture IV – 'Our Lord's Divinity as witnessed by his consciousness – St John 10.33' – with its uncompromising assertion, 'The "Christ of history" none other than the "Christ of dogma"'). But it was also true of Schleiermacher's very different presentation of Jesus' divine sonship in his *Life of Jesus*,[1] which nevertheless rested equally on the assumption that the consciousness of Jesus is truly reflected in the Fourth Gospel. However, with the increasing recognition of the theological character of the Fourth Gospel's presentation of Jesus (in the second half of the nineteenth century), it became less and less possible for would-be Life of Jesus historians to use the Johannine discourses as the expression of the historical Jesus' self-consciousness: at best they were Johannine meditations on the significance of Jesus in the light of Easter faith using some authentic Jesus-tradition as starting point; at worst they were the total creation of the author's faith with no anchor point in history. Either way the crucial passages like John 8.58 and 10.30 had to be accounted to the side of John's theology and not to the side of the historical Jesus (see above pp.27, 75f.).

In the hundred years since then NT researchers have been confronted with three alternatives in the main.

(*a*) The most popular alternative in the latter decades of the nineteenth century was to let the Jesus of history and the Christ of dogma/faith fall apart and to abandon the latter for the former. Many Liberal Protestant scholars despaired of rooting the kerygma of early Christianity in Jesus' own ministry and settled for the gospel *of* Jesus – a gospel where Jesus himself played no role such as was ascribed to him by post-Easter faith, a gospel where the self-consciousness of Jesus was much less exalted than that represented in the Fourth Gospel. In other words, they settled for a gospel where Jesus was simply the first to proclaim and live by the ideals which the nineteenth century had (at last) recognized to be of enduring value. They settled for a christology where Jesus was *the great exemplar*, in effect, the first Christian.[2] This alternative is still favoured by some who want to present Jesus merely as the prototype revolutionary, the exemplary man for others, the model for secular man, and so on.

(*b*) The second alternative is to attempt to blur again the distinction between the gospel of Jesus and the kerygma of Paul. One way to do this is to claim that *the kerygmatic Christ is the only one with whom we have to deal*, and that it is neither necessary nor possible to get behind the kerygmatic Christ to a historical Jesus. This in substance was the thesis argued by Martin Kähler at the end of the nineteenth century,[3] and his thesis had considerable influence on the whole biblical theology movement which dominated the first half of the twentieth century. In effect it was an attempt to reinstate traditional christology on a sounder theological and exegetical footing. The other not independent but rather different way is so to reinterpret the kerygma(ta) of the early church(es) that the centrality of Christ in it (them) is *demythologized*. That is to say, the role given to Christ becomes a history- and culture-conditioned expression of some other message – for example, the possibility of authentic existence – a message which is also found to be the (demythologized) message of the historical Jesus. In other words, the kerygma of Christianity becomes a kind of all purpose message whose proclamation of Jesus and/or by Jesus is in the last analysis an accident of history. For all his protests, Bultmann's christology is in constant danger of succumbing to this kind of reductionism.[4]

(*c*) The third alternative is to attempt to uncover or trace out some link or links between the message of Jesus and the kerygma about Christ. It believes that enough of the message of the historical Jesus can be recovered by us today to give us its characteristic notes and emphases, and it endeavours to discover whether any of these are sufficient to explain some or part of the characteristic christological emphases of the early kerygmata. This investigation has been a dominant concern of Gospel research over the past 30 years or so. It has concentrated for the most part on two aspects of Jesus' message – its forward looking emphasis and its realized eschatological element – both of which can be interpreted as containing an implicit claim to christological or eschatological significance, a claim which provides at least some correlation between the Christ-centred kerygma of early Christianity and the proclamation of Jesus himself.

On the one hand, some have recognized in Jesus' proclamation of the *coming* kingdom a claim that the coming kingdom was in some way *dependent on his proclamation* or would constitute a *vindication* of his mission – whether because he saw himself as the Elijah of the end-time, the forerunner of the divine intervention,[5] or because he believed that the Son of Man (a heavenly figure other than himself) would judge men by reference to his mission and message (particularly Luke 12.8f.; Mark 8.38),[6] or because in more general terms his whole work aimed at and remained open to the eschatological verification of his present claims, a hope in which he went to his death and which found answer in his resurrection.[7] This last in particular offers the possibility of a very direct and substantial continuity between Jesus' proclamation of the kingdom and the post-Easter proclamation of the risen Christ, and we shall have to examine it more closely below.

On the other hand some have argued that Jesus' proclamation of the kingdom's *presence* involved *an implicit christological claim*, for in proclaiming that the eschatological 'shift in the ages' was already taking place he was claiming in effect that it was taking place precisely in and through his own ministry, or that his ministry, even he himself, was the sign of what was already in train.[8] An important variation of this view is that of W. Marxsen who also wants to diminish the christological break between the pre-Easter proclamation by Jesus and the post-Easter proclamation about Jesus: the break between proclaimer and proclaimed does not lie in Easter – it comes 'at the point where a believer proclaims Jesus' words and deeds'; continuity between the message of Jesus and the kerygma of the first Christians lies in the fact that already before Easter some had been brought to faith by Jesus and proclaimed *Jesus'* words and deeds, and were thus proclaiming Jesus.[9] In other words, the link between Jesus the proclaimer and Jesus the proclaimed, is *Jesus proclaimed as the proclaimer*. The same basic point can be put in more general terms: Jesus so proclaimed God that his hearers knew Jesus himself to be the one through whom God comes to expression.[10]

In effect winding up the 'new quest' L. E. Keck attempted to synthesize these two approaches (of Ebeling and Pannenberg – nn. 7 and 10): 'To trust Jesus is to appropriate him as the index of God'; 'Whom God vindicates discloses the character of God'.[11]

Of the three alternatives outlined above the first two have in effect given up any hope of rooting the kerygma of Christianity in the historical Jesus: one opts for a historical Jesus who in the end of the day has a much lesser significance than that characteristically ascribed to him by Christianity; the other opts for a kerygmatic Christ who in his central significance has no discernible connection with the historical Jesus. But has first-century christology lost touch with the historical reality so completely? If it has, then Christianity is something other than it has always claimed to be. If it has, then the one unifying element which we have found to hold together the diversities of first-century Christianity will have shattered in our hands, leaving Christianity as a whole without a unifying centre. Only the third alternative offers the possibility of a more positive answer – of a continuity between the message of Jesus and the kerygmata of earliest Christianity which provides an anchor point for the early churches' claims about Christ in the history of the man Jesus of Nazareth, of a unity between kerygmatic Christ and historical Jesus which alone can hold the diverse forms of Christianity together as one. The claims made under the third alternative are relatively modest, but only if such building blocks provide a solid foundation can there be any hope of building something more upon them.

50.2   *Can we then speak meaningfully of a continuity and unity between the kerygmatic Christ and the historical Jesus?* Our own study of the early Christian kerygmata posed the problem for us in chapter II. It was posed afresh in chapter IV by our recognition that the 'Jesus-tradition is cited by Paul only in matters ethical and with reference to the Lord's Supper, whereas the kerygmatic tradition as such uses only the tradition of Jesus' death and resurrection' (p. 78); that is to say, *the kerygma was not intended (simply) to reproduce the teaching of Jesus*, and the problem of relating Jesus' proclamation to the message of cross and resurrection remains unresolved. Our study of the sacraments in first-century Christianity illustrated the issue from another angle: for while there was some continuity between the table-fellowship practised by Jesus and the common meals of the earliest Christian communities in Palestine, the more both baptism and Lord's Supper came to be seen as distinct ritual acts representing the death of Christ the less they had in common with the actual disciple-ship to which Jesus called men and women during his ministry.

At the same time in chapter III we discovered a marked degree of continuity between, on the one hand, Jesus' own distinctive self-understanding (particularly *bar 'enāšā* and *abba*) and the recognition accorded to him (hailed as Messiah, authority as teacher), and, on the other, the explicit language of (confessional) faith which developed after Easter (Son of Man, Son of God, Messiah, Lord). And in chapter IX we noted some features of Jesus' own experience which closely paralleled those of early Christian experience and which therefore also suggest themselves as worthy of further investigation. In the light of the variations of the third alternative outlined above (§50.1) therefore it would appear that some lines of continuity can be exposed further to view, some building blocks picked out as offering a historical foundation for christological theologizing. There are three in particular which seem to offer the best prospect.

50.3 *Jesus' expectation of vindication.* It is very probable that Jesus foresaw the suffering that would be his lot and that his ministry would be brought to a violent end in death. Even apart from the more disputed passion sayings (Mark 8.31; 9.31; 10.33f.; also 2.20), there are clear indications of this in Mark 10.38f., 14.8, 22–24, 27, 35f. Following as he did consciously in the prophetic tradition (see above pp.185f. and §45.3) he almost certainly regarded martyrdom in Jerusalem as part of his prophetic role (Mark 12.1–9 pars.; Matt. 23.29–36/Luke 11.47–51; Luke 13.33; Matt. 23.37/Luke 13.34). And he must have known that his action in 'cleansing the temple' was a challenge to and condemnation of the religious establishment which they could hardly ignore and which in the event seems to have been the spur which goaded the authorities into using the ultimate sanction to silence him.[12]

If then Jesus anticipated a violent death, at least some time before his last journey to Jerusalem, *it is scarcely conceivable that he failed to tie this into his belief in the presence of the kingdom and its imminent consummation* (see above §§3.1,2). A theological rationalization of Jesus' death is not necessarily a *post-eventum* construction. As A. Schweitzer pointed out to W. Wrede, the fact that Jesus' resolve to suffer and die in Mark is a dogmatic formulation does not mean that it is unhistorical; on the contrary, *the dogma may be Jesus' own*, grounded in his own eschatological conceptions.[13] In such a case he could scarcely have thought of his death as a calamity, as marking the failure and nullification of his mission (otherwise he would not have gone up to Jerusalem); on the contrary, *he must have looked beyond his death to some sort of vindication*, God's ratification of what he had said and done.

This inherently plausible conclusion is supported by several exegetical considerations. (1) Jesus probably thought his death would fulfil the Baptist's expectation that the end-time would be introduced by a fiery baptism (Luke 12.49f. – see above pp.153, 154, and below pp.319f.); that is, his suffering and death would be the beginning of *the messianic woes* which would anticipate and therefore precipitate the establishment of the messianic kingdom (hence the vow of abstinence in Mark 14.25 and the shuddering horror of Mark

14.33–36). (2) In so far as Jesus did use a *bar⁺nāš* form of expression both in self-reference and with allusion to Dan. 7.13 (see above p. 40), then it becomes immediately relevant to recall that the man-like figure of Dan. 7 appears as 'the representative of God's chosen people, destined through suffering to be exalted'. (3) It is not at all implausible that Jesus could have been influenced here by a firm belief in the vindication of the suffering righteous man (see especially Wisd. 2–5),[14] or even by the martyr theology already current to the effect that a martyr's death both has vicarious value for Israel's salvation and ends in the vindication of resurrection (II Macc. 7.14, 23, 37f.). Indeed a direct influence of Isa. 53 on Jesus is not at all out of the question – the possibility being strengthened by the direct quotation of Isa. 53.12 in Luke 22.37, although the verse may very well have been added to what certainly appears to be authentic (and enigmatic) Jesus-tradition.[15] The point is of course that Isa. 53 includes the thought both of vicarious suffering, and, more prominently, of the vindication of the sufferer. (4) It is even possible that Jesus expressed his hope of vindication in terms of *resurrection* (cf. II Macc. 7.11, 23; 14.46) – that is, the general resurrection when the kingdom would come in its fullness, beginning the final judgment and the messianic age. Such a hope is certainly implied in Mark 10.37–40, 12.25, 14.25, Matt. 19.28/Luke 22.28–30. To correlate such an expectation with the idea of the Son of Man coming in glory is a difficult problem but not insuperable.

In short, there are not insubstantial grounds for the conclusion that Jesus looked on his approaching death as a vicarious suffering which would issue in divine vindication. This means that his message about the imminent kingdom embodied *a claim about himself* which remained open and subject to future verification. The precise character of the verification he expected is no longer clear to us; in our sources it is couched too much in terms of what actually transpired;[16] and we should not exclude the possibility that Jesus himself was not clear about what would happen (cf. Mark 13.32; Luke 11.29–32/Matt. 12.39–42, 16.4). But at least we can say that in this expectation of Jesus we have a substantial line of continuity between Jesus' own message and the kerygma about the risen Christ – that *the resurrection of Jesus was in a very real sense the fulfilment of Jesus' own expectation*, that however different or not it was from his own expectation *it provided in the event the vindication that Jesus had looked for.*

50.4 *Jesus' sense of sonship.* We have seen above how fundamental to Jesus' own understanding of himself and of his mission was his experience of God as Father (§45.2). What we must now note is that Jesus sought to bring his disciples into the reality of the *same* experienced relationship; that is, he encouraged his disciples to address God with the same boldness and intimacy – 'Abba' (particularly Luke 11.2/Matt. 6.9). Moreover, it was apparently *only his own disciples* that he so encouraged to live out of this relationship (Mark 11.25 par.; Matt. 5.48/Luke 6.36; Matt. 6.32/Luke 12.30; Matt. 7.11/Luke 11.13; Luke 12.32). There is no evidence that he preached a much wider message of divine fatherhood and human brotherhood – such a summary arises more from the timeless ideals of nineteenth-century Liberal Protestantism than from the eschatological 'Either-or' of Jesus' message. In other words, *Jesus seems to have seen a link between his disciples' sonship to God and their discipleship of him*; their use of *abba* was somehow *dependent* on their relationship with him; their 'Abba' was somehow *derived* from his 'Abba', their sonship from his.

If this is a fair characterization of pre-Easter discipleship, then it becomes at once noteworthy that in the post-Easter situation sonship appears again as an important way of describing the believer's relationship to God (Matt. 23.8f.; Rom. 8.14–17, 29; Gal. 4.6–7; Col. 1.18; Heb. 2.11–17; I John 3.1f.; Rev. 1.5) – the continued use of the Aramaic 'Abba' in the Greek speaking churches (Rom. 8.15; Gal. 4.6) showing how deeply rooted both experience and expression were in the primitive community. More important, these references indicate with sufficient clarity that *the sonship thus experienced was understood as determined by Jesus' own sonship*: they cried 'Abba' just as he did, and in conscious dependence on the Spirit *of Christ* (Rom. 8.9, 15–17; Gal. 4.6f.). Indeed the explicit allusion to Jesus' own sonship (thereby they show themselves to be 'fellow-heirs with Christ' – Rom. 8.17; it is precisely 'the Spirit of the Son' who cries 'Abba, Father' – Gal. 4.6) strongly implies that those who so prayed knowingly traced both experience and expression back to the distinctive prayer style and experience of Jesus while on earth.

Here is a point of no little significance: that in this one expression of prayer experience so widespread in early Christianity we see clearly visible the unity and continuity between earthly Jesus and exalted Christ, with the link firmly bonded *at both ends*. At the one end the prayer is inspired by the Spirit of the exalted Christ, the prayer which was so distinctively the prayer of Jesus of Nazareth. At the other it is the prayer, the same prayer, which Jesus taught his own disciples to pray during his own ministry. The point is that *at both ends* the prayer and the relationship it brings to expression are understood as *only possible in dependence on Jesus and as derived from Jesus' own sonship*. We are of course not talking about the public proclamation of either Jesus or the early churches, but more at the level of the presupposition of proclamation – the relationship out of which the proclamation sprang as it was explicated within the circle of discipleship. But we can say that at that deeper level of self-understanding, both of Jesus and of the earliest Christians, the role of Jesus was alike central on both sides of Easter. And thus we are given a further strand of continuity between the pre-Easter call to discipleship and the post-Easter call to faith.

50.5   *Jesus' experience of the kingdom and of the Spirit of God*, or more accurately his *understanding* of the kingdom and of his experience of the Spirit, provides us with one further anchor point within the history of Jesus for another element in the first Christians' self-understanding. For it is fairly clear that Jesus experienced and understood the kingdom as *an eschatological tension* – that is, a tension between an eschatological reality already experienced and a consummation of the kingdom imminent and longed for but not yet realized (cf. e.g. Matt. 11.5/Luke 7.22; Matt. 13.16f./Luke 10.23f. with Matt. 6.10/Luke 11.2; Mark 14.25 pars. – see further above §§3.1, 2). Moreover, this eschatological tension was *a function of the Spirit*: because he experienced a plenitude of the Spirit, because he understood his exorcisms as the effect of divine power working in him and through him, he concluded that this was a manifestation of the end-time rule of God, a manifestation of the kingdom (Matt. 12.28; see above p.188); and since the end-time Spirit was already active, the end itself could not long be delayed – the rout of Satan was anticipated and already in train though not yet complete (Luke 10.18; Mark 3.27). This also means that in Jesus' understanding, his own experience of the Spirit and his ministry in the power of the Spirit was something *unique*: his was not just the inspiration of a prophet, but the anointing of the end-time Spirit (Isa. 61.1f. – see above p.189); only in *his* exorcisms was the kingdom manifested, precisely because his exorcistic power was that of the eschatological Spirit – that is, a power which he alone experienced (Matt. 12.27f.). But this in turn involves a certain interdependence and interchange between Jesus and the eschatological power of his mission: opposition to this ministry was opposition to the Spirit (Mark 3.28f. pars.); he himself was part of the eschatological offence of his own mission (Matt. 11.5f./Luke 7.22f.; cf. Luke 12.8f. pars.). *He who understands himself as endowed in unique degree by the Spirit also understands the Spirit as uniquely his.*

In the first-century Christianity most clearly represented in Paul we see the same kind of eschatological tension, between the *already* of the grace already given and the *not yet* of a kingdom inheritance still to be fully realized. Not only so, but this post-Easter eschatological tension is also understood as a function of the Spirit: in the Pauline churches the Spirit is understood precisely as the first instalment of that kingdom inheritance which guarantees its full realization in the resurrection of the body (Rom. 8.10f., 15–23; I Cor. 6.9–11; 15.45–50; II Cor. 4.16–5.5; Gal. 4.6f.; 5.16–24; Eph. 1.13f.). More important, the Spirit thus experienced is experienced as the Spirit of Jesus – the power of the crucified and risen one which manifests itself precisely as it did in him, as power in weakness, as life through death (see above §46.4). That is to say, there is a certain merging or fusing of the role of the Spirit with the exalted Christ (I Cor. 15.45) so that the presence and work of the Spirit is determined and defined by its relation to Christ, that is, by whether or not it manifests the same character as was manifested in the ministry of Jesus.[17]

Here again then we have a parallel between the self-understanding of Jesus and that of the first Christians. But more than that, we have *an explication of their experience by the first Christians which is rooted in Jesus' own explication of his experience.* The unique relation between Jesus and the Spirit which was a presupposition of their gospel proclamation is in the end of the day nothing but an elaboration and development (in the light of his resurrection) of Jesus' own presupposition of a unique inspiration by the eschatological Spirit. To be sure there is no clear evidence that Jesus looked for an outpouring of the Spirit on his disciples for which he would be responsible – although such a tradition quite possibly underlies the Paraclete passages of John 14–16 which are at least paralleled in the testamentary disposition regarding the kingdom in Luke 22.29, and he did seem to embrace the other aspect of the Baptist's prediction regarding the ministry of the Coming One (above p.210).[18] Be that as it may, the point is that once again we have a strand of continuity which runs *through* Easter – experience which is attributed to the exalted Christ, which is similar to Jesus' own experience as he himself interpreted it, and whose distinctive features were already determined by the character of Jesus' mission as he himself understood it and lived it out.

I need merely add briefly that a closely related point emerges from a comparison of Jesus' and Paul's attitudes to *the law*.[19] For I would wish to argue that Paul's view of Jesus as 'the end of the law' (Rom. 10.4) is rooted not only in his understanding of Jesus' death and resurrection but also in his awareness of Jesus' own freedom with regard to the law and supremely authoritative interpretation of the law (see above pp.97f., 186); compare particularly Mark 7.19b and note the centrality of the love command for both (Mark 12.31 par.; Rom. 13.8–10; Gal. 5.14).[19a] That is to say, Jesus' sovereign handling of the law in the light of the coming kingdom and as expression of his own eschatological (self-)consciousness provides another anchor point within the ministry of the historical Jesus for Paul's teaching on the righteousness of God in the light of Good Friday and Easter.

50.6   To sum up, it appears that we can speak meaningfully of a unity and continuity between the historical Jesus and the kerygmatic Christ – a unity and continuity which is not merely a post-Easter theological creation, but which has sufficiently firm anchor points in the pre-Easter history of Jesus. This does *not* mean that the proclamation of Jesus and the kerygmata of the first Christians are one and the same, or that their presuppositions are one and the same. It does not mean that the post-Easter disciples simply revived and repeated the message Jesus himself had preached with little change of any importance (above p.209). Nothing of what we have said above diminishes *the central significance of Easter in decisively determining and shaping the post-Easter kerygmata*. The vindication which resurrection actually achieved for Jesus was not altogether the vindication which Jesus had anticipated (the general resurrection and judgment following) – though his expectation was not all that precisely formulated. And certainly, on the other two points of continuity, the first Christians were quite clear that what they experienced was not simply a relation or experience *like* that of Jesus, or even simply one *determined* by the ministry of the earthly Jesus, but a relation and an experience brought about by the risen Jesus and deriving immediately from his resurrection.

In other words, the unity and continuity we have discovered between historical Jesus and kerygmatic Christ does not diminish the significance of Easter in shaping the kerygma and self-understanding of earliest Christianity. But *neither does the importance of Easter diminish the central role already filled by Jesus even before Easter in his own proclamation and self-understanding*. Already before Easter the eschatological nearness of God as Father was seen to be somehow dependent on him. Already before Easter the imminent consummation was understood to be somehow determined in relation to him. Already before Easter the eschatological Spirit and the already/not yet tension was thought of as somehow bound up with him. Already before Easter freedom with respect to the law was recognized to be a feature and consequence of his ministry. In short, *there are sufficiently clear foreshadowings of the centrality of the kerygmatic Christ in the self-understanding of Jesus during his ministry for us to recognize the kerygmata of the early churches as a development from Jesus' own proclamation in the light of his resurrection.* As Christianity could properly claim to be a legitimate interpretation of the OT in the light of Jesus, so the kerygmatic Christ can claim to be a legitimate interpretation of the historical Jesus in the light of Jesus' resurrection.

§51. 'ONE JESUS, MANY CHRISTS?'

If we recognize the continuity between the historical Jesus and the kerygmatic Christ we must also recognize that there are *many kerygmatic Christs*. That is to say, it is no single coherent understanding or presentation of Christ which meets us after Easter. 'The kerygmatic Christ' is a convenient shorthand to distinguish Jesus as the object of historical research from Jesus as the object of faith, the historical Jesus from the proclaimed Christ. But if 'the NT kerygma' is an oversimplification, so is 'the kerygmatic Christ'; if we have to speak of NT kerygmata (ch. II above), so we have to speak of kerygmatic Christs – diverse understandings and presentations of 'the Christ of faith' within first-century Christianity. We have already seen something of this in chapter III, where we traced the main features of development in the first-century Christians' confessional faith in Jesus as Son of Man, Messiah, Son of God and Lord. Now I want to illustrate this diversity further by highlighting what is probably *the chief contrast within NT christology* – namely, that between the christology of the very first Christians and the christology that began to develop as Christianity began to adopt (and adapt to) more of the conceptualizations of the wider religious philosophy of the time. Then by way of summary we will briefly compare the different evaluations of the dimensions and stages of 'the Christ event'. In this whole field there are many passages whose original life-setting and reference is disputed. But even without coming to a firm opinion on most of them a sufficiently clear picture emerges.

51.1   *The christology of earliest Christianity* seems to have been *essentially forward looking*. This is evident from what are probably the earliest post-Easter uses of the four main christological titles (above ch. III). The hope that Jesus as the Son of Man would soon return must have been a dominant expectation: the 'coming of the Son of Man' sayings form the largest homogeneous group among the Son of Man logia; only in the eschatological fervency of the first few years would it have been meaningful to preserve (or create) and circulate Matt. 10.23; and no Son of Man saying seems to have been subjected to such reflection (at a very early stage) as Luke 12.8f./Matt. 10.32f./Mark 8.38/Luke 9.26 (see also below p.323). As for Jesus as Messiah, Acts 3.19–21 apparently embodies what is probably a fragment of earliest Christian preaching, where the promise is explicitly held out that if men repent and turn again, the Lord (= God) would send Jesus the Christ from heaven once again. On Son of God, one of the earliest formulations links Jesus' installation as Son of God (in power) with 'the resurrection of the dead' (Rom. 1.3f. – see further below p.217; cf. I Thess, 1.10). And of course the earliest post-Easter designation of Jesus as Lord preserved in the Pauline letters is I Cor. 16.22, an invocation vibrant with longing for Christ's return – 'Our Lord, come!' (cf. Rev. 22.20; of a sense of Christ's *coming* to or in the Lord's Supper there is no evidence[20]).

At the same time we must not ignore the central emphasis given to the resurrection of Christ, as is reflected particularly in the early kerygmatic traditions (see above p.22, also pp.45f. and 51). This was certainly seen as a vindication of his ministry and claims (cf. above §50.3 and below p.219), in particular as his installation or adoption to a new and exalted status (Acts 2.36; 13.33; Rom. 1.3f.; Heb. 5.5; cf. Phil. 2.9–11; see also above pp.45f. and below p.243). But it was also seen as *an eschatological event foreshadowing the consummation*, the beginning of the end, the first act in the general resurrection. This is clearly indicated by the (obviously early) description of Jesus' resurrection as the 'first fruits', that is, as part of and beginning of the general resurrection (I Cor. 15.20, 23). The same understanding is preserved in the reference to Jesus' resurrection *as* the (general) resurrection *of* the dead (Rom. 1.4) and in the ancient tradition preserved in Matt. 27.52f. Since the resurrection had begun in Jesus, the 'last days' were already in progress. The resurrection announced both his exaltation and the imminent consummation. If there is any truth at all in the suggestion that the parousia hope developed out of the belief in Jesus' ascension,[21] the development must have taken place within a very short time since the evidence otherwise is clear that the parousia hope was part and parcel of the earliest community's fervent eschatological expectation (see further below §67.3). In short, *the resurrection of Jesus was significant for the first Christians both for what Jesus had become thereby and for what it foreshadowed*. That is to say, the resurrection of Jesus was significant as an anticipation of the future and as a promise of Jesus' role in that future, as the beginning of what was soon to be completed.[21a]

So too we are not surprised to find that at this earliest stage *no real thought seems to have been given to the role of the exalted Jesus between his resurrection-exaltation (-outpouring of the Spirit) and his parousia*. Even in Acts the only function attributed to Jesus between Pentecost and his final role as judge (10.42; 17.31) is his appearance in a number of visions (7.55f.; 9.10; 18.9; 22.17f.; 23.11; 26.16, 19). And though the use of the name of the exalted Jesus invokes his power by its use, the name itself serves more as a *surrogate* for Jesus (as with the name of Yahweh in contemporary Judaism) and so underscores the *lack* of his personal presence (Jesus is present only in his name – cf. particularly 4.10, 12; see also above p. 19). Furthermore, it is probably significant that the tradition of Jesus' sayings has not been elaborated at this point: no attempt has been made to fill in the gap between Jesus' hoped for resurrection and his promised parousia; the two elements remain unrelated within the Jesus-tradition. Perhaps here too we have a partial reflection of that period when no real gap between exaltation and parousia was yet envisaged: to speak of Jesus' resurrection and to speak of his parousia were more or less alternative ways of saying the same thing – that Jesus had been exalted (to pour out the Spirit and) to return in eschatological consummation. consummation.

All this does not mean that the earliest believers were uninterested in other aspects of 'the Christ event'. As we have seen they soon began to wrestle with the problem of a crucified Messiah (§10.2). But how soon the death of Christ became the focus of soteriological reflection is not clear, for the evidence is capable of different interpretations. On the one hand the idea of Jesus' death as (the new) covenant sacrifice may well be part of the earliest tradition of the words spoken at the last supper (see above pp.166f.), though the eschatological note probably rang loudest in the common meals of the earliest community (above pp.163, 168); and in the very early tradition of I Cor. 15.3 Jesus' death is confessed as 'for our sins', though in the extended formula of I Cor. 15 the main emphasis is on Jesus' resurrection appearances, and I Cor. 15 itself is an exposition of Jesus' resurrection as the prototype of the general resurrection. On the other hand, there is the almost complete lack of any concern with Jesus' passion in the Q sayings; and in the sermons in Acts the death of Jesus is mentioned only as part of the suffering-vindication theme, as the rejection of Christ prior to his resurrection, and not in terms of vicarious suffering – though this is probably a reflection of Lukan theological emphasis as much as anything else (see above pp.17f.). Perhaps the simplest solution of this conflict of evidence is that the death of Jesus was reflected on *christologically* (as Jesus' humiliation before his vindication) before its meaning was developed *soteriologically*, and that initially the imminent parousia was seen as the decisive act of salvation (cf. Acts 3.19f.; I Thess. 1.10; 5.8f.).[22]

Interest in the earthly teaching and ministry of Jesus is implied as soon as we have a concern to preserve the traditions about Jesus. Such a concern is minimal in the sermons of Acts (2.22; 10.36–39 – see above p.17), but clearly lies behind the compilation of Q, though we should at once recall the strong forward looking christology of Q (see further below p.286). And Paul certainly takes very seriously the ethical traditions which, as we saw, probably largely referred back to the life and teaching of Jesus (above §17.3) – though here it is interesting to note that he appeals to this Jesus-tradition in II Thessalonians *against* something like the eschatological fervency which must have characterized the earliest Palestinian community (II Thess. 3.6–12; cf. Acts 2.44f.; 4.32–35). So too it may be relevant to recall that at Corinth an interest in Jesus as *miracle worker* may well have been wedded to a *realized* eschatology which left no room for hope of a future resurrection (see above pp.179f., and below pp.278f.). All this suggests again that initially interest in the earthly teaching and ministry of Jesus was subordinate to the parousia hope and that the Jesus-tradition served in part at first as a kind of counterbalance to (over)enthusiastic imminent expectation.

In short, so far as we can tell, the christology (and soteriology) of the first Christians seems to have been essentially forward looking.

51.2 *The developments in christology* after this earliest period can be characterized as *the beginning of a shift of the decisive 'christological moment'*[23] *backwards in time from the eschatological double event of resurrection-exaltation-parousia*. We perhaps see something of this already in the pre-Pauline formula of Rom. 8.34, where the (lengthening) gap between Jesus' exaltation and parousia is understood to be filled by Jesus' role as intercessor. Still more so in Hebrews: Jesus' exaltation is still central (his highpriestly entry into the heavenly sanctuary), but the emphasis falls markedly on Jesus' *present* continuing role as forerunner into and intercessor in heaven where believers can already enter in (1.3; 2.10; 4.14–16; 6.19f.; 7.25; 8.1f.; 9.24; 10.19–22; 12.22–24), whereas the parousia hope, while still present, receives little attention.

A certain shift in the christological moment seems to be bound up with *the crystallization of the account of Jesus' encounter with John at Jordan and of his anointing with the Spirit there.* The explicit use of Ps. 2.7b (in part in Mark/Matthew, in whole in what is probably the original Lukan text, and possibly Q) suggests that for some at least this was the point in time when Jesus became Messiah and Son. Here the same verse (Ps. 2.7 – 'You are my son, today I have begotten you'), which seems to have expressed the earliest community's 'adoptionist' view of the resurrection of Jesus (Acts 13.33; Heb. 5.5; see above pp.45f., 217), has been referred to the starting point of Jesus' ministry. Behind this presumably lies a concern to include Jesus' whole earthly ministry within the salvation-history events now recognized as decisive both for Christ's status and for man's salvation. Perhaps also bound up with this was the interest in Jesus as a miracle-worker which, as we have seen, was probably an element in the situations addressed by II Cor. 10–13 and by Mark and in the fragmentary miracle source used by the Fourth Evangelist in John 2.1–11 and 4.46–54 (above pp.70f., 179f. and below pp.302f.). Such an evaluation of Christ would presumably have attached no little significance to Jesus' baptism as the moment of endowment with these supernatural powers (the Corinthians at least seem to have accorded baptism some such significance – see above §39.5). Paul and Mark, as we have seen, responded by focusing the decisive soteriological moment on Jesus' death and resurrection and by emphasizing Jesus' suffering more than his miracles (above pp.71, 195). John responded by rebuking the faith which depends on signs (2.23–25; 4.48) and by emphasizing that the miracles of his Gospel are significant because they foreshadow the hour of Jesus' death-glorification (see further below p.303). Matthew and Luke incidentally also effectively counter a christology wrongly based on Jesus' baptism and mighty works by interposing the fuller Q account of Jesus' temptations between Jesus' baptism and the start of his ministry in such a way that they qualify both.

Much the most important shift in the christological moment is heralded by the introduction of *the language of pre-existence* into the talk about Christ. When this development first took place is not clear; even if the idea of pre-existent entities or beings is more typical of Greek than of Hebraic thought, pre-Christian Judaism was already familiar with it – particularly in its speculation about Wisdom (Prov.

3.19; 8.22–31; Wisd. 7.22–8.1; 9.1f.; Ecclus. 24.1–22). So we need not assume that the category of pre-existence entered Christian theology only when the new sect encountered Hellenistic philosophy for itself. It is quite possible indeed that it was first used as a corollary to a fuller appraisal of the significance of Jesus' resurrection-exaltation.[24] Be that as it may, it would appear that *the thought of pre-existence initially entered early christology by the application of Wisdom terminology to Christ.* So far as we can now tell, Jesus thought of himself as Wisdom's *messenger* – a self-understanding reflected particularly in Q (Matt. 11.25–27; Luke 7.31–35; 11.49–51). That is to say, there is no evidence that Jesus thought of himself as pre-existent Wisdom, and nothing in the traditions of Q and Mark which implies that the thought of pre-existence was present (either to Jesus or to Q and Mark).[25] The idea of pre-existence first entered by way of implication with the *identification* of Christ with *Wisdom herself*. This identification was certainly made by Matthew (see below pp.258f.); but already, earlier, Paul had left the matter in no doubt (I Cor. 1.24, 30); nor had he hesitated to ascribe to Christ the role of pre-existent Wisdom (particularly I Cor. 8.6; Col. 1.15–17).

Now here we must recall that within Judaism Wisdom was only a way of speaking about God's action in creation, revelation and redemption without actually speaking about God. Wisdom, like the name of God, the Spirit of God, the Logos, etc., denotes the *immanent* activity of God, without detracting from God's wholly other transcendence. For pre-Christian Judaism Wisdom was neither an inferior heavenly being (one of the heavenly council) nor a divine hypostasis (as in the later Trinitarian conception of God); such a development would have been (and in the event was) unacceptable to Judaism's strict monotheism. Wisdom in fact is no more than *a personification of God's immanence*, no more to be regarded as a distinct person within the Godhead than the rabbinic concept or talk of a pre-existent Torah. The probability then is that Paul in applying Wisdom language to Christ is in effect simply saying: that which you have hitherto ascribed to Wisdom, we see most fully expressed and embodied in Christ; that same power and wisdom you recognize to be manifested in God's creative, revelatory and redemptive purpose, we now see manifested finally and exclusively in Jesus Christ our Lord.[26] This would also explain why Paul never used the name 'Jesus' alone for the pre-existent one: Jesus was not himself pre-existent; he was the man that pre-existent Wisdom became.[27]

However, as the last sentence indicates, with the use of the language of pre-existence the concept of *incarnation* becomes part of christology. And the door is thereby opened to that christology which sees Jesus not only as the incarnation of divine Wisdom or divine Logos, but which also reckons the incarnation as the decisive moment in salvation – the taking of humanity into the godhead and thereby sanctifying it. In such a case Jesus' death, resurrection and parousia become in effect not much more than a ratification of what had already been achieved in principle; and christology becomes a matter of trying to understand the human(ity of) Jesus in the light of what must be true of the pre-existent Logos, rather than a matter of trying to understand the exalted Christ in the light of the traditions about Jesus of Nazareth. Of course, all this has not yet happened in the NT writings, but *already we see beginning to emerge in the NT the tendency for the* impersonal *pre-existent intermediary figure to be thought of as a* personal *pre-existent divine being whose decision to become incarnate has already determined man's salvation and its means*. Perhaps it is present as early as the Phil. 2.6–11 hymn; though I suspect that Paul's thought is dominated at this point by *the Adam/Christ parallel*.[28] In which case Jesus' earthly career is expressed in language appropriate to the archetypal man, Adam: like Adam he was made in the image of God (cf. Gen. 1.26f.; 2.7), but unlike Adam he did not grasp after equality with God (cf. Gen. 3.5); like Adam he surrendered his privileged status and embraced its human antithesis (cf. Gen. 3.17–19), but unlike Adam he did this freely and not as punishment, willingly submitting even to the shameful death of the cross, and thus he attained an honour higher than the honour God had first intended for man. If this line of interpretation adequately represents Paul's mind in Phil. 2.6–11 (and it does accord quite closely with Rom. 5.14b–19), then we must question whether there is any real thought of personal pre-existence here.[29] Besides, there is no question that for Paul the decisive event for both christology and soteriology was Jesus' death and resurrection (so also Phil. 2.8f.; and note how the 'sending' formulations of Rom. 8.3 and Gal. 4.4 are at once elaborated by reference to Jesus' death – Rom. 8.3c, Gal. 4.5a).[30] Prior to his death Jesus was wholly one with man, first Adam (Rom. 8.3; Phil. 2.7f.); only with the resurrection did Jesus become representative of a new humanity, last Adam (Rom. 8.29; Col. 1.18; and particularly I Cor. 15.20–23, 45).

If we are looking for the earliest appearance of the thought of personal pre-existence in relation to Jesus a stronger candidate is the letter to the Hebrews. Like Paul the writer describes Jesus in the language of pre-existent Wisdom (1.2f.); but in addition the thought of personal pre-existence may be implied in the argument of 7.3

(Jesus qualifies as a Melchizedek priest because like Melchizedek he has 'neither beginning of days nor end of life', or more precisely, because his resurrection demonstrates the indestructible quality of his life – 7.16), and in 10.5 (cf. 1.8, 2.14 and 13.8 – see below p.260). Yet we should not fail to notice that this is accompanied by some of the *strongest adoptionist language* to be found in the NT (see below pp. 259f.), and there is little doubt that for Hebrews too the christological moment focuses firmly on Jesus' death and entry into the heavenly sanctuary (1.3f.; 2.9f.; 5.5–10; 6.20; 7.15f., 26–28; etc.). Equally significant is Hebrews' exegesis of Ps. 8.4–6, where Jesus is represented as the man who fulfilled the divine programme for man, which had hitherto remained unfulfilled, and so as the pioneer who leads the way and makes it possible for his brother men to follow him through the programme to its intended end (2.5–18) – a christology not so very far removed from Paul's Adam/last Adam christology in Rom. 8.3 and I Cor. 15.[31]

It is only really in John's Gospel, towards the end of the first century, *that we see the shift in the christological moment actually beginning to take place* – where Jesus is presented as *conscious* of a *personal* pre-existence (particularly 8.58), and the talk of ascent is set in counterpoise with the talk of a prior descent (3.13; 6.33, 38, 41f., 50f., 58, 62). Yet even here (as with Paul), Jesus is more precisely to be thought of as the man that pre-existent Logos became (1.14), that is, the man who brings God to expression more clearly than any of God's previous acts (1.18); and the divine glory which was discernible to the eye of faith in the earthly Jesus (1.14) is pre-eminently the glorification of death-resurrection-ascension (7.39; 12.16, 23; 17.1, 5). Moreover, the soteriological moment remains firmly centred on this salvation climax to Jesus' ministry; for the flesh which the Logos became (1.14) is of no avail 6.63; cf. 3.6); it is only the Jesus given over to death, lifted up on the cross and in resurrection who thereby becomes the source of the life-giving Spirit, of life for the world (3.13–15; 6.51, 62f.; 7.38f.; 19.30, 34; 20.22).

In short, as the first century draws to a close we seem *but a step away from an incarnation-centred christology*. In John the decisive *soteriological* moment is still that of *death-resurrection-ascension*. But the christological moment is split between the descent of a pre-existent Logos in incarnation and the ascent whence he was before through the counterpoised uplifting in the glorification of cross and exaltation. This is still a far cry from the idea of redemption by means of incarnation, such as we find later particularly in Gregory of Nyssa,[32] where however much Christ's death and resurrection are stressed, the decisive christological and the decisive soteriological moment are both focused on the incarnation. But it is also significantly different from the christology of some 40 or 50 years earlier with its forward-looking focus on the Jesus now risen to become Messiah, Son of God and Lord and soon to return again.

51.3   We can demonstrate *the diversity of first-century christology* very simply from another angle in more summary fashion. The development which we have traced in first-century christology (ch. III and above §§51.1, 2) is reflected in *the diverse evaluations of the different stages of 'the Christ event'* which we find within the NT. Thus next to nothing is made of the *ministry* of Jesus in the Acts sermons and in Paul, whereas certain elements within Hellenistic Christianity seem to have focused attention on Jesus as the great miracle worker (the so-called 'divine man' christology), and there is a strand of *imitatio Christi* running through much of the NT which Liberal Protestantism was able to elaborate with considerable effect, though less justification (e.g. Mark 8.34; Luke 9.57f.; John 13.13–16; I Cor. 11.1; Heb. 12.1f.; I Peter 2.21). As regards the *death* of Jesus: Jesus himself probably regarded it as the beginning of the messianic woes which would bring in the eschaton, the final rule of God; the earliest churches and/or Luke apparently made little of it as a soteriological factor; whereas Paul in particular developed a theology of the suffering and death of Christ probably partly at least in response to a 'gospel' of Christ the miracle working Son of God (Mark and John somewhat similarly).

Popular ideas of the *resurrection* of Jesus are largely determined by Luke's presentation in Luke 24 and Acts 1. But 'resurrection' was in fact only one way of speaking about what had happened to Jesus after his death, only one way of interpreting their post-Easter experience of Jesus. Mark's account of the empty tomb could possibly have been interpreted in terms of a translation of Jesus from earth to heaven (like those of Enoch and Elijah). Elsewhere in the NT, resurrection, exaltation, ascension are all equivalent forms of expression (Hebrews never really speaks of Jesus' resurrection as such – the nearest is 13.20); whereas Luke envisages a two-stage process with resurrection clearly distinguished from ascension. Similarly the resurrection appearances are differently interpreted – by Paul in terms of a spiritual body from heaven, by Luke particularly in very physical and earthy terms (Luke 24.39).

What of *Jesus' present role* now that he has been raised/exalted? In earliest Christianity, in the Synoptic tradition and in Acts hardly any role is attributed to the exalted Christ. Whereas Hebrews focuses attention precisely at this point – on Jesus' continuing role as high priest interceding on our behalf in the very presence of God (cf. Rom. 8.34; I John 2.1). In Paul there is a strange ambivalence since he speaks of the exalted Lord both as an exalted being in heaven (e.g. Rom. 8.34; I Cor. 15.25; Phil. 2.9–11), as the Spirit who gives life to man on earth (I Cor. 15.45), and as the community of believers (I Cor. 12.12). In fact, it is not in the end clear how Paul conceived of the exalted Christ and how he conceived of Christ's present role in relation to believers ('in Christ').

As for the *parousia*, the harsh reality is that the imminent parousia hope of (Jesus and) the first Christians did not materialize – Jesus did not return in glory within the life-span of his own generation.[33] And most students of the NT readily recognize the problems which the delay of the parousia caused particularly to Luke, John and II Peter (see below §§71.2–4). To be sure, it is possible to escape the christological problem of Jesus' being mistaken about the imminent parousia, by arguing that the original hope was not of parousia at all: it was of a coming (parousia) all right, but of a coming in the clouds of heaven to the Ancient of Days (Dan. 7.13) rather than a coming again to earth; that it was the hope of exaltation rather than of return (Mark 14.62).[34] But if this was the case (and personally I remain unconvinced) then the parousia hope itself is a secondary development and we have an important further element of diversity.

What finally of *pre-existence* and *deity*? There is no good evidence that Jesus thought of himself as a pre-existent being.[35] Certainly the earliest christology seems to have been distinctly 'adoptionist' in character (even if the description is somewhat anachronistic); indeed, I would find it very hard to escape that conclusion (see above pp.20, 45f., 51, 217, 223). It was probably only when the Jesus-tradition was put together as a kind of 'life of Jesus' that the emphasis in the apologetic use of Ps. 2.7 swung from Jesus' resurrection to his experience at Jordan. The thought of pre-existence first came in through a Wisdom christology, where Jesus was understood as the embodiment and fullest expression of Wisdom. Initially the language of pre-existence probably referred only to Wisdom as such and the man Jesus was what Wisdom became. But in the Fourth Gospel the concept of a personal pre-existence of Jesus himself begins to emerge. How this squares with the idea of a virgin birth as in Matthew (and Luke) is not clear; though the concepts of incarnation and virgin birth are not necessarily incompatible.[36] Be that as it may, it is not an unfair summary to say that while for Mark the beginning of the Christ event is the baptism of John (Mark 1.1), for Matthew and Luke it is Jesus' conception by Mary, whereas John sets it before creation itself (John 1.1f.).

Similarly the thought of Jesus' *deity* seems to be *a relatively late arrival* on the first-century stage. Paul does not yet understand the risen Christ as the *object* of worship: he is the theme of worship, the one for whom praise is given, the one whose risen presence in and through the Spirit constitutes the worshipping community, the one *through* whom the pray-er prays to God (Rom. 1.8; 7.25; II Cor. 1.20; Col. 3.17), but not the object of worship or prayer. So too his reticence about calling Jesus 'God'. Even the title 'Lord' becomes a way of distinguishing Jesus from God rather than of identifying him with God (Rom. 15.6; I Cor. 8.6; 15.24–28; II Cor. 1.3; 11.31; Eph. 1.3, 17; Phil. 2.11; Col. 1.3). Paul was and remained a monotheist (see above p. 53). That reticence in calling Jesus 'God' is only really overcome towards the end of the first century with the Pastorals (Titus 2.13) and again with the Fourth Gospel (John 1.1, 18; 20.28).[37]

In short, *'the kerygmatic Christ' is no single or simple formulation, but a fairly wide diversity of formulations which embrace quite a broad spectrum of different understandings of 'the Christ event', which are not always wholly compatible with each other, and which change and develop as the first century progresses.*

§52. CONCLUSIONS

52.1   *Diversity.* After such a catalogue as outlined above (§51.3) one might be tempted to ask, 'Will the real christology please stand up'! The fact is that *there was no one christology in first-century Christianity but a diversity of christologies.* There is no single christology to which we can point and say, 'That is *the* view of Christ which the churches of the first century recognized as orthodox'. There are of course formulations which Paul and the Johannine writers all reject (II Cor. 11.4; I John 4.2f. – see further below §§62.3, 64.3), but no single orthodoxy, and certainly no single comprehensive orthodoxy. Indeed, what many Christians both past and present have regarded as orthodox christology may be represented (not altogether unfairly) as a curious amalgam of different elements taken from different parts of first-century Christianity – personal pre-existence from John, virgin birth from Matthew, the miracle-worker from the so-called 'divine man' christology prevalent among some Hellenistic Christians, his death as atonement from Paul, the character of his resurrec-

tion from Luke, his present role from Hebrews, and the hope of his
parousia from the earlier decades. Well might a recent writer entitle
his essay, 'One Jesus, many Christs?'[38] – though it would be more
accurate to speak of 'one Jesus, many christologies'.

52.2   *Unity.* Within this diversity however a unifying element is
regularly discernible: namely, *the affirmation of the identity of the man
Jesus with the risen Lord,* the conviction that the heavenly reality known
in kerygma and scripture, in community, worship and religious
experience generally is one and the same Jesus of whom the Jesus-
tradition speaks. So for Paul, the Risen One is precisely the Crucified
One, the last Adam who shared the fleshness of the first Adam; and
the Spirit is precisely the Spirit of Jesus who enables the believer to
echo the prayer of the earthly Jesus – 'Abba, Father'. For Mark the
gospel is of the Son of God, but also of the suffering Son of Man. In
Luke the unity is less clear, but he too certainly wants to hold Jesus
the man and Jesus the Lord together as one, for he himself calls the
Jesus of his narratives 'Lord' (e.g. Luke 7.19; 10.1) and he evidently
regards his second volume as complementary to his first (Acts
1.1f.).[39] The same consciousness that Jesus of Nazareth is the
heavenly presence in worship comes through in Matthew, particularly in 11.28–30 and 18.20, which are probably words of the exalted
Christ but attributed without sense of inconsistency to the earthly
Jesus (see above p.74). In Hebrews the key point of his argument is
that Jesus is *now* high priest in the heavenly sanctuary, only because
he *was* and *is* man; only because he knows human weakness from the
inside, only because he was made 'perfect through suffering', is he
qualified as priest, can he serve as priest (2.6–18; 4.14–5.10). When
I Peter speaks to those faced with persecution it is the one Jesus who
provides both an example by his own patience in suffering (2.21–23;
4.1, 13f.; 5.1) and the hope of glory to come by his resurrection (1.7,
11, 21; 4.13; 5.1, 4, 10). In Revelation the central image for Christ is a
lamb 'standing as though slain' (5.6; cf. 5.9); the glorified Christ is
precisely the lamb who was slain, and who still bears the mark of the
fatal wound (see also below pp.333f.).

Above all there is John. The inspired genius of John is most clearly
seen in the way he weaves into one the two strands of the basic
christological affirmation – he who was, *is* – or perhaps better, he
who is, was. Thus he presents the earthly Jesus *already* in terms of his
exalted glory. Thus in the great bread of life discourse (John 6), the
bread of life is precisely the incarnate one, but the incarnate one who
died, was exalted and now ministers to his own through the Spirit

(6.51, 62f.). Thus the whole Gospel seeks to present the climax of Jesus' ministry precisely as a unity of death and exaltation – a single upward sweep of the pendulum lifting up Jesus on the cross in ascension and glorification (see above p.75 and n.22). Thus the Spirit is precisely the other Paraclete, the *alter ego* of the incarnate Logos, whose coming is Jesus' return to indwell his own. And thus the future life, judgment, resurrection are already anticipated in the here and now of Christ (3.18f.; 5.24.; 11.25f.) – past, present and future tied together in a glorious unity.

We must add of course that from very early on the first believers found it necessary to speak of Christ in the language of pre-existence. The reality of Christ could not be comprehended adequately in talk simply of resurrection and exaltation. Jesus himself had to be understood not merely as the eschatological proclaimer of God's kingdom and as the one through whom men now come to God, but as himself the expression of God's revelation and redemptive purpose, as the embodiment of the divine wisdom that had always been manifest in all God's works. And this conviction developed through the use of more traditional wisdom language in Paul and Hebrews to John's bold presentation of Jesus as the incarnate Logos conscious of a personal pre-existence. Thereafter, if I may summarize so briefly, the christological moment began to centre more and more on the incarnation while the soteriological moment swung between incarnation and atonement. But ultimately all such reflection stems from a realization that the man who is thus exalted must at the same time have been more than man from the beginning – not just representing, embodying man (Adam, 'man' of Ps. 8), but somehow also representing God, embodying the wisdom of God. So ultimately it all stems from the primary affirmation that Jesus the man has been exalted after death.

52.3   We can affirm also *a unity between the historical Jesus and the kerygmatic Christ*. That is to say, the identity between the man Jesus and the proclaimed Christ unites not only the diverse kerygmata in one, but *unites also the pre-Easter proclamation of Jesus with the post-Easter kerygma of the first Christians*. Two firm strands of continuity bind the before and after of Easter into one. (1) There is a close similarity between *the relation with God* into which Jesus sought to bring his disciples and that which the kerygma of the earliest believers sought to realize (the *abba* relationship, through the power of the eschatological Spirit). Not only so, but on both sides of Easter bound up with this is a recognition that this relationship is *dependent on Jesus* – a sonship which Jesus himself sought to share with his disciples (Luke 11.2), and one which the early Christians recognized as a sharing in Jesus' own sonship (Rom. 8.15–17); the Spirit/power which the first Christians regarded as peculiarly his own ('Spirit of Jesus') was already so in Jesus' own mind (Matt. 12.28). (2) There is a *forward lookingness* in Jesus' own ministry which reaches forward through Easter, just as there is a *backward lookingness* in the first Christians' proclamation which reaches back through Easter, and these together provide a double clamp which holds the two firmly joined. In other words, Jesus looked forward to a future vindication which was not so very far removed in conceptualization from the vindication which the first Christians believed he had received through the resurrection; and the first-century Christians look back to the earthly Jesus and to the character of his life and ministry and count that, together with the proclamation of his death and resurrection, as the chief criteria by which to test the claims of new revelation and of their own understanding and practice of 'the faith of Christ' (§48.3). In short, *the identity of historical Jesus with kerygmatic Christ is the one basis and bond of unity which holds together the manifold diversity of first-century Christianity*; that is, the continuity between the message of Jesus and the post-Easter proclamation, and the agreement of the different kerygmata in affirming that Jesus of Nazareth and the exalted Christ are one and the same, is the unifying core round which the diversity of NT Christianity coheres. Or to put the same point in a way which evokes older discussions: even in Jesus' own mind and ministry he never simply stood as man before God; and in the post-Easter christology he never simply stood as God before man. There was an element of divine otherness even in his own ministry, just as the exalted Christ never ceased to be Jesus of Nazareth for any NT writer. On both sides of Easter elements of the divine and the human belong firmly together – in different ways and with different 'weighting', but always together.

52.4   It is important to reaffirm the point which we stressed at the end of chapter II (§7.1) – that *this unifying core is an abstraction*. When we look at any of the areas examined in the preceding chapters, the particular self-understanding which becomes apparent in proclamation, confession, apologetic, worship, etc., is always fuller than the unifying core itself. The leading NT theologians (Paul and the Johannine school most explicitly) are sufficiently self-conscious about the basic unifying core to revert to it when a criterion for faith and conduct is required. But when they attempt to put Christianity into words at any particular point, it is always a much fuller formulation which they use – inevitably so if they were to speak clearly and meaningfully to their own situations and their potential readerships. But this also means that as soon as we move beyond the unifying core, the self expressions of Christian faith, worship and life multiply and diversify. Indeed the diversity is much more obviously a feature of the beginnings of Christianity than the unity. Moreover, many of the differences which become immediately apparent are in fact integral to these different self expressions. *Diversity is as integral to first-century Christianity as unity*. In short, *there is no single closely defined Christianity or christology in the NT*; and if we recognize the unifying christological strand in first-century Christianity we must recognize also the many different strands which are woven in with it at different points to form the diverse patterns which are first-century Christianity. We must explore the ramifications and repercussions of this conclusion more fully in our final chapter below.

52.5   Of the three main questions posed in the penultimate paragraph of §49 above we have dealt only with the first two in any detail. We can make only a few remarks on the third, since it raises issues which go far beyond the scope of the present study. But clearly there is a problem of considerable dimensions here: *granted the unity and diversity which we have discovered in NT christology, what are we to say about traditional christology?* How are we to correlate the two? How well rooted in the NT is the latter? The problem can perhaps be illustrated by recalling how the original World Council of Churches confession of 'our Lord Jesus Christ as God and Saviour' was expanded by the New Delhi Assembly in 1961 by the addition of the phrase 'according to the Scriptures' and by an explicit Trinitarian formula. Quite properly the scriptures are here regarded as providing Christians with the normative definition of Christian faith (see further below ch. XV). But what about the *diversity* of NT christology? What if it is the case that the title 'God' only began to be attributed to Jesus in the latest writings of the NT? that a full-blown Trinitarian understanding of God was only one possible interpretation of much more ambivalent language and thought in Paul, John, etc.? Does it matter that of the NT writings only the Pastorals and II Peter show much enthusiasm for the title 'Saviour'?[40] What if it is the case that the shift of the christological moment from resurrection-exaltation to incarnation, a shift which made possible the full flowering of Logos and Alexandrian christology in the subsequent centuries, was only beginning to take place in the last of the four Gospels and one of the last of the NT writings? Then to be sure traditional christology can claim to have some sort of foothold in the NT – at least one of the diverse strands which gathered round the unifying strand provides a guideline which leads forward into the formulations of later centuries. But what of the other diverse strands? What of earliest Christianity's 'adoptionism'? What of Paul's unwillingness to pray to Jesus and reservation about calling Jesus 'God'? What of the central christological and soteriological significance of Jesus' death and resurrection – so much more characteristic of the NT writers at large than any thought of the incarnation of pre-existent deity? What of the more limited claims involved in the earliest Wisdom christology and the fact that Jesus seems to have thought of himself only as Wisdom's messenger? What indeed of the limitations of the historical Jesus' own self-understanding? – was Jesus much, much more than even he himself sensed? In short, how typical of first-century Christianity is the World Council's present confession of Christ? How truly can it claim to be 'according to the Scriptures'? Should there be room for a greater diversity of expression, or at least for a greater hesitation or uncertainty than these firm assertions seem to allow?[41] Of course we may well wish to argue that the first Ecumenical Councils recognized what strand of NT christology was the one that really mattered – that out of the diverse half-formed ideas and faith formulations of first-century Christianity they grasped and elaborated the one that had most truly perceived the reality that was (and is) Christ. But then that is a christology which is not simply 'according to the Scriptures', but according to *one particular interpretation of the scriptures* – an interpretation which came to dominate and triumph over the other interpretations which could claim also to be justifiable interpretations of the scriptures, but which the winning orthodoxy branded as heresies. A Jew could of course make the same criticism of NT interpretation of the Jewish scriptures. But it does raise crucial questions about the locus and norm of revelation and authority – some of which will become clearer in the course of Part II and to which we must return in chapter XV.[42]

PART TWO

DIVERSITY IN UNITY?

XI

JEWISH CHRISTIANITY

§53. INTRODUCTION

If we may claim to have discovered the unity within the diversity of first-century Christianity we can now go on to examine the range of diversity round that unity. *Just how diverse was the diversity of first-century Christianity?* We have discovered the centre of the circle of first-century Christianity. Now we must inquire whether there was also a circumference to that circle – and if so whether it was clearly marked or barely discernible, or whether perhaps it only began to emerge in the second, third or subsequent generations of Christianity.

How can we best pursue this second main line of inquiry? Perhaps it is simplest to take a lead from later developments. For we know that from the second half of the second century onwards clear boundaries were being drawn, marking off the emerging great Church from its competitors – particularly the various Jewish Christian sects, the different varieties of Gnostic Christianity and the Marcionites, and the enthusiastic apocalypticism of Montanism. We may pose our question this way: Are similar or equivalent boundaries already being drawn within the NT period? Or do some of the features, some of the emphases within first-century Christianity lie in the areas that were later excluded by developing orthodoxy? Are there elements in the NT writings themselves which give more scope to the later Jewish Christian, Gnostic and apocalyptic sects than orthodoxy in the event allowed? How far does the diversity of first-century Christianity extend? Where did acceptable diversity fall over into unacceptable diversity?

Developments in the latter decades of the second century thus suggest four main areas in which we might hope to find answers to these questions. For want of better titles I will head these chapters simply Jewish Christianity, Hellenistic Christianity, Apocalyptic

Christianity, and Early Catholicism. None of these is very satisfactory and they are liable to provoke dispute, so I should perhaps stress at once that (1) they do not denote mutually exclusive segments of first-century Christianity – rather they denote dimensions and emphases within first-century Christianity which all overlap and interact to some degree, but which can nevertheless be subjected to separate analysis without resorting to unacceptable oversimplification; (2) they do not presuppose any particular relation or continuity between these dimensions and emphases of first-century Christianity and the more clearly defined sects and 'heresies' of the second and third centuries onwards.

The difficulty in nomenclature is highlighted by the phrase 'Jewish Christianity'. 'Jewish Christian' can be used quite appropriately to describe all the NT writings, since they are all in greater or less degree dependent on and expressive of Christianity's Jewish heritage (see above p.81); or it can be restricted to the first generation Christians who remained in Jerusalem (and Palestine), particularly those who, according to Eusebius (*HE*, III.5.3), fled from Jerusalem during the 60s across the Jordan to Perea (and their successors); or again it can be confined to the four or so more clearly distinguished Jewish Christian sects of the second and third centuries who were attacked by several early Fathers as heretical (see below p.239 n.5).[1] In the present study I use the title in a blanket way covering particularly the last two more restricted senses, but more to provoke the question as to what their relation to each other was, not to specify any particular relation.

Similarly 'Hellenistic Christianity' could embrace the whole of first-century Christianity since more or less all Palestine and all Jewish life and thought was to greater or less degree influenced by Hellenism,[2] so that, for example, Matthew is described more accurately as a Hellenistic Jewish Christian document than simply as a Jewish Christian document. But here we will have to use 'Hellenistic Christianity' in a more restricted sense to denote Christianity as it spread beyond Palestine and Judaism, the Christianity of the Gentile mission, Christianity as it came into increasing contact with the philosophical speculations, mystery cults and gnostic tendencies of the wider oriental-hellenistic syncretism of the Eastern Mediterranean (including influences from Judaism), since alternative shorthand titles like 'Gentile Christianity' and 'Gnostic Christianity' are too narrow and if anything even more misleading.

The last two titles are no less contentious – 'Apocalyptic Christianity' denoting the influence within first-century Christianity of

Jewish apocalyptic thought and provoking the questions: How integral was apocalypticism to earliest Christianity? How distinctive was earliest Christian apocalyptic eschatology? Did it do enough to guard itself against the fanaticism which later on brought apocalyptic enthusiasm into such disrepute in the eyes of the orthodox?' 'Early catholicism' turns the questioning around and asks whether and to what extent the hallmarks of emerging catholic orthodoxy are already present in the NT. When do the bulwarks of later orthodoxy begin to appear?

These four titles are of course not meant to be a definitive or exhaustive description of the total phenomenon of first-century Christianity. Others could be coined, other emphases highlighted. But our task here is the limited one of investigating the diversity of earliest Christianity by focusing attention on those areas and movements within earliest Christianity wherein that diversity came to clearest expression and where we may have good hope of discovering where acceptable diversity fell over into unacceptable diversity.

We begin in this chapter by comparing the earliest form of Christianity with the Jewish Christianity which came to be regarded as heretical in the late second and third centuries, to investigate the similarity and possible continuity between the two. We then turn to the intervening period to find out if we can where the acceptable diversity of Jewish Christianity within the NT differs from the unacceptable diversity of the Ebionites.

§54. HOW 'ORTHODOX' WAS EARLIEST PALESTINIAN CHRISTIANITY?

54.1   *The first Christians were Jews.* Even accepting Luke's account of the range of nationalities present at Pentecost, they were all 'Jews and proselytes' (Acts 2.10). And even though they believed that Jesus was Messiah and risen from the dead, that did not alter their standing or outlook as Jews, although to be sure their belief in a *crucified* Messiah and a resurrection *already* begun or past would be regarded as eccentric by most other Jews (cf. I Cor. 1.23). They constituted a small messianic conventicle or eschatological sect within Judaism, but they continued to think and act as Jews in all matters most characteristic of Judaism. This can be demonstrated with sufficient probability.

(*a*) They evidently regarded themselves as the climax of Judaism, what Paul later called 'the Israel of God' (Gal. 6.16): thus 'the 'twelve' presumably constituted the earliest community's focal point in their role as representatives of eschatological Israel (Matt. 19.28/Luke 22.29f.; Acts. 1.21f.; I Cor. 15.5; see above p.108); [3] so too the earliest function of the Lord's Supper was probably as the meal of the new covenant (see above §40.4, and further below p.323).

(*b*) They apparently continued to observe the law without question, not interpreting their traditions of Jesus' words and actions in a manner hostile to the law. Hence the Pharisees seem to have seen in them little or nothing of the threat which Jesus had posed (Acts 5.33–39) and not a few became members of the Jesus-sect while still remaining Pharisees (Acts 15.5; 21.20); hence too the shock of the Cornelius episode to the Jerusalem believers – it had not occurred to them that faith in Jesus the Christ might make the purity law irrelevant (Acts 10.14, 45; 11.2f.; see further above §16.3).

(*c*) They evidently continued to be firmly attached to the temple, attending daily at the hours of prayer (Acts 2.46; 3.1), regularly coming together there for mutual support and in order to teach and evangelize (5.12, 20f., 25, 42). Luke's account of the earliest period in the life of the new community ends with them never having stirred from Jerusalem and still largely centred on the temple (5.42). Moreover, the fact that Matt. 5.23f. was preserved in the Jesus-tradition suggests that it had continuing relevance for the first Christians – that is, they continued to use and be part of the sacrificial cultus; note the similar implication of Acts 21.24 (see also above p.127).

(*d*) Their belief in the imminent parousia of Jesus, the Son of Man, Messiah and Lord (see above pp.40, 43, 51f., 216ff. and below p.323) seems to have stayed within the framework of Jewish eschatological hope. This is probably the chief reason why they remained so firmly rooted in Jerusalem and centred on the temple, for the temple was the obvious focal point of the imminent consummation, as Mal. 3.1 clearly indicated; and the tradition of the mysterious word of Jesus about destroying and rebuilding the temple (Mark 14.58; 15.29; John 2.19 – see above p.74) certainly testifies that the hope of a renewed cultus in the eschatological temple was cherished among the first Christians (see further below p.324).

(*e*) This would also explain why there was such a lack of concern for the Gentiles or for mission outside Jerusalem among the earliest Jerusalem community. They were still thinking only in terms of Israel (Acts 1.6, 21f.; 2.39 – 'all that are far off' = Jews of the diaspora; 3.25; 5.31; cf. Matt. 10.5f., 23; 15.24).[3a] In so far as the Gentiles entered into their thinking it would probably be in terms of the long cherished hope that in the new age the Gentiles would flock to Mount Zion (with the diaspora Jews) to worship God there as eschatological proselytes (e.g. Ps. 22.27; Isa. 2.2f.; 56.6–8; Zeph. 3.9f; Zeh. 14.16; Tobit 13.11; T.Ben. 9.2; Ps.Sol. 17.33–35; Sib.Or. III.702–18, 772–76) – a perspective and a hope which Jesus himself may well have shared (Matt. 10.5f., 23; 15.24; together with Matt. 8.11f./Luke 13.28f. and Mark 11.17 = Isa. 56.7 – a word spoken in the Court of the Gentiles).[4]

In short, it is evident that *the earliest community in no sense felt themselves to be a new religion, distinct from Judaism*. There was no sense of a boundary line drawn between themselves and their fellow Jews. They saw themselves simply as a fulfilled Judaism, the beginning of eschatological Israel. And the Jewish authorities evidently did not see them as anything very different from themselves: they held one or two eccentric beliefs (so did other Jewish sects), but otherwise they were wholly Jewish. Indeed we may put the point even more strongly: since Judaişm has always been concerned more with ortho*praxy* than with ortho*doxy* (right *practice* rather than right *belief*) the earliest Christians were not simply Jews, but in fact continued to be quite 'orthodox' Jews.

Notice then, that this is the group with whom Christianity proper all began. Only their belief in Jesus as Messiah and risen, and their belief that the last days were upon them mark them out as different from the majority of their fellow Jews. None of the other great Christian distinctives that come to expression in and through Paul are present. The Lukan psalms were probably used from earliest days in this community, and we have already seen how undistinctively Christian they are (see above §35.1). Altogether it is a form of Christianity which we today would scarcely recognize – *Jewish* Christianity indeed, or perhaps more precisely, a form of Jewish messianism, a messianic renewal movement within pre-70 Judaism.

54.2   If we now shift our glance from the beginning of Christianity forward 150 years or so into the second century and beyond, it at once becomes evident that the situation has significantly altered: Jewish Christianity, far from being the only form of Christianity, is now beginning to be classified as unorthodox and heretical. There seem to have been several groups of Jewish Christians (four anyway)[5] whose beliefs put them beyond the pale of the emerging great Church. One at least preserved an ancient title for early Christians – Nazareans (cf. Acts 24.5) – the name probably embodying a claim to preserve the true tradition against the antinomian (in Jewish Christian eyes) Christian communities elsewhere. The best known sect, whose name became a kind of stereotype in great Church polemic against Jewish Christian heresy, was the *Ebionites*.[6]

Three significant characteristics distinguish heretical Jewish Christianity so far as we can now tell – though of course we should not assume that the different Jewish Christian groups were uniform in all three respects (see e.g. below p.258).

(*a*) *Faithful adherence to the law.* Justin Martyr knew of Jews who believed in Christ and who kept the law without insisting that all Christians should. But he also knew others who not only kept the law themselves, but who also compelled Gentile believers to keep it too: either the Gentile believers 'live in all respects according to the law given by Moses' or else the Jewish believers withheld full fellowship from them.[7] Of the Nazareans Epiphanius says:

> Only in this respect they differ from the Jews and Christians: with the Jews they do not agree because of their belief in Christ, with the Christians because they are trained in the law, in circumcision, the sabbath and the other things.[8]

Likewise the Ebionites, according to Irenaeus:

> They practise circumcision, persevere in the customs which are according to the Law and practise a Jewish way of life, even adoring Jerusalem as if it were the house of God.[9]

In the Jewish Christian view which comes to strongest expression in the pseudo-Clementines and the underlying material known as the *Kerygmata Petrou* (Preaching of Peter, *c*. AD 200?), Jesus was the greatest of 'the true prophets', last in a line of succession going back to Adam, and including, of course, most eminently, Moses. The true prophet was the bearer of divine revelation, namely the law. That is to say, Jesus had no wish to suppress or abandon the law – that was the charge laid at Paul's door; on the contrary, Jesus upheld the law, and reformed it by bringing it back to the true ideas of Moses.[10]

(*b*) *Exaltation of James and denigration of Paul.* The exaltation of James is not such a prominent feature as the first. It is clearest in the pseudo-Clementine literature where James appears as the head of the Jerusalem church from the first, 'ordained bishop in it by the Lord' (*Recog.*, I.43). As for Peter, he and the other apostles are shown as subordinate to James and must give account of their work to him (see e.g. *Recog.*, I.17, 72; IV.35; *Hom.*, I.20; XI.35). Thus the Clementines are introduced by a letter wherein Peter addresses James as 'the lord and bishop of the holy Church'. Likewise Clement addresses his letter to

James, the lord and the bishop of bishops, who rules Jerusalem, the holy church of the Hebrews, and the churches everywhere excellently founded by the providence of God . . . .

Jerome preserves a fragment of the Gospel of the Hebrews which has significance here; it occurs 'after the account of the resurrection of the Lord':

But the Lord after he had given his linen cloth to the servant of the priest went to James and appeared to him (for James had sworn that he would not eat bread from the hour in which he drank the cup of the Lord until he had seen him rising again from those who sleep) . . . .

Notice how James is given special prominence: he was present at the last supper; and the risen Jesus appeared first to him (not to Peter or the twelve). This Gospel obviously stems from a community where James was the most significant figure of the earliest church: by implication, continuity with Jesus was through James (he was present at the last supper), and he was the authoritative guarantor of the resurrection of Jesus (the first appearance was to James). Two other passages are perhaps worthy of mention. According to Epiphanius the Ebionites wrote books which they passed off 'as if these were from the hands of James, Matthew and the other disciples' – note the two who are named. Finally we may observe that Marius Victorinus links the origin of the (Jewish Christian) sect called the Symmachians with James.[12]

Exaltation of James is accompanied by denigration of Paul. Irenaeus, Origen, Eusebius and Epiphanius number rejection of Paul as one of the characteristics of Ebionism and of the other Jewish Christian sects.[13] In the pseudo-Clementines Paul is violently attacked (under the figure of Simon Magus). Peter calls him 'the man who is my enemy' (*Epistula Petri*, 2.3), and dismisses his claim to have seen the risen Christ: Peter's experience at Caesarea Philippi (Matt. 16.16f.) taught him that 'revelation is knowledge gained without instruction, and without apparitions and dreams'.

The statements to a friend are made face to face, openly and not through riddles and visions and dreams, as to an enemy. If, then, our Jesus appeared to you in a vision, made himself known to you, and spoke to you, it was as one who is enraged with an adversary (*Hom.*, XVII.18–19).[14]

For Jewish Christianity in general Paul was the arch enemy, responsible for the rest of Christianity's rejection of the law and himself an apostate from the law.

(c) *Adoptionism*. One of the most frequently attested features of Ebionite christology is their affirmation that Jesus' birth was wholly natural − he was the natural son of Joseph and Mary.[15] In this connection it should be noted that they used only the Gospel of Matthew,[16] and that according to Epiphanius it was an incomplete, mutilated version, wholly lacking the first two chapters; that is to say, the Ebionites had removed both genealogy and account of Jesus' birth from a virgin.[17]

The clearest expression of Ebionite adoptionism is found in Epiphanius:

> Christ they call the prophet of truth and 'Christ, the Son of God' on account of his progress (in virtue) and the exaltation which descended upon him from above . . . . They want him to be only a prophet and man and Son of God and Christ and mere man, as we said before, who attained by a virtuous life the right to be called Son of God.[18]

That is to say, Jesus was named both Christ and Son of God because the Spirit/Christ descended upon him at Jordan and because he kept the law.[19] This must be the significance of the Ebionite Gospel of Matthew's account of Jesus' baptism:

> And when he came up from the water, the heavens opened and he saw the Holy Spirit in the form of a dove coming down and *entering into him*. And a voice from heaven said, 'You are my beloved Son, in you I am well pleased'; and again, 'This day I have begotten you'.[20]

Perhaps also significantly, John the Baptist's recognition of Jesus (Matt. 3.14) has been transposed to follow the descent of the Spirit and the heavenly voice.[21]

How the relation between Christ and Jesus in Ebionite thought is to be more fully understood is not entirely clear. Epiphanius reports the Ebionites' claim that Christ was 'not begotten by God the Father, but created as one of the archangels . . . and that he is Lord over the angels . . .'.[22] This could match the pseudo-Clementine belief that the Spirit of Christ was manifested in repeated incarnations of the true prophet from Adam onwards (see particularly *Clem.Hom.*, III.20). Presumably Jesus was the final reincarnation since their hope now centred on the second coming of Jesus as the Christ (*Recog.*, I.49, 69).[23]

54.3   If these are indeed the three principal features of heretical Jewish Christianity, then a striking point immediately emerges: *heretical Jewish Christianity would appear to be not so very different from the faith of the first Jewish believers.*

(*a*) We have already noted that the first Christians remained loyal to the law (above p.238). And as the Christian gospel began to

spread outside Palestine it was the Jewish Christian desire to maintain their observance of circumcision, the sabbath and the purity law
which lay at the root of some of the most serious problems and
disputes (cf. Acts 15.1ff.; Rom. 14.1–5; Gal. 2.4f., 12f.; 4.10; 5.2ff.;
6.12ff.; Phil. 3.2; Col. 2.16f., 20–22). Notice also that the earliest
Christian preaching seems to have included the claim that Jesus was
the prophet like Moses, whose coming Moses himself had promised
(Deut. 18.15f.; so Acts 3.22; 7.37; cf. Luke 1.68–79 – see above
pp.132f.).

(*b*) When we first meet James, the brother of Jesus, in the earliest
Christian literature, he is already among the leadership of the
Jerusalem church (Gal. 1.19), and very soon thereafter he stands at
the head of the community eclipsing even Peter in importance (Gal.
2.9, 12; Acts 12.17; 15.13ff. – see above p.109). As for hostility to
Paul, we know from his own account in Galatians how unpopular
Paul quickly became with Jewish believers, an antagonism so sharp
that Luke makes little attempt to disguise it (Acts 15.1f.; 21.20f. – see
further below §56.3).

(*c*) The adoptionist christology of the Ebionites too seems to have
a firm anchor point in the earliest Christian attempts to express faith
in Jesus the Christ (Acts 2.36; 13.33; Rom. 1.3f.; Heb. 5.5; cf. Phil.
2.9–11 – see above pp.45f., 217). Note also Acts 2.22 – 'Jesus of
Nazareth, a man attested to you by God . . .'; and 10.38 – able to do
good and heal, 'for God was with him' (see above pp.19f.). It may
also be significant that the earliest NT writings (Paul and Mark)
seem to know nothing, or at least say nothing about any virgin birth
tradition. Indeed both Mark and the kerygma of the Acts sermons
make the starting point of the gospel about Jesus the ministry of John
the Baptist (Mark 1.1ff.; Acts 10.36f.; 13.24f.) – like the Gospel of the
Ebionites.

Only at one point do the second-century Ebionites seem to stand
apart from the first believers in Jerusalem, for the Ebionites were
markedly hostile to the sacrificial cult of the temple.[24] This does not
seem to reflect the views of the first Christians (see above p.238),
particularly Matt. 5.23f. and Acts 3.1 (where 'the hour of prayer' =
the hour of evening sacrifice), though it is possible that the sacrificial
cult was of secondary importance to them (reflected perhaps in the
absence of sacrificial language in the early understanding of Jesus'
death – see above pp.17f., 218f.). On balance however it is more
probable that the Ebionite hostility dates back ultimately to the
Jewish Christians' flight from Jerusalem in the 60s and the increasing influence of Essene thought in the transjordan settlements after

the destruction of the temple.[25] It is less likely to stem from Stephen's rejection of the temple (see below pp.271f.). Such animadversion to the cult was hardly possible for a Jewish Christianity so long as it remained centred in Jerusalem.[26]

In short, apart from the different attitudes to the temple cult, the measure of agreement between the earliest Jerusalem believers and Ebionites is quite striking. *The heretical Jewish Christianity of the second and third centuries apparently has no closer parallel than the earliest Christian community in Jerusalem.* Indeed, on the basis of this evidence, *the heretical Jewish Christianity of the later centuries could quite properly claim to be more truly the heir of earliest Christianity than any other expression of Christianity.*

However, that is only one side of the picture; to leave such a claim unchallenged would give a false impression. For there are two other important differences between Ebionism and earliest Christianity. The first we might call the difference in *tone*. The faith and practice of the primitive Jerusalem community was not something thought out, clearly crystallized in debate; it was simply the first stage in the development from a form of Jewish messianism to Christianity proper, from Jewish faith with some peculiarities to a distinctively Christian faith. Consequently an important difference between the two forms of Jewish Christianity does emerge: the practice and beliefs of the primitive Jerusalem community were marked by development and transition, there was nothing fixed and final, everything was fluid; whereas Ebionism is a self-conscious faith, held in opposition to other expressions of Christian faith (notably Paul), thought out and clearly articulated. A link can certainly be traced between the two, a continuity of tradition; but Ebionism has hardened and petrified a tradition that was initially fluid and developing.

The second difference follows from the first – a difference in *time*. The primitive Jerusalem faith and practice was the first tentative attempt to express the newness of belief in Jesus as Messiah, risen and coming again – to express it, that is, in a totally Jewish environment. Ebionism came to expression in quite different circumstances – when Christianity had expanded right out of Judaism, had become predominantly Gentile – and, most importantly, after at least several crucial debates and controversies on the relationship between the new faith and the Judaism which cradled it in infancy. In other words, we might justifiably conclude that *Ebionism was rejected because in a developing situation where Christianity had to develop and change, it did not!*

Here then is an interesting definition of heresy. Heretical Jewish Christianity could claim a direct line of continuity with the most primitive form of Christianity. It could certainly claim to be more in accord with the most primitive faith than Paul, say. If the earliest church is the norm of orthodoxy, then Ebionism measures up pretty well; if primitiveness means purity, then Ebionism can claim to have a purer faith than almost any other. But Ebionism was rejected – why? Because its faith did not develop as Christianity developed. It clung to an expression of Christian faith which was acceptable at the beginning of Christianity in a context of Judaism. In the wider environment of the second and third centuries, with the formative documents of Christianity already written, the simple Jewish messianism was no longer adequate. In short, *heretical Jewish Christianity was a form of stunted, underdeveloped Christianity*, rigid and unfitted to be the mouthpiece of the gospel in a new age.[27]

54.4   So far we have studied the Jewish Christianity of two periods – the Christianity of the earliest years in Palestine, and the Jewish Christian sects of the second and third centuries. What about the intervening period? How did primitive Jewish Christianity shape up to the developments which moulded Christianity in a non-Jewish fashion during the rest of the first century? What were the events and controversies which prepared the way for Ebionism? Where and why did simple Jewish messianism cease to be adequate? If the answer is to be found at all it will be found within the NT. We proceed then by measuring various NT writings and passages against the check list of the three characteristic features of second- and third-century Jewish Christianity.

§55. JEWISH CHRISTIANITY WITHIN THE NEW TESTAMENT: (1) ADHERENCE TO THE LAW

We know from Galatians and Acts in particular that the question of whether the law was binding on all believers became a central area of controversy within first-century Christianity – Paul maintaining against many, probably most of the Jerusalem based believers, that those in Christ have been liberated from the yoke of the law. We shall return to this below (§56). One of the key factors in Peter's loss of influence in Jerusalem was very probably his greater ambivalence or openness on this issue (cf. above p.109 and below p.385).

What is more interesting is the fact that we have among the NT

documents themselves two writings which give clear expression to a
Jewish Christian attitude to the law (in contrast to the Pauline view)
– Matthew and James.

55.1   *Matthew's attitude to the law* comes to clearest expression in
5.17–19. These were probably three independent logia which
Matthew himself has joined together, though possibly vv.18–19
were already linked in the (more conservative?) tradition on which
he was drawing. Whatever their original meaning, Matthew clearly
understands them in terms of continuing *loyalty* to the law, that is, for
him, *the law as interpreted by Jesus*.[28] Whatever Jesus himself may have
meant by any talk of fulfilling the law, he is not to be understood as
superseding it, or leaving it behind. On the contrary, 'fulfilment' is
defined by the antithesis with 'destroy': Jesus came not to abolish
(the affirmation is repeated) but to fulfil – that is, presumably, to
realize or complete the law and *thus* to establish it, set it on a firmer
basis (5.17). The point is strengthened by linking the saying with
v.18 by the explanatory 'for': Jesus came not to destroy but to fulfil,
'for so long as heaven and earth endure, not one dot not one letter
will disappear from the law until everything has happened'. That is
to say, the law will remain inviolate, imperishable until the end of the
age, or until the will of God has been fully accomplished. And what
that means is clarified in turn by setting out v.19 as a corollary:
'Therefore whoever relaxes (or sets aside) even the least of these
commandments and teaches others to do the same, he shall be called
least in the kingdom of heaven' (note, not excluded from the kingdom, but definitely a second rate citizen); whereas 'whoever keeps
the commandments and teaches others so will be called great in the
kingdom of heaven'. Here clearly the law as 'realized' by Jesus
retains *an unconditional validity for those who belong to the kingdom of heaven*;
and here too is a firm rebuke to other members of the kingdom (other
Christians – Matt. 8.11) who were more liberal in their attitude to
the law. A similar emphasis is evident in 23.3 – 'Whatever the
scribes and Pharisees tell you practise and observe'; also 23.23 – you
should practise the weightier matters of the law (justice, mercy and
faith) without neglecting the lesser matters (tithing mint, dill and
cummin).
   Matthew's high regard for the law is also expressed in two words
distinctive in his vocabulary. The godlessness against which he
contends in his gospel he characterizes as *anomia* – 'lawlessness,
rejection of the law'. The word occurs in Matthew more often than in
any other NT document, and Matthew is the only evangelist to use it

(7.23; 13.41; 23.28; 24.12) – clearly, then, his own formulation and expressive of his own understanding of Jesus' message as advocating continuing faithfulness to the law. The same point is implied in the second distinctively Matthean word – *dikaiosunē*, 'righteousness' (7 times in Matthew;[29] elsewhere in the Gospels only in Luke 1.75 and John 16.8, 10). Its use in Matt. 5.20 indicates that Matthew understands 'righteousness' in terms of keeping the commandments (note again the explanatory 'for' linking vv.19 and 20): 'unless your righteousness exceeds that of the scribes and Pharisees, you will never enter the kingdom of heaven' (cf. 6.1 and contrast Luke 18.9–14). We could perhaps just mention also the emphasis Matthew places on the disciples 'doing' (*poiein*). The verb occurs about 40 times in Matthew's special material, and 22 times in the Sermon on the Mount alone: only he who *does* the will of Jesus' Father in heaven will enter the kingdom of heaven (see particularly 5.19; 7.21, 24; 12.50; 19.16f.; 25.40, 45).[30]

Further confirmation of Matthew's Jewish Christian attitude to the law may be found at one or two points in his redaction of Mark. For example, the question about divorce: in Mark 10.2 the question reads simply, 'Can a man divorce his wife?'; but Matthew reformulates it, 'Can a man divorce his wife *for any cause*?' Thereby he transforms a general question and sets it within the rabbinic debate between the schools of Hillel and Shammai; the Matthean formulation in fact presupposes the then current practice of divorce and asks Jesus for a verdict on the then dominant Hillelite position (divorce permissible for any cause). With the same effect the unconditional ruling of Jesus in Mark 10.11 is amended by Matthew to allow the possibility of divorce in cases of unchastity – the more rigorous position of Shammai (19.9; so 5.32). Jesus is thus shown as engaging in a current rabbinic debate and as favouring the stricter viewpoint of the Shammaites.[31]

Again, Matthew's redaction of Jesus' words about true cleanliness is significant (Matt. 15.17–20/Mark 7.18–23). Mark reads, ' "Do you not see that whatever goes into a man from outside *cannot defile him*, since it enters, not his heart but his stomach, and so passes out into the drain?" (*Thus he declared all foods clean*)'. Matthew was evidently unhappy with Mark's presentation at this point, for he omits the two key phrases: ' "Do you not see that whatever goes into the mouth passes into the stomach and so is discharged into the drain?" '. He could not escape the force of the tradition itself (15.11 – 'not what goes into the mouth defiles a man . . .'), but (1) he softens Mark's version (Mark 7.15) – he was not prepared to have Jesus affirm that unclean foods *cannot* defile; (2) he completely omits Mark's interpretation that Jesus' saying implied annulment of the law on clean and unclean foods; and (3) by his additions of 15.12–14 and particularly 15.20b (summarizing the teaching) he attempts to direct the force of Jesus' words into a rejection of the rabbinic elaboration of the law (rather than of the law itself – 'to eat with unwashed hands does not defile a man'). From this we may deduce that *Matthew was less than willing to abandon the dietary laws himself and less than happy with the suggestion that Jesus' words amounted to an abrogation of the law.*[32]

In addition a noticeable feature of Matthew's Gospel is his presentation of Jesus as the fulfilment of OT revelation – most clearly seen in the 'fulfilment quotations' so distinctive of Matthew (1.22f.; 2.5f., 15, 17f., 23; 4.14–16; 8.17; 12.17–21; 13.35; 21.4f.; 27.9f. – note also 5.17; 26.54, 56), and in his suggestion that Jesus' teaching was the climax of the prophetic interpretation of the law ('the law *and* the prophets' – 5.17; 7.12; 11.13; 22.40). There is possibly something of a parallel here with the more distinctive second- and third-century Jewish Christian idea of Jesus as the climax of prophetic revelation (above p.240). If so, this parallel may be strengthened by the element of Moses typology which is fairly clearly discernible in Matthew's Gospel. I am thinking here especially of the (deliberate) parallel between the 'slaughter of the innocents' in Matt. 2.16ff. and Ex. 1.22, of the evocation of the sojourn in Egypt and of the Exodus in Matt. 2.13–15, and of the similar evocation of the wilderness wanderings and Moses' 'forty days and forty nights' on Sinai in Matt. 4.1–11.[33] Like Moses, Jesus dispenses both blessing and curse (5.3ff.; 23.13ff.). Perhaps most striking of all, Matthew seems deliberately to have gathered together Jesus' teaching into five blocks (5–7; 9.36–10.42; 13.1–52; 17.22–18.35; 23–25), each block preceded by narrative material and its conclusion marked by the repeated formula, 'When Jesus finished these words/parables/teaching . . .' (a feature which can hardly be accidental – 7.28; 11.1; 13.53; 19.1; 26.1). A not implausible explanation of this feature is that Matthew intends thereby to suggest that Jesus' teaching parallels the five books of Moses.[34] In particular it can hardly be coincidence that Matthew specifically has Jesus deliver his first block of teaching on a mountain (whereas Luke speaks of 'a level place') – again an allusion to the giving of the law from Mount Sinai is strongly implied.[35]

All this reinforces the view that *Matthew stands firmly within the mainstream of Jewish Christianity*: whether, like the Ebionites, he saw Moses and Jesus as the two greatest prophets is not so clear,[36] but *he certainly understood the revelation given by Jesus to be continuous with and a faithful realization of the law first given through Moses.*

55.2   Matthew's attitude to the law comes into still clearer perspective when we take into account two further strands of evidence which seem to indicate that *Matthew was seeking to defend the law from abuse on two fronts*. On the one hand there is his polemic against *anomia*, lawlessness – in particular against what he considers to be charismatic antinomianism (7.15–23; 24.10ff.). Notice the *contrast* between reliance on prophetic inspiration and spiritual powers on the one hand, and doing God's will on the other; those who rely on their charismata are called 'workers of lawlessness'. Quite possibly then there were some enthusiastic Christians in or around the communities addressed by Matthew, who believed that their spiritual experience and charismata put them on a plane where they were (wholly) liberated from the law. Against them Matthew insists that *doing God's will means precisely keeping the law*.

On the other hand, Matthew seems to be fighting against too *legalistic* an understanding of the law – an attitude probably coming to ever clearer expression in the rabbinic Judaism of his own day. Hence presumably the strong attacks on the Pharisees for what Matthew counts as in fact failure to keep the law (3.7–10; 5.20; 15.12–14; 16.12; 21.28–32, 33–46; and particularly 23.1–36). The critical question at this point concerns the law's interpretation. And here he shows Jesus frequently confronting Pharisaism with a new and deeper understanding of the law – in three ways. (1) In a manner unparalleled in other Gospels, Matthew draws on Jesus' teaching to underscore his conviction that the commandment of *love* is the heart and essence of the law, in contrast to Jewish legalism (5.43–48; 7.12; 12.1–8, 9–14 – love determines how the law is to be obeyed; 18.12–35; 22.34–40). (2) So too in a manner unparalleled in the other Gospels Matthew presents Jesus' interpretation of the law as continuous with and the climax of the prophetic protest against mere law-observance; note particularly the repeated appeal to Hos. 6.6 against the Pharisees (Matt. 9.13; 12.7; and see again the emphasis on 'the law and the prophets' – 5.17; 7.12; 11.13; 22.40). (3) Other passages indicate Matthew's conviction that Jesus did not set himself against the law, but against the rabbinic tradition – the multiplying scrupulosity of the oral tradition. Thus particularly the great antitheses of 5.21–48: Matthew clearly intends his readers to understand Jesus' teaching as a repudiation of the oral tradition, not of the law itself (5.17–19 determines the interpretation of what follows); in

these sharp edged sayings Jesus returns to the original commandment and exposes its deeper meaning. And thus also 5.20: obedience
at this deeper level exceeds the Pharisees' casuistic obedience to the
oral tradition (see also 15.1–20). In short, Matthew agreed with
rabbinic Judaism in holding fast to the whole law; but where they
interpreted the law by elaborating its rulings, he shows Jesus standing within the prophetic tradition and interpreting the law by love –
and in this way 'fulfilling the law'.[37]

It appears then that Matthew is attempting to steer his readers
between the two extremes of antinomianism and Pharisaism: *the whole
law has an abiding validity, but it expresses the will of God only when
interpreted by love – only then do we penetrate to its real meaning.*

At this point therefore *Matthew stands wholly within the stream of
Jewish Christianity which flows from the earliest Jerusalem community.* His
position is not so very different from that of the first Christians,
though obviously more self-conscious and more fully thought
through. Certainly his attitude to the law is far more conservative
than Paul's (or Mark's, say) – though there is no evidence that he
attacks Paul as such.[38] And quite clearly he represents a form of
Jewish Christianity which Paul would probably regard as still un-
liberated from the law, though nevertheless as valid. On only one
related issue does he seem to have moved out beyond the earliest
unthought-out Jewish Christianity of the first believers – in reference
to mission. By way of concession to that more limited view of mission
he retains the tradition that (the pre-Easter) Jesus envisaged only a
mission to Israel (10.5f., 23; 15.24). But he qualifies this with the
universal commission of the risen Christ in 28.18–20. Similarly his
redaction of Mark 11.17 probably signifies his abandonment of the
view that 'all the nations' will flock to Mount Zion in the last days
(see above p.239) in favour of the view that the gospel must first be
taken out to 'all the nations' (28.19; cf. the Matthean additions
12.18–21; 21.43; 24.14).

Does Matthew therefore provide us with something of a link
between the Jewish Christianity of the earliest church in Jerusalem
on the one hand and later Ebionism on the other? There is a
continuity of attitude towards the law. In particular Matthew shares
a similar loyalty to the law (cf. Matt. 5.18 with *Clem.Hom.*, VIII.10 –
'eternal law'). And he shares too something of the Ebionite belief
that Jesus came as the fulfiller of OT revelation, to restore the true
meaning of the law. Yet at the same time his 'intensifications' of the
law (Matt. 5.21–48) are of a different order from those of the Ebionites,[39] and he shows an awareness of the dangers of a casuistic legalism

which is lacking in Ebionism. Perhaps therefore we could go so far as to say that however 'Ebionite' Matthew is at this point, it is his insistence on love as the determining factor in how the law is to be obeyed which keeps him wholly within the mainstream of developing Christianity.

55.3 *The letter of James is the most Jewish, the most undistinctively Christian document in the NT.* The name 'Christ' appears in only two places – at points where it could easily have been added (1.1; 2.1). Otherwise no explicit reference is made to the life, death or resurrection of Jesus. When an example of patience under suffering is sought, it is found in the OT prophets and Job (5.10f.), not in Jesus (contrast I Peter 2.21ff.). The Jewish and undistinctively Christian character of the letter is such that some have been able to argue, not implausibly, that James was originally a Jewish document taken over with little alteration by an early church.[40] However, there are a number of features which seem to require a Christian author – in particular, the reference to birth through the word (1.18; cf. I Cor. 4.15; I Peter 1.23; I John 3.9) and not a few echoes of Jesus' teaching as preserved most noticeably in the (Hellenistic) Jewish Christian Gospel, Matthew (e.g. James 1.5, 17 = Matt. 7.7ff.; James 1.22f. = Matt. 7.24ff.; James 4.12 = Matt. 7.1; James 5.12 = Matt. 5.34–37).[41] So James is best understood as belonging to the same stream of Jewish Christianity as the Lukan psalms and Matthew. The faith he gives expression to is one which seeks to live according to the teaching of Jesus within a wholly Jewish framework of belief and practice – *Christian at significant points but more characteristically Jewish in sum.*

The most striking passage in James is 2.14–26, his polemic against the doctrine of faith without works. This seems to be directed against the Pauline expression of the gospel, or more precisely, against those who have seized on Paul's slogan, 'justification by *faith* (*alone*)'. It was Paul who first expressed the gospel in this way (particularly Rom. 3.28); so the view which James attacks certainly goes back to Paul. That Paul's argument *is* in view is also indicated by the fact that James in effect refutes the Pauline exegesis of Gen. 15.6: 'Abraham believed God and it was reckoned to him as righteousness'. This, affirms James, was 'fulfilled' in Abraham's *work*, not in his faith – that is, not in 'faith alone' (contrast Rom. 4.3–22, particularly vv. 3–8; Gal. 3.2–7; cf. above pp. 87f.).[41a]

It is obvious then that what is reflected here is *a controversy within Christianity* – between that stream of Jewish Christianity which was represented by James at Jerusalem on the one hand, and the Gentile churches or Hellenistic Jewish Christians who had been decisively influenced by Paul's teaching on the other. It is precisely this exaltation of the law – 'the perfect law' (1.25), 'the law of liberty' (1.25; 2.12), 'the royal law' (2.8) – in reaction against Paul, which marks out Ebionism. James however does not attack Paul as such, only a one-sided influence of Paul, a Pauline slogan out of context. So at most he represents only a halfway stage towards Ebionism – but very definitely a Jewish Christianity which remained loyal to the law and consequently was sharply critical of the faith-and-not-works emphasis so distinctive of the Gentile mission.

§56. JEWISH CHRISTIANITY WITHIN THE NEW TESTAMENT: (2) EXALTATION OF JAMES AND DENIGRATION OF PAUL

These twin emphases are complementary to the first, for in Jewish Christianity Paul was denigrated precisely because he was considered 'an apostate from the law',[42] and James was exalted precisely because of his exemplary fidelity to the law.[43] Within the NT itself this latter emphasis is not so clearly articulated, though we should note Acts 15.20, where significantly it is James who lays down the minimal requirements of law which he expects all Christians to observe, and we should recall that the NT document which shows itself in most explicit disagreement with Paul is attributed specifically to this same James (above §55.3). Apart from these there are three passages in particular which give us as it were soundings at three points along the stream of Jewish Christianity in or about the middle of the first century, and which give some indication of the way in which Jewish Christian antagonism against Paul gathered strength even during Paul's lifetime – Gal. 2, II Cor. 10–13 and Acts 21.

56.1   *Gal. 2.* We know from Gal. 2.4, not to mention Acts 15.1 and Phil. 3.2ff., that there was a strong party in the Palestinian churches, a powerful force in the Christianity of Jerusalem and Palestine, which insisted on circumcision for all converts. Paul calls them some very rude names – 'false brethren' (RSV), 'sham Christians, interlopers' (NEB – Gal. 2.4), 'dogs' (Phil. 3.2) (see also above pp.23f.). But it is quite clear, from Gal. 2 and Acts 15 at least, that they were Jewish Christians – that is to say, a force *within* the Jerusalem community who could with justice claim to speak for Jewish believers in Judea. Moreover, they obviously saw it as their task to undo the evil which they thought Paul was doing with his law-free gospel; for evidently they set themselves deliberately against Paul and what he stood for.[44] Here at once we recognize *a form of Jewish Christianity which stands within the Christian spectrum at the time of Paul's missionary work, but which manifests a character very similar to that of later Ebionism.*

If the controversy in Jerusalem was relatively straightforward (whether Gentile converts should be circumcised) and its resolution amicable, the same cannot at all be said for the subsequent dispute at *Antioch* (Gal. 2.11–14). Here is one of the most tantalizing episodes in the whole of the NT. If we could only uncover the full picture of what happened here, what led up to it and what its sequel was, we would have gained an invaluable insight into the development of earliest Christianity. Instead we have to be content to make what we can of the clues and hints Paul gives us – the problem being, of course, that we have only one side of the dispute, Paul's, and just how one-sided it is we are not fully able to judge.[44a]

Who was at fault in the incident? The likelihood is that the earlier agreement implied in Gal. 2.7–10 (cf. Acts 15.22–29) included some ruling (possibly not explicit) about the mutual relations of Jews and Gentiles within mixed Christian communities – probably to the effect that Jewish Christians should continue to regard the law as obligatory among themselves without forcing it upon the Gentile Christians. In the strongly (perhaps predominantly) Gentile church at Antioch (Acts 11.20–24) the diaspora Jewish Christians no doubt felt it appropriate to be less rigorous in their practice of ritual purity (Gal. 2.12a, 14b). But when a party of Jewish Christians came down from Jerusalem 'from James' they presumably felt that the positions were reversed and consequently expected the Gentiles at Antioch to exercise *their* liberty in turn and to accept the Jewish dietary laws for as long as James's people were present. Otherwise they would be requiring Jews to 'Hellenize', to abandon something integral to their faith (something their ancestors had resisted to the death), they would be threatening the whole Jewish Christian understanding of Christianity as a fulfilled Judaism (see above §54.1), indeed they would be threatening the very existence of the Jewish communities within Palestine. Thus for the sake of Christianity in Palestine the agreement had to be observed, and the Gentile Christians could be expected to see this and to respond in a free and considerate manner, as the Jewish Christians had done in the earlier situation. Whether this was Peter's line of reasoning or not, we have certainly to reckon

with some such considerations, weighty enough to explain the
actions of Peter and of so many other Jewish Christians, including
Barnabas, who, after all, had been as much identified with the
Gentile mission as Paul.

If the events leading up to the confrontation between Paul and
Peter are obscure, so also is its sequel. We naturally tend to assume
that Paul made his point and won the day – Peter admitting his
mistake, and the previous practice being resumed. But Paul does not
actually say so, and his upbraiding of Peter tails off into a defence of
his own position to the Galatians. Yet if Paul had won, and if Peter
had acknowledged the force of his argument, Paul would surely have
noted this, just as he strengthened his earlier position by noting the
approval of the 'pillar apostles' in 2.7–10. Moreover, the line Paul
takes in 2.11–14 is a very hard one – Peter 'stands condemned', the
rest of the Jews including Barnabas 'acted hypocritically', 'their
conduct did not square with the truth of the gospel', Peter was
forcing Gentiles to 'judaize' – an attitude in fact which contrasts
quite sharply with the flexibility of Peter! In the circumstances then,
it is quite likely that Paul was defeated at Antioch, that the church as a
whole at Antioch sided with Peter rather than with Paul.[45] This
episode would thus mark the end of Paul's specific association with
Antioch and his emergence as a fully independent missionary
(according to Acts he visited Antioch only once more during his life –
18.22); it was also probably a decisive factor in bringing Paul and
Barnabas to the parting of the ways (cf. Acts 15.36–40); and no
doubt it caused Paul to redefine his position on the mutual responsibilities of Jewish and Gentile Christians within a mixed Christian
community – for it can hardly go unnoticed that Paul's advice to
such communities in I Cor. 8, 10.23–11.1, and Rom. 14.1–15.6 (not
to mention his own practice according to Acts 21.20–26) is more in
line with the policy of Peter and Barnabas at Antioch than in accord
with his own strongly worded principle in Gal. 2.11–14![46]

Whatever the precise facts of the matter then it is evident that *there
was a much deeper divide between Paul and the Jewish Christianity emanating
from Jerusalem than at first appears*. It is probable indeed that Paul was
much more isolated in the strong line he maintained at Antioch than his
own version of the episode admits. Not only so, but the fierceness of
his response to Peter at Antioch and elaborated in Galatians may
well have been a contributing factor of some significance in fuelling
the antagonism of Jewish Christianity towards Paul.

56.2   The situation is if anything more serious, the tone more strident in *II Cor. 10–13*. It would appear that some missionaries had arrived in Corinth where they proceeded to attack Paul in no uncertain terms. Who these missionaries were is not entirely clear; but the best explanation is that they were Jewish Christians from Jerusalem (note particularly 11.22), presenting themselves in a way that would most commend them to the gnostically influenced Corinthians.[47] Whoever they were, they obviously claimed to be Christians and were accepted as such (10.7). Paul calls them 'super-apostles' (11.5; 12.11); but also 'false apostles', 'servants of Satan' (11.13–15)! Obviously then they claimed to be much superior to Paul: they were the true apostles, 'apostles of Christ' (11.13), beside whom Paul did not begin to count as an apostle – *he* was the false apostle, the servant of Satan. Presumably in their eyes only the original apostles (the twelve?) and those properly accredited by the mother church (that is, by James?) at Jerusalem could claim to be 'apostles of Christ' – and Paul had no such credentials, he was quite unqualified, wholly lacking in authority (II Cor. 3.1f., 5f.). Paul also accuses them of preaching another Jesus, of having a different spirit, of proclaiming a different gospel (11.4). No doubt they made precisely the same accusation against Paul!: it was he who preached another Jesus (not the Jesus whose teaching was echoed in the letter of James); it was Paul who proclaimed a different gospel, who had perverted the original message of Jesus' words and deeds in an antinomian and obscurantist sense (cf. 4.2f.).

Here then is evidence of *a deepening rift between Paul and the Jerusalem church* – with each disputing the other's authority, and each attributing the other's gospel to Satan. It may be, of course, that the 'super-apostles' had exceeded their brief from Jerusalem; but almost certainly they claimed Jerusalem's authority and must have represented a very significant body of opinion within Jewish Christianity which denounced Paul as an upstart, traitor and false teacher. II Cor. 2.17 indeed suggests that the *majority* of evangelists or (Jewish) missionaries were opposed to Paul.[48] An alternative and very plausible explanation is that the 'false apostles' and the 'super-apostles' were two different groups, and that by 'super-apostles' Paul means in fact the pillar apostles or the twelve at Jerusalem.[49] If that was the case, then *the sharpness of the antagonism between Paul and Jerusalem can hardly be overstated.* Barrett puts Paul's point of view on this thesis in these terms: 'He (Paul) was obliged to recognize that the point of origin from which Christianity was disseminated into the world had come to be a source of perversion'.[50] If that truly represents Paul's attitude as expressed in II Corinthians, then no doubt there was equal and very likely even stronger animosity on the side of the Jerusalem Christians (cf. particularly I Cor. 15.8 – 'abortion' looks like a sharp-ended jibe directed against Paul). But even if that is an overstatement, II Cor. 10–13 remains a strong testimony to a depth of division between Paul and Jerusalem which helps considerably towards explaining later Jewish Christianity's loathing for Paul the apostate.

56.3   *Acts 21* tells of Paul's last journey to Jerusalem and his reception there. Several features are rather striking for the careful reader. At Tyre a prophecy in the assembly warned Paul against going to Jerusalem – an utterance regarded as an authoritative word of the Spirit (21.4). Caesarea was the last community to welcome him. There he stayed with Philip (21.8), one of the leaders of the Hellenists in the initial schism within the Jerusalem community (Acts 6–8; see below §60). There Agabus prophesied a hostile reception from the Jews in Jerusalem; Agabus had just come from Judea and knew how strong was the feeling against Paul (21.10f.). There Paul expressed his willingness to die in Jerusalem (21.13). For his time in Jerusalem, with whom did he stay? – not James, nor one of the leaders of the Jerusalem community (as Philip evidently was at Caesarea) – but with 'Mnason of Cyprus, an early disciple', that is, in all probability, a Hellenist (21.15f.). When Paul met with James and the elders immediately they pointed out how zealous for the law were the great bulk of the Christian community, they repeated the hostile reports of Paul which were being passed around the Jerusalem church, and at once they put pressure on him to reaffirm his loyalty to the law, to demonstrate that those reports were groundless and that he himself still lived in observance of the law. Obviously Paul was widely regarded as a renegade for abandoning the law, and it would seem that little or nothing had been done within or by the Jerusalem church to defend him on this score (21.20–24; despite 16.3 and 18.18). Then when Paul was arrested and put on trial we hear nothing of any Jewish Christians standing by him, speaking in his defence – and this despite James's apparent high standing among orthodox Jews (above p.252 n.43). Where were the Jerusalem Christians? It looks very much as though they had washed their hands of Paul, left him to stew in his own juice. If so it implies *a fundamental antipathy on the part of the Jewish Christians to Paul himself and to what he stood for.*

Most striking of all, Luke says nothing of the *collection* which Paul had been making for the church in Jerusalem; even in 24.17 the word 'collection' is avoided, and without Paul's letters we would hardly recognize the allusion here – indeed the allusion may only be to his act of piety in 21.26. Yet we know from Paul's correspondence how important the collection was for him (Rom. 15.25–32; I Cor. 16.1–4; II Cor. 8–9). Luke does mention seven delegates from the churches (Acts 20.4f.), but he fails to mention why they travelled with Paul – namely, to deliver the collection. This was obviously *Paul's* chief concern in going to Jerusalem, but Luke fails to mention that too. Why? The answer lies probably in Paul's reason for making the collection in the first place: for Paul it was an expression of unity, unity between the churches he had established and the churches of Judea. The reason why Luke omits to mention it therefore is most likely because *the Jerusalem church refused to accept the collection* – something which Paul himself had feared might happen (Rom. 15.30f.). For the Jerusalem Christians acceptance of the collection would, or would be seen to mean declaring their agreement with Paul's mission, approving the attitude Paul had adopted towards the law. And this would destroy their own position among their fellow Jews, inevitably so in a period of mounting Jewish nationalism. So most likely they chose to *reject* the collection, thereby symbolizing their disapproval of Paul and his methods. Probably the rejection was not quite so abrupt as it seems at first: the course of action which James urged upon Paul may well have been one which would have allowed the Jerusalem Christians to accept Paul's gift, once Paul had proved his good Jewish faith. But the plan went very badly wrong and in the ensuing confrontation and crisis Paul seems hardly to have been supported, let alone his collection accepted by the local Christians. Luke evidently chose to omit this whole side of the episode, since it was hardly the sort of picture of the early church which he would wish to preserve (see below §72.2).[51]

If all this is a fair reconstruction of Paul's final close encounter with the Jewish Christianity of Jerusalem it shows how wide and deep the split between Jewish Christianity and the Gentile congregations had become, how sharp and bitter was the antagonism of Jewish Christians towards Paul. *A Jewish Christianity which had aligned itself so firmly with its Jewish heritage and which had set its face so firmly against Paul and the law-free Gentile mission was well on the way to Ebionism*.

§57. JEWISH CHRISTIANITY WITHIN THE NEW TESTAMENT: (3) ADOPTIONIST CHRISTOLOGY

So far we have uncovered evidence of a Jewish Christianity within the NT period which has some striking resemblances to the second- and third-century Jewish Christianity which emerging orthodoxy condemned as heretical. But now with this third feature we can for the first time draw a fairly distinct line between later Ebionism and the Jewish Christian documents of the NT itself. James is no help on this issue – he can hardly be said to have a christology as such. But what about the others?

57.1 *Matthew*. As we have already seen there is one possible important link between Matthew's christology and that of Ebionism – namely, the Moses typology evident in the construction of Matthew. On the other hand, Matthew does not give much weight to the idea of Jesus as a prophet. He reports it as the opinion of the crowds (16.14; 21.11, 46; and see above p.248), but as a recognition of Jesus' significance it falls far short of the designation, 'the Christ, the Son of the living God' (16.15–17). The Fourth Gospel, it is perhaps worth mentioning, sharpens this implied antithesis considerably: Jesus is called 'prophet' by those on the way to faith (4.19; 9.17) and by the fickle wavering crowd (6.14; 7.40), but the title completely fails to express the significance of him who already was, long before Abraham or any prophet appeared (8.52–59).[52]

More important, Matthew contains a birth narrative: clearly in Matthew's intention Jesus' experience of the Spirit at Jordan must be understood in the light of his virgin birth. Now, as we saw above (p.242), it was precisely the birth narratives which the Ebionites had excised from Matthew, enabling them to give a more 'adoptionist' weighting to the Jordan episode. Thus the account of the virgin birth indicates with sufficient clarity that *Matthew's christology had already developed beyond the point at which Ebionite christology 'seized up'*; and the Ebionite mutilation of Matthew likewise indicates a self-conscious retreat from or rejection of the christology of the Jewish Christianity which finds expression in Matthew.

One further point of contrast should be noted. According to Origen some Ebionites did accept the virgin birth; but these, adds Eusebius, 'refused to confess that he was God, Word and Wisdom'.[53] The point is that besides the virgin birth narrative, *Matthew also identifies Jesus with Wisdom*. This is clearly to be seen in his redaction of

Q. Luke 7.35 reads, 'Yet Wisdom is justified by all her *children*', where Jesus (and John the Baptist) are evidently called Wisdom's children. But Matt. 11.19 has altered this Q saying to read, 'Yet Wisdom is justified by her *deeds*', where the 'deeds' are obviously to be understood as the 'deeds' and 'mighty works' of *Jesus* (11.2, 20ff.). Similarly the saying attributed by Luke 11.49–51 to 'the Wisdom of God' is specifically attributed to Jesus by Matt. 23.34–36. And in Matt. 11.28–30 Matthew has probably appended to Q material a typically Wisdom utterance where Wisdom calls men to accept her yoke (cf. particularly Ecclus. 51.23–27); but again Matthew presents it as a saying of Jesus – Jesus not merely counsels men to accept the yoke of Wisdom but issues Wisdom's own invitation (see above p.74). In other words, in each case Jesus is portrayed by Matthew not merely as Wisdom's messenger but as Wisdom herself.[54] So here again Matthew seems already to have advanced in his christology even beyond the modified Ebionism of which Origen and Eusebius testify; and that Ebionism seems to have made a dogma of the more inchoate and less developed christology of pre-Matthean Jewish Christianity.

In short, Matthew's virgin birth narrative and his Wisdom christology provide us with clear points at which any tendency towards Ebionism in first-century Jewish Christianity began to diverge from the Jewish Christianity which remained within the spectrum of acceptable diversity of first-century Christianity.

57.2 *Hebrews* has obvious claims to be considered among the more Jewish documents of the NT, and its argument that Jesus' death and entry into the heavenly sanctuary has brought the (earthly) temple cult to an end (Heb. 10.1–18) has obvious parallels with the Ebionite hostility to the sacrificial cult (see above pp.243f.). More to our present point, however, the distinctive highpriestly christology of Hebrews seems at first glance to offer few contacts with Ebionism. But a careful reading of the text soon uncovers *quite a remarkable amount of adoptionist language*. In particular we might note 1.4 – by his passion and exaltation he has *become* superior to the angels and inherited a title superior to theirs; 1.5, 5.5 – likewise by his exaltation he was *begotten* as God's Son and *appointed* God's high priest; 1.9 – because he loved right and hated wrong, *therefore* God *anointed* him above his fellows; 2.6–9 – he was the one man in whom the divine programme for humanity has been fulfilled – he alone of all men had been *crowned* with glory and honour *because* he suffered death; 2.10 – he was *made perfect* through suffering; 3.2f. – like Moses he was faithful to him who *appointed* him, but he has been *deemed worthy* of greater honour than Moses; 5.7ff. – *because* of his humble submission his prayer was heard – he *learned* obedience through what he suffered – and being thus *made perfect* he was designated high priest after the order of Melchizedek.[55] Here then are not a few points of contact with the adoptionist christology of second- and third-century Jewish Christianity. One might even say that 9.14 is not so far from the Ebionite idea of Jesus' mission being made effective through the Spirit who as the eternal Spirit manifested himself in earlier revelations, particularly Melchizedek (in the case of Hebrews): as Melchizedek had 'neither beginning of days nor end of life' (7.3), so Jesus attained to that priesthood by demonstrating the indestructible quality of his life in his resurrection (7.15f.).

On the other hand, we have already noted (above p.222) that Hebrews, like Paul, identifies Jesus with pre-existent Wisdom (1.2f.). Not only so, but Heb. 1.8f. refers Ps. 45.6f. to the exalted Son, and thereby addresses him as 'God'. Whether the writer intended this in the hyperbolic sense of the psalmist's original address to the king or not (cf. Ps. 82.6f.; John 10.34f.), the fact remains that in these opening verses Hebrews has more or less explicitly affirmed of Jesus two of the very titles which, according to Eusebius, even the more moderate Ebionites denied to Jesus (God, Wisdom – see above p.258). Indeed, if we look more carefully at the initial development of Hebrew's whole argument in this light it almost reads like *a polemic against Ebionite christology*. If Ebionism regarded Jesus chiefly as a prophet, the writer to the Hebrews begins by setting Jesus in a category apart: the prophets made God known 'in fragmentary and varied fashion', but now God has spoken through a *Son*, a Son who 'reflects the glory of God and bears the very stamp of his nature' (1.1–3). If Ebionism evaluated Jesus or the Christ as an angel or archangel (see above p.242), the writer to the Hebrews, still in his opening sentence, moves on to dismiss the view that the Son is even comparable to the angels: on the contrary he has a rank and title far superior to those of any angel – 'To what angel did God ever say . . .?' (1.4–2.18). If Ebionism attributed to Jesus the significance of another Moses figure, Hebrews concludes its opening theological exposition (1.1–3.6) by comparing and contrasting Moses with Jesus as equally faithful in God's service but of quite different rank and status – Moses a servant, Jesus the Son (3.1–6). It is only when he has dismissed these Ebionite-like views as wholly inadequate to express the significance of Jesus the Son of God that he goes on in his subsequent argument to develop his more distinctive high-priesthood christology.

How the author of Hebrews managed to maintain the tension between these two sides of his christology – the adoptionist language, together with his anti-Ebionite stance (if we may so put it) – is not at all clear. But what does seem to be clearly implied is that Hebrews stands within the developing stream of Jewish Christian christology, that already some of the characteristic features of later Ebionite christology have become an issue *within* Jewish Christianity, and that the writer to the Hebrews while maintaining his adoptionist language is unwilling to freeze it within Ebionite-like limitations. It would appear in fact as though *Hebrews, like Matthew, marks a parting of the ways of the two main currents within Jewish Christianity*, the one remaining as an element within the acceptable diversity of Christianity, the other veering off into the unacceptable diversity of second- and third-century Jewish Christianity. If this is a fair assessment then the point to note is that *we do not need to wait until the late second century and the emergence of orthodoxy to find a denial of the christology which was to characterize Ebionism; that denial had already been made within the first century and came from within Jewish Christianity itself.*

§58. CONCLUSIONS

58.1   *There is a significant similarity, possibly even continuity between the Jewish Christianity evident in the NT and the Jewish Christianity adjudged heretical by the emerging great Church in the late second and third centuries.* The three most characteristic features of the latter – their faithful adherence to the law, their exaltation of James and denigration of Paul, and their 'adoptionist' christology – are all present in the Christianity which centred on Jerusalem during the first decades of the new sect's existence. Indeed *the earliest form of Christianity is almost more like second- and third-century Ebionism than anything else* – though it must at once be added that the earliest Christian community was only beginning to express their faith and reformulate their life-style, whereas Ebionism was much more carefully thought out, much more a reaction to developments elsewhere in Christianity and in Judaism. But even in the Jewish Christian documents and the Pauline correspondence in the second half of the first century we see clear indications of the way in which Jewish Christianity was developing; *even within the NT itself* we see signs of that reaction to the law-free Gentile mission, and a certain clinging to the early christological formulations which became so characteristic of Ebionism. So if there is a continuity between Jerusalem Christianity and later

Ebionism then perhaps we have to conclude that something of this development within Jewish Christianity can be traced in part by means of the NT documents and in part *through the NT documents themselves*.

58.2   *It is however also possible to draw a firm line of distinction between the Jewish Christianity of the NT and the Jewish Christianity deemed heretical by the great Church in later centuries.* Such a line cannot be drawn in terms of law: James and Matthew are in some ways nearer to the Ebionites than they are to Paul as regards the status and role they attribute to the law – though Matthew's emphasis on love (the love shown by Jesus) as the means of interpreting the law does mark off his attitude as more distinctively Christian than Jewish, or better Pharisaic. Such a line certainly cannot be drawn between first-century Jerusalem Christianity's attitudes to James and Paul and later Jewish Christianity's attitudes to James and Paul – each seems to be almost as deferential to the former and certainly as hostile to the latter as the other. In other words, on these two issues we are not really in a position to mark off heretical Jewish Christianity from the Jewish Christianity which was an acceptable part of the Christian spectrum; *Jewish Christianity could take up a very conservative stance towards the law and a very antagonistic stance towards Paul and still be recognized as a valid expression of faith in Jesus the Christ.*

Where the line of distinction is firmly drawn is in *the assessment of Jesus.* Second- and third-century Jewish Christianity regarded Jesus as a prophet, as the greatest of the prophets, who was adopted as God's Son and Christ by the descent of the Spirit or Christ (= angel?) and by virtue of his obedience to the law. But already within the NT, and indeed within the Jewish Christianity of the NT, such views of Jesus were being rejected as inadequate – he was Son in a unique sense, Wisdom itself and not just her mouthpiece, in a class apart from and immeasurably superior to prophet, angel or Moses. That is to say, *already within the first century Jewish Christians were setting themselves against assessments of Jesus which became characteristic of Ebionism*, already within the NT *Jewish* Christians were defining the limits of valid Jewish Christianity.

The significance of this point should be underlined: just as the *unity* of Christianity was defined in terms of Jesus, so now we see that *the diversity of Jewish Christianity is being defined also in terms of Jesus*. As the exaltation of Jesus and the unity between the man of Nazareth and the exalted one present to the first Christians in their worship and service was the strand which united the diverse kerygmata, confessions, worship, etc., so the exaltation of the man Jesus, the affirmation that the man Jesus was in fact God's Wisdom, the assertion of his (in the end) unquantifiable superiority over prophet, angel, Moses and priest, becomes the dividing line where the acceptable diversity of first-century Jewish Christianity falls over into the unacceptable diversity of later Ebionism, where faith in Jesus falls short of Christian faith.

58.3   When we talk of Jewish Christianity we are talking about a *spectrum*. Jewish Christianity was not just a point on the spectrum of first-century Christianity; it was itself a spectrum, *a diverse phenomenon*. At one end of that spectrum Jewish Christianity falls over into the unacceptable beliefs that were to characterize Ebionism. But also *within acceptable* Jewish Christianity there was diversity; even within the NT Jewish Christian writings themselves we can see that *they do not all represent a single uniform type of faith*. The opponents of Paul whom we met in Gal. 2, II Cor. 10–13 and Acts 21 are in the end of the day not easy to differentiate from the later Ebionites. The letter of James and the Lukan psalms are characteristically Jewish but hardly yet distinctively Christian. The Gospel of Matthew is more discriminating and more interesting, for he seems to be steering a middle course between a more conservative (Ebionite-like?) Jewish Christianity and a more liberal Hellenistic Jewish Christianity: on the one hand, he affirms the inviolability of the law, while on the other he emphasizes that the law must be interpreted by love and not by multiplying halakic rulings; again, on the one hand, he preserves sayings of Jesus which limited mission to Israel, while on the other he emphasizes that Jesus' message is for all nations – almost as though he was saying to the conservative, 'The gospel is for all, Gentile as well as Jew', and to the liberal, 'Remember that Jesus himself confined his mission within the boundaries of Israel' (see above §§55.1, 2).

To locate *Hebrews* within the spectrum of Jewish Christianity is even more fascinating. For Hebrews seems to belong chiefly to that type of Hellenistic Jewish Christianity which we first meet in Stephen (see below §60 and p.275).[56] It does not take issue over the law (except perhaps for Heb. 13.9), but deals almost exclusively with the question of the traditional cult: priesthood, tabernacle, sacrifice – do they continue in Christian Judaism in some sense, or have they been superseded? Otherwise the law does not seem to have posed any problems.[57] At the same time, Hebrews has been influenced to a considerable extent by Greek philosophic thought, in particular the

Platonic world view of two worlds, where the world of ideals/ideas is the real world, and our world is the world of copies/shadows; the writer develops his theme by a fascinating combination of the Jewish belief in two ages with that Platonic belief in two worlds.[58] From this we can build up a picture of the Jewish Christian community to which Hebrews was written: it was not involved in dispute about the whether-or-not of law observance, and so was probably a fairly homogeneous Jewish Christian community untouched by the sort of questions Paul raised; but probably it did hanker after the tangibility of the temple cult, such as the primitive Jerusalem community had enjoyed; and it was familiar with Platonic philosophic thought – quite likely then a rather special form of Jewish Christianity or particular group of Jewish Christians in the diaspora, hankering after the primitive simplicities of earliest Christianity. Perhaps therefore Hebrews represents *a developing type of Jewish Christianity whose development both reflects something of the influences which made for Ebionism and also embodies the growing convictions which caused Christianity later to reject Ebionism.* Thus, on the one hand, the author seems to regard the sort of loyalty to the traditional cult which we find in the earliest Jerusalem church as a childish stage of faith which should have been outgrown. But on the other, while he retains the sort of strong adoptionist language which must have remained most congenial to Ebionite christology, it is clear that already his own faith has begun to transcend what in fact became the chief categories of Ebionite christology. If this is so, then *Hebrews represents a kind of middle path or indeed a turning point in the development of Jewish Christianity,* where it has turned its back both on the primitive formulations and loyalties of the first stage of Christianity as outmoded and on the otherwise conservative developments which led to Ebionism.

We should perhaps just note that the Gospel of John can be regarded as a more developed expression of roughly the same attitude. A major concern of the Fourth Evangelist is to present Jesus as the fulfilment of Judaism – its law (4.10, 14; 6.27, 30–32, 48, 58, 63), its temple (2.13–22; 4.20–24), its festivals (particularly 1.29; 7.37–39; 10.22, 36; 19.33–36) and its rites (2.6; 3.25) – and not least Jesus as the one whose revelation has superseded that of Moses (1.17). Note particularly that John is the only Evangelist to attribute to Jesus himself the saying about the temple which evidently prompted Stephen's rejection of the temple (John 2.19; Acts 6.14; see above pp.98, 131). At the same time his assessment of Jesus leaves far behind the tentative formulations of Hebrews not to mention the ossified categories of later Ebionism. John indeed is so far along the spectrum of Jewish Christianity from Ebionism that he is best considered under the heading of Hellenistic Christianity – though he does serve to remind us that these classifications are not at all mutually exclusive or rigid.

If all this is a fair representation of these NT writings then we can represent the spectrum of Jewish Christianity diagrammatically, the broad vertical line marking the point at which acceptable diversity falls over into unacceptable diversity.

JEWISH CHRISTIANITY

John	Hebrews	Matthew	Lukan psalms	James	Opponents of Paul in Galatians 2 etc.	Ebionites

But even if there remains much that is open to question in the above analysis, there can be little doubt that *Jewish Christianity in the first century did comprise a wide diversity*: Jewish Christians who had abandoned the law and the cult and devoted themselves to a universal mission and who had been influenced by wider Hellenistic culture and thought in varying degrees; Jewish Christians who were variously questioning the narrower view of mission, the continuing validity of the cult, and some, but by no means all, the continuing validity of the law; Jewish Christians who were unhappy with the law-free Gentile mission, and who saw the law as having a continuing validity for Christians – some continuing to regard the temple as of central significance; and Jewish Christians who were opposed to the Gentile mission, hostile to Paul and devout in their observance of the whole law – Christian Jews rather than Jewish Christians, many of them the direct forerunners of the later Ebionites.[59]

58.4   To sum up. *Two, possibly three criteria of unity and diversity* seem to have emerged from this chapter. First, Matthew's insistence that the law must be interpreted by love may provide one: Jewish Christianity was counted unacceptable when it *began to regard strict observance of the law as more important than the spontaneity of love*. More clearly, second, Jewish Christianity was counted unacceptable when it *persisted in clinging to a limited view of Jesus and his role*. It could claim support for this conservatism from some of the earliest expressions of Christian faith. But since the spread of Christianity outside Palestine and the controversies of the first few decades caused these early, more fluid and provisional formulations to be left behind as inadequate, *the Jewish Christianity of the second and third centuries represents in the end a reactionary attempt to restrict the Christian estimate of Jesus within the limitations and confines of traditionally conceived Jewish thought and practice.* Third, Jewish Christianity was counted unacceptable when it *failed to develop*, when it hardened the inchoate expressions of the earliest days into a system, when it lost the flexibility and openness to a new revelation which questions of law and mission demanded in a developing situation, when it became rigid and exclusive. *One of the earliest heresies was conservatism.*[60] In short, the failure of heretical Jewish Christianity was that it neither held to the unity (the exaltation of Jesus showing Jesus to be the unique expression of God) nor allowed for the diversity (of developing Christianity).

XII

HELLENISTIC CHRISTIANITY

§59. INTRODUCTION

So far we have explored something of the overlap between Christianity and Judaism, something of the interaction within Jewish Christianity between the emphases of emerging (rabbinic) Judaism and those of developing Christianity, something of first-century Jewish Christianity's attitude towards the tendencies which may have grown into the distinctive beliefs of later Ebionism. But Christianity of course soon spread outside Palestine and came into interaction with other beliefs and ideas within the syncretistic milieu of the eastern Mediterranean, speculations and cults themselves shaped in greater or less degree by a wide range of religious and philosophical influences (including those from Palestine itself). It was from this first-century melting pot that Gnosticism emerged in the second century, Christianity's most dangerous rival for several decades at least, though as is now generally recognized individual ideas and emphases which became characteristic of second-century Gnosticism were already current in the first century (I will speak of these as 'gnostic' or 'pre-Gnostic').[1]

Our question is simply posed: How was first-century Christianity affected by these various influences and ideas? How open were the early Christians to them? How widely ranging was the diversity of first-century Christianity on this broad front? Did first-century Christianity embrace within its acceptable diversity anything that might properly be called *gnostic* Christianity? Or were the boundaries drawn in the latter decades of the second century to separate Christianity and Gnosticism already being drawn in the first century?

We start with the 'Hellenists' of Acts 6. Not only does their very name indicate that we can quite properly speak of a Hellenistic

Christianity in some distinction from Jewish Christianity (the 'Hebrews' of Acts 6.1 – see below §60), but, more to the point, the Hellenists mark the first significant broadening out of primitive Christianity: it was they who evidently began the large scale movement of Christianity towards 'the Greeks' (Acts 11.20); and it was they who thereby in effect began to open up Christianity to the wider range of influences prevalent within Greek religion and culture. We will then focus attention on the growing edge of Christianity as it began to compete more and more effectively with the ancient Graeco-Roman religions, the mystery cults and the philosophical speculations current in the major centres of the area. Here we must ask: To what extent were the earliest Christian communities emerging from the Gentile mission affected by these wider influences? To what extent (if at all) does first-century Christianity on these frontiers manifest a syncretistic character, manifest tendencies which became distinctive of later Gnosticism? In particular, twentieth-century research into the history of religions in this period forces us to ask whether any of the NT documents themselves (or their immediate sources) express what can properly be called gnostic features, or leave themselves open to gnosticizing interpretation and use. Here the discussion will focus on the Synoptic source Q, on Paul, and on the Fourth Gospel.

§60. 'THE FIRST CONFESSIONAL SCHISM IN CHURCH HISTORY'

Who were the 'Hellenists'? Most likely *Hellēnistai* signifies Jews who used or could use only Greek as their *lingua franca* and who had been influenced to a significant extent by Greek culture.[2] The majority of these would probably be Jews of the diaspora who had settled in Jerusalem (cf. Acts 2.9–11; 6.9), though no doubt there were not a few local Jews who associated with them, seeking to cultivate the more sophisticated Greek customs. So too the 'Hebrews' probably denote those who retained Aramaic (or Hebrew) as their daily tongue even in the diaspora and who had been educated to remain defiantly Jewish through and through in the face of pressure to relax their loyalty to Torah and temple (cf. II Cor. 11.22; Phil. 3.5). Whatever the precise facts, the clear implication of Acts 6 is that the Jerusalem Hellenists maintained separate synagogues where no doubt the common language of teaching and worship was Greek

(6.9). Obviously many Hellenists had been converted and identified themselves with the new sect of the Nazarene.

One conclusion follows almost immediately: that *the earliest Christian community embraced two fairly distinct groups more or less from the first* – Hebrews who spoke Aramaic (or Hebrew) as a badge of their Jewishness, and Hellenists who preferred to or who could converse only in Greek, presumably as the language more appropriate to a faith that made universalistic claims. Moreover, the Hellenists must have lived rather apart from the rest; otherwise how could the Christian widows have been so completely neglected (6.1) – not just some of them, but the whole group? This strongly suggests that Hebrews and Hellenists were somewhat isolated from each other, the Hellenists probably living in a particular section of the city, a fairly distinctive social quarter.[3] The relationships between the two groups would be complicated by the fact that the thoroughly orthodox very probably tended to regard the Hellenists as religiously inferior: their embracing of Greek customs would certainly feed the suspicion that they were lax in their observance of the law; proselytes, inferior to Hebrews born and bred, would naturally associate more with the Hellenists (cf. 6.5); and from the time of the Maccabees 'Hellenist' probably contained 'a disparaging nuance'[4] – where the Sadducees had collaborated with alien forces politically, the Hellenists had compromised culturally.

These latent tensions within the earliest Christian community came to a head in the failure of the 'community of goods' – the separateness of the two groups resulting in the Hellenist widows being missed out in the daily distribution from the common fund (6.1). Luke's narrative suggests that the only problem was a temporary breakdown in the community's administration which was soon put right. But almost certainly the failure to cater for the Hellenists and the subsequent complaints of the Hellenists were only the surface expressions of these latent tensions, *the symptoms of a deeper division*. The case for seeing this confrontation as the beginning of 'the first confessional schism in church history' (to use E. Haenchen's too formal phrase)[5] is a cumulative one, but here can be stated only briefly.

(*a*) The implications of the names, 'Hebrews' and 'Hellenists', and (*b*) the indications of the fuller circumstances surrounding the Hellenists' complaints (6.1) have already been drawn out.

(*c*) The seven who were elected in 6.5 were probably all Hellenists, since all have Greek names. Of course Greek names were not so uncommon among Palestinian Jews – two of the twelve had Greek names, after all (Andrew and Philip). But Stephen and Philip, the first two of the seven named, were certainly Hellenists, and Nicolaus, the last named, 'a proselyte from Antioch', would also rank among the Hellenists. More than likely then the middle four were Hellenists too. But even if our conclusion here runs beyond the immediate evidence, the astonishing fact remains that among the seven chosen, not one non-Greek name appears. How odd that the group elected to administer the common fund for the *whole* community should be composed (almost?) entirely of Hellenists! It is more plausible, I think, that the seven were all Hellenists and that they were elected as spokesmen for the Hellenist believers, presumably to represent the Hellenists at city level as the twelve represented (in effect only) the Hebrews. Very likely indeed they were already the *de facto* leaders of the Hellenist Christians, perhaps the emerging leaders of the Hellenistic house groups.[6] In such a case their election would simply be a *recognition* of the leadership qualities they *already* displayed – as in fact the narrative suggests (6.3,5).

(*d*) According to Luke the seven were elected 'to serve tables', to leave the twelve free to preach the word of God (6.2). But in the following narratives the ones depicted as preaching the word of God are precisely Stephen and Philip (6.8–8.13). That is to say, they act as initiators and evangelists taking the gospel to those whom the Hebrews had tended to neglect – the Hellenists in Jerusalem and the half-breed Samaritans. Is there here implied *a different attitude to mission?* The local Jerusalem Christians as we have seen had little thought of going out with the gospel; if anything they expected diaspora and heathen to come to them, to worship in the temple in the end-time (see above pp.238f.). Quite likely the Hellenists with their background of diaspora Judaism tended more or less from the first to be much more outward going in their understanding of the gospel and of evangelism.

(*e*) This last speculation gains support from the most striking evidence of all – namely, *the attitude to the temple* which is credited to Stephen in Acts 6 and 7. The discussion here is complicated by the question of the historical trustworthiness of the Lukan narrative and of the speech attributed to Stephen. Suffice it to say that the speech is so distinctive within Acts and chapters 6–8 contain such distinctive features that the most plausible view is that Luke is here drawing on a source which has preserved quite accurately the views of the Hellenists or even Stephen in particular with regard to the temple. Certainly the whole narrative explains the subsequent persecution of the Hellenists so well that there is no real reason to doubt its essential historicity. The point then is that Stephen was accused of speaking against the temple and the customs handed down by Moses (Acts 6.13f.). And this accusation is borne out by the speech which follows.

Far from being a dull, straightforward recital of Israel's history of no immediate bearing on the situation envisaged, as it at first seems, the speech attributed to Stephen is a subtly slanted presentation which climaxes in *an outspoken attack on the temple*. It concentrates on the period prior to Israeli settlement in the promised land, prior, that is, to Jerusalem's becoming the national and religious capital of Israel. The underlying theme of the first half is the presence of God with his people outside Judea (note particularly vv.2, 5, 8, 9, 16, 20, 30–33). Then the climax quickly builds up, composed of two antiphonal themes. The first is the *contrast* between the tabernacle and the temple: the tabernacle typified the time of the wilderness wanderings when the congregation (*ekklēsia*) received the living oracles and the angel of the presence was with them (v.38), it was made according to the pattern shown to Moses on Sinai (v.44), it symbolized God's presence moving with them in the period of the conquest (v.45), it provided no permanent place of worship during Israel's golden age (v.46); whereas the house which Solomon provided for God was fixed and rooted in one spot (vv.48ff.). The second is the direct line of *apostasy* which the speech draws from Israel's rejection of Moses for the tangible idolatry of the golden calf (vv.39–41), through the idolatry of the worship of the planetary powers which resulted in the exile to Babylon (vv.42–43), to the climax of the present idolatry of the temple (vv.48f.). This is the most astonishing feature of the speech – its outspoken attack on the temple itself. The key word here is Stephen's description of the temple as 'made with hands' (*cheiropoiētos*). It was a word used by more sophisticated Greek thinkers in criticism of idolatry. But, more important, it was regularly used by Hellenistic Jews in their condemnation of paganism – the word itself often serving to characterize both the idol itself and the Jewish scorn of idolatry from the time of the LXX on (see e.g. Lev. 26.1; Isa. 46.6; Sib.Or. III.605f., 618; IV.8–12; Philo, *Vit.Mos.*, I.303; II.165, 168; Apoc. Peter 10; cf. Acts 7.41; 17.24). But Stephen uses this adjective of the temple in Jerusalem – *he calls the temple an idol!* – and compounds his blasphemy by quoting Isa. 66.1–2, one of the few OT passages which seem to denounce the temple root and branch (vv. 49–50; cf. *Barn.* 16.2).

The significance of the views expressed here should not go unmarked. (1) Stephen's rejection of the temple meant in effect also *a rejection of the local Christians' attitude to the temple*. As we have seen, the bulk of the new community apparently continued to worship at the temple and probably looked to the temple as the locus of the Son of Man's return and the focus of God's eschatological action (see above pp.238f.). Stephen's speech was in fact a sharp-edged criticism of the narrow cultic nationalism of his fellow believers in Jesus the Christ. In other words, the speech confirms the suggestion made above that the breakdown of the community of goods was only symptomatic of a deeper division between Hebrew and Hellenist within the earliest Christian community. (2) The emphasis on God's presence outside Judea and the evidence that the speech shows influence of distinctively Samaritan views,[7] may also confirm the further suggestion made above (*d*), that Stephen and the Hellenists were *more outward going* in their understanding of the demands of the gospel, and consequently critical of the stay-in-Jerusalem attitude of the Hebrews. (3) Since the accusation against Stephen in Acts 6.14 so clearly echoes the saying attributed to Jesus by the false witnesses in Mark 14.58[8] and attributed to Jesus by John 2.19, the most obvious implication is that Stephen's view of the temple was greatly influenced by this particular Jesus-tradition (see above pp.74, 98). In which case we see here *the first instance of Christians differing (and differing sharply) in their interpretation of Jesus' teaching*. In fact, Jesus' views about the temple were neither so uncritical as the Hebrew Christians' practices implied, nor so hostile as Stephen's ('my Father's house' – see above §34.1). As with his attitude to mission, so here, there were strands in his teaching which could be followed in different directions. The earliest believers evidently opted for an essentially conservative interpretation of those parts of the Jesus-tradition which might have caused unnecessary friction with the Jerusalem authorities. Whereas Stephen seems to have seen the significance of this neglected strand (see also above §34.2). The point is that he did not hesitate to emphasize this side of Jesus' teaching and to elaborate it even though it meant being (sharply) critical of his fellow (Hebrew) Christians and provoking the hostility of the more orthodox Jews.

(4) We should perhaps simply note that there is no indication in the speech of Acts 7 that Stephen or the Hellenists were at this stage attacking the *law* as well as the temple: the speech hardly plays down the importance of Moses (see particularly vv. 17, 20, 22, 36–38) or of the law (particularly vv. 38, 53) – there is no Pauline antithesis here between the covenant given to Abraham (v.8) and the 'living oracles' given to Moses (v.38). The accusations of 6.13–14 may have been expressed in general terms by Luke, or 'the law' and 'the

customs delivered to us by Moses' may have referred solely in the first instance to the law relating to the temple and the cult. Of course, since so much of the law was bound up with the sacrificial system, a rejection of the temple was bound to lead sooner or later to a questioning of the law as a whole. And it was evidently zeal for the law and the traditions which made Paul a persecutor of the Hellenists (Gal. 1.13f.; Phil. 3.5f.). But when it was that the continuing authority of the law as such came into question is not clear. Stephen himself probably did not yet consider his position as constituting a breach with Judaism and the law; he may indeed have believed that Jesus' coming and exaltation as the prophet like Moses (Acts 7.37) constituted a call to return to the authentic religion of Moses, stripped of all its later idolatrous abuses and corruptions (sacrifices, ritual and temple).[9] If so, the point is that *the first attempt to broaden Christianity began in a division within Judaism.*

(*f*) Stephen's views seem to have led directly to *an open split within the earliest community of Christians*; the differences which first became visible in Acts 6.1 now deepened into a more obvious and clear-cut division. The depth of this division is indicated by the account of Stephen's trial and death. The Hebrew Christians seem to have shown no solidarity with or support for Stephen in his trial (despite Peter and John's earlier boldness in face of the same Sanhedrin – 4.13). Had Stephen gone too far for them in attacking the temple so fiercely? Luke's silence is ominous. Similarly the account of Stephen's burial is probably significant – 'devout men (*eulabeis*) buried Stephen' (8.2). Who were the *eulabeis*? The word is used elsewhere in the NT only of devout Jews, that is, devout in their attendance on the temple (Luke 2.25), in their pilgrimages to Jerusalem (Acts 2.5), in their observance of the law (Acts 22.12). Does the word then indicate men who agreed with Stephen's execution, orthodox Jews noted for their pious good deeds (acting in obedience to Deut. 21.22f.)? If so, why them? Why not 'believers' or 'young men' as in 5.6, 10? Why does Luke say that (only) they 'made great lamentation over Stephen' and not 'the church'? Why not 'the apostles' if indeed they were the only ones spared in the persecution following Stephen's death (8.1)? Is Luke perhaps trying to cloak the fact that the Hebrew Christians had virtually *abandoned* Stephen, so antagonized were they by his views on the temple? Perhaps they believed that Stephen had brought his fate upon his own head, even that his death was just reward for the extremeness of his views. At any rate it looks rather as though Stephen's views had at least lost him the sympathy of the local Hebrew Christians, who may well have felt that Stephen had gone much too far, and had jeopardized the very existence of the whole new sect; by tacitly repudiating Stephen's views they made possible their continuing presence within Jerusalem.[10] If this is the case then the ramifications of this first confessional schism become more apparent – the Hebrew Christians seeking to preserve their position within Judaism and thereby drawing away in the opposite direction from their fellow believers who were more outward going and more ready to pursue the implications of Jesus' teaching even when it meant a radical reappraisal of the new sect's understanding of and relation towards Judaism as a whole.

(g) Finally we may note that the persecution following Stephen's death seems to have affected only or principally the Hellenist Christians. Stephen's initial evangelism and disputation was evidently carried on within the Hellenist synagogues (6.9f.). His views on the temple would naturally cause deep offence to those who had abandoned homes in the diaspora precisely in order to live in Jerusalem, the city of the temple; Stephen's attitude to the temple may indeed partly be explained as the reaction of an 'angry young man' to his elders' over-valuation of the temple cult. At all events it was the Hellenists who engineered the accusation against Stephen and his arrest (6.11ff.), and significantly the leading part in the subsequent persecution was played by Saul, a Jew of the diaspora (Gal. 1.13, 23; Phil. 3.6; Acts 8.3; 9.1ff.). In other words the persecution has the marks of an intra-Hellenist conflict. This strongly suggests that *the chief, perhaps sole targets of the persecution were the renegade (that is Christian) Hellenists*, and that the Hebrew believers were caught up in it only incidentally or only for a brief time. Luke maintains that the whole church was scattered abroad, 'except the apostles' (8.1); but that persecuting authorities would concentrate on the numerous followers and ignore the leaders of any proscribed movement is very hard to accept and contrary to obvious pogrom strategy (cf. 12.1–3). Besides, in Jerusalem the Hellenists would stand out and be easily recognized, and the Hellenist Christians who shared Stephen's views would have few friends to shelter them; whereas local Hebrew Christians still loyal to temple and law would be relatively secure.[11] Whatever the actual scope of the persecution the fact seems to be that the Hellenists were almost wholly driven out of Jerusalem (8.4ff.; 11.19ff.), and thereafter the Jerusalem church consisted almost entirely of Hebrews, the bastion of the more conservative Jewish Christianity in the subsequent disputes over the Gentile mission (see above §56; cf. *Clem.Hom.*,XI.35 – James, leader of 'the church of the Hebrews in Jerusalem'). In that case the persecution following Stephen's death simply pushed *further apart* the two sides of the schism which Stephen's views had already brought about.

Here then is *a considerable element of diversity within Christianity almost at the very beginning of its existence*, in fact *a schism within the first Christian community*. In effect we have uncovered in part at least the first division between two types of Christian – conservative and liberal (to use broad and recognizable categories) – the one holding fast to tradition, the other sitting loose to it in the light of changing circumstances. The local Hebrew believers thought it more important to remain within the already existing pattern of Judaism – as Jesus himself had, of course. But the Hellenist believers evidently began to place more importance on those elements in the Jesus-tradition which could not find continuing expression within the pattern of Judaism then prevailing: the new material was beginning to rend the old garment, the new wine to burst the old bottles – as Jesus also had foreseen (Mark 2.21f.).

§61. GNOSTIC TENDENCIES WITHIN FIRST-CENTURY CHRISTIANITY

If Christianity broadened out so quickly as a result of the Hellenists' views and consequent persecution (Acts 8.4ff.; 11.19ff.), how far could it broaden out before it lost effective contact with its roots in Judaism and its centre in Christ? How diverse did Christianity become in the missionary churches which sprang from the Hellenists' work[12] and from Paul's apostolic labours? How syncretistic or gnostically inclined were the churches addressed within the NT? In this section we begin our attempt to answer these questions by examining those Christian communities or sections of Christian churches which seem to have been most open to and influenced by categories and concepts characteristic of the full blown Gnostic systems of the second century and beyond.[13]

61.1 *The church at Corinth*. I Corinthians provides the clearest evidence in the NT of a division within a Christian community.

> I appeal to you, brethren, by the name of our Lord Jesus Christ, that all of you agree and that there be no dissensions among you, but that you be united in the same mind and the same judgment. For it has been reported to me by Chloe's people that there is quarreling among you, my brethren. What I mean is that each one of you says, 'I belong to Paul', or 'I belong to Apollos', or 'I belong to Cephas', or 'I belong to Christ'. Is Christ divided? Was Paul crucified for you? Or were you baptized in the name of Paul? (I Cor. 1.10–13).

This passage has been frequently understood to mean that there were four parties in Corinth – a Paul party, an Apollos party, a Peter party and a Christ party – the first three expressing loyalty to a significant figure in the early mission of Christianity, and the Christ party presumably decrying such factionalism but in a rather supercilious, perhaps exclusive manner, claiming loyalty to Christ alone, but in such a way as to make themselves a fourth party.[14] J. Munck, on the other hand, has argued that there were in fact no 'parties' or factions in Corinth, only bickerings provoked by a wrong evaluation of wisdom.[15] The best explanation is probably that of N. A. Dahl:[16] there were not four different factions but only *two* – a pro-Paul party and a faction hostile to Paul. This is most clearly indicated by three features. (1) There are no traces of *three* opposing viewpoints in the rest of the letter: all the troubles seem to have arisen from a single diverse form of teaching which clashed with Paul's at various points. There were certainly Jewish Christians in Corinth (as the dimensions of the problem tackled in I Cor. 8–10 make clear), but they do not seem to have been hostile to Paul, and probably did not form a coherent party as such, though it is quite possible that one or two of them offered the slogan, 'I am of Cephas' as a sort of protest against the two more distinct factions. (2) In the opening section dealing with the factionalism Paul does not in fact deal with various groups: the whole section, 1.10–4.21, is an apology by Paul for himself, his conduct and ministry, an attempt to re-establish his authority against the attacks made on it. (3) In the immediate response to the different slogans Paul poses his question in terms of only two parties – those who claimed allegiance to himself, and those who claimed allegiance to Christ. Had there been an Apollos or Cephas party distinct from the Christ party Paul's questions would probably have embraced them too – 'Was Apollos crucified for you?', or 'Were you baptized in the name of Cephas?' Similarly in II Cor. 10.7 he confronts only those who claim to be Christ's in an exclusive manner – no other parties are envisaged.

Why then four different slogans in 1.12? Dahl answers this question adequately:

> Those who said 'I belong to Paul' were proud of him and held that his excellence surpassed that of Apollos or Cephas. The other slogans are all to be understood as declarations of independence from Paul. Apollos is mentioned as the most outstanding Christian teacher who had visited Corinth after Paul. Cephas is the famous pillar, the first witness to the resurrection, an apostle before Paul. The slogan 'I belong to Christ' is not the motto of a specific 'Christ-party' but simply means 'I belong myself to Christ – and am independent of Paul'.[17]

Who then were Paul's opponents in Corinth? The best explanation is that they were Christians heavily influenced by the sort of thought which was to characterize later Gnosticism, and enthusiastic in expression (see above p.179). Indeed many scholars would be prepared to call them Gnostics as such,[18] though there is no evidence in the Corinthian letters of a complete Gnostic system, particularly in the area of christology.[19]

(a) It is clear, particularly from 2.6–3.4, that Paul was confronting in Corinth those who called themselves pneumatics, spiritual ones (*pneumatikoi*) – a key gnostic word; indeed, in all three instances where Paul uses the word in I Corinthians he seems to be picking up the language of his opponents (2.13, 15; 3.1; 12.1; 14.1, 37; 15.44, 46). With this self-esteem was linked a high evaluation of what they called 'wisdom' (*sophia*). As pneumatics and wise they despised Paul for the naivety of his teaching, both its manner and content (1.17–2.5); they had left behind the milk of his teaching for the solid meat of deeper wisdom (3.1f.). Already they had attained fullness, already they were rich, already reigning, and consequently they could look down on their fellow believers with inflated pride and arrogance and on Paul as the teacher of an inferior brand of Christianity (4.6, 8, 10, 18). Clearly then they saw Christianity as a form of wisdom and themselves as possessing a deeper wisdom, a higher spirituality; in contrast to other believers they were mature, the spiritual ones. The parallels here with later Gnostic thought are striking. The Gnostic systems differed at many points, but typically Gnostic was the division of men into two (or three) classes, with pneumatics inherently superior to the rest.[20] Wisdom (*sophia*) played an important role in their understanding of salvation.[21] And the cross was an embarrassment for some at least.[22]

(b) The questions of immorality and marriage treated in I Cor. 5–7 may also reflect early gnostic or pre-Gnostic thought. As is well known, Gnostic dualism of spirit and body could lead to either promiscuity or asceticism. If the spirit is alone good and the body evil, despised 'mud', a prison incarcerating the divine spark in matter, then logically it is really of no great consequence how the body is treated: it can be either indulged even in the grossest sensuality (the spirit being unaffected)[23] or starved.[24] So the immorality of I Cor. 5–6 may well be the corollary of gnostic ideas about the body, combined with the social pressures of a Corinth notorious for its social licence (hence the argument of 6.15–20). So too if I Cor. 7.36–38 reflects an ascetic or spiritual marriage, this could also just possibly be a consequence of the same basic gnostic ideas, possibly combined with a reaction against the immoral laxity of Corinth and with the expectation of an imminent consummation.[25]

(c) The tension in the Corinthian community between meat-eaters and vegetarians looks very much like a division between gnostics and others (8–10). The 'men of knowledge' obviously made much of their knowledge (*gnōsis*), their superior insight and understanding (8.1, 7, 10, 11), in a manner very similar to later Gnosticism.[26] 'We have knowledge', was obviously their proud claim (8.1, 10) – probably also, 'We know God and are known by him' (8.3 – cf. *Gosp. of Truth*, 19.33). Consequently they thought nothing of idols and felt wholly free to join in and enjoy feasts that took place in the temples – again just like those who made the same claim in the second century.[27]

(d) The spiritual conceit of the pneumatics (they would have said knowledge of the true state of affairs) is probably reflected behind several of the other disputes that racked the Corinthian church – though not all. It came to clear expression in their conduct at the common meal and Lord's Supper (11.17–22, 33): one section of the community made it an occasion for a good meal and ignored the poorer members who had little food or who came late. Almost certainly the former were the same group whose superior knowledge enabled them to enjoy the good things of life – they were treating the common meal and Lord's Supper like the idol feasts they attended (cf. 10.19–21).[28] The same spiritual conceit is again evident in the matter of spiritual gifts (12–14): they were clearly proud of their spiritual gifts (*pneumatika*), particularly their experiences of ecstatic inspiration when they spoke in tongues (14.12, 23, 33), regarding such experiences as a manifestation of their superior spirituality, and disregarding those with less striking gifts as worthy of little esteem (12.21). It may even be that in 12.3 we have one of the earliest formulations of a distinctively Gnostic christology – the *earthly* Jesus was of no account, it was the *heavenly* Christ alone that counted.[29]

(e) A striking feature of the later Gnosticism was their conviction that having been given knowledge of the true state of things and of themselves they were thereby already 'perfect'.[30] Analogously we see in the Corinthian faction opposing Paul an overemphasis on the 'already' and a neglect of the 'not yet' of eschatological salvation. Hence the inflated language of 4.8: 'Already you are filled! Already you have become rich! Without us you have become kings!' So too the whole point of 10.1–12 was obviously to warn those who thought they had already arrived (presumably by virtue of their participation in the sacraments);[31] on the contrary they were still on the way, and might well come to grief as a result of their inflated self-confidence – the example of what happened to the Israelites between the Red Sea and Jordan providing an awful precedent. Probably the clearest example of the 'already' mentality of the Corinthian pneumatics was their attitude to the resurrection (15). They are most obviously to be identified as the group in the Corinthian church who affirmed 'that there is no resurrection of the dead' (15.12). What presumably they meant was that there was no *future* resurrection, no resurrection still to come: *already* they were raised, experiencing through their participation in the life-giving Spirit participation in the resurrection of him who by resurrection had become life-giving Spirit (15.45). In denying resurrection of the dead, they meant denying resurrection of the (dead) body: salvation did not depend on what happened to the body at or after death – indeed resurrection of the (material) body would have been incomprehensible to a gnostic, a contradiction of his fundamental dualism between spirit and matter; on the contrary, salvation was already secured, resurrection was already theirs in the resurrection Spirit.[32] Here once more then we have an affirmation typical of later Gnosticism.[33]

To sum up, the root of the trouble facing Paul at Corinth was almost certainly the strong influence of gnostic (or pre-Gnostic) ideas on a large section of the Christian community. The situation was undoubtedly more complicated than we have been able to show, but enough has been done to demonstrate that what may properly be called 'gnostic tendencies' were present within the church at Corinth. The point which we must take note of is *the diversity within that one congregation*: there was a division in the community, but both factions were still recognized as belonging to the community; one end of the spectrum of Corinthian Chrisitianity was familiar with and relished concepts and categories drawn from the wider syncretistic mix of Hellenistic culture and religious philosophy, but that did not exclude them from the community. In other words, *there were gnostics within the church at Corinth, and Paul did not denounce them as non-Christian, sham believers*. He rebuked them for their pride and lack of love, but he nonetheless recognized them to be members of the body of Christ. In short, we are only half way through the first century, but already we can see an early form of gnostic or pre-Gnostic Christianity gaining ground – *not* as a threat or attack from outside the church, but as *part of the spectrum of Christianity itself*.[33a]

61.2   When we look elsewhere in the NT it is not too difficult to find evidence of the pressure of gnostic tendencies within the growing Hellenistic edge of early Christianity.

(a) The situation involving the church at *Philippi* was rather complex, to our view at least. By 'mirror reading' the evidence we can deduce that, like the Corinthian faction, many in the Philippian congregation believed that they had already reached the ultimate, were already perfect and fulfilled (3.12–15; cf. 1.6, 11) so that talk of a salvation still to be worked out left them unmoved (2.12) and talk of a still future resurrection was irrelevant (3.10f., 20f.). Like the Corinthians their beliefs made them conceited, they disregarded others and concerned themselves only with their own higher affairs (2.3f.). Probably the antinomian corollaries to such beliefs were already being drawn out by them – at least such seems to be implied by the emphases in 2.12, 14, 3.16, and 4.8f. Consequently the Philippians were ready prey to those against whom Paul warns in 3.17–19. Who were this latter group? Clearly they were libertines who boasted of their (gross) sensuality ('their god is their belly, and they glory in their shame'). Probably, like the Corinthian gnostics they thought the message of the cross was folly ('enemies of the cross of Christ, whose end is destruction' – cf. I Cor. 1.18). Probably too they boasted of their knowledge of heavenly matters ('with minds set on earthly things' being a derisive parody). So, most likely they were libertines with marked gnostic tendencies.[34]

What is most interesting for us is their relationship to the church at Philippi. Evidently Paul regarded them as not members of the church, as is implied by the distinction between the 'many' and the 'brethren' in 3.17f. and between 'them' and 'us' in 3.19f. But probably they thought of themselves as Christians (they had a theology of the cross, their teaching was very attractive to the Philippians, and note the parallel verbs in vv.16–18). They may even have been members of the church at Philippi in the beginning (why else would Paul speak of them 'with tears'?). If so their libertine attitudes must have quickly emerged (or been brought in with them) and presumably Paul quickly saw the danger they posed and had them 'disfellowshipped' or expelled (cf. I Cor. 5.2–13). At all events they had been in or near the Philippian congregation for a long time (Phil. 3.18), and the attractiveness of their life style to the Philippians had if anything increased in the interim. Here then we may have *a good example of the effect and interaction of gnostic or syncretistic tendencies with and within one of the churches which Paul regarded most highly.*

(b) *Colossae.* Evidently there were those in the Colossian church (not necessarily a coherent faction) who might 'delude' the rest 'with specious arguments' (2.4) – proponents of what Paul calls 'hollow and delusive speculations, based on traditions of man-made teaching and centred on the elemental spirits of the world' (2.8), who probably regarded Jesus as one intermediary heavenly figure among many (cf. 2.9, and see below p.294). Apparently they were strictly ascetic: they demanded observance of festivals, new moon and sabbath (2.16); they laid down regulations about food (2.16, 21); their self denial was aimed at mortifying the flesh (2.20–23). Quite probably they called for 'worship of angels' (and of other spiritual beings – 2.8?), and made much of visions they had experienced, as a sign that they had attained to a higher stage of spirituality (2.18 – though the precise meaning of the verse is obscure).[35] How this kind of teaching is to be designated is not clear. Bearing in mind that the eastern Mediterranean was at this time a melting pot of a whole variety of religious concepts and practices, it looks very much as though we have to do here with a syncretistic teaching which drew together elements of Judaism, mystery cults, Christianity and probably more characteristically gnostic ideas – combining in a single system, its proponents would no doubt claim, the best from different quarters. If so we have a good illustration of the nature of the growing edge of Christianity in Asia Minor, of *how blurred was the border of Hellenistic Christianity* and how subtle the attraction for the first Christians of moulding their new faith and worship into more impressive syncretistic or gnostic forms.

(c) *Pastorals.* When we move on a generation or so, we find a situation not very much changed, though to be sure warnings against false teaching are more emphatic and more frequently reiterated than before. The false teaching in question was fairly clearly a kind of Jewish Christian *gnosis* not unlike that encountered above at Colossae. The writer refers to them as 'the circumcision party' (Titus 1.10) who had a high regard for the law and argued for its validity (I Tim. 1.7; Titus 1.14f.; 3.9). But 'gnosis' was obviously also a key word (I Tim. 6.20), and in propagating it they occupied themselves 'with myths and endless genealogies . . .' (I Tim. 1.4; 4.7; Titus 3.9). They were markedly ascetic in practice (I Tim. 4.3; Titus 1.14f.). And, most striking of all perhaps, they believed that the resurrection was already past (II Tim. 2.18). Most likely then it was a teaching which saw redemption in terms of the spiritual man's knowledge of the true state of affairs concerning both the cosmos and himself, and which came to expression in an acute disdain for things material. But the point is, this teaching is envisaged as not coming from without. It is a teaching which was propagated *within* the community (I Tim. 1.3f.; II Tim. 2.16ff.; 3.5; Titus 1.13f.; 3.9f.), and which had already so captivated some that they had had to be 'disfellowshipped' or expelled (I Tim. 1.19f.; Titus 3.10f.; cf. I Tim. 1.6f.; 6.20f.; II Tim. 2.18; 4.14). That is to say, even in a second (or third) generation situation where 'the faith' was more clearly outlined and defined (see above §17.4), *the actual boundaries of the communities themselves were not so clearly defined.* The gnostic teaching was condemned, but it was still argued for within the churches and many had obviously found it attractive. Here again then we see the same kind of diversity as before, present within communities near the turn of the first century.

(d) The churches addressed in *Rev. 2–3* were clearly a very mixed bag. Most noticeably the church of Thyatira 'tolerated' a prophetess, 'that Jezebel . . . who by her teaching lures my servants into fornication and into eating food sacrificed to idols' (Rev. 2.20; so Pergamum – 2.14f.; contrast Ephesus – 2.6). Moreover her followers gloried in deeper spiritual experiences – 'what they like to call the deep secrets of Satan' (2.24 – though it may well be the seer who added or changed the last word into 'Satan'). Probably therefore we have to do with a kind of libertine Gnosis – though since the seer is so morally strict himself (14.4) we may have to discount some of his description as an over-conservative reaction to what was simply a more liberal form of Christianity. Whatever the precise facts the point is that the teaching rejected by the seer and by the church at Ephesus was being entertained ('tolerated' is the seer's word) by the churches at Pergamum and Thyatira. In them at least *clear limits* marking off orthodox from heretic, Christian from non-Christian, *still had to be drawn.*

(e) The epistle of *Jude* also opposes what is clearly a form of libertine pre-Gnostic spirituality: v.19 – 'These men draw a line between spiritual and unspiritual persons, although they are themselves wholly unspiritual' (NEB). Obviously they were pneumatics who considered their own inspiration (in dreams or visions) superior to any other authority (v.8). They were proud of their ideas and boasted about their spiritual superiority (v.16). This pride in spiritual knowledge was combined with uninhibited indulgence of the body: they perverted the grace of God into debauchery (v.4); like the Corinthian gnostics they were completely selfish in their behaviour at the common meals (v.12); they indulged in sexual immorality and unnatural lust (vv.7f.); they acted like brute beasts, following their godless passions (vv.10, 18). Here then we are certainly dealing with a form of gnostic teaching, very much like that referred to above (pp. 277f. nn. 23, 27), where the body was thought to have so little integral relation to the Spirit within that it could be freely indulged without harming the spirit. The important verse for us is v. 12 – 'These men are a blot on your lovefeasts'. That is to say, the gnostics were not outsiders trying to subvert and draw away the true believers, they were *inside* the community, they took part in the common love feasts.[36] Moreover Jude, like the Pastorals, does not make any real attempt to answer the challenge of this teaching; and though he threatens them with God's judgment (vv. 5–7, 13, 15), he does not call for them to be expelled from the community. In other words, *the Christianity which Jude addressed was not a pure unadulterated faith, but a Christianity which contained within itself some gnostic-like (or pre-Gnostic) elements.* A similar conclusion would have to be drawn from *II Peter* since the key chapter (II Peter 2) is so heavily dependent on Jude.

61.3   Here then are Christian communities at different times in the first century and probably into the second century as well, which contained a considerable degree of diversity – a spectrum of diversity which stretches right over into faith and conduct which the later Church found thoroughly unacceptable – a trajectory (if the metaphor is not too misleading) whose outer edge continually merged into the sort of gnostic beliefs and practices which later orthodoxy condemned out of hand as heretical. There are various attempts made by the letter writers to achieve a clearer idea of what is acceptable diversity and what beliefs and conduct *ought* to be *un*acceptable. But *in the communities themselves a considerable spectrum of diversity was evidently counted acceptable* – a diversity which embraced within itself elements which later characterized full-blown Gnosticism, the gnostics participating in the inner life of the church as fully accepted members. In other words, we do not at this stage see a church, far less *the* Church with a full(y) Christian system of faith and order, where the only false teachers come from outside and are clearly recognized as such. On the contrary, the fact that only a modest system of discipline and expulsion had been attained even in the Pastorals implies that *there were as yet no well defined or unanimous views regarding orthodoxy and heresy,* and that these were only beginning to become appropriate concepts as the first century drew to a close.[37]

§62. THE 'GNOSTICIZING PROCLIVITY' OF Q?

J. M. Robinson, elaborating some hints from Bultmann, has pointed out that the nearest parallels to the literary form of Q are on the one hand the collections of Wisdom sayings such as we find in Proverbs and on the other the collection of sayings of Jesus presented to us in the Oxyrhynchus Papyri and the Gospel of Thomas. He designates the *Gattung, Logoi Sophōn* – 'Sayings of the Sages', or 'Words of the Wise' – and suggests consequently that Q lies on a trajectory from Jewish Wisdom to Hellenistic Gnosticism in which a gnosticizing tendency is at work. H. Koester, following up Robinson's thesis, has qualified it by arguing that the Gospel of Thomas is derived from pre-Q traditions (some of the Thomas logia appear to be more primitive than the Q version) – pre-Q traditions 'in which the apocalyptic expectation of the Son of man was missing' – and that Q has introduced this apocalyptic element 'to check the gnosticizing tendencies of this sayings gospel'.[38] Can we then properly speak of the 'gnosticizing proclivity' of Q? Do we have to place Q on a 'gnosticizing trajectory'?

62.1   Several considerations could be taken to indicate a positive answer to this question.

(*a*) About a quarter of the 114 Thomas sayings are paralleled in whole or in part by Q tradition.[39] If we included in the comparison Q material which has been reproduced by only Matthew or only Luke or likely (pre-)Q material from only Thomas, the proportion would rise to nearer one third. Clearly then, there is *a continuity between the tradition which Q has preserved and the Gospel of Thomas*, and Thomas is ultimately dependent on that tradition to quite a marked degree. One example with only slight modification is Logion 86 – interesting as being the only Son of Man saying preserved in Thomas: 'Jesus said: (Foxes have their holes) and birds have (their) nests, but the Son of man has nowhere to lay his head (and) to rest' (cf. Matt. 8.20/Luke 9.58) – only the last two words having been added (cf. Logia 50, 51, 60, 90).

(*b*) One of the most noteworthy features of Q has always been *the absence of any interest in Jesus' suffering or death* – that is, not merely the lack of any passion narrative, which would be understandable in a collection of sayings, but also the absence of any of the passion predictions which receive such emphasis in the latter half of Mark (Mark 8.31; 9.31; 10.33f., 45). As we noted above (p.40 n.19), the thought of suffering and rejection is not entirely absent from Q, but it is hardly obvious, and the sayings in question could be otherwise interpreted. The only ones which Thomas used are Logion 55 (Matt. 10.38/Luke 14.27) and Logion 86 (quoted just above); but these were probably understood in a Gnostic sense of Sophia's and the spiritual man's wandering existence with no home in this world, no rest or acceptance within the material creation.

(c) Finally we might note *how strong is the wisdom influence within Q*. It does not appear as though Jesus is yet identified with Wisdom.[40] But Jesus is certainly presented by Q as a teacher of wisdom.[41] Taken together with the last point therefore, it looks rather as though the Q tradition presents Jesus' teaching as guidance for living in the last days rather than as kerygma, with Jesus understood as one whose words have eschatological significance quite apart from any question of his dying or rising. When we turn to the Gospel of Thomas we find a significant parallel, in so far as many of the same sayings together with all the rest are presented as the words of 'the living Jesus' who thus gives life *through his teaching* (cf. Logion 52); 'faith is understood as belief in Jesus' words', which disclose 'eternal wisdom about man's true self'.[42]

Here then are some possible grounds for seeing Q as located earlier on the same gnosticizing Wisdom trajectory to which Thomas belongs.

62.2   On the other hand we cannot ignore at least two other factors.

(a) *There is nothing distinctively Gnostic in Q*, whereas the Gospel of Thomas has typically Gnostic features. See particularly

Logion 29 – Jesus said: If the flesh has come into existence because of spirit, it is a marvel; but if spirit (has come into existence) because of the body, it is a marvel of marvels. But I marvel at how this great wealth has settled down in this poverty.

Logion 50 – Jesus said: If they say to you, Whence have you come? say to them, We have come from the light, (from) the place where the light came into existence through itself alone . . .

Logion 77 – Jesus said: I am the light which is over everything. I am the All; the All came forth from me and the All has reached to me. Split the wood; I am there. Lift up the stone, and you will find me there.[43]

Moreover, Thomas was able to use early Q-type material precisely by reading it as gnosis or elaborating it in a Gnostic direction. Thus, as we saw above, only two of the few Q sayings which could be readily interpreted as allusions to Jesus' suffering and rejection have been retained in Thomas, in one case with a small but significant addition to give it a more Gnostic-like tinge (Logion 86). Two other examples are

Logion 2 – Jesus said: He who seeks must not stop seeking until he finds (cf. Logion 92; Matt. 7.7/Luke 11.9); and when he finds, he will be bewildered; and if he is bewildered, he will marvel, and will be king over the All.

Logion 3 – . . . But the kingdom is within you and outside you (cf. Luke 17.21). When you know yourselves, then you will be known; and you will know that you are the sons of the living Father. But if you do not know yourselves, then you are in poverty, and you are poverty.

(b) The most striking difference between Q and Thomas is in the area of *eschatology*. For Q is thoroughly eschatological and is characterized to a significant degree by the expectation of the soon coming of the Son of Man;[44] whereas in Thomas eschatological interest is almost wholly absent, and the Synoptic-like material which it has preserved has been thoroughly de-eschatologized. Thus, for example,

Logion 10 – Jesus said: I have cast fire upon the world (note the past tense – cf. Luke 12.49), and behold, I guard it until it is ablaze.

Logion 18 – The disciples said to Jesus: Tell us in what way our end will take place. Jesus said: Have you indeed uncovered the beginning so that you may seek the end? For in the place where the beginning is, there shall the end be. Blessed is he who will stand at the beginning, and he will know the end and will not taste death.

Logion 46 – . . . But I have said that whoever among you will become a little one will *know* the kingdom and will be greater than John (cf. Matt. 18.3; Matt. 11.11/Luke 7.28).

See also the realized emphasis in 1, 3, 11, 19, 35, 37, 51, 59, 111, 113, and notice how the parables of crisis have become advice to prudence rather than to watchfulness for the eschaton (21, 103), and how the parables of the kingdom have become wisdom sayings (8, 76, 109). Koester argues that Thomas reflects a stage of the Q tradition when the emphasis was wholly realized; but I do not think the future eschatology in Jesus' teaching can be sloughed off quite so readily (see below §67.2) – so that Q is almost certainly earlier and nearer to Jesus' emphasis than any non-eschatological version of the Jesus-tradition. More to the present point, the Thomas material in these logia just mentioned looks much more like *de-eschatologized* tradition rather than pre-eschatologized tradition – with the eschatology of Logion 57 seen as an unremoved residue rather than as the forerunner of a more thorough eschatologizing.

62.3   To sum up, we must not overemphasize the wisdom character of Q. If the eschatological element was as strong as it appears then Q was certainly not content to portray Jesus simply as the teacher of wisdom who lives on in and through his words; on the contrary, the soon coming of Jesus as the Son of Man was integral to its christology and its message. Yet at the same time the fact remains that Q was not retained by the early Christian churches as it stood (as they retained the other source of Matthew and Luke – Mark); they retained it only as wedded to, inserted within a Markan framework – that is, only when firmly united to the passion narrative, only when set in conjunction with and in the context of Jesus' total ministry, his life and death and resurrection. *The early churches did not choose to preserve and use Jesus' teaching in isolation from his death; Q in itself was apparently not treated as gospel by most of the early Christians.* Quite possibly they recognized the danger of presenting Jesus simply as a revealer and teacher of wisdom. And it is not impossible that some even saw the danger of Q being swept up into the trajectory of gnosticizing Wisdom – although in this case at least the trajectory metaphor itself suggests a firmer connection and continuity with *later developments* than the evidence really allows. In short, there is nothing overtly gnostic in Q itself, not even a recognizable 'gnosticizing proclivity'; but perhaps we have also to say that by their failure to include any of Jesus' forebodings of his suffering and death (except five or six more allusive references) the compilers of Q left its traditions somewhat exposed to the sort of interpretation which was perhaps inevitable once the parousia hope had faded and which subsequently came to full expression in the Gospel of Thomas – the sort of interpretation which was impossible once the Q tradition had been firmly wedded to the Markan passion story.

But this means that once again it is *the unity and continuity of the man Jesus with the exalted Christ which was crucial for Christianity even in its earliest use of the Jesus-tradition.* It was not the earthly Jesus alone or his teaching by itself which the first Christians valued, but the teaching of him who was the soon coming Son of Man (so Q). And even the Q combination and balance of tradition was, on reflection, found inadequate to serve as an expression of the Christian gospel, since it lacked precisely the emphasis that Jesus is the crucified and risen one as well as the teacher of wisdom and Son of Man coming in glory.

One other point is perhaps worth making. Christian Gnosticism usually attributed its secret teaching of Jesus to discourses delivered by him, so they maintained, in a lengthy ministry after his resurrection (as in *Thomas the Contender* and *Pistis Sophia*). The Gospel of Thomas is unusual therefore in attempting to use the Jesus-tradition as the vehicle for its teaching. Indeed, it rather looks as though the attempt to treat Jesus' teaching as 'sayings of the wise' was found wanting in Gnostic circles, despite the freedom they exercised in redacting and adding to the Jesus-tradition, and was abandoned in favour of the complete freedom provided by the literary form of 'resurrection dialogues'.[45] Perhaps Gnosticism abandoned the Gospel of Thomas format because it was to some extent subject to check and rebuttal from Jesus-tradition preserved elsewhere: the more thorough their redaction of the Jesus-tradition, the less credible it became; whereas there were no such checks with the resurrection dialogues. At all events, *Gnosticism was able to present its message in a sustained way as teaching of Jesus only by separating the risen Christ from the earthly Jesus and by abandoning the attempt to show a continuity between the Jesus of the Jesus-tradition and the heavenly Christ of their faith.*

In short, the 'criterion' of the unity of the man Jesus and the exalted Christ suggests in part how the Q tradition became vulnerable to gnostic redaction, and Q suggests in part why the criterion began to take the shape it did in Mark as unity not just between Jesus the teacher and the coming Son of Man but as the unity of the Son of Man who must suffer and die before he is raised and exalted.

§63. PAUL – 'THE GREATEST OF ALL THE GNOSTICS'?

63.1   R. Reitzenstein's description of Paul (which heads this section)[46] comes as something of a shock to those familiar only with the Paul of ecclesiastical tradition, held in honour by the great Church as a staunch defender of orthodoxy more or less since Irenaeus. But in fact, *at not a few points Paul affirmed views which commended him more to the heretical Gnostics than to the orthodox Fathers.* Let me illustrate this at a number of key points.

(a) *The Valentinians firmly maintained that their theology was based on Paul* and that he

> made use of the basic concepts of their system in his letters in a manner sufficiently clear to anyone who can read . . . The teaching of Valentinus is just as inconceivable without the letters of Paul as without the prologue to the Fourth Gospel, and it is no accident that Paul is preferred by all Valentinians as the preacher of the hidden wisdom who speaks out most clearly.[47]

Thus they could appeal to Gal. 1.12, 15f., where Paul affirms that his gospel was revealed directly to him by immediate revelation from God and was not received from men. This firm assertion of Paul that his gospel was not ultimately dependent on the Jerusalem apostles and their tradition is used to justify the second-century Gnostics' appeal to their revelation over against the ecclesiastical tradition of the orthodox Fathers (cf. Eph. 3.3). Similarly Valentinian exegetes could enlist Paul's support (I Cor. 2.13f.) for their distinction between *pneumatikoi* and *psychikoi*. Moreover they were able to cite

Paul's claim that, contrary to the jibes of his Corinthian opponents he *did* speak wisdom among the mature (I Cor. 2.6; cf. II Cor. 12.4), as justification of the secret wisdom which they taught their initiates.[48] W. Schmithals is not altogether unjustified therefore when he says of Gal. 1.12, 'This argument is genuinely Gnostic. The Gnostic apostle is not identified by means of a chain of tradition, by the apostolic succession, but by direct pneumatic vocation';[49] and of the I Corinthian passage – 'What is found in 2.6–3.1 could be the precise exposition of a Gnostic'.[50] Similarly the Valentinians valued Ephesians as unfolding 'the mystery of the pneumatic redemption',[51] and seem to have attributed their speculation about the aeons to Ephesians and Colossians.[52]

(*b*) The greatest Paulinist in the early centuries was *Marcion* – some would say the greatest Paulinist of all time, at least in the sense of one who acknowledged the greatest debt to Paul. At any rate he was 'the first systematic collector of the Pauline heritage'.[53] Now a key element in Marcion's theology, probably *the* key to his whole system, was his antithesis between law and gospel.[54] *This antithesis he derived directly from Paul*. And there can be no doubt that Paul expressed the antithesis between law and gospel, between faith and works very sharply in several places – particularly II Cor. 3.6 – 'the written code kills, but the Spirit gives life' (see also e.g. Rom. 5.20; 7.6; Gal. 3.2f.). It is this contrast between the old covenant as a dispensation of condemnation and death and the new covenant of grace and life which served as the springboard for Marcion's radical hostility to the OT, its law, its religion, its God (cf. II Cor. 4.4 – 'the god of this world').[55] Not so far from the mark then is J. W. Drane's claim that 'Paul's statements on the law in Galatians can with a great deal of justification be called blatantly Gnostic'.[56]

(*c*) We have already identified the anti-Paul faction at Corinth as a gnostically inclined group within the Christian church of that city (above §61.1). The striking fact which must now be noted is that at several points *Paul is plainly in sympathy with the views of the Corinthian gnostics*. In particular, he agrees with those who 'have knowledge' that idols are nothing and that Christians are at liberty to eat anything (10.26; cf. Rom. 14.14, 20), though he is willing to restrict his liberty for the sake of the 'weak' (I Cor. 8.13; 10.28f.; cf. Rom. 14.13–21). He places a high value on spiritual gifts (*pneumatika*), though his preferred word is *charismata*, and he thinks the Corinthians have greatly overestimated the benefit of glossolalia (I Cor. 12–14). And he wants to call himself *pneumatikos*, to affirm that he does speak wisdom among the mature, denying such a title to other members of the community, though on rather different grounds from the gnostics (2.6–3.4). Perhaps it is also relevant to note that Paul was himself pronouncedly ascetic in his attitude to marriage and to his body (I Cor. 7; 9.27), an asceticism perhaps shared by some of the Corinthian gnostics. In addition we should recall that while Paul obviously does not share the predominant Corinthian view of baptism (see above §39.5) he does not argue against it or condemn it (see above p.24) – and that he is quite prepared to speak of the Lord's Supper as 'participation' in the body and blood of Christ (10.16). Indeed the evidence of I Corinthians is such that J. C. Hurd has been able to argue that the Corinthians against whom Paul now writes had simply remained faithful to the more enthusiastic emphases of Paul's original preaching, when Paul had presented the gospel in terms of 'knowledge' and 'wisdom' and had himself valued glossolalia much more highly.[57] If that conclusion goes beyond the evidence, at least we have to accept that the Corinthian errors were to a very large extent simply unbalanced developments of views that Paul himself held.[58]

(d) In particular, when viewed from a second-century perspective, *Paul's teaching on the resurrection body in I Cor. 15 and II Cor. 5 seems to be more gnostic than orthodox*. It is probable that his distinction between the natural (psychic) body and the spiritul (pneumatic) body (I Cor. 15.44ff.), and his strong assertion that '*flesh* and blood *cannot* inherit the kingdom' (15.50), was both something of an advance from the earlier, more physical understanding of Jesus' resurrection body and a deliberate concession to Hellenistic aversion to the material flesh – an attempt to make the Christian understanding of the resurrection more meaningfully acceptable to Greek thought, without abandoning the more Hebraic affirmation of the wholeness of salvation: thus, *bodily* resurrection (not immortality of the soul), but resurrection of the whole man as a *spiritual* body (not resurrection of the physical body, the flesh).[59] What is even more striking, however, is that in the subsequent decades and disputes about the resurrection body *it was the Gnostics who often remained more faithful to Paul's view than the orthodox Fathers*: for when the Christian Gnostics came to express their understanding of the pneumatic's mode of existence after his release from the flesh they quite often used language denoting some kind of spiritual body;[60] whereas the early Fathers retreated from Paul's position and reaffirmed that it was precisely the physical body, precisely the flesh that was raised (see further below p.292).[61]

(e) Finally we might note that *Paul's christology was vulnerable at a key point to Gnostic interpretation.* I refer to Paul's view of the earthly Jesus, of Jesus as a man. For one thing, he seems so unconcerned with the earthly life of Jesus and wholly preoccupied with the exalted Christ; moreover, to affirm that no longer (that is, since the 'revelation of Jesus Christ' to him outside Damascus), no longer did he know Christ 'according to the flesh' (II Cor. 5.16) was in effect an open invitation to a Gnostic evaluation of Christ 'according to the Spirit'.[62] And for another, Paul twice speaks of Jesus coming in the 'likeness' (*homoiōma*) of flesh or of men (Rom. 8.3; Phil. 2.7), which the Gnostics were able readily to cite as evidence that the Saviour took upon him only the appearance of a human body.[63]

Small wonder then that Tertullian called Paul 'the apostle of the heretics'.[64]

63.2   Paul's amenability to a gnosticizing interpretation can also be illustrated from the other side – namely, from *the Fathers' own treatment of Paul in response to such Gnostic interpretations.* Faced with the very real threat of a Marcionite and Valentinian 'take over' of Paul, they had to demonstrate Paul's orthodoxy on the points at dispute, but in the event could only use Paul in defence of orthodoxy at (most of) these points by *abusing* him.

(*a*) As we have seen the Gnostics were able to use Galatians in asserting their own independence from the ecclesiastical tradition of emerging orthodoxy – including Gal. 2.5: '. . . to them we did not yield submission even for a moment, that the truth of the gospel might be preserved for you'. In attempting to refute the heretics' exegesis of this passage both Irenaeus and Tertullian rejected the usual reading of the text and followed an infrequent variant reading which *omits* the negative: 'to them we yielded submission for a time . . .'. In other words, with this exegesis they were able to bolster their claim that Paul did after all submit to the authority of the Jerusalem apostles[65] – a claim which, as we have seen, must be regarded as a misinterpretation both of history and of Paul's letters themselves.

(*b*) The Fathers were generally embarrassed by the strength of Paul's contrast between law and gospel, works and faith, and were prepared to welcome any exegetical device, however far-fetched, which would prevent Paul being understood in a Marcionite sense. Cyril of Jerusalem, for example, declared that Paul remained a persecutor of the Church so long as he believed that Christianity abrogated the law rather than fulfilled it, and Pelagius argued that Paul wrote ten letters (including Hebrews, but excluding Philemon and the Pastorals) in order to signify his basic accord with the law of

Moses.[66] More usually however they attempted to win their case by emphasizing (we should say, overemphasizing) the Pauline idea of the law as a kind of tutor until Christ came (Gal. 3.24), and by introducing the distinction between the moral and the ceremonial law into Paul's thought (a distinction not drawn from Paul himself).[67] So too the majority of the Fathers were able to soften the sharpness of Paul's antithesis between faith and works by reading Paul through the eyes of the author of James, but all too often at the cost of emptying the Pauline understanding of grace and faith of its richness and power.[68]

(c) The Gnostic dualism between God and the world and its consequent disjunction between creation and redemption was able to draw too much strength from the Pauline view of the resurrection body. Recognizing this the Fathers sought to interpret Paul in conformity with their own belief in the resurrection of the flesh – but again, inevitably, it involved some exegetical contortions. Irenaeus and Tertullian, for example, were clearly concerned at the capital which their opponents were able to make out of I Cor. 15.50, but their attempts to wrest a favourable meaning from it are hardly convincing.[69] And Epiphanius rants at the Valentinians, somewhat amusingly at this point for us, in the following terms:

> They deny the resurrection of the dead, saying something mysterious and ridiculous, that it is not this body which rises, but another one rises from it, which they call spiritual[70] (but cf. I Cor. 15.35–50).

In short, at all these critical points in the debate between Gnosticism and emerging orthodoxy *the Fathers were only able to retain Paul within the great Church by* mis*interpreting him.*

63.3   Is Reitzenstein's description of Paul therefore justified? Was Paul so much a part of a gnosticizing trajectory that the heretics had a better claim to him than the orthodox? Was Marcion simply taking Paul's reasoning to its logical conclusion so that the great Church would have shown a better historical judgment if they had rejected him along with Marcion instead of holding on to him on their own terms? There is, fortunately, another side to the story.

(a) If the Fathers subjected Paul to exegetical violence, *the same is true of the Gnostics*. The technique of the Valentinians, for example, was simple: by reading different passages symbolically as references to the demiurge or the pleroma, to psychics or pneumatics (or hylics), they were able to achieve the appropriate meaning in every case. The result was a very plausible exegesis of such passages as

Rom. 7.14–25 and Gal. 4.21–26,[71] but in passages like I Cor. 1.1ff., 1.22, 15.20–23 and Eph. 5.22–32 the distinction between psychic and pneumatic became very forced and artificial.[72] And, rather significantly, in interpreting I Cor. 4.8 they ignored the obvious irony and read it as a positive assertion of the criteria by which pneumatics could recognize their election.[73] Marcion's technique was simpler. Although he appealed solely to Paul and allowed into his canon only those writings which conformed with Paul, there were passages even in Paul which he could not accept. These he simply regarded as judaizing falsifications; consequently he saw it as his task to remove these interpolations, and thus to restore the genuine Paulinism which he regarded as the true gospel. In the event, not surprisingly, the verses which were excised as non-Pauline were the very passages which showed that the Pauline antithesis between law and gospel should not be read as antithesis between Old Testament and New, between creation and redemption (for example he struck out Rom. 1.19–2.1, 3.31–4.25, 8.19–22, 9.1–33, 10.5–11.32; the phrases 'which I also received' and 'according to the scriptures' in I Cor. 15.3f.; and Col. 1.15–17 was left reading 'he is the image of the invisible God, and he is before all things').[74]

(b) More important for our purposes are *the lines of demarcation which Paul himself drew* between his own message and practice and that of his gnosticizing opponents. In I Corinthians Paul's chief criticism is the Corinthian faction's *failure of love*, their lack of concern for their fellow believers and for the edification of the whole community. Any claims to wisdom or knowledge or gifts which caused believers to think of themselves as superior and of others as inferior he roundly rebuked: '"Knowledge" breeds conceit; it is love that edifies' (I Cor. 8.1; cf. e.g. 3.3f.; 10.23; 12.21ff.; 13). The strength of Paul's relationship with his communities was precisely the breadth of his love. If the compulsion of Christ's love led him to become as one outside the law in order to win those outside the law, it also led him to become as one under the law in order to win those under the law (I Cor. 9.20f.). The welfare of the *whole* congregation was his concern – weak as well as strong, but strong as well as weak (Rom. 14.1–15.6; I Cor. 8–10; Gal. 5.13–6.5). He would not stand for Jewish Christians narrowing down Christian liberty into legalism (Gal. 5.1ff.; Phil. 3.2ff.); but neither would he stand for Gentile Christians perverting Christian liberty into licence and. elitism (Rom. 16.17f.; I Cor. 5–6; 8–10; cf. II Thess. 3.6, 14f.).[74a]

(c) The other and more striking line of demarcation which Paul drew was the *christological* one. Where the Corinthian would-be-wise evidently made much of their experience of relationship with the pneumatic Christ and of resurrection already realized (cf. I Cor. 1.12; 2.16; 4.8; 15.12, 45), Paul emphasized that his kerygma was the folly of Christ *crucified*, proclaimed in the same weakness (I Cor. 1.18–25; 2.1–5, 8b), and he strongly asserted that the mark of the Spirit was the confession of the man Jesus as Lord (12.3). Against the false apostles of II Corinthians who, as we have already suggested (above pp.70f., 179f., 255 n.47) probably adapted their message and missionary style to strengthen their appeal to the Corinthian gnostics, Paul argued that the mark of pneumatic maturity was not simply a ministering of Christ's life but a sharing also in his death (II Cor. 4.10f.), was to be evaluated not simply in terms of power, the power of the risen Christ, but in terms also of weakness, the weakness of the crucified Christ (12.1–10; 13.3f.). Likewise against the perfectionist tendencies at Philippi (above p.280) he emphasized that knowing Christ was not simply a matter of knowing the power of his resurrection but also of sharing in his sufferings, becoming like him in his death (Phil. 3.10) (see also above §46.4).

The thrust of Colossians is significantly different – which suggests either a different authorship, or, more likely, that the syncretistic mix confronting Paul at Colossae included different gnostic elements. I am thinking here, on the one hand, of the much stronger realized emphasis of 1.13, 2.12, 2.20–3.3 (see below p. 345), which would have been welcomed by his gnosticizing opponents in Corinth and Philippi. And on the other, of the emphasis on the primacy of the exalted Christ, which is such a mark of the Colossian hymn: note the repeated uses of 'all' – 'firstborn of all creation . . . in him all things were created . . . all things were created through him and for him. He is before all things, and in him all things hold together . . . that in everything he might be pre-eminent . . . in him all the fullness of God was pleased to dwell . . . through him to reconcile to himself all things' (1.15–20). Here evidently what is under attack (at least by implication) is that other aspect of pre-Gnostic teaching which tended to view Jesus as one intermediary within what became in developed Gnosticism a whole hierarchy of divine beings distancing the pleroma from humankind.[75] Paul's emphasis then is clear-cut: the believer's relation with God through Christ is direct and complete and through Christ alone; or, as Paul puts it emphatically in his own words, 'in Christ lie hidden all the treasures of wisdom and knowledge . . . in him dwells embodied the complete pleroma of deity . . . he is the head of all rule and authority' (2.3, 9f.). But in addition he retains the christological emphasis of the earlier letters and rules out of court any potential gnostic dualism between an impassible heavenly Christ and a human Jesus who dies: he adds (probably) to the hymn the phrase 'by the blood of his cross' (1.20) – he 'who is the image of the invisible God' is also the crucified one; he underlines the fact that the Son accomplished his reconciling work 'in his body of flesh by his death' (1.22); and 1.24 echoes the II Corinthian and Philippian theme of (apostolic) ministry as a sharing in Christ's sufferings (see also 2.11f., 20).

In short, *it is this strong affirmation that Jesus the Lord is Christ the crucified, so consistent in Paul,*[76] *which cuts at the nerve of Christian Gnosticism.* It is this which prevents Paul, for all his openness to Hellenistic thought, from being absorbed into Christian Gnosticism. It is this which in particular makes it impossible for the Gnostic interpretation of Rom. 8.3 and Phil. 2.7 to be counted as a fair representation of Paul's thought: he who came 'in the (very) likeness of sinful flesh' *came for sin* (that is, probably as a sin offering) to condemn (to death and by death) sin in the flesh (Rom. 8.3); he who 'became in the (very) likeness of men' *humbled himself to death*, death on a cross (Phil. 2.7f.).[77] Thus once again it is the unity between human Jesus and exalted Lord which marks the boundary of acceptable diversity. Once again, *the refusal to let worship through and union with the glorified Christ fall apart from the historical reality of the man from Nazareth marks the point at which a gnosticizing Christianity diverges from the Christianity proclaimed and taught by Paul.*

63.4   *It was probably inevitable that Paul should become associated with a Gnostic anti-Judaism.* For Paul played the principal role during the first decades of Christianity in disengaging faith in Christ from Judaism. But after his death, and after AD 70, Judaism began to withdraw into itself, and the danger that Christianity would remain a dependent sect of Judaism or be confused with Jewish nationalism began to recede. Now the principal danger came to be perceived as posed from the other side – the danger that Christianity would become separated from its Jewish heritage, would become too hellenized. The process of disengagement from Judaism and from the OT law could be and was reversed; the now predominantly Gentile Church began consciously to appropriate its Jewish heritage in a more comprehensive manner, its organizational structure (see above p.115), its liturgy[78] and fasting practice (see Didache 8.1) and especially the OT (see I Clement, Barnabas, Justin's *Dialogue with Trypho*).[79] In this reverse process Paul was bound to appear in the wrong light and a genuinely Pauline emphasis and balance would

easily become identified with the forces of Gnosticism. Thus it was
that in the second century Paul's influence was more detectable on
Valentinus and Marcion than on the theologians of the great
Church, and it was only with Irenaeus that orthodoxy began to make
a determined effort to wrest Paul's theology from the embrace of the
heretics.[80] But it was the Paul of the Pastorals, the Paul of Acts who
emerged[81] – a Paul who opposed heresy with the weight of ecclesiastical tradition, a Paul who readily acknowledged the authority of the
twelve and knew no breach with Jerusalem, a Paul whose antithesis
between law and gospel was muted, whose central teaching on
justification by grace through faith alone was scarcely to be seen. In
short, as Bauer puts it, 'the price the Apostle to the Gentiles had to
pay to be allowed to remain in the church was the complete surren-
der of his personality and historical peculiarity'.[82]

The fact is that *Paul did not belong wholeheartedly to any one of the main
second- and third-century camps contesting the title of Christian*: he was
rejected totally by the Jewish Christians, and he was misinterpreted
to the point of abuse by both Gnostic and orthodox. The author of
the Pauline epistles was too big for the narrowing pigeonholes of
the second century, his theology too dynamic, too open-ended to be
compressed within the constrictive categories of later orthodoxy.
Paul owned but one Lord, Jesus Christ – that was the focus of unity
for him. Christ apart he acknowledged no other loyalty – that was his
greatness. But it was also his undoing, for in the controversies of later
centuries when the party men could not win his vote on his terms
they seized it anyway on their own.

§64. WAS JOHN 'GUILTY' OF 'NAIVE DOCETISM'?

64.1   As Paul was the Gnostic apostle, so John was the Gnostic
gospel. As we have seen, Paul was almost taken over completely by
the second-century Gnostics; the Fourth Gospel almost suffered the
same fate. Where the Ebionites used only an abbreviated Matthew,
and Marcion only a mutilated Luke, the Gnostics, particularly the
Valentinians, centred their attention on and made copious use of
John.[83] The first commentary we know to have been written on the
Gospel was by Heracleon, a Valentinian.[84] So much indeed was the
Fourth Gospel capable of being identified with a Gnostic standpoint
that the Alogi (second half of second century) and the Roman
presbyter Caius (early third century) both ascribed it to the Gnostic
Cerinthus. But again, as with Paul, it was Irenaeus who stemmed
the tide and rescued John for orthodoxy, so that from the third

century onwards John became increasingly the source book and scriptural keystone of orthodox christology.[85]

The question of John's relation with Gnosticism was however far from closed, and in the past century or so it has once again become a front line issue. In the middle of the nineteenth century A. Hilgenfeld, a follower of the Tübingen school, maintained the view that John was a product of Gnosticism, full of Gnostic teaching about sons of God and sons of the devil (see particularly 8.44) and riddled through and through with Gnostic conceptions of the world.[86] G. Volkmar, another Tübinger, argued more extravagantly that the Gospel started from 'the dualistic anti-Judaical Gnosis of Marcion'![87] All this involved the Tübingen school's thesis that the Gospel first appeared about the middle of the second century (Hilgenfeld himself argued for a date between 120 and 140) – a dating soon shown to be implausible, in view of second-century writers' knowledge of John (quite likely as early as Ignatius), and finally rendered virtually impossible by the discovery of the Rylands papyrus 457 (p^{52}) in Egypt, an early second-century fragment containing a few verses of John 18 (first published in 1935).

But that did not resolve the issue of John's relation to Gnosticism either. For already the History of Religions researchers had begun to demonstrate that Gnosticism was not merely a second-century Christian heresy, but an altogether much older phenomenon, probably in its earliest forms as old (or older) than Christianity itself. Consequently the possibility emerged with renewed force that John was dependent on or at least influenced by a form of pre-Christian Gnosis. It was R. Bultmann in particular who first attempted by using Mandaean writings to construct the Gnostic myth which he believed the Fourth Evangelist had utilized;[88] more specifically in his commentary on John (1941) he argued that the Gnostic influence on the Fourth Gospel had come through a revelatory speech source which John had used as the basis for the discourses of Jesus. This particular attempt too has gained little favour. Few now would accept the hypothesis of a discourse source – the speeches in the Fourth Gospel are all so distinctively Johannine in character that the demonstration of such a source is not possible. And the theory of a pre-Christian Gnostic redeemer myth suffers from the fact that it depends wholly on documents dated after the first century AD (often much later); Bultmann's own chief evidence in reconstructing the myth seems to have been the Johannine discourses themselves![89] The more plausible conclusion is that whatever elements of the myth were already in circulation before Christianity, the synthesis is itself strictly speaking a *post-Christian* development in which the more distinctively Christian belief in Christ as redeemer played a decisive role.[90]

The discovery of the Qumran scrolls and the Nag Hammadi writings gave a new twist to the debate. On the one hand, the former demonstrated that several features of the Fourth Gospel which had previously been regarded as typical of oriental Gnosticism, particularly its dualism, were after all thoroughly rooted in the Palestine of Jesus – albeit in a form of sectarian Judaism (see below n.95). But the latter have begun to expose a number of significant parallels with Johannine thought, as in the case of the 'I ams' and the coming of the Son from the Father into the world and back again.[91] More important, both sets of discoveries have strengthened the case for viewing the background of John not simply as an either-or of Palestinian Judaism or gnosticizing Hellenism, but as an extremely *syncretistic* milieu which had absorbed influences particularly from the Wisdom speculation of Hellenistic Judaism and the mythological soteriology typical of early or proto-Gnosticism. There is indeed a growing consensus among NT scholars that influences from some kind of very syncretistic (or gnosticizing) Judaism have to be assumed if the character of the Fourth Gospel is to be explained and understood (though the precise nature of these influences is greatly disputed).[92]

All this poses some very obvious questions. If a movement or tendency towards Gnosticism is discernible within and through the syncretistic 'mix' of the period, is John part of that movement? Does the Fourth Gospel belong to a broad gnosticizing trajectory, together with Hellenistic Jewish Wisdom, the Dead Sea scrolls, the Hermetic and Mandaean literature and now also the Nag Hammadi Coptic documents (though presumably not all in a direct line)? And if an affirmative answer is at all appropriate, did the Fourth Gospel *increase* the gnosticizing tendency of this trajectory, or did it *resist* that tendency, or was it simply at the mercy of the concepts and forms it had chosen for other reasons to use? In other words, E. Käsemann's claim that the Fourth Evangelist presents his understanding of Christ 'in the form of a naive docetism' only serves to give sharper point to *an issue which is forced upon us anyway by any attempt to understand the Fourth Gospel against its historical background.*

64.2 *Is John then 'guilty' of 'naive docetism'?* Did he begin to lose the distinctiveness of the Christian proclamation by merging it into the language and thought forms of syncretistic Judaism, by surrendering it to words and conceptualizations over which in the end of the day he had too little control? Did he take a decisive step forward in the process of mythicizing the Jesus-tradition?

Most of the older indices do not help us much here. The parallels with Hellenistic Jewish Wisdom and the Qumran scrolls on the one hand and with the Mandaean, Hermetic and Nag Hammadi texts on the other, indicate only that John belongs somewhere within the same broad cultural context, *but do not tell us where*: if one parallel commends itself as more distinctively 'Gnostic' to some, another commends itself as quite properly 'Jewish' to others. Thus the fact that the verb *ginōskein* (to know) occurs more frequently in the Johannine writings (John's Gospel 56, Johannine Epistles 26) does not help us very much, especially since the total avoidance of the noun *gnōsis* (knowledge) seems also to be deliberate. The revelatory discourses of John can indeed be paralleled at quite a number of individual points in the Odes of Solomon and the Mandaean literature, as Bultmann showed (above n.88), but in overall content the Wisdom literature offers better parallels[93] and the form of the speeches is much nearer that of a Jewish midrash (as most obviously in John 6 – see above p.87). Again the Johannine dualism between light and darkness, above and below, spirit and flesh, etc. (1.5; 3.6, 19, 31; 6.63; 8.12, 23; 12.35, 46) can readily be paralleled in Gnosticism,[94] though John's is not so much a cosmological dualism (note particularly 1.3; 3.16) as a dualism of decision and the parallels with Qumran are closer.[95] Closely related to John's dualism is a certain element of predestinarianism or determinism (as in 8.42ff.; 10.26–28; 12.39–41; 17.22f. – see also above pp.28f.), where again the parallels on both sides are not dissimilar in strength.[96] The logos of the Johannine prologue has parallels in the variously named intermediary figure(s) of developed Gnosticism,[97] though John's use of it is more firmly and more immediately rooted in Hellenistic Jewish speculation about Wisdom (cf. Wisd. 1.4–7; 9.9–12; 18.14–16; Ecclus. 24; 1QH 1.7f.).[98] Similarly the nearest parallels to John's talk of the Son of Man's descent and ascent (3.13; 6.62; 20.17) are to be found in Wisdom on the one hand (note particularly I Enoch 42.1f.) and in the later Gnostic redeemer myth on the other.[99]

However, the case for recognizing a naive docetism in John does not rest on any specific features in the Fourth Gospel so much as on the overall impact of John's christology. Nor does its strength depend on the amassing of particular parallels with later Gnostic literature so much as on *the sharpness of the contrast between John's presentation of Jesus and that of the Synoptics*. For anyone familiar with the Fourth Gospel we need only recall some of the points we have mentioned before (pp.27, 75f., 223) – the exalted self-knowledge of the 'I ams', the assertion of complete and unbroken oneness with the Father, the unclouded (*un*kenotic) consciousness of divine pre-existence, the parody of prayer in 11.42 and 12.27–30 (cf. 6.6). Can this be a human being who so speaks, or are we here encountering rather the Son of God, fully conscious of his divine origin and glory, debating with others from the vantage point of heaven, wholly master of events and of men? Käsemann is not without some justification when he exclaims:

> Not merely from the prologue and from the mouth of Thomas, but from the whole Gospel he (the reader) perceives the confession, 'My Lord and my God'. How does all this agree with the understanding of a realistic incarnation? Does the statement 'The Word became flesh' really mean more than that he descended into the world of man and there came into contact with earthly existence, so that an encounter with him became possible? Is not this statement totally over-shadowed by the confession 'We beheld his glory', so that it receives its meaning from it . . . The Son of Man is neither a man among others, nor the representation of the people of God or of the ideal humanity, but God, descending into the human realm and there manifesting his glory.[100]

All this strongly suggests that *John has so elaborated the Jesus-tradition that the historical Jesus has been very largely hidden behind the bold presentation of the divine Son of God*. And if so, then John *is* moving in the direction of docetism, of presenting a Jesus who for all his human traits (like hunger and grief) is in the end of the day more god than man – divine certainly, human only to outward view.

However, that is not the whole story. Käsemann's argument is heavily lopsided at several points. Here I can elaborate only the two main deficiencies.[100a]

(*a*) 1.14a – 'the Word became flesh'. This is *a clear assertion of the historicity and reality of the incarnation*. It is not possible to weaken its force to that of a divine appearance among men (so Käsemann). The ancient world was quite familiar with that idea, and could express it in various ways. John chooses none of them. Instead he affirms simply and pointedly, 'The Word (the same Word as in 1.1–3) *became* flesh – not appeared as or 'came down into', but 'became' – a confession which 'can only be understood as a protest against all other religions of redemption in Hellenism and Gnosticism'.[101] Nor is it possible to weaken the force of 1.14a by referring to the divine glory visible in and through the incarnate Word, for the noun is deliberately chosen too – that which the Word became was '*flesh*'; and for John 'flesh' signifies human nature in absolute contrast and antithesis to God (1.13; 3.6; 6.63; 8.15). John underscores the shocking nature of his assertion in 6.51–63: to believe in Jesus is to crunch or chew his flesh and drink his blood. This was a scandalous claim, as John well knew (6.60): the very idea of attaining eternal life by feeding upon flesh would horrify John's Hellenistic readers and most of all any docetists. But John's choice of words is clearly deliberate (he substitutes 'flesh' for 'bread' and 'chew' for 'eat' in 6.51, 54); such otherwise needlessly offensive language can only be understood as deliberately and provocatively directed against any docetic spiritualization of Jesus' humanity, *an attempt to exclude docetism by emphasizing the reality of the incarnation in all its offensiveness* – 6.51–58 thereby simply bringing into sharper focus what was already implicit in 1.14 (cf. again 3.6; and see above p.170).

(b) *The central importance of Jesus' death in John's theology*: the incarnate Logos *dies* – something the docetists sought at all costs to deny (see above p.277 n.22). Käsemann attempts to weaken the force of this point by arguing that 'apart from a few remarks that point ahead to it, the passion comes into view in John only at the very end' (p.7). This is a serious misinterpretation of the Fourth Gospel. Far from bringing it into view only at the very end, on the contrary, John *continually* points forward towards the climax of Jesus' death, resurrection and ascension. We have previously noted the dramatic forward looking effect he achieves by the frequent talk of Jesus' 'hour' or 'time', like a steady drum beat heralding the hour of his passion (see above p.75). Here we need simply list the various sayings which appear from the first chapter onwards and which on every occasion draw the reader's thoughts towards the same climax – 1.29, (51), 2.19ff., 3.13f., 6.51, 53ff., 62, 7.39, 8.28, 10.11, 15, 17f., 11.16, 50, 12.7, 16, 23f., (28), 32, etc. Notice particularly that the motif of Jesus' glory plays a significant role in this dramatic crescendo. It was precisely by means of Jesus' *death* and resurrection-ascension (not by his resurrection-ascension alone) that Jesus was to be glorified: the hour of his greatest glory was the hour of his passion! (most clearly 12.23f., 17.1). 'We beheld his glory' (1.14) therefore cannot be taken to imply that Jesus' flesh was only a kind of thin insubstantial covering barely cloaking his heavenly glory (his whole life a perpetual transfiguration). *In John's presentation Jesus' glory was revealed not so much in his life as in his death-resurrection-ascension*; and it was manifested in his signs and words only in so far as they pointed forward to that climax (2.11; 7.37–39; 11.4).

Above all there is 19.34f., where John goes out of his way to emphasize the historical veracity of the account of the blood and water coming from the side of the crucified Jesus after the spear thrust. The sufficiently close parallel with I John 5.6 tells us why. John wishes to give convincing proof that the incarnate Logos really died, that his body was not simply a phantom, his death simply an elaborate confidence trick – look, real blood![102] In other words, it seems to me to be excessively difficult to avoid the conclusion that *there is a deliberate anti-docetic polemic intended here.* Since Käsemann would regard 6.51–58 and 19.34–35 as the work of an ecclesiastical redactor, I should simply add that I find this an unnecessary and unjustified hypothesis. There is no *prima facie* literary or textual evidence for the thesis; and the Gospel hangs together well as a *theological* whole – in particular, 6.63 creates more problems if 6.51–58 is attributed to an ecclesiastical redactor than if it is taken together with 6.51–58 as an expression of the same author's intention (even if in a final revision). And since the whole can be shown to give a consistent meaning in serving a single author's joint concern about docetism and sacraments (above §41 and pp.300f.). these verses (6.51–58; 19.34–35) can be excluded only at the risk of misinterpreting the whole (as Käsemann's thesis shows).

In short, it is not necessary to demonstrate that the anti-docetic polemic is a major plank in the construction of the Fourth Gospel. It was not. But the conclusion remains firmly grounded in the text that *at two points in particular John wished to guard against a docetic interpretation of his Gospel* – the very points which docetism sought to deny – *the reality of the eternal Word's becoming flesh, and the reality of his death.*

64.3   How then are we to reconcile these twin features in the Fourth Gospel – the powerful presentation of the divine Son of God on earth (so amenable to Gnostic interpretation), and the firm refusal to draw the docetist corollary? One answer which suggests itself is that *John was deliberately attempting to portray Jesus in a manner as attractive as possible to would-be (Christian) Gnostics, while at the same time marking out the limits he himself imposed on such a presentation.* This suggestion, plausible in itself in the light of the evidence reviewed above, may appeal for further support to John's relationship on the one hand with his putative *signs source* and on the other with *I John*.

(*a*) Of the various written sources suggested for John only one has a real plausibility – a Signs Source.[103] The extent of it is far from clear (Fortna's and Teeple's reconstructions are over bold); but certainly there are sufficient indications of a source behind at least 2.1–11, 4.46–54 and probably 6.1–21; and almost certainly it did not include a passion narrative. The point for us is that John seems both to have used this source and to have qualified or *corrected* it. The clearest indication of this is 4.48, an awkward insertion intended to counter what was probably the source's aim – namely, to recount Jesus' miracles as an encouragement to faith (contrast 2.11, 4.53 with particularly 2.23–25, 4.48 and 6.25–36).[104] This suggests in turn that the source saw Jesus pre-eminently as a miracle worker and invited faith in him on that basis – an attitude which both Paul (II Cor.) and Mark probably encountered and sought to refute with their own respective theologies of the cross (see above pp.70f., 179f.). If so, then it would appear that John took account of the attitude represented in the Signs Source and sought to present Jesus in a way that would make the greatest appeal to those who saw Jesus primarily as the miracle working Son of God. At the same time he sought to counter their inadequate christology and gospel by affirming that the primary function of the signs was to point forward to the life-giving effect of his death-resurrection-ascension. Signs thus seen in their full significance did provide a basis for faith (cf. 2.11; 6.26; 9.35–39; 12.37; 20.30f.); but faith in the signs/miracles themselves was defective faith, the shallow affirmation of the fickle crowd, faith in Jesus as a mere miracle worker (2.23–3.2; 4.48; 6.2, 14, 30; 7.31; 9.16; cf. 20.29). In other words, if a naive docetism or gnosticizing tendency is detectable within the Fourth Gospel's material, *it is a feature of John's miracle source rather than of John's Gospel itself*; John used this source (and to that extent was influenced by it), but evidently he was well aware of its vulnerability to docetic interpretation and sought both *to correct his source and to safeguard his own work* at precisely this point.[105]

(*b*) Two features of I John are of particular significance for us. First, it presents a much blunter, more explicit rebuttal of docetic christology (4.1–3; 5.5–8). Second, it indicates that there had been a split in the community – a number of its erstwhile members had withdrawn (2.19). The point is that these two features are evidently linked – those who 'went out' are identified with the 'antichrists' who deny that Jesus is the Christ, that Jesus Christ came in the flesh (2.18, 22; 4.3; II John 7). In other words, it looks as though there had been a 'showdown' over christology; the issue of docetism had come into the open, and an irreconcilable confrontation was the result.[106] We should note also that in the view of the author those who went out were probably guilty of a failure in *love* as well; the words 'love' (noun and verb) appear more frequently in I John than anywhere else in the NT (46 times). Presumably the author regarded their claim to a higher anointing and fuller knowledge (attacked in 2.20) as a failure to love and respect their brothers – and how could anyone claim to love God when he despised his brother?

All this suggests that *the Fourth Evangelist was dealing with a community which in part at least had become fascinated by a gnosticizing understanding of Christ*. He therefore wrote his Gospel largely, but not wholly with this in view – that is, to present Jesus in such a way as to attract and hold such believers within the community (John 20.30f.). Thus he used language and ideas which were meaningful to would-be Gnostics, he painted a portrait of the earthly Jesus in colours they would appreciate and respond to, he took over as much as possible of their sort of understanding of Jesus, but *without going the whole way* with them. How successful he was we cannot now know. But if I John was written subsequently to John's Gospel and to the same community (as seems quite probable), it would appear that his apologetic attempt failed, or was only partly successful. The situation apparently deteriorated from one of acceptable diversity into an open rift. While many of those addressed were prepared to draw the line at the points the Fourth Evangelist had indicated, others found it necessary to go the whole way into outright docetism and to withdraw from the community. With such an outcome the author of I John was able to *draw back from the rather more exposed christology of the Gospel* and to *lay down the borders of acceptable diversity explicitly and emphatically*.

64.4   If there is anything in this last suggestion (§64.3) then the Fourth Gospel is to be seen as a classic example of the challenge and danger of translating the good news of Jesus Christ into the language and thought patterns of other cultures – the challenge of translating with as little loss from or gain to the original, the danger that the good news will be absorbed wholly into these thought patterns and lose both its distinctive otherness and its power to change them. This apparently was the challenge and danger that confronted the Fourth Evangelist. In order to speak effectively to his syncretistic society, in order to meet the the challenge of a Christian community influenced by gnosticizing tendencies, he presented Jesus as the incarnate Logos, the divine Son of God in full awareness of his deity and in perfect union with the Father. He almost paid the price: he sailed as close as possible to the wind of early Gnosticism and was almost swept away by it! He skirted the last border with emerging Gnosticism and was almost dragged over by the Gnostics! To win would-be Gnostics he almost became a Gnostic and was almost branded by emerging orthodoxy as a heretic!

But – and this is the significant fact – he himself saw these dangers.

He did *not* go all the way with (some of) those for whom he wrote. He did not go as far as he might quite well have done. On the contrary, he opposed the developing (proto-)Gnosticism of his time at the decisive point. If then he interacted with a broad gnosticizing tendency of his time, *at the crucial point he distanced himself from it*. And that point is again Jesus; and again it is *the refusal to let go the unity between the historical man Jesus and the glorified Christ*, the refusal to dissolve the history of Jesus in the acidic categories of a transcultural myth. Jesus is indeed presented in godly garb in the Fourth Gospel, but it is the Logos who *became flesh* who is so presented, the one on whose *flesh and blood* humanity faith depends, the one who *really died* on the cross and who only thus gave forth the life-giving Spirit. Once again therefore it is the identity of earthly Jesus with exalted Christ which not only *marks out the unity* but also *marks off the limits of acceptable diversity* of first-century Christian faith.

§65. CONCLUSIONS

65.1   If Jewish Christianity was characterized by its loyalty to the traditions of Christianity's mother faith, Hellenistic Christianity was characterized by its readiness to pull free from the apron strings, by its willingness to leave behind the earlier formulations of the new faith, by its desire to let its experience of the exalted Christ shape its faith and life into whatever language and life-style was most appropriate to its several situations and societies. This was true of Stephen, who saw it as essential that he should develop and propagate an interpretation of Jesus' teaching sharply at odds with the current practice of most of his fellow believers. It was true in excessive measure of the various churches briefly reviewed above in §61, many of whose members evidently thought that the Christian gospel was about liberty before anything else; at the growing edge of Christianity there was no clear margin between Christianity and the surrounding syncretism and there must have been not a few whose faith was not so very different from that of men like Hymenaeus and Philetus (II Tim. 2.17f.) but who were fully active members of the local church. It was true of Paul, noted as he was for his insistence on the significance of his own revelatory experience of Christ, for his role in liberating Christianity from the tutelage of Judaism, and for his unwillingness to denounce and condemn outright ideas with which he disagreed (only gross sensuality consistently earned his condemnation – Rom. 16.17f.; I Cor. 5–6; II Cor. 12.21; Phil.

3.18f.). And it was true of John in his readiness to present the earthly
Jesus in the full light of his exalted glory as the divine Son of God,
even at some risk of mythicizing the Jesus-tradition. It is perhaps
worth noting in addition that Paul in particular is nowhere so
violently polemical against gnosticizing tendencies as he was against
the Judaizers – *the insistence on a strict conformity to a single authority and
tradition (Jerusalem) he evidently regarded as more dangerous than the radical
openness of diverse nonconformity*. There is no question of course that
Paul and John (and no doubt Stephen too) stood four square within
the circle of Christianity and held firmly to Jesus Christ at the centre.
The point is however that they were open to new and different ways
of looking at the centre and of bringing the centre into interaction
with the various other circles of faith round about it. Such a policy is
always a dangerous one, open to misunderstanding, exposed to
attack from those who value tradition more than liberty, to abuse
from those who value liberty more than love; but ultimately it is
probably the most Christian position of all.

65.2   While gnostic tendencies and concepts are already clearly
evident in the churches of the first century, *no NT document can properly
be described as gnostic in character*. For all their openness to new
developments the NT writers most caught up in the broadening out
of Christianity were conscious that *a line had to be drawn at some point* –
that there could and should be a wide ranging diversity round the
centre, but that a circumference had to be sketched in at certain
points and some expressions of Christianity adjudged to have
pushed out beyond it. Thus we saw that some attempted formulations of the Christian message were early on judged to be *less than
adequate* in themselves, too vulnerable to abuse. This in effect was the
judgment of Matthew and Luke on Q, and indeed of all the churches
who retained Q only as absorbed into Matthew and Luke and not in
its own right. Others were judged to be *wrongheaded*: however attractive their presentation of the gospel in some respects, they had
ignored an indispensably integral emphasis. This in effect was the
judgment of Paul (particularly II Corinthians and Philippians),
Mark and John (in relation to their miracle sources). In both cases
the criterion was the same: *does this new formulation hold together the
crucified Christ and the exalted Lord and Son of God?* In other words,
already within the first-century period a stand was being taken by
Hellenistic Christians against what would become integral to the
distinctive christology of (second-century) Gnosticism. As the more
characteristically Jewish Christian documents in the NT drew a line

of demarcation between the acceptable diversity of Jewish Christianity and (what later became) unacceptable Ebionism – and that line is Christ, that the historical Jesus is truly exalted *Lord*, the embodiment of Wisdom, exalted to an incomparable status before God; so the more broadly ranging Hellenistic Christian documents in the NT drew a line of demarcation between the acceptable diversity of Hellenistic Christianity and (what later became) unacceptable Gnosticism – and that line also is Christ, that the glorified Lord, the one mediator between God and man is *Jesus*, who ascended to glory by being lifted up on a cross.

It is again perhaps worth noting that so far as we know *Paul was the first to formulate this absolutely fundamental christological criterion*. For it was precisely this Pauline emphasis which Mark transposed into the format of a 'Gospel': confronted (probably) by a teaching similar to that which Paul faced at Corinth (presenting Jesus primarily as a wielder and dispenser of power) Mark so constructed his Gospel as to focus attention most fully on Jesus as the suffering Son of Man (see above pp.39, 71, 180). It was this Markan definition of 'gospel format' which became the pattern for Matthew and Luke. And it was the insertion of Q material into a Markan framework which counteracted most effectively any vulnerability to gnostic interpretation inherent in its format. Similarly the Fourth Evangelist, apparently confronted with a similar challenge as faced Mark (a Signs Source presenting Jesus' miracles as a basis for faith), met it in a way ultimately the same as Mark's – that is, by setting the miracle working Jesus in the shadow of the passion. Finally we may note that the equivalent emphasis in Hebrews and I Peter were quite probably due ultimately to Pauline influence. Christianity's indebtedness to Paul at this point therefore is considerable.[107]

In short, once again it becomes evident that *for the NT writers not only the unity but also the diversity of Christianity was determined by reference to Christ – the centrality and primacy of the exalted Lord, and the identity of the crucified Jesus with the exalted Son of God – this is the decisive mark of* Christian *faith*.

65.3   As with Jewish Christianity so in the case of Hellenistic Christianity, we are dealing with *a diverse phenomenon*, or in oversimplified terms, a spectrum. At one end of the spectrum, Hellenistic Christianity falls over into the unacceptable diversity of Gnosticism. But also *within acceptable Hellenistic Christianity there was a considerable diversity* – from the libertines tolerated by churches addressed by the seer of Revelation and Jude at one end, to Paul (and Mark) at the other. There was no single form of acceptable Hellenistic Christianity in the first century. If the oversimplification can be tolerated (that is, reducing the diversity to a single straight line), perhaps we could most easily represent this diversity thus – the broad vertical line again marking out where acceptable diversity falls over into unacceptable diversity.

HELLENISTIC CHRISTIANITY

Paul John Q	Opponents attacked in I Corinthians, Philippians, Colossians, Pastorals, Revelation, Jude	Proponents of miracle man christology	Those referred to in I John 2.19	Gnosticism proper

65.4   To sum up, *two criteria* for distinguishing unacceptable from acceptable diversity again seem to have emerged. First, Hellenistic Christians became unacceptable when they ceased to *love* other Christians, when they claimed a spiritual superiority and failed to respect the knowledge and spiritual experience of other believers. When no christological issue was at stake (as apparently in I Corinthians) right relationships were regarded by Paul as more important than right belief. Second, Hellenistic Christianity became unacceptable when its liberalism became detached from the centre, when its diversity began to reduce the significance of the exalted Christ or to pull apart the unity of earthly Jesus and exalted Lord. Christian liberty is not limitless: it is always to be constrained by love of others in its conduct and by belief in Christ as man and Lord in its faith, otherwise it ceases to be *Christian*.

XIII

APOCALYPTIC CHRISTIANITY

§66. WHAT IS 'APOCALYPTIC'?

66.1 Apocalyptic Christianity has been both historically and theologically one of the most striking and important expressions of Christian faith. Despite this the main body of Christian tradition has largely ignored the phenomenon of apocalyptic Christianity: because of its highly charged spiritual enthusiasm the great Church has usually been embarrassed by it; because of its tendency to fanaticism the major churches have frequently suppressed it. But in fact Christianity first emerged in a context of apocalyptic thought, as is now generally recognized. Moreover, in the beginning, Christianity was itself in large measure an eschatological and enthusiastic movement with marked apocalyptic traits, as we shall see. And from the first century to the beginning of the Middle Ages it produced an extensive apocalyptic literature. Indeed no 'trajectory' is more clearly visible in historical Christianity than that which runs from the apocalyptic expectations of the later Jewish prophets, through the earlier Jewish apocalyptic literature, Qumran, John the Baptist, Jesus, the primitive Palestinian community, the early Paul, the book of Revelation, early Montanism and the various Jewish and Christian apocalypses of the first two or three centuries of the Christian era, and on through the medieval millenarian sects, to leave its clearest mark in 1534 in the messianic reign of John of Leyden at Münster. From there the influence of apocalyptic thought can be traced in different directions – in religious movements like Jehovah's Witnesses and Pentecostalism on the one hand, and in the totalitarian movements of Communism and National Socialism on the other. Recognition of its historical importance has been one of the major factors in bringing an apocalyptic perspective back into the centre of biblical and theological study in recent years.[1]

But what is 'apocalyptic?' Most of twentieth century discussion has been confused, with the force and scope of the key word 'apocalyptic' unclear. Can it be used as a noun, or only as an adjective? Does it refer only to literature, a classification of genre? Or can it also describe beliefs and ideas characteristic of such literature, but present elsewhere? Or is it primarily a sociological category – an apocalyptic (= millenarian) movement? The most recent scholarship has in fact abandoned the use of 'apocalyptic' as a noun and distinguishes between *apocalypse* as a literary genre, *apocalypticism* as a social ideology, and *apocalyptic eschatology* as a set of ideas present in other genres and social settings.[2] More important, should 'apocalyptic' be used primarily or exclusively for *mode* of revelation (*apokalypsis* = unveiling of heavenly mysteries), or for the *content* of such revelation. C. Rowland in particular has pointed out that what has often been described as 'apocalyptic' (= revelation of final events) is better classified under the heading 'eschatology', and that while apocalypses typically have a very strong interest in 'the end events', that is by no means the exclusive focus of their interest; 'apocalyptic' and 'eschatology' are not synonymous.[2a]

The following analysis reflects some of the earlier difficulties and confusions. Since there is no standard type of apocalypse, the features picked out in the next section do not constitute a description of the genre but simply highlight the most striking of the features which appear frequently in 'apocalypses'. And the list of theological characteristics likewise focuses more on apocalyptic *eschatology* than on 'apocalyptic' as a broader category.[3] Together they provide a clear enough picture of what we have already called, for want of a better title, 'apocalyptic Christianity'. Our question is simple. To what extent were Jesus and the first Christians apocalyptic in outlook and message? To what extent is an apocalyptic eschatology integral to earliest Christianity so that without it Christianity becomes something qualitatively other than that movement which began in Palestine nineteen and a half centuries ago?

66.2   *Literary characteristics of apocalypses.* Apocalypses are 'revelatory writings which disclose the secrets of the beyond and especially of the end of time'.[4] The chief characteristics of such writings are as follows.

(*a*) *Pseudonymity.* It is typical of the apocalyptist that he did not use his name but set out his writing under the name of some famous individual from the past (e.g. Peter or Paul, Moses or Ezra, Enoch or Adam). Presumably he used this device as a way of stressing his claim to stand in continuity with and to be the authoritative interpreter of one who by common consent had been highly favoured with divine revelation.[4a]

(*b*) *Visions and symbolism.* The apocalyptist usually received his revelation in visions, sometimes through dreams, often full of bizarre symbolism and heavenly portents – for example, Daniel's visionary dream of the four beasts which came up out of the sea (Dan. 7), or IV Ezra's dream: 'Lo! there came up from the sea an eagle which had twelve(?) feathered wings, and three heads' (IV Ezra 11). At other times the visions came while the apocalyptist was awake – an experience of visionary ecstasy; this, for example, was how the NT seer received his visions – 'After this I looked, and lo, in heaven, an open door! . . . At once I was in the Spirit, and lo, a throne stood in heaven . . .' (Rev. 4.1f.). Angels regularly feature as the intermediary who explains and interprets the vision. To what extent the visionary form derived ultimately from a genuine religious experience or was simply a literary device remains in most cases an open question.

(*c*) *Survey of history as from a perspective in the past.* One feature of pseudonymity is that the apocalyptist was able to represent himself as standing at an earlier point in history. He then presented the course of history from his pseudonymous standpoint up to his actual standpoint in the form of prophecy, usually allegorical prophecy: for example, the image of different metals or the four beasts in Dan. 2 and 7, or the elaborate dream vision of world history in I Enoch 85–90. The allegorical prophecy was then continued down into the real author's future, depicting the events of the end, the decisive divine intervention into the course of history which he believed was about to take place. As C. K. Barrett points out: 'This method often permits the dating of apocalypses; the point at which the history loses precision and accuracy is the moment of writing'.[5]

(*d*) *Esoteric character* – a corollary to the bizarre symbolism and allegorical prophecy form. It is not always clear what the dreams and visions meant, or what dating was intended by the division of history into days and weeks. The survey of history was in code form, its information about the future was something to be kept from general knowledge, something to be handed down in secret. Thus, for example, Daniel is instructed to 'seal up the vision', to 'keep the vision secret, for it points to days far ahead' (8.26), and at the end is told, 'Go your way Daniel, for the words are kept secret and sealed till the time of the end' (12.9). Similarly Enoch is told at the beginning that he writes not for this generation but for a generation far distant in the future (I Enoch 1.2).

(*e*) *'Underground literature'.*[6] Apocalyptic literature was very often faith's response to a situation of crisis[6a] – a looking to God to intervene in a situation where human resources were failing and the men of faith were in danger of being destroyed by faith's enemies. Thus, for example, Daniel seems to have been written to stir up resistance to Antiochus Epiphanes' attempt to impose Hellenistic practices and worship upon the Jews (c. 167 BC); the War Scroll of the Qumran sect gives the battle orders for the imminent final conflict between the sons of light and the sons of darkness (1QM); IV Ezra reflects something of the crisis which Judaism underwent after the fall of Jerusalem in AD 70; and Revelation seems to have been called forth partly at least by the threat of persecution under Emperor Domitian about AD 95.

(f) *Ethical exhortations*. Apocalypses typically exhort their readers to repent and convert in view of the imminent End and the coming judgment, and include also more traditional exhortations – woes and warnings against unrighteousness as well as urgings to righteous living. Moral strictness is a regular feature of the trajectory of apocalypticism.

66.3   *Theological characteristics of apocalyptic eschatology.*

(a) *The two ages.* 'The Most High has made not one age but two' (IV Ezra 7.50). Apocalyptic eschatology shares the Hebraic view of history – a view almost unique in antiquity – that is, of history as a linear rather than circular progression, moving forward rather than repeating itself, and moving forward towards a definite end and goal. Where apocalyptic is distinctive within Hebraic thought in turn is in the sharp break it envisages in this line of history, the break between this age and the age to come. This age and the age to come are not simply consecutive segments of the same line of history: at the end of this age the line breaks off; the new age starts as a new line, something quite different. Often this age is divided into a number of periods (4, 7, 10, 12, 70), but the age to come is something wholly other.

> The dualism of the Two-Ages doctrine recognizes no continuity between the time of this world and that which is to come: 'For behold, the days are coming when everything that has come into being will be given over to destruction, and it will be as if it had never been' (II Bar. 31.5). Between the two Ages there is a qualitative difference, and this comes to clearest expression in Dan. 7 with the contrast of the beasts rising from the sea and the 'man' coming from heaven (cf. also IV Ezra 7.52–61).[7]

(b) *Pessimism and hope.* The discontinuity between the two ages is also clearly expressed in the apocalyptists' very different attitude to the two ages. Towards the present age their attitude is one of unrelieved pessimism: it is degenerate; it has grown old; it stands under the domination of Satan and hostile powers; it is defiled with evils, an age of ills, full of affliction and sorrow; there is no hope for it. But the black picture of the present is more than compensated for by the glory of the age to come – a new creation, a new heaven and earth, a heavenly Jerusalem, Paradise restored. One of the most grandiose, even grotesque expressions of this hope is in II Bar. 29.5:

> The earth also shall yield its fruit ten thousandfold and on each vine there shall be a thousand branches, and each branch shall produce a thousand clusters, and each cluster a thousand grapes, and each grape produce a cor of wine (cor = 120 gallons!).

(c) *The eschatological climax* – messianic woes, judgment (on God's enemies), salvation (for Israel), and resurrection. A frequent feature of apocalyptic thought is that the ending of the old age and introduction of the new will be marked by a period of severe distress such as the world has never known – sometimes thought of as a heightening of ordinary woes or under the figure of childbirth, sometimes in terms of military conflict and war, sometimes in terms of supernatural cosmic portents and catastrophes, often with a combination of different metaphors and images. An early foreboding along these lines is Jub. 23.13 –

> . . . For calamity follows on calamity, and wound on wound, and tribulation on tribulation, and evil tidings on evil tidings, and illness on illness, and all evil judgments such as these, one with another, illness and overthrow, and snow and frost and ice, and fever, and chills, and torpor, and famine, and death, and sword, and captivity, and all kinds of calamities and pains . . .[8]

The messianic woes culminate in the divine intervention which brings in the new age – the age of bliss for Israel, or at least for the righteous remnant. As to the Gentiles, opinions differed. In some writings, particularly the early ones, it is anticipated that the Gentiles will be brought in to share the blessings of Israel – for example, the Sibylline Oracles:

> Then all the isles and the cities shall say, How doth the Eternal love these men! . . . Let us make procession to his temple, for he is the sole Potentate . . . And from every land they shall bring frankincense and gifts to the house of the great God . . . (III.710f., 718, 772f.).

But the more usual tone, particularly of the later writings, is that any nations which have shown hostility to Israel will be destroyed, whether by the sword, or by the direct act of God. There is some hope for the innocent or repentant nations; but, though spared, their role in the new age would be one of subserviency to Israel.[9]

Part of this eschatological hope is expressed in terms of resurrection; the concept of the resurrection of the dead comes from apocalyptic eschatology. The righteous dead would be restored to life in order to share the blessings of the new age; less frequently expressed is the belief that the wicked too would be raised, in order to be judged. An early formulation of this expectation is Dan. 12.2f.: '(Many of) those who sleep in the dust of the earth shall awake, some to everlasting life, and some to shame and everlasting contempt'.[10]

(d) *Imminence of the End*. Apocalyptic eschatology is born of crisis and is characterized by a longing for the End, the end of the present evil world, its suffering and affliction, and a longing for the new. This anxious yearning expresses itself in an impatient questioning: 'How long? How long?'; (Dan. 8.13; 12.5ff.; IV Ezra 4.33f.; 6.59; II Bar. 26; 81.3; etc.). Some at least of the apocalyptists were conscious that the End could not be hastened – God's purpose must be fully worked out (so particularly IV Ezra 4.33–37).[10a] But more typical is the sense of tip-toe expectancy, the conviction that the End itself could not be long delayed. The very fact that these secret revelations which the men of old sealed up for the end of time were now being made known was itself a sure sign that the End was near. The survey of past history in prophetic form arose from the conviction that the final acts of history were about to take place: the stone hewn from the mountain without hands would soon shatter the iron and clay feet of the idol (Dan. 2). The present age could be divided into periods because its climax was near – writer and reader, Jew and Gentile together stood already in the final period before the End. God's purpose had first to be fulfilled, of course, but that fulfilment was almost complete, the consummation was at hand (IV Ezra 4.33–50; 8.61; 11.44).

> For the youth of the world is past, and the strength of the creation is already long ago at an end, and the advance of the ages is almost here and even past. For the pitcher is nearly to the fountain, the ship to the harbour, the caravan to the city, and life to its conclusion (II Bar. 85.10).

(e) *Supernatural and cosmic dimensions*. Characteristic of the apocalyptist is the fact that his vision of reality is not confined merely to Israel, it embraces the whole world, and not just the whole earth, but heaven and the underworld as well. Even apocalypses with strong Jewish nationalist colouring think of the events of the End as affecting the whole of mankind; resurrection, world judgment and world dissolution in particular are on a cosmic scale. And if the cosmos is the stage the actors are not just men, but divine beings – angels and spirits. Behind the evil of earth stand the fallen angels and demons,

represented above all by Satan or anti-Christ (see particularly
I Enoch 6–11; 16; 21; 54–6; etc.; Sib.Or. III.63ff.). This of course is
why the saints of the Most High are helpless in the face of evil – why
they have to wait for and depend on the intervention of God. In
prophetic works the agent of divine purpose is classically thought of
as the Messiah – a human figure. But the classical expression in
apocalyptic literature is in terms of the Son of Man – a transcendent,
almost divine being (Dan. 7.13–14; I Enoch 48; 69.26–29; 71.14–17;
Mark 13.24–27; Rev. 14.14ff.; probably IV Ezra 13).

(f) *Divine sovereignty and control.* Overarching all is the faith that
God is in control, that God is in control of history – it is moving
towards *his* goal. This faith is most clearly evident in the picture of
future history as already written down in a scroll (Dan. 8.26; 12.4, 9;
Rev. 5–8).[10b] The message is plain: all that is to happen is foreknown,
it has all been determined beforehand. Likewise the apocalyptist
looks to God alone to bring in the new age. It is not something which
will grow out of the present age, or something which will be achieved
by human activity. Only God can wind up the old age; the new age will
come only through divine, supernatural intervention. This is why
hope can rise above pessimism. The apocalyptist does not dwell on
the appearances, or the reality of the present; he looks beyond to God
and sees it as his task to present to his readers his understanding of
the fuller, cosmic reality and his vision of God's imminent intervention.

66.4   We can sum up our findings and perhaps further clarify the
distinctive character of apocalyptic eschatology by comparing and
contrasting it briefly with prophecy, out of which it probably
developed. Clearly there is a fair amount of overlap between the two.
Isaiah, for example, looked forward to a future when men would live at
peace, when nature would be transformed, the wolf dwelling with the
lamb, the leopard lying down with the kid, and the whole earth filled
with the knowledge of Yahweh (Isa. 2; 11). Ezekiel experienced
visions and used the sort of fantastic imagery which we more
naturally associate with apocalypses – 'the four living creatures', four
wheels whose rims were 'full of eyes round about', etc. Particularly in
the post-exilic period there is discernible a development within
prophecy towards apocalypticism – with the picture of divine judgment on the nations and of deliverance and vindication for the
righteous remnant, leading to a new golden age of justice, peace and
infinite bliss. But in apocalyptic eschatology the picture is painted on
a larger canvas, with bolder brush strokes. At each of the character-

istic points of apocalypticism there is a radical heightening of the eschatology which leaves prophecy behind. The discontinuity between old age and age to come is much sharper there than anything we find in prophecy. The utter pessimism with regard to the present is much more radical. The end-time suffering is more terrible, the judgments and salvation are final, the End much closer, the reliance on divine intervention by a divine agent more absolute. Likewise the esoteric character of so many apocalypses, the elaboration of the idea of a pre-determined history, the cosmic dimensions . . . These can all be seen as extensions of prophecy, but also mark the boundary between prophecy and apocalypse. H. H. Rowley sums up the difference thus: 'Speaking generally, the prophets foretold the future that should *arise out* of the present, while the apocalyptists foretold the future that should *break into* the present'.[11]

If then we have done enough to clarify the distinctive character of 'apocalyptic', we can now go on to examine the beginnings of Christianity and its writings to ascertain whether and to what extent we can speak of first-century Christianity as 'apocalyptic Christianity'.

§67. 'APOCALYPTIC – THE MOTHER OF ALL CHRISTIAN THEOLOGY'?

Jewish apocalyptic writing extends from late third century BC to second century AD. The apocalyptic writings which we have fall into two roughly equal halves on either side of Jesus. This means that Jesus stands in the middle of a period when apocalypticism was one of the most important forces in Jewish religious thought. The full significance of this was first brought home to NT scholarship by the work of J. Weiss and A. Schweitzer at the turn of the century, who argued that Jesus was strongly influenced by apocalyptic eschatology and that his proclamation of the kingdom and understanding of his mission was constitutively stamped with the characteristics of apocalypticism and cannot be understood apart from the apocalyptic thought world. In a very real and important sense *almost all historical Jesus research since then has been an attempt to escape from or at least to soften this evaluation of Jesus*, not least in many instances because of the christological corollaries that follow in its train. There have been fewer inhibitions about dubbing the earliest Christian community 'apocalyptic', despite the lack of supporting evidence in Acts. Either way E. Käsemann's claim that 'apocalyptic was the mother of all Christian theology'[12] becomes a characterization which can hardly be ignored, and whose importance for our understanding of first-century Christianity has still to be fully appreciated. If Christianity first emerged out of an apocalyptic thought world, as an apocalyptic sect, what does that tell us about Christianity?

67.1   We know too little about *John the Baptist* to reconstruct an elaborate account of his work and preaching. But what we have shows clearly enough that *his preaching was greatly influenced by apocalyptic eschatology*. His message was predominantly one of judgment (Matt. 3.7–12/Luke 3.7–9, 15–18), but, more to the point, of *final* judgment – the final verdict on the vineyard (every unfruitful tree cut down and thrown on the bonfire), the final harvest (wheat gathered into the granary, chaff burned with 'unquenchable fire'). Not only so, but the judgment was *imminent*: those who had come out to hear him were fleeing from the (eschatological) wrath about to begin; '*Already* the axe is laid at the root of the trees'; the shovel was ready in hand to begin the winnowing of the threshing floor.

John's imagery of judgment is typical of apocalyptic eschatology. The metaphor of the harvest is common to both prophecy and apocalypse (cf. Joel 3.13; IV Ezra 4.30). But the idea of judgment by *fire*, the dominant feature of (what we have of) the Baptist's message (Matt. 3.10, 11, 12) is more distinctively apocalyptic (see e.g. I Enoch 10.6, 13; 90.24ff.; 100.9; 102.1; Test.Jud. 25.3; Sib.Or. III.542ff.; IV.176ff.; II Bar. 48.39, 43; 59.2; IV Ezra 7.36ff.; 1QH 6.18f.). Even more striking is John's use of *baptism*, the rite which was his own hallmark, as a metaphor for this divine judgment – 'he will baptize with Spirit and fire' (Matt. 3.11/Luke 3.16). John here had probably picked up the apocalyptic symbol of judgment as a river of fire (Isa. 30.27f.; Dan. 7.10; I Enoch 14.19; 17.5; 67.7, 13; 71.2; II Enoch 10.2; Sib.Or. III.54; IV Ezra 13.10f.; 1QH 3.29ff.). And since he evidently envisaged both unrepentant *and* repentant as being baptized in this stream of fiery *pneuma*, he must have understood it as both destructive for the former (cf. Matt. 3.10, 12/Luke 3.9, 17) and purgative for the latter (see above p.153 n.6). In other words, his metaphor is best understood as a variant on the apocalyptic theme which we know as 'the messianic woes' – that end-time tribulation and catastrophe which would both destroy and purify as the old age gave way to the new (above pp.153 and 313).

We should notice also the combination of *pessimism and hope* in John's message. So far as we can tell, he gave no weight to the view that faithful observance of the law could win God's favour, and he explicitly attacked the closely related view that descent from

Abraham (including circumcision) even began to satisfy God. Only those who repented genuinely and wholeheartedly could hope to survive the baptism in Spirit and fire, and even then only at the cost of every taint and mark of the present age being burned up in the stream of fiery *pneuma*. But those who did repent and survived the winnowing of the messianic woes would then be as the good grain in the granary of the new age.

It is not clear who John thought of as the agent of divine judgment: all we hear of is 'one who comes after me, who is greater than me' (Mark 1.7 pars.). Possibly he thought in terms of a human figure endowed with divine authority. But it is more probable that he envisaged a heavenly being, perhaps in human form; and indeed it is just conceivable that John was here influenced by the apocalyptic imagery of the man-like figure or Son of Man;[12a] notice particularly how the (Son of) Man and the stream of fire belong together in the vision of Dan. 7.9–14 and even more closely in the vision of IV Ezra 13.10f. (cf. also Rev. 14.14 with the Baptist's harvest metaphors).

Despite the lack of material therefore we have enough to substantiate the case that John the Baptist belonged firmly within the broad trajectory of first-century apocalyptic thought.

67.2   What then of *Jesus*? We have already summarized Jesus' proclamation (above §3); here we need only focus on the salient points of comparison. It will be simplest if we follow the rough sketch of theological characteristics outlined above in §66.3.

(*a*) It is quite likely that Jesus used the language of the two ages (Mark 3.29/Matt. 12.32; Mark 10.30/Luke 18.30; Mark 11.14/Matt. 21.19; cf. Mark 4.19/Matt. 13.22; Matt. 13.39f., 49; Luke 16.8; 20.34f.). More characteristic however is his talk of 'the kingdom of God'. This is not a regular apocalyptic phrase, but it can certainly be regarded quite properly as a variation on the two-ages motif– that is, as Jesus' way of speaking about the age to come. And almost certainly Jesus did so use it (Matt. 6.10/Luke 11.2; Matt. 8.11/Luke 13.28f.; Matt. 10.7/Luke 10.9, 11; Mark 9.1 pars.). Here the insight of Weiss still stands: the kingdom of God cannot be conceived as something which develops out of and in this world, but only as 'a radically superworldly entity which stands in diametric opposition to this world'.[13] Even though Jesus understood the power of the end-time to be already present in and through his own ministry (see above §§3.2, 50.5 and below pp.321f.), it was precisely as *the power of the age to come* that he perceived it – so distinctively supernatural and eschatologically wholly other that it allowed no comparison and resistance to it imperilled one's place in the age to come (Matt. 12.27f./Luke 11.19f.; Mark 3.28f. pars.). The discontinuity between the present age and the coming kingdom is further indicated by the different kind of sustenance and relationships of the latter (Matt. 6.11/Luke 11.3 – eschatological bread; Mark 12.25 pars – 'like angels in heaven'), by the complete reversal of this-worldly values (Luke 6.20/Matt. 5.3; Mark 10.29f., 31 pars.; Luke 12.16–21), by the different kind of temple (eschatological – cf. Mark 14.58; John 2.19; see above p.42), and particularly by the fact that the final judgment would mark the beginning of the age of the kingdom (Matt. 19.28/Luke 22.29f.).

(b) The pessimism-hope dualism typical of apocalypses is not so marked in Jesus – principally because Jesus saw the eschatological hope already being fulfilled in his ministry (see below pp. 321f.). But the fulfilment was precisely the power of the *future* kingdom already *breaking into* the present age, it did not emerge from the present age. On the contrary, like John the Baptist, Jesus saw little to encourage him from within the present age: it stood under the sway of evil spirits and demons, a kingdom opposed to God's (Mark 1.23–27, 34; 3.22–26; etc.; cf. Matt. 4.8–10/Luke 4.5–8; Matt. 6.10b); without repentance there was no hope for men or cities, Jews or not (Matt. 11.21–24/Luke 10.13–15; Matt. 12.41f./Luke 11.31f.; Luke 13.1–5); Israel as a whole was like one of the unfruitful trees of which the Baptist had spoken (Mark 11.12–14 pars.; Luke 13–9); even Jerusalem, 'the city of the great king', stood under divine judgment (Matt. 23.37–39/Luke 13.34f.).

(c) In Jesus' conception of the events of the End apocalyptic influence is again evident. He anticipated a time of suffering and tribulation, the time of *eschatological trial* prior to the End (Matt. 5.11f./Luke 6.22f.; Matt. 6.13/Luke 11.4; Mark 10.39; Matt. 10.23, 24f.; Mark 13.7f., 14–20); it would probably be marked by unnatural enmity (Matt. 10.34–36/Luke 12.51–53; Mark 13.12/Matt. 10.21 – as in I Enoch 100.2; IV Ezra 5.9), and probably also by cosmic catastrophe (Mark 13.24f.; as in Ass. Mos. 10.5); and as with John the Baptist the imagery of fire in the tradition of Jesus' teaching denotes not only final judgment (Mark 9.43, 48 par.; Matt. 5.22; 7.19; 13.40, 42, 50; 25.41), but also the fiery purification through which the repentant must go if they would enter the kingdom (such is the implication of the various 'fire-logia' – Mark 9.49; Luke 12.49; Gosp.Thomas 10, 16, 82; cf. Luke 9.54). Indeed (as we have seen above pp.154, 210), it is probable that Jesus used the Baptist's fire imagery as a way of understanding his own anticipated death – that is, as suffering the messianic woes (Luke 12.49f./Mark 10.38f.; so also the imagery of the cup of God's wrath – Mark 10.38f.; 14.36; cf. 14.27); that is to say, he quite probably saw his death as the necessary antecedent to the coming of the kingdom (cf. Mark 14.25 pars.).

In addition Jesus seems to have seen eschatological salvation as primarily *Israel centred* (Matt. 10.5f., 23; 15.24), though he fully expected that the Gentiles would be brought into the kingdom in the End, and by no means necessarily on inferior terms (Matt. 8.11f./Luke 13.28f.; Mark 11.17 pars. = Isa. 56.7). So too the hope of the end events typical of apocalypses are again not so marked in Jesus' teaching. However, in view of the evident influence of apocalyptic thought on Jesus' expectations for the future, there is no real reason why he should not have expressed his hope of his own vindication a short time after his death in terms of resurrection also (Mark 8.31; 9.31; 10.34; see further above p.211) – that is, as part of the beginning of the resurrection of the dead at the end of time ushering in the new age (see also below p.323).

(*d*) It also looks very much as though Jesus thought the End was *imminent* (Mark 1.15; Matt. 10.7/Luke 10.9, 11), within the lifetime of his own generation (Mark 9.1 pars.; 13.30 pars. – where 'this generation' can only refer to the contemporaries of Jesus), before the disciples had completed the round of preaching to Israel (Matt. 10.23).[14] Hence the sense of urgency and crisis in so many of Jesus' sayings and parables (Mark 13.28f. pars.; 13.34–36 pars.; Matt. 5.25f./Luke 12.58f.; Matt. 8.22/Luke 9.60; Matt. 24.43f./Luke 12.39f; Matt. 24.45–51/Luke 12.42–46; Matt. 25.1–12; Luke 9.61f.; 10.4; 12.36; 13.1–5; 18.7f.; see above p.73), and the vow to fast in Mark 14.25 (see above p.162). It is not possible to excise such a well rooted strand without seriously distorting the Jesus-tradition. The counter emphasis of Mark 13.10 is about as clear an example of an interpretative addition in the light of a changed perspective as we could expect to find in the Synoptic tradition (see above p.74).

(*e*) The *supernatural and cosmic dimensions* of the end events are again not so clearly marked in Jesus' teaching as in apocalyptic. However, it is significant that in the only really clear allusion to Jesus as a visionary, Jesus 'saw Satan fall like lightning from heaven' (Luke 10.18). The only other possible candidates for visions of Jesus are his experience at Jordan, the account of which uses the apocalyptic imagery of the heavens opening to afford a heavenly revelation (Mark 1.10f. pars.), and the temptation narrative in which Jesus again sees, encounters and defeats Satan (Matt. 4.1–11/Luke 4.1–12; see also above pp.184f.). Moreover, Jesus evidently understood events on earth as reflecting supernatural conflict, at least to the extent that he regarded his casting out of demons as the beginning of Satan's eschatological defeat (Mark 3.27 pars.). And he probably saw the climax of the end events as the coming from heaven of (himself as) the Son of Man, deliberately echoing the apocalyptic language of Dan. 7 (Mark 8.38 pars.; etc.). Note also the language of Mark 13.24–27 which probably belongs to the earliest stratum of the Mark 13 discourse, the so-called 'little apocalypse'.

(*f*) Finally we need simply note that Jesus' technical term 'the kingdom *of God*' in itself underlines his belief not only in its transcendent character, but also in the divine sovereignty which controls events leading to its full establishment (cf. also e.g. Matt. 6.9–13/Luke 11.2–4; Mark 14.36 pars.).

In short, it is difficult to avoid the conclusion that *Jesus' expectation of the future kingdom was apocalyptic in character*. However, there are two features of Jesus' preaching at this point which mark Jesus' apocalypticism off from more typical contemporary apocalypses. First, there was what we might call a *cautionary note* in his teaching on the future. That is to say, like some apocalyptists, he seems to have contemplated an interval of time before the End, during which several decisive developments had still to take place – not least his own death and vindication, his disciples' final appeal to Israel, their persecution and the end-time tribulation.[15] But in addition Jesus did not follow typical apocalyptic practice in drawing up a calendar (of days or weeks) of the End. On the contrary, he specifically denied the possibility of calculating such a timetable – 'Of that day or that hour *no one* knows . . . only the Father' (Mark 13.32). In other words, for Jesus there was an element of unknowability and therefore of uncertainty about the End; its coming was not so rigorously predetermined as most apocalyptists seem to have believed. As God could shorten the period of eschatological distress (Mark 13.20 par.; Luke 18.7f.) so it was conceivable that he could lengthen the time of respite, the final period of grace, the last chance to repent (Luke 13.6–9).[16] This does not alter the conclusion that Jesus expected the End as imminent, but it does qualify it to some extent.

Second, what marks Jesus' teaching off most distinctively from other apocalyptic eschatology is its clear note of *realized eschatology* – that the eschatological kingdom was already in some sense present and active in and through his ministry. This forms a decisive break with the apocalypticism of Jesus' time. Käsemann indeed believed that this is so much *the* distinctive feature of Jesus' teaching that it sets Jesus wholly *outside* the framework of apocalyptic thought: 'His own preaching was not constitutively stamped by apocalyptic but proclaimed the immediate nearness of God'. The passages in the Synoptic tradition which speak of an imminent End belong not to the message of Jesus, but to the preaching of the primitive Christian community, to the post-Easter enthusiasm for the parousia, wherein the primitive community resorted again to apocalyptic terms and 'in a certain sense' supplanted Jesus' preaching of 'the nearness of God'.[17]

Käsemann however has undoubtedly overstated his case. Such a complete discontinuity between an *apocalyptic* John the Baptist, a *non*-apocalyptic Jesus, and an *apocalyptic* primitive community is scarcely credible.[18] Moreover, the apocalyptic language and imagery is so pervasive in the Jesus-tradition, as we have seen above, that it can hardly be removed, just as it could hardly have been added, without altering the character of Jesus' message drastically and completely (not merely 'in a certain sense'). The fact is that Käsemann has failed to grasp the nature of the present-future tension in Jesus' preaching. The 'immediate nearness of God' is not something other than the presence of the kingdom in eschatological blessing, and the presence of the kingdom was precisely the end-time power already entering the present age and presaging the imminent coming of the kingdom in eschatological finality (see also above pp.14f., and 213).

To sum up then, we must resist the temptation to cut and run in the face of the challenge which Weiss and Schweitzer still pose to twentieth-century theology, the temptation to resort to a neo-Liberalism which stresses only that strand in Jesus' teaching which is most easily translatable into modern terms. Dogmatic theologizing and contemporary apologetic must not dictate to historical research what its findings should be, but must do their best with what historical research does find. And at this point the conclusion is to be neither weakened nor avoided that *Jesus not only proclaimed God's eschatological power as already active but proclaimed also the final consummation of God's purpose for the world as imminent and did so in the language of apocalyptic eschatology.* To that extent the message of Jesus is part of the trajectory linking Jewish and Christian apocalypticism.

67.3 *The primitive Christian community.* The earliest days of Christianity proper were marked by a high degree of eschatological fervency, as most historical researchers agree. This is less easy to document than the eschatological character of Jesus' message (§67.2) or of the early preaching of Paul (§68.1). For his own reasons Luke has chosen to ignore or suppress this important aspect of earliest Christianity (see below pp.347f.) – so, for example, there were many visionaries and visions (not least of angels) in the first few years, but in Luke's account only a handful could begin to warrant the description 'apocalyptic' (Acts 1.9–11; 7.55f.; cf. 2.2f.; 10.10–16; 26.13–19). Nevertheless there are sufficient other indications of the apocalyptic enthusiasm of the first Christians.[19]

(*a*) It cannot be insignificant that *they found it necessary to use the apocalyptic category of resurrection to express their new faith* (see above p.217). Evidently they believed that Jesus' resurrection was *the beginning of the resurrection of the dead*, the first sheaf of the eschatological harvest now being reaped (Rom. 1.3f.; I Cor. 15.20, 23; cf. Matt. 27.52f.) – a belief and metaphor (first fruits) which Paul can hardly have coined for the first time twenty years after the event and which must have been part of the initial enthusiasm: Jesus has been raised from the dead – the resurrection of the dead has begun.[20] Thus they believed also that they stood in 'the last days', leading up to the last day, as predicted by Joel (Acts 2.17f.; Joel 2.28–32). They had reached the climactic point of God's purpose for Israel: they were the eschatological Israel, the people of the new covenant inaugurated by the death and resurrection of Jesus (Mark 14.22–25 pars.; I Cor. 11.23ff.); their representatives, 'the twelve' (reconstituted with the election of Matthias in Judas's place – Acts 1.15–26), would soon take up their role as judges of Israel in the final judgment itself (Matt. 19.28/Luke 22.29f.).

(*b*) Evidently too they lived in *daily expectation of the parousia of Jesus*. This is clearly implied: by the primitive invocation preserved by Paul in its original Aramaic in I Cor. 16.22 – 'Our Lord, come! (cf. James 5.7f.; Rev. 22.20); by the primitive kerygmatic formulation embedded in Luke's account of Peter's second sermon – if his hearers repented God would send the Christ from heaven (Acts 3.19–21); and by the hope of the soon coming of Jesus as the Son of Man preserved in Q (Luke 12.8f./(Matt. 10.32f.); Luke 11.30/(Matt. 12.40); Matt. 24.27/Luke 17.24; Matt. 24.37/Luke 17.26; Luke 17.30/(Matt. 24.39); Matt. 24.44/Luke 12.40). The degree of reworking to which this Son of Man tradition has been subjected (cf. above pp.36, 217) indicates that it was a topic of vital interest and concern in the earliest churches; it is not without significance that according to tradition both Stephen and James (the brother of Jesus) summed up their faith at the point of crisis by reference to the (coming) Son of Man (Acts 7.56; Eusebius, *HE*, II.23.13). Similarly the more likely it is that Mark 13 is the product of a lengthy development, the dominant view in recent redactional studies,[21] the more difficult it is to escape the conclusion that there was a continuing eschatological speculation of considerable vigour and influence within earliest Christianity. It is almost certainly within the context of such eschatological enthusiasm that we have to understand the so-called 'community of goods' (Acts 2.44f.; 4.32–37) – that is, not as a careless enterprise (they disposed of their capital goods, not merely their income) on the part of those who anticipated many years of evangelism ahead of them, but as a policy which disdained the needs of the present age in view of the imminent End of the present age itself.

(c) Finally we might recall to what extent the earliest community's common life seems to have revolved round the temple (above pp.238f.). Evidently the first Christians' hope for eschatological renewal centred on Mount Zion and on an eschatologically renewed or rebuilt temple (as in Tob. 14.4f.; I Enoch 90.28f.; 91.13; Test. Ben. 9.2; Sib. Or. III.718, 772ff.; Ass.Mos. 1.17f.; II Bar. 4.2–7; 6.7f.; IV Ezra 7.26; 8.52; 10.25–57; and at Qumran[22]). This no doubt is the significance they attached to Jesus' 'cleansing of the temple' (Mark 11.17 = Isa. 56.7; Mal. 3.1) and why the puzzling word of Jesus about the destruction and rebuilding of the temple (Mark 14.58; 15.29; John 2.19) was preserved among the first Christians – an important part of their self-understanding as the representatives of eschatological Israel. This is no doubt why too they evidently did not stir from Jerusalem in the early months and why Stephen's alternative interpretation of that saying met with such hostility from them (see above pp. 271ff.). The same Israel centredness of their eschatological concern is also reflected in the question preserved in Acts 1.6 – 'Lord, will you at this time restore the kingdom to Israel?' – a question which has an odd ring in the context of Luke's de-eschatologized history, but which rings true in the circumstances as we have outlined them above; and note again Matt. 10.23.

In short, the perspective of the earliest Christian church(es) seems to have been very narrow indeed: they were already in the last days leading up to the last day, they stood in the final climactic period of history, at the edge of the End, the final swing of the pendulum had already begun. To the extent that they looked back to the resurrection as already begun in the resurrection of Jesus, and to Jesus as Messiah and Son of Man already during his earthly ministry, to that extent the note of realized eschatology so distinctive of Jesus was certainly present;[23] on the other hand, so far as we can tell, the cautionary note also present in Jesus' teaching seems to have been almost wholly swamped by the eschatological fervour for the imminent End. It is well to remind ourselves that we are talking here of the mother church of all Christianity – that *Christianity began as an eschatological sect within Judaism, a sect which in its apocalypticism was in substantial continuity with the messages both of John the Baptist and of Jesus.* And since this is where Christianity all began, to that extent Käsemann is correct: 'apocalyptic *was* the mother of all Christian theology'.

§68. APOCALYPTIC LITERATURE IN THE NEW TESTAMENT

The trajectory of apocalyptic Christianity is most easily traced through the first century by referring to the literature which makes up the NT. It has left a literary deposit at three points in particular – I and II Thessalonians, the so-called Markan apocalypse (Mark 13) and the apocalypse of John (Revelation).

68.1 *I and II Thessalonians.* It will occasion no surprise, in view of §67 above, that (probably) the earliest NT documents, though not apocalypses as such, have characteristic apocalyptic features (see particularly I Thess. 1.9f.; 413–5.11, 23; II Thess. 1.4–10; 2.1–12). It is not to be disputed that *in Thessalonica at least Paul's preaching was marked by apocalyptic eschatology* – as Paul himself reminds his Thessalonian converts in II Thess. 2.5 (see further below). In particular, the expectation of an *imminent parousia* was a prominent feature: it was well known that the Thessalonians' turning to God had been a turning to await the parousia, the coming of Jesus which would deliver them from the eschatological wrath and judgment of God (I Thess. 1.9f.). Evidently Paul's proclamation had led his converts to believe that the eschatological climax was very imminent indeed. That was why the death of some of the Thessalonian Christians since Paul's visit was causing some bewilderment. So far as Paul personally was concerned there was no real problem, and his own expectation of an imminent End was scarcely diminished: many of them, he was clearly convinced, would still be alive to greet Christ on his return (I Thess. 4.15, 17; 5.23).

The parousia itself he describes in distinctive apocalyptic language – as a descending from heaven, with archangels and clouds, with loud shouts and trumpet blasts,[24] and the resurrection of the dead (I Thess. 4.16f.); it would come without warning, bringing destruction for the unprepared, sudden and terrible, the birth pangs of the new age, 'and there will be no escape' (I Thess. 5.2f.). We may note also how much of this apocalyptic anticipation seems to have been fed by prophecy (I Thess. 5.19f.), and that 'the word of the Lord' in 4.15 was in all probability itself a prophetic utterance in a Pauline assembly, an oracle which clarified the apocalyptic hope in relation to those converts who had already died. In short, not only does the oldest text in the NT itself demonstrate distinctively apocalyptic features, but it also reveals clearly how markedly apocalyptic was the teaching and hope of the early Pauline churches. If I Thessalonians is not necessarily wholly typical at this point, it cannot be wholly untypical either; *apocalyptic eschatology was an integral feature of the early Christian expansion beyond the confines of Palestine.*

II Thessalonians is even more interesting. Paul (and I see no significant reason to deny the letter to Paul)[25] reaffirms his expectation of an imminent parousia and again paints it in apocalyptic colours (II Thess. 1.4–10). Notice particularly, he seems to think that the suffering his Thessalonian converts were *already* experiencing was part or *the beginning of the messianic woes* (so also I. Thess. 3.3f.) – the tribulation believers must endure before the kingdom, the new age fully comes – at which time the Lord would be revealed from heaven with his mighty angels in blazing fire, bringing relief to the believers and inflicting vengeance upon all who had persecuted them and refused to acknowledge God or obey his gospel.

II Thess. 2.1–12 holds the chief interest for us, since it demonstrates both the extent to which Paul at this stage was prepared to think and teach in typically apocalyptic language, and also how conscious Paul was of the danger of eschatological enthusiasm getting out of hand. Evidently prophecies had been made in the Thessalonian assemblies and reports or letters received to the effect that the day of the Lord was already present (2.2). What the Thessalonians understood this to mean is far from clear, and Paul's initial response is a tantalizingly unfinished sentence (2.3). But the result seems to have been quite a feverish frenzy and alarm (2.2), with many of the new converts abandoning their work and employment (so as to be ready? – 3.6–12). Paul's response has three strands. First, he warns them that prophecy can deceive and correspondence be forged – don't accept uncritically all you hear or read, however inspired sounding or authoritatively written! Second, he reminds them of what he had already told them – that there would be a necessary *interval* before the End: the opposition to God which they were already experiencing (1.5ff.) must first rise to a climax with the appearance of 'the man of lawlessness' (2.3f.). It was true that 'the mystery of lawlessness' ('the secret power of wickedness' – NEB) was already present (2.7); the last revolt against God was already under way – the End *was* imminent. But the rebellion against God had still to come to full expression – there was a 'restraining hand' (*to katechon*) which held back the full intensity of the flood of wickedness and end-time tribulation (2.6f.).[26] Only when it had been removed would the lawless man appear in all his power and deceit (2.9f.) and be destroyed by the parousia (2.8). Third, Paul insists that the normal business of life must be pursued while the parousia is awaited: those who refuse to work – that is, presumably, who insist on standing around in readiness for the End – must not expect support from any common funds (3.10).

Particularly striking in this passage is the strong influence of classical Jewish apocalyptic imagery. (*a*) 'The man of lawlessness', 'the son of perdition' reflects a Jewish apocalyptic world view, where the eschatological opposition to God was often represented by a single figure – Satan, or a dragon, or in human form as a tyrant or prophet hostile to God (the closest parallel is Sib.Or. III.63–70). In II Thessalonians 'the man of lawlessness' is the Christian equivalent. We should notice that he is not properly speaking an anti-Christ figure, the opponent and opposite pole to Christ; in II Thess. 2 he opposes God. Here Christian thought has taken over the Jewish concept, but has not yet developed it into the more distinctively Christian idea of anti-Christ; that idea as such only appears in the Johannine letters and Revelation (I John 2.18, 22; 4.3; II John 7; cf. Rev. 13; 17).

(*b*) The supreme blasphemy of 'the man of lawlessness' is his taking his seat in the temple of God and proclaiming himself to be God (II Thess. 2.4). In Jewish thought the classical type of opposition to God was the desecration of the temple by Antiochus Epiphanes (Dan. 9.27; 11.31; 12.11; I Macc. 1.54). It is evidently this that Paul has in mind, a the probable allusion to Dan. 11.36 confirms. Here then is Christianity, already spread into Europe, but still depicting the final rebellion in terms of Jewish apocalyptic fears regarding the Jerusalem temple.

(*c*) Also very marked is the esoteric character – a typical apocalyptic stylistic feature, as we saw above (p.311). 'The man of lawlessness' is obscure enough, but 'that which restrains' (*to katechon*) and 'the restrainer' (*ho katechōn*) are obviously a deliberately veiled reference which the readers presumably could decode without too much difficulty, but which we certainly cannot.

(d) Finally we might note the ethical exhortations in view of the imminent denouement (I Thess. 5.1–11; II Thess. 2.15; 3.6–13) – another feature characteristic of Jewish apocalypses (p. 312). The eschatological hope should *not* mean a slackening of moral effort; on the contrary it should mean all the greater watchfulness. *It is this combination of imminent expectation and moral earnestness which marked off the enthusiasm of apocalyptic Christianity so clearly from the enthusiasm of Hellenistic Christianity*.

In short, here we have a Christian document, about twenty years after the first burst of apocalyptic enthusiasm which launched the new sect in Jerusalem, and with the Gentile mission already well under way, and the hope of an imminent end still burns brightly and is still expressed in language and imagery typical of Jewish apocalyptic.

At the same time distinctively Christian features have clearly emerged (1) Notice particularly that the divine agent who will bring about the End is identified with *Jesus*. This is what distinguishes Christian from Jewish apocalyptic eschatology. In the latter the same obscurity veils the apocalyptist's vision of the agent of God as veils his vision of the opponents of God. But in the apocalyptic expectation of I and II Thessalonians the vision has come to focus and no doubt remains – the one who will intervene to institute judgment, destroy the man of lawlessness and save his persecuted people is a heavenly figure whose identity is already known as one who previously walked this earth, 'the Lord Jesus'. (2) The element of realized eschatology is not prominent; presumably the expectation of an imminent parousia drowned its note – though in Paul's later writings it comes to steadily increasing prominence (see below §71.1). But the *cautionary* note of Jesus' preaching is certainly present: *to katechon* is still operative; the flood of end-time evil and tribulation is still quite a way short of its peak; Paul refuses to be drawn into speculation about the dates and times of the end events (I Thess. 5.1). This note of sobriety remains an integral part of apocalyptic thought within the NT. At the same time we should note the significance of the fact that Paul does not meet the Thessalonian abuse of eschatology by abandoning eschatology, but simply by spelling out the apocalyptic hope more fully. At this stage anyway (nearly twenty years after his conversion) *apocalyptic eschatology remained integral to his message and his hope*.[27]

68.2   *Mark 13* is not an apocalypse either but a composite of individual sayings of Jesus and interpretative and editorial additions, infused with an apocalyptic eschatology (see above pp. 323f.

n.21). How much goes back to Jesus is a matter of considerable dispute (cf. §67.2 above); but here we are concerned with the passage as a complete whole. Mark presents the whole discourse as an elaboration of Jesus' prophetic utterance concerning the destruction of the temple – 'Not one stone will be left upon another; all will be thrown down' (13.2). The disciples then ask, 'When will this happen? What will be the sign when the fulfilment of all this is at hand?' (13.4). The discourse is Jesus' reply.

(a) Notice *the typical apocalyptic elements*: v.4 – 'when all these things are to be accomplished (*sunteleisthai*)?', where the equivalent noun phrase, *sunteleia* (*tou aiōnos*), as in Matt. 24.3, is a technical apocalyptic term, particularly in Daniel and the Testaments of the Twelve Patriarchs, to denote the End;[28] vv. 7–8 – world-wide turmoil, wars and natural disasters, 'the beginning of the birth pangs (of the new age), that is, the messianic woes;[29] vv.9–13 – severe affliction and persecution for the disciples, including the characteristic apocalyptic foreboding of internecine family strife (references above p.319); v.14 – the esoteric sign, 'the desolating sacrilege', an allusion again to Antiochus Epiphanes' profanity in erecting an altar to Zeus in the temple in 168 BC (references above p.327) – notice Mark's cryptic decoding signal ('let the reader understand'); vv.14–20 – the urgency and unprecedented anguish of the final tribulation; vv.24–27 – the cosmic dimensions of the messianic woes, the whole of creation in labour to bring the new age to birth, including the coming of the Son of Man 'in clouds with great power and glory' (cf. Dan. 7.13f.); vv.28–30 – the imminence of these events of the End, 'at the very gates', within this very generation; vv.33–37 – exhortations to be ready.

(b) It is fairly clear from this chapter that Mark saw the destruction of Jerusalem and the temple as part of the messianic woes, the birth pangs of the new age (probably reflecting and elaborating Jesus' own expectations about the End – above §67.2). The dating of the Gospel is uncertain, but the strongest probability remains that Mark was writing prior to the fall of Jerusalem, though at a time when this catastrophe was beginning to loom large on the horizon – that is, about the middle of the 60s. In which case, *he evidently anticipated that the desecration of the temple would mark the beginning of the End*. Notice, for example, the warnings against false prophets and false messiahs which take up such a prominent place in the discourse (vv.5f., 21f.); the fact that Mark places these warnings first and then repeats them implies that this was a real and pressing threat; and we know from Josephus that not a few such claimants disturbed and

incited Palestine in the 50s and 60s.[30] Likewise vv.9ff. in Mark's
mind probably refer to the very bitter antagonism which grew up
between the different parties within Judaism as the national crisis
heightened. We do not know what role, if any, the Christian communities in Palestine played in all this, but it is likely that they were
caught up in the cross-fire to some extent at least. Some no doubt
favoured the militants, but others would be more quietist in their
apocalyptic hope of Jesus' return, and consequently leave themselves open to the charge of being unpatriotic, etc. Notice particularly v.13b – in Mark's presentation the suffering referred to would
continue right to the End; in effect the passage is saying, 'Hang on!
the End is near!'. Verses 14ff. obviously refer to the inevitable attack
on Jerusalem. And, above all, v.24 links all this firmly with the
cosmic catastrophes of the End itself – 'But in those days (which
cannot refer to anything other than the events described in the first
half of the chapter – note particularly vv.17, 19f.), after that tribulation, the sun will be darkened . . .' and the Son of Man come. In
short, Mark, in typical apocalyptic fashion, writes in a context of
mounting crisis which he sees as building up to the final crisis of the
End, and his purpose here at least is to warn and encourage his
readers to recognize the true nature of the crisis and to endure to the
End.

(c) At the same time we can see the same two distinctively Christian elements as we noticed in II Thessalonians. First, the apocalyptic expectation is related to *Christ*. It is *his* prediction; warnings
against false christs are given a prominent position and repeated; the
Son of Man is obviously in Mark's mind to be identified with Christ;
and 'the desolating sacrilege' (a neuter concept to which he attaches
a masculine participle) he probably associated with anti-Christ –
'The verse evidently treats of an adversary raised to titanic proportions, in contrast to which the false messiahs (vv.21–22) are, so to
speak, but "forerunners" '.[31]

Second, the apocalyptic enthusiasm is kept within firm bounds;
there is *a distinct cautionary note* in the whole discourse which is
designed to prevent the reader from building his hopes too high.
Verse 7 – ' . . . but the end is not yet'; v.8 – 'these are the beginning of
the sufferings/messianic woes' – the final events are beginning, but
only *beginning*; v.10 – 'the gospel must first be preached to all nations'
(a task already well under way but not yet complete); v.24 – 'after
that tribulation'; v.32 – 'of that day or that hour no one knows, not
even the angels in heaven, nor the Son, but only the Father'. Within
this generation, yes (v.30), but not necessarily immediately. The

recognition of this cautionary note incidentally helps us to understand the function of all the various 'signs of the End' in Mark 13. They were *not* given to enable the reader to compute the date and hour of the Son of Man's coming; they were listed rather to encourage the reader who was already in the midst of these tribulations, to assure him that his sufferings were part of the messianic woes, that the End could not be too far distant – 'Hold on! Endure to the End!'

The importance of the cautionary element is of course given added point by the fact that Jerusalem fell and the temple was destroyed (AD 70) and yet the End did *not* come. This would obviously cause problems for the later Evangelists in their use of Mark 13. In particular we shall see below how Luke reinterpreted Mark 13 by disentangling what for Mark (and probably Jesus) were a single complex of events (destruction of temple and parousia) and by separating them into two distinct events (p.347). In other words, for Luke there was both an element of *fulfilment* of the earlier apocalyptic hope: Jerusalem had fallen, the temple had been destroyed – 'the desolating sacrilege' had been decoded by the event as the siege of Jerusalem by (Roman) armies (Luke 21.20). At the same time the apocalyptic hope is *reaffirmed afresh*: the cautionary element already present in Mark is extended to break the link between the destruction of Jerusalem and the parousia precisely so that the parousia hope can be reaffirmed afresh (21.27f., 31f.; note also 17.22–18.8).[32] The point which we must note now is that despite the lack of fulfilment of the apocalyptic hope of Mark (and of Jesus) *Luke does not abandon the apocalyptic discourse*; rather he reinterprets it in the light of unfulfilled expectation without abandoning the hope it expresses.

68.3   *Revelation.* (a) The Apocalypse of John obviously stands firmly within the tradition of apocalyptic literature. It is essentially a transcript of John's *visions*, and is built round three seven-fold visions – seven seals (5.1–8.1), seven trumpets (8.2–9.21, 11.15–19) and seven bowls (15–16). Note also the repeated phrase 'in the Spirit' (1.10; 4.2; 17.3; 21.10). It is full of *fantastic imagery* typical of apocalypses: for example, 1.16 – 'one like a son of man' (Dan. 7.13) holding seven stars in his hand, and with a two edged sword coming from his mouth; 4.6 – round the throne four living creatures covered with eyes in front and behind; 5.6 – a lamb with seven horns and seven eyes; 9.7ff. – most fearsome locusts; 9.17ff. – apocalyptic horsemen; etc. Prominent also are visions of world wide turmoil and cosmic catastrophe – particularly the visions of the trumpets (8) and the bowls (16). *Numbers* obviously play an important role, particularly the number seven – seven seals, seven trumpets, seven bowls, etc.; but also three, four and twelve; 666, the number of the beast (13.18); and 1260 days = 42 months = 3½ years (11.2f.; 12.6, 14; 13.5) – by now a stereotyped apocalyptic number which goes back to Dan. 12.7.

Revelation is firmly in the tradition of apocalyptic literature too in that it has clearly been born out of *crisis*. John believed that the final tribulation was already upon them: it had already claimed not a few victims (2.13; 6.9), and it would soon reach world wide proportions (3.10; cf. 2.10; 6.10; 16.6; 18.24; 19.2; 20.4). He was most probably referring to the increasingly sharp confrontation between Christianity and the imperial cult which marked the final years of Emperor Domitian's reign (AD 93–96). Emperor worship had been practised in Asia Minor since the time of Augustus, but it was only under Domitian, who took his divinity more seriously than most of his predecessors, that Christians (and others) began systematically to be persecuted for failure to pay him the divine honours he required of his subjects.[33] Most commentators recognize this as the most likely background to Revelation, with Rome and the emperor pictured in terms of a fearsome beast who demanded men's worship (13.4, 12–15; 14.9, 11; 16.2; 19.20). Whether we should actually identify Domitian as the eighth king of 17.11 is a much more disputed issue, but one whose outcome does not affect the point here. The point is that John writes against the backcloth of a mounting persecution which he believed was building up to the final climax of evil and tribulation.

One thing does distinguish Revelation from earlier apocalypses – namely the fact that the author writes under his own name – he does not use a pseudonym (1.1, 4, 9; 22.8). This may be because, unlike his predecessors, he is not attempting to survey past history from an even earlier standpoint – although 17.10 could be read as an attempt to present his writing as contemporaneous with an earlier emperor, probably Vespasian (AD 69–79), and the bulk of the book does appear to consist of three or four surveys of the End period, from the first advent of Jesus to his final triumph (6.1–8.1; 8–11; 12–14; 15–16). But John evidently saw himself as nearing the climax of the End and was not disposed to cloak that fact. Hence too there is no command to seal up the revelation, 'till the time of the End', as in Dan. 8.26, 12.9 – the crisis was too pressing, too final for such artifice, the End was already at hand (Rev. 22.10). And similarly he is not concerned to veil his meaning by using elaborate symbolic visions which only the initiated could decipher; to be sure we today have little certainty about the precise reference of the beast whose number is 666 (13.18), but the woman on the beast is clearly Rome and John does not care who knows it (17.9, 18).

Nevertheless, other characteristics of apocalyptic literature are so marked that it would be pusillanimous to deny Revelation's place within the apocalyptic *genre*.[33a]

(*b*) The main *theological* characteristics of apocalyptic are also present in Revelation. This will already be sufficiently obvious from the details given above. Here we need only highlight a few others. (1) Notice particularly the *apocalyptic dualism*. The real struggle is not so much between the churches and the pagan powers as between Christ and Satan. Moreover, John has no hope for this world; all he foresees for it is destruction. His own hope is focused in heaven, and on the new heaven and the new earth, on the new Jerusalem which will come down from heaven (21–22). The theme is not unfamiliar to apocalyptic eschatology (see above p. 324), but more clearly than any other apocalyptist John has transfigured the hope of an eschaton focused on Mount Zion into the vision of a heavenly Jerusalem, representative of the rebirth of the whole of creation. (2) The *messianic woes*, the tribulation of the saints, are a feature to which we have already alluded (above p.332). The present persecution suffered or about to be suffered by John and his readers is 'the great tribulation' (7.14; see also e.g. 11.7f.; 13.7), the great tribulation of the end-time. But fear not, comforts John, the seal of God is upon you (7.1–8; 9.4). (3) The expectation of the End as *imminent* is given particular emphasis by its prominence at both beginning and end: 1.1 – 'what must shortly take place'; 1.3 – 'the time is near', 1.7 – 'he is coming with clouds'; 3.11 – 'I am coming soon'; 22.10 – 'the time is near'; 22.20 – 'He who testifies to these things says, "Yes, I am coming soon". Amen! Come, Lord Jesus!' (4) Perhaps most striking of all is the way in which John expresses *his confidence in God's sovereign control*. 'The plan of God for history is unalterably laid down in the "book with seven seals" and, after the opening of this, it is unfolded without obstruction'.[34]

John's message is therefore very simple. To those already enduring persecution, or under the threat of persecution, he says, 'Do not be distracted by what is happening on earth. The End is near. God is in control. Your present tribulations foreshadow God's intervention. Your enemies will shortly be utterly routed and destroyed, and you will soon enjoy the life of heaven in the new creation'.

(*c*) The distinctive Christian features are more prominent here than in Mark 13 and I and II Thess. First, its *Christ-focus*. 5.5 – no one else is worthy to open the scroll of the End, only the Lion of Judah, the Root of David, he it is who has won the right to open the scroll and break the seven seals; that is to say, only he can accomplish God's purposes, can initiate the events of the End. Notice particularly how closely the thought of this authority is linked to Jesus' death and resurrection: it is precisely the lamb who has been killed who takes the scroll and opens the seals (5.6, 9, 12). So too it is the 'first born from the dead', he who once died but is now alive for evermore (1.5, 18), who grants John the revelation of what is and what is to come. The whole apocalypse in fact moves between the victory of the risen Jesus and his coming again: as his victory qualifies Jesus to open the scroll, to initiate the final acts, so his parousia is the climax of the whole – ' "I am coming soon". Amen! Come, Lord Jesus!' (22.20). In short, the seer of the apocalypse holds together the historical Jesus, the exalted Christ and the soon coming Lord as firmly and as clearly as any other NT writer (see also above p.227).

Second, *the cautionary element* of Christian apocalyptic eschatology is preserved. The note of imminence never becomes a definite prediction. The 42 months = 3½ years is a standard number which was hardly intended to provide a timetable on which the events of the End could be calculated. The letters of Rev. 2–3 have exhortations which imply that the End is not just yet – for example, the ten days of tribulation to come (2.10) and the frequent calls to endure and conquer. John certainly sees the beginning of the persecution under Domitian as the beginning of the final period of tribulation. But how long he expects these tribulations to last is something he does not really attempt to specify. There is no call here to be caught up in an apocalyptic frenzy of expectation. It is enough for John to know that the sufferings of the present are those which will precede the soon coming of the Lord.

§69. CONCLUSIONS

69.1   Our method in this chapter has been different from that of the last two chapters. This is principally because apocalyptic Christianity has generally been regarded in a different and a dimmer light. No one doubts that Christianity's attempts to understand itself within the context of its Jewish heritage and in face of the manifold challenges of the syncretism of the age were central and fundamental aspects of first-century Christianity – so our task there was to explore the dimensions of this quest for self-understanding, to demonstrate how far first-century Christianity's diversity overlapped with surrounding faiths, to investigate the extent to which the first-century Christians were of the fringe as well as of the centre. But apocalyptic Christianity is usually regarded as something which by definition belongs to the fringe from the start, and has been so treated in history as well as in modern theology.[35] So our task here has been rather to show how central to earliest Christianity was apocalyptic hope and expression, to show that apocalyptic eschatology is as fundamental to the diversity of first-century Christianity as the Christianity of Matthew and James or the Christianity of Corinth and of John.

This we have demonstrated. There can now be no doubt that *apocalyptic eschatology had an integral part in first-century Christianity*.[36] We can ignore it or remove it only by distorting the historical reality of Christianity's beginnings (and distorting thereby the whole of Christian theology).[37] Christianity emerged from an environment strongly oriented to an apocalyptic perspective; the preaching of its Baptist herald was apocalyptic in content. Jesus' own expectation for the future can hardly avoid being described as apocalyptic; and the earliest Christian community in Palestine was thoroughly apocalyptic in character and self-understanding. Similarly the kerygma of the early Gentile mission was strongly marked by apocalyptic features. One of the earliest, perhaps the earliest, collections of sayings of Jesus into a larger discourse, (what became) the eschatological discourse of Mark 13, indicates the apocalyptic expectations of Jesus to be one of the areas of most vigorous theological concern in the earliest decades of Christianity. And the Revelation of John shows how little the fires of apocalyptic expectancy had faded in the latter decades of the first century, and how quickly they flared up again when Christians were confronted with the crisis alternatives of submission to the imperial cult or bloody persecution.

69.2   Granted then that earliest Christianity and some of the NT literature belong firmly within an apocalyptic trajectory stretching from the apocalypses of early Judaism to second-century Montanism and beyond, what are the distinctive or characteristic features of earliest apocalyptic Christianity? The present chapter has brought to light three such features which mark off earliest Christian apocalyptic eschatology from what went before.

(a) It was *Christ-centred*. Where the hope of Jewish eschatology was undefined or was left in purely symbolic language, the Christian apocalyptic hope crystallized round a particular man whom many of the first Christians had already encountered in history. That hope came to classical expression in the expectation of the parousia of this Jesus now exalted. Demythologized we may re-express it thus: the transcendent power which is shaping history and which will bring history to an end has the 'shape' and character of Jesus of Nazareth. Or, in more traditional terms, the exalted Jesus will intervene in future history as he did in past history, but next time his intervention will be of *immediate* and *final* significance for the world as a whole.

(*b*) *The already/not yet tension.* The future hope was linked with events in the past; the divine climax was seen in terms of *Jesus*, the future resurrection in terms of Jesus' resurrection. The hope for the future arose out of what had happened in the past. The Christian apocalyptist looked *both* ways. This characteristic was also expressed in the belief that Christians live in the overlap of the ages; that the event of Jesus (his life, death and resurrection) was *decisive* for the future; that the last days were already here, the Spirit being the first instalment of eschatological salvation. In other words, *God's interven-tion in the past had already determined the End*; however long delayed it might be, the power already operative in believers was the same power which would bring about the End, was already working towards that End.

(*c*) A *cautionary note.* The first-century Christian apocalyptic writ-ings never allowed enthusiasm to get out of hand; they deliberately set their face against speculating about dates and times; always the note of the not yet was present to prevent hope becoming too detailed, too certain about the details of God's future. This was true also of Jesus' apocalyptic expectation, so far as we can tell, though the hope of the earliest Jerusalem community seems to have been less inhibited, and some of the Thessalonian Christians apparently abandoned themselves to their hope without reservation. But other-wise the emphasis on the already, the looking to the past as well as to the future, prevented the looking to the future becoming too frenzied and so inevitably disappointed. As Cullmann has well expressed the point:

> The hope of Paul suffered no loss either in intensity or in its firm anchorage, because from the outset its starting point had been that *the centre, the fixed point of orientation*, lies not in the future but in the past, and accordingly *in an assured fact which cannot be touched by the delay in the Parousia*.[38]

Of these characteristic features of Christian apocalypticism only the third is readily paralleled in Jewish apocalypticism (see above p. 314). This means that it is the Christ-centredness, the already emphasis centred on the man of Nazareth, his life, death and resurrection, which alone clearly distinguishes Christian from Jewish apocalyptic eschatology. It is the realized character Jesus stamped on Jewish eschatology and the centrality of Jesus himself in earliest Christian apocalyptic eschatology which determines its nature. That is to say, Christian apocalyptic eschatology is formed not only by the application of Jewish apocalyptic hope to Jesus, but even more distinctively by the reinterpretation of Jewish apocalyptic hope in the light of the Christ event – both his own proclamation and his resurrection.[39] In other words, once again *the distinctiveness of Christianity at this point boils down to the unity between the man of Nazareth and the soon coming Christ*, the continuity between Jesus' own proclamation (both its realized and future emphasis) and the resurrection faith and parousia hope of the first Christians.

69.3 It is also worth drawing attention to *the distinctiveness of apocalyptic Christianity within earliest Christianity*. Apocalyptic Christianity was essentially *a form of Jewish Christian enthusiasm*, the combination of Jewish apocalypticism and a broadening Christian perspective. Thus it was able to retain its fervour even when Christianity moved outside of Palestine and its Jewishness became more diluted with elements from a wider spectrum. For example, Luke retained Jesus' and Mark's apocalyptic expectation, but separated it from the fall of Jerusalem. And Revelation retained the idea of a Jerusalem centred consummation, but, writing in Asia Minor, expressed it in terms of a *heavenly* Jerusalem, a new Jerusalem coming down out of heaven from God – Jewish nationalist apocalypticism had been internationalized, reinterpreted in cosmic terms.

At the same time Christian apocalypticism did retain its Jewishness over against the other principal form of enthusiasm within early Christianity, the more gnostic type of enthusiasm which came to clear expression in the Corinthian church, at two points. First, apocalyptic enthusiasm is essentially *future*-oriented, while more gnostically influenced Christianity has an essentially *realized* emphasis (see above pp.278f.); where gnostic enthusiasm stressed the already, apocalyptic enthusiasm stressed the not yet (and the imminence of its realization). At this point Paul in particular stands more under the banner of Jewish Christian apocalypticism than under that of gnostic enthusiasm.[40] Second, apocalyptic enthusiasm was marked off from gnostic enthusiasm by its *moral earnestness*. Gnostic Christian stress on the freedom already achieved led all too easily and quickly to ethical laxity and licence in all too many instances.

Apocalyptic eschatology, looking for the End, spelt out firmly what manner of life the Christian ought to lead in view of this hope. Thus, for example, Matthew retained the apocalyptic hope of Mark 13, but wedded it to some very forceful attacks on an antinomian enthusiasm (note particularly Matt. 7.23; 24.11f; see above p.249). And the seer of Revelation took a very firm stand against the moral laxity of some of the churches to which he wrote. This combination of ethical strictness and apocalyptic enthusiasm was to be a feature of many apocalyptic movements in later centuries, from Montanism to classical Pentecostalism.[41]

69.4   There is in no sense an apocalyptic orthodoxy; there never was and there never could be. Its visions and its hope are too relative, too bound up with the period of history which called them forth, to allow any standardized interpretation or expression of apocalyptic hope. This means inevitably that *apocalyptic eschatology has never fitted very comfortably into the orthodoxy of the great Church*. The whole trajectory of apocalyptic Christianity has skirted along the edges of orthodoxy, giving too much scope to unbridled enthusiasm for churchmen like Dionysius of Alexandria and Martin Luther, both of whom were more than a little unhappy about accepting Revelation into the NT canon. Yet the surprising thing about apocalyptic Christianity is *its extraordinary vitality*. Repeated disappointments have not dimmed the apocalyptic fervour of fresh generations. Matthew and Luke did not wholly abandon the apocalyptic expectation of Jesus and of Mark, despite its lack of fulfilment; they reinterpreted it and hoped afresh. And, despite the failure of the new heaven and new earth to appear 'soon', Revelation *did* find a place within the NT canon.

This means that apocalyptic eschatology has a *valid* and *important* place within Christianity – despite its dangers and failures. Attempts to exclude it from the more sophisticated great Church have simply resulted in it springing up afresh outside the great Church and robbing the great Church of the vitality and enthusiasm it brings. Since nineteenth-century Liberal Protestantism's aversion to apocalypticism remains influential, it is worthwhile reminding ourselves of the significance and continuing relevance of apocalyptic Christianity.

(*a*) It sees reality on a wide canvas – history, past, present and future, as involving not only men and nations, but *God*. It affirms that God is not distant from or unconcerned about the world, but has a part in the spiritual forces operating 'behind the scenes' – the decisive part.[41a] This means, inevitably, that humanity is responsible in some way before God – a belief classically expressed in the apocalyptic vision of the last judgment. 'To keep alive this sense that life is charged with responsibility, and that we are responsible unto God, is to render a lasting service to men'.[42]

(*b*) It sees history as having a *purpose*, a goal. It is not only *God* oriented, it is *future* oriented. Fundamental within Christian apocalyptic eschatology is *hope* – not a hope based on a naive optimism in human progress, but a hope based on the belief that the forces of history are ultimately in God's control and are driving towards *his* goal. This hope, expressed in the NT in terms of Jesus' second coming, is integral to the gospel of first-century Christianity: 'to reject this hope is to mutilate the NT message of salvation'.[43]

(*c*) These two beliefs have two results. First of all, to enable believers to give *a proper evaluation to the present*. They cherish no allusions about the present and its possibilities. In particular, they are able to adopt a positive atttitude towards *suffering*. The suffering of the present is in some way an inevitable phase in the movement of history towards God's goal, in some sense a necessary preparation for and antecedent to the greater, richer future of God. As F. C. Burkitt noted, 'The Gospel is the great protest against the modern view that the really important thing is to be comfortable'.[44]

(*d*) Second, apocalyptic hope should bring believers *a new sense of responsibility towards the world*. They cease to be dependent on the world for value and hope, but they become more responsible for it – to live and work *in* the world for the hastening of God's purposed End. Notice that the apocalyptic hope as such is *not* one which ignores or turns its back on the world – although it has been all too often interpreted in that way down through the centuries. Certainly it ceases to find its value and meaning in the world, and it is pessimistic towards the future of the world itself. But it does not opt out of this world: it has been born of suffering in the world, and it holds itself responsible both to declare to the world the true state of reality, the true course of history, and to work *in* the world so far as it is possible to hasten the coming of God's kingdom from beyond. Moreover, it is able to persevere in this mission, despite persecution and disappointment, precisely because it is not dependent on this world for recognition and value. This is why apocalyptic eschatology contains *seeds of revolution*, and has in fact been the basic inspiration for many revolutionary movements in European history.

The role of apocalyptic Christianity is therefore to resist all or any temptation to abandon hope for the 'realities' of the present, or to abandon the present for the vision of the future, but instead to relate the two to each other, *to understand the present in the light of the future and the future in the relation to the present*. This is an ongoing task, the responsibility of each generation to work out afresh. The new generation must not confuse the hope for the future with the particular expression of earlier generations; it must not abandon the hope because a particular expression of it was too much bound up with events and personalities now past. Rather it must recognize the relativeness of *any* expression of apocalyptic hope, it must reinterpret the present in the light both of the past (the already) and the future (the not yet), and it must reaffirm the future as God's and hope afresh.

In short, the problem of apocalyptic Christianity is how both to *retain* it and to *restrain* it: To retain its hope of God's imminent intervention and the enthusiasm it brings, and to restrain it from becoming detailed, too certain of its particular expression, too dependent on a particular fulfilment of that hope. Apocalyptic Christianity is confronted by the constant danger of 'accelerating expectations',[45] the problem of retaining hope without letting it get out of hand. Such conflicting currents have been an integral and important part of the broad stream of Christianity from the earliest days till now.

XIV

EARLY CATHOLICISM

§70. WHAT IS 'EARLY CATHOLICISM'?

To what extent are the features which characterize catholic Christianity from the (late) second century already present in the NT? When did it become inevitable that (Western) Christianity was going to become the catholic orthodoxy of Cyprian and Leo? Was catholicism a post-apostolic development, a falling away from the primeval purity and simplicity of the first century? – as some Protestants have argued. Or was it simply the natural unfolding of what had belonged to the essence of Christianity from the first? – as many Catholics have maintained. Or does the answer lie somewhere in between? – perhaps in a decisive development (or several such) during the first century; perhaps in the dominance of one view over others towards the end of the first century; perhaps in the slow coming together of different elements into a coherent whole which had more lasting power than alternative views and structures; perhaps by way of reaction to other first-century developments. And if any of the latter alternatives better represent the facts than the rest, can we then speak of an 'early catholicism' within the NT? Are there NT writings which are primarily centred on the 'trajectory' of emerging catholic orthodoxy?

The phrase 'early catholicism' (*Frühkatholizismus*) itself seems to have been coined round about the turn of the century. But the issues involved in it go back at least to the middle of the nineteenth century and the Tübingen school of F. C. Baur.[1] For Baur and particularly his pupil A. Schwegler argued in effect that 'catholicism' first emerged in the second century as a *compromise* between the two rival factions which had dominated first- and early second-century Christianity – Jewish (Petrine) Christianity and Gentile (Pauline) Christianity. This compromise first appeared in conciliatory documents like Acts, Philippians, I Clement (Rome) and Hebrews (Asia Minor), which attempt to mediate between the two parties and to play down disagreements between their representative heroes; and it was consolidated in the later second-century works, the Pastorals and the letters of Ignatius (Rome) and the Gospel of John (Asia Minor).[2]

The beginning of the end of the Tübingen school was marked by the publication of the second edition of A. Ritschl's, *Die Entstehung der altkatholischen Kirche*.[3] In this he demonstrated that early Christian history was not simply a case of two monolithic blocks grinding against each other: Peter (and the original apostles) were to be distinguished from the Jewish Christians (Judaizers), and there was a Gentile Christianity distinct from Paul and little influenced by him. More to the point for us, he insisted that Catholicism was not the consequence of a reconciliation between Jewish and Gentile Christianity, but was in fact 'only a stage of Gentile Christianity', the development of a popular Gentile Christianity independent of Paul.

This thesis was in turn taken up by his protégé, A. Harnack, with his understanding of the essence of Catholicism as the '*Hellenizing*' of Christianity. As Harnack himself later defined it:

> [Catholicism] is the Christian preaching influenced by the Old Testament, lifted out of its original environment and plunged into Hellenic modes of thought, that is, into the syncretism of the age and the idealistic philosophy.'

In an important sense then, on this view the movement towards catholicism was *inherent* in Gentile Christianity,

> . . . . for the Greek spirit, the element which was most operative in Gnosticism, was already concealed in the earliest Gentile Christianity itself . . . . The great Apostle to the Gentiles himself, in his epistle to the Romans and in those to the Corinthians, transplanted the Gospel into Greek modes of thought . . .[5]

But the 'influx of Hellenism, of the Greek spirit' only happened in a significant way in the second century (Harnack can even date it specifically to about AD 130), and catholicism proper, the Church of established doctrine and fixed form, only emerged in the struggle with Gnosticism, in the conflict between Hellenization and 'radical Hellenization'.[6]

This view of the matter was questioned from two sides. In the History of Religions school the Hellenization which is the foundation of 'catholicism' was identified more precisely as the *sacramentalism* which intruded from the religious environment of the Gentile mission into early Christian understanding of baptism and the Lord's Supper. Catholicism here is defined in terms of reliance upon the outward and visible ritual act and ordinance, an attitude already present in Paul's letters (so *early* catholicism), even though it was in conflict with Paul's own understanding of faith.[7]

On a different tack completely R. Sohm took Luther's distinction between the visible and invisible Church as his starting point rather than Hellenistic thought, societies or religions. He defined 'the essence of Catholicism' as

> . . . the refusal to make any distinction between the Church in the religious sense [the Church of Christ] and the Church in the legal sense [the Church as a legally constituted entity]. The teaching of the visibleness of the Church of Christ . . . is the basic dogma on which the whole history of Catholicism rests from the first.[8]

Catholicism then first emerged when the charismatic organization which characterized the earliest Church gave way to *institutionalization*, where the institution was identified as Church with all which that meant in terms of authority of office and ecclesiastical law. The decisive step here was taken in I Clement which thus marks the rise of catholicism. In the subsequent debate on the relation between charisma and office those who accept that there was a transition from one to the other would see it as having already happened within the NT, with the Pastorals providing the primary evidence and the position of Acts disputed.

The one major new element to be introduced into the debate since then is 'the delay of the parousia'. If earliest Christianity was apocalyptic enthusiastic in character, then 'early catholicism' can be defined precisely in terms of the recognition by the Church that the End is not yet, that it must therefore settle down to a protracted period of waiting with all which that involves in more stable patterns of organization geared to preserving the Church's identity with the past and its continuity into the future. M. Werner indeed argued that the change in presupposition consequent on the delay of the parousia was 'the turning point' which set Christianity's face towards early catholicism.

> The rise of Christian doctrine, i.e. the transformation of the Primitive Christian faith into the doctrine of early Catholicism, was achieved as a process of the de-eschatologizing of Primitive Christianity in the course of its Hellenization.[9]

E. Käsemann has contributed most to this debate in the post-war decades; he defines early catholicism thus:

> Early catholicism means that transition from earliest Christianity to the so-called ancient Church, which is completed with the disappearance of the imminent expectation . . . there is a characteristic movement towards that great Church which understands itself as the *Una Sancta Apostolica*.[10]

So too in effect he redefines the earlier thesis of Heitmüller: catholicism does not emerge from the 'enthusiastic-mystic' sacramental piety of Hellenistic Christianity, but is to be understood precisely as *a reaction against all 'enthusiasm'*, both Hellenistic enthusiasm and (in my own terms) apocalyptic enthusiasm.

In the light of all this it becomes fairly clear what we are looking for. Early catholicism can be distinguished by three main features:[11]

(a) *The fading of the parousia hope*, 'the disappearance of the imminent expectation (*Naherwartung*)', the slackening of the eschatological tension between the already of Christ's earthly ministry and the not yet of his imminent reappearing to bring in the End.

(b) *Increasing institutionalization*: this would include some or all of the following features – the emergence of the concept of office, of a distinction between clergy and laity, of a priestly hierarchy, of 'apostolic succession', of sacramentalism, of an identification between church and institution so ordered.

(c) *Crystallization of the faith into set forms*, the emergence of a 'rule of faith', with the specific aim of providing a bulwark against enthusiasm and false teaching – the sense that the founding era of revelation was now past, with the correlatives that the responsibility of the present becomes the preservation of the faith from the founding fathers for the future, and that claims to new revelation from the prophetic Spirit become more the mark of the enthusiast and heretic than of the church.[12]

These were certainly the features which distinguished emerging catholic orthodoxy in the second century when it sought to ward off the challenges of Gnosticism and Montanism (see also above §26). The question which now confronts us is, To what extent are these features already visible in the NT writings themselves? To what extent can we properly speak of an early catholic element within the NT? When does the trajectory of (early) catholicism first appear? Our earlier investigations have already touched on these issues at several points, so in this chapter we will be able to gather up a few loose ends.

§71. THE FADING OF THE PAROUSIA HOPE, 'THE IMMINENT EXPECTATION'

As we saw in ch. XIII the expectation of an imminent parousia was integral to earliest Christianity and was a strong feature of Christian self-understanding during the first generation of Christianity. To

that extent early catholicism is almost inevitably a second generation development at best and cannot be traced back to the beginnings of Christianity; for early catholicism is not simply about
organization, but about organization *that will last*; early catholicism
is properly defined as, in part at least, *a reaction consequent upon the
failure of the parousia hope.* Where then in the NT do we find evidence
of the fading of the parousia hope?[12a]

71.1   *The later Paul and the Pastorals.* In §68.1 above we noted how
apocalyptic categories featured strongly in Paul's (early) preaching
and teaching in the Gentile mission. So far as the expectation of
an imminent End is concerned we might have referred also to
I Cor. 7.26–31 and 15.51f., or to Paul's powerful conviction of the
eschatological significance of his apostleship – that his mission to the
Gentiles was the last act in the history of salvation before the End
(Rom. 11.13ff.; 15.15ff.; I Cor. 4.9).[13] There is evidence however
that *this imminent expectation had begun to fade somewhat before the end of his
life.*

The earliest indication of such a change in perspective may be
I Cor. 15.51f. itself, where, although the parousia is still expected
within his own generation, death prior to the parousia has become
more the norm. Even less specific is Rom. 13.11f., for all the intensity
of its hope – near? yes; but how near?[14] And by the time we reach the
later letters of Paul the contrast with the eschatological enthusiasm of
I and II Thessalonians is clear. In *Phillipians* the parousia hope itself
is still strong (Phil. 1.6, 10; 2.16; 3.20; 4.5), but Paul is no longer
confident that he himself will still be alive when 'the day of Christ'
comes (Phil. 1.20ff.), as he evidently was in I Thess. 4.15–17 (see
also above pp.25f.).

In *Colossians* there is only one explicit reference to the coming of
Christ (Col. 3.4), but there is no sense of imminence or urgency (cf.
1.5, 12, 23, 27; 3.6, 24). Moreover, as we noted above (p.294), there
is a much stronger realized emphasis in 1.13 and 2.12, 2.20–3.3:
where in the earlier Pauline epistles inheritance of and entry into the
kingdom of God is something still outstanding (I Cor. 6.9f.; 15.50;
Gal. 5.21; I Thess. 2.12; II Thess. 1.5), in Col. 1.13 Paul speaks of
believers as having already been transferred into the kingdom of the
Son (at conversion); and where in Rom. 6.5 and 8.11 Paul spoke of
resurrection with Christ as something future, part of the not yet
consummation, in Col. 2.12 and 3.1 resurrection with Christ is
something already accomplished, part of the already. Is the implication not fairly clear that in Colossians we see Paul turning away from

the urgent hope of an imminent parousia which previously drove him on, to a more tranquil and settled hope which now reckoned with a longer interval before the parousia, with more continuing human relationships (3.18–4.1), and so focused attention more on what Christ had already accomplished? Here, it could justly be argued, we see the first movement towards early catholicism in Paul himself.

In *Ephesians* the same sense of hope deferred comes through even more strongly. There is still a forward looking to a future consummation (Eph. 1.14, 18, 21; 4.4, 30; 5.5) and also an urgency of exhortation which recalls the earlier Paul (5.16). But otherwise the expectation of an imminent End is wholly lacking and the parousia is not even mentioned (cf. 5.27). Instead Paul seems to envisage a much longer period on the earth lasting several generations before the End finally comes (2.7; 3.21; 6.3); the already of new life and salvation is strongly emphasized (2.1, 5f., 8; 5.8); and the hope of consummation and completion in Christ in 2.19–22 and 4.13–16 has been stripped of every apocalyptic feature (though an apocalyptic residue is still evident in 1.10, 20–23). Whether this shift in perspective postdates Paul or not, it is from such a shift in perspective that early catholicism emerged.

With the *Pastorals* the position is not so very different. The belief in the day of the Lord is still strong (II Tim. 1.12, 18; 4.8) and in 'the appearing of our Lord Jesus Christ' (I Tim. 6.14; II Tim. 4.1, 8; Titus 2.13). It may even be that the author believes he and his readers are (still) in the last days (I Tim. 4.1; II Tim. 3.1), although II Tim. 4.3 could indicate that for the author the last days have not yet begun. Either that or 'the last days' has become something of a formal phrase lacking its original eschatological fervency, for clearly in II Tim. 2.2 the perspective has perceptively lengthened, and other future looking statements are much more like the language of later piety which holds a doctrine of 'the Last Things' but lacks the urgency of an imminent End expectation (I Tim. 4.8; 5.24; 6.7; II Tim. 2.10ff.; 4.18). So here again we see evidenced that shift in perspective, that disappearance of eschatological tension which is part and parcel of early catholicism.

71.2 *Luke-Acts.* The disappointment of the earliest Christians' 'imminent expectation' is perhaps nowhere so clearly marked in the NT as in Luke-Acts. The most striking evidence of this is Luke's redaction of the Markan apocalypse and his presentation of the earliest Jerusalem community in Acts.

(a) It very much appears as though Luke, writing in the period after the fall of Jerusalem (AD 70), was faced with the problem of what to do with Mark 13, in which, as we saw above (§68.2), the destruction of Jerusalem was seen as part of the messianic woes, the beginning of the End. For when we compare Mark 13 with Luke 21 it becomes increasingly evident that Luke has carefully separated these two elements (fall of Jerusalem and parousia), and that he has extended Mark's cautionary note to embrace a further (and lengthy) period of time. Luke 21.8 – in Mark the false prophets say only, 'I am he' (Mark 13.6); Luke adds another oracle, 'The time (End) is at hand'; proclamation of the imminence of the End has become a false prophecy! Mark had spoken of the world-wide turmoil as 'the beginning of the messianic woes' (Mark 13.8); Luke omits the phrase altogether (Luke 21.11). Mark had said, 'He who endures to the end shall be saved (Mark 13.13); Luke omits the reference to the end (Luke 21.19 – 'By your endurance you will gain your lives') – the suffering connected with the fall of Jerusalem is not to be linked with the tribulation of the last days. Mark thought of the suffering caused by the siege and fall of Jerusalem as the eschatological distress – so severe that God would have to shorten it for the sake of the elect (Mark 13.20); Luke completely separates the fall of Jerusalem from the End – 'Jerusalem will be trodden down by the Gentiles, until the times of the Gentiles are fulfilled' (Luke 21.24). Mark had firmly linked the destruction of Jerusalem with the cosmic upheavals of the End – 'in those days . . .' (Mark 13.24); Luke just as firmly cuts the link by omitting the phrase altogether (Luke 21.25). As we also noted above (p.331), part of Luke's object in thus severing Mark's imminent expectation of the parousia from the destruction of Jerusalem and its temple was that he might *reaffirm* the parousia hope *despite* the failure of Mark's expectation. But the point we must note here is that *he was able to reaffirm the parousia only by effectively denying its immediate imminence for Jesus* and by 'postponing' it (for another generation?), to the far end of a further stage or epoch of history ('the times of the Gentiles' = the age of the church).[15] Here then is hope deferred, 'imminent expectation' faded.

(b) As we demonstrated above (§67.3) the primitive Christian community in Jerusalem must have been markedly apocalyptic in its thought and self-understanding. We can scarcely begin to understand how a key concept like Jesus' resurrection and the gift of the Spirit as the 'first fruits' of the end-time harvest emerged, or how a phrase like 'Maranatha' ('Our Lord, come!') became established in the language of worship (I Cor. 16.22), or how such an improvident practice as the community of goods (selling off capital) swept the new sect off its feet, *unless* they were all more or less spontaneous expressions of a dominant conviction that the end-time had begun, the parousia would take place very soon, the End was imminent. And yet this sense of tip-toe expectancy is completely absent from the account in Acts. *Nothing* of the 'Maranatha' invocation finds expression in Acts. There is still talk of parousia (Acts 1.11), but attention is focused rather on the responsibility for world-wide mission (1.6–8), and the sense of imminence is barely preserved in Luke's use of the early material in Acts 3.20f. There is talk too of the day of judgment (Acts 10.42; 17.31; 24.25), but only as a still distant threat (the last things) and no longer as something pressingly close. The apocalyptic language of Joel 2.28–32 is quoted, including the cosmic signs (Acts 2.17–21), but as a prophecy *already* fulfilled at Pentecost. Otherwise no vestige of primitive Christianity's apocalyptic fervour remains – and the same is true of the early Paul's imminent expectation, even though Luke gives some details of Paul's missionary work in Thessalonica (Acts 17). There can be only one explanation, for Luke can hardly have been unaware that earliest Christianity ran a high eschatological temperature: Luke must have decided to ignore or suppress this feature (even at the cost of making the community of goods seem more an act of complete irresponsibility than an act of zealous faith). To present such a picture of first generation Christianity, so even temperatured from beginning to end, so remarkably *un*apocalyptic, could certainly constitute a qualification for the title 'early catholic'.

We need simply add that, as has been widely recognized in the past thirty years, the very act of writing a history of earliest Christianity (rather than an apocalypse) was an admission that the earliest parousia hope was mistaken and that the parousia hope itself had faded. When Luke wrote not only a 'life of Jesus', but also a history of the Church, he was in effect interposing a whole new epoch between the resurrection/ascension of Jesus and the parousia. Jesus' death and resurrection could no longer be regarded as the beginning of the End, the (final) eschatological climax, as Jesus and the first Christians had understood it, but rather as the mid-point of history, with an epoch stretching forward into the future on one side as well as one stretching back into the past on the other. It is unnecessarily confusing, indeed it is misleading, to say that Luke substituted the idea of salvation history for the earlier eschatology, as a way of resolving the problem posed by the delay of the parousia.[16] Imminent eschatology and salvation history are by no means contradictory or mutually exclusive understandings: the salvation history perspective is fairly basic to all the main NT writers and the already/not yet tension is almost always present in NT eschatological.[17] But *in Luke–Acts the eschatological tension has certainly been slackened to a significant extent*; and for Acts in particular the hoped for parousia is a reality only as the still distant climax at the far end of the age of the Church. In thus presenting Christianity as faced with the need to organize itself for a longer term future Luke had certainly opened the door to early catholicism.

71.3   We cannot ignore the fact that *the strongest expression of realized eschatology in the NT is to be found in John's Gospel.* Its most prominent features are the conviction that judgment is something which has *already* taken place in the coming of Jesus as the light of the world and in human reaction to him (John 3.19), that those who hear and believe the truth of Jesus 'do not come into judgment, but have (already) passed from death to life' (5.24), that Jesus himself is both the resurrection and the life – to know him is to know eternal life, resurrection life here and now (11.25f.). When John says 'we beheld his glory' (1.14), in a real sense he has collapsed the past and future glory of the Son of God into the period of his earthly ministry with its climax of cross and resurrection; and the resultant faith which the Gospel seeks to engender is a believing in one who can no longer be seen, on the testimony of those who did see his glory, and without any forward glance to its future manifestation (20.29–31). Or again, when the Johannine Jesus speaks of his imminent departure and reappearance (14.18; 16.16–22) what is fairly clearly in mind is the coming of the Paraclete (14.15–26; 16.7); in a real sense the parousia of the Paraclete, the life-giving Spirit, has so filled Jesus' place that there is little cause to think of a still future parousia.

It would not be true however to say that there is no future eschatology in John; passages like 5.28f., 6.39f., 12.48 (cf. I John 2.18, 28; 3.2; 4.17) cannot simply be consigned to a redactor and conveniently passed over. But the hope they express is much less immediate than the hope of the first Christians. John 14.1–3 is probably the one passage in the Fourth Gospel itself which does speak of the second coming of Christ as such, but it is more the sort of passage which (rightly) comforts the hearts of the bereaved than one which conveys any sense of the pressing imminence of the End. And in the epilogue in John 21 the final little episode climaxing in v.23 seems to have been included in order to meet the problem caused by John's dying prior to the parousia. In short, it is almost as though *the forward movement of salvation history in John has been suspended in a timeless eschatological 'now'*, where all that matters is the individual's response to the words of Jesus which are Spirit and life (4.23; 5.25; 6.63). Whether this is a theology that properly can be called 'early catholic' is another question to which we will return below.

Not so very far removed from John's eschatology is that of *Hebrews*. To be sure the writer of the letter maintains a more vivid expectation of the imminent parousia (10.25, 37; cf. 1.2; 6.18–20; 9.27f.). But his eschatology has been significantly modified by merging the Jewish (apocalyptic) doctrine of the two ages with the Platonic distinction between the heavenly world of the real and the earthly world of shadow (see above pp.263f. and n.58). By so doing he has to some extent detached the hope of full participation in the heavenly reality from the belief in a still future consummation (4.14–16; 7.19; 10.19–22; 12.22–24). In this way he is able to encourage his readers in their striving and suffering and 'to impress upon believers the nearness of the invisible world without insisting on the nearness of the parousia'.[18]

71.4   We must also mention *II Peter*, probably the latest of the NT writings. The striking feature about its eschatology is its somewhat hollow 'orthodoxy'. It is 'orthodox' enough in its talk of entering into 'the eternal kingdom of our Lord and Saviour Jesus Christ' (II Peter 1.11), of the day of judgment (2.9, 17; 3.7), of scoffers 'in the last days' (3.3), of the day of the Lord coming like a thief in the night (3.10), of a future cosmic dissolution in vivid apocalyptic colours (3.10, 12), and of the coming of new heavens and a new earth (3.13). But the delay of the parousia has clearly become a major stumbling block – 'Where is the promise of his coming? . . .' (3.4). The author's response is for the most part traditional in character – the argument from the purpose of God in salvation history (3.5–7); the argument that the delay is the mercy of God giving time for repentance (3.9), and so on. The somewhat hollow ring comes in the argument of 3.8 – the rather unsatisfactory consideration that concepts of time are inadequate when thinking of an act of God – 'with the Lord one day is as a thousand years, and a thousand years as one day'. That is, he denies that the Christian can relate hope to any events of the present; man's time and God's promise are not so readily correlated. This inevitably imparts a degree of arbitrariness into the action of God (at least from the human standpoint) and cuts away at the nerve of apocalyptic eschatology.[19] He who argues thus has lost all hope of an imminent parousia and would not be surprised if *centuries* (even one or two millennia) elapsed before the traditional parousia hope was realized. In short, in II Peter the original language of apocalyptic fervour has become the more dogmatically calculated language of 'the last things'. *If 'early catholicism' is a reaction to the repeated disappointment of apocalyptic hope, then II Peter is a prime example of early catholicism.*[19a]

The later Paulines and the Pastorals, Luke-Acts, John and II Peter – these are the NT writings which most clearly reflect the changes in emphasis and self-understanding which the delay of the parousia forced upon the early Christians in the second half of the first century and beyond. These examples are sufficient to demonstrate the point that *if early catholicism is defined*, in part at least, *by the fading of the imminent parousia hope, then early catholicism is already well established within the NT.*

§72. INCREASING INSTITUTIONALIZATION

Increasing institutionalization is the clearest mark of early catholicism[20] – when church becomes increasingly identified with institution, when authority becomes increasingly coterminous with office, when a basic distinction between clergy and laity becomes increasingly self-evident, when grace becomes increasingly narrowed to well defined ritual acts. We saw above that such features were absent from first generation Christianity (chs VI and VIII), though in the second generation the picture was beginning to change.

72.1   *Ephesians and Pastorals.* The strongest evidence that an early catholic perspective manifests itself already in Ephesians is the use of *ekklēsia* and Eph. 2.20. Whereas in the earlier Paul *ekklēsia* (church) almost always denotes all the Christians living or gathered in one place, in Ephesians *ekklēsia* is used exclusively of the universal Church (1.22; 3.10, 21; 5.23–25, 27, 29, 32; contrast even Col. 4.15f.). And Eph. 2.20 is easily read as an expression of second generation veneration of first generation leaders. Yet, on the other hand, there are strong parallels between the image of church order in Eph. 4 and the body metaphor in Rom. 12 and I Cor. 12. So we cannot be certain on internal evidence alone whether Ephesians is the work of Paul enlarging his vision of the local church as charismatic community to cosmic dimensions (Eph. 1.22f.; 2.19–22; 3.10; 5.23–32; cf. Col. 1.18, 24), or the work of a second generation disciple of Paul beginning to think of ministry in terms of offices valid throughout the universal Church.[21] Even in the latter case, the absence of any mention of bishops or elders makes it very arguable that the author is *resisting* early catholicizing pressures as much as anything else.[22]

With the Pastorals the position is clearer. I need only refer to the evidence presented above (§30.1). Notice particularly how the concept of *office* has already clearly emerged: elders, overseers (bishops) and deacons are all titles for well established offices (I Tim. 3.1 – 'office of overseer'). Even more striking are the respective positions of Timothy and Titus. They are obviously not simply emissaries from Paul visiting one of his churches as his spokesman, as in days of yore (I Cor. 4.17; Phil. 2.19; I Thess. 3.2, 6; II Cor. 7.13f.; 12.18). Rather they begin to assume something of the role of *monarchical bishops*, with authority *over* the community and its members concentrated in them: theirs is the responsiblity to keep the faith pure (I Tim. 1.3f.; 4.6ff., 11–16; etc.), to order the life and relationships of the community (I Tim. 5.1–16 – Timothy has the authority to enrol a widow or to refuse enrolment, apparently without reference to others; 6.2, 17; Titus 2.1–10, 15 – 'with all authority'), to exercise discipline and mete out justice not least in the case of elders (I Tim. 5.19ff. – Timothy is the court of appeal, above the eldership), to lay on hands (I Tim. 5.22 – a function already reserved to Timothy?), and to *appoint* elders (Titus 1.5). There is also a concept of 'apostolic succession' beginning to emerge – Paul to Timothy to 'faithful men' to 'others', though whether the succession is yet conceived in formal terms, from office to office, is not clear (II Tim. 2.2). Also unclear is whether a kind of sacramentalism has begun to emerge: the 'faithful saying' of Titus 3.5–7 is not significantly different from the (earlier) Pauline understanding of baptism (see above p.159), though it is possible that the metaphor of 'washing' was now equated with the water of baptism by the author. This is rather more likely than the saying itself suggests since elsewhere in the Pastorals a clear theology of ordination has emerged, with *charisma* no longer a free manifestation of the Spirit through any member of the church, but the power of office bestowed through the laying on of hands (I Tim. 4.14; II Tim. 1.6.[23] With such evidence it would be difficult to deny that the Pastorals are already some way along the trajectory of early catholicism.

72.2   *Luke–Acts.* The evidence suggesting early catholic tendencies in Luke–Acts at this point is not difficult to gather together (cf. above pp. 106f.), although there is another side to the picture. In the first place it is fairly clear that *Luke has attempted to portray earliest Christianity as much more unified in spirit and uniform in organization than was in fact the case.*

(*a*) Consider first the way *he has cloaked the very serious and deep divisions between the Jewish Christians centred on Jerusalem and the expanding Gentile mission.* He has presented the initial schism between Hebrews and Hellenists as merely an administrative hitch (Acts 6), whereas the reality was evidently much more serious (see above §60). The disagreement over circumcision between Paul and Barnabas and 'some men' from Judea was serious, but amicably and *unanimously* resolved at the Jerusalem council (Acts 15). But we hear nothing in Acts of the subsequent confrontation between Paul and Peter at Antioch (involving 'some men from James'), which Paul obviously regarded with the utmost seriousness (Gal. 2), nor of the depth of hostility between Paul and the apostles from Palestine in II Cor. 10–13, not to mention the violent explosions of Gal. 1.6–9, 5.12 and Phil. 3.2ff. or their causes. Similarly his account of Paul's last visit to Jerusalem in Acts 21 successfully ignores the purpose of Paul's visit (to deliver the collection) and so draws a veil over what was probably the saddest breach of all between Paul and the Jerusalem leadership (see above §56). All this gives added weight to the observations about Acts familiar since they were first documented by M. Schneckenburger, *Über den Zweck der Apostelgeschichte*:[24] namely the parallelism between the activity of Peter and of Paul (cf. particularly 3.1–10 with 14.8–10; 5.15 with 19.12; 8.14–24 with 13.6–12; 9.36–41 with 20.9–12); the portrayal of Paul as one who fulfilled the law's requirements (note particularly 16.1–3; 18.18; 20.16; 21.20–26; and cf. 23.6; 24.17; 25.8; 26.5; 28.17), and who showed due respect for the Jerusalem apostles (9.27; 15; 16.4; 21.26); and the character of the sermons attributed to Paul in Acts which are more like the sermons in the first half of Acts and contain little that is distinctively Pauline (cf. particularly 2.22–40 with 13.26–41). In all this Luke has hardly given an unbiased and fully rounded picture even of the episodes and areas he has chosen to cover. It is not necessary to conclude that Luke has invented all or even many of these details; nor need we assume that Paul's own treatment of the issues between him and the Jerusalem church is wholly objective and fair. But if Paul's treatment is one-sided, so certainly is Luke's. At the very least Luke has rubbed off the sharp angles of Paul's personality and polemic as much as was necessary to fit him comfortably into his unified picture of earliest Christianity. Is this not a kind of early catholic papering over the first-century cracks?

(*b*) We should note how cleverly *Luke has focused this unity of the early Church on Jerusalem as the fountainhead.* His Gospel begins in the temple and the Lukan birth narratives end in the temple (Luke 1–2), just as the climax to the Lukan version of the temptations of Jesus is set on the temple (Luke 4.9ff.). More than a third of this Gospel is presented in the framework of a journey from Galilee to Jerusalem (Luke 9.51–19.46). And the Gospel ends where it began, with the disciples 'continually in the temple blessing God' (Luke 24.53). Most striking of all is the way in which Luke has concentrated all the resurrection appearances in Jerusalem. By a simple redaction he omits all reference to resurrection appearances in Galilee. Where Mark reads, 'Go, tell his disciples and Peter that he is going before you to Galilee; there you will see him, as he told you' (Mark 16.7, with reference back to 14.28), Luke reads instead, 'Remember how he told you, *while he was still in Galilee*, that the Son of Man must be delivered into the hands of sinful men . . .' (Luke 24.6f., with Mark 14.28 simply omitted). Evidently then, Luke wished to present Jerusalem as the fountainhead of the gospel, the undisputed birthplace and mother church of Christianity. Thus it is no accident that the programme of his history has the gospel going out from Jerusalem in ever widening circles till it reaches Rome (Acts 1.8; 28.30f.). In the early stages he is able to show the leading figures in Jerusalem supervising the decisive stages of the widening mission (8.14ff.; 11.1ff., 22ff.). And in the latter half where the focus is exclusively on Paul he achieves his end by presenting Paul as a regular visitor to Jerusalem and his mission in effect as a series of missionary journeys out from and back to Jerusalem (9.28; 12.25; 15.2; 18.22 – the church of Jerusalem is 'the church'; 20.16; 21.17).[25] All this is historically grounded at least to the extent that Paul acknowledged a certain primacy of Jerusalem (Rom. 15.27). But Luke has clearly slanted his material by portraying earliest Christianity as a unified whole with the progress of the gospel from Jerusalem to Rome backed by the resources of a Church united round Jerusalem and threatened in a serious or lasting way only from without – very much the sort of presentation that we would expect from an early catholic historian.

(*c*) Luke also endeavours to *focus the unity of the first generation Church in the twelve apostles at Jerusalem and to depict the earliest churches as uniform in organization.* As we saw above, 'the twelve' and 'the apostles' were not initially the same group (p.107); and whereas the Jerusalem church evidently gathered round the twelve in the first stages of its life (p.108), the earliest outreach beyond Palestine and to the Gentiles probably focused round the apostles, with 'apostleship' presumably reckoned in terms of mission (p.107). But Luke has in effect merged these two (overlapping) groups and made them synonymous – the focus of unity for the whole Church worldwide (note particularly Luke 6.13; Acts 1.21–26; 2.42f.; 4.33; 6.2, 6; 8.14; 9.27; 11.1; 15.22f.; 16.4). This has had two curious corollaries. First, in 8.1 he portrays the whole church in Jerusalem as scattered throughout Judea and Samaria (cf. 1.8) – that is, all *except* 'the apostles'. In preserving apostolic continuity in and with Jerusalem Luke wholly abandons the earlier sense of apostle = missionary, and depicts the apostles in Jerusalem as the representative, or should we say institutional centre of the whole growing Church. More important, second, by using 1.21f. as his definition of an apostle – one who accompanied Jesus from the beginning of his ministry and witnessed his resurrection and ascension – he effectively *excludes Paul from this central group of apostles, the twelve*.[26] Presumably it is for the same reason that he treats the appearance of Jesus to Paul on the Damascus road as simply a 'vision' (so specifically in 26.19) and not therefore as a (very tangible) resurrection appearance like those which the apostles enjoyed and which qualified for apostleship (cf. particularly Luke 24.39). Here again we see Luke the apologist for Paul nevertheless so anxious to portray the Church of first generation Christianity as unified and in accord that he is willing to concede one of the points which the historical Paul argued for most vehemently over against (at least some) Jewish Christians (Gal. 1.1, 15–17; I Cor. 9.1–6; 15.7–9). *Luke achieves the rapprochement with Jerusalem which eluded Paul in the end, but only by blurring his differences with Jerusalem and by presenting him as one with and in effect subordinate to the Jerusalem apostles.*

The same effect is achieved in the area of 'church government' – for he depicts Paul as appointing elders in all his churches (14.23) – an act and an office of which we nowhere find mention in the Pauline letters and which would have run counter to his vision of the church as charismatic community (see above pp.107f. and §29) – but an act and an office which made the Pauline churches accord with the Jerusalem pattern of government from the first (see above p.109). Note also the use of 'overseers' (20.28) = elders (20.17) – a usage and equation foreshadowing the post-Pauline merging of the developed order of the Pauline churches and the Jerusalem form of church government, and again implying a higher degree of uniformity than was evidently the case (above §30). Again it is not necessary to conclude that Luke's account is wholly fabricated, since most of the functions which came to be concentrated on overseers and elders in the post-Pauline situation had very probably been fulfilled from the first by diverse members (charismatically) in the Pauline churches. But we have to say that Luke's account is at least anachronistic and involves what can properly be called an early catholic tidying up of the intial rather diverse forms into the more uniform pattern of later decades (cf. I Clem. 42.4).

A rather striking conclusion emerges from all this – namely, that F. C. Baur's understanding of Acts was not so far from the truth after all, despite its dogmatic overstatement. *Luke's picture of earliest Christianity and of Paul's role in it is after all something of a compromise between Jewish and Gentile Christianity*, a smoothing of the wrinkles and a disguising of the tears that disfigured the cloth of first generation Christianity and made up into a suit which both might find reasonably acceptable.[27] The compromise, however, is not so much between Peter and Paul, as Baur argued, as between *James* and Paul, with Peter in effect the median figure to whom both are subtly conformed (James – see Acts 15.13ff.; Paul – see above p. 353).[28] Is this not justifiably to be designated 'early catholic'? But there is yet more to be said.

(*d*) We must remind ourselves at this point that we have already described Luke as an *enthusiast* (§44.3), and that early catholicism has to be understood in part at least precisely as a reaction to enthusiasm, an attempt 'to throw up a dam against the flood of enthusiasm'.[29] What are we to make of this surprising paradox? The fact is that *much though Luke wants to present earliest Christianity as a unified whole, he also wants to demonstrate the sovereign freedom of the Spirit over the Church*. Hence even more than the completion of the twelve apostles, the mission of the Church must await the coming of the Spirit (Acts 1–2). Hence even more than the official teaching of the apostles the prophetic inspiration of the Spirit is emphasized (p.182). Hence even more than the supervision of Jerusalem in the Church's mission the direction of the Spirit and of ecstatic vision is given prominence (Acts 1.8; 8.29, 3; 10.19; 13.2–4; 16.6f.; 19.21; 20.22; and see above p.181). Hence, above all, it is the gift of the Spirit which is decisive for entry into Christianity, not approval or ratification by Jerusalem and the apostles; these are not opposites for Luke, of course (8.14–17), but where the primary emphasis lies is clear enough from the episodes of the Ethiopian eunuch (8.38f. – no ratification here), Paul's conversion (9.10–19 – Ananias is described as a devout Jew, 22.12, but no attempt is made to tie him in with Jerusalem or to represent him as Jerusalem's agent), Cornelius and his friends (10.44–48, 11.15–18; 15.7–9) and Apollos (18.25f. – Priscilla and

Aquila are as independent of Jerusalem as Ananias, and add nothing fundamental to Apollos's Christianity).

These episodes also underline the point that there is *no developed sacramentalism* in Acts. There is no dependence of the Spirit on baptism in Acts 8, 10 or 19; rather the clear message is that the gift of the Spirit is the one thing that matters above all else (8.12–17; 19.2), and that where the Spirit is already given baptism serves primarily as acknowledgment of God's prior act and rite of entry into the church (10.44–48).[30] To be sure Luke does speak of the Spirit as 'given through the laying on of the apostles' hands' (8.18; cf. 5.12; 14.3; 19.11), but the sequel at once rules out a sacramentalist interpretation (8.19ff.), and elsewhere in Acts laying on of hands is a wholly charismatic act, the spontaneous act of identification and prayer for the appropriate gift of grace (see particularly 3.6f.; 6.6; 9.17; 13.3; 19.6; 28.8). Käsemann's attempt to bulldoze this evidence into conformity with his understanding of Luke as early catholic through and through strains the evidence of Acts beyond endurance.[31] Similarly with his attempt to argue that in Acts 'the word' has been subordinated to the Church.[32] Not so! – a central theme of Acts is the free and victorious progress of the word of God. It is not so much a case of the Church carrying the word from Jerusalem to Rome as the word carrying the Church to Rome (see particularly 6.7; 12.24; 13.49; 19.20).[33]

I therefore see nothing for it but to accept that *Luke is both early catholic and enthusiastic in outlook* – however strange the paradox. Perhaps he is able to hold the two contrasting strands together because he writes in a second generation situation when enthusiasm had greatly receded and early catholic attitudes had become more dominant. But in so far as Luke has refused to subordinate Spirit to sacrament, or word to Church, and so refused also to portray the earliest Christian ministry as a kind of priesthood, to that extent he cannot be designated 'early catholic'. The description of Luke the early catholic has to be qualified by the description of Luke the enthusiast – and vice-versa. It could be argued, of course, that his presentation implies a confining of 'enthusiasm' to the idealized primitive past. But the fact that he at the same time plays down the parousia hope of the first Christians suggests rather that he wanted to portray earliest Christianity in its life and mission as something of a model for his own time. And since he could just as easily have played down or ignored the other enthusiastic features of the earliest period, the fact that he did not do so (rather the reverse – see above §44.3) leads us back to the conclusion that Luke was himself an enthusiast. In short, if we have to conclude that early catholic tendencies were operative in Luke's writing of Acts, we have also to conclude that his own enthusiasm provided an effective brake on these tendencies.

72.3   The Pastorals and Luke–Acts are the only serious NT candidates for the title 'early catholic' in respect of increasing institutionalization, though II Peter 1.19–21 can be understood as restricting exegesis of the scriptures to an official teaching ministry.[34] Matthew and John could also just possibly be considered, if only because both of them do speak in one passage of the Church as universal, the *Una Sancta* (Matt. 16.18; John 17.20–23). But as we have already seen, their ecclesiology is actually much less institutionalized, much more individualistic, than that of the Pastorals (see above §§30.3, 31.1), and their emphasis on the universal Church is in fact much closer to that of Ephesians than to the early catholicism of the Pastorals. A similar judgment would have to be made, *mutatis mutandis*, with regard to I Peter, Hebrews and Revelation (see above §§30.2, 31.2, 3), and no clear impression can be gained from Jude on this point (though Jude 20ff. has strong Pauline echoes). Nor is any sacramentalism evident in these writings. Matthew 28.19 probably envisages a more formal baptismal ceremony, but gives no hint of a sacramentalist view of baptism. I Peter 3.21 defines baptism as the expression of faith (not as a channel of grace), and no other reference in I Peter (or James) involves a reference to baptism. Hebrews 10.22 describes baptism only as a washing of the body with pure water and so puts baptism on the same level as Jewish washings (also 6.2). And a passage like Rev. 7.14 hardly refers to baptism (washed in blood).[35]

In particular, John's individualism is very plausibly to be understood precisely as a *protest* against the kind of institutionalizing trends so evident in Pastorals (above pp.119f., cf. again Hebrews and Revelation – §§31.2, 3). Likewise the Johannine writings seem if anything to be opposed to the kind of sacramentalism which is already clearly established in the early catholicism of Ignatius ('the medicine of immortality' – *Eph.*, 20.2) (see above §41). Most intriguing of all is the attack of 'the elder' on Diotrephes in III John 9f. Diotrephes was clearly in control of this church at least: not only was he able to refuse a welcome to visiting Christians, but he also 'expels from the church' those who crossed him. Diotrephes, in other words, was acting with the authority of a monarchical bishop (cf. Ignatius, *Eph.*, 6.1; *Trall.*, 7.2; *Smyrn.*, 8.1f.), and it was against this lust for ecclesiastical prominence and power (*philoprōteuōn*) that 'the elder' wrote. In other words, assuming that III John comes from the same circle as I and II John, it is best seen as the response of a kind of convention or conventicle Christianity, an anti-institutional and individualistic pietism, protesting against the increasing influence of early catholicism.[36]

In short, *if the increasing institutionalization of early catholicism begins to emerge within the NT itself*, in part in Luke–Acts and most strikingly in the Pastorals, *so too does a protest against early catholicism*, in part in Hebrews and Revelation, in part even in Acts, more strongly in John's Gospel and the Johannine epistles, and most strongly probably in III John.

§73. CRYSTALLIZATION OF THE FAITH INTO SET FORMS

We need not delay long in this area since ch. IV above has covered most of the ground already, and the findings there bear directly upon our question here. It is quite clear of course that there was a tendency to formulate Christian faith into particular statements more or less from the beginning (e.g. Rom. 1.3f.; 10.9; I Cor. 15.3ff.; II Tim. 2.8). But we were forced to conclude from our study of the role of tradition in first-century Christianity that in Paul and John at least tradition was not something which, once put into words, set fast in unyielding forms which were simply passed from apostle to new church, from teacher to taught. For both Paul and John faith was living faith, tradition was pneumatic tradition, and teaching was as much (or more) charisma as craft. So, for example, the gospel which Paul proclaimed to the Galatians was not simply a series of traditional formulations passed on to him from the Jerusalem apostles, but the kerygma interpreted by him in a way which caused offence to many Jewish Christians (though the pillar apostles accepted the interpretation). And in I Cor. 15 the argument he uses is not simply a repetition of the tradition about the death and resurrection appearances of Jesus, but an interpretation of that tradition which ran counter to the interpretation (of the same tradition) maintained by the Corinthian gnostics (I Cor. 15.12). Likewise John's Gospel is hardly simply the literary deposit of traditions of Jesus which have remained fixed from the first, but his own inspired reproclamation, that is reinterpretation of earlier traditional material. Just as the formula with which the docetists are denounced in I John is not an original tradition, but the early faith interpreted and reformulated in the face of the new challenge (see further above §§17.1, 18.4, 19.3; also 47.3, 64.3). So it is clear at this point at least that early catholicism has no real anchor point in Paul and John, for the mark of early catholicism is not simply the framing or passing on of tradition, but the crystallization of tradition into set forms, with liberty to reinterpret and recast these forms either denied or strictly limited to a selected few. Where then in the NT is there evidence of such an attitude to tradition?

(a) We saw above that a more conservative attitude towards the traditions of Judaism was a mark of the earliest Jerusalem community and indeed of Jewish Christianity in general (§§16.3, 54.2, 55). An obvious question therefore is whether any of the more distinctively Jewish Christian writings in the NT demonstrate early catholic traits in respect of Christian tradition. Neither James nor Hebrews shows any real sign of early catholicism at this point; Hebrews' urging of its readers to hold fast their confession is about as near as we get (3.1; 4.14; 10.23), and that is hardly close. But there is perhaps some more positive evidence in *Matthew*. I am thinking here particularly of Matt. 16.19, 18.18, 24.35 and 28.20.[37] Matthew 24.35 speaks of the timeless validity of Jesus' words, and, though the saying is taken over without alteration from Mark 13.31, it may be intended by Matthew to denote a fixity of the Jesus-tradition similar to that of the law in Matt. 5.18. Matthew 28.20 formulates the final commission to the disciples in terms of 'making disciples . . . and teaching them to observe all that I have commanded you' – in some contrast to the nearest parallel in Luke (Luke 24.47). Most striking of all is the use of the language of 'binding' and 'loosing' in Matt. 16.19 and 18.18 – material peculiar to Matthew; for most probably Matthew has in mind here the technical Aramaic terms for the verdict of a doctor of the law who pronounces something forbidden (bound) or permitted (loosed), the judgment being made in the light of the oral law[38] – the implication being that the teaching of Jesus has taken the place of the oral law.

On the other hand, we have also noticed that Matthew's own presentation of Jesus' teaching is itself a development and interpretation of the Jesus-tradition (cf. §§18.1–3), though of course it is always possible that he hoped his representation of the Jesus-tradition would be the lasting and determinative one (hence perhaps his presentation of Jesus' teaching in five blocks in echo of the Pentateuch – see above p.248). We saw too that Matthew himself seems to have set his face against the oral tradition of the rabbis and insisted that Christians must interpret the law by love (§55.2); for Matthew the teaching of Jesus had not become part of the law, so as to share its fixed and inviolate nature, but provided an extended illustration of how Christians should interpret the law by love. And finally we should recall that for Matthew the authority to bind and loose was not restricted to Peter or to some ecclesiastical hierarchy, but was precisely the prerogative of every member in the community (§30.3). We must conclude therefore that while there are expressed in Matthew attitudes which could develop into an early catholic view of the faith, Matthew himself hardly qualifies even as a candidate for the title 'early catholic'.

(b) The other most conservative attitude to tradition was that of the *Pastorals*. And here indeed we have *the strongest evidence in the NT of an early catholic attitude to Christian tradition*. As we noted above (§17.4), in the Pastorals a coherent body of tradition has already crystallized into set forms and serves as a well defined touchstone of orthodoxy – 'the faith', 'sound teaching', 'that which has been entrusted', etc. The possibility of this tradition being (radically) recast or moulded into fresh formulations is nowhere envisaged, and indeed is almost certainly excluded. The role of the church hierarchy is to preserve, cling to, protect the tradition (I Tim. 6.14, 20; II Tim. 1.14; Titus 1.9), not to reinterpret or refashion it. Prophecy, which Paul had always prized more highly than teaching (Rom. 12.6; I Cor. 12.28; 14.1; Eph. 4.11), is evidently seen by the author as belonging more to the past than the present, or it may conceivably have been reduced to a formalized element within the ritual of ordination (I Tim. 1.18; 4.1, 14).[39] At any rate it no longer stands in dynamic interaction with the earlier tradition, as in Paul and John, and the possibility of new revelations which could call in question the established formulations of 'the teaching' is hardly envisaged, or else such questionings are already condemned as idle speculations, so-called knowledge, stupid controversies and the like (I Tim. 1.4; 6.20; Titus 3.9). Even Paul is himself depicted more as the keeper of tradition than its creator, and the Spirit as the preserver of the past tradition rather than as the one who leads into new truth (I Tim. 1.11; II Tim. 1.12–14; Titus 1.3). If in Paul's letters enthusiasm was contained, in the Pastorals it is wholly excluded (above §47.2). Early catholicism indeed!

(c) Elsewhere in the NT the only real evidence of the development of an early catholic 'rule of faith' comes in *Jude*, where false teaching is not argued against but simply confronted with the established formulations of the faith – 'the faith which was once for all delivered to the saints' (Jude 3; cf. v.17)[39a] – and *II Peter*, where again we see the concept already developed of a clearly defined and authoritative body of truth passed on from the prophets and apostles of an earlier generation (II Peter 1.12; 3.2; cf. 2.2, 21; also 3.15f. – Paul now a somewhat awkward part of the sacred inspired tradition).

There is however, no real sign in *Acts* of a similar crystallization of the faith into set forms, despite the claims once again of Käsemann.[40] To be sure Luke presents a picture of 'the (authoritative) teaching' of the apostles in Acts 2.42 (cf. 1.21f.; 6.2, 4), and speaks readily of 'the faith' in 6.7 and 13.8 (cf. 14.22; 16.5); but to say that 'this principle of tradition and legitimate succession runs like a red thread through the fabric of the whole first section of Acts'[41] is a conclusion which far outruns the evidence. There is a certain fixing of tradition in the threefold repetition of the key episodes of Paul's conversion (Acts 9; 22; 26) and Cornelius's conversion (10; 11; 15.7–11), just as the repeated emphases in many of the sermons in Acts presumably indicate what Luke considers should be the character and central content of evangelistic preaching in his own day.[42] And in 20.29f. there appears the typical view of later orthodoxy (cf. above pp.2f.), that heresy is (by definition) a post-apostolic development. Yet at the same time the sermons are by no means repeated stereotypes: not one is parallel to another throughout, each has its own distinctive elements (e.g. 2.14–21; 10.34–39; 13.16–25), and the speeches of Acts 7 and 17 are quite unlike any of the rest.[43] Similarly the three accounts of Paul's conversion differ significantly in detail. In neither case can we really speak of Luke fixing the tradition into set forms. Nor is there any attempt by Luke to portray an 'apostolic succession', or instruction in the faith as a transmission of apostolic tradition in the manner suggested by the Pastorals, Jude and II Peter – not even in Acts 20.18–35;[44] Luke 1.1ff. certainly need not be so interpreted, and Acts 16.4, the most plausible case in point, is better understood as part of Luke's attempt to show the unity of earliest Christianity and does not represent an early catholicizing of tradition (see further above p.353). Once again therefore Acts fails to fulfil the criterion which would require us to designate it 'early catholic'. Only the Pastorals, Jude and II Peter pass muster on this point.

§74. CONCLUSIONS

74.1   It can hardly be disputed that *early catholicism is to be found already in the NT*, that there are clear-cut tendencies evident in some

NT writings which developed directly into the catholicism of later centuries, that the trajectory of early catholicism begins within the first century and some NT documents lie firmly on it. The clearest examples are the Pastorals: in them the parousia hope is a faded shadow of its earliest expression, in them institutionalization is already well advanced, in them Christian faith has already set fast in fixed forms. The question of whether Ephesians should also be classified as early catholic depends on the interpretation of one or two key passages, that is to say it depends on whether Ephesians is regarded as Pauline or post-Pauline in origin: if Pauline, then the passages are better interpreted as a development of the Pauline understanding of the church which does not significantly depart from his vision of the church as charismatic community; if post-Pauline, then they could be interpreted as a movement (an unwilling movement? – see above p. 352 n. 22) towards the early catholicism of the Pastorals. The other clearest example of early catholicism within the NT is II Peter, in virtue particularly of its treatment of the parousia and of its appeal to the sacred tradition from the founding era of Christianity now past. Jude also probably qualifies if only because for it too 'the faith' has already become fixed and established – though there is also evidence in Jude of a livelier and less for-malized experience of the Spirit than would be typical of early catholicism (Jude 19f.).

John's Gospel and I–III John should *not* be regarded as early catholic. Despite the evidence of some reaction against an imminent parousia hope, these Johannine writings are better understood as *a reaction also against early catholicism itself*. The Pastorals and the Johannine circle are in fact sharply contrasting ways of meeting the same problem of the delay of the parousia. Finally Luke–Acts, the most intriguing NT documents on the question of early catholicism, are best understood as an attempt at *a sort of merger* between an early catholic perspective and the enthusiasm of the first Christians. Baur was on the right lines when he saw Acts as a compromise between Jewish and Gentile Christianity, and such a compromise is the basis of the early catholic view of the *Una Sancta Apostolica*. But Luke was evidently aware of the danger of squeezing out the spirit, of subor-dinating him to a church hierarchy, of confining him within set forms and rites, and so wrote as one who wanted to see the church of his own day both unified and open to the Spirit – open to the Spirit in the way the first Christians had been, unified in a way they had not.

74.2 In terms of historical origin within the first century, *early catholicism was a late starter*. Christianity, as we saw above (§67.3), began as an enthusiastic apocalyptic sect, and early catholicism has all the marks of subsequent reaction in face of the disappointments and excesses of such enthusiasm. Early catholicism is the typical second generation solidifying and standardizing of forms and patterns which were much more spontaneously diverse in the enthusiasm of the first generation, so that, for example, the institutionalization of the Pastorals is the post-Pauline reaction to the failure of the Pauline vision of charismatic community to provide an enduring structure of internal and inter-church relationships.

This judgment has to be qualified in one respect, since it is clear that the organization of the Jerusalem church which developed under James (still in the first generation) was in many ways more conducive to early catholicism than the Pauline 'model' – particularly in so far as the synagogue pattern of government and the Jewish Christian respect for tradition provided for an easier transition to early catholicism. It is precisely the merger of the Jerusalem pattern and the post-Pauline form which constitutes some of the clearest evidence of early catholicism in Acts and the Pastorals (Acts 14.23; 20.17, 28 – see above p. 355; I Tim. 3.1–7; 5.17, 19; Titus 1.5, 7ff.). This being so, then in view of the theses of Harnack and Heitmüller mentioned above (pp. 342f.), it is worth noting that *if anything, early catholicism was rooted more in the conservatism of Jewish Christianity than in the syncretism of Hellenistic Christianity*.[44a]

74.3   *Early catholicism was not the only trajectory or form of Christianity to emerge from the first century*. It is the one which became dominant in later decades, but at the turn of the century it was not yet dominant. And if judgment was to be made solely in terms of the NT alone there would be nothing to suggest that it should become the normative expression of Christianity. Unfortunately however the other main alternatives at the end of the first century were not so well constituted to provide a pattern of church life that would endure. Apocalyptic Christianity, almost by definition, is unable to outlive any more than one generation; failure of the parousia hope, if it did not destroy the faith which bore it, would in most cases result in a reaction into some kind of early catholicism; imminent End expectation is hardly a tradition which can be passed from one generation to another, but can only be reborn afresh as something wholly new in succeeding generations.[44b] As for Jewish and Hellenistic Christianity, early catholicism may be understood precisely as that compromise between the two which absorbed the most enduring elements of both

and which left second- and third-century Christians a choice between the large middle ground now occupied by early catholicism or
the radical alternatives of Ebionism and Christian Gnosticism. The
Johannine alternative to early catholicism has in fact prospered
after a fashion, but (in the West) only as confined to the mystical
tradition within Christianity, or squeezed out to the fringes of
Christianity to emerge sporadically as the conventicle or camp-
meeting protest against the authoritarianism of the great Church.
And the attempt of Acts to provide a lasting balance between the
early catholic vision of the *Una Sancta* and the enthusiasm of
Christianity's beginnings has also been a failure, since subsequent
interpreters looking for a model of churchmanship have usually
failed to recognize the Lukan balance and have been captivated
either by his early catholicism (the catholic tradition of interpretation) or by his enthusiasm (the Pentecostal tradition of interpretation). Thus it was that early catholicism became increasingly the
dominant trajectòry as Christianity moved through the second and
third centuries, became indeed the flight path of orthodoxy, so that
the price which such as Paul had to pay in order to be included
within the canon was their conformity to that norm (see above
§63.4).

74.4   An intriguing question arises from all this: whether, from the
perspective of Christian origins, early catholicism should have been
seen to be capable of *heretical* expression? Jewish Christianity,
Hellenistic Christianity, Apocalyptic Christianity were all widely
recognized to have tendencies within them which when unchecked
led into heresy (Ebionism, Gnosticism, Montanism). That is to say,
it was widely recognized that there were elements in each which
could be overemphasized and cause the whole to become unacceptably lopsided. Would it not have been better if equivalent tendencies
had been (more widely) recognized as present within early catholicism? May it not be that among those who eventually laid the most
effective claim to the title 'orthodox' there was too little recognition
that catholicism could become similarly lopsided? – in particular,
too little recognition of how integral a lively eschatological hope
is to lively Christianity,[45] of the importance of maintaining the
eschatological tension, too little recognition that church life and
organization could be grievously overstructured, the Spirit bottled
up in office and ritual, too little recognition that faith could be *reduced*
to formulae and stifled within set forms, not just crystallized but
petrified. Luke and John both sounded warnings against such
developments, but they went largely unheeded. Subsequently the

only really effective protests, in Western Christianity at least, were to be found in monasticism, in the rise of the orders and in the Reformation. Perhaps then the tragedy of early catholicism was its failure to realize that the biggest heresy of all is the insistence that there is only one ecclesiastical obedience, only one orthodoxy.

CONCLUSION

XV

THE AUTHORITY OF THE NEW TESTAMENT

§75. SUMMARY

75.1   The task we set ourselves at the beginning of this book was to investigate the unity and diversity of first-century Christianity and of its literary deposit, the New Testament. I think it can justly be said that we have discovered *a fairly clear and consistent unifying strand* which from the first both marked out Christianity as something *distinctive* and different and provided the *integrating centre* for the diverse expressions of Christianity. That unifying element was the unity between the historical Jesus and the exalted Christ, that is to say, the conviction that the wandering charismatic preacher from Nazareth had ministered, died and been raised from the dead to bring God and man finally together, the recognition that the divine power through which they now worshipped and were encountered and accepted by God was one and the same person, Jesus, the man, the Christ, the Son of God, the Lord, the life-giving Spirit. Whether we looked at the proclamation of the first churches, at their confessional formulae, at the role of tradition or their use of the OT, at their concepts of ministry, their practice of worship, their developing sacraments, their spiritual experience – the answer came out consistently in more or less the same terms: the cohesive focal point was Jesus, the man, the exalted one. Even when we probed more deeply into the most difficult area of all – the relation between the message of Jesus and the messages of the first Christians – the same answer began to emerge: the continuity between Jesus the man and Jesus the exalted one was not simply assumed or read back as a *post eventum* theological insight, but was rooted in Jesus' own understanding of his relationship with God, with his disciples and with the kingdom. So, that there is a fundamental unifying strand running through earliest Christianity and the NT can hardly be doubted, and that unifying strand – Jesus himself.

What about other unifying elements? At various stages in our investigation we have noted several such features which would have been (or should have been) common to all or most of first-century Christian communities. In particular, the diverse kerygmata called for the same faith and made the same promise (forgiveness, salvation, Spirit) (above p.30); first-century Christianity was uniformly monotheistic (above p.53); kerygmatic and Jesus traditions could be appealed to as common property (above p.76); the Jewish scriptures provided a common basis for all first-century believers (above p.81); the sense that Christianity is the continuation and eschatological fulfilment of Israel, the people of God, is widespread within the NT (above p.122 n.26); all Christians practised baptism in the name of Jesus and joined in the common meals from which emerged the Lord's Supper as such (above p.172); experience of the Spirit was a *sine qua non* of belonging to Christ (pp.199f.); love of neighbour is regularly the touchstone of conduct pleasing to God from Jesus to I John (pp.265, 308); and all first-century Christians looked for the parousia of Christ albeit with varying degrees of fervent expectancy (p.335). It would be quite possible to seize on one (or more) of these and to make that the central unifying focus of first-century Christianity and the NT writings – for example, on salvation-history,[1] on faith or the self-understanding of faith (see above p.4), or on love of neighbour.[2] But in fact again and again the unifying element in these other features of earliest Christianity narrows back down to Christ; that which really *distinguishes* Christianity from its first-century rivals is Jesus the man and exalted one, Christ crucified and risen marking out both centre and circumference. The faith called for by the kerygmata is faith *in Christ*, the promise held out in effect the promise of grace *through Christ*. What marks Christian monotheism off from Judaism's monotheism is the Christian conviction that the one God is precisely to be recognized as *the Father of our Lord Jesus Christ*. The kerygmatic and Jesus traditions are unifying precisely because *they focus on Jesus*, on the significance of his death and resurrection, on the words of the earthly Jesus which continue to express the mind of the exalted Lord. Beyond that no one kerygma provided common ground on which all were content to stand, no one confession served as a banner which all waved with equal fervency, and even the Jesus-tradition was not interpreted uniformly across the spectrum of first-century Christianity. The Christian OT is in the end of the day something other than the Jewish Bible, for the simple reason that the effective Christian OT is the Jewish Bible *interpreted in the light of the revelation of the Christ event*; and here too the application of the same hermeneutic principle led in the event to diverse interpretations of particular passages. The Christian concept of salvation-history is distinct from the Jewish in its conviction that God's purpose for Israel has climaxed in *Jesus* and that the whole present and future of that purpose revolve round *Jesus* – Christ the mid-point of time, the parousia of Christ the end of time. So too the Gentiles can be included within the people of God only by regarding them as heirs of God's promise *in and through Christ*. Beyond that the actual outworking of this conviction resulted in very different concepts and practices of mission, ministry and worship. As for the sacraments, they are a force for unity precisely because *they focus the unity and continuity of the Lord we now encounter with Jesus of Nazareth* the crucified and risen. Beyond that the way in which they do this and enable the encounter is a matter of continuing dispute. In particular, although the eating of bread and drinking of wine was common to all, the form which that eating and drinking took was developing right through our period (so too the accompanying words), so that again the really unifying factor was neither form nor formula so much as the recognition that in these words and actions the common faith in Jesus the man and exalted one came to expression and was strengthened. Experience of the Spirit was only a force for unity when the spirit in question could be recognized precisely as *the Spirit of Jesus*; beyond that attitudes to religious experience and enthusiasm quickly diversify. And the Christian motivation and practice of love of neighbour is distinctive in its conviction that this love was nowhere so clearly enunciated or embodied as in *Jesus*, that this love is enabled in the present precisely by the Spirit of *the same Jesus*. The unity of the NT writings then is not simply faith, but faith in this Christ, not simply the self-understanding of faith, but that self-understanding which measures itself by the cross and resurrection of Christ and which receives and understands the experience of grace precisely as mediated through that Christ, 'the grace of our Lord Jesus Christ'.

In short, our study has shown *the surprising extent to which the different unifying factors in first-century Christianity focus again and again on Christ, on the unity between Jesus the man and Jesus the exalted one*. And when we ask in addition what both unifies *and* marks out the distinctiveness of first-century Christianity, the unifying strand narrows again and again to Christ alone. As soon as we move beyond it, as soon as we begin to attempt to fill it out in word or practice, diversity quickly becomes as prominent as unity. And the more we attempt to add to it, the more disagreement and controversy we find ourselves caught up in. In the final analysis then, the unity of first-century Christianity focuses (often exclusively) on Jesus the man now exalted, Christ crucified but risen.

75.2   Our study has also forced us to recognize *a marked degree of diversity* within first-century Christianity. We can no longer doubt that there are many *different expressions of Christianity within* the NT. No form of Christianity in the first century consisted simply and solely of the unifying strand outlined above. In different situations and environments that strand was woven into more complex patterns, and when we compare these patterns we find that by no means did they always complement each other; on the contrary, they not infrequently clashed, sometimes fiercely. To put it another way, the same faith in Jesus man and exalted one had to come to expression in words in a variety of different individuals and circumstances. Inevitably the language forms, even when shaped primarily by that faith, were shaped also in part at least by each individual's own distinctive experience and by the circumstances in relation to which the words were framed or repeated. And so the language forms were different, often so different that the words of one believer could not serve as the vehicle for the faith of another, or even for him/herself in different circumstances. And not infrequently the differences were so sharp that they provoked disagreement, dispute and even some conflict. This was the picture which emerged again and again from our study, whether we looked at the language of faith in proclamation or confession or tradition or worship, or whether we turned rather to the attitudes and actions of faith expressed in ministry, in worship or in sacrament. So, if we have been convinced of the unity of first-century Christianity we can hardly be less convinced of its diversity.

We should also remind ourselves of just *how diverse the diversity* has proved to be. When we compare the unifying strand with the claims of other contemporary religions and sects the differences between them are clear and undisputable. But when we compare the elaborated pattern, Christianity as it actually was within its different first-century historical contexts, when we set the diverse expressions of first-century Christianity against their religious cultural backgrounds, then we have to confess that the margins become blurred, there is no clearly agreed outline to be discerned. Earliest Jewish Christianity was not so very different from the Judaism out of which it grew; the Jewish Christianity of which we hear in the letters of Paul was evidently anxious to remain as closely linked with Judaism as possible; and the most Jewish Christian of the NT writings evince the same concern to maintain continuity with the religion of the law and to avoid that breach which would show Christianity to be something wholly distinct. So too when we looked across the diversity to the edges of Hellenistic Christianity the same picture emerged – the churches of the Gentile mission often a very mixed bag, subject to gnosticizing pressures within and with no clear margin (baptism notwithstanding) marking off their beliefs and religious practices from those of the surrounding syncretistic cults. Not only so, but key figures like Paul and John were open to ways of presenting their faith in Jesus the man now exalted which seemed to others to hazard the distinctiveness of that faith. That is to say, even when we look at the writings of the NT themselves the margin (or better margins) between accepted Christianity and its competitors are not so easy to draw, are neither clear nor constant. The unifying strand remains distinctive, but the more it was elaborated the less distinctive it appears to have been. Not only so, but when we compare Jewish Christianity and Hellenistic Christianity with each other we see that diversity meant also disagreement, that the nearer we draw towards the blurred margin of each in its environment the further each draws apart from the other, and the sharper the disagreement becomes. As for enthusiastic Christianity and apocalyptic Christianity, they almost by definition are impossible to retain within fixed boundaries since their high surges of devotion and excitement almost inevitably carry them into some excess or other, even while holding firmly to the unifying centre. On the other hand, early catholicism certainly began to draw firmer and clearer boundaries, to define 'the faith' more precisely and safeguard its ministration, and that already before the first century had drawn to a close. But so far as first-century Christianity itself is concerned and so far as the NT is concerned, early catholicism was only one part of the diversity which was first-century Christianity, which is the NT.

We must conclude therefore that *there was no single normative form of Christianity in the first century*. When we ask about the Christianity of the NT we are not asking about any one entity; rather we encounter different types of Christianity, each of which viewed others as too extreme in one respect or other – too conservatively Jewish or too influenced by antinomian or gnostic thought and practice, too enthusiastic or tending towards too much institutionalization. Not only so, but each 'type' of Christianity was itself not monochrome and homogeneous, rather more like a spectrum. Even when we looked at individual churches the picture was the same – of diversity in expression of faith and life-style, of tension between conservative and liberal, old and new, past and present, individual and community.

In short, if the distinctive unifying strand running through the NT and first-century Christianity is narrow, the surrounding diversity is broad and its outer margins not always readily discernible. An identifiable unity, yes; but orthodoxy, whether in concept or actuality, no.

§76. HAS THE CANON A CONTINUING FUNCTION?

A crucial issue emerges from all this – the issue of the NT *canon*. In view of this sharply contrasting picture (minimal unity, wide-ranging diversity), *what continuing value has the canon*? Since the NT is not a homogeneous collection of neatly complementary writings can we any longer speak of 'the NT teaching' on this or that? Is the phrase 'the NT says' any longer meaningful except when speaking of the central unifying factor? Must we not rather talk in terms of '*Jesus*' teaching', '*Paul* says', and so on? Since the NT writings do not speak with a united voice, where does that leave the authority of the NT? The orthodoxy of later centuries tried to read catholic tradition, order, liturgy back into the beginnings of Christianity; the sectarian response was to pursue the vision of the purity of the primitive church unsullied by the post-apostolic fall. The NT justifies neither expediency but bears witness to a diversity and disagreement within Christianity more or less from the first. So how does the NT function as a 'canon', as a criterion for orthodoxy, as a norm for Christians of later generations?[3] These are questions which require a much fuller discussion than is appropriate here. All that I can do is outline a number of points which highlight the relevance of the present study for such a fuller discussion.

76.1 *Canon within canon.* We must observe first the historical fact that no Christian church or group has in the event treated the NT writings as uniformly canonical. Whatever the theory of canonicity, the reality is that *all Christians have operated with a canon within the canon.* Any who use their NT a great deal will at once acknowledge that some pages are more grubby with finger marks than others; (how many sermons has the average 'man in the pew' heard on Heb. 7, say, as against Matt. 5–7 or Acts 2?). All Christians no doubt operate on the principle of interpreting the unclear passages by means of the clear; but, of course, a passage which gives a clear meaning to one is precisely the unclear passage for another, and vice-versa. This we may recall includes the first-century Christians themselves who used the passages which spoke most clearly to their own faith in and experience of God through Jesus the Christ to interpret others which provided the basis for emerging Judaism (see above §24). It is hardly too much of an oversimplification to say that (until recently) the effective NT canon for Roman Catholic ecclesiology has been Matt. 16.17–19 and the Pastoral Epistles;[4] the canon for Protestant theology has clearly been the (earlier) letters of Paul (for many Lutherans indeed 'justification by faith' is the real canon within the canon);[5] Eastern Orthodoxy and the mystical tradition within Western Christianity draw their principal NT inspiration from the Johannine writings; while Pentecostalism looks for its authentication to Acts. Or again, the canon for nineteenth-century Liberal Protestantism was the (so-called) historical Jesus, whereas after the first World War the focus of authority for many Christian theologians became 'the kerygma', while more recently others have sought to orient themselves in relation to 'the apostolic witness'.[6] Perhaps most arresting of all, we must remind ourselves that since early catholicism was only one strand within the NT, consequently *orthodoxy itself is based on a canon within the canon*, where the lack of clarity of a Paul or a John (cf. II Peter 3.15f.) has been interpreted into a conformity with that single strand (cf. above particularly §63.4). Like it or not, then, all Christians have operated and continue to operate with a canon within the NT canon. Since the NT in fact enshrines such a diversity of first-century Christianity it cannot be otherwise. It is inevitable that one should find Paul most congenial, while another recoils from Paul and relaxes with John, while yet another turns in puzzlement from both to the simplicities of Acts or the orderliness of the Pastorals. To recognize the reality that each does in fact operate with a canon within the canon should not cause embarrassment or shame; it simply means accepting that Christians are no different in their diversity from their fellow believers of the first century.

Granted then that each Christian operates with a different canon within the canon, is there no *one* canon within the canon that would serve as the norm for all (like the 'historical Jesus' for the Liberal Protestants and 'justification by faith' for so many Lutherans)? Granted the diversity of the NT, does the unity within the NT not offer itself as *the* canon within the canon? Our study would point towards an affirmative answer, since we found that a common faith in Jesus-the-man-now-exalted was the consistent focus of unity throughout Part I, and in Part II we came to realize that that nuclear faith served not only as the centre of unity but also to mark out the circumference of acceptable diversity. Certainly, if the NT serves *any* continuing usefulness for Christians today, *nothing less than that canon within the canon will do*. Christianity begins from and finally depends on the conviction that in Jesus we still have a paradigm for our relationship to God and to one another, that in Jesus' life, death and life out of death we see the clearest and fullest embodiment of divine grace, of creative wisdom and power, that ever achieved historical actuality, that Christians are accepted by God and enabled to love God and their neighbours by that same grace which we now recognize to have the character of that same Jesus. This conviction (whether in these or in alternative words)[7] would appear to be the irreducible minimum without which 'Christianity' loses any distinctive definition and becomes an empty pot into which people pour whatever meaning they choose. But to require some particular elaboration of it as the norm, to insist that some further assertion or a particular form of words is also fundamental, would be to move beyond the unifying canon within the canon, to erect a canon on only one or two strands within the NT and no longer on the broad consensus of the NT writings as a whole. It would be divisive rather than unifying. It would draw the circumference of acceptable diversity far more tightly than the canonical writings themselves justify.[8]

In short, the canon of the NT still has a continuing function in that *the NT in all its diversity still bears consistent testimony to the unifying centre*. Its unity canonizes Jesus-the-man-now-exalted as the canon within the canon. Its diversity prevents us from insisting on a larger or different canon within the canon (see further below §76.5).

76.2   The canon of the NT has a continuing function also in that *it recognizes the validity of diversity*; it canonizes very different expressions of Christianity. As E. Käsemann pointed out in that lecture already cited (above p.122) which gave ecumenical thinking such a jolt:

> the New Testament canon does not, as such, constitute the foundation of the unity of the church. On the contrary, as such (that is, in its accessibility to the historian) it provides the basis for the multiplicity of the confessions.[9]

In other words the canon is important not just because it canonizes the unity of Christianity, but also because *it canonizes the diversity* of Christianity – not only the liberalism of Jesus but also the conservatism of the first Jerusalem Christians, not only the theological sophistication of Paul but also the uncritical enthusiasm of Luke, not only the institutionalization of the Pastorals but also the individualism of John. To put it another way: despite Ebionism the letter of James gained a place in the canon; despite Marcion the letters of Paul were accepted as canonical; despite Montanism the book of Revelation was accorded canonical status. If we take the canon of the NT seriously therefore we must take seriously the diversity of Christianity. We must *not* strive for an artificial unity – a unity based on our own particular canon within the canon, or on some intricate meshing of traditions, hoping that somehow we can cajole the others into line whether by claiming a monopoly of the Spirit or by the expedients of ecclesiastical blackmail. There never was such a unity which could truly claim to be rooted in the NT; the unity of the great Church in earlier centuries owed more to social factors than to theological insights and could be justified theologically only by ignoring or suppressing alternative but equally valid expressions of Christianity (valid in terms of the diverse forms of Christianity preserved in the NT). Such 'orthodoxy' is usually the worst heresy of all, since its narrow rigidity and intolerant exclusiveness is a standing denial of the love of God in Christ.

To recognize the canon of the NT is to affirm the diversity of Christianity. We cannot claim to accept the authority of the NT unless we are willing to accept as valid *whatever* form of Christianity can justifiably claim to be rooted in one of the strands that make up the NT. To put it another way, we must take with renewed seriousness the famous precept of Peter Meiderlin, quoted so often in ecumenical circles:

> In essentials, unity;
> in non-essentials, liberty;
> in all things, charity.[10]

If the conclusions of this study are sound the only way we can take it seriously is by recognizing how *few* the essentials are and how *wide* must be the range of acceptable liberty. We must recognize that the Rom. 14 paradigm of 'the weak' and 'the strong', conservative and liberal, to which we alluded above (p.79), is of wider application than merely to matters of conduct and tradition. That is to say, we must recognize that other theological claims and ecclesiastical forms which embody the unifying faith in Jesus the man now exalted, or which truly spring from the diversity of the NT, are authentic and valid expressions of Christianity, even when they cross and conflict with some of the cherished claims and forms which we also derive from the NT. 'Conservatives' who want to draw firm lines of doctrine and practice out from the centre in accordance with their particular tradition's interpretation of the NT, and 'liberals' who want to sit loose to all but the central core, must both learn to *accept* the other as equally 'in Christ', must learn to *respect* the other's faith and life as valid expressions of Christianity, must learn to *welcome* the other's attitude and style as maintaining the living diversity of the faith. The conservative must not condemn the liberal simply because the latter does not conform to the former's particular canon within the canon. And liberals must not despise conservatives simply because the latter tend to count some non-essentials among their own personal essentials (cf. Rom. 14.3). If 'canon' is to remain meaningful it must be the *whole* NT canon; each must avoid confusing their own tradition's interpretation of the NT with the NT itself, of confusing their own canon within the canon with the canon proper.[11] There are obvious corollaries that follow from all this for our understanding of 'the visible unity of the Church'; but to explore them here would take us too far beyond the proper scope of this study.

In short, whoever accepts the authority of the NT cannot ask less than the NT's own unifying canon within the canon as the basis for unity; but neither can we ask more without failing to respect *the canonical diversity of Christianity*.[12]

76.3   The NT also functions as canon in that *it marks out the limits of acceptable diversity*. As we noted above in chs XI and XII, even within the first century there were those who recognized that not all expressions of Christianity were to be accepted as equally valid. Already within the NT writings themselves the limits of acceptable Jewish Christianity and Hellenistic Christianity were being firmly drawn (see above §§58.2, 65.2). So too the character and limits of Christian apocalypticism were being defined (§69.2), though, unfortunately, not the limits of early catholicism (§74.4). The criterion we saw in these chapters was basically two-fold: diversity which abandons the unity of the faith in Jesus the man now exalted is unacceptable; diversity which abandons the unity of love for fellow believers is unacceptable. In other words, where the conviction had been abandoned that worship of God was determined by Jesus of Nazareth and his resurrection, was now 'through' Jesus, then diversity had gone too far; or where the conviction had been abandoned that the one encountered in worship now was not really fully one with, continuous with Jesus the man, then diversity had gone too far; or again, where diversity meant a breach in love towards those who also called upon the name of this Jesus, then diversity had gone too far. *The centre also determined the circumference.*

Thus since the NT shows not only how diverse was first-century Christianity but also where that diversity lost its hold on the centre, then the NT can be said to function as canon by defining both the breadth and the boundaries of the word 'Christian'. Of course, to accept the NT as canon is not simply a matter of restricting the adjective 'Christian' only to the actual Christianity witnessed to by the NT (see also below pp. 381f.); but it does mean that any claimants to the title 'Christian' who cannot demonstrate their substantial dependence on and continuity with the NT (in its unity as well as its diversity) thereby forfeit their claim.

That such judgments (about acceptable and unacceptable diversity) were not lightly or easily achieved may perhaps be indicated, for example, by the difficulty which both James and Hebrews and in a different way Paul and John experienced in achieving canonicity; that is to say, the great Church consciously drawing the lines of orthodoxy more strictly was not wholly comfortable with precisely those writings which were exploring the frontiers of Christianity and drawing in boundaries in a day when the border area was much more of a no man's land. In effect we continue to explore this twofold criterion of acceptable diversity and the difficulty of its application in the following three paragraphs – the interaction between the unity and diversity of faith in Jesus in §§76.4 and 76.5, and the interaction between diversity and the unity of love in §76.6.

76.4   The NT canon also canonizes the *development* of Christian faith and practice, both the *need* for faith in Jesus the man now exalted to take new forms in new situations, and the *way* in which the NT witness to Christ has continually to be brought into interaction with the changing world in which faith must live its life. The NT shows Christianity always to have been a living and developing diversity and provides some sort of norm for the ongoing process of interpretation and reinterpretation.

The *need* for development is plain. For example, as we saw above, faith's talk of Jesus as the Christ had in other circumstances to be supplemented, in effect superseded, by the confession of Jesus as the Son of God, while in still other circumstances it was the (new) confession that Jesus Christ came in the flesh which became the vital expression of living faith (see above p.58). Again, those who framed the hymns used in Philippians and Colossians, etc., evidently found it important and necessary to develop an expression of worship which spoke meaningfully in the language and thought forms of contemporary speculation. Later on we saw that the Jewish Christianity which failed to be canonized by the NT was precisely that form of primitive Christianity which *failed* to develop. Or to put the point the other way round, it was only Matthew's and Hebrews' more *developed* christologies which countered the *more primitive* christology retained by the Ebionites; just as it was I John's more developed confession of Jesus Christ come in the flesh which countered interpretations which could be drawn from the more ambiguous Son of God confession. The fact is that no NT document as such preserves or embodies Christianity as it actually was in the very beginning; rather each shows us Christianity in a different place and at a different time, and consequently in a different and developed form.

As to the '*how*' of such development, two points of clarification are necessary. When I talk here of development, I am not thinking of the developments within the NT as a straight line, of one development growing out of another, of Newman's idea of evolutionary development, whereby doctrinal developments can be justified as an organic growth from NT shoots.[13] I am not arguing, for example, that the Johannine christology of the personal pre-existence of the Son is simply the fuller apprehension of what had always been true, the making explicit of what had always been implicit in earlier formulations (or that the orthodox Trinitarianism of the Councils was simply the inevitable progressive unfolding of what had always been integral to the whole of NT theology).[13a] That would be to make John, or a particular doctrine of revelation, or a particular doctrinal formulation the effective canon within the canon, rather than one deriving from historical critical exegesis (as above §76.1). For if the canon is the NT as such, then why should the earlier, less developed expressions of faith not be equally normative, normative in their very uncertainty or unwillingness or refusal to head in the direction John followed so boldly? To argue that only one development within the NT is canonical is to fail to recognize the diversity of development within the NT. Indeed to argue that only one development within the NT is canonical is in fact to *deny* canonicity to the NT (where the elimination of elements unacceptable to later orthodoxy is far from complete) and actually shifts canonical authority to the great Church's *interpretation* of the NT writings from the late second century onwards – no longer a canon within the canon, but *a canon outside the canon*. In the NT picture each development is less like another length of pipeline, and more like another radius of a sphere (or spheroid), formed by immediate interaction between the unifying centre and the moving circumference. Alternatively, the diverse developments of the NT are somewhat like a series of branches (to be sure often intertwined) growing out of the trunk of the unifying centre, with *nothing in the NT itself* to justify the claim that only the branch of early catholicism should become the main (far less normative) line of growth.

The second clarification is that the NT functions as canon at this point in that it shows us the *how* of development, but not the *what* of development. If the NT canon does not support the sole legitimacy of only one of the subsequent developments (catholic orthodoxy), neither does it restrict legitimacy only to the developments which are actually enshrined within its pages. We must not absolutize the particular forms which Christianity took in the NT documents; we must not make the NT into law. The NT as canon demonstrates how the unifying centre of Christian faith came to diverse expression in the diverse circumstances of the first century; it does not dictate what the expression of Christian faith should be in any and every circumstance.

The *how* of development can be characterized as the *interaction* between my or a church's faith in the Jesus of the NT and my or a church's perception of the diverse challenges and needs confronting that faith as it seeks contemporary expression, or in shorthand, as a *dialogue* between the historical Christ-event and the present Spirit. Christianity cannot be Christianity unless it lives out and expresses in its daily life the creative tension between the givenness of the historical past of its founding era and the vitality of the present Spirit. The more we believe that the Spirit of God inspired the writers of the NT to speak the word of God to people of the 60s, 70s, 80s or 90s of the first century AD, reinterpreting faith and life-style diversely to diverse circumstances, the more acceptance of the NT canon requires us to be open to the Spirit to reinterpret in similar or equivalent ways in the twentieth century. Consequently, to accept the NT as canon means wrestling with such questions as these: if Matthew is canonical, who went so far as he did in presenting Jesus' attitude to the law so conservatively, what does Matthew's canonicity say concerning those who want to remain in close dialogue with their own religious traditions? If John is canonical who went so far as he did in open dialogue with emerging (proto-)Gnosticism, what does John's canonicity say concerning those who seek dialogue with the equivalent ideologies and (quasi-)religious philosophies of the twentieth century? If Revelation is canonical and retained apocalyp-

tic eschatology as part of NT Christianity even when the parousia had
already been long delayed, what does that say about the character
and form of Christian hope in the twentieth century? If the Pastorals
are canonical, and show us early catholicism already within the first
century, what does that say about the necessity for form and structure in community, about the desirability or inevitability of a growing conservatism in community leadership? I should perhaps underline the point that by dialogue I mean *dialogue* – neither side dictating
to the other, past to present, or present to past, but a critical
interaction between the NT in all its first-centuriness and me and the
church in all our twentieth-centuriness – using all the tools of historical critical exegesis to enable us to hear the words of the NT writings
as they were heard by their first readers, to catch the full meaning
intended by the writers, but always with an ear cocked for the
unexpected word of God through the witness of the NT challenging
our twentieth-century presuppositions and perceptions.[14]

76.5   In this dialogue the NT canon has an indispensable function,
in that *only through the NT have we access to the past, to the other pole of the
dialogue* – to Jesus as he was encountered in the hills and streets of
Palestine, to the initial encounters with the risen Jesus which from
the first have been recognized as definitive for faith in Jesus as the
exalted one; or, in other words, only through the NT canon do we
have access to the historical actuality of the Jesus who himself
constitutes the unifying centre of Christianity, to the first and
definitive witness to the wholeness of the Christ-event.

Here we must revert to our earlier talk of canon *within* the canon
(§76.1) and define the concept more carefully, for in fact Jesus-the-
man-now-exalted is *the Jesus of the NT*: he is not separable from the
NT, the diverse NT witness to him cannot be peeled away like a husk
leaving an easily detachable Jesus-kernel. In other words, in Jesus as
the centre we have not so much a canon *within* the canon, as a canon
through the canon, a canon embodied in and only accessible through
the NT. *It is not possible to hold to Jesus the centre without also holding to the
NT witness to the centre*, for so far as the Jesus of first-century history
and faith is concerned we are always like Zacchaeus, standing
behind the crowd of first-century disciples, dependent on what those
in the crowd nearest to us report of this Jesus whom we too would
see. It is not possible to hear Jesus of Nazareth except in the words of
his followers. It is not possible to encounter the Jesus of history
except in the words of the NT.

All this of course does not mean that the NT writings become themselves the Christ-event. As we have already noted, they are themselves products of a dialogue between Christ-event and present Spirit already begun. But without the NT it is not possible to recognize him we now encounter as Jesus, not possible to recognize the God and Father of our Lord Jesus Christ to be such. The Christ-event always meets us in the NT clothed in particular forms and language culturally and historically conditioned (that is why historical critical exegesis is necessary, that is why it must be a dialogue rather than a fundamentalist subserviency); but without the NT we have no possible way of tying our faith into the Christ-event, no possible way of carrying forward the dialogue of faith for ourselves.

Nor does what I say mean that God's word cannot and does not come to expression apart from these writings – otherwise Christian belief in the Spirit would be without meaning. Revelation takes place every time God encounters us. But if Jesus is determinative for Christian faith, then, I say again, the NT is indispensable, because only through the NT writings have we access to the historical events involving Jesus and the first faith in him as risen. If we do not recognize Jesus and the character of Christian faith here, then we have no standard or definition, no criterion by which to recognize Jesus and the character of Christianity anywhere.

That is of course why the traditions of the NT have a normative authority which cannot be accorded to later church traditions (contrary to Roman Catholic dogma), for the NT is the primary source for the original traditions whose interpretation and reinterpretation is the purpose of the dialogue, the NT is the initial statement (complex in itself) of the theme on which all that follows are but variations. Later traditions can and should play a part in the dialogue, of course, for they demonstrate how the dialogue has been carried forward in other ages and situations, they provide many an object lesson on the 'hows' and 'how nots' of that dialogue. But the primary dialogue must be with the original traditions, for only they can serve as a norm for the authenticity of what we call Christian, only they can fill the word 'Jesus' with authoritative meaning. If I may put it thus: with *only* the NT and without all the rest of Christian history and documentation, we should have more than enough to serve as chart and compass as Christianity presses into the unknown future. But with *all* the confessions, dogmas, traditions, liturgies of church history and without the NT, we would be lost, with no clear idea of what Christianity should be or of where it should be going.

76.6   One final reason why the NT writings can continue to function as canon is suggested by the fuller appreciation we have begun to achieve in this study of the role played by the NT writings themselves within the diversity of first-century Christianity – prompted particularly by the observation above (pp.47f.) that some at least of the NT documents served as *bridge builders or connecting links* between different strands within first-century Christianity. That is to say, their canonicity is a recognition not that they served as a founding charter for one kind of Christianity over against another, but *a recognition rather of their eirenical spirit, that for all their diversity they served also to promote the unity of the first-century churches*. Thus Matthew and Hebrews served not so much as Jewish Christian party statements, but rather as bridges between a more narrowly conceived Jewish Christianity and a Jewish Christianity much more influenced by Hellenistic thought (above pp.47f., 263f.). Similarly Mark and Paul seem to be fulfilling a similar function, holding together Gentile Christianity and diaspora Jewish Christianity. To be sure Galatians or II Cor. 10–13 in particular can hardly be called eirenic, but the canonicity of Paul at this point is a function not so much of any one letter (though Romans would most nearly fill the bill) as of the whole Pauline corpus (particularly when the Pastorals are included); for here within these thirteen letters we have embraced the whole sweep of Christianity from apocalyptic enthusiasm to early Catholicism, from deep Jewish sympathies to whole hearted commitment to the Gentiles, from fervent insistence on the immediacy of revelation to complete subserviency to the inherited tradition, etc. Again Acts and John in different ways serve as bridges between the origins of Christianity and the situations facing Christianity towards the end of the first century – Acts serving as Luke's attempt to hold together the initial enthusiasm of Christianity with the growing influence of early catholicism, and the Johannine writings serving as a bridge between the message given 'from the beginning' and the challenge facing Jewish Christians within the wider oriental-Hellenistic syncretism of the time. Even Revelation can be seen as a bridge in the way it sought to internationalize Jewish apocalypticism, that it might serve as a vehicle for the hopes of all Christians. Perhaps most striking of all, particularly in view of the tensions of second-century Christianity, is the function fulfilled by I Peter, in so far as in its theology and traditional authorship it serves to bring Paul and Peter together.

To explore this thesis in adequate detail would take far longer than is appropriate here. But perhaps I should just point out that this bridge building function of the NT writings should not in any way be taken as a denial of the diversity of first-century Christianity explored above in Part II, nor of the full sweep of diversity embodied in the NT writings themselves. Those who explore the vague boundary areas between Christianity and the competing religious claims and languages round about, and who seek to let the central faith in Jesus determine where in any one instance the boundary line should be drawn, also show their concern thereby to hold fast links with their fellow Christians who wish to remain much further back from the boundary areas. It is precisely because the NT documents as a whole both represent such a wide ranging diversity *and* built bridges linking up and overlapping with each other that the *whole* NT canon can serve as canon for the *whole* Church.

One further very tentative thought is perhaps worth outlining briefly. If bridge building is a central reason for the canonicity of many of the NT writings, then perhaps this explains more fully why it was Peter who became the focal point of unity in the great Church, since *Peter was probably in fact and effect the bridge-man who did more than any other to hold together the diversity of first-century Christianity*. James and Paul, the two other most prominent leading figures in first-century Christianity, were too much identified with their respective 'brands' of Christianity, at least in the eyes of Christians at the opposite end of this particular spectrum. But Peter, as shown particularly by the Antioch episode in Gal. 2, had both a care to hold firm to his Jewish heritage which Paul lacked, and an openness to the demands of developing Christianity which James lacked. John might have served as such a figure of the centre holding together the extremes, but if the writings linked with his name are at all indicative of his own stance he was too much of an individualist to provide such a rallying point. Others could link the developing new religion as or more firmly to its founding events and to Jesus himself. But none of them, including none of the rest of the twelve, seem to have played any role of continuing significance for the whole sweep of Christianity (though James the brother of John might have proved an exception had he been spared). So it is Peter who becomes the focal point of unity for the whole Church – Peter who was probably the most prominent among Jesus' disciples, Peter who according to early traditions was the first witness of the risen Jesus, Peter who was the leading figure in the earliest days of the new sect in Jerusalem, but Peter who also was concerned for mission, and who as Christianity broadened its outreach and character broadened with it, at the cost to be sure of losing his leading role in Jerusalem, but with the result that he became the most hopeful symbol of unity for that growing Christianity which more and more came to think of itself as the Church Catholic.

76.7   To sum up then, how meaningful is the concept of a NT canon, and has the NT canon a continuing function? I have not tried to explain or defend the canon in the traditional terms of 'apostolicity', for I do not think it can be done. We cannot ignore the overwhelming conclusions of NT scholarship that some at least of the NT writings were not composed by 'apostles' and are second (or even third) generation in their origin. And if 'apostolicity' is broadened to a concept like 'the apostolic faith', that does not help much since it tends to cloak the fact that the apostles did not all preach the same message and disagreed strongly on several important points. Nor have I said, nor would I want to say, that the NT writings are canonical because they were *more inspired* than other and later Christian writings. Almost every Christian who wrote in an authoritative way during the first two centuries of Christianity claimed the same sort of inspiration for their writing as Paul had for his.[15] And I would want to insist that in not a few compositions Martin Luther and Charles Wesley, for example, were as, if not more inspired, than the author of II Peter. Nor certainly would I attempt to define NT canonicity in terms of some kind of *orthodoxy*, for our findings are clearly that no real concept of orthodoxy as yet existed in the first century and that in terms of later orthodoxy the NT writings themselves can hardly be called wholly 'orthodox'. Nor can I enter here into the question of the limits of the canon which all this inevitably raises – whether, for example, II Peter should have been excluded from the NT canon and Didache or I Clement included – for that would take us too far beyond the already extended limits of the present study.

Nevertheless if the conclusions drawn in the last few pages are sound, then the NT does have a continuing function as canon. (1) It canonizes the *unity* of Christianity. It embodies, albeit in diverse expressions, the unifying centre of Christianity. It shows how small and how basic that canon within the canon actually is. It is a striking fact that all the *diversity* of the NT can claim to be justifiable interpretations of the Christ-event – James as well as Paul, Revelation as well as the Pastorals. (2) It canonizes the *unity* of Christianity. It shows just how diverse, sometimes dangerously diverse the expressions of that unifying faith could be. It is a standing corrective to each individual's, each church's more limited, more narrowly circumscribed perception of Christianity. To all who would say of only one kind of NT Christianity, 'This alone is Christianity', the NT replies, 'And that, and that too is Christianity'. (3) It canonizes the range of acceptable diversity but also the *limits* of acceptable diversity. It recognizes the Gospel of Matthew, but not the Gospel of the Ebionites, the Gospel of John but not the Gospel of Thomas, the Acts of the Apostles but not the Acts of Paul, the Apocalypse of John but not the Apocalypse of Peter. If the conviction that God meets us now through the one who was Jesus of Nazareth marks the beginning and heart of Christianity it also marks the limits and edge of Christianity. (4) It canonizes the *development* of Christianity and provides the norm for the 'how' of development, for the way in which the unifying centre should be brought into interaction with the moving circumference, particularly at the points of pressure or of possible expansion. It shows us how genuine and deeply penetrating the dialogue between past and present must be, neither permitting a clinging to forms or formulations that are not meaningful to the contemporary situation nor allowing the contemporary situation to dictate the message and perspectives of its faith. (5) It serves as canon in that through it *alone* we have *access* to the events which determined the character of Christianity. The portraits of Jesus and statements about Jesus which we find in the NT are normative, not in themselves but in the sense that only in and through these portraits can we see the man behind them, only in and through these statements can we encounter the original reality of the Christ-event. (6) It serves as a canon because of the *eirenic* character of so many of the NT writings themselves, each maintaining the twofold tension between the (common) past and the particular present, but also between the resultant form of Christianity and the diverse forms of others. The NT is canonical not because it contains a rag bag of writings documenting or defending the diverse developments of the first century, not because it contains a cross section of first-century 'party manifestoes', but because the interlocking character of so many of its component parts hold the whole together in the unity of a diversity which acknowledges a common loyalty.

The NT does not of course function in the same way in each of these different roles. For example in (1) and (5) James and Jude do not add anything to the Gospels; but in (2) James and Revelation would be more important than Luke, while in (3) Hebrews could be more important than Matthew. Or again in (4) Galatians and John would probably in most circumstances be more important than the Pastorals, whereas in (6) Matthew could provide more guidelines than Galatians. The point is of course that only when we recognize the full *diversity of function* of the canon as well as the full diversity of the NT material, only then can the NT canon as a *whole* remain viable. Or, more concisely, only when we recognize the unity in diversity of the NT and the diversity in unity of the NT and the ways they interact, only then can the NT continue to function as canon.

NOTES

Chapter I Introduction

1a. In an unsympathetic review B. Meyer *The Early Christians* pp. 194–5 takes these questions (somewhat tendentiously edited) as a definition or description of 'orthodoxy'. It should be clear however that the questions are simply a way of setting up the issue – my normal style, in fact. I fully accept, however, that a discussion of orthodoxy and heresy would require fuller and more nuanced treatment than I provide here.

1. W. Bauer, *Orthodoxy and Heresy in Earliest Christianity*, 1934, [2]1964, ET Fortress 1971 and SCM Press 1972.

2. See particularly the forcible presentation of W. Wrede, 'The Task and Methods of "New Testament Theology"' (1897), ET in R. Morgan, *The Nature of New Testament Theology*, SCM Press 1973, pp. 68–116, especially pp. 95–103.

3. R. Bultmann, *Theology of the New Testament*, ET SCM Press, Vol. I, 1952; Vol. II, 1955.

4. Bultmann, *Theology*, II, p. 135. See further below pp. 30, 370.

5. 'The Meaning of New Testament Christology', *God and Christ: Existence and Province*, ed., R. W. Funk, *JThC*, 5, 1968, p. 118. See further below p. 371.

6. *The Testament of Jesus*, 1966, ET SCM Press 1968, I. See further below §64.2.

7. 'Ketzer und Zeuge: zum johanneischen Verfasserproblem' (1951), *Exegetische Versuche und Besinnungen*, Göttingen, Vol. I, 1960, pp. 168–87. See further below pp. 358f.

8. '*Gnomai Diaphoroi*: the Origin and Nature of Diversification in the History of Early Christianity', *HTR*, 58, 1965, reprinted in *Trajectories through Early Christianity*, ed., J. M. Robinson and H. Koester, Fortress 1971, p. 117. Cf. H. D. Betz, 'Orthodoxy and Heresy in Primitive Christianity', *Interpretation*, 19, 1965: 'The Christian faith did not exist in the beginning. In the beginning there existed merely the "heretical" Jew, Jesus of Nazareth. Which of the different interpretations of Jesus are to be called authentically Christian? And what are the criteria for making that decision? This seems to me the cardinal problem of New Testament studies today' (p. 311).

9. H. E. W. Turner, *The Pattern of Christian Truth*, Mowbray 1954.

10. J. Charlot, *New Testament Disunity: its Significance for Christianity Today*, Dutton 1970, p. 111.

11. *Trajectories*, pp. 14ff., 69.

Chapter II   Kerygma or Kerygmata?

1. Statistically *euaggelion* (gospel) and *marturia* (witness) are more important than *kerygma* in the NT. But 'kerygma' has been the dominant term in the debate covering the last 40 years, and it serves to pose the issues for us most clearly, without restricting the subsequent discussion in any way.

2. C. H. Dodd, *The Apostolic Preaching and its Developments*, Hodder & Stoughton 1936, reprinted 1963.

3. Bultmann, *Theology* I, p. 307.

4. The Fourth Gospel does not use the words *kērussō*, *kērygma*, *euaggelizomai* or *euaggelion*. For this and other reasons (see below pp. 27, 75f.) we shall confine our analysis of the kerygma of Jesus to the first three Gospels.

5. See E. Kränkl, *Jesus der Knecht Gottes*, Regensburg 1972, pp. 102–29.

6. It is probably significant in this connection that the one other passage in the Synoptic Gospels where a clear theology of the death of Jesus is present is once again textually confused in Luke (Luke 22.19f.).

7. E. Lohse, *Märtyrer und Gottesknecht*, Göttingen 1955, p. 71.

8. C. F. D. Moule, 'The Christology of Acts', *SLA*, speaks appropriately of Acts' 'absentee Christology' (pp. 179f.). See also below p. 218.

9. Acts 1.5, 11.16 is easier to fit into *Luke's* reconstruction of Jesus' life as the stage in salvation history prior to the age of the Church (see further below pp. 348f.), than into the teaching of the historical Jesus as we are able to reconstruct it now. On the references in John's Gospel see below pp. 76 and 214.

10. See J. D. G. Dunn, *Jesus and the Spirit*, SCM Press 1975, §53; also 'Rom. 7.14–25 in the Theology of Paul', *TZ*, 31, 1975, pp. 257–73.

10a. Along with some others, Meyer, *Early Christians* objects to talk of three gospels here. For Paul there is only one gospel (pp. 185–6). I would not quarrel with the point so long as *the depth of disagreement* between Christians as to what that gospel meant in practice is acknowledged (Gal. 1.6–7; 2.11–14). To speak of 'three gospels' is simply a way of sharpening the point. Meyer's Paul at this point is the Paul of Acts (both ignore Gal. 2.11–14).

10b. Meyer pp. 196–9 seems not to recognize that the main emphasis here is to contrast the *relative* restraint in Paul's attack in I Cor. 15 with the fierceness of his denunciations in Galatians and II Cor. 10–13 (above §5.2).

11. In view of our later discussion (§§55 and 56) it is worth noting at this point that the closest parallels between Matthew and Paul come precisely in Romans 2; see C. H. Dodd, 'Matthew and Paul' (1947), *New Testament Studies*, Manchester University Press 1953, pp. 63f.

12. Though note C. F. D. Moule, 'The Influence of Circumstances on the Use of Eschatological Terms', *JTS* ns, 15, 1964, pp. 1–15; reprinted in *Essays in New Testament Interpretation*, Cambridge University 1982, pp. 184–99.

13. For the sense in which I use 'Jewish Christian' here see below p. 236.

14. See e.g. F. Mussner, *The Historical Jesus in the Gospel of St John*, Herder 1967; O. Cullmann, *The Johannine Circle*, SCM Press 1976, pp. 14ff.; D. M. Smith, 'The Presentation of Jesus in the Fourth Gospel', *Interpretation* 31, 1977, pp. 367–78; J. D. G. Dunn, *The Evidence for Jesus*, SCM Press/Westminster 1985, ch. 2.

Chapter III Primitive Confessional Formulae

1. See e.g. E. Stauffer, *New Testament Theology*, 1941, ET[5] SCM Press 1955, chs 62–5.

2. A. Seeberg, *Der Katechismus der Urchristenheit*, 1903, München 1966.

3. See further M. Hengel, 'Christology and New Testament Chronology', *Between Jesus and Paul*, SCM Press/Fortress 1983, pp. 30–47.

4. W. Bousset, *Kyrios Christos*, 1914, [2]1921, ET Abingdon 1970, p. 51.

5. E. Lohmeyer, *Galiläa und Jerusalem*, Göttingen 1936, pp. 68–79.

6. H. E. Tödt, *The Son of Man in the Synoptic Tradition*, 1959, ET SCM Press 1965, pp. 232–69; cf. P. Hoffmann, *Studien zur Theologie der Logienquelle*, Münster 1972, pp. 142–58.

7. S. P. Vielhauer, 'Gottesreich und Menschensohn in der Verkündigung Jesu' (1957), *Aufsätze zum Neuen Testament*, München 1965, pp. 55–91.

8. See my 'Prophetic "I" -Sayings and the Jesus-tradition: the Importance of Testing Prophetic Utterances within Early Christianity', *NTS* 24, 1977–78, pp. 175–98.

9. The opposing viewpoints are too well known to require documentation. See e.g. I. H. Marshall, 'The Synoptic Son of Man Sayings in Recent Discussion', *NTS* 12, 1965–66, pp. 327–51; R. Pesch and R. Schnackenburg, hrsg., *Jesus und der Menschensohn: Für Anton Vogtie*, Freiburg 1975; C. C. Caragounis, *The Son of Man*, WUNT 38, Tübingen 1986, pp. 19–33.

10. For one possible schema see N. Perrin, *Rediscovering the Teaching of Jesus*, SCM Press 1967, pp. 164–85; also *A Modern Pligrimage in New Testament Christology*, Fortress 1974, chs. II, III, V.

11. See particularly M. Casey, *Son of Man*, SPCK 1979, ch. 9; 'The Jackals and the Son of Man (Matt. 8.20/Luke 9.58)', *JSNT* 23, 1985, pp. 3–22.

12. See e.g. Koester, *Gnomai Diaphorai'*, *Trajectories*, pp. 129–32.

13. Cf. further below p. 307. Perrin argues that 'the evangelist Mark is the major figure in the creative use of the Son of Man traditions in the New Testament period' (*Modern Pilgrimage*, pp. 77–93).

14. The most recent study here is that of F. J. Moloney, *The Johannine Son of Man*, Rome 1976, [2]1978, with full bibliography.

15. See on the one hand G. Vermes in M. Black, *An Aramaic Approach to the Gospels and Acts*, Oxford University Press [3]1967, pp. 310–30; also his *Jesus the Jew*, Collins 1973, pp. 163–8, 188–91; Casey (above n. 11); on the other J. A. Fitzmyer, review of Black in *CBQ*, 30, 1968, pp. 424–8; also 'Methodology in the Study of the Aramaic Substratum of Jesus' Sayings in the New Testament', in J. Dupont, *Jésus aux origines de la christologie*, Gembloux 1975, pp. 92–4.

16. See Dunn, *Jesus*, pp. 49–52.

17. Was it the recognition of the breadth of the *bar ˀnāšā* usage which suggested the use of Ps. 110.1, linked as it is not only with Ps. 8 (Mark 12.36; I Cor.

15.25–27; Eph. 1.20–22 – note particularly Ps. 8.6), but also with Dan. 7.13 (Mark 14.62)?

18. So C. F. D. Moule, 'Neglected Features in the Problem of "the Son of Man"', *NTK*, pp. 413–28; reprinted in *Essays in New Testament Interpretation.* Cambridge University 1982, pp. 75–90. In the past 20 or so years see also M. D. Hooker, *The Son of Man in Mark* SPCK 1967; W. G. Kümmel, *The Theology of the New Testament*, 1972, ET SCM Press 1974, pp. 76–90; B. Lindars, 'Re-Enter the Apocalyptic Son of Man', *NTS*, 22, 1975–76, pp. 52–72; J. Bowker, 'The Son of Man', *JTS*, 28, 1977, pp. 19–48; S. Kim, '*The "Son of Man"' as the Son of God*, WUNT 30, Tübingen 1983; Caragounis, *Son of Man.*

19. See particularly B. Lindars, *Jesus Son of Man*, SPCK 1983, ch. 4. The thought of suffering and rejection is probably present in other Son of Man sayings preserved in Q (Matt. 8.20/Luke 9.58; Matt. 10.32f./Luke 12.8f.; Luke 11.30/Matt. 12.40; Luke 22.28–30/Matt. 19.28. See also Matt. 10.38/Luke 14.27; Matt. 23.37–39/Luke 13.34f.

20. See O. Betz, *What do we Know about Jesus?*, 1965, ET SCM Press 1968, pp. 83–93.

21. The longer text of Mark 14.62 is probably original – 'You say that I am'. It explains the divergent versions of Matthew and Luke; a scribal abbreviation to the briefer, unequivocal 'I am' is more likely than the reverse alteration. So e.g., V. Taylor, *The Gospel according to St Mark*, Macmillan 1952, p. 568; O. Cullmann, *The Christology of the New Testament*, 1957, ET SCM Press 1959, pp. 118f.

22. C. Burger, *Jesus als Davidssohn: eine traditionsgeschichtliche Untersuchung*, Göttingen 1970, p. 41.

22a. J. D. G. Dunn, 'Jesus – Flesh and Spirit: an Exposition of Rom. 1.3–4', *JTS* ns, 24, 1973, pp. 40–68.

23. See more fully W. Kramer, *Christ, Lord, Son of God*, 1963, ET SCM Press 1966, §§2–8; K. Wengst, *Christologische Formeln und Lieder des Urchristentums*, Gütersloh 1972, pp. 27–48, 55–104.

24. See particularly J. L. Martyn, *History and Theology in the Fourth Gospel*, Harper 1968, Abingdon [2]1979; and further J. D. G. Dunn, 'Let John be John', *Das Evangelium und die Evangelien*, hrsg. P. Stuhlmacher, WUNT 28, Tübingen 1983, pp. 309–39; cf. W. C. van Unnik, 'The Purpose of St John's Gospel', *Studia Evangelica*, I, Berlin 1959, pp. 382–411.

25. Conveniently set out in Vermes, *Jesus*, p. 198. Cf. E. Lovëstam, *Son and Saviour: a Study of Acts 13.32–37*, Lund 1961; E. Schweizer, 'The Concept of the Davidic "Son of God" in Acts and its Old Testament Background', *SLA*, pp. 186–93.

26. J. A. Fitzmyer, 'The Contribution of Qumran Aramaic to the Study of the New Testament', *NTS*, 20, 1973–74, pp. 382–407, here pp. 391ff.; reprinted in *A Wandering Aramean. Collected Aramaic Essays*, Scholars 1979, ch. 4, here pp. 102ff.

27. Vermes, *Jesus*, pp. 206f.; M. Hengel, *The Son of God*, 1975, ET SCM Press 1976, pp. 42f.; cf. K. Berger, 'Die königlichen Messiastraditionen des Neuen Testament', *NTS*, 20, 1973–74, pp. 1–44.

28. See further Dunn, *Jesus*, §§4–6; *Christology in the Making*, SCM Press [2]1989, §4; and below §§45.2, 50.4.

28a. Though note the caution with regard to the use of the word 'adoptionist' in my *Christology*, p. 62.

29. That 'suffering Servant' language was used of Jesus by the first Christians is probable (see e.g. R. N. Longenecker, *The Christology of Early Jewish Christianity*,

SCM Press 1970, p. 104–9, and references there), but initially in the service of a humiliation-vindication theme (see above p. 17). There is no evidence of any early Christian confession of the form, 'Jesus is the Servant of God'.

30. See E. Best, *The First and Second Epistles to the Thessalonians*, A. & C. Black 1972, pp. 85ff. and those cited there.

31. See J. Jeremias, *The Prayers of Jesus*, 1966, ET SCM Press 1967, pp. 29–35.

32. See also J. D. Kingsbury, *Matthew: Structure, Christology, Kingdom*, Fortress 1975, and SPCK 1976 chs II–III.

33. For my use of 'Hellenistic Christianity' see below p. 236.

34. Paul's relative disinterest in this title ('Son of God' 3 times, 'the Son' 12 times) may in part reflect a similar misuse of the title in the Gentile mission (see below pp. 70f.); but the overwhelming dominance of the *kyrios* confession in Paul (see below p. .50) may be explanation enough.

35. It has been argued that the Aramaic *mara* had a much more restricted range than the Greek *kyrios* – that while it was regularly used by Aramaic speaking Jews in addressing human authorities it was hardly used at all in reference to God and never in the absolute form 'the Lord' (S. Schulz, 'Maranatha und Kyrios Jesus', *ZNW*, 53, 1962, p. 125–44; followed by P. Vielhauer, 'Ein Weg zur neutestament-lichen Christologie?', *EvTh*, 25, 1965, pp. 28–45; H. Boers, 'Where Christology is Real', *Interpretation*, 26, 1972, pp. 315f.). However the Qumran scrolls give a fuller and rather different picture of first-century Aramaic use of *mara*, and we now have to hand not a few instances where *mar*, including both the absolute and the emphatic form, is used of Yahweh (see particularly 1QGen.Ap. 20.12–16; 4QEn[b] 1.iii.14 (Enoch 9.4); 4QEn[b] 1.iv.5 (Enoch 10.9); 11Qtg Job 24.6–7; 26.8) (see Vermes, *Jesus*, pp. 111–14; M. Black. 'The Christological Use of the Old Testament in the New Testament', *NTS*, 18, 1971–72, p. 10; Fitzmyer (as n. 26 above), p. 387ff., also 'The Semitic Background of the New Testament *Kyrios*-Title'. *A Wandering Aramean*, Scholars 1979, pp. 115–42. For the Enoch fragments see J. T. Milik, *The Books of Enoch: Aramaic Fragments of Qumran Cave 4*, Oxford University Press 1976).

36. Vermes, *Jesus*, pp. 118f.

37. Moule, 'Christology of Acts', *SLA*, pp. 160f.

38. V. Taylor, *The Names of Jesus*, Macmillan 1953, p. 43.

39. Cf. B. Lindars, *New Testament Apologetic*, SCM Press 1961, pp. 45–9; Perrin, *Teaching*, pp. 175ff.

40. A. E. J. Rawlinson, *The New Testament Doctrine of the Christ*, Longmans 1926; '"Teacher, come!" is an impossible rendering (of I Cor. 16.22); the phrase means, and can only mean, "Come, Lord!"' (p. 235).

41. It hardly features in the pre-Pauline kerygmatic formulae noted above (p. 22 – Kramer, *Christ*, §§8g, 12e).

42. See particularly D. M. Hay, *Glory at the right Hand: Psalm 110 in Early Christianity*, SBL Monograph 18, Abingdon 1973; W. R. G. Loader, 'Christ at the right hand – Ps. 110.1 in the New Testament', *NTS* 24, 1977–78, p. 199–217.

43. The Hebrew of Ps. 110.1 uses two different words – Yahweh and Adonai. How the verse would have been read in Aramaic is the subject of dispute (*Mara mari?*)

44. II Cor. 12.8 use the word meaning 'beseech' (or even 'exhort'); it is not the typical language of prayer (e.g. Rom. 1.10; Eph. 1.16f.). I Cor. 16.22 is more of an invocation than a prayer.

45. See particularly H. von Campenhausen, 'Das Bekenntnis im Urchristentum', *ZNW*, 63, 1972, pp. 226–34; also below §36.2.

46. Cf. C. F. D. Moule, 'A Reconsideration of the Context of *Maranatha*', *NTS*, 6, 1959–60, pp. 307–10; reprinted in *Essays in New Testament Interpretation*, Cambridge University 1982, pp. 222–6; Wengst, *Formeln*, pp. 52–4.

47. So H. Lietzmann, *Mass and Lord's Supper*, 1926, ET Leiden 1954, p. 186.

48. V. Neufeld, *The Earliest Christian Confessions*, Leiden 1963, p. 11.

Chapter IV   The Role of Tradition

1. Cf. the restatement of Vatican II: 'Both sacred tradition and sacred scripture are to be accepted and venerated with the same sense of devotion and reverence. Sacred tradition and sacred Scripture form one sacred deposit of the word of God, which is committed to the Church' (*Dei Verbum*, II.9–10).

2. Cf. F. F. Bruce, *Tradition Old and New*, Paternoster 1970, pp. 13–18.

3. 'The Pharisees had passed on to the people certain regulations handed down by former generations and not recorded in the Laws of Moses, for which reason they are rejected by the Sadducean group, who hold that only those regulations should be considered valid which were written down, and that those which had been handed down by former generations need not be observed' (Josephus, *Ant.*, XIII.x.6 (297)).

4. 'Whatever an acute disciple shall hereafter teach in the presence of his Rabbi has already been said to Moses on Sinai' (j.Peah ii.5; cited by R. T. Herford, *The Pharisees*, 1924, Beacon 1962, p. 85).

4a. See particularly J. Neusner in New Foreword n. 7, also chs. 1–3 in my *Jesus, Paul and the Law*, SPCK 1990.

5. Mishnah, Shabbath 7.2. See further my 'Mark 2.1–3.6: a Bridge between Jesus and Paul on the Question of the Law', *NTS* 30, 1984, pp. 395–415, reprinted in *Law* (above n. 4a) ch. 1, which, inter alia, notes how well developed the sabbath halakah was by the time of Jesus.

5a. See further my 'Jesus and Ritual Purity: a study of the tradition history of Mark 7.15', *A Cause de l'Evangile*, Cerf 1985, pp. 251–76; reprinted in *Law* (above n. 4a) ch. 2.

6. See particularly L. Goppelt, 'Tradition nach Paulus', *KuD*, 4, 1958, pp. 213–33; K. Wengst, 'Der Apostel und Die Tradition', *ZTK*, 69, 1972, pp. 145–62. See further on the complementary functions of prophet and teacher in the Pauline communities in Dunn, *Jesus*, pp. 186f., 282ff.

7. See further below §40. Cf. the way in which he adds his own resurrection appearance to the list of witnesses handed down in I Cor. 15.3–7.

8. Cf. O. Cullmann, 'The Tradition' (1953), *The Early Church*, ET SCM Press 1956, pp. 66–9; F. F. Bruce, *Paul and Jesus*, Baker 1974, p. 43.

9. I am not including here the household regulations of Colossians and Ephesians or the lists of vices and virtues which are not called tradition, nor are they distinctively Christian (probably ultimately Stoic in origin).

10. On Rom. 6.17 see below (pp. 144f.). On Phil. 2.5 see C. F. D. Moule, 'Further Reflections on Philippians 2.5–11', *AHGFFB*, pp. 264ff.

11. See also D. L. Dungan, *The Sayings of Jesus in the Churches of Paul*, Blackwell 1971; J. W. Fraser, *Jesus and Paul*, Marcham 1974, ch. 6; Bruce, *Paul*, ch. 5; J. D. G. Dunn, 'Paul's Knowledge of the Jesus Tradition: the Evidence of Romans',

Christus bezeugen. Festschrift für W. Trilling, Leipzig 1989, pp. 193–207, with further bibliography.

12. Cf. C. H. Dodd, 'Ennomos Christou', *More New Testament Studies,* Manchester University Press 1968, pp. 134–48; R. N. Longenecker, *Paul Apostle of Liberty,* Harper 1964, pp. 187–90; J. Barclay, *Obeying the Truth. A Study of Paul's Ethics in Galatians,* T. & T. Clark 1988, pp. 125–42. Otherwise V. P. Furnish, *Theology and Ethics in Paul,* Abingdon 1968, pp. 59–65.

13. See Dunn, *Jesus,* §40.5.

14. See also K. Wegenast, *Das Verständnis der Tradition bei Paulus und in den Deuteropaulinen,* Neukirchen 1962, pp. 139–43.

15. See e.g. D. Georgi, *The Opponents of Paul in Second Corinthians,* 1964, ET Fortress 1986 (on Mark, pp. 170–3); L. E. Keck, 'Mark 3.7–12 and Mark's Christology', *JBL,* 84, 1965, pp.341–58; Koester, 'One Jesus and Four Primitive Gospels', *HTR,* 61, 1968, and reprinted in *Trajectories,* pp. 187–91; P. J. Achtemeier, 'The Origin and Function of the Pre-Marcan Miracle Catena', *JBL,* 91, 1972, pp. 198–221; R. P. Martin, *Mark: Evangelist and Theologian,* Paternoster 1972, ch. VI; E. Trocmé, *Jesus and his Contemporaries,* 1972, ET SCM Press 1973, ch. 7. See also below pp. 179f., and cf. p. 39 n. 13.

16. See J. M. Robinson, 'Kerygma and History in the New Testament' (1965), *Trajectories,* pp. 46–66 and ch. 7; and see further below pp. 302f. and ch. XII n. 103.

16a. See also my *The Evidence for Jesus,* SCM Press 1985, ch. 1; also *The Living Word,* SCM Press 1987.

17. See J. Jeremias, *Unknown Sayings of Jesus,* [3]1963, ET SPCK [2]1964, pp.61–73; O. Hofius, 'Unbekannte Jesusworte', *Das Evangelium und die Evangelien,* WUNT 28, Tübingen 1983, pp. 355–82.

18. Cf. T. W. Manson, *The Teaching of Jesus,* Cambridge University Press 1931, pp. 75–80.

19. C. H. Dodd, *The Parables of the Kingdom,* 1935, Nisbet 1955, ch. V; J. Jeremias, *The Parables of Jesus,* [6]1962, ET SCM Press 1963, pp. 48–63; see also C. E. Carlston, *The Parables of the Triple Tradition,* Fortress 1975; and see further below p. 320.

20. The thesis argued by B. Gerhardsson, *Memory and Manuscript,* Lund 1961; cf. earlier, H. Riesenfeld, *The Gospel Tradition and its Beginnings,* Mowbray 1957. On the possibility that Matthew intended his Gospel as a more fixed form of Jesus' teaching, see below pp. 360f.

21. R. E. Brown, 'The Problem of Historicity in John', *CBQ,* 24, 1962, reprinted in *New Testament Essays,* Chapman 1965, ch. IX; C. H. Dodd, *Historical Tradition in the Fourth Gospel,* Cambridge University Press 1963; L. Morris, *Studies in the Fourth Gospel,* Eerdmans 1969, ch. 2; Dunn, *Evidence,* ch. 2.

22. 'hour' – 2.4; 7.6, 8, 30; 8.20; 12.23, 27; 13.1; 16.25, 32; 17.1.
'glorify' – 2.11; 7.39; 11.4; 12.16, 23, 28; 13.31f.; 17.1, 4f.
'lift up' – 3.14; 8.28; 12.32, 34.
'ascend' – 3.13; 6.62; 20.17.

23. C. H. Dodd, *The Interpretation of the Fourth Gospel,* Cambridge University Press 1953, pp. 344–89; see also J. Blank, *Krisis: Untersuchungen zur johanneischen Christologie und Eschatologie,* Freiburg 1964.

24. Cf. R. Schnackenburg, *Thge Gospel according to St John,* Vol. I, 1965, ET Herder 1968: 'The technique of the "parabolic discourses" also displays the method of concentric thinking which progresses in new circles: a meditative way of thought which uses few arguments but goes deeper and deeper into its subject to gain better and higher understanding of it' (p. 117).

25. Cf. the role of tradition in Eastern Orthodoxy: 'Loyalty to tradition means not only concord with the past but in a certain sense freedom from the past. Tradition is not only a protecting, conservative principle, it is primarily the principle of growth and regeneration. . . . Tradition is the constant abiding of the Spirit, and not only the memory of words. Tradition is a charismatic, not an historical principle' (G. V. Florovsky, 'Sobornost: The Catholicity of the Church', *The Church of God*, ed., E. Mascall, SPCK 1934, pp. 64f.).

26. To that extent C. H. Dodd's distinction between *kerygma* and *didache* (teaching) is soundly based. See also J. I. H. McDonald, *Kerygma and Didache*, SNTSMS 37, Cambridge University 1980.

27. See further Dunn, *Romans*, pp. 802ff.; R. Jewett, *Christian Tolerance. Paul's Message to the Modern Church* Westminster 1982.

28. See further Dunn, *Living Word*, ch. 6.

Chapter V   The Use of the Old Testament

1. C. H. Dodd, *According to the Scriptures*, Nisbet 1952, p. 127, my italics. See also D. Juel, *Messianic Exegesis*, Fortress 1988.

2. See e.g., J. Barr, 'Which Language did Jesus Speak? – Some Remarks of a Semitist', *BJRL*, 53, 1970, pp. 9–29; J. A. Emerton, 'The Problem of Vernacular Hebrew in the First Century AD and the Language of Jesus', *JTS* ns, 24, 1973, pp. 1–23.

3. See R. le Déaut, *Introduction à la littérature targumique*, Prem. part., Rome 1966; J. W. Bowker, *The Targums and Rabbinic Literature*, Cambridge University Press 1969; M. McNamara, *Targum and Testament*, Irish University Press and Eerdmans 1972.

4. J. F. Stenning, *The Targum of Isaiah*, Oxford University Press 1949, pp. 178, 180. See also W. Zimmerli and J. Jeremias, *The Servant of God*, ET revised SCM Press 1965, pp. 67–77. For other more detailed examples see D. Patte, *Early Jewish Hermeneutic in Palestine*, SBL Dissertation 22, 1975, ch. IV.

5. B. Gerhardsson, *The Testing of God's Son (Matt. 4.1–11 and par.)*, Coniectanea Biblica, Lund 1966, p. 14; see further R. Bloch, 'Midrash', *Approaches to Ancient Judaism: Theory and Practice*, ed. W. S. Green, Brown Judaic Studies 1, Scholars 1978, pp. 29–50.

6. See H. L. Strack, *Introduction to the Talmud and Midrash*, 1931, Harper 1965, pp. 93–8.

7. According to E. E. Ellis, 'the distinctiveness of the Qumran *pesher* is not in its structure nor in its specific subject matter but in its technique and, specifically, its eschatological perspective', ('Midrash, Targum and New Testament Quotations', *Neotestamentica et Semitica: Studies in Honour of M. Black*, ed., E. E. Ellis and M. Wilcox, T. & T. Clark 1969, p. 62). For Patte the distinctiveness of the Qumran pesher is that it treats the scriptural text like a dream or vision, a riddle to be 'unriddled' (*Hermeneutic*, pp. 299–308).

8. F. F. Bruce, *Biblical Exegesis in the Qumran Tests*, Tyndale Press 1960, pp. 7–11. See further M. P. Horgan, *Pesharim, Qumran Interpretations of Biblical Books*, CBQMS 8, Catholic Biblical Association of America 1979; W. H. Brownlee, *The Midrash Pesher of Habakkuk*, SBLMS 24, Scholars 1979.

9. K. Stendahl, *The School of St Matthew*, Lund 1954, [2]1968, pp. 191f.

10. Texts cited in D. S. Russell, *The Method and Message of Jewish Apocalyptic*, SCM Press 1964, pp. 283f.

11. Examples in S. G. Sowers, *The Hermeneutics of Philo and Hebrews*, Zürich 1965, pp. 29–34.

12. R. Williamson, *Philo and the Epistle to the Hebrews*, Leiden 1970, pp. 523–8.

13. See P. Borgen, *Bread from Heaven*, SNT, X, 1965.

13a. See further my *Romans*, Word Biblical Commentary 38, Word 1988, p. 196–8.

14. See J. D. G. Dunn, 'II Cor. 3.17: "The Lord is the Spirit"', *JTS* ns, 21, 1970, pp. 309–18.

15. See particularly J. W. Bowker, 'Speeches in Acts: A Study of Proem and Yellammedenu form', *NTS*, 14, 1967–68, pp. 96–111.

16. Paul's pesher is quite probably modelled on a current Jewish paraphrase still preserved in the recently discovered Neofiti Targum (see M. McNamara, *The New Testament and the Palestinian Targum to the Pentateuch*, Rome 1966, pp. 73–7); Dunn, *Romans*, pp. 603–6.

17. Cf. e.g., A. T. Hanson, *Studies in Paul's Technique and Theology*, SPCK 1974, pp. 159–66.

18. There is no reference to or thought of Christ as pre-existent here. Verse 4c is not intended as a historical statement but as the interpretative key to understanding the allegory: 'the rock represented/stands for Christ'. Similarly in Gal. 4.24 – 'Sinai is (= represents/stands for) Hagar'; and II Cor. 3.17 – '"The Lord is (= represents/stands for) the Spirit'. The use of a past tense in I Cor. 10.4c, as opposed to the present tenses of the two parallel passages, does not disturb the parallel: 'Sinai' and 'the Lord' are present (as well as past) realities to Paul, whereas 'the rock' belonged solely to the historical past. See further Dunn, *Christology*, pp. 183–4.

19. Cf. R. N. Longenecker, *Biblical Exegesis in the Apostolic Period*, Eerdmens 1975, pp. 127ff. A close parallel to the allegorical method of Gal. 4.22–31 in contemporary Judaism is CD 6.3–11 (I owe this reference to my colleague Dr G. I. Davies).

20. There is some dispute as to whether the same is true of the Qumran text of Habakkuk, or whether the Qumran text is simply derived from divergent versions of the Hebrew. See e.g., Stendahl, *Matthew*, pp. 185–90; J. A. Fitzmyer, 'The Use of explicit Old Testament quotations in Qumran literature and in the New Testament', *NTS*, 7, 1960–61, reprinted in *Essays on the Semitic Background of the New Testament*, Chapman 1971, ch. 1; Longenecker, *Biblical Exegesis*, pp. 39f.; Horgan, *Pesharism*, p. 245; Brownlee, *Midrash Pesher* pp. 31–4.

21. McNamara, *Palestinian Targum*, pp. 78–81.

22. For other examples of modification of a text for the sake of interpretation see Lindars, *Apologetic*, p. 284; and for later examples of gnosticized pesher quotation of sayings of Jesus see the Gospel of Thomas (below §62).

23. E. Schweizer, 'Er Wird Nazaräer heissen', *Neotestamentica*, Zürich 1963, pp. 51–5.

24. See e.g., R. S. McConnell, *Law and Prophecy in Matthew's Gospel: the Authority and Use of the Old Testament in the Gospel of St Matthew*, Basel 1969, particularly pp. 135–8; E. D. Freed, *Old Testament Quotations in the Gospel of John*, SNT, XI, 1965; E. E. Ellis, *Paul's Use of the Old Testament*, Eerdmans 1957 – nearly 20 OT citations seem to be 'a deliberate adaptation to the NT context' (p. 144); S. Kistemaker, *The Psalm Citations in the Epistle to the Hebrews*, Amsterdam 1961.

25. Lindars, *Apologetic*, p. 18.

26. Perrin, *Teaching*, pp. 173–84.

27. Hay, *Glory*, pp. 155–88; Dunn, *Christology*, pp. 108–110. For further examples cf. Lindars, *Apologetic*, summary on pp. 251–9.

27a. See my 'Jesus and Ritual Purity' (above ch. IV n. 5a).

28. See e.g., Bousset, *Kyrios Christos*, pp. 109–15.

29. See e.g., the discussion in Lindars, *Apologetic*, ch. V; R. E. Brown, *The Virginal Conception and Bodily Resurrection of Jesus*, Chapman 1973, ch. 1; also *The Birth of the Messiah*, Chapman 1977, pp. 517–33; J. A. Fitzmyer, 'The Virginal Conception of Jesus in the New Testament', *Theological Studies*, 34, 1973, pp. 541–75; J. D. G. Dunn (with J. P. Mackey), *New Testament Theology in Dialogue*, SPCK 1987, pp. 65–71. On the possibility that 'on the third day' of I Cor. 15.4 was shaped by or even derived from current Jewish exposition of Hos. 6.2, see H. K. McArthur, 'On the Third Day', *NTS*, 18, 1971–72, pp. 81–6.

30. M. Dibelius, 'Gethsemane', *Botschaft und Geschichte*, I, Tübingen 1953, pp. 258–71. But see also D. J. Moo, *The Old Testament in the Gospel Passion Narratives*, Almond 1983, pp. 245–6.

31. Cf. B. Lindars, 'The Place of the Old Testament in the Formation of New Testament Theology', *NTS*, 23, 1976–77: 'The place of the Old Testament in the formation of New Testament theology is that of a servant, ready to run to the aid of the gospel whenever it is required, bolstering up arguments, and filling out meaning through evocative allusions, but never acting as the master or leading the way, nor even guiding the process of thought behind the scenes. God's new word, the "yes", the "now", of the gospel is Jesus, who demotes the scriptures from master to servant, as much as he changes the basis of religion from law to grace' (p. 66).

Chapter VI   Concepts of Ministry

1. See O. Linton, *Das Problem der Urkirche in der neuren Forschung*, Uppsala 1932.

2. For the debates and disagreements lying behind §§27, 28, 29, 30.1 and 31.1 below, see the notes in Dunn, *Jesus*, particularly §§13.4, 32.3, ch. IX and §§57.3 and 58.3 respectively.

2a. 'Community' is a far from ideal word for this discussion, but it is difficult to find a better; 'congregation' or 'sect' suffer from even greater weaknesses. The question being asked here is whether the discipleship to which Jesus called involved not merely relations of mutual acceptance, forgiveness and service, but a more structured organization with clear boundaries and demarcation of function (such as we find in the post-Easter churches). The best single treatment of the theme is G. Lohfink, *Jesus and Community*, Fortress/SPCK 1985. See also my *Jesus and Discipleship*, Cambridge University 1990.

3. J. Jeremias, *New Testament Theology: Vol. I – The Proclamation of Jesus*, 1971, ET SCM Press 1971, pp. 174–8.

4. E. Schweizer, *Church Order in the New Testament*, 1959, ET SCM Press 1961, §2c.

5. It is unlikely that the earliest Jerusalem church was influenced by the Qumran community to any significant extent, if at all. The differences in organization and order greatly outweigh the parallels.

6. The memory of who 'the twelve' actually were has already become confused by the time it was written down in the traditions used by the Synoptics (Mark

3.16–19/Matt. 10.2–4/Luke 6.14–16).

7. See Dunn, *Jesus*, ch. VIII (summary §43), and below p. 191.

8. Gal. 2.1–10 was hardly a case of Paul 'throwing his weight around'; rather of his refusing to yield submission in matters concerning his own 'sphere of influence' to those in Jerusalem who insisted in effect on Jerusalem having universal oversight or at least on the Jerusalem pattern of membership being the norm for all. On the subsequent Antioch incident (Gal. 2.11ff.) see below §56.1.

9. H. von Campenhausen, *Ecclesiastical Authority and Spiritual Power in the Church of the First Three Centuries*, 1953, ET A. & C. Black 1969; pp. 70f.

10. If either or both 'overseers and deacons' at Philippi were responsible for raising and transmitting the Philippians' financial gift to Paul (Phil. 4.10–18), then Paul's commendation of their generosity (II Cor. 8.1–7; Phil. 4.14–18) may have been taken as implying a commendation of their organization.

11. The presentation of the early church in Acts requires a fuller treatment which we will reserve for ch. XIV (§72.2).

12. Cf. H. Goldstein, *Paulinische Gemeinde im Ersten Petrusbrief*, Stuttgarter Bibelstudien 80, 1975, particularly ch. I.

13. Contrast Jewish Christianity (below pp. 240f., 252); and cf. below p. 385.

14. Cf. the overbold suggestion of E. Trocmé that Mark's Gospel was written partly to attack the power of James and the twelve in the Jerusalem church and to defend a movement which had broken away from the mother church of Jerusalem and had launched out into a large scale missionary venture (*The Formation of the Gospel according to Mark*, 1963, ET SPCK 1975, pp. 130–37 and ch. 3). More extreme and fanciful is W. Kelber, *The Oral and the Written Gospel*, Fortress 1983, pp. 91–105.

15. 18.12f., 18 could be read as addressed to a special group singled out as leaders; but in the context of the whole passage (addressed to 'the disciples') the 'you' would most probably be taken as referring to every member throughout (otherwise R. Schnackenburg, *The Church in the New Testament*, ET Herder 1965, pp. 74f.).

16. Cf. Matt. 28.10 where Matthew does not follow Mark 16.7 in distinguishing Peter from the rest of the disciples. In recent literature cf. P. Hoffmann, 'Der Petrus-Primat im Matthäusevangelium', *NTK*, pp. 94–114; J. P. Martin, 'The Church in Matthew', *Interpretation*, 29, 1975, pp. 54f. Earlier references in R. E. Brown, K. P. Donfried and J. Reumann, *Peter in the New Testament*, Chapman 1974, p. 14 n. 29.

17. 'Elder' in Matthew is used only of the Jewish authorities hostile to Jesus.

18. See further E. Schweizer, *Matthäus und seine Gemeinde*, Stuttgarter Bibelstudien 71, 1974, particularly ch. X; ET in G. Stanton, ed., *The Interpretation of Matthew*, SPCK/Fortress 1983, pp. 129–55.

19. R. E. Brown, 'The Kerygma of the Gospel According to John', *Interpretation*, 21, 1967, reprinted in *New Testament Issues*, ed., R. Batey, SCM Press 1970, p. 213.

20. Only in the appendix added to the Gospel subsequent to its composition is there any thought of a particular pastoral ministry exercised within the community (21.15–17).

21. Note again, the discussion is in terms of ministry, not of community as such. On 'the elder' of II John and III John see below pp. 358f.

22. Schweizer, *Church Order*: '. . . Hebrews combats the institutional Church' (§10c).

23. See further A. Satake, *Die Gemeindeordnung in der Johannesapokalypse*, Neukirchen 1966.

24. A nickname in the UK for one of the most complex motorway interchanges.

25. E. Käsemann, 'The New Testament Canon and the Unity of the Church' (1951), *ENTT*, p. 103.

26. Had we widened our study to include an examination of the various concepts of church (as well as of ministry) we would be able to point to another important unifying strand – continuity with Israel: the conviction that those who believed in Christ, Gentile as well as Jew, constituted a renewed or even a new Israel. This was particularly important within the earliest community, in Matthew, Paul and Hebrews, and is prominent also in different ways in Luke, the Fourth Gospel, I Peter and Revelation. But, of course, for Gentile Christians (and so for the unity of Christianity) this continuity with Israel was possible only through Jesus and faith in him – as the fundamental argument of Gal. 3 and Rom. 4 makes very clear.

Chapter VII Patterns of Worship

1. So F. Hahn, *The Worship of the Early Church*, 1970, ET Fortress 1973, pp. 23–30. On the last supper and its relation to the passover see below pp. 162f.

2. Jeremias, *Prayers*, p. 75.

3. The parallels between the first two petitions of the Lord's prayer and what is probably the earliest form of the *Kaddish* are striking (see Jeremias, *Prayers*, p. 98).

4. The variation in the wording of Deut. 6.5 in Mark 12.30, 33 pars. suggests to Jeremias that 'the Greek *Shema* was not a regularly recited liturgical text for any of the three Synoptic evangelists' (*Prayers*, p. 80); but cf. the variation in the wording of the Lord's prayer (Matt. 6.9–13/Luke 11.2–4).

5. Two or three gathered even informally were sufficient to provide a focus for worship (Matt. 18.20), whereas according to later specification Jewish worship required the presence of ten men (Meg. 4.3; b.San. 7a).

6. In this paragraph I am largely summarizing the fuller discussion below on pp. 270–73.

6a. However, one of my doctoral students, John Chow, argues that the leaders could not provide the answer because they were the problem!

7. On I Peter see below (§36) and on Revelation see below §35.2.

8. In the Samaritan Pentateuch Moses' command to set up an altar on entering Canaan refers to Mount Gerizim (Deut. 27.4f.). The Massoretic text's reading of 'Mount Ebal' may in fact be an anti-Samaritan correction of the original preserved by the Samaritans. The Samaritan temple on Mount Gerizim was destroyed by John Hyrcanus in 128 BC.

9. Cf. D. R. Jones, 'The Background and Character of the Lukan Psalms', *JTS* ns, 19, 1968, pp. 19–50.

10. E. Lohmeyer, *Kyrios Jesus: eine Untersuchung zu Phil. 2.5–11*, Heidelberg 1928, ²1961.

11. R. P. Martin, *Carmen Christi: Philippians 2.5–11*, Cambridge University Press 1967, p. 38. More recent discussion is reviewed in the revised edition, Eerdmans 1983. The following two paragraphs have been substantially altered from the first edition of *U&D* in the light of my further analysis of the Philippian hymn in *Christology*, pp. 114–21.

12. See particularly E. Käsemann, 'A Critical Analysis of Phil. 2.5–11' (1950), *God and Christ*, *JThC*, 5, 1968, pp. 45–88; Wengst, *Formeln*, pp. 149–55. But see also

D. Georgi, 'Der vorpaulinische Hymnus Phil. 2.6–11', *Zeit und Geschicte: Dankesgabe an R. Bultmann*, ed. E. Dinkler, Tübingen 1964, pp. 263–93; O. Hofius, *Der Christushymnus Philipper 2.6–11*, Tübingen 1976; Dunn, *Christology*, pp. 114–21.

13. E. Norden, *Agnostos Theos*, 1913, reprinted Stuttgart 1956, pp. 250–4.

14. E. Käsemann, 'A Primitive Christian Baptismal Liturgy' (1949), *ENTT*, pp. 154–9. For the earlier history of the investigation of Col. 1.15–20 see H. J. Gabathuler, *Jesus Christus: Haupt der Kirche – Haupt der Welt*, Zürich 1965. For further bibliography see P. T. O'Brien, *Colossians, Philemon*, Word Biblical Commentary 44, Word 1982, pp. 31–2.

14a. See further Dunn, *Christology*, pp. 165–6, 187–94.

15. The question of reconstructing the original form of the poem is too complex to go into here. A basic outline of Stanza I vv. 1, 3, Stanza II, vv. 4–5, (9), Stanza III, vv. 10–12b, Stanza IV, vv. 14, 16, (with several insertions), seems to be most plausible.

16. R. Bultmann, *The Gospel of John*, 1964, ET Blackwell 1971, pp. 25ff., 61ff.

17. See particularly the commentary of R. E. Brown, *The Gospel according to John*, Vol. 1, Anchor Bible 29, Chapman 1966; Dunn, *Christology*, pp. 239–45.

18. E. Käsemann, 'The Structure and Purpose of the Prologue to John's Gospel' (1957), *NTQT*, ch. VI, ends the hymn with v. 12. J. T. Sanders, *The New Testament Christological Hymns*, Cambridge University Press 1971, pp. 20–24, ends it with the rejection of v. 11, which seems most improbable.

18a. See further Dunn, *Christology*, pp. 166, 206–9.

19. A recent study of these two passages is C. Burger, *Schöpfung und Versöhnung: Studien zum liturgischen Gut im Kolosser-und Epheserbrief*, Neukirchen 1975.

20. R. Deichgräber, *Gotteshymnus und Christushymnus in der frühen Christenheit*, Göttingen 1967, ch. II.

21. P. Carrington, *The Primitive Christian Catechism*, Cambridge University Press 1940, p. 90.

22. E. G. Selwyn, *The First Epistle of St Peter*, Macmillan 1947, p. 363–466.

23. H. Preisker, revision of H. Windisch, *Die katholischen Briefe*, HNT, [3]1951, pp. 156–62; F. L. Cross, *I Peter – A Paschal Liturgy*, Mowbray 1954. See also M. E. Boismard, 'Une liturgie baptismale dans la Prima Petri', *RB*, 63, 1956, pp. 182–208; A. R. C. Leaney, 'I Peter and the Passover: an Interpretation', *NTS*, 10, 1963–64, pp. 238–51.

24. J. C. Kirby, *Ephesians: Baptism and Pentecost*, SPCK, 1968, pp. 150, 170.

25. A. T. Hanson, *Studies in the Pastoral Epistles*, SPCK 1968, ch. 7.

26. P. Vielhauer, 'Das Benedictus des Zacharias (Luke 1.68–79)', *ZTK*, 49, 1952, pp. 255–72.

27. Martin, *Carmen Christi*, pp. 81f., 292–4; see particularly J. Jervell, *Imago Dei*, Göttingen 1960, pp. 206–9.

28. Käsemann, *ENTT*, pp. 149–68.

29. G. Bornkamm, 'Das Bekenntnis im Hebräerbrief', *Studien zu Antike und Urchristentum: Gesammelte Aufsätze*, II, München 1963, pp. 196f.

30. G. Friedrich, 'Ein Tauflied hellenistischer Judenchristen I Thess. 1.9f.', *TZ*, 21, 1965, pp. 502–16.

31. G. Schille, *Frühchristliche Hymnen*, Berlin 1965, p. 43.

32. W. Nauck, *Die Tradition und der Charakter des ersten Johannesbriefes*, Tübingen 1957, p. 96.

33. P. von der Osten-Sacken, 'Christologie, Taufe, Homologie: ein Beitrag zu Apc. Joh. 1.5f.', *ZNW*, 58, 1967, pp. 255–66. On attempts to read an order of service

out of the Revelation of John see K. P. Jörns, *Das hymnische Evangelium: Untersuchungen zu Aufbau, Funktion und Herkunft der hymnischen Stücke in der Johannesoffenbarung*, Gütersloh 1971, pp. 180–84.

34. P. Carrington, *The Primitive Christian Calendar*, Cambridge University Press 1952. But see W. D. Davies, 'Reflections on Archbishop Carrington's *The Primitive Christian Calendar*', *BNTE*, pp. 124–52.

35. G. D. Kilpatrick, *The Origins of the Gospel according to St Matthew*, Oxford University Press 1946, ch. V.

36. M. D. Goulder, *Midrash and Lection in Matthew*, SPCK 1974; *The Evangelists Calendar. A Lectionary Explanation of the Development of Scripture*, SPCK 1978.

37. A Guilding, *The Fourth Gospel and Jewish Worship*, Oxford University Press 1960, pp. 54, 57. But see also L. Morris, *The New Testament and the Jewish Lectionaries*, Tyndale Press 1964.

38. B. Reicke, *The Disobedient Spirits and Christian Baptism*, Copenhagen 1946, pp. 191–5.

39. Cf. D. Daube, 'A Baptismal Catechism', *The New Testament and Rabbinic Judaism*, London 1956, pp. 106–40.

40. Cf. W. Robinson, 'Historical Survey of the Church's Treatment of New Converts with reference to Pre- and Post-baptismal Instruction', *JTS*, 42, 1941, pp. 142–5.

40a. See also my *Living Word*, ch. 2.

41. J. Munck, *Paul and the Salvation of Mankind*, 1954, ET SCM Press 1959, p. 18 n. 1.

42. W. C. van Unnik, 'Dominus Vobiscum: the background of a liturgical formula', *NTETWM*, p. 272.

43. See further C. F. D. Moule, 'The Nature and Purpose of I Peter', *NTS*, 3, 1956–57, pp. 1–11, reprinted in *Essays in New Testament Interpretation*, Cambridge University 1982, pp. 133–45; T. C. G. Thornton, 'I Peter, A Paschal Liturgy?', *JTS* ns, 12, 1961, pp. 14–26. The baptismal liturgy thesis attracts no support from recent commentators – L. Goppelt, *Der erste Petrusbrief*, KEK, Göttingen 1978, pp. 38–40; N. Brox, *Der erste Petrusbrief*, EKK, Benziger/Neukirchener 1979, pp. 19–23; J. R. Michaels, *I Peter*, Word Biblical Commentary 49, Word 1988, pp. xxxviii – xxxix.

Chapter VIII Sacraments

1. These references are drawn from G. D. Henderson, *Church and Ministry*, Hodder & Stoughton 1951, p. 38.

2. *Church Dogmatics*, I/1, ET T. & T. Clark 1936, p. 98.

3. I confine my discussion in this chapter to the two 'ecumenical sacraments'.

4. See e.g., the discussion in G. R. Beasley-Murray, *Baptism in the New Testament*, Macmillan 1963, pp. 15–18, 39–43; Paternoster 1972.

5. Much of what follows in §§39.1, 2 is an attempt to summarize discussion contained in J. D. G. Dunn, *Baptism in the Holy Spirit*, SCM Press 1970, chs II and III.

6. See J. D. G. Dunn, 'Spirit and Fire Baptism', *NovTest* 14, 1972, pp. 81–92.

7. See further Strack-Billerbeck, I.950; IV. 977–86; and n. 8 below.

8. See more fully J. D. G. Dunn, 'Baptized in Spirit: the Birth of a Metaphor', forthcoming in *ExpT* 89, 1977–78, pp. 134–8, 173–5.

9. See J. Weiss, *Earliest Christianity*, 1914, ET 1937, Harper 1959, pp. 50f.; F. J. Foakes Jackson and K. Lake, *The Beginnings of Christianity: Part I: The Acts of the Apostles*, Macmillan, Vol. I, 1920, pp. 332–44.

9a. The Rubicon was a small stream that separated Cisalpine Gaul from Italy during the Roman Republic. The decision of Julius Caesar to 'cross the Rubicon' with his army in 49 BC amounted to a declaration of war against the Roman Senate. Hence the Rubicon has become a metaphor for the boundary by crossing which one makes a decisive, no-turning-back commitment to an enterprise.

10. Cf. particularly W. Heitmüller, *Taufe und Abendmahl im Urchristentum*, Tübingen 1911, pp. 18–26. For what follows see also my *Romans*, pp. 305ff.

11. The structure of thought here is disputed. For fuller exegesis see Dunn, *Baptism*, pp. 154ff.

12. The 'Do you not know . . . ?' of Rom. 6.3 may very well be simply the polite teacher's manner of passing on new knowledge (see Dunn, *Baptism*, p. 144 n. 17).

13. In this section I am particularly indebted to E. Schweizer, *The Lord's Supper according to the New Testament*, 1956, ET Fortress Facet Book 1967, and W. Marxsen, *The Lord's Supper as a Christological Problem*, 1963, ET Fortress Facet Book 1970.

13a. See further my 'Jesus, Table-Fellowship and Qumran', *Jesus and the Dead Sea Scrolls*, ed. J. H. Charlesworth, Doubleday 1990.

14. See particularly J. Jeremias, *The Eucharistic Words of Jesus*, ³1960, ET SCM Press 1966, ch. I.

15. Cf. the helpful discussions in Schweizer, *Lord's Supper*, pp. 29–32; B. Klappert, 'Lord's Supper', *NIDNTT*, II, pp. 527ff.; I. H. Marshall, *Last Supper and Lord's Supper*, Paternoster 1980, pp. 57–75.

16. See Dunn, *Jesus*, §29 and below §67.3.

17. Origen, *in Matt. comm. ser.*, 79; Epiphanius, *Pan.*, 30.16.1.

18. *Not* that each is a sacrificial meal; see e.g. W. G. Kümmel, *An die Korinther, HNT*, 1949, pp. 181f.; C. K. Barrett, *The First Epistle to the Corinthians*, A. & C. Black 1968, pp. 235ff. See also below n. 21.

19. Schweizer, *Lord's Supper*, pp.5f.

20. See e.g. E. Käsemann, 'The Pauline Doctrine of the Lord's Supper' (1947–48), *ENTT*, pp. 108–35; J. Héring, *The First Epistle of Saint Paul to the Corinthians*, 1948, ET Epworth 1962, p. 120.

21. See e.g. A. J. B. Higgins, *The Lord's Supper in the New Testament*, SCM Press 1952, pp. 72f.; Kümmel, *Theology*, pp. 221f.

22. Though the longer text is probably original in Luke – see particularly H. Schürmann, 'Lk 22.19b–20 als ursprüngliche Textüberlieferung' (1951), *Traditionsgeschichtliche Untersuchungen zu den synoptischen Evangelien*, Düsseldorf 1968, pp. 159–92; Jeremias, *Eucharistic Words*, pp. 139–59.

23. G. Bornkamm, 'Lord's Supper and Church in Paul' (1956), *Early Christian Experience*, ET SCM Press 1969, pp. 134ff.; Schweizer, *Lord's Supper*, pp. 10–17; Marxsen, *Lord's Supper*, pp. 5–8; F. Lang, 'Abendmahl und Bundesgedanke im Neuen Testament', *EvTh*, 35, 1975, pp. 527f.; H. Merklein, 'Erwägungen zur Überlieferungsgeschichte der neutestamentlichen Abendmahlstraditionen', *BZ*, 21, 1977, p. 94–8; Marshall, *Last Supper*, pp. 43–51; otherwise Klappert, *NIDNTT*, II, pp. 524ff.

24. E.g., O. Cullmann, *Early Christian Worship*, 1950, ET SCM Press 1953, ch. 2; A. Corell, *Consummatum Est*, 1950, ET SPCK 1958, ch. 3.

25. E.g., R. Bultmann, *John*, pp. 138 n. 3, 234–7, 677f.; Käsemann, *Testament*, pp. 32f.

26. E.g., Beasley-Murray, *Baptism*, pp. 216–32; R. E. Brown, 'The Johannine Sacramentary', *New Testament Essays*, Chapman 1965, ch. IV; H. Klos, *Die Sakramente im Johannesevangelium*, Stuttgarter Bibelstudien 46, 1970.

27. See J. D. G. Dunn, 'A Note on *dorea*', *ExpT*, 81, 1969–70, pp. 349–51.

28. The 'flesh' reference in 6.63 makes it very difficult to accept the view that these verses were a later addition.

29. See more fully J. D. G. Dunn, 'John 6 – A Eucharistic Discourse?', *NTS*, 17, 1970–71, pp. 328–38.

30. For discussion of the relevant passages in I John see Dunn, *Baptism*, ch. XVI.

31. To what extent the last supper was a continuation of Jesus' normal pattern of table fellowship, and to what extent a departure from it is an important question, but one almost impossible to answer. However, the two should not be separated as much as they usually are; somewhat surprisingly, the eucharistic echoes in the bread of life discourse of John 6 are set in the context of an open meal.

Chapter IX   Spirit and Experience

1. S. Tugwell, *Did you Receive the Spirit?*, Darton, Longman & Todd 1972, pp. 52ff.

2. R. A. Knox, *Enthusiasm*, Oxford University Press 1950, pp. 152, n. 3, 410.

3. J. Wesley, *Forty-four Sermons*, X. 'The Witness of the Spirit', Epworth 1944, p. 115.

4. L. Newbigin, *The Household of God*, SCM Press 1953, pp. 87f.

5. G. Williams, *The Radical Reformation*, Weidenfeld & Nicolson 1962, p. 822.

6. Cited by Knox, *Enthusiasm*, p. 450.

7. Article on 'Experience, Religious', in *A Dictionary of Christian Theology*, ed., A. Richardson, SCM Press 1969, p. 127.

8. What follows is in large part a summary of Dunn, *Jesus*, where the discussion with other viewpoints is fully documented.

9. So Knox, op. cit., pp. 4ff.

10. See more fully Dunn, *Jesus*, ch. V. Cf. most recently W. L. Craig, *Assessing the New Testament Evidence for the Historicity of the Resurrection of Jesus*, Edwin Mellen 1989.

11. It is hardly possible that Luke understood the Samaritans to have already received the Spirit and only to lack the *manifestations* of the Spirit. Luke thinks of the Spirit precisely as that power which manifests itself clearly and tangibly to the observer – no manifestations, no Spirit (see above pp. 180f. and more fully Dunn, *Baptism*, ch. V.).

11a. According to Mark 3.20 those close to Jesus thought he was out of his mind (literally 'ecstatic').

12. See J. Klausner, *Jesus of Nazareth*, Allen & Unwin 1925, pp. 18–47; H. van der Loos, *The Miracles of Jesus*, *SNT*, VIIII, 1965, pp. 156–75; J. D. G. Dunn and G. H. Twelftree, 'Demon-Possession and Exorcism in the New Testament', *Churchman* 94, 1980, pp. 210–25.

13. See E. Käsemann, 'The Problem of the Historical Jesus' (1954) *ENTT*, pp. 37–42; Jeremias, *Theology*, I, pp. 35f.

14. Jeremias, *Prayers*, pp. 57–62; though see also the important qualifications of

G. Vermes, *Jesus and the World of Judaism*, SCM Press 1983, pp. 41f.; J. A. Fitzmyer, 'Abba and Jesus' Relation to God', *A Cause de l'Evangile*, J. Dupont Festschrift, Cerf 1985, pp. 15–38; J. Barr, 'Abba isn't "Daddy"', *JTS* 39, 1988, pp. 28–47.

14a. See further my 'Matthew 12.28/Luke 11.20 – A Word of Jesus?', *Eschatology and the New Testament*, G. R. Beasley-Murray Festschrift, ed. W. H. Gloer, Hendrickson 1988, pp. 29–49.

15. Fuller details in Dunn, *Jesus* §38.1.

16. Paul did not however regard the resurrection appearance of Jesus to him at his conversion as a vision; it was something unique and unrepeated (I Cor. 15.8 – 'last of all').

17. See also J. D. G. Dunn, 'Discernment of Spirits – A Neglected Gift', *Witness to the Spirit*, ed. W. Harrington, Irish Biblical Association/Koinonia 1979, pp. 79–96.

18. See further Dunn, 'Rom. 7.14–25', pp. 257–73.

18a. Although I use 'charisma' in Paul's more than Weber's sense, Weber's description of the process by which a charismatic group develops its doctrine, cult and organization as 'the routinization of charisma' is pertinent here.

18b. Meyer, *Early Christians*, pp. 174–81, rightly emphasizes the 'experiential roots of (Christian) identity'.

19. Koester, '*Gnomai Diaphoroi*', *Trajectories*, p. 117.

20. Cf. Käsemann, 'Blind Alleys in the "Jesus of History" Controversy', *NTQT*, pp. 47f.

Chapter X   Christ and Christology

1. F. D. Schleiermacher, *Life of Jesus*, 1864, ET Fortress 1975.

2. A Harnack's famous presentation of liberal Christianity, *What is Christianity?*, 1900, ET 1901, reprinted Benn 1958, can be summed up at this point in two famous sentences: 'The Gospel, as Jesus proclaimed it, has to do with the Father only and not with the Son'; 'True faith in Jesus is not a matter of credal orthodoxy but of doing as he did' (Lecture 8 and contents summary).

3. M. Kähler, *The So-called Historical Jesus and the Historic Biblical Christ*, 1892, ET ed., C. E. Braaten, Fortress 1964.

4. Cf. particularly Braun, 'New Testament Christology', *JThC*, 5, 1968, pp. 89–127; and the criticisms of Bultmann by S. M. Ogden, *Christ without Myth*, Harper 1961, pp. 76–94.

5. Cf. J. A. T. Robinson, 'Elijah, John and Jesus', *NTS*, 4, 1957–58, pp. 263–81, reprinted in *Twelve New Testament Studies*, SCM Press 1962, pp. 28–52; cf. also J. Becker, 'Das Gottesbild Jesu und die älteste Auslegung von Ostern', *JCHT*, pp. 105–26.

6. So particularly Tödt, *Son of Man*, and F. Hahn, *The Titles of Jesus in Christology*, 1963, ET Lutterworth 1969, pp. 28–34.

7. U. Wilckens, 'The Understanding of Revelation within the History of Primitive Christianity', *Revelation as History*, ed., W. Pannenberg, 1961, ET Macmillan 1968, pp. 57–121; W. Pannenberg, *Jesus God and Man*, 1964, ET SCM Press 1968, pp. 53–66; cf. N. A. Dahl, 'The Problem of the Historical Jesus' (1962), *The Crucified Messiah and other essays*, ET Augsburg 1974: 'Either the events of Easter and Pentecost are the preliminary fulfilment of Jesus' eschatological promise, or this promise, at the heart

of his message, remained unfulfilled' (p. 83). See also C. K. Barrett, *Jesus and the Gospel Tradition*, SPCK 1967, ch. 3; A. Strobel, *Kerygma und Apokalyptik*, Göttingen 1967.

8. Initially argued by E. Käsemann, 'Problem', *ENTT*, particularly pp. 42f., and G. Bornkamm, *Jesus of Nazareth*, 1956, ET Hodder & Stoughton 1960, particularly pp. 67–9. More recently P. Stuhlmacher, 'Jesus als Versöhner', *JCHT*, pp. 95–7. We should not forget Bultmann's own earlier formulation in 'The Significance of the Historical Jesus for the Theology of Paul' (1929), *Faith and Understanding*, ET SCM Press 1969, pp. 237f.: 'Such a call to decision in the light of his person (Luke 12.8f.) *implies* a christology' (p. 237).

9. W. Marxsen, *The Beginnings of Christology*, ET Fortress 1969, particularly ch. 5; also 'Die urchristlichen Kerygmata und das Ereignis Jesus von Nazareth', *ZTK*, 73, 1976, p.42–64; see also H. Schürmann, 'Die vorösterlichen Anfänge der Logientradition', *Der historische Jesus und der kerygmatische Christus: Beiträge zum Christusverständnis im Forschung und Verkündigung*, ed. H. Ristow and K. Matthiae, Berlin 1961, pp. 362–8; J. Ernst, *Anfänge der Christologie*, Stuttgarter Bibelstudien 57, 1972, pp. 125–61.

10. Cf. G. Ebeling, *Theology and Proclamation*, 1962, ET Collins 1966, p. 79; E. Jungel, *Paulus und Jesus*, Tübingen ³1967, pp. 280–83.

11. L. E. Keck, *A Future for the Historical Jesus*, SCM Press 1972, pp. 183, 235. For other literature on the three alternative positions outlined above, see S. Schulz, 'Der historische Jesus: Bilanz der Fragen und Lösungen', *JCHT*, pp. 21ff. The 'new quest' has now been superceded by the 'third quest' (see above New Foreword n. 9), which is in effect an extension of (c) with particular concern to set Jesus as fully as possible within his Jewish context.

12. See further Jeremias, *Theology*, I, pp. 277–86; H. Schürmann, 'Wie hat Jesus seinen Tod bestanden und verstanden?', *Orientierung an Jesus: Für Josef Schmid*, ed., P. Hoffmann, Herder 1973, pp. 325–63; V. Howard, 'Did Jesus speak about his own death?', *CBQ* 39, 1977, pp. 515–27.

13. A. Schweitzer, *The Quest of the Historical Jesus*, ET A. & C. Black 1910, pp. 385, 390.

14. See particularly E. Schweizer, *Erniedrigung und Erhöhung bei Jesus und seinen Nachfolgern*, Zürich ²1962, §§2–3. See also G. W. E. Nickelsburg, *Resurrection Immortality, and Eternal Life in Intertestamental Judaism*, Harvard 1972. And note the important qualification of Schweizer's thesis by L. Ruppert, *Jesus als der leidende Grechte?*, Stuttgarter Bibelstudien 59, 1972, that it was Jesus himself who brought together at this point strands of OT and intertestamental thought which were previously unrelated. Cf. Stuhlmacher (above n. 8) p. 102.

15. See further J. Jeremias (with W. Zimmerli), *Servant*, pp. 99–106; Cullmann, *Christology*, pp. 60–69; otherwise M. D. Hooker, *Jesus and the Servant*, SPCK 1959; Hahn, *Titles*, pp. 54–67.

16. In Mark 8.31, 9.31 and 10.33f., the language suggests nothing beyond an individual resurrection of Jesus. But the earliest understanding was evidently of Jesus' resurrection as the beginning of the general resurrection (Rom. 1.3f.; I Cor. 15.20, 23; cf. Matt. 27.52f.); see also below §67.3. For the whole issue see now H. F. Bayer, *Jesus' Predictions of Vindication and Resurrection*, WUNT 2.20, Tübingen 1986.

17. See further J. D. G. Dunn, 'I Corinthians 15.45 – Last Adam, Life-giving Spirit', *CSNT*, pp. 127–41.

18. On Acts 1.5 see Dunn, *Jesus*, ch. VI, n. 60 (p. 398) and above p. 21 n. 9.

19. See R. Bultmann, *Faith and Understanding*, pp. 223–35; Jungel, *Paulus*, pp. 268–73; R. Banks, *Jesus and the Law in the Synoptic Tradition*, Cambridge University Press 1975, p. 245 n. 4.

19a. See further my 'Pharisees, Sinners and Jesus', *The Social World of Formative Christianity and Judaism*, H. C. Kee Festschrift, ed. J. Neusner et al., Fortress 1988, pp. 264–89, here pp. 282–3; reprinted in my *Jesus, Paul and the Law*, SPCK 1990.

20. Cf. C. F. D. Moule, 'A Reconsideration of the Context of *Maranatha*', *Essays in New Testament Interpretation*, Cambridge University 1982, pp. 222–6. Against Cullmann, *Christology*, pp. 211f.; B. Sandvik, *Das Kommen des Herrn beim Abendmahl im Neuen Testament*, Zürich 1970. See also above pp. 55f.

21. Cf. J. A. T. Robinson, *Jesus and his Coming*, SCM Press 1957; Perrin, *Teaching*, pp. 164–85. See also n. 34 below.

21a. For the importance of the resurrection in the earliest stage of Christian theologizing see P. Pokorny, *The Genesis of Christology*, T. & T. Clark 1987.

22. In primitive Christianity 'salvation' is primarily a future, eschatological term (W. Foerster, '*sōzō*', *TDNT*, VII, pp. 992ff.).

23. By 'christological moment' I mean that event which is seen as defining and determining the character and status of Christ. Similarly, by the phrase 'soteriological moment' I mean that event which is seen as decisive for salvation.

24. J. Knox, *The Humanity and Divinity of Christ*, Cambridge University Press 1967, p. 11; cf. G. Schneider, 'Praexistenz Christi', *NTK*, pp. 405, 408f., 412. But see my *Christology*, p. 63.

25. There is no evidence that Jesus' use of *bar* ˣnāšā implied a consciousness or conviction of pre-existence. The thought of the Son of Man's pre-existence first emerged in I Enoch 48.6, 62.7, but these passages are part of the only section of Enoch (the Similitudes or Parables – I Enoch 37–71) which has failed so far to appear among the Dead Sea Scrolls – a fact suggesting that the Similitudes were added to I Enoch at a date subsequent to Qumran (finally destroyed AD 68) (see further particularly Milik, *Enoch*, pp. 89–98). Pre-existence is implied neither in Dan. 7.13, nor in the Synoptic Son of Man material (cf. Tödt, *Son of Man*, p. 300; otherwise R. G. Hamerton-Kelly, *Pre-existence, Wisdom and the Son of Man*, Cambridge University Press 1973, whose firm conclusions on pp. 67, 102, go beyond even his own evidence – cf. eg., the earlier conclusion on p. 47). See further my *Christology*, p. 29.

26. The same applies to Rom. 8.3 and Gal. 4.4; cf. Wisd. 9.10 (also to Rom. 10.6f. if an allusion to Wisdom is intended there – cf. Bar. 3.29); see particularly E. Schweizer, 'Zur Herkunft der Präexistenzvorstellung bei Paulus', *Ev Th*, 19, 1959, pp. 65–70; reprinted in *Neotestamentica*, pp. 105–9; also 'Zum religionsgeschichtlichen Hintergrund der "Sendungsformel" Gal. 4.4f., Rom. 8.3f., John 3.11f., I John 4.9', *ZNW*, 57, 1966, pp. 199–210. The description of the pre-existent one as 'God's Son' does not advance the discussion in either direction, since Wisdom is also hailed as God's child and Philo can call the Logos God's 'eldest and first born son' while also calling the (visible) world God's 'younger son' (Philo, *De Conf. Ling.*, 62f.; *Quod Deus Imm.*, 31f.; cf. *De Ebr.*, 30). See further my *Christology*, ch. VI.

27. The oddly literalist thesis of A. T. Hanson, *Jesus Christ in the Old Testament*, SPCK 1965, that Paul and the other NT writers understood not a few OT passages either to refer to the pre-existent Jesus or to have been spoken *by* the pre-existent Jesus(!) has very little to commend it. The lynch-pin text, I Cor. 10.4, is, as we have seen, probably an explanatory or decoding note to explain Paul's typological-allegorical interpretation (above p. 90 n. 18), though many scholars do take it as

another instance of Christ being accorded a role elsewhere attributed to Wisdom (cf. Philo, *Leg. Alleg.*, II.86; *Quod.Det.*, 115–18).

28. Cf. e.g. Cullmann, *Christology*: 'All the statements of Phil. 2.6ff. are to be understood from the standpoint of the Old Testament history of Adam' (p. 181); C. H. Talbert, 'The Problem of Pre-existence in Philippians 2.6–11', *JBL*, 86, 1967, pp. 141–53; J. Murphy–O'Connor, 'Christological Anthropology in Phil. 2.6–11', *RB*, 83, 1976, pp. 25–50. Note also Schweizer, *Erniedrigung*, p. 96 n. 383; M. D. Hooker, 'Philippians 2.6–11', *JuP*, pp. 160–4. See further above p. 135.

29. Cf. J. A. T. Robinson, *The Human Face of God*, SCM Press 1973, pp. 162–6 and those cited there; otherwise Hamerton-Kelly, *Pre-existence*, pp. 156–68. See also above p. 135f. The rich/poor antithesis of II Cor. 8.9 need not be intended as a pre-existence/incarnation antithesis, but may be simply a fulsome contrast between the sinless life of Jesus and the humiliation of the cross (cf. II Cor. 5.21, and Dunn, *Christology*, pp. 121–3).

30. See E. Schweizer, *Jesus*, 1968, ET SCM Press 1971, pp. 84f.

31. J. Knox assesses the christology of Hebrews as 'a close approximation to a pure kenoticism' (*Humanity*, p. 43); but he has not demonstrated that the thought of a personal pre-existence of the Son is present in Hebrews; and even if it can be argued for in 7.3 and 10.5 it is hardly as strong or as persistent as the adoptionist language (see below pp. 259f.).

32. Gregory of Nyssa, *contra Eunomium*, 5.5, 12.1; *oratio catechetica*, 26 (ET in H. Bettenson, *The Later Christian Fathers*, Oxford University Press 1970, pp. 137, 142–5). Cf. Leo's fifth Christmas sermon (in J. P. Jossua, *Le salut incarnation ou mystère pascal*, Paris 1968, p. 363 – I owe these references to my colleague S. G. Hall); cf. also Harnack's comment on Athanasius (*History of Dogma*, [3]1894, ET Williams & Norgate 1897, III, p. 292f).

33. Cf. the biting judgment of H. S. Reimarus: 'Now if the apostles had at that time said that it would be about seventeen, eighteen, or several hundred years before Christ would return in the clouds of heaven and begin his kingdom, people would simply have laughed at them, and would naturally have thought that by their placing the fulfilment of the promise far beyond the lives of so many men and generations, they were only seeking to hide their own and their master's disgrace . . . If Christ neither has nor does come again to reward the faithful in his kingdom, then our belief is as useless as it is false' (*Fragments*, 1778, ed., C. H. Talbert, SCM Press 1971, pp. 215, 228).

34. T. F. Glasson, *The Second Advent*, Epworth 1945, pp. 64f.; Robinson, *Jesus and his Coming*, pp. 43–58. See also n. 21 above.

35. The evidence reviewed above (§§6.2, 18.4) is decisive against the view that John is attempting to present Jesus 'as he actually was' in such passages as John 8.58 and 10.30.

36. More difficult is the question whether the concepts of incarnation and virgin birth are finally compatible with the full humanity of Jesus. Cf. e.g., Brown, *Virginal Conception*, pp. 45–7; Knox, *Humanity*, pp. 61f., 68, 73, etc. In the revision of *U&D* I have been conscious that too little is said about the virgin birth. But see R. E. Brown, *The Birth of the Messiah*, Chapman 1977.

37. Possibly as early as Rom. 9.5 – but if so only as an isolated instance. See now my *Romans*, pp. 528–9.

38. D. Cupitt, in *Christ Faith and History: Cambridge Studies in Christology*, ed., S. W. Sykes and J. P. Clayton, Cambridge University Press 1972, pp. 131–44.

39. Note e.g. the deliberate parallels between the Gospel and Acts listed in

G. Stählin, *Die Apostlegeschichte*, NTD, 5, [10]1962, pp. 13f.

40. For possible reasons see Foerster, '*soter*', *TDNT*, VII, pp. 1020f.

41. Cf. the comments of Knox and K. Rahner cited by Knox, *Humanity*, pp.56f.

42. When I returned to these questions and subjected the NT data to much more careful scrutiny I was interested to find that my respect for the subsequent Trinitarian formulations was considerably strengthened – rather to my surprise (see *Christology*, pp. 262–3, 266–8, and New Foreword to Second Edition pp. xxviii – xxxii). But since a large part of the task of this present book is to stimulate questioning and provoke theological reflection I decided to leave the questions of §52.5 as originally posed and unchanged for the second edition.

Chapter XI   Jewish Christianity

1. Cf. J. Danielou, *The Theology of Jewish Christianity*, 1958, ET Darton, Longman & Todd 1964, pp. 7ff.; S. K. Riegel, 'Jewish Christianity: Definitions and Terminology', *NTS* 24, 1977–78, pp. 410–5.

2. 'From about the middle of the third century BC *all Judaism* must really be designated "*Hellenistic Judaism*" in the strict sense' (M. Hengel, *Judaism and Hellenism*, ET SCM Press 1974, Vol. I, p. 104.)

3. See also C. K. Barrett, 'Paul and the "Pillar" Apostles', *Studia Paulina in honorem J. de Zwaan*, Haarlem 1953, pp. 1–19.

3a. See also Deut. 30.1–10; the 10th of the 18 Benedictions; and the material surveyed by E. P. Sanders, *Jesus and Judaism*, SCM 1985, particularly pp. 79–86, 96–8.

4. At all these points the evidence from Acts is sufficiently consistent with itself at the historical level and with the evidence from elsewhere in the NT for us to conclude that Luke is drawing on good historical tradition (see also above pp. 64, 127).

5. A. F. J. Klijn and G. J. Reinink, *Patristic Evidence for Jewish–Christian Sects*, Leiden 1973, p. 71. On the significance and diversity of second- and third-century Jewish Christianity see G. Strecker, 'On the Problem of Jewish Christianity', in Bauer, *Orthodoxy*, pp. 241–85.

6. In what follows I will frequently use 'Ebionite', 'Ebionism' to denote the characteristic emphases of heretical Jewish Christianity, without forgetting or denying thereby that the reality was much more complex.

7. Justin, *Dial.*, 47.

8. Epiphanius, *Pan.*, 29.7.5.

9. Irenaeus, *adv.haer.*, I.26.2. See also Tertullian, *de prae.haer.*, 32.5; Origen, *hom.in Gen.*, III.5; *comm.in Matt.*, XI.12; *in Matt.comm.ser.*, 79; *cont.Cels.*, II.1; Epiphanius, *Pan.*, 30.2.2; 30.26.1–2; *Epistula Petri*, 2.4–5 (Hennecke, *Apocrypha*, II, p. 112).

10. See e.g., *Clem.Recog.*, I.44; V.10; X.51; *Clem.Hom.*, II.38; III.49–51; VIII.7. See further H. J. Schoeps, *Theologie und Geschichte des Judenchristentums*, Tübingen 1949, ch. 3; also *Jewish Christianity*, 1964, ET Fortress 1969, ch. 5.

11. Jerome, *de vir.ill.*, II.

12. Epiphanius, *Pan.*, 30.23.1; Marius Victorinus, *in ep.ad Gal.*, 4.12; cf. 1.15. See also Epiphanius, *Pan.*, 30.2.6, and cf. 30.13.3. And note the striking saying in the Gospel of Thomas: 'Jesus said to them, In the place to which you have come, you

will go to James the Just, for whose sake heaven and earth came into existence' (Logion 12); see further J. Doresse, *The Secret Books of the Egyptian Gnostics*, 1958, ET Hollis & Carter 1960, p. 237.

13. Irenaeus, *adv.haer.*, I.26.2; Origen, *cont.Cels.*, V.65; Eusebius, *HE*, VI.38; Ephiphanius, *Pan.*, 28.5.3; 30.16.8–9.

14. See also Schoeps, *Theologie*, pp. 418–34; *Jewish Christianity*, pp. 51–5; Hennecke, II, pp. 121–3.

15. See e.g. Irenaeus, *adv.haer.*, III.21.1; V.1.3; Tertullian, *de virg.vel.*, 6.1; *de car.Chr.*, 14; Origen, *hom.in Luc.*, XVII; Ephiphanius, *Pan.*, 30.2.2; 30.3.1.

16. Irenaeus, *adv.haer.*, I.26.2; III.11.7; Epiphanius, *Pan.*, 30.3.7.

17. Epiphanius, *Pan.*, 30.13.2; 30.14.3.

18. Epiphanius, *Pan.*, 30.18.5–6. Cf. Justin, *Dial.* 48.

19. See also Hippolytus, *Ref.*, VII.34.1–2; Eusebius, *HE*, III.27.1–2; Epiphanius, *Pan.*, 30.14.4; 30.16.3; *Clem.Recog.*, I.48.

20. Epiphanius, *Pan.*, 30.13.7.

21. Epiphanius, *Pan.*, 30.13.8.

22. Epiphanius, *Pan.*, 30.16.4; see also 30.3.4. Also Tertullian, *de car.Chr.*, 14.5; though see Klijn and Reinink, pp. 21f.

23. For further discussion see Klijn and Reinink, pp. 33f.; Danielou, *Theology*, ch. 4; Longenecker, *Christology*, pp. 26ff.; Schoeps, *Theologie*, pp. 78–82; *Jewish Christianity*, pp. 62ff.

24. Epiphanius, *Pan.*, 19.3.6; 30.16.5, 7; *Recog.*, I.35ff.; *Hom.*, III.45.

25. So Danielou, *Theology* p. 64 (citing particularly Cullmann).

26. Against Schoeps, *Theologie*, pp. 440–8; *Jewish Christianity*, pp. 42–4.

27. Cf. Bauer, *Orthodoxy*, p. 236; H. Koester, 'The Theological Aspects of Primitive Christian Heresy', *FRP*, p. 83; Schoeps, *Jewish Christianity*: 'The delay of the Parousia made possible the development of the Catholic church, but the Ebionite communities which derived from the primitive church in Jerusalem were not to survive this brute fact since they had deliberately remained at a more primitive stage of christology, a stage based on the expectation of the Son of man' (p. 65).

28. See further R. Banks, 'Matthew's Understanding of the Law: Authenticity and Interpretation in Matthew 5.17–20', *JBL*, 93, 1974, pp. 226–42; also *Jesus and the Law*, pp. 203–26; R. A. Guelich, *The Sermon on th Mount*, Word 1982, pp. 134–74; U. Luz, *Das Evangelium nach Matthaus*, EKK 1/1, Benziger/Neukirchener 1985, pp. 241–2.

29. Matt. 3.15; 5.6, 10, 20; 6.1, 33; 21.32.

30. See A. Sand, *Das Gesetz und die Propheten: Untersuchungen zur Theologie des Evangeliums nach Matthäus*, Regensburg 1974, ch. 7.

31. See D. R. Catchpole, 'The Synoptic Divorce Material as a Traditio-historical Problem', *BJRL*, 57, 1974, pp. 93ff.; J. A. Fitzmyer, 'The Matthean Divorce Texts and some new Palestinian Evidence', *Theological Studies*, 37, 1976, pp. 197–226.

32. For other examples of Matthew's 'casuistic' redaction of Mark see C. E. Carlston, 'The Things that Defile (Mark 7.14) and the Law in Matthew and Mark', *NTS*, 15, 1968–69, pp. 86ff. See further my 'Jesus and Ritual Purity: a study of the tradition history of Mk 7.15', *Jesus, Paul and the Law*, SPCK 1990, ch. 2.

33. As noted above (p. 88), Gerhardsson has argued plausibly that Matt. 4.1–11 is a midrash on Deut. 6–8. Here the Israel typology is stronger than the specific Moses typology.

34. Though see Banks, *Jesus and the Law*, pp. 230ff.

35. For various expositions of this Moses typology motif in Matthew see those cited in Sand, *Gesetz*, pp. 101ff., Dunn, *Jesus*, III n. 19, and Banks, *Jesus and the Law*, p. 230 n. 1.

36. The echo of Deut. 18.15 in the transfiguration scene (Matt. 17.5 – 'Hear him') is simply taken over from Mark 9.7.

37. See particularly G. Barth in G. Bornkamm, G. Barth and H. I. Held, *Tradition and Interpretation in Matthew*, 1960, ET SCM Press 1963, pp. 62–105; Sand, *Gesetz*.

38. See W. D. Davies, *The Setting of the Sermon on the Mount*, Cambridge University Press 1964, p. 316–41. Notice also that it is Peter who is given prominence rather than James (see above §30.3).

39. See Schoeps, *Theologie* pp. 188–218; *Jewish Christianity*, pp. 99–109.

40. See W. G. Kümmel, *Introduction to the New Testament*, revised 1973, ET SCM Press 1975, pp. 406f.

41. See further J. B. Mayor, *The Epistle of St James*, Macmillan ²1897, pp. lxxxivff.; F. Mussner, *Der Jakobusbrief*, Herder ²1967, pp. 47–51.

41a. See further my *Romans*, p. 197.

42. Irenaeus, *adv.haer.*, I.26.2; Epiphanius, *Pan.*, 28.5.3; 30.16.9.

43. Eusebius, *dem.ev.*, III.5 – James 'whom those formerly living in Jerusalem called "the righteous one" because of the excellencies of his virtue'; Marius Victorinus, *in ep.ad Gal.*, 4.12. See also Danielou, *Theology*, pp. 370f.

44. Cf. Bauer, *Orthodoxy*: 'Paul was the only heresiarch known to the apostolic age – the only one who was so considered in that period at least from one particular perspective (p. 236).

44a. I have written a good deal more on this passage since *U&D* (see my *Jesus, Paul and the Law*, SPCK, 1990); but I have left the text here unaltered as my earliest statement on a theme which came increasingly to occupy my attention in the 1980s. See also P. J. Achtemeier, *The Quest for Unity in the New Testament Church*, Fortress 1987.

45. It may just be relevant that in later tradition (as early as Origen) Peter was regarded as the first bishop of Antioch (see O. Cullmann, *Peter: Disciple, Apostle, Martyr*, ET SCM Press ²1962, p. 54 n. 60); perhaps also indicative is the fact that the next letter we know of to have been addressed to the churches in Galatia is attributed to Peter!

46. Cf. E. Haenchen, *The Acts of the Apostles*, ET Blackwell 1971, pp. 475ff.; Koester, *'Gnomai Diaphoroi'*, *Trajectories*, pp. 121f.; and the general thesis of J. W. Drane, *Paul, Libertine or Legalist?*, SPCK 1975.

47. See especially E. Käsemann, 'Die Legitimität des Apostles', *ZNW*, 41, 1942, pp. 33–71; reprinted separately as a booklet in 1956 (Darmstadt); and again in K. H. Rengstorf, *Das Paulusbild in der neuren deutschen Forschung*, Darmstadt 1969, pp. 475–521; C. K. Barrett, 'Christianity at Corinth', *BJRL*, 46, 1964, pp. 286–97; 'PSEUDAPOSTOLOI, II Cor. 11.13', *MBBR*, pp. 377–96; 'Paul's Opponents in II Corinthians', *NTS*, 17, 1970–71, pp.233–54; (all three essays reprinted in Barrett's *Essays on Paul*, SPCK 1982); *II Corinthians*, A. & C. Black 1973, pp. 5–10, 28–32, 277f. See also above pp. 70f., 179f.

48. Barrett, 'Pseudapostoloi', pp. 384f.

49. So Käsemann and Barrett. Paul had, after all, already been somewhat dismissive of the 'pillar apostles' in Gal. 2.6, 9.

50. Barrett, *II Corinthians*, p. viii.

51. See also Haenchen, *Acts*, pp. 611–14; O. Cullmann, 'Dissensions within the Early Church', *New Testament Issues*, ed., R. Batey, SCM Press 1970, pp. 124ff.;

A. J. Mattill, 'The Purpose of Acts: Schneckenburger Reconsidered', *AHGFFB*, pp. 115ff.; Achtemeier, *Quest.*

52. Matt. 13.57 and John 4.44 have the character more of a proverbial saying than of a christological affirmation.

53. Origen, *cont. Cels.*, V.61; Eusebius, *HE*, III.27.3.

54. See M. J. Suggs, *Wisdom, Christology and Law in Matthew's Gospel*, Harvard 1970, pp. 55–61, 95–100; Dunn, *Christology*, pp. 197–206.

55. See J. A. T. Robinson, *Human Face*, pp. 156ff.

56. For possible links between Stephen and Hebrews see W. Manson, *The Epistle to the Hebrews*, Hodder & Stoughton 1951, ch. II.

57. It is difficult to imagine a *Gentile* Christian community where both the argument of Hebrews was directly relevant and questions of law observance were of little moment. The problems seem to be more those of a distinctive Jewish Christian group in a post-AD 70 context. Otherwise, Kümmel, *Introduction*, pp. 398ff.

58. See further above pp. 89f. Hebrews technique here is helpfully set out by G. Vos, *The Teaching of the Epistle to the Hebrews*, Eerdmans 1956, pp.56f.

59. Cf. R. E. Brown, 'Not Jewish Christianity and Gentile Christianity, but Types of Jewish/Gentile Christianity', *CBQ* 45, 1983, pp. 74–9; also (with J. P. Meier) *Antioch and Rome*, Chapman 1983, pp. 2–8.

60. Cf. R. Murray's review: 'it is inaccurate to refer to conservatism as a "heresy"; rather it is one of the seed beds, always pathetic, sometimes tragic, of heresy' (*Heythrop Journal* 20, 1979, pp. 194f.; referring to his own 'Tradition as Criterion of Unity' in *Church Membership and Intercommunion*, ed. J. Kent and R. Murray, London, 1973, pp. 251–80, especially 257–71).

Chapter XII   Hellenistic Christianity

1. On distinctions in terminology (Gnosticism, Gnosis; proto-Gnostic, pre-Gnostic) see U. Bianchi (ed.), *Le Origini dello Gnosticismo*, Leiden 1967, pp. xxviff. The best collection of texts on and from Gnosticism is W. Foerster, *Gnosis*, 2 vols, Oxford University Press 1972, 1974. For the Nag Hammadi texts see J. M. Robinson, *The Nag Hammadi Library in English*, third revised edition, Brill 1988.

2. So e.g. N. A. Dahl, *Das Volk Gottes*, 1941, Darmstadt [2]1963, p. 193; M. Simon, *St Stephen and the Hellenists in the Primitive Church*, Longmans 1958, pp. 11ff.; F. F. Bruce, *New Testament History*, Nelson 1969, pp. 217f.

3. W. L. Knox, *St Paul and the Church of Jerusalem*, Cambridge University Press 1925, p. 48 n. 2. Social factors would be important here too. Since the hellenization of the region, in the wake of Alexander the Great's conquests, embracing of Greek language and customs had always been a mark of the upper class, better educated, well to do. In this case Barnabas (Acts 4.36) and John Mark (Acts 12.12.25) would have to be included in their number.

4. Simon, *Stephen*, p. 12.

5. E. Haenchen, 'The Book of Acts as Source Material for the History of Early Christianity', *SLA*, p. 264.

6. Cf. L. Goppelt, *Apostolic and Post-Apostolic Times*, 1962, ET A. & C. Black 1970, pp. 54f.; M. Hengel, 'Between Jesus and Paul', *Between Jesus and Paul*, SCM Press/Fortress 1983, pp. 13–16.

7. See particularly A. Spiro, 'Stephen's Samaritan Background', in J. Munck, *The Acts of the Apostles*, Anchor Bible 31, Doubleday 1967, pp. 285–300; M. H. Scharlemann, *Stephen: A Singular Saint*, Analecta Biblica 34, Rome 1968, pp. 36–51; C. H. H. Scobie, 'The Origins and Development of Samaritan Christianity', *NTS*, 19, 1972–73, pp. 391–400. Spiro greatly overstates his case and Scharlemann also makes too much of the Samaritan influence on Stephen; note also the cautionary comments of R. Pummer, 'The Samaritan Pentateuch and the New Testament', *NTS*, 22, 1975–76, pp. 441–3; E. Richard, 'Acts 7: An Investigation of the Samaritan Evidence', *CBQ*, 39, 1977, pp. 190–208.

8. Note how Mark also uses the same blasphemous description (*cheiropoiēton*) for the temple in his version of this obscure saying of Jesus (Mark 14.58).

9. Simon, *Stephen*, pp. 45ff.

10. Note the Jerusalem Christians' anxiety to refute the same accusation (of changing or abandoning 'the customs' handed down from Moses) against Paul (Acts 21.21; cf. 6.14); see also above §56.3.

11. Knox, *Jerusalem*, p. 57 n. 42.

12. For possible direct influence of Stephen's views see above p. 263 n. 56. Other suggestions include G. Friedrich, 'Die Gegner des Paulus im II Korintherbrief', *Abraham unser Vater*, O. Michel Festschrift, ed., O. Betz, M. Hengel, P. Schmidt, Leiden 1963, pp. 181–215, who argues for a link between Stephen and Paul's opponents in II Cor., and Cullmann, *Johannine Circle*, who suggests a link between the Hellenists and the circle from which the fourth Gospel emerged.

13. We will pass by Hebrews here, though in some ways it is the most Hellenistic of the NT writings in its use of the Platonic world view (see above pp. 263f.).

14. See J. C. Hurd, *The Origin of I Corinthians*, SPCK 1965, ch. 4, for the different theories on this point.

15. Munck, *Paul*, ch. 5.

16. N. A. Dahl, 'Paul and the Church at Corinth in I Cor. 1.10–4.21', *Christian History and Interpretation: Studies Presented to John Knox*, ed., W. R. Farmer, C. F. D. Moule and R. R. Niebuhr, Cambridge University Press 1967, pp. 313–35.

17. Dahl, op. cit., p. 322.

18. See e.g. Kümmel, *Introduction*, pp. 274f. and those cited by him there. The strongest proponent of the thesis that Paul's opponents were Gnostics is W. Schmithals, *Gnosticism in Corinth*, [2]1965, ET Abingdon 1971.

19. See those cited by E. Yamauchi, *Pre-Christian Gnosticism*, Tyndale Press 1973, pp. 39–43. See further below n. 58. If indeed the II Cor. 10–13 'false apostles' did present Jesus as a supreme miracle worker (see above pp. 70f., 179f.), then we must infer that the Corinthian delight in the miraculous had taken a more explicitly christological turn by the time Paul wrote II Cor. 10–13 (see further below pp. 293f.).

20. See particularly Irenaeus, *adv.haer.*, I.5.4–6.2, 4; 7.5; 8.3; Clement, *Exc.Theod.*, 2f.; 53–58; *Hypostasis of the Archons*, 87.18.

21. Particularly in the very elaborate Valentinian system: see e.g. Irenaeus, *adv.haer.*, I.7.1; 21.5; Clement, *Exc.Theod.*, 44f., 53. Note the certain identification in Valentinian thought between Wisdom and the Spirit (Irenaeus, *ad.haer.*, I.4.1; Hippolytus, *Ref.*, VI.34.1; 35.3f., 7).

22. So Cerinthus, Basilides and the Valentinians (Irenaeus, *adv.haer.*, I.26.1; I.24.4; I.7.2; Clement, *Exc.Theod.*, 61.6).

23. Irenaeus, *adv.haer.*, I.6.2; 25.3f.; Clement, *Strom*, III.10.1; Hippolytus, *Ref.*, VI.19.5; Epiphanius, *Pan.*, 40.2.4.

24. Irenaeus, *adv.haer.*, I.24.2; Hippolytus, *Ref.*, V.9.11; Epiphanius, *Pan.*, 45.2.1–3.

25. Cf. particularly Irenaeus, *adv.haer.*, I.6.3.

26. Basilides – 'The gospel is, according to them, the knowledge of the super-mundane things' (Hippolytus, *Ref.*, VII.27.7). Valentinians – 'The end will come when all that is spiritual is shaped and perfected through knowledge . . .'; 'They claim that they have more knowledge than all others, and that they alone have attained the greatness of the knowledge of the ineffable power'; 'The inner, spiritual man is redeemed through knowledge' (Irenaeus, *adv.haer.*, I.6.1; 13.6; 21.4). See also Hippolytus, *Ref.*, V.6.4, 6; Epiphanius, *Pan.*, 26.10.7–9; 31.7.8f.; *Poimandres*, 26f., 32, etc.

27. Irenaeus, *adv.haer.*, I.6.3; 24.5.

28. On the Corinthians' attitude to baptism and the Lord's Supper see further above §39.5 and pp. 165, 167f.

29. See the brief discussion in Dunn, *Jesus*, pp. 234f. and nn. 176, 177 and 180.

30. As in Irenaeus, *adv.haer.*, I.6.4; 13.6; Clement, *Strom.*, III.1 (Basilides, *Fragments*, 8.3); Hippolytus, *Ref.*, V.8.9, 29; *Acts of Thomas*, 18.34; 36.20; 42.28; 43.20; *Gosp. of Philip*, 31, 100; *Thomas the Contender*, 140.10f.; 145.17.

31. See above §39.5. Cf. *Acts of Thomas*, 26 – 'The apostle said to them: "I am glad and I entreat you to receive this seal and partake with me in this eucharist and praising of the Lord and be perfected by it"'.

32. See J. H. Wilson, 'The Corinthians who say there is no resurrection of the dead', *ZNW*, 59, 1968, pp. 90–107, and those cited by him on pp. 95ff.; also Barrett, *I Corinthians*, pp. 347f.; Robinson, *Trajectories*, pp. 33ff.; J. H. Schütz, *Paul and the Anatomy of Apostolic Authority*, Cambridge University Press 1975, pp. 85f.

33. II Tim. 2.18; Justin, *Dialogue* 80; Irenaeus, *adv.haer.*, I.23.5; II.31.2; Tertullian, *de praes.haer.*, 33.7; *de res.car.*, 19; *Acts of Paul and Thecla*, 14; *Letter to Rheginos*, 49.15ff.; *Gosp. of Philip*, 21, 63, 90, 95. But see further below p. 290.

33a. Further studies have highlighted other, particularly social factors (G. Theissen, *The Social Setting of Pauline Christianity*, 1979, ET Fortress/T. & T. Clark 1982; P. Marshall. *Enmity in Corinth: Social Conventions in Paul's Relations with the Corinthians*, WUNT 2.23. Tübingen 1987); but this simply underlines the complexity of the 'mix' at Corinth, including syncretistic religious elements (especially 'knowledge') which point towards the subsequently fully developed Gnostic systems.

34. See particularly R. Jewett, 'Conflicting Movements in the Early Church as Reflected in Philippians', *NovTest*, 12, 1970, pp. 362–90; Martin, *Philippians*, pp. 22–36. I would probably wish to qualify this conclusion now; see my *Romans*, p. 903; cf. G. F. Hawthorne, *Philippians*, Word Biblical Commentary 43, Word 1983, pp. xliv–xlvii.

35. See e.g. W. L. Knox, *St Paul and the Church of the Gentiles*, Cambridge University Press 1939, p. 170, and the discussion in E. Lohse, *Die Briefe an die Kolosser und an Philemon*, KEK 1968, pp. 173–8. But see also F. O. Francis in F. O. Francis and W. A. Meeks, *Conflict at Colossae*, Scholars 1975; P. T. O'Brien, *Colossians, Philemon*, Word Biblical Commentary 44, Word 1982, pp. 141–6.

36. F. Wisse, 'The Epistle of Jude in the History of Heresiology', *Essays on the Nag Hammadi Texts in Honour of A. Böhlig*, ed., M. Krause, Leiden 1972, pp. 133–43, denies that Jude has a particular historical situation in mind, though he fails to explain how Jude could still envisage such people as accepted participants in Christian love feasts. But see R. J. Bauckham, *Jude, II Peter*, Word Biblical Commentary 50, Word 1983, pp. 11–13.

37. Cf. A. D. Nock, 'Gnosticism', *Essays on Religion and the Ancient World*, ed., Z. Stewart, Oxford University Press 1972: 'What we call Gnosticism seems to me to be the aggregate of a series of individualistic responses to the religious situation – the responses, moreover, of men *who in many cases cannot have thought of themselves as in any way deviationist*. The crystallization of what came to be orthodoxy was a gradual process, a progressive elimination of ideas which proved unacceptable' (p. 954 – my emphasis).

38. J. M. Robinson, '*Logoi Sophon*: on the *Gattung* of Q', *Trajectories*, ch. 3; also in *FRP*, ch. 5; H. Koester, '*Gnomai Diaphoroi*', *Trajectories*, ch. 4 (here see particularly pp. 126–43); also 'One Jesus', *Trajectories*, ch. 5 (here pp. 166–87 – quotation from 186f.) For the relationship of the Oxyrhynchus fragments with Thomas see Hennecke, *Apocrypha*, I, pp. 97–113.

39. 6b, 16, 21b, 26, 33a, 33b, 34, 36, 39a, 44, 45, 46, 47a, 54, 55, 64, 68, 69b, 73, 76b, 78, 86, 89, 91(?), 92a, 94, 95(?), 96, 101, 103, 106b(?), 107.

40. See above pp. 221, 258f.; also G. N. Stanton, 'On the Christology of Q', *CSNT* pp. 36ff.

41. See particularly R. A. Edwards, *A Theology of Q*, Fortress 1976, ch. V.

42. Koester, '*Gnomai Diaphoroi*', *Trajectories*, pp. 138f.; 'One Jesus', *Trajectories*, p. 186.

43. Other good examples of logia manifestly Gnostic in character include 39, 60 and 87.

44. See Edwards, *Q*, pp. 37–43 and those cited by him there; Koester, *Introduction*, vol. 2, p. 148.

45. Robinson *Trajectories*, pp. 82–5, 102f.; cf. J. D. Turner, 'A New Link in the Syrian Judas Thomas Tradition', *Essays on the Nag Hammadi Texts in Honour of A. Böhlig*, ed., M. Krause, Leiden 1972, pp. 115f. See also S. Kloppenborg, *The Formation of Q*, Fortress 1987.

46. *The Hellenistic Mystery-Religions*, [3]1927, ET Pickwick 1978, p. 84.

47. T. Zahn, cited by Bauer, *Orthodoxy*, pp. 224f. See also E. H. Pagels, *The Gnostic Paul*, Fortress 1975, pp. 1ff. The Valentinians were the most important of the second and third century Gnostic systems.

48. Pagels, *Paul*, pp. 57f., 101ff., 121. See also B. A. Pearson, *The Pneumatikos-Psychikos Terminology in I Corinthians*, SBL Dissertation Series 12, 1973, pp. 59, 66f., 71, 80f.; 'By far the most important apostolic authority for the Christian Gnostics was the apostle Paul' (p. 84).

49. W. Schmithals, *Paul and the Gnostics*, ET Abingdon 1972, p. 29.

50. Schmithals, *Gnosticism*, p. 151.

51. Pagels, *Paul*, p. 115.

52. Bauer, *Orthodoxy*, p. 234. We may also recall that the Jewish Christian pseudo-Clementines attacked Paul under the figure of Simon Magus (above p. 241) – the very one whom Justin, Hegesippus and Irenaeus regarded as the earliest Gnostic.

53. Bauer, *Orthodoxy*, p. 221.

54. Tertullian, *adv.Marc.*, – 'Marcion's special and principal work is the separation of the law and the gospel' (1.19).

55. See also E. C. Blackman, *Marcion and his Influence*, SPCK 1948, p. 107.

56. Drane, *Paul*, p. 112; see also pp. 100, 112f., 114, 119. Drane does not make this comment with Marcion in mind; and it is disputable whether Marcion should properly be called a Gnostic; but Marcion does hold several ideas which are also present in Gnosis. Cf. also H. D. Betz. 'Spirit, Freedom and Law: Paul's Message to

the Galatian Churches', *Svensk Exegetisk Arsbok*, 39, 1974, pp. 159–61.

57. Hurd, *I Cor.*, ch. 8; cf. Drane's suggestion that Paul's Corinthian opponents 'had actually quoted his statements in Galatians to prove their own point of view' (p. 61). This thesis too, though containing valuable insights, goes beyond the evidence.

58. It is unlikely that Paul was indebted to a more developed Gnosticism in the form of a Sophia myth in I Cor. 2 (see above n. 19); and if I Cor. 15.44ff. shows any awareness of Primal man speculation (but see my *Christology*, pp. 123–5), Paul seeks to correct it rather than simply to draw on it. See the full discussions of L. Schottroff, *Der Glaubende und die feindliche Welt*, Neukirchen 1970, chs 4–5; cf. Pearson, *Pneumatikos-Psychikos*, ch 3–4.

59. See Dunn, *Jesus*, §21, particularly pp. 120f.

60. See texts in M. L. Peel, 'Gnostic Eschatology and the New Testament', *NovTest* 12, 1970, pp. 159–62; also *The Epistle to Rheginos*, SCM Press 1969, pp. 146–9.

61. See e.g. Luke 24.39; Ignatius, *Smyrn.*, 3; II Clement 9; Apoc. Peter 4, 17; Tertullian, *de res.car.*; and the Old Roman Creed's belief in 'the resurrection of the flesh'. But note also the view of Origen and the impact it had (see J. N. D. Kelly, *Early Christian Doctrines*, A. & C. Black [2]1960, pp. 470–2, 474–9).

62. Cf. *Exc.Theod.*, 23.2–3, cited by Pagels, *Paul*, p. 14.

63. So apparently the Valentinian, Alexander, attacked by Tertullian, *de car.Chr.*, 16. See also Tertullian, *adv.Marc.*, V.14.1–3, and other passages cited by M. F. Wiles, *The Divine Apostle*, Cambridge University Press 1967, pp. 81f.

64. Tertullian, *adv.Marc.*, III.5.

65. Pagels, *Paul*, p. 104.

66. Cited by Wiles, *Apostle*, pp. 49f.

67. Wiles, *Apostle*, p. 133.

68. Wiles, *Apostle*, p. 136; see also T. F. Torrance, *The Doctrine of Grace in the Apostolic Fathers*, Oliver & Boyd 1948.

69. Irenaeus, *adv.haer.*, V.9.4; Tertullian, *de res.car.*, 49–50. See also Wiles, *Apostle*, pp. 4ff.

70. Epiphanius, *Pan.*, 31.7.6.

71. Pagels, *Paul*, pp. 32f., 110.

72. Pagels, *Paul*, pp. 53, 55f., 82, 126f.

73. Pagels, *Paul*, p. 63. See further R. McL. Wilson, *Gnosis and the New Testament*, Blackwell 1968, ch. III.

74. See A. Harnack, *Marcion*, Leipzig [2]1924, pp. 45–51; Blackman, *Marcion*, pp. 44f.

74a. This moral/ethical boundary drawn by Paul should have been given more prominence; see pp. 305f.

75. See references in index, 'Pleroma', of Foerster, *Gnosis*, II, p. 337.

76. Cf. Dunn, *Jesus*, §55 and above p. 195.

77. Marcion followed Paul in placing a high value on Christ's death (Harnack, *Marcion*, pp. 131ff.), but this was wedded to an explicitly docetist understanding of the incarnation (pp. 124f.); so his christology has only an apparent contact with Paul's kerygma of Christ crucified.

78. W. O. E. Oesterley, *The Jewish Background of the Christian Liturgy*, Oxford University Press 1925.

79. Cf. Bauer, *Orthodoxy*, pp. 238f.

80. Cf. H. Schneemelcher, 'Paulus in der griechischen Kirche des zweiten

Jahrhunderts', *ZKG*, 75, 1964, pp. 1–20; E. Dassmann, *Der Stachel im Fleisch. Paulus in der frühchristlichen Literatur bei Irenaus*, Aschendorff 1979. A. Lindemann, *Paulus im altesten Christentum*, Tübingen 1979, does not carry his analysis through as far as Irenaeus.

81. See Irenaeus, *adv.haer.*, praef.; III. 13.3; 14.1–4 (referred to by Pagels, *Paul*, p. 161).

82. Bauer, *Orthodoxy*, p. 227; as further illustration of the point he refers to the *Acts of Paul*, and *Epistula Apostolorum*. Cf. Bousset who talks of 'the ecclesiastically tempered Paulinism, the Paulinism that has been divested of all Gnostic dangers and tendencies' (*Kyrios Christos*, p. 21). Note also the slightly more qualified judgment of C. K. Barrett, 'Pauline Controversies in the Post-Pauline Period' *NTS*, 20, 1973–74, pp. 229–45.

83. Irenaeus, *adv.haer.*, III.11.7. See J. N. Sanders, *The Fourth Gospel in the Early Church*, Cambridge University Press 1943, pp. 55–66.

84. See E. H. Pagels, *The Johannine Gospel in Gnostic Exegesis: Heracleon's Commentary on John*, SBL Monograph 17, Abingdon 1973.

85. Sanders, *Fourth Gospel*, pp. 65–84.

86. A. Hilgenfeld, *Das Urchristenthum*, Jena 1855, cited by H. Harris, *The Tübingen School*, Oxford University Press 1975, p. 225.

87. Cited by H. A. W. Meyer, *The Gospel of John*, ET 1874, p. 40.

88. R. Bultmann, 'Die Bedeutung der neuerschlossenen mandäischen und manichäischen Quellen für der Verständnis des Johannesevangeliums', *ZNW*, 24, 1925, pp. 100–146, reprinted in *Exegetica*, Tübingen 1967, pp. 55–104; see also his *Primitive Christianity in its Contemporary Setting*, ET Thames & Hudson 1956, pp. 163f.

89. R. H. Fuller, *The New Testament in Current Study*, SCM Press 1963, p. 136.

90. See those cited by Yamauchi, *Pre-Christian Gnosticism*, pp. 164–9.

91. G. W. MacRae, 'The *Ego*-Proclamation in Gnostic Sources'. *The Trial of Jesus*, ed., E. Bammel, SCM Press 1970, pp.122–34; R. Schnackenburg, *Das Johannes evangelium*, Part II, Herder 1971, pp. 162–6.

92. See e.g., those cited by Wilson, *Gnosis*, pp. 45f.; R. Kysar, *The Fourth Evangelist and his Gospel*, Augsburg 1975, pp. 102–46. After further study I would now place John's Gospel still more firmly within a broad (and diverse) Jewish milieu, wherein apocalyptic and mystical concerns were particularly prominent, which *inter alia* provides a fuller explanation of the important descending/ascending motif in John. See further my 'Let John be John', *Das Evangelium und die Evangelien*, hrsg. P. Stuhlmacher, Mohr: Tübingen, 1983, pp. 309–39. But the first paragraph of §64.2 can remain unaltered.

93. See Brown, *John*, pp. cxxiiff.

94. See e.g. the indices in Foerster, *Gnosis*.

95. See particularly J. H. Charlesworth, 'A Critical Comparison of the Dualism of 1QS 3.13–4.26 and the "Dualism" Contained in the Gospel of John', *NTS*, 15, 1968, pp. 389–418; reprinted in *John and Qumran*, ed., J. H. Charlesworth, Chapman 1972, pp. 76–106. The earlier discussion is reviewed by H. Braun, *Qumran und das Neue Testament*, Tübingen 1966, II, pp. 119–23.

96. For Qumran see e.g. 1QS 3.13–4.26; CD 2.11–3; IQM 13.9–13; 1QH 7.6–12; 14.13–6; 15.13–22. For Gnosticism see e.g. the discussion in Pagels, *Heracleon's Commentary*, ch. 6.

97. Bultmann, *John*, pp. 24–31; S. Schulz, *Das Evangelium nach Johannes*, NTD 1972, pp. 26–9. The parallels are assessed also by Schnackenburg, *John*, I, pp. 489ff.

98. See e.g., Dodd, *Interpretation of the Fourth Gospel*, pp. 274f.; Brown, *John*,

pp. 521ff.; Dunn, *Christology*, pp. 239–45; and cf. G. W. MacRae, 'The Jewish Background of the Gnostic Sophia Myth', *NovTest*, 12, 1970, particularly pp. 88–94.

99. Irenaeus, *adv.haer.*, I.15.3; 30.12, 14; Hippolytus, *Ref.*, V.12.6. 'The decisive factor in this is that the concept of the descent and ascent of the redeemer, which is of fundamental importance for John, cannot be demonstrated in Judaism but is characteristic of Gnosticism' (Kümmel, *Introduction*, p. 227); cf. Schnackenburg, *John*, I, pp. 550–53. But see C. H. Talbert, 'The Myth of a Descending-Ascending Redeemer in Mediterranean Antiquity', *NTS*, 22, 1975–76, pp. 418–40; J. A. Bühner, *Der Gesandte und sein Weg im 4. Evangelium*, Tübingen 1977; and see also above n. 92.

100. Käsemann, *Testament*, pp. 9f., 13; cf. the equivalent presentation of Bousset, *Kyrios Christos*, pp. 217ff.; S. Angus, *The Religious Quests of the Graeco-Roman World*, Murray 1929, pp. 389ff.; and the more extreme theses of Schulz, *Johannes*, especially pp. 211f., and Schottroff, *Glaubende*, pp. 268–96.

100a. See also particularly M. M. Thompson, *The Humanity of Jesus in the Fourth Gospel*, Fortress 1988.

101. Schnackenburg, *John*. I, p. 268; cf. C. Colpe, 'New Testament and Gnostic Christology', *Religions in Antiquity: Essays in Memory of E. R. Goodenough*, ed., J. Neusner, Leiden 1968. pp. 233f., 236f. See also Dunn, *Christology*, particularly p. 347 n.104.

102. The water from Jesus' side represents a fulfilment of 7.38f. (see Dunn *Baptism*, pp. 187f.; and above p. 169); the Spirit for John is precisely the Spirit of the crucified one (cf. 19.30).

103. See particularly R. T. Fortna, *The Gospel of Signs. A Reconstruction of the Narrative source Underlying the Fourth Gospel*, Cambridge University Press 1970; also *The Fourth Gospel and its Predecessor. From Narrative Source to Present Gospel*, T. & T. Clark 1989; W. Nicol, *The Sēmeia in the Fourth Gospel*, *SNT*, XXXII, 1972; H. M. Teeple, *The Literary Origin of the Gospel of John*, Evanston 1974.

104. See further, e.g. Nicol, *Sēmeia*, pp. 99–106.

105. Cf. G. Bornkamm, 'Zur Interpretation des Johannes-Evangeliums', *Geschichte und Glaube*, I, München 1968, pp. 115ff.; J. Becker, 'Wunder und Christologie', *NTS*, 16, 1969–70, pp. 136–48; Fortna, *Signs*, p. 224; Schottroff, *Glaubende*, pp. 245–68; Koester and Robinson, *Trajectories*, pp. 188f., 238–60.

106. See further R. E. Brown, *The Community of the Beloved Disciple*, Chapman 1979, pp. 109–23.

107. The same is true of the ethical principles and guidelines drawn by Paul (pp. 293, 305f.), since the primary emphasis falls on a walk in accordance both with the Spirit of Christ (Rom. 8.4–6, 12–14; Gal. 5.16–25) and with the traditions of Christ's ethical teaching (above p. 68), particularly love of neighbour as fulfilling the law (Rom. 13.8–10; Gal. 5.14).

Chapter XIII   Apocalyptic Christianity

1. See e.g. R. W. Funk, ed., *Apocalypticism*, *JThC*, 6, 1969; K. Koch, *The Rediscovery of Apocalyptic*, 1970, ET SCM Press 1972; J. Barr, 'Jewish Apocalyptic in Recent Scholarly Study', *BJRL*, 58, 1975–76, pp. 9–35. See also nn. 2–3 below. C. Rowland, *Radical Christianity. A Reading of Recovery*, Polity 1988, highlights the continuing

influence of apocalyptic thought in later centuries. For the investigation of apocalypticism prior to 1947 see J. M. Schmidt, *Die jüdsiche Apokalyptik*, Neukirchen 1969.

2. See particularly P. D. Hanson, *The Dawn of Apocalyptic*, Fortress 1975, [2]1979, pp. 10–12, 429ff.; J. J. Collins, ed., *Apocalypse. The Morphology of a Genre. Semeia 14*, 1979, pp. 1–19; J. J. Collins, *The Apocalyptic Imagination*, Crossroad 1984, ch. 1 especially p. 2. This clarification hopefully meets the most important of the objections to the continued use of the word by T. F. Glasson, 'What is Apocalyptic?', *NTS*, 27, 1980–81, pp. 98–105.

2a. C. Rowland, *The Open Heaven. A Study of Apocalyptic in Judaism and Early Christianity*, SPCK 1982; also *Christian Origins*, SPCK 1985, pp. 56–64.

3. For convenience I draw particularly on P. Vielhauer's analysis in Hennecke, *Apocrypha*, II, pp. 582–94. See also particularly W. Bousset and H. Gressmann, *Die Religion des Judentums im späthellenistischen Zeitalter*, Tübingen [4]1966, ch. XIII; C. K. Barrett, *The New Testament Background: Selected Documents*, SPCK 1956, pp. 227–55; Russell, *Apocalyptic*; Koch, *Apocalyptic*, pp. 23–33. See also Foreword, p. xxviii.

4. Vielhauer in Hennecke, *Apocrypha*, II, p. 582. It should be noted that this definition is quite acceptable to Rowland (above n. 2a).

4a. See D. G. Meade, *Pseudonymity and Canon*, WUNT 39, Tübingen 1986.

5. Barrett, *Background*, p. 231. E.g. cf. Ass.Mos. 7.1ff. with 2–6; Sib.Or. IV before and after line 134.

6. D. N. Freedman, 'The Flowering of Apocalyptic', in Funk, *Apocalypticism*, p. 173.

6a. Collins, *Imagination*, p. 31.

7. Vielhauer in Hennecke, *Apocrypha*, II, p. 588.

8. Other references in Bousset-Gressmann, *Religion*, pp. 250f.; Strack-Billerbeck, IV.977–86; Russell, *Apocalyptic*, pp. 272–6; W. Schmithals, *The Apocalyptic Movement: Introduction and Interpretation*, 1973, ET Abingdon 1975, pp. 25f.; and above p. 153.

9. See Russell, *Apocalyptic*, pp. 297–303.

10. See further Dunn, *Jesus*, pp. 117f.

10a. See further W. Harnisch, *Verhangnis und Verheissung der Geschichte. Untersuchungen zum Zeitnund Geschichtsverstandnis im 4. Buch Ezra und in der Baruch-Apokalypse*, Göttingen 1969, especially pp. 268–321; C. L. Holman, *Eschatological Delay in Jewish and Early Christian Apocalyptic Literature*, PhD thesis, Nottingham 1982.

10b. Cf. Jub. 32.21; also Dan. 2.21; Ass.Mos. 12.4f.; I Enoch 39.11; 92.2; IQS III.15f.

11. H. H. Rowley, *The Relevance of Apocalyptic*, Lutterworth, 1944, [3]1963, p. 38 (my emphasis). See further Hanson, *Dawn of Apocalyptic*.

12. 'The Beginnings of Christian Theology', in Funk, *Apocalypticism*, p. 40; also *NTQT*, p. 102.

12a. But see Dunn, *Christology*, p. 304 n. 139.

13. J. Weiss, *Jesus' Proclamation of the Kingdom of God*, 1892, ET SCM Press 1971, p. 114. Cf. particularly Sib. Or., III. 46f., 767; Ass. Mos., 10.1ff.; IQM 6.6; 12.7.

14. See particularly W. G. Kümmel, 'Eschatological Expectation in the Proclamation of Jesus' (1964), *FRP*, pp. 29–48.

15. See particularly W. G. Kümmel, *Promise and Fulfilment*, [3]1956, ET SCM Press [2]1961, pp. 64–83.

16. Jeremias, *Theology*, I, pp. 139f.; cf. A. L. Moore, *The Parousia in the New*

Testament, SNT, XIII, 1966, p. 205f.

17. Käsemann in Funk, *Apocalypticism,* p. 40, and *NTQT,* p. 102; Cf. E. Linnemann, 'Zeitansage und Zeitvorstellung in der Verkündigung Jesu', *JCHT,* pp. 237–63.

18. Koch, *Apocalyptic,* p. 78; W. Schmithals, 'Jesus und die Apokalyptik', *JCHT,* pp. 64–9.

19. See more fully Dunn, *Jesus,* pp. 158–62. The preceding sentence betrays the older definition of 'apocalyptic' on which the chapter was originally structured; all visions of heaven or of heavenly beings can properly be described as 'apocalyptic' (Rowland).

20. Cf. W. Pannenberg, *Revelation as History,* 1961, ET Macmillan 1968, pp. 141ff.

21. See particularly L. Hartmann, *Prophecy Interpreted,* Uppsala 1966; J. Lambrecht, *Die Redaktion der Markus-Apokalypse,* Analecta Biblica 28, Rome 1967; R. Pesch, *Naherwartungen: Tradition und Redaktion in Markus 13,* Dusseldorf 1968; L. Gaston, *No Stone on Another, SNT,* XXIII, 1970, ch. II; though see also D. Wenham, *The Rediscovery of Jesus' Eschatological Discourse,* JSOT Press 1984.

22. See J. T. Milik, *Ten Years of Discovery in the Wilderness of Judaea,* 1957, ET SCM Press 1959, pp. 41f.

23. See also W. Thüsing, *Erhöhungsvorstellung und Parusieerwartung in der ältesten nachösterlichen Christologie,* Stuttgarter Bibelstudien 42, 1969. But I. H. Marshall, 'Is Apocalyptic the Mother of Christian Theology?', *Tradition and Interpretation in the New Testament,* E. E. Ellis Festschrift, ed. G. F. Hawthorne, Eerdmans 1987, pp.33–42, discounts the evidence overmuch in his attempt to dispute the intensity of the imminent expectation of the earliest believers.

24. On the eschatological significance of the trumpet see G. Friedrich, *TDNT,* VII, p. 84.

25. See particularly Kümmel, *Introduction,* pp. 264–9; R. Jewett, *The Thessalonian Correspondence,* Fortress 1986. Otherwise see now particularly G. S. Holland, *The Tradition that You Received from Us: 2 Thessalonians in the Pauline Tradition,* Tübingen 1988.

26. It is far from clear what *to katechon, ho katechōn* mean; suggestions include the Roman state, a divine or heavenly power, the gospel, and even (very unlikely) Paul himself. See particularly C. H. Giblin, *The Threat to Faith: an exegetical and theological re-examination of II Thessalonians 2,* Analecta Biblica 31, Rome 1967, pp. 167–242; Best, *Thessalonians,* pp. 295–302.

27. On I Cor. 15.20–28 see the most recent studies of E. Schweizer, 'I Korinther 15.20–28 als Zeugnis paulinischer Eschatologie und ihrer Verwandschaft mit der Verkündigung Jesu', *JuP,* pp. 301–14; J. Baumgarten, *Paulus und die Apokalyptik,* Neukirchen 1975, pp. 99–106; L. J. Kreitzer, *Jesus and God in Paul's Eschatology,* JSOT Press 1987.

28. See G. Dalman, *The Words of Jesus,* ET T. & T. Clark 1902, pp. 155f.; G. Delling, *TDNT,* VIII, pp. 65f. On the echoes of Daniel in Mark 13 see Hartman, *Prophecy,* ch. V.

29. Cf. Strack-Billerbeck, I, p. 950.

30. Josephus, *Bell.,* II.258–63; VI.285–315.

31. W. Marxsen, *Mark the Evangelist,* 1956, ET Abingdon 1969, pp. 185f.

32. Cf. E. Franklin, *Christ the Lord: a Study in the Purpose and Theology of Luke–Acts,* SPCK 1975, pp. 12–21. Other references in C. H. Talbert, 'Shifting Sands: the Recent Study of the Gospel of Luke', *Interpretation,* 30, 1976, p. 386 n. 38.

33. Dio Cassius 67.14.1–3; Eusebius, *HE,* IV.26.9.

33a. Cf. Hanson, *Dawn* pp. 428–9; A. Y. Collins in Collins, ed., *Apocalypse* pp. 70–72.

34. Vielhauer in Hennecke, *Apocrypha*, II, p. 624.

35. Cf. the protest of Koch, *Apocalyptic*.

36. Despite the various hesitations (at points justified) of e.g. G. Ebeling, 'The Ground of Christian Theology' (1961), ET in Funk, *Apocalypticism*, pp. 47–68; E. Lohse, 'Apokalyptik und Christologie', *ZNW*, 62, 1971, pp. 48–67; W. G. Rollins, 'The New Testament and Apocalyptic', *NTS*, 17, 1970–71, pp. 454–76; L. Morris, *Apocalyptic*, Tyndale Press 1973.

37. Cf. Käsemann's concluding remarks (Funk, *Apocalypticism*, p. 46, and *NTQT*, p. 107).

38. O. Cullmann, *Christ and Time*, 1946, ET SCM Press ²1962, p. 88; cf. the thesis of Baumgarten that Paul 'de-apocalypticizes' the eschatological content of the gospel (*Paulus*, pp. 232ff.). See also E. S. Fiorenza, *The Book of Revelation*, Fortress 1985, p. 3.

39. Cf. Ebeling, in Funk, *Apocalypticism*, pp. 53–9.

40. Cf. E. Käsemann, 'On the Topic of Primitive Christian Apocalyptic', (1962), ET in Funk, *Apocalypticism*, pp. 126ff., and *NTQT*, pp. 131ff. See more generally Beker (n. 41a below); L. E. Keck, 'Paul and Apocalyptic Theology', *Interpretation* 38, 1984, pp. 229–41.

41. Note here R. M. Grant's thesis that 'Gnosticism originated out of the failure of the apocalyptic hope' (*Gnosticism and Early Christianity*, 1959, Harper ²1966, p. 38).

41a. Hence the title of J. C. Beker's study of Pauline theology – *Paul the Apostle. The Triumph of God in Life and Thought*, Fortress/T. & T. Clark 1980.

42. Rowley, *Relevance*, p. 189.

43. Cullmann, cited by Rowley, *Relevance*, p. 164.

44. Quoted by Rowley, *Relevance*, p. 181.

45. Freedman in Funk, *Apocalypticism*, p. 173.

Chapter XIV   Early Catholicism

1. Cf. K. H. Neufeld, '"Frühkatholizismus" – Idee und Begriff', *ZKT*, 94, 1972, pp. 1–28. Cf. also S. Schulz, *Die Mitte der Schrift*, Stuttgart 1976, pp. 29–84, though Schulz finds the recognition of early catholicism in the NT foreshadowed in Luther's setting Hebrews, James, Jude and Revelation apart from the rest of the canon (pp. 14–28).

2. A. Schwegler, *Das nachapostolische Zeitalter in den Hauptomomenten seiner Entwicklung*, Tübingen 1846 – usefully summarized in Harris, *Tübingen School*, pp. 202–7.

3. A. Ritschl, *Die Entstehung der altkatholischen Kirche*, Bonn ¹857.

4. A. Harnack, *The Constitution and Law of the Church in the First Two Centuries*, 1910, ET Williams & Norgate 1910, p. 254.

5. Harnack, *History of Dogma*, Vol. I, p. 218. But see also pp. 56f.

6. Harnack, *What is Christianity?*, 1900, ET Williams & Norgate 1901, Lecture XI. Harnack defined Gnosticism as 'the radical (or acute) hellenizing of Christianity' (*Dogma*, I, p. 227).

7. Heitmüller, *Taufe*, pp. 18–26, E. Troeltsch, *The Social Teaching of the Christian Churches*, 1911, ET Allen & Unwin 1931, I, pp. 95f.

8. R. Sohm, *Wesen und Ursprung des Katholizismus*, [2]1912, Darmstadt 1967, pp. 13, 15.

9. M. Werner, *The Formation of Christian Dogma*, 1941, ET A. & C. Black 1957, pp. 25, 297.

10. E. Käsemann, 'Paul and Early Catholicism' (1963) *NTQT*, p. 237.

11. Cf. now G. Strecker, *Die Johannesbriefe*, KEK Göttingen, 1989, pp. 348–54. Cf. F. Hahn, 'Frühkatholizismus als ökumenisches Problem', *Exegestische Beiträge zum ökumenischen Gespräch*, Göttingen 1986, pp. 66–75. Schulz works with a maximizing list of early catholic characteristics (including 'the misunderstanding of the Pauline message of justification as the theology of the cross' and 'the unpauline understanding of the law' – *Schrift*, p. 80) so that 'early Catholicism' in Schulz's discussion becomes too broad a concept embracing whatever is not in accord with the Paulinism of the principal Pauline letters (he finds early catholic tendencies and characteristics in no less than 20 of the 27 NT writings). Far too little consideration is given to the other forces and considerations which shaped much of the nonpauline material (particularly the more specifically Jewish Christian documents); see e.g. his treatment of Matthew and the law (pp. 183–9) and his description of Luke–Acts as 'anti-enthusiastic' (pp. 153–5). For an alternative schematization of early catholicism see U. Luz, 'Erwägungen zur Entstehung des "Frühkatholizismus", Eine Skizze', *ZNW* 65, 1974, pp. 88–111. Hahn properly points out that 'the designation Frühkatholizismus is useable only as a partial concept for individual phenomena, not as a complete description of a period of early church history continuous with primitive Christianity' (Das Problem des Frühkatholizismus', *Beiträge* p. 49). See also the disclaimers of §53 above. The debate, including Schulz's contribution in particular, has been reviewed by J. Rohde, 'Die Diskussion um den Frühkatholizismus im Neuen Testament, dargestellt am Beispiel des Amtes in den spätneutestamentlichen Schriften', in J. Rogge and G. Schille, *Frühkatholizismus im ökumenischen Gespräch*, Berlin 1983, pp. 27–51.

12. See M. Hornschuh in Hennecke, *Apocrypha*, II, pp. 74–9.

12a. Cf. what follows with P. J. Achtemeier, 'An Apocalyptic Shift in Early Christian Tradition: Reflections on Some Canonical Evidence', *CBQ* 45, 1983, pp. 231–48.

13. Cf. Dunn, *Jesus*, §20.2.

14. Cf. particularly G. Klein, 'Apokalyptische Naherwartung bei Paulus', *Neues Testament und christliche Existenz: Festschrift für Herbert Braun*, ed., H. D. Betz and L. Schottroff, Tübingen 1973, pp. 244–58. See also above pp. 25, 336 n. 38.

15. He achieves the same effect by his introduction to the parable of the pounds – Luke 19.11; and his redaction of Mark 12.1 (Luke 20.9 – 'for a long time'); cf. Luke 17.20f.; 22.69 (par. Mark 14.62).

16. So P. Vielhauer, 'On the "Paulinism" of Acts' (1950, ET 1963), *SLA*, pp. 45–8; H. Conzelmann, *The Theology of St Luke*, 1953, [2]1957, ET Faber & Faber 1961, pp. 131f.; E. Käsemann, 'New Testament Questions of Today' (1957), *NTQT*, pp. 21f.; Schulz, *Schrift*, p. 134.

17. O. Cullmann, *Salvation in History*, 1965, ET SCM Press 1967; and above pp. 242f.

18. C. K. Barrett, 'The Eschatology of the Epistle to the Hebrews', *BNTE*, p. 391; cf. H. Conzelmann, *An Outline of the Theology of the New Testament*, [2]1968, ET SCM Press 1969, pp. 312f.

19. Cf. E. Käsemann, 'An Apologia for Primitive Christian Eschatology' (1952) *ENTT*, p. 194.

19a. But see also R. J. Bauckham, *Jude, II Peter*, Word Biblical Commentary 50, Word 1983, pp. 151–4.

20. See e.g. H. Conzelmann, *RGG*[3], III.139; F. Mussner, *LTK*, VI.89f. See further New Foreword on ch. VI (n. 24).

21. See further Dunn, *Jesus*, p. 346f.

22. Cf. K. M. Fischer, *Tendenz und Absicht des Epheserbriefes*, Göttingen 1973, pp. 21–39.

23. See further Dunn, *Jesus*, pp. 348f.

24. M. Schneckenburger, *Über den Zweck der Apostelgeschichte*, Bern 1841; summarized in W. W. Gasque's useful study, *A History of the Criticism of the Acts of the Apostles*, Tübingen 1975, pp. 34ff. See also Mattill, 'Purpose of Acts' (Bruce Festschrift), pp. 108–22.

25. See further G. W. H. Lampe, *St Luke and the Church of Jerusalem*, Athlone Press 1969.

26. Luke does call Paul and Barnabas 'apostles' in Acts 14.4, 14, but only in the 'missionary journey' which was immediately and directly sponsored by the church at Antioch (13.1–3), so that 'apostle' in these two passages is used in the earlier sense of 'missionary' = apostle from Antioch, and does not carry the same weight as 'apostle' when used of the twelve in Jerusalem (cf. II Cor. 8.23; Phil. 2.25).

27. 'The historical study of the last 100 years has not shown that the conflicts, tensions, and resolutions described by F. C. Baur are imaginary; it has shown that they belong to earlier dates than those to which Baur assigned them' (Barrett, 'Pauline Controversies', p. 243).

28. Peter *had* a very significant role to play in preserving the unity of earliest Christianity (see further below p. 385). But if the above presentation is at all securely grounded it becomes impossible to trace back early catholicism, or in particular, the (Roman) Catholic concept of Petrine primacy, apostleship and apostolic succession, either to the beginnings of Christianity or to the intention of Jesus (see also above ch. VI; against such theses as those of P. Batiffol, *Primitive Catholicism*, [5]1911, ET Longmans 1911, and O. Karrer, *Peter and the Church*, ET Herder 1963).

29. Käsemann, *NTQT*, p. 22.

30. See further Dunn, *Baptism*, ch. IX and above pp. 156f.

31. Käsemann, 'The Disciples of John the Baptist in Ephesus' (1952), ET *ENTT*, pp. 136–48.

32. Käsemann, *NTQT*, p. 22.

33. See also C. K. Barrett, *Luke the Historian in Recent Study*, Epworth 1961, and Fortress Facet Book 1970, pp. 68, 70–76; Haenchen, *Acts*, p. 49; H. Conzelmann, 'Luke's Place in the Development of Early Christianity', *SLA*, p. 304.

34. Käsemann, 'Apologia', *ENTT*, pp. 187–91.

35. See Dunn, *Baptism*, chs XVII–XVIII.

36. Cf. e.g. von Campenhausen, *Authority*, pp. 122f.; Kümmel, *Introduction*, p. 448; J. Lieu, *The Second and Third Epistles of John*, T. & T. Clark 1986, pp. 162–3; and the extremer thesis of Käsemann (above p. 5). Some discern 'early catholic' traits in the Johannine epistles, particularly in the emphasis on tradition and truth; but see C. C. Black, 'The Johannine Epistles and the Question of Early Catholicism', *NovTest* 28, 1986, pp. 131–58; Strecker, *Johannesbriefe* pp. 351–4.

37. On Matthew's attitude to charismatic enthusiasm, including the immediacy of inspiration, see above pp. 180, 196, 249.

38. Dalman, *Words*, pp. 214f.

39. Dunn, *Jesus*, ch. XI, n. 14.

39a. Disputed by Bauckham, *Jude* pp. 8–11, who also notes the extent to which Jude is dependent on the *apocalyptic* writings, I Enoch and Ass.Mos.

40. Käsemann, 'Ministry', *ENTT*, pp. 89ff.; 'Ephesians and Acts', *SLA*, p. 290.

41. Käsemann, 'Ministry', *ENTT*, p. 89.

42. Cf. Schweizer, 'Concerning the Speeches in Acts' (1957), ET *SLA*, pp. 208–16; and above §4. But see also Schweizer, *Jesus*, pp. 147–51.

43. Cf. further W. W. Gasque, 'The Speeches of Acts: Dibelius Reconsidered', *New Dimensions in New Testament Study*, ed., R. N. Longenecker and M. C. Tenney, Zondervan 1974, pp. 247–9.

44. See H.-J. Michel, *Die Abschiedsrede des Paulus an die Kirche Apg. 20.17–38*, München 1973, pp. 91–7; otherwise H.-F. Weiss, '"Frühkatholizismus" im Neuen Testament?', in J. Rogge and G. Schille, *Frühkatholizismus im ökumenischen Gespräch*, Berlin 1983, pp. 18–20. The earlier debate is helpfully reviewed by E. Grässer, 'Acta Forschung seit 1960', *ThR*, 41, 1976, pp. 275–86 (here particularly pp. 281–3).

44a. Cf. W. Wiefel, 'Frühkatholizismus und synagogales Erbe', in J. Rogge and G. Schille, hrsg., *Frühkatholizismus im ökumenischen Gespräch*, Berlin 1983, pp. 52–61.

44b. As has been demonstrated in the twentieth century by the successive waves of early Pentecostalism, 'Latter Rain', neo-Pentecostalism, and Charismatic Movement.

45. 'Prophecy and imminent expectation belong together' (U. B. Müller, *Prophetie und Predigt im Neuen Testament*, Gütersloh 1975, p. 238).

Chapter XV   The Authority of the New Testament

1. E.g. A. M. Hunter, *The Unity of the New Testament*, SCM Press 1943.

2. Cf. H. Braun, 'The Problem of a New Testament Theology' (1961), ET in *The Bultmann School of Biblical Interpretation: New Directions*, J. M. Robinson, et al., *JThC*, 1, 1965, pp. 169–83.

3. Cf. Koester, *Trajectories*: 'The term *canonical* loses its normative relevance when the New Testament books themselves emerge as a deliberate collection of writings representing various divergent convictions which are not easily reconciled with each other (p. 115). Cf. Käsemann, *Testament*, p. 76.

4. Cf. H. Küng, *The Church*, 1967, ET Burns & Oates 1968, p. 179.

5. See e.g. I. Lönning, '*Kanon im Kanon*', Oslo 1972, p. 272; Schulz, *Schrift*, pp. 429ff.; E. Käsemann, *Das Neue Testament als Kanon*, Göttingen 1970, p. 405. But Käsemann goes on, 'Every christology which is not oriented to the justification of the godless, abstracts from the Nazarene and his cross. Every proclamation of justification which does not remain anchored christologically and continuously drawn back to the Lordship of Jesus Christ ends in an anthropology or ecclesiology, or possibly in religious doctrine which can also be legitimated in other ways . . .' (p. 405). See also A. Stock, *Einheit des Neuen Testaments*, Zürich 1969, pp. 20ff.

6. W. Marxsen, *The New Testament as the Church's Book*, 1966, ET Fortress 1972. 'The locus of the canon . . . can only be the earliest traditions of Christian witness accessible to us today by historical-critical analysis of those writings. Specifically the canon of the church . . . must now be located in what form critics generally speak

of as the earliest layer of the Synoptic tradition, or what Marxsen in particular refers to as "the Jesus-kerygma" . . .' (S. M. Ogden, 'The Authority of Scripture for Theology', *Interpretation*, 30, 1976, p. 258); this becomes the hermeneutical basis of Ogden's *The Point of Christology*, SCM Press 1982. I have suggested that the first Christians in effect used such a 'canon' themselves in determining what properly belonged within the Jesus-tradition, that is, in judging whether a prophetic utterance was a word of (the exalted) Jesus or not (see above p. 36 n. 8).

7. Cf. e.g. Luther: 'The proper touchstone by which to find out what may be wrong with all the books is whether or not they treat of Christ. Whatever does not touch Christ is not apostolic, even if Peter or Paul teaches it. On the other hand, whatever preaches Christ, that is apostolic, even if it is done by someone like Judas, Annas, Pilate or Herod' (Preface to James, 1522, cited by Kümmel, *Introduction*, p. 505); J. Denney, *Jesus and the Gospel*, Hodder & Stoughton 1908, [4]1911, who suggested that the confession, 'I believe in God through Jesus Christ his only Son, our Lord and Saviour' would 'safeguard everything which is vital to New Testament Christianity . . . include everything which ought to have a place in a fundamental confession of faith, and . . . (provide) the only basis of union broad enough and solid enough for all Christians to meet upon' (pp. 398ff.).

8. Even the Lutheran canon within the canon in effect de-canonizes James (as Luther found).

9. Käsemann, 'Canon', *ENTT*, p. 103. In *Kanon* he puts the point more sharply still: The canon 'also legitimizes as such more or less all sects and false teaching' (p.402)!

10. R. Rouse and S. C. Neill, *A History of the Ecumenical Movement 1517–1948*, SPCK 1954, [2]1967, p. 82.

11. 'One must not make the canon in the canon into the canon' (Lönning, p. 271).

12. Cf. Käsemann, 'Is the Gospel Objective?', *ENTT*: 'Those who seek to maintain the identification of the Gospel with the canon are delivering Christendom over to syncretism or, on the other wing, to the hopeless conflict between the Confessions' (p. 57).

13. J. H. Newman, *Essay on the Development of Christian Doctrine* (1845), Penguin Books 1974.

13a. But see ch. 10 n. 42.

14. See further my *The Living Word*, SCM Press/Fortress 1987. Cf. Käsemann, 'Canon', *ENTT*: 'The canon is not the word of God *tout simple*. It can only become and be the Word of God so long as we do not seek to imprison God within it; for this would be to make it a substitute for the God who addresses us and makes claims upon us . . . The Spirit does not contradict the "It is written . . ." but manifests himself in Scripture. But Scripture itself can at any moment become "the letter" and indeed does so as soon as it ceases to submit to the authorization of the Spirit and sets itself up as immediate Authority, seeking to replace the Spirit. The tension between Spirit and Scripture is constitutive . . .' (pp. 105f.). See also *NTQT*, pp. 8ff.; *Kanon*, pp. 407ff.

15. See A. C. Sundberg, 'The Bible Canon and the Christian Doctrine of Inspiration', *Interpretation*, 29, 1975, pp. 364–71. Of course inspiration has not only to be *claimed* but also *recognized* and *acknowledged* by the churches (see also New Foreword p. xxxi).

BIBLIOGRAPHY

General Bibliography and Select Bibliography on individual chapters. Other references are contained in the Notes. It is assumed that readers wishing further bibliography will refer to such works as *ABD (The Anchor Bible Dictionary)*, *ANRW (Aufstieg und Niedergang der Römischen Welt)*, *IZBG (Internationale Zeitschrift für Bibelwissenschaft und Grenzgebiete)*, *TDNT*, and *TRE (Theologische Realenzyklopädie)*.

General

Balthasar, H. U. von, 'Einheit und Vielheit neutestamenlicher Theologie', *Communio* 12, 1983, pp. 101–9

Bauer, W., *Orthodoxy and Heresy in Earliest Christianity*, 1934 [2]1964, ET Fortress 1971, and SCM Press 1972

Baur, F. C., *Vorlesungen über neutestamentliche Theologie*, 1864, Neudruck, Darmstadt 1973

Betz, H. D., 'Orthodoxy and Heresy in Primitive Christianity', *Interpretation*, 19, 1965, pp. 299–311

Betz, O., 'The Problem of Variety and Unity in the New Testament', *Horizons in Biblical Theology* 2, 1980, pp.3–14

Blank, J., 'Zum Problem "Haresie und Orthodoxie" im Urchristentum', *Zur Geschichte des Urchristentums*, hrsg. G. Dautzenberg et al., Freiburg 1979, pp. 142–60

Boers, H., *What is New Testament Theology?* Fortress 1979

Braun, H., 'The Meaning of New Testament Christology' (1957), ET in *God and Christ: Existence and Providence*, *JThC*, 5, 1968, pp. 89–127

— 'The Problem of a New Testament Theology' (1961), ET in *The Bultmann School of Biblical Interpretation: New Directions?*, *JThC*, 1, 1965, pp. 169–83

Brown, R. E., *The Churches the Apostles Left Behind*, Chapman 1984

Bultmann, R., *Primitive Christianity in its Contemporary Setting*, 1949, ET Thames & Hudson 1956

— *Theology of the New Testament*, 1948–53, ET 2 vols, SCM Press 1952, 1955

Charlot, J., *New Testament Disunity: its Significance for Christianity Today*, Dutton 1970

Clavier, H., *Les Variétés de la Pensée Biblique et le Problême de son Unité*, *SNT*, XLIII, 1976

Cohen, S. J. D., *From the Maccabees to the Mishnah*, Westminster 1987

Collins, J. J., *Between Athens and Jerusalem. Jewish Identity in the Hellenistic Diaspora*, Crossroad 1983

Congar, Y., *Diversity and Communion*, Twenty-Third Publications 1985

Conzelmann, H., *An Outline of the Theology of the New Testament*, [2]1968, ET SCM Press 1969

—*History of Primitive Christianity*, 1969, ET Abingdon, and Darton, Longman & Todd 1973

Cullmann, O., *Unity through Diversity*, Fortress 1988

Dix, G., *Jew and Greek: a Study in the Primitive Church*, Dacre Press 1953

Dunn, J. D. G., *The Evidence for Jesus*, SCM Press/Westminster 1985

— 'Die Instrumente kirchlicher Gemeinschaft in der frühen Kirche', *Una Sancta* 44.1, 1989, pp. 2–13

Ehrhardt, A., 'Christianity Before the Apostles' Creed', *HTR*, 55, 1962, reprinted in *The Framework of the New Testament Stories*, Manchester University Press 1964, pp. 151–99

Evans, C. F., 'The Unity and Pluriformity of the New Testament', *Christian Believing* (A Report by The Doctrine Commission of the Church of England), SPCK 1976, pp. 43–51

Fiorenza, E. S., *In Memory of Her. A Feminist Theological Reconstruction of Christian Origins*, SCM Press 1983

Forkman, G., *The Limits of the Religious Community: Expulsion from the religious community within the Qumran sect, within Rabbinic Judaism, and within primitive Christianity*, Lund 1972

Gager, J. G., *Kingdom and Community: the Social World of Early Christianity*, Prentice-Hall 1975

Gloer, W. H., 'Unity and Diversity in the New Testament. Anatomy of an Issue', *Biblical Theology Bulletin 13*, 1983, pp. 53–8

Goguel, M., *The Birth of Christianity*, 1946, ET Allen & Unwin 1953

Goppelt, L., *Apostolic and Post-apostolic Times*, 1962, ET A. & C. Black 1970

—*Theologie des Neuen Testaments*, 2 vols., Göttingen, 1975, 1976; ET *Theology of the New Testament*, Eerdmans 1981, 1982

— 'The Plurality of New Testament Theologies and the Unity of the Gospel as an Ecumenical Problem', *The Gospel and Unity*, ed. V. Vajta, Augsburg 1971, pp. 106–30

Grabbe, L. L., 'Orthodoxy in First Century Judaism. What are the Issues?', *JSJ* 8, 1977, pp. 149–53

Grant, F. C., *An Introduction to New Testament Thought*, Abingdon 1950

Guelich, R. A., ed., *Unity and Diversity in New Testament Theology*, Eerdmans 1978

Hahn, F., *Exegetische Beiträge zum ökumenischen Gespräch. Gesammelte Aufsätze Band I*, Göttingen 1986

— *Mission in the New Testament*, 1963, ET SCM Press 1965

Harnack, A., *What is Christianity?*, 1900, ET Putnam 1901

Harrington, D. J., 'The Reception of Walter Bauer's *Orthodoxy and Heresy in Earliest Christianity* during the Last Decade', *HTR* 73, 1980, pp. 289–98; reprinted in *Light of All Nations. Essays on the Church in New Testament*

Research, Glazier 1982, pp. 162–73

Hawkin, D. J., 'A Reflective Look at the Recent Debate on Orthodoxy and Heresy in Earliest Christianity', *Eglise et Theologie* 7, 1976, pp. 367–78

Hoskyns, E., and Davey, N., *The Riddle of the New Testament*, Faber 1931

Hunter, A. M., *The Unity of the New Testament*, SCM Press 1943

Jeremias, J., *The Central Message of the New Testament*, SCM Press 1965

Jewett, R., *Christian Tolerance: Paul's Message to the Modern Church*, Westminster 1982

Käsemann, E., 'New Testament Questions of Today' (1957), ET in *NTQT*, pp. 1–22

— *Jesus Means Freedom*, [3]1968, ET SCM Press 1969

— 'The Problem of a New Testament Theology', *NTS*, 19, 1972–73, pp. 235–45

Kinnamon, M., *Truth and Community. Diversity and its Limits in the Ecumenical Movement*, World Council of Churches/Eerdmans 1988

Knox, J., *The Early Church and the Coming Great Church*, Abingdon 1955

Koester, H., 'Häretiker im Urchristentum', *RGG*[3], III 17–21

— *Introduction to the New Testament*, 2 vols., Fortress 1982

— 'The Theological Aspects of Primitive Christian Heresy', *FRP*, pp. 65–83

— 'Variety in New Testament Theology' (Society for New Testament Studies Conference Paper, 1975)

Kraft, R. A., 'The Development of the Concept of "Orthodoxy" in Early Christianity', *Current Issues in Biblical and Patristic Interpretation: Studies in Honour of M. C. Tenney*, ed., G. F. Hawthorne, Eerdmans 1975, pp. 47–59

Kümmel, W. G., 'Urchristentum', *RGG*[3], VI, 1187–93

— *The New Testament: the History of the Investigation of its Problems*, 1970, ET SCM Press 1973

— *The Theology of the New Testament: According to its Major Witnesses, Jesus-Paul-John*, 1972, ET SCM Press 1974

— *Introduction to the New Testament*, revised edition 1973, ET SCM Press 1975

Ladd, G. E., *A Theology of the New Testament*, Eerdmans 1974, Lutterworth 1975

Lohse, E., 'Die Einheit des Neuen Testaments als theologisches Problem. Uberlegungen zur Aufgabe einer Theologie des Neuen Testaments', *EvTh*, 35, 1975, pp. 139–54; reprinted in *Die Vielfalt des Neuen Testaments*, Göttingen 1982, pp. 231–46

Loisy, A., *The Birth of the Christian Religion*, 1933, ET Allen & Unwin 1948

Luz, U., 'Einheit und Vielfalt neutestamentlicher Theologie', *Die Mitte des Neuen Testaments. Einheit und Vielfalt neutestamentlicher Theologie*, E. Schweizer Festschrift, hrsg. U. Luz & H. Weder, Göttingen 1983, pp. 142–61

Macquarrie, J. M., *Christian Unity and Christian Diversity*, SCM Press 1975

Markus, R. A., 'The Problem of Self-Definition: From Sect to Church', *Jewish and Christian Self-Definition. Vol. 1. The Shaping of Christianity in the Second and Third Centuries*, ed., E. P. Sanders, Fortress/SCM Press 1980, pp. 1–15

Marshall, I. H., 'Orthodoxy and Heresy in Earlier Christianity', *Themelios* 2, 1976, pp. 5–14

Marxsen, W., *Introduction to the New Testament*, 1964, ET Blackwell 1968

— 'Das Neue Testament und die Einheit der Kirche' *Der Exeget als Theologie: Vorträge zum Neuen Testament*, Gütersloh 1968, pp. 183–97

McEleney, N. J., 'Orthodoxy and Heresy in the New Testament', *Proceedings of the Catholic Theological Society of America*, 25, 1970, pp. 54–77

— 'Orthodoxy in Judaism of the first Christian Century', *JSJ* 4, 1973, pp. 19–42

Meeks, W. A., *The First Urban Christians. The Social World of the Apostle Paul*, Yale University 1983

Meyer, B., 'Identity and Development', *The Early Christians. Their World Mission and Self-Discovery*, Glazier 1986, pp. 172–207

Morgan, R., *The Nature of New Testament Theology*, SCM Press 1973

Moule, C. F. D., *The Birth of the New Testament*, A. & C. Black 1962

Murray, R., 'Tradition as Criterion of Unity', *Church Membership and Intecommunion*, ed. J. Kent and R. Murray, Darton 1973, pp. 251–80

Neill, S., *The Interpretation of the New Testament 1861–1961*, Oxford University Press 1964; revised by T. Wright 1988

— *Jesus Through Many Eyes: Introduction to the Theology of the New Testament*, Lutterworth 1976

Norris, F. W., 'Ignatius, Polycarp and I Clement: Walter Bauer Reconsidered', *Vigiliae Christianae* 30, 1976, pp. 23–44

Perrin N. and Duling, D. C., *The New Testament. An Introduction*, Harcourt Brace Jovanovich ²1982, especially ch. 3

Riesenfeld, H., 'Zur Frage nach der Einheit des Neuen Testaments, *Jesus in der Verkündigung der Kirche*, hrsg. A. Fuchs, Linz 1976, pp. 9–25

Robinson, J. M. and Koester, H., *Trajectories through Early Christianity*, Fortress 1971

— 'The Future of New Testament Theology (1973), ET in *Religious Studies Review*, 2:1, 1976, pp. 17–23

Robinson, T. A., *The Bauer Thesis Examined. The Geography of Heresy in the Early Christian Church*. Edwin Mellen 1988

Rowland, C., *Christian Origins. An Account of the Setting and Character of the Most Important Messianic Sect of Judaism*, SPCK 1985

Rowley, H. H., *The Unity of the Bible*, Carey Kingsgate Press 1953

Schlier, H., 'The Meaning and Function of a Theology of the New Testament', *The Relevance of the New Testament*, 1964, ET Herder 1968, pp. 1–25

Schnackenburg, R., *New Testament Theology Today*, 1961, ET Chapman 1963

Schweizer, E., *Theologische Einleitung in des Neuen Testaments*, Göttingen 1989

Scott, E. F., *The Varieties of New Testament Religion*, Scribners 1943

Simon, M., 'From Greek Hairesis to Christian Heresy', *Early Christian Literature and the Classical Intellectual Tradition*, R. M. Grant Festschrift, ed. W. R. Schoedel and R. L. Wilken, Paris 1979, pp. 101–16

Stock, A., *Einheit des Neuen Testament*, Zürich 1969

Trilling, W., *Vielfalt and Einheit im Neuen Testament*, Einsiedeln 1968
Turner, H. E. W., *The Pattern of Christian Truth*, Mowbray 1954
Weiss, J., *Earliest Christianity: A History of the Period AD 30–150*, 1914, ET 1937, reprinted Harper 1959
Wilken, R. L., *The Myth of Christian Beginnings*, SCM Press 1979

Chapter II   Kerygma or Kergymata?

Beker, J. C., *Paul the Apostle. The Triumph of God in Life and Thought*, Fortress/ T. & T. Clark 1980
Bornkamm, G., *Jesus of Nazareth*, [3]1959, ET Hodder & Stoughton 1960
— *Paul*, 1969, ET Hodder & Stoughton 1971
Brown, R. E., 'The Kerygma of the Gospel according to John', *Interpretation*, 21, 1967, pp. 387–400, reprinted in *New Testament Issues*, ed., R. Batey, SCM Press 1970, pp. 210–25
— *The Community of the Beloved Disciple*, Chapman 1979
Bruce, F. F., *Paul, Apostle of the Free Spirit*, Paternoster 1977
— 'The Speeches in Acts – Thirty Years After', *Reconciliation and Hope: New Testament Essays on Atonement and Eschatology*, L. L. Morris Festschrift, ed., R. J. Banks, Paternoster 1974, pp. 53–68
Buck, C. H. and Taylor, G., *St Paul: A Study in the Development of his Thought*, Scribners 1969
Bultmann, R., *Jesus and the Word*, 1926, ET Scribners 1934, Fontana 1958
Dodd, C. H., *The Apostolic Preaching and its Developments*, Hodder & Stoughton 1936
Evans, C. F., 'The Kerygma', *JTS*, 7, 1956, pp. 25–41
Green, M., *Evangelism in the Early Church*, Hodder & Stoughton 1970
Hengel, M., *Acts and the History of Earliest Christianity*, SCM Press/Fortress 1979, ch. 1
Jeremias, J., *New Testament Theology Vol. I – The Proclamation of Jesus*, 1971, ET SCM Press 1971
Kränkl, E., *Jesus der Knecht Gottes: die heilsgeschichtliche Stellung Jesu in den Reden der Apostelgeschichte*, Regensburg 1972
Kysar, R., *The Fourth Evangelist and his Gospel: an Examination of Contemporary Scholarship*, Augsburg 1975
Meyer, B. F., *The Aims of Jesus*, SCM Press 1979
Mounce, R. H., *The Essential Nature of the New Testament Preaching*, Eerdmans 1960
Mussner, F., *The Historical Jesus in the Gospel of St John*, 1965, ET Herder 1967
Oepke, A., *Die Missionspredigt des Apostels Paulus*, Leipzig 1920
Rensberger, D., *Johannine Faith and Liberating Community*, Westminster 1988/SPCK 1989
Ridderbos, H., *Paul: An Outline of his Theology*, 1966, ET Eerdmans 1975
Sanders, E. P., *Jesus and Judaism*, SCM Press/Fortress 1985
Schnackenburg, R., 'Revelation and Faith in the Gospel of John', *Present*

and Future: Modern Aspects of New Testament Theology, Notre Dame 1966, pp. 122–42

Schulz, S., 'Die Anfänge urchristlicher Verkündigung. Zur Traditions- und Theologiegeschichte der ältesten Christenheit', *Die Mitte des Neuen Testaments. Einheit und Vielfalt neutestamentlicher Theologie*, E. Schweizer Festschrift, hrsg. U. Luz & H. Weder, Göttingen 1983, pp. 254–71

Schweizer, E., 'Concerning the Speeches in Acts' (1957), ET *SLA*, pp. 208–16

Smith, D. M., 'Johannine Christianity: Some Reflections on its Character and Delineation', *NTS*, 21, 1974–75, pp. 222–48; reprinted in *Johannine Christianity. Essays on its Setting, Sources and Theology*, University of South Carolina 1984, pp. 1–36

— 'The Presentation of Jesus in the Fourth Gospel', *Interpretation* 31, 1977, pp. 367–78, reprinted in *Johannine Christianity*, pp. 175–89

Stanton, G. N., *Jesus of Nazareth in New Testament Preaching*, Cambridge University Press 1974

Sweet, J. P. M., 'The Kerygma', *ExpT*, 76, 1964–65, pp. 143–7

Wilckens, U., *Die Missionsreden der Apostelgeschichte*, Neukirchen 1961

Ziesler, J., *Pauline Christianity*, Oxford 1983

Chapter III   Primitive Confessional Formulae

Bauckham, R., 'The Sonship of the Historical Jesus in Christology', *SJT* 31, 1978, pp. 245–60

Boers, H., 'Where Christology is Real: a Survey of Recent Research on New Testament Christology', *Interpretation*, 26, 1972, pp. 300–27

Bousset, W., *Kyrios Christos*, [2]1921, ET Abingdon 1970

Campenhausen, H. von, 'Das Bekenntnis im Urchristentum', *ZNW*, 63, 1972, pp. 210–53

Caragounis, C. C., *The Son of Man. Vision and Interpretation*, WUNT 38, Tübingen 1986

Casey, M., *Son of Man. The Interpretation and Influence of Daniel 7*, SPCK 1979

Cullmann, O., *The Earliest Christian Confessions*, 1943, ET Lutterworth 1949

— *The Christology of the New Testament*, 1957, ET SCM Press 1959

Dahl, N. A., 'The Crucified Messiah' (1960), 'The Messiahship of Jesus in Paul' (1953), *The Crucified Messiah and Other Essays*, ET Augsburg 1974, pp. 10–47

Dunn, J. D. G., *Christology in the Making. An Inquiry into the origins of the Doctrine of the Incarnation*, SCM Press, Westminster 1980, [2]1989

Fitzmyer, J. A., 'New Testament Kyrios and Maranatha and their Aramaic Background', *To Advance the Gospel: New Testament Studies*, Crossroad 1981, pp. 218–35

Foakes Jackson, F. J. and Lake, K., *The Beginnings of Christianity Part I: The Acts of the Apostles*, Macmillan, Vol. I, 1920, pp. 345–418

Foerster, W., '*kurios*', *TDNT*, III, pp. 1039–95

Fuller, R. H., *The Foundations of New Testament Christology*, Lutterworth 1965, Fontana 1969

Hahn, F., *The Titles of Jesus in Christology*, 1963, ET Lutterworth 1969

Hengel, M., '"Christos" in Paul', *Between Jesus and Paul*, SCM Press/ Fortress 1983, p. 65–77

— *The Son of God: The Origin of Christology and the History of Jewish–Hellenistic Religion*, 1975, ET SCM Press 1976

Hooker, M. D., *The Son of Man in Mark*, SPCK 1967

Kelly, J. N. D., *Early Christian Creeds*, Longmans 1950

Kramer, W., *Christ, Lord, Son of God*, 1963, ET SCM Press 1966

Lindars, B., *Jesus Son of Man. A Fresh Examination of the Son of Man Sayings in the Gospels*, SPCK 1983

Longenecker, R. N., *The Christology of Early Jewish Christianity*, SCM Press 1970

Marshall, I. H., *The Origins of New Testament Christology*, Inter-Varsity Press 1976

Moule, C. F. D., 'The Influence of Circumstances on the Use of Christological Terms', *JTS*, 10, 1959, pp. 247–63

— *The Origin of Christology*, Cambridge University 1977

Neufeld, V., *The Earliest Christian Confessions*, Leiden 1963

Perrin, N., *A Modern Pilgrimage in New Testament Christology*, Fortress 1974

Schillebeeckx, E. and Metz, J.-B., ed., *Jesus, Son of God?*, *Concilium* 153, T. & T. Clark 1982

Schweizer, E., *Erniedrigung und Erhöhung bei Jesus und seinen Nachfolgern*, Zürich ²1962 ET of first edition, *Lordship and Discipleship*, 1955, SCM Press 1960

Seeberg, A., *Der Katechismus der Urchristenheit*, 1903, München 1966

Stauffer, E., *New Testament Theology*, 1941, ET SCM Press 1955, Part III

Tödt, H. E., *The Son of Man in the Synoptic Tradition*, 1959, ET SCM Press 1965

Vermes, G., *Jesus the Jew*, Collins 1973

Vielhauer, P., 'Gottesreich und Menschensohn in der Verkündigung Jesu', 'Jesus und der Menschensohn', 'Ein Weg zur neutestamentlichen Christologie?', in *Aufsätze zum Neuen Testament*, München 1965, pp. 55–198

Wengst, K., *Christologische Formeln und Lieder des Urchristentum*, Gütersloh 1972

Chapter IV The Role of Tradition

Banks, R., *Jesus and the Law in the Synoptic Tradition*, Cambridge University Press 1975

Bruce, F. F., *Tradition Old and New*, Paternoster 1970

— *Paul and Jesus*, Baker 1974

Bultmann, R., *The History of the Synoptic Tradition*, 1921 ³1958, ET Blackwell 1963

Campenhausen, H. von, 'Tradition and Spirit in Early Christianity', *Tradition and Life in the Church*, 1960, ET Collins 1968, pp. 7–18

Carlston, C. E., *The Parables of the Triple Tradition*, Fortress 1975

Congar, Y., *Tradition and Traditions*, 1960, 1963, ET Burns & Oates 1966

Cullmann, O., 'The Tradition' (1953), *The Early Church*, ET SCM Press 1956, pp. 59–75

Davies, W. D., *The Setting of the Sermon on the Mount*, Cambridge University Press 1964

Dibelius, M., *From Tradition to Gospel*, 1919, [2]1933, ET Nicholson & Watson 1934; James Clarke 1971

Dodd, C. H., '*Ennomos Christou*' (1953), *More New Testament Studies*, Manchester University Press 1968, pp. 134–48

Dungan, D. L., *The Sayings of Jesus in the Churches of Paul*, Blackwell 1971

France, R. T. and Wenham, D., ed., *Gospel Perspectives. Studies of History and Tradition in the Four Gospels*, especially vols. 1 and 2, JSOT 1980, 1981

Fraser, J. W., *Jesus and Paul*, Marcham 1974

Gerhardsson, B., *Memory and Manuscript*, Lund 1961

— *The Origins of the Gospel Traditions*, Fortress/SCM Press 1979

Goppelt, L., 'Tradition nach Paulus', *KuD*, 4, 1958, pp. 213–33

Hahn, F., 'Das Problem "Schrift und Tradition" im Urchristentum', *EvTh* 30, 1970, pp. 449–68

Hanson, R. P. C. *Tradition in the Early Church*, SCM Press 1962

Herford, R. T., *Pirke Aboth: The Ethics of the Talmud: Sayings of the Fathers*, 1945, Schocken 1962

Hunter, A. M., *Paul and his Predecessors*, SCM Press [2]1961

Jeremias, J., *The Parables of Jesus*, [6]1962, ET SCM Press 1963

Longenecker, R. N., *Paul Apostle of Liberty*, Harper 1964

McDonald, J. I. H., *Kerygma und Didache*, SNTSMS 37, Cambridge University 1980

Müller, P. G., *Der Traditionsprozess im Neuen Testament*, Freiburg 1981

Neusner, J., 'Scripture and Tradition in Judaism', *Approaches to Ancient Judaism* II, ed., W. S. Green, Brown Judaic Studies 9, Scholars 1980, pp. 173–93

Riesenfeld, H., *The Gospel Tradition and its Beginnings*, Mowbray 1957, reprinted in *The Gospel Tradition*, Fortress 1970, and Blackwell 1971, pp. 1–29

Riesner, R., *Jesus als Lehrer. Eine Untersuchung zum Ursprung der Evangelien-Überlieferung*, WUNT 2.7, Tübingen 1981

Taylor, V., *The Formation of the Gospel Tradition*, Macmillan [2]1935

Trocmé, E., *Jesus and his Contemporaries*, 1972, ET SCM Press 1973

Wegenast, K., *Das Verständnis der Tradition bei Paulus und in den Deuteropaulinen*, Neukirchen 1962

Wengst, K., 'Der Apostel und die Tradition', *ZTK*, 69, 1972, pp. 145–62

Zimmermann, A. F., *Die urchristlichen Lehrer*, WUNT 2.12, Tübingen 1984

Chapter V The Use of the Old Testament

Baker, D. L., *Two Testaments, One Bible*, IVP 1976

Barrett, C. K., 'The Interpretation of the Old Testament in the New', *The Cambridge History of the Bible Vol I: from the Beginnings to Jerome*, ed., P. R. Ackroyd and C. F. Evans, Cambridge University Press 1970, pp. 377–411

Barth, M., 'The Old Testament in Hebrews' *CINTI*, p. 53–78

Barton, J., *Oracles of God*, Darton, Longman & Todd 1986

Black, M., 'The Christological Use of the Old Testament in the New Testament', *NTS*, 18, 1971–72, pp. 1–14

Brooke, G. J., *Exegesis at Qumran*, JSOT Press 1985

Bruce, F. F., *Biblical Exegesis in the Qumran Texts*, Tyndale Press 1959

Carson, D. A. and Williamson, H. G. M., *It is Written: Scripture Citing Scripture*, B. Lindars Festschrift, Cambridge University 1988

Chilton, B., *A Galilean Rabbi and his Bible. Jesus' Own Interpretation of Isaiah.* SPCK 1984

Dodd, C. H., *According to the Scriptures*, Nisbet 1952; Fontana 1967

Ellis, E., E., *Paul's Use of the Old Testament*, Eerdmans 1957

—*Prophecy and Heremeneutic in Early Christianity*, Tübingen/Eerdmans 1978

Fitzmyer, J. A., *Essays on the Semitic Background of the New Testament*, Chapman 1971, chs 1 and 2

France, R. T., *Jesus and the Old Testament*, Tyndale Press 1971

Freed, E. D., *Old Testament Quotations in the Gospel of John*, SNT, XI, 1965

Goppelt, L., *The Typological Interpretation of the Old Testament in the New*, 1939, ET Eerdmans 1982

Hanson, A. T., *The New Testament Interpretation of Scripture*, SPCK 1980

— *The Living Utterances of God. The New Testament Exegesis of the Old*, Darton, Longman & Todd 1983

Harris, R., *Testimonia*, 2 vols, Cambridge University Press 1916, 1920

Juel, D., *Messianic Exegesis. Christological Interpretation of the Old Testament in Early Christianity*, Fortress 1988

Kistemaker, S., *The Psalm Citations in the Epistle to the Hebrews*, Amsterdam 1961

Lindars, B., *New Testament Apologetic*, SCM Press 1961

Lindars, B. and Borgen, P., 'The Place of the Old Testament in the Formation of New Testament Theology: Prolegomena and Response' *NTS*, 23, 1976–77, pp. 59–75

Longenecker, R. N., *Biblical Exegesis in the Apostolic Period*, Eerdmans 1975

McConnell, R. S., *Law and Prophecy in Matthew's Gospel: the Authority and Use of the Old Testament in the Gospel of Matthew*, Basel 1969

McNamara, M., *The New Testament and the Palestinian Targum to the Pentateuch*, Analecta Biblica 27, Rome 1966

Michel, O., *Paulus und seine Bibel*, Gütersloh 1929

Miller, M. P., 'Targum, Midrash and the Use of the Old Testament', *JSJ*, 2, 1971, pp. 29–82

Moo, D. J., *The Old Testament in the Gospel Passion Narratives*, Almond 1983

Neusner, J., *Midrash in Context. Exegesis in Formative Judaism*, Fortress 1983

Patte, D., *Early Jewish Hermeneutic in Palestine*, SBL Dissertation Series 22, 1975

Smith, D. M., 'The Use of the Old Testament in the New', *The Use of the Old Testament in the New and Other Essays*, ed., J. M. Efird, Duke University Press 1972, pp. 3–65

Sowers, S. G., *The Hermeneutics of Philo and Hebrews*, Zürich 1965

Stendahl, K., *The School of St Matthew and its Use of the Old Testament*, Lund 1954, ²1968

Westermann, C., ed., *Essays on Old Testament Interpretation*, SCM Press 1963

Chapter VI Concepts of Ministry

Banks, R., *Paul's Idea of Community*, Paternoster 1980

Barrett, C. K., *Church, Ministry, and Sacraments in the New Testament*, Paternoster 1985

—— *The Signs of an Apostle*, Epworth 1970

Brockhaus, U., *Charisma und Amt: die paulinische Charismenlehre auf dem Hintergrund der frühchristlichen Gemeindefunktionen*, Wuppertal 1972

Brown, R. E., 'The Unity and Diversity in New Testament Ecclesiology', *NovTest*, 6, 1963, pp. 298–308, reprinted in *New Testament Essays*, Chapman 1965, pp. 36–47

Campenhausen, H. von, *Ecclesiastical Authority and Spiritual Power in the Church of the First Centuries*, 1953, ET A. & C. Black 1965

Davies, W. D., 'A Normative Pattern of Church Life in the New Testament?' (1950), *Christian Origins and Judaism*, Darton, Longman & Todd 1962, ch. IX

Dunn, J. D. G., *Jesus and the Spirit*, SCM Press 1975

—— 'Models of Christian Community in the New Testament', *Strange Gifts*, ed. D. Martin and P. Mullen, Blackwell 1984, pp. 1–18

Ellis, E. E., *Pauline Theology. Ministry and Society*, Eerdmans 1989

Evans, C. F., 'Is the New Testament Church a Model?', *Is 'Holy Scripture' Christian? and Other Questions*, SCM Press 1971, pp. 78–90

Farrer, A. M., 'The Ministry in the New Testament', *The Apostolic Ministry*, ed., K. E. Kirk, Hodder & Stoughton 1946, ch. 3

Haacker, K., *Jesus and the Church in John*, Tübingen 1971

Hahn, F., 'Die Einheit der Kirche und Kirchengemeinschaft in neutestamentlicher Sicht', *Beiträge* pp. 116–58

Harnack, A., *The Constitution and Law of the Church in the First Two Centuries*, 1910, ET Williams & Norgate 1910

Hengel, M., *The Charismatic Leader and his Followers*, 1968, T. & T. Clark 1981

Käsemann, E., 'Ministry and Community in the New Testament', *ENTT*, ch. III

—— 'Unity and Multiplicity in the New Testament Doctrine of the Church',

NovTest, 6, 1963, pp. 290–7, reproduced in *NTQT*, ch. XIII

Kertelge, K., hrsg., *Das kirchliche Amt im Neuen Testament*, Darmstadt 1977

Knox, J., 'The Ministry in the Primitive Church', *The Ministry in Historical Perspective*, ed., H. R. Niebuhr and D. D. Williams, Harper 1956, ch. I

Küng, H., *The Church*, ET Burns & Oates 1968

Lightfoot, J. B., 'The Christian Ministry', *St Paul's Epistle to the Philippians*, Macmillan 1868, pp. 179–267

Linton, O., *Das Problem der Urkirche in der neuren Forschung*, Uppsala 1932

Lohfink, G., *Jesus and Community. The Social Dimension of Christian Faith*, SPCK/Fortress 1985

Manson, T. W., *The Church's Ministry*, Hodder & Stoughton 1948

Perkins, P., *Ministering in the Pauline Churches*, Paulist 1982

Ramsey, A. M., *The Gospel and the Catholic Church*, Longmans 1936, second edition 1956

Schillebeeckx, E., *Ministry*, SCM Press 1981; revised as *The Church with a Human Face*, SCM Press 1985

Schlier, H., 'The Unity of the Church according to the New Testament', *The Relevance of the New Testament*, ET Herder 1967, pp. 193–214

Schnackenburg, R., *The Church in the New Testament*, ET Herder 1965

Schweizer, E., *Church Order in the New Testament*, 1959, ET SCM Press 1961

— 'The Concept of the Church in the Gospel and Epistles of St John', *NTETWM*, pp. 230–45

Sohm, R., *Kirchenrecht*, Leipzig 1892

Streeter, B. H., *The Primitive Church*, Macmillan 1930

Trilling, W., 'Zum "Amt" im Neuen Testament. Eine methodologische Besinnung', *Die Mitte des Neuen Testaments. Einheit und Vielfalt neutestamenlicher Theologie*, E. Schweizer Festschrift, hrsg. U. Luz and H. Weder, Göttingen 1983, pp. 317–44

Witherington, B., *Women in the Earliest Churches*, SNTSMS 59, Cambridge University 1988

Chapter VII   Patterns of Worship

Carrington, P., *The Primitive Christian Catechism*, Cambridge University Press 1940

Cross, F. L., *I Peter – A Paschal Liturgy*, Mowbray 1954

Cullmann, O., *Early Christian Worship*, 1950, ET SCM Press 1953, ch. I

Dalman, G., *Jesus-Jeshua*, 1922, ET SPCK 1929, ch. VII

Deichgräber, R., *Gotteshymnus und Christushymnus in der frühen Christenheit*, Göttingen 1967

Delling, G., *Worship in the New Testament*, 1952, ET Darton, Longman & Todd 1962

Dodd, C. H., 'The Primitive Catechism and the Sayings of Jesus', *NTETWM*, pp. 106–18

Dunn, J. D. G., 'The Responsible Congregation (I Cor. 14.26–40)', *Charisma und Agape (1 Ko 12–14)*, hrsg. L. De Lorenzi, Rome 1983, pp. 201–36

Goulder, M. D., *Midrash and Lection in Matthew*, SPCK 1974

Guilding, A., *The Fourth Gospel and Jewish Worship*, Oxford University Press 1960

Hahn, F., *The Worship of the Early Church*, 1970, ET Fortress 1973

Hanson, A. T., *Studies in the Pastoral Epistles*, SPCK 1968

Hengel, M., 'Hymns and Christology', *Between Jesus and Paul*, SCM Press/Fortress 1983, pp. 78–96

Hurtado, L. W., *One God, One Lord. Early Christian Devotion and Ancient Jewish Monotheism*, Fortress/SCM Press 1988

Jeremias, J., *The Prayers of Jesus*, 1966, ET SCM Press 1967, chs II and III

Jones, D. R., 'The Background and Character of the Lukan Psalms', *JTS*, 19, 1968, pp. 19–50

Kirby, J. C., *Ephesians: Baptism and Pentecost*, SPCK 1968

Lohmeyer, E., *Lord of the Temple: A Study of the Relation between Cult and Gospel*, 1942, ET Oliver & Boyd 1961

Macdonald, A. B., *Christian Worship in the Primitive Church*, T. & T. Clark 1934

Martin, R. P., *Worship in the Early Church*, Marshall 1964

— *Carmen Christi: Phil. 2.5–11 in recent interpretation and in the setting of early Christian worship*, Cambridge University Press 1967, revised Eerdmans 1983

— *The Spirit and the Congregation. Studies in I Corinthians 12–15*, Eerdmans 1984

Morris, L., *The New Testament and the Jewish Lectionaries*, Tyndale Press 1964

Moule, C. F. D., 'Use of Parables and Sayings as Illustrative Material in Early Christian Catechesis', *JTS*, 3, 1952, pp. 75–9

— *Worship in the New Testament*, Lutterworth 1961

Norden, E., *Agnostos Theos: Untersuchungen zur Formgeschichte religiöser Rede*, 1913, reprinted Stuttgart 1956

Oesterley, W. O. E., *The Jewish Background of the Christian Liturgy*, Oxford University Press 1925

Petuchowski, J. J. and Brocke, M., *The Lord's Prayer and Jewish Liturgy*, Burns & Oates 1978

Reicke, B., 'Some Reflections on Worship in the New Testament', *NTETWM*, pp. 194–209

Rordorf, W., *Sunday: the History of the Day of Rest and Worship in the Earliest Centuries of the Christian Church*, 1962, ET SCM Press 1968

Rowley, H. H., *Worship in Ancient Israel*, SPCK 1967

Sanders, J. T., *The New Testament Christological Hymns: their historical religious background*, Cambridge University Press 1971

Selwyn, E. G., *The First Epistle of St Peter*, Macmillan 1947, pp. 363–466

Wengst, K., *Christologische Formeln und Lieder des Urchristentums*, Gütersloh 1972, Dritter Teil

Chapter VIII Sacraments

Barrett, C. K., *Church, Ministry and Sacraments in the New Testament*, Paternoster 1985

Barth, G., *Die Taufe in frühchristlicher Zeit*, Neukirchen 1981

Barth, K., *Church Dogmatics*, IV/4, ET T. & T. Clark 1970

Barth, M., *Rediscovering the Lord's Supper*, John Knox 1988

Beasley-Murray, G. R., *Baptism in the New Testament*, Macmillan 1963; Paternoster 1972

Bornkamm, G., 'Baptism and New Life in Paul' (1939), 'Lord's Supper and Church in Paul' (1956), *Early Christian Experience*, ET SCM Press 1969, chs V and IX

Brown, R., E., 'The Johannine Sacramentary', 'The Eucharist and Baptism in John', *New Testament Essays*, Chapman 1965, chs 4 and 5

Brown, S., '"Water-Baptism" and "Spirit-Baptism" in Luke–Acts', *Anglican Theological Review* 59, 1977, pp. 135–51

Corell, A., *Consummation Est*, 1950, ET SPCK 1958

Cullmann, O., 'The Meaning of the Lord's Supper in Primitive Christianity' (1936), ET in O. Cullmann and F. J. Leenhardt, *Essays on the Lord's Supper*, Lutterworth 1958, pp. 5–23

— *Baptism in the New Testament*, 1948, ET SCM Press 1950

— *Early Christian Worship*, 1950, ET SCM Press 1953, ch. 2

Dinkler, E., 'Die Taufaussagen des Neuen Testaments', *Zu Karl Barths Lehre von der Taufe*, ed., K. Viering, Gütersloh 1971, pp. 60–153

Dix, G., *The Shape of the Liturgy*, Dacre Press, A. & C. Black 1945

Dunn, J. D. G., *Baptism in the Holy Spirit*, SCM Press 1970

— 'John 6 – a Eucharistic Discourse?' *NTS*, 17, 1970–71, pp. 328–38

— 'The Birth of a Metaphor – Baptized in Spirit', *ExpT* 89, 1977–78, pp. 134–8, 173–5

Flemington, W. F., *The New Testament Doctrine of Baptism*, SPCK 1948

George, A., et al., *Baptism in the New Testament*, 1956, ET Chapman 1964

Jeremias, J., *The Eucharistic Words of Jesus*, [3]1960, ET SCM Press 1966

Käsemann, E., 'The Pauline Doctrine of the Lord's Supper' (1947–48), *ENTT*, pp. 108–35

Klappert, B., 'Lord's Supper', *NIDNTT*, II, 1976, pp. 520–38

Lampe, G. W. H., *The Seal of the Spirit*, SPCK 1951, [2]1967

Leon-Dufour, X., *Sharing the Eucharistic Bread. The Witness of the New Testament*, 1982, ET Paulist 1987

Lietzmann, H., *Mass and Lord's Supper: a Study in the History of Liturgy*, 1926, ET Leiden 1954

Lindars, B., 'Word and Sacrament in the Fourth Gospel', *SJT*, 29, 1976, pp. 49–63

Marshall, I. H., *Last Supper and Lord's Supper*, Paternoster 1980

Marxsen, W., *The Lord's Supper as a Christological Problem*, 1963, ET Fortress Facet Book 1970

Parratt, J. K., 'Holy Spirit and Baptism', *ExpT*, 82, 1970–71, pp. 231–5, 266–71

Reumann, J., *The Supper of the Lord. The New Testament, Ecumenical Dialogues, and Faith and Order on Eucharist*, Fortress 1985

Saldarini, A. J., *Jesus and Passover*, Paulist 1984

Schnackenburg, R., *Baptism in the Thought of St Paul*, 1961, ET Blackwell 1964

Schweizer, E., *The Lord's Supper according to the New Testament*, 1956, ET Fortress Facet Book 1967

Wagner, G., *Pauline Baptism and the Pagan Mysteries*, 1962, ET Oliver & Boyd, 1967

Wedderburn, A. J. M., *Baptism and Resurrection. Studies in Pauline Theology against its Graeco-Roman Background*, WUNT 44, Tübingen 1987

Chapter IX Spirit and Experience

Barrett, C. K., *The Holy Spirit and the Gospel Tradition*, SPCK 1947

Beasley-Murray, G. R., 'Jesus and the Spirit', *MBBR*, pp. 463–78

Brown, R. E., 'The Paraclete in the Fourth Gospel', *NTS*, 13, 1966–67, pp. 113–32

Cerfaux, L., *The Christian in the Theology of St Paul*, 1962, ET Chapman 1967, chs 8 and 9

Chevallier, M.-A., *Souffle de Dieu. Le Saint-Esprit dans le Nouveau Testament*, Beauchesne 1978

Congar, Y., *I Believe in the Holy Spirit*, Seabury/Chapman, 3 vols., 1983

Deissmann, A., *Paul: A Study in Social and Religious History*, [2]1925, ET 1927, Harper 1957

Dunn, J. D. G., 'I Corinthians 15.45 – Last Adam, Life-giving Spirit', *CSNT*, pp. 127–41

—*Jesus and the Spirit: a Study of the Religious and Charismatic Experience of Jesus and the first Christians as Reflected in the New Testament*, SCM Press 1975

—'Rom. 7.14–25 in the Theology of Paul', *TZ*, 31, 1975, pp. 257–73

—'Rediscovering the Spirit (2)', *ExpT* 94, 1982–83, pp. 9–18

—'The Spirit of Jesus', and 'The Spirit and Body of Christ', *The Holy Spirit: Renewing and Empowering Presence*, ed., G. Vandervelde, Wood Lake 1989, pp. 11–43

Gaventa, B. R., *From Darkness to Light. Aspects of Conversion in the New Testament*, Fortress 1986

George, A., *Communion with God in the New Testament*, Epworth 1953

Gunkel, H., *Die Wirkungen des heiligen Geistes nach der populären Anschauung der apostolischen Zeit und nach der Lehre des Apostels, Paulus*, Göttingen 1888

Hamilton, N. Q., *The Holy Spirit and Eschatology in Paul*, *SJT*, Occasional Papers no. 6 1957

Heron, A. I. C., *The Holy Spirit*, Marshall 1983

Hopwood, P. G. S., *The Religious Experience of the Primitive Church*, T. & T. Clark 1936

Hull, J. H. E., *The Holy Spirit in the Acts of the Apostles*, Lutterworth 1967

Isaacs, M. E., *The Concept of Spirit*, Heythrop Monograph 1, 1976

Jeremias, J., *The Prayers of Jesus*, 1966, ET SCM Press 1967, ch. I

Küng, H. and Moltmann, J., ed., *Conflicts about the Holy Spirit*, *Concilium* 128, Seabury/T. & T. Clark 1979

Lampe, G. W. H., 'The Holy Spirit in the Writings of St Luke', *Studies in the Gospels*, ed., D. E. Nineham, Blackwell 1955, pp. 159–200

Lindblom, J., *Gesichte und Offenbarungen*, Lund 1968

Montague, G. T., *The Holy Spirit: Growth of a Biblical Tradition*, Paulist 1976

Otto, R., *The Idea of the Holy*, 1917, ET Oxford University Press 1923

Potterie, I. de la and Lyonnet, S., *The Christian Lives by the Spirit*, 1965, ET Society of St Paul 1971

Robeck, C. M., ed., *Charismatic Experiences in History*, Hendrickson 1985

Robinson, H. W., *The Christian Experience of the Holy Spirit*, Nisbet 1928

Schillebeeckx, E., *Christ. The Christian Experience in the Modern World*, SCM Press 1980

Schweizer, A., *The Mysticism of Paul the Apostle*, ET A. & C. Black 1931

Schweizer, E., *The Holy Spirit*, SCM Press/Fortress 1978

Smart, N., *The Religious Experience of Mankind*, 1969, Fontana 1971, chs I and 7

Tannehill, R. C., *Dying and Rising with Christ*, Berlin 1967

Taylor, J. V., *The Go-Between God*, SCM Press 1972

Wikenhauser, A., *Pauline Mysticism: Christ in the Mystical Teaching of St Paul*, ²1956, ET Herder 1960

Chapter X Christ and Christology

Balz, H. R., *Methodische Probleme der neutestamentlichen Christologie*, Neukirchen 1967

Barrett, C. K., *Jesus and the Gospel Tradition*, SPCK 1967

Brown, R. E., *Jesus God and Man*, Chapman 1968

Bultmann, R., 'The Significance of the Historical Jesus for the Theology of Paul' (1929), 'The Christology of the New Testament', *Faith and Understanding: Collected Essays*, ET SCM Press 1969, pp. 220–46, 262–85

— 'The Christological Confession of the World Council of Churches' (1951), *Essays Philosophical and Theological*, ET SCM Press 1955, pp. 273–90

— 'The Primitive Christian Kerygma and the Historical Jesus' (1961), *The Historical Jesus and the Kerygmatic Christ*, ed., C. E. Braaten and R. A. Harrisville, Abingdon 1964, pp. 15–42

Caird, G. B., 'The Development of the Doctrine of Christ in the New Testament', *Christ for us Today*, ed., N. Pittenger, SCM Press 1968, pp. 66–80

Casey, M., 'Chronology and the Development of Pauline Christology', *Paul and Paulinism*, C. K. Barrett Festschrift, ed. M. D. Hooker and S. G. Wilson, SPCK 1982, pp. 124–34

Cupitt, D., 'One Jesus, many Christs?', *Christ, Faith and History: Cambridge Studies in Christology*, ed., S. W. Sykes and J. P. Clayton, Cambridge University Press 1972, pp. 131–44

Ebeling, G., *Theology and Proclamation*, 1962, ET Collins 1966

Ernst, J., *Anfänge der Christologie*, Stuttgarter Bibelstudien 57, 1972

Fuller, R. H. and Perkins, P., *Who is this Christ? Gospel Christology and Contemporary Faith*, Fortress 1983

Furnish, V. P., 'The Jesus–Paul Debate: from Baur to Bultmann', *BJRL*, 47, 1964–65, pp. 342–81

Hamerton-Kelly, R. G., *Pre-existence, Wisdom and the Son of Man: A Study of the Idea of Pre-existence in the New Testament*, Cambridge University Press 1973

Hanson, A. T., *Grace and Truth: A Study in the Doctrine of the Incarnation*, SPCK 1975

— *The Image of the Invisible God*, SCM Press 1982

Hurst, L. D. and Wright, N. T., ed., *The Glory of Christ in the New Testament. Studies in Christology in Memory of G. B. Caird*, Clarendon 1987

Hurtado, L. W., *One God, One Lord. Early Christian Devotion and Ancient Jewish Monotheism*, Fortress/SCM Press 1988

Jewett, R., ed., *Christology and Exegesis: New Approaches, Semeia 30*, 1984

de Jonge, M., *Christology in Context. The Earliest Christian Response to Jesus*, Westminster 1988

Jungel, E., *Paulus und Jesus: eine Untersuchung zur Präzisierung der Frage nach dem Ursprung der Christologie*, Tübingen 1962, ³1967

Käsemann, E., 'The Problem of the Historical Jesus' (1954), *ENTT*, pp. 15–47

— 'Blind Alleys in the "Jesus of History" Controversy', *NTQT*, pp. 23–65

Keck, L. E., *A Future for the Historical Jesus*, SCM Press 1972

— 'Toward a Renewal of New Testament Christology', *NTS* 32, 1986, pp. 362–77

Knox, J., *The Humanity and Divinity of Christ: a Study of Pattern in Christology*, Cambridge University Press 1967

Marxsen, W., *The Beginnings of Christology*, 1960, ET Fortress Facet Book 1969

McCaughey, J. D., *Diversity and Unity in the New Testament Picture of Christ*, University of Western Australia 1969

Moule, C. F. D., *The Phenomenon of the New Testament*, SCM Press 1967

— *The Origins of Christology*, Cambridge 1977

— 'Jesus of Nazareth and the Church's Lord', *Die Mitte des Neuen Testaments. Einheit und Vielfalt neutestamentlicher Theologie*, E. Schweizer Festschrift, hrsg. U. Luz and H. Weder, Göttingen 1983, pp. 176–86

Pannenberg, W., *Jesus God and Man*, 1964 ET SCM Press 1968

Pokorny, P., *The Genesis of Christology. Foundation for a Theology of the New Testament*, T. & T. Clark 1987

Robinson, J. A. T., *The Human Face of God*, SCM Press 1973

Robinson, J. M., *A New Quest of the Historical Jesus*, SCM Press 1959

Schillebeeckx, E., *Jesus: an Experiment in Christology*, Collins 1979

Schnackenburg, R., 'Paulinische und johanneische Christologie', *Die Mitte des Neuen Testaments. E. Schweizer Festschrift*, hrsg. U. Luz and H. Weder, Göttingen 1983, pp. 221–37

Schweizer, E., *Jesus*, 1968, ET SCM Press 1971

Strecker, G., ed., *Jesus Christus in Historie und Theologie: Neutestamentliche Festschrift für Hans Conzelmann*, Tübingen 1975

Taylor, V., *The Person of Christ in New Testament Teaching*, Macmillan 1958

Wainwright, A. W., *The Trinity in the New Testament*, SPCK 1962

Chapter XI Jewish Christianity

C. K. Barrett., 'Paul's Opponents in II Corinthians', *NTS*, 17, 1970–71, pp. 233–54

Barth, G., in G. Bornkamm, G. Barth and H. J. Held, *Tradition and Interpretation in Matthew*, 1960, ET SCM Press 1963

Brandon, S. G. F., *The Fall of Jerusalem and the Christian Church*, SPCK 1951

Brown, R. E. & Meier, J. P., *Antioch and Rome. New Testament Cradles of Catholic Christianity*, Chapman 1983

Cullmann, O., 'Dissensions within the Early Church' (1967), *New Testament Issues*, ed., R. Batey, SCM Press 1970, pp. 119–29

Danielou, J., *The Theology of Jewish Christianity*, 1958, ET Darton, Longman & Todd 1964

—*Judéo-christianisme. Recherches historiques et théologiques offertes au Cardinal Jean Danielou*, Paris 1972

Davies, W. D., *Paul and Rabbinic Judaism*, SPCK 1948

—*The Setting of the Sermon on the Mount*, Cambridge University Press 1964

Dunn, J. D. G., *Jesus, Paul and the Law. Studies in Mark and Galatians*, SPCK 1990

Elliott-Binns, L. E., *Galilean Christianity*, SCM Press 1956

Foakes Jackson, F. J. and Lake, K., *The Beginnings of Christianity Part I: The Acts of the Apostles*, Macmillan, Vol. I 1920, pp. 300–20

Hooker, M. D., *Continuity and Discontinuity. Early Christianity in its Jewish Setting*, Epworth 1986

Kaufman, Y., *Christianity and Judaism. Two Covenants*, Jerusalem 1988

Klijn, A. F. J. and Reinink, G. J., *Patristic Evidence for Jewish–Christian Sects*, *SNT*, XXXVI, 1973

Klijn, A. F. J. 'The Study of Jewish Christianity', *NTS*, 20, 1973–74, pp. 419–31

Maier, J., *Jüdische Auseinandersetzung mit dem Christentum in der Antike*, Darmstadt 1982

Martyn, J. L., *History and Theology in the Fourth Gospel*, Harper 1968; revised Abingdon 1979

Meeks, W. A., '"Am I a Jew?" Johannine Christianity and Judaism', *Christianity, Judaism and Other Greco–Roman Cults*, M. Smith Festschrift, ed. J. Neusner, Part One, Brill 1975, pp. 163–86

Meeks, W. A. and Wilken, R. L., *Jews and Christians in Antioch in the First Four Centuries of the Common Era*, Scholars 1978

Munck, J., *Paul and the Salvation of Mankind*, 1954, ET SCM Press 1959

—'Jewish Christianity in Post-Apostolic Times', *NTS*, 6, 1959–60, pp. 103–16

Murray, R., 'Jews, Hebrews and Christians: Some Needed Distinctions',
    NovT 24, 1982, pp. 194–208
Neusner, J. and Frerichs, E. S., ed., '"*To See Ourselves as Others See Us*".
    Christians, Jews and "Others" in Late Antiquity, Scholars 1985
Osten-Sacken, P. von der, *Christian–Jewish Dialogue. Theological Foundations*,
    1982, ET Fortress 1986
Richardson, P., *Israel in the Apostolic Church*, Cambridge University Press 1969
Sanders, E. P. *Paul and Palestinian Judaism. A Comparison of Patterns of Religion*,
    SCM Press/Fortress 1977
Sandmel, S., *Judaism and Christian Beginnings*, Oxford University 1978
Schiffman, L. H., 'At the Crossroads: Tannaitic Perspectives on the Jewish–
    Christian Schism', *Jewish and Christian Self-Definition Vol. 2. Aspects of
    Judaism in the Graeco–Roman World*, ed. E. P. Sanders, Fortress/SCM Press
    1981, pp. 115–56
Schmithals, W., *Paul and James*, 1963, ET SCM Press 1965
Schoeps, H., *Theologie und Geschichte des Judenchristentums*, Tübingen 1949
—*Paul: the Theology of the Apostle in the Light of Jewish Religious History*, 1959, ET
    Lutterworth 1961
—*Jewish Christianity: Factional Disputes in the Early Church*, 1964, ET Fortress
    1969
Segal, A. F., *Rebecca's Children. Judaism and Christianity in the Roman World*,
    Harvard University 1986
Simon, M., *Verus Israel. A study of the relations between Christians and Jews in the
    Roman Empire (AD 135–425)*, 1948, ET Oxford University 1986
Stanton, G., 'The Gospel of Matthew and Judaism', *BJRL* 66, 1984,
    pp. 264–84
Strecker, G., 'On the Problem of Jewish Christianity', in W. Bauer, *Orthodoxy
    and Heresy in Earliest Christianity*, ET Fortress 1971, and SCM Press 1972,
    pp. 241–85
Vielhauer, P., 'Jewish–Christian Gospels', Hennecke, *Apocrypha*, I,
    pp. 117–65

Chapter XII   Hellenistic Christianity

Barrett, C. K., 'Pauline Controversies in the Post-Pauline Period', *NTS*, 20,
    1973–74, pp. 229–45
Bianchi, U., ed., *Le Origini dello Gnosticismo*, Leiden 1967
Cullmann, O., *The Johannine Circle*, 1975 ET SCM Press 1976
Dassmann, E., *Der Stachel im Fleisch. Paulus in der frühchristlichen Literatur bis
    Irenaus*, Aschendorff 1979
Drane, J. W., *Paul, Libertine or Legalist?*, SPCK 1975
Foerster, W., *Gnosis: I Patristic Evidence*, 1969; *II Coptic and Mandaic Sources*,
    1971, ET Oxford University Press 1972, 1974
Grant, R. M., *Gnosticism and Early Christianity*, 1959, Harper ²1966
Hengel, M., 'Between Jesus and Paul', *Between Jesus and Paul*, SCM Press/
    Fortress 1983, pp. 1–29

Käsemann, E., *The Testament of Jesus*, 1966, ET SCM Press 1968, ch. II

Kloppenborg, J. S., *The Formation of Q. Trajectories in Ancient Wisdom Collections*, Fortress 1987

Knox, W. L., *St Paul and the Church of the Gentiles*, Cambridge University Press 1939

Koester, H., *Introduction to the New Testament. Vol. 2. History and Literature of Early Christianity*, Fortress/de Gruyter 1982

Meeks, W. A., 'The Man from Heaven in Johannine Sectarianism', *JBL* 91, 1972, pp. 44–72

Nock, A. D., 'Early Gentile Christianity and its Hellenistic Background', *Essays on the Trinity and the Incarnation*, ed., A. E. J. Rawlinson, 1928, pp. 51–156, reissued separately Harper 1964, and reprinted in his *Essays on Religion and the Ancient World*, ed., Z. Stewart, Oxford University Press 1972, pp. 49–133

—'Gnosticism', *HTR*, 57, 1964, reprinted in *Essays*, pp. 940–59

Pagels, E., *The Gnostic Gospels*, Random House/Weidenfeld 1979

Pagels E. H., *The Johannine Gospel in Gnostic Exegesis: Heracleon's Commentary on John*, SBL Monograph Series 17, Abingdon 1973

—The Gnostic Paul: *The Gnostic Exegesis of the Pauline Letters*, Fortress 1975

Pearson, B. A., *The Pneumatikos-Psychikos Terminology in I Corinthians*, SBL Dissertation Series 12, 1973

Perkins, P., 'Gnostic Christologies and the New Testament', *CBQ* 43, 1981, pp. 590–606

Piper, R. A., *Wisdom in the Q-Tradition. The Aphoristic Teaching of Jesus*, SNTSMS 61, Cambridge University 1989

Puech, H. C., in Hennecke, *Apocrypha*, I, pp. 231–362

Quispel, G., *Gnostic Studies*, Istanbul, Vol. I 1974, Vol. II 1975

Reitzenstein, R., *The Hellenistic Mystery-Religions. Their Basic Ideas and Significance*, Pickwick 1978

Robinson, J. M., 'Logoi Sophon: On the Gattung of Q', *FRP*, pp. 84–130, reprinted in *Trajectories*, pp. 71–113

—ed., *The Nag Hammadi Library in English*, revised Brill 1988

Rudolph, K., *Gnosis: the Nature and History of an Ancient Religion*, 1977, ET T. & T. Clark 1983

Sanders, J. N., *The Fourth Gospel in the Early Church*, Cambridge University Press 1943

Schmithals, W., *Gnosticism in Corinth*, ³1969, ET Abingdon 1971

—Paul and the Gnostics, 1965, ET Abingdon 1972

Schneemelcher, W., 'Paulus in der griechischen Kirche des zweiten Jahrhunderts', *ZKG*, 75, 1964, pp. 1–20

Schottroff, L., *Der Glaubende und die feindliche Welt: Beobachtungen zum gnostischen Dualismus und seiner Bedeutung für Paulus und das Johannesevangelium*, Neukirchen 1970

Scroggs, R., 'The Earliest Hellenistic Christianity', *Religions in Antiquity: Essays in Memory of E. R. Goodenough*, ed., J. Neusner, Leiden 1968, pp. 176–206

Simon, M., *St Stephen and the Hellenists in the Primitive Church*, Longmans 1958

Smalley, S. S., 'Diversity and Development in John', *NTS*, 17, 1970–71, pp. 276–92

Tröger, K. W., hrsg., *Gnosis und Neues Testament: Studien aus Religionswissenschaft und Theologie*, Gütersloh 1973

Tuckett, C., *Nag Hammadi and the Gospel Tradition. Synoptic Tradition in the Nag Hammadi Library*, T. & T. Clark 1986

Wedderburn, A. J. M., *Baptism and Resurrection. Studies in Pauline Theology against its Graeco–Roman Background*, WUNT 44, Tübingen 1987

Wilson, R. M., *Gnosis and the New Testament*, Blackwell 1968

Yamauchi, E., *Pre-Christian Gnosticism*, Tyndale Press 1973

Chapter XIII   Apocalyptic Christianity

Barrett, C. K., *The New Testament Background: Selected Documents*, SPCK 1956, pp. 227–55

Baumgarten, J., *Paulus und die Apokalyptik*, Neukirchen 1975

Beasley-Murray, G. R., *The Kingdom of God*, Paternoster 1986

Brown, C., 'The Parousia and Eschatology in the New Testament', *NIDNTT*, II, 1976, pp. 901–35

Bultmann, R., *History and Eschatology*, Edinburgh University Press 1957

Cohn, N., *The Pursuit of the Millenium*, Secker & Warburg 1957

Collins, A. Y., *Crisis and Catharsis. The Power of the Apocalypse*, Westminster 1984

Collins, J. J., ed., *Apocalypse. The Morphology of a Genre*, Semeia 14, 1979

Collins, J. J., *The Apocalyptic Imagination. An Introduction to the Jewish Matrix of Christianity*, Crossroad 1984

Cullmann, O., *Christ and Time*, 1946, ET SCM Press ²1962

— *Salvation in History*, 1965, ET SCM Press 1967

Davies, W. D., 'Apocalyptic and Pharisaism', *ExpT* 59, 1947–48, pp. 233–7, reprinted in *Christian Origins and Judaism*, Darton, Longman & Todd 1962, pp. 19–30

Fiorenza, E. S., *The Book of Revelation. Justice and Judgment*, Fortress 1985

Funk, R. W., ed., *Apocalypticism, JThC*, 6, 1969

Grässer, E., *Die Naherwartung Jesu*, Stuttgarter Bibelstudien 61, 1973

Hanson, P. D., *The Dawn of Apocalyptic. The Historical and Sociological Roots of Jewish Apocalyptic Eschatology*, Fortress 1975, ²1979

Hellholm, D., ed., *Apocalypticism in the Mediterranean World and the Near East*, Tübingen 1983

Jewett, R., *The Thessalonian Correspondence. Pauline Rhetoric and Millenarian Piety*, Fortress 1986

Käsemann, E., 'The Beginnings of Christian Theology' (1960), 'On the Subject of Primitive Christian Apocalyptic' (1962), *NTQT*, chs 4 and 5, also in Funk, *Apocalypticism*

Keck, L. E., 'Paul and Apocalyptic Eschatology', *Interpretation* 38, 1984, pp. 229–41

Koch, K., *The Rediscovery of Apocalyptic*, 1970, ET SCM Press 1972

Kümmel, W. G., *Promise and Fulfilment*, [3]1956, ET SCM Press [2]1961

Laws, S., 'Can Apocalyptic be Relevant?' *What about the New Testament? Essays in Honour of Christopher Evans*, ed., M. Hooker and C. Hickling, SCM Press 1975, pp. 89–102

Marshall, I. H., 'Is Apocalyptic the Mother of Christian Theology?', *Tradition and Interpretation in the New Testament*, E. E. Ellis Festschrift, ed. G. F. Hawthorne, Eerdmans 1987, pp. 33–42

Moltmann, J., *Theology of Hope*, [5]1965, ET SCM Press 1967

Moore, A. L., *The Parousia in the New Testament*, *SNT*, XIII, 1966

Morris, L., *Apocalyptic*, Tyndale Press 1973

Pannenberg, W., *Revelation as History*, 1961, ET Macmillan 1968

Robinson, J. A. T., *Jesus and his Coming*, SCM Press 1957

Rollins, W. G., 'The New Testament and Apocalyptic', *NTS*, 17, 1970–71, pp. 454–76

Rowland, C., *The Open Heaven. A Study of Apocalyptic in Judaism and Early Christianity*, SPCK 1982

Rowley, H. H., *The Relevance of Apocalyptic*, Lutterworth 1944, [3]1963

Russell, D. S., *The Method and Message of Jewish Apocalyptic*, SCM Press 1964

Schmithals, W., *The Apocalyptic Movement: Introduction and Interpretation*, 1973, ET Abingdon 1975

Schnackenburg, R., *God's Rule and Kingdom*, 1959, ET Herder 1963

Schweitzer, A., *The Quest of the Historical Jesus*, ET A. & C. Black 1910, third edition 1954

Vielhauer, P., et al., in Hennecke, *Apocrypha* II, Part C

Weiss, J., *Jesus' Proclamation of the Kingdom of God*, 1892, ET SCM Press 1971

Chapter XIV   Early Catholicism

Barrett, C. K., *Luke the Historian in Recent Study*, Epworth 1961; Fortress Facet Book 1970

— *New Testament Essays*, SPCK 1972, chs 5–7

Batiffol, P., *Primitive Catholicism*, [5]1911, ET Longmans 1911

Bauer, W. and Hornschuh, M., in Hennecke, *Apocrypha*, II, pp. 35–87

Brown, R. E., Donfried, K. P., and Reumann, J., *Peter in the New Testament*, Chapman 1974

Conzelmann, H., *The Theology of St Luke*, 1953 [2]1957, ET Faber & Faber 1961

Cullmann, O., *Peter: Disciple, Apostle, Martyr*, 1952 [2]1960, ET SCM Press [2]1962

Drane, J. W., 'Eschatology, Ecclesiology and Catholicity in the New Testament', *ExpT*, 83, 1971–72, pp. 180–4

Ehrhardt, A., *The Apostolic Ministry*, *SJT*, Occasional Papers no. 7, 1958

Elliott, J. H., 'A Catholic Gospel: Reflections on "Early Catholicism" in the New Testament', *CBQ*, 31, 1969, pp. 213–33

Ellis, E. E., *Eschatology in Luke*, Fortress Facet Book 1972

Fuller, R. H., 'Early Catholicism. An Anglican Reaction to a German Debate', *Die Mitte des Neuen Testaments*, E. Schweizer Festschrift, hrsg. U. Luz and H. Weder, Göttingen 1983, pp. 34–41

Gasque, W. W., *A History of the Criticism of the Acts of the Apostles*, Tübingen 1975, Eerdmans 1975

Goppelt, L., 'The Existence of the Church in History according to Apostolic and Early Catholic Thought', *CINTI*, pp. 193–209

Grässer, E., *Das Problem der Parusieverzögerung in den synoptischen Evangelien und in der Apostelgeschichte*, Berlin 1957, [2]1960

Hahn, F., 'Das Problem des Frühkatholizismus', and 'Frühkatholizimus als ökumensiches Problem', *Exegetische Beiträge zum ökumenischen Gespräch*, Göttingen 1986, pp. 39–56 and 57–75

Holmberg, B., *Paul and Power. The Structure of Authority in the Primitive Church as Reflected in the Pauline Epistles*, CWK Gleerup 1978

Karrer, O., *Peter and the Church: an Examination of Cullmann's Thesis*, ET Herder 1963

Käsemann, E., 'The Disciples of John the Baptist in Ephesus' (1952), 'An Apologia for Primitive Christian Eschatology' (1952), *ENTT*, chs VI and VIII

— 'Paul and Early Catholicism' (1963), *NTQT*, pp. 236–51

— *The Testament of Jesus*, 1966, ET SCM Press 1968, chs III and IV

Keck, L. E. and Martyn, J. L., ed., *Studies in Luke Acts*, Abingdon 1966; SPCK 1968

Kümmel, W. G., 'Current Theological Accusations against Luke' (1970), ET in *Andover Newton Quarterly*, 16, 1975–76, pp. 131–45

Küng, H., *Structures of the Church*, ET Burns & Oates 1965, pp. 135–51

Luz, U., 'Erwägungen zur Entstehung des "Frühkatholizismus". Eine Skizze'. *ZNW* 65, 1974, pp. 88–111

MacDonald, D. R., *The Legend and the Apostle. The Battle for Paul in Story and Canon*, Westminster 1983

MacDonald, M. Y., *The Pauline Churches. A Socio-historical study of institutional-ization in the Pauline and Deutero-Pauline writings*, SNTSMS 60, Cambridge University 1988

Maddox, R., *The Purpose of Luke–Acts*, T. & T. Clark 1982

Marshall, I. H., '"Early Catholicism" in the New Testament', *New Dimensions in New Testament Study*, ed., R. N. Longenecker and M. C. Tenney, Zondervan 1974, pp. 217–31

Mattill, A. J., 'The Purpose of Acts: Schneckenberger Reconsidered', *Apostolic History and the Gospel: Biblical and Historical Essays Presented to F. F. Bruce*, ed., W. W. Gasque and R. P. Martin, Paternoster 1970, pp. 108–22

Neufeld, K. H., '"Frühkatholizismus" – Idee und Begriff', *ZKT*, 94, 1972, pp. 1–28

Schulz, S., *Die Mitte der Schrift: der Frühkatholizismus im Neuen Testament als Herausforderung an die Protestantismus*, Stuttgart 1976

Sohm, R., *Wesen und Ursprung des Katholizismus*, [2]1912, Darmstadt 1967

Strecker, G., 'Frühkatholizismus', *Die Johannesbriefe*, *KEK*, Göttingen 1989, pp. 348–54

Troeltsch, E., *The Social Teaching of the Christian Churches*, 1911, ET Allen & Unwin 1931, pp. 89–200

Weiss, H.-F., '"Frühkatholizismus" im Neuen Testament? Probleme und Aspekte', in J. Rogge & G. Schille, hrsg., *Frühkatholizismus im ökumenischen Gespräch*, Berlin 1983, pp. 9–26

Werner, M., *The Formation of Christian Dogma*, 1941, ET A. & C. Black 1957

Chapter XV   The Authority of the New Testament

Aland, K., *The Problem of the New Testament Canon*, Contemporary Studies in Theology 2, Mowbray 1962

Barr, J., *Old and New in Interpretation*, SCM Press 1966

— *The Bible in the Modern World*, SCM Press 1973

Barrett, C. K., 'The Centre of the New Testament and the Canon', *Die Mitte des Neuen Testaments. Einheit und Vielfalt neutestamentlicher Theologie*, E. Schweizer Festschrift, hrsg. U. Luz and H. Weder, Göttingen 1983, pp. 5–21

Best, E., 'Scripture, Tradition and the Canon of the New Testament', *BJRL* 61, 1979, pp. 258–89

Brown, R. E., *The Critical Meaning of the Bible*, Chapman 1982

— *Biblical Exegesis and Church Doctrine*, Chapman 1985

Bruce, F. F., 'New Light on the Origins of the New Testament Canon', *New Dimensions in New Testament Study*, ed., R. N. Longenecker and M. C. Tenney, Zondervan 1974, pp. 3–18

— 'Some Thoughts on the Beginning of the New Testament Canon', *BJRL* 65, 1983, pp.37–60

Campenhausen, H., von, *The Formation of the Christian Bible*, 1968, ET A. & C. Black 1972

Childs, B. S., *The New Testament as Canon. An Introduction*, SCM Press 1984

Cullmann, O., 'The Plurality of the Gospels as a Theological Problem in Antiquity' (1945), 'The Tradition' (1953), *The Early Church: Historical and Theological Studies*, ET SCM Press 1956, pp. 39–54, 75–99

Dodd, C. H., *The Authority of the Bible*, Nisbet 1929

Doty, W. G., *Contemporary New Testament Interpretation*, Prentice-Hall 1972

Dungan, D. L., 'The New Testament Canon in Recent Study', *Interpretation*, 29, 1975, pp. 339–51

Dunn, J. D. G., *The Living Word*, SCM Press/Fortress 1987

Dunn, J. D. G. and Mackey, J. P., *New Testament Theology in Dialogue*, SPCK/Westminster 1987

Farmer, W. R. and Farkasfalvy, D. M., *The Formation of the New Testament Canon*, Paulist 1983

Fazekas, L., 'Kanon im Kanon', *TZ* 37, 1981, pp. 19–34

Gamble, H. Y., *The New Testament Canon. Its Making and Meaning*, Fortress 1985

Hahn, F., 'Die Heilige Schrift als älteste christliche Tradition und als Kanon', *Exegetische Beiträge zum ökumenischen Gespräch*, Göttingen 1986, pp. 29–39

Hanson, P. D., *The Diversity of Scripture. A Theological Interpretation*, Fortress 1982

Käsemann, E., 'Is the Gospel Objective?' (1953), 'The Canon of the New Testament and the Unity of the Church' (1951), *ENTT*, pp. 48–62, 95–107

— 'Thoughts on the Present Controversy about Scriptural Interpretation' (1962), *NTQT*, pp. 260–85

— ed., *Das Neue Testament als Kanon*, Göttingen 1970

Kelsey, D. H., *The Uses of Scripture in Recent Theology*, Fortress and SCM Press 1975

Küng, H., '"Early Catholicism" in the New Testament as a Problem in Controversial Theology', *The Living Church*, ET Sheed & Ward 1963, pp. 233–93; (published in USA under the title *The Council in Action: Theological Reflections on the Second Vatican Council*)

Lönning, I., *'Kanon im Kanon'. Zum dogmatischen Grundlagenproblem des neutestamentlichen Kanons*, Oslo 1972

Marxsen, W., *The New Testament as the Church's Book*, 1966, ET Fortress 1972

Meade. D. G., *Pseudonymity and Canon. An Investigation into the Relationship of Authorship and Authority in Jewish and Earliest Christian Tradition*, Tübingen/Eerdmans 1986

Mildenberger, F., 'The Unity, Truth and Validity of the Bible', *Interpretation*, 29, 1975, pp. 391–405

Murray, R., 'How did the Church determine the Canon of Scripture?', *Heythrop Journal*, 11, 1970, pp. 115–26

Nineham, D. E., *The Use and Abuse of the Bible*, Macmillan 1976

Ogden, S. M., 'The Authority of Scripture for Theology', *Interpretation*, 30, 1976, pp. 242–61

Pannenberg, W., *Basic Questions in Theology*, Vol. I, 1967, ET SCM Press 1970

Pedersen, S., 'Die Kanonfrage als historisches und theologisches Problem', *Studia Theologica* 21, 1977, pp. 83–136

Robinson, J. M., *The New Hermeneutic*, Harper 1964

Sanders, J. A., *Canon and Community. A Guide to Canonical Criticism*, Fortress 1984

Schürmann, H., 'Auf der Suche nach dem "Evangelisch Katholischen". *Zum Thema "Frühkatholizismus im ökumenischen Gespräch*, Berlin 1983, pp. 71–107

Schweizer, E., 'Scripture – Tradition – Modern Interpretation' *Neotestamentica* Zürich 1963, pp. 203–35

Sheppard, G. T., 'Canonization. Hearing the Voice of the Same God through Historically Dissimilar Traditions', *Interpretation* 36, 1982, pp. 21–33

Stendahl, K., 'One Canon is Enough', *Meanings. The Bible as Document and as Guide*, Fortress 1984, pp. 55–68

Wall, R. W., 'The Problem of the Multiple Letter Canon of the New Testament', *Horizons in Biblical Theology* 8, 1986 pp. 1–31

Wiles, M. F., 'The Uses of "Holy Scripture"', *What about the New Testament? Essays in Honour of Christopher Evans*, ed., M. Hooker and C. Hickling, SCM Press 1975, pp. 155–64

Zahn, T., *Geschichte des neutestamentlichen Kanons*, 4 vols, Leipzig 1888–92

INDEXES

Throughout the indexes references to the text are cited by page number and are given first. References to notes are cited by chapter and note number.

INDEX OF BIBLICAL AND ANCIENT WRITINGS

I OLD TESTAMENT

II   OLD TESTAMENT APOCRYPHA AND PSEUDEPIGRAPHA

III DEAD SEA SCROLLS, PHILO, JOSEPHUS AND RABBINIC TEXTS

DEAD SEA SCROLLS

IV   NEW TESTAMENT

V EARLY CHRISTIAN, GNOSTIC AND OTHER ANCIENT WRITINGS

INDEX OF MODERN AUTHORS

(*Italics* indicate that a new title appears for the first time)

INDEX OF SUBJECTS